FARM JOURNAL'S COUNTRY COOKBOOK

Edited by NELL B. NICHOLS
Food Editor, FARM JOURNAL

Photography Supervised by AL J. REAGAN
Art Director, THE FARMER'S WIFE

DOUBLEDAY & COMPANY, INC.
Garden City *New York*

Library of Congress Catalog Card Number 59–6414

Printed in the United States of America

How This Book Came To Be

It's with real pride that we present this COUNTRY COOKBOOK. We've been working up to it for twelve years! All during this time the readers of THE FARMER'S WIFE magazine within FARM JOURNAL have inspired us—and often pushed us a little.

Certainly hardly a week has passed without some farm homemaker urging us to collect THE FARMER'S WIFE recipes between two covers. Often it was a lost favorite from five or even ten years ago that gave her the idea: "Back in 1946, you printed a recipe for chocolate cake. I've used it all these years and it's my 'reputation cake.' Now I've lost the recipe."

Or: "This is just the kind of day my husband is likely to say 'What about some of your brown sugar cookies?' It's a FARM JOURNAL recipe, really, and I've mislaid it! Can you help me out?"

And, even as I write this, a letter arrives requesting our prize recipe for Pumpkin Pie. The homemaker added this postscript: "Also if Nell Nichols has any books other than her GOOD HOME COOKING I should like to hear about them. . . ."

Actually, it was when Nell Nichols joined us as Food Editor several years ago that we began seriously to plan to publish a cookbook. For editing a cookbook takes special skill. It takes a lot of food judgment to cull through years of excellent recipes and select those that have stood the test of time and taste—and practicality.

As you know, farm life has changed in the past decade or two; so have ingredients on the grocers' shelves. So have pots and pans and equipment! The cellar pantry has been replaced by a refrigerator and, in half the farm homes of the U.S., a freezer or locker space, too. Mixers, griddles, electric skillets—there are all kinds of new appliances and improvements in large pieces of equipment. Methods of mixing recipes have changed—FARM JOURNAL has improved its style of recipe writing several times. So each of the thousands of recipes had to be evaluated and adjusted down to the last half-teaspoonful!

Mrs. Nichols, who is not only our Food Editor but also a combination of home economist, journalist, homemaker, and traveling food explorer, was just the right person to select the more than one thousand best recipes. For she has crisscrossed the country over and over, talking with women of all ages about their cooking and recipes; she may have visited you! Already the author of an earlier book (GOOD HOME COOKING ACROSS THE U.S.A.), she has a nationwide reputation as a food expert.

Besides, she's a farm product—grew up on a ranch in the wide open spaces around Dodge City, Kansas. We believe that it takes a country girl really to know good country cooking—and the kinds of dishes that are practical and have appeal. Mrs. Nichols is at home in farm and ranch kitchens. She loves good food and she likes to search for it, cook it, talk about it—and eat it!

We feel that publishing this cookbook has been a command performance—you asked for it, and you helped us build it. We hope the book will make cooking more enjoyable and creative for all homemakers—both farm and city. Won't you write and tell us how you like it?

GERTRUDE DIEKEN
Editor, THE FARMER'S WIFE

How This Book Is Different

COUNTRYSIDE KITCHENS
FARM JOURNAL
PHILADELPHIA, PENNSYLVANIA

DEAR FRIEND:

I wish I could stop by to visit you the first time you open your new COUNTRY COOKBOOK. I'd love to hear your comments and take you on a grand tour through the twenty-five chapters to point out some of our favorite recipes. There are those Lemon-Coconut Squares, delightful, praise-winning cookies; Sally Lunn, the bread that's so delicious hot from the oven; Crusty Fried Chicken, with its keep-them-guessing seasonings. But I fear I'd overstay my welcome, for we have hundreds of pets among the more than a thousand tested recipes, FARM JOURNAL's best.

You will notice right away that this is not a standard cookbook. We believe there are plenty of those already. The COUNTRY COOKBOOK is different. It's a collection of recipes that have helped make country cooking the nation's finest—recipes that have stood the test of practical use and that have been most praised by our readers through the years. About half of them came from farm kitchens across the country; the other half were developed by home economists in our Countryside Kitchens. But every recipe has been many times tested in our Test Kitchens and in farm homes.

After we planned what we believed most country cooks want in a cookbook, we sent our blueprint to 500 farm women, members of FARM JOURNAL's Family Test Group, to obtain their reactions. With their guidance, we started to put together the *Cookbook* you hold in your hands. There's never been one like it.

You'll find the chapters or groups of recipes divided in just the way country women think of food. We start with dishes to fix for guests, for if there ever is a time when you want your table to make a good showing, it's when there's company. These chapters deal with reputation-building dishes we call *Company Specials, Dishes To Tote* to covered-dish suppers (good travelers), homey foods for the *Coffee Break, Eating Outdoors,* and *Cooking for a Crowd* (for church club suppers and community barbecues).

Next come the recipes using staple farm foods like *Meats, Chicken and Other Poultry, Potatoes, Eggs, Apples, Milk and Cheese,* and *Butter and Cream.* These are some of the ingredients responsible for the country-good taste. And because you are the greatest cookie bakers on earth, we devote a whole chapter to cookie recipes. Some of the treats made with natural sweetenings like honey, maple sugar or syrup, caramelized sugar, and molasses get together in a chapter, as do recipes based on nature's bounty *From Stream and Field*—fish and game.

Vegetables have a glorious inning in our *From the Garden* chapter. Foods to freeze and bring out in a hurry have their own chapter titled *From the Freezer*. And because you tell us there is nothing like a homemade relish to set off a meal, we devote a section to these treats.

We know how busy you are, and to help you stretch time we put the spotlight on two important groups of foods: *Make Ahead Dishes* and *Quick and Easy Cooking*. Because our *Master Recipes* with variations have continuously enjoyed such an enthusiastic reception, we include some of them—recipes that by simple substitutions or additions make several different dishes. It's like changing a basic dress with accessories. You'll find that all through the COUNTRY COOKBOOK we offer variations for hundreds of recipes to multiply their usefulness.

Some of you tell us you earn money by selling homemade foods; so we include a full chapter on *Money Makers*. All these recipes are from farm women who have best sellers—foods that win new customers and keep old ones coming back.

You'll find directions for some of the dishes that Mother and Grandmother used to make—old-fashioned ones too tasty to forget. There's a chapter on the specialties of different parts of the country and another filled with recipes from our *Guest Cooks*. They are the farm women who come to our Test Kitchens to show us how they make dishes that have won them reputations as their neighborhoods' best cooks.

I wish you could visit our Countryside Kitchens, too. We have four complete kitchens in which our home economists test all recipes printed in FARM JOURNAL and in which we try new food products and appliances.

The skills and talents of many people were brought together in this COUNTRY COOKBOOK. The Food Department wishes to thank the hundreds of farm women who shared their recipes with us. We are grateful to the members of FARM JOURNAL'S Family Test Group for their assistance in organizing a book that will be of limitless service. We appreciate the contributions which all members of the food staff made during the twelve years when these recipes were first appearing in FARM JOURNAL. And we acknowledge the willing help of members of the editorial staff of THE FARMER'S WIFE who pitched in and helped us make this cookbook come true.

If you enjoy using the recipes in the COUNTRY COOKBOOK, we'll be happy. And if your friends use them, too, we know that country cooking will continue to rate first in good eating.

Sincerely yours,
NELL B. NICHOLS
Food Editor

Contents

	How This Book Came to Be	iii
	How This Book Is Different	v
CHAPTER 1.	Company Specials	1
CHAPTER 2.	Dishes to Tote	25
CHAPTER 3.	Eating Outdoors	41
CHAPTER 4.	Cooking for a Crowd	55
CHAPTER 5.	Coffee Break	75
CHAPTER 6.	The Cookie Jar	85
CHAPTER 7.	Meats	101
CHAPTER 8.	Chicken and Other Poultry	127
CHAPTER 9.	Potatoes	143
CHAPTER 10.	Eggs	157
CHAPTER 11.	Butter and Cream	171
CHAPTER 12.	Milk and Cheese	185
CHAPTER 13.	Apples	203
CHAPTER 14.	Special Sweetenings	215
CHAPTER 15.	From the Garden	227
CHAPTER 16.	From the Freezer	249
CHAPTER 17.	Homemade Relishes	261

CHAPTER 18. From Stream and Field 273

CHAPTER 19. Make-Ahead Dishes 285

CHAPTER 20. Quick and Easy Cooking 299

CHAPTER 21. Master Recipes 315

CHAPTER 22. Money-Maker Recipes 333

CHAPTER 23. Old-Fashioned Recipes 345

CHAPTER 24. Regional Dishes 357

CHAPTER 25. Guest Cooks in Our Test Kitchens 371

Index 379

COLOR PHOTOGRAPHS
BY

Robert E. Coates

Peter Dant Studio

Hoedt Studios

George Lazarnick

Mel Richman

Paul Wing

FARM JOURNAL'S
COUNTRY COOKBOOK

1

Company Specials

Come on over to our house!

If you're forever making such tempting suggestions to friends, this chapter is for you. It's a star-studded recipe collection—some of Farm Journal's best. They're the kind of dishes you'll be proud to spring on guests—not all easy to fix, but all superior. And if there's ever a time when you wish to put exceptionally tasty food on the table, it's when friends are gathered around. Many of these company specials you can make ahead and freeze to have on hand for unexpected drop-in guests.

You will find more desserts than other dishes in this chapter. That's partly because we've put our best chicken, meat, bread and vegetable recipes in other chapters in this cookbook. But good cooks know that a super dessert is a meal's climax—that it can transform a plain-Jane menu into a glamorous company meal.

Our cakes are dazzling—they make cake-talkers out of everyone who sees and tastes them. No Farm Journal recipe has won more bouquets through the years than our magnificent Fudge Cake. It came to us from the Golden West, a Montana ranch kitchen, but by requests from readers has spread to every state.

The Ambrosia Chiffon Cake is another wonder—it brings sunshine and spring to the table even if the windows are frosted. Our Pumpkin Cake suggests the gold-and-bronze season when Thanksgiving dinner plans invade your dreams. It's a cake with a slightly coarse grain because of the pumpkin, but it's luscious down to the last forkful.

Our pie recipes hold their own with the cakes. This chapter includes a de luxe cherry pie, the cover selection for this cookbook and a Farm Journal 5-star recipe. It's a jackpot of good eating, the tart-sweet, juicy filling contrasting with an extra-flaky, tender pastry. There's an Apricot Meringue Pie with tall meringue tinged with gold; also blueberry, raisin and strawberry-pineapple pies that we have given high scores.

Our party-pink Strawberry Parfait Ring is a spectacular dessert. And Chocolate Angel Pie is correctly named—perfect to tote to covered-dish suppers. It's just one of the recipes in our prized collection of favorite chocolate desserts in this chapter.

You can use these recipes knowing that you'll win a reputation as a good cook with them. Such confidence in the food you're serving will make you a relaxed hostess. You'll find your guests will catch your spirit—everyone will have a happy time.

Hostess Cakes

While there are dozens of recipes for superb cakes in this cookbook, these are the stand-outs our readers have most generously praised as assets to any hostess. The cakes are tender and light—the kind you eat slowly to savor between sips of hot tea or coffee. They're guaranteed to bring compliments—and to be good to the last crumb.

FUDGE CAKE

A Farm Journal 5-star recipe

¾ c. butter or margarine
2¼ c. sugar
1½ tsp. vanilla
3 eggs
3 (1 oz.) squares unsweetened chocolate, melted
3 c. sifted cake flour
1½ tsp. baking soda
¾ tsp. salt
1½ c. ice water

• Cream butter, sugar and vanilla with mixer. Add eggs, beating until light and fluffy. Add melted chocolate and blend well.
• Sift together dry ingredients; add alternately with water to chocolate mixture. Pour batter into three 8" layer pans which have been greased and lined with waxed paper. Bake in moderate oven (350°) 30 to 35 minutes. Cool. Put layers together with Date Cream Filling. Frost with Fudge Frosting.

Date Cream Filling:

1 c. milk
½ c. chopped dates
1 tblsp. flour
¼ c. sugar
1 egg, beaten
½ c. chopped nuts
1 tsp. vanilla

• Combine milk and dates in top of a double boiler.
• Combine flour and sugar and add beaten egg, blending until smooth. Add to hot milk. Cook, stirring, until thick. Cool.
• Stir in nuts and vanilla. Spread between layers.

Fudge Frosting:

2 c. sugar
1 c. light cream
2 (1 oz.) squares unsweetened chocolate, grated

• Combine all ingredients in a heavy saucepan. Boil over high heat 3 minutes without stirring. Reduce heat and continue cooking until it reaches soft ball stage (238°). Cool.
• Beat until creamy and of spreading consistency. Add cream if too thick.
• Spread on sides of cake first and a little over the top edge; frost top last. Makes 8 to 10 servings.

PUMPKIN CAKE

A Farm Journal 5-star recipe

½ c. shortening
1 c. sugar
1 c. brown sugar, firmly packed
2 eggs, beaten
1 c. cooked, mashed pumpkin or winter squash
3 c. sifted cake flour
4 tsp. baking powder
¼ tsp. baking soda
½ c. milk
1 c. chopped walnuts
1 tsp. maple extract

• Cream shortening and slowly add sugars, eggs and pumpkin.
• Sift together flour, baking powder and soda; add alternately with milk to mixture. Fold in walnuts and extract.

• Pour into 3 greased 8″ layer cake pans. Bake in moderate oven (350°) 30 minutes. Cool and frost with Harvest Moon Frosting.

Harvest Moon Frosting:

3 eggs whites, unbeaten
1½ c. brown sugar, firmly packed
Dash of salt
6 tblsp. water
1 tsp. vanilla

• Combine in double boiler eggs, sugar, salt and water. Beat well; place over rapidly boiling water. Cook 7 minutes, beating constantly, or until frosting will stand in peaks. Remove from boiling water; add vanilla. Beat until thick enough to spread.
• Put cake layers together with frosting. Frost sides, bringing frosting slightly over top edge. Frost top. Makes enough frosting for a 3-layer cake.

POPPY SEED LAYER CAKE

A Farm Journal 5-star recipe

¼ c. poppy seeds
1 c. milk
⅔ c. shortening
1½ c. sugar
1 tblsp. baking powder
3 c. sifted cake flour
1 tsp. salt
4 egg whites, stiffly beaten

• Add poppy seeds to milk. Let stand 1 hour.
• Cream shortening with sugar until light and fluffy.
• Sift baking powder with flour and salt. Add dry ingredients and poppy seed milk alternately to creamed mixture.
• Fold in egg whites, half at a time. Pour into two 8″ waxed paper-lined layer pans.
• Bake in moderate oven (375°) 30 minutes. Remove from pans to cool. Frost with Sour Cream Frosting.

Sour Cream Frosting:

1 c. dairy sour cream
1½ c. sugar
¼ c. water
1 tsp. vanilla
3 tblsp. dairy sour cream
½ c. whole nuts

• Combine the 1 c. sour cream and sugar in saucepan; blend together and add water. Cook to soft ball stage (235°), stirring constantly. Remove from heat.
• Cool slightly. Add vanilla and the 3 tblsp. sour cream; beat 5 minutes with rotary beater until creamy.
• Spread quickly. Decorate top with nuts. Makes enough to frost 2 (8″) layers.

TEA-TIME CUPCAKES

Dainty, pretty—the tasty flavor is an orange and coconut combination

1 loaf-size (10 oz.) pkg. white cake mix
2 egg whites
½ c. (about) orange juice
1½ tsp. grated orange rind
Confectioners sugar frosting
Food colors
1 (3½ oz.) can flaked coconut

• Prepare cake batter according to package directions, using orange juice instead of water and adding orange rind.
• Half fill tiny (1¾″) greased cupcake pans. Bake in moderate oven (350°) 15 to 20 minutes. Cool.
• Divide into thirds frosting made with 1½ c. sifted confectioners sugar, 2 tblsp. cream and 3 tblsp. butter. Tint each with a little food color (red, green and yellow) to make pastel pink, green and yellow frosting. Dip tops of cakes in frosting. While still moist, sprinkle with coconut. Let frosting set before storing. Makes 28 cupcakes.

AMBROSIA CHIFFON CAKE

A Farm Journal 5-star recipe

5 egg yolks
1 c. egg whites (8 or 9 eggs)
2¼ c. sifted cake flour
1½ c. sugar
1 tblsp. baking powder
1 tsp. salt
½ c. oil
¼ c. water
½ c. orange juice
1 tblsp. grated orange rind
½ tsp. cream of tartar
1 c. flaked or shredded coconut

• Bring eggs to room temperature.
• Sift flour with 1 c. sugar, baking powder and salt.
• Measure into mixing bowl egg yolks, oil, water, orange juice and rind. Add sifted dry ingredients. Beat until smooth, about ½ minute at low speed of mixer, or 75 strokes by hand.
• Add cream of tartar to egg whites. Beat until soft peaks form. Gradually add remaining ½ c. sugar, beating until mixture stands in very stiff peaks. Do not underbeat.
• Chop or cut coconut into shorter lengths. Fold into egg whites with a large spoon or rubber scraper. Then gently fold egg yolk mixture into whites.
• Pour into ungreased 10" tube pan. Bake in moderate oven (325°) 1 hour or until surface springs back when touched lightly.
• Invert pan to cool. A good way is to place tube of pan over inverted funnel. When cool, loosen sides with a spatula and turn out. Frost.
• Makes 16 to 20 servings.

Orange Satin Frosting:

2 egg whites
1½ c. sugar
1½ tsp. light corn syrup
⅓ c. orange juice
Dash of salt
1 tsp. grated orange rind
8 marshmallows, cut in pieces
Yellow food color

• Combine in top of double boiler egg whites, sugar, corn syrup, orange juice and salt. Beat 1 minute with electric or rotary hand beater.
• Cook mixture over boiling water, beating constantly until mixture forms peaks (about 7 minutes).
• Remove from heat. Add orange rind, marshmallows and enough yellow food color to tint delicately. Beat 1 or 2 minutes, until partially cooled. Spread over top and sides of cake. For a festive touch, add border of coconut shreds around rim of cake.

HOLIDAY CAKE SPECIAL

The fruit goes between the layers and on top of this Farm Journal 5-star dessert

3¼ c. sifted flour
3½ tsp. baking powder
¾ tsp. salt
1 c. butter or margarine
2 c. sugar
1 tsp. vanilla
1 c. milk
8 egg whites (use yolks in filling)

• Sift together flour, baking powder and salt.
• Cream butter; add sugar, then vanilla, beating until light and fluffy.
• Add dry ingredients alternately with milk, beating after each addition.
• Beat egg whites until stiff, but not dry. Fold into batter.
• Pour into 4 well greased 9" round layer pans. Bake in moderate oven (375°) 15 minutes.
• Remove from oven. Let stand 5 minutes. Turn out on racks to cool.
• When cool, spread Fruit Filling between layers and on top of cake. Cake tastes best when stored several days in airtight container in cool place.

Fruit Filling: Beat 8 egg yolks slightly. Blend in ½ c. soft butter or margarine. Add 1¼ c. sugar. Place over medium heat; cook, stirring constantly, 5 to 10 minutes, until sugar is dissolved and mixture slightly thickened and glossy. Remove from heat; add 1 c. chopped pecans, 1 c. finely chopped raisins, 1 c. flaked coconut, 1 c. finely chopped candied cherries, ¼ tsp. salt and ⅓ c. pineapple juice. Cool. Spread on cake.

WHITE FRUIT CAKE

Traditional and time-consuming but a Farm Journal 5-star recipe

2 lbs. white raisins, chopped
2 c. orange juice
4½ c. sifted cake flour
¼ tsp. baking powder
½ tsp. salt
1 lb. diced candied cherries
1 lb. diced candied pineapple
½ lb. diced preserved citron
¼ lb. diced candied lemon peel
¼ lb. diced candied orange peel
1 lb. almonds, blanched and slivered
2 c. butter or margarine
2¼ c. sugar
8 to 10 medium eggs (1 lb.)
1 fresh coconut, grated or shredded

• Wash raisins; chop. Combine with 1 c. orange juice; let stand overnight.
• Save 1½ c. flour to mix with candied fruit and nuts. Sift remaining 3 c. with baking powder and salt.
• Mix candied fruit and nuts with 1½ c. flour.
• Cream butter, add sugar; beat well. Add eggs, one at a time, beating well after each addition.
• Gradually add dry ingredients, beating after each addition. Add coconut, floured fruit and nuts, raisins and remaining orange juice. Beat well.
• Divide batter evenly in 2 well greased 9″ or 10″ tube pans. Bake in very slow oven (250°) about 2½ hours, or until done. Or, bake in 4 greased, paper-lined 9×5×3″ pans at the same temperature and for same length of time.
• Cool 30 minutes. Remove from pans; cool completely. Wrap in waxed paper or aluminum foil; store in air-tight container in a cool place or freeze.
• To prepare fresh coconut, pierce eyes of shell with ice pick; drain out milk. Heat in moderate oven (350°) 30 minutes. Cool, break shell—meat falls free. Peel off all the crisp brown skin. Grate or shred.

APPLESAUCE CAKE A LA MODE

Fruity cake squares with glistening nut frosting and spoonfuls of ice cream

2 c. sifted cake flour
1¼ c. sugar
½ tsp. baking soda
1 tsp. baking powder
1½ tsp. salt
½ tsp. each: allspice, cinnamon, nutmeg, cloves
½ c. shortening
1½ c. thick applesauce
2 eggs, unbeaten
½ c. currants or raisins
½ c. dates, cut in small pieces
¾ c. walnuts, cut and toasted

• Sift flour, sugar, soda, baking powder, salt and spices into mixing bowl.
• Add shortening and applesauce; beat 2 minutes. Add eggs; beat 2 minutes more. Blend in fruits and nuts.
• Bake in greased 8×12×2″ pan in moderate oven (350°) 55 to 60 minutes. Makes 12 servings.

Quick Frosting: It's optional, but adds crunchiness and flavor. Bring to boil in saucepan: ⅓ c. butter, ¾ c. brown sugar (firmly packed), ¼ tsp. salt and 3 tblsp. milk. Cook 1 minute. Remove from heat; add ¾ tsp. vanilla and 1½ c. coarsely chopped walnuts. Spread over cake. Cut in squares and top with vanilla ice cream.

Variation: Omit frosting and top with banana or coffee ice cream instead of vanilla.

Perfect Pies

Pies score high in all country dessert popularity contests. Every pie and tart in this hostess collection make good eating.

CHERRY PIE SPECIAL

A Farm Journal 5-star recipe

2 (1 lb.) cans pitted tart red cherries (water pack)
2½ tblsp. quick-cooking tapioca
¼ tsp. salt
¼ tsp. almond extract
1 tsp. lemon juice
4 drops red food color
1¼ c. sugar
Rich Pastry (recipe follows)
1 tblsp. butter or margarine

• Drain cherries. Measure ⅓ c. liquid into mixing bowl. Add tapioca, salt, almond extract, lemon juice and food color, then cherries and 1 c. sugar. Mix and let stand while making pastry.
• Fit pastry into bottom of 9" pie pan. Trim ½" beyond outer rim of pan. Fill with cherry mixture. Dot with butter. Sprinkle with remaining sugar. Moisten rim with water.
• To make crisscross top interlace 14 strips, pressing ends against moistened rim and folding lower crust up over them. Moisten rim again and circle it with remaining 4 strips. Press down firmly. Sprinkle top with sugar.
• To keep high rim from browning faster than crisscross strips, circle pie with a stand-up foil collar. Fold foil over rim and leave on during entire baking.
• Bake in hot oven (425°) 40 to 45 minutes. Serve warm.

Rich Pastry:

2¼ c. sifted flour
1 tsp. salt
1 tblsp. sugar
¾ c. vegetable shortening
1 egg yolk
1 tblsp. lemon juice
¼ c. milk

• Sift flour with salt and sugar. Cut in shortening until mixture resembles fine crumbs.
• Beat together egg yolk and lemon juice. Blend in milk. Add to dry ingredients, tossing with fork into a soft dough.
• Divide dough in half. Form each into ball. Flatten each on lightly floured surface. Roll to about ⅛" thickness. Use half for bottom crust. Cut second half into 18 strips with sharp knife or pastry wheel. Use as directed in cherry pie recipe.

GOOSEBERRY PIE

Old-fashioned fruit in rich almond pastry

⅔ c. water
2 c. sugar—or less according to sweetness of berries
1½ qts. fresh gooseberries
¼ c. cornstarch
Almond Pastry for 2-crust (9") pie, baked as shell, rim trim and "diamonds"
Whipped cream (optional)

• Cook ⅓ c. water and sugar in saucepan over low heat 2 to 3 minutes. Add berries. Simmer gently about 5 minutes, until cooked but still whole.
• Using small strainer, remove berries from syrup. Place in pie shell.
• Dissolve cornstarch in remaining ⅓ c. water. Stir into syrup. Cook over moderate heat until thick and clear, stirring constantly, about 3 minutes.
• Cool to lukewarm. Pour over berries.
• Decorate with diamond-shaped pieces of pastry. To serve, cut into wedges with "diamond" centering each. Serve with puff of whipped cream or ice cream, if desired. Makes 6 servings.

Almond Pastry:

1½ c. sifted flour
1 tblsp. sugar
⅔ c. butter or other shortening
2 tsp. almond extract
2 to 3 tblsp. water

• Mix flour and sugar; cut in butter until mixture resembles coarse meal.
• Sprinkle almond extract, then water, 1 tblsp. at time, over mixture, tossing quickly with fork until dough forms ball. (Use only enough water for mixture to just cling together—should not be wet or slippery.)
• Form dough into smooth ball between palms of hands. Wrap, and chill at least 30 minutes for easier handling. Makes 6 tart shells or one 8" or 9" pie shell and decorative trim.

RASPBERRY TARTS

One of those wonderful à la mode desserts

1 c. sugar (approximately)
1½ to 2 tblsp. quick-cooking tapioca
½ tsp. cinnamon
3 c. firm raspberries, not too ripe
6 unbaked tart shells (see Almond Pastry recipe)
⅓ c. currant jelly, melted
Whipped cream or ice cream—vanilla or fruit flavor

• Mix sugar, tapioca and cinnamon; sprinkle over berries. Mix gently to keep berries whole. Place in tart shells, molded in muffin pans or other baking cups.
• Bake in moderate oven (375°) 20 minutes, until almost done.
• Carefully spoon melted jelly over berries. Return to oven.
• Bake 5 to 10 minutes longer, until baked and "set." Cool.
• Serve with scoops of ice cream for real eating pleasure. Makes 6 servings.

RAISIN PIE

Pies made from seedless and seeded raisins taste different—why not try both

2 c. raisins (seedless or seeded)
2 c. boiling water
⅓ c. granulated sugar
⅓ c. brown sugar
2¼ tblsp. cornstarch
⅛ tsp. salt
2 tsp. grated lemon rind
½ tsp. grated orange rind
2 tblsp. lemon juice
1 tblsp. orange juice
Pastry for 2-crust (9") pie
2 tblsp. butter or margarine

• Add raisins to water; simmer until tender (3 to 5 minutes). Combine sugars, cornstarch and salt; stir into hot raisins. Cook slowly, stirring constantly, to full rolling boil; boil 1 minute. Remove from heat.
• Blend in fruit rinds and juices. Pour hot filling into pastry-lined pie pan; dot top with butter. Cover with remaining pastry.
• Bake in hot oven (425°) 30 to 40 minutes. Serve slightly warm, plain or with scoops of lemon sherbet.

Variations: Use a lattice pastry top or cook filling in saucepan until it thickens; partly cool and pour into a baked pie shell. Spread with meringue and bake in moderate oven (350°) until delicately browned, 12 to 15 minutes. Or omit meringue and at serving time spread on thin layer of whipped cream.

Tips From Good Cooks: After rinsing in warm water, spread raisins in a flat pan. Cover and heat slowly in moderate oven (350°) until they become plump. To obtain full flavor, cut raisins in halves with your kitchen scissors.

STRAWBERRY-PINEAPPLE PIE

If there's a spring song in pies, here it is—bright and delicious

Pastry for 2-crust (9″) pie
1 (10 oz.) pkg. frozen strawberries
1 (13½ oz.) can frozen pineapple chunks
3 or 4 tblsp. quick-cooking tapioca
½ c. sugar
¼ tsp. salt
2 tblsp. butter or margarine

• Line 9″ pie pan with half of pastry made from pie crust mix or your favorite recipe. Defrost fruit just enough to separate.
• Combine tapioca, sugar and salt. Mix with fruit and let stand at least 15 minutes.
• Place fruit mixture in pastry-lined pan; dot with butter. Cover top with remaining pastry; turn and flute edges. Cut top so steam can escape.
• Bake in hot oven (425°) 40 to 50 minutes, or until thoroughly baked.
• For a special party, roll out leftover pastry and cut into small strawberry and pineapple shapes. Brush with egg yolk "paint" (recipe follows).
• Bake in slow oven (325°) about 8 to 10 minutes, using care not to let pastry brown. Garnish pie for a party with these miniature pastry fruits.

Egg yolk "paint": Blend 1 egg yolk and 1 tsp. cold water; divide in 3 parts, tint one red, one yellow and one green. To paint pastry, use a clean watercolor brush for each color.

FRESH BLUEBERRY PIE

Awakens laggard appetites

1 baked (9″) pie shell
4 c. fresh (or frozen) blueberries
1 c. sugar
3 tblsp. cornstarch
¼ tsp. salt
¼ c. water
1 tblsp. butter or margarine

• Line cooled pie shell with 2 c. blueberries.
• To make sauce, cook remaining berries with sugar, cornstarch, salt and water over medium heat until thickened. Remove from heat, add butter and cool.
• Pour over berries in shell. Chill until serving time. If desired, serve with whipped cream.

APPLE-ORANGE PIE

A real favorite in the South

6 c. tart apples, sliced thin (6 or 7 medium apples)
½ c. orange juice
½ to ¾ c. sugar
¼ c. brown sugar
½ tsp. ground cinnamon
2 tblsp. butter or margarine
Pastry for 2-crust (9″) pie

• Place apples, juice and sugars in saucepan. Add water barely to cover. Cook gently until apples are just tender. Remove apples and cook juices until syrup thickens. Add cinnamon.
• Place apples in pastry-lined pie pan; add syrup and dot with butter. Cover with remaining pastry; flute rim. Bake in hot oven (425°) about 40 minutes.

PUMPKIN PIE

Blue ribbon winner in a famous Ohio Pumpkin Show

1½ c. cooked or canned pumpkin
¼ c. white corn syrup
2 eggs
½ c. evaporated milk
2 tblsp. butter or margarine
½ c. hot milk
½ c. brown sugar, firmly packed
½ tsp. salt
1½ tsp. cinnamon
½ tsp. nutmeg
¼ tsp. ginger
⅛ tsp. cloves
1 unbaked (9″) pie shell

- Combine pumpkin, corn syrup, eggs and evaporated milk.
- Stir butter into hot milk.
- Combine brown sugar, salt and spices. Mix until well blended.
- Combine all three mixtures; pour into pastry-lined pie pan. (For crisp crust, brush pastry with egg white or melted butter.)
- Bake in hot oven (425°) 15 minutes, then reduce heat to moderate oven (350°) and bake 35 minutes longer or until knife inserted comes out clean.
- Just before serving, garnish, if you wish, with dollops of whipped cream topped with slivered, candied ginger.

MINIATURE PECAN TARTS

Watch everyone choose this famous Southern delicacy

1 (10 oz.) pkg. pastry mix
2 eggs
½ c. sugar
¼ tsp. salt
¼ c. butter or margarine
¾ c. dark corn syrup
¾ c. small pecan halves
1 tsp. vanilla

- Prepare dough from pastry mix according to package directions. Roll thin and cut out 3 dozen 2½" circles. Fit into tiny muffin pans (1¾" measured across top of cup).
- Beat together, with rotary beater, eggs, sugar, salt, butter and corn syrup. Stir in pecans and vanilla.
- Pour into unbaked tart shells, ¼" from top. Bake in moderate oven (350°) 25 to 30 minutes until filling is set and pastry is lightly browned. Makes about 3 dozen.
- If you don't have small muffin pans you can make tins from heavy aluminum foil as follows: With 3" round cutter, mark 3 dozen circles on foil. Cut out and shape over bottom of a 1½" round spice can. Save to re-use.

PRUNE-APRICOT TARTS

Grandmother's prize turnovers often were fat with this luscious fruit filling

1½ c. dried prunes
1 c. dried apricots
½ c. sugar
½ tsp. salt
1 tsp. cinnamon
½ tsp. nutmeg
¾ c. prune liquid
Pastry for 2-crust (9") pie

- Rinse, drain prunes. Cook in boiling water to cover, about 15 minutes; drain. Remove pits.
- Rinse and drain apricots; but do not cook.
- Chop and combine fruits; add sugar, salt, spices and prune liquid; bring to boil. Simmer until thickened, about 5 minutes.
- Roll out pastry (one pkg. pie crust mix or pastry recipe based on 2 c. flour) and cut into 5" circles. Place about 2 tblsp. filling in center of each circle. Moisten edges and pinch together in about 6 or 7 pleats. (Or for Grandmother's old-fashioned turnovers, place filling on half pastry circle, fold over and seal edges with tines of fork or handle of teaspoon.) Bake in hot oven (425°) 15 to 18 minutes. Makes about 9 turnovers or tarts, or 1 pie.

Variation: To dress up tarts for special guests, whip ½ c. heavy cream; fold in ¼ c. sieved cottage cheese. Add ¼ tsp. grated orange rind. Chill. Spoon on tarts just before serving.

Hostess Tip: Keep these baked turnovers in the freezer to bring out and heat in a moderate oven (350°) to serve with coffee when friends stop by.

APRICOT MERINGUE PIE

Wonderful dessert from the golden fruit

Meringue Shell:

4 egg whites
¼ tsp. salt
¼ tsp. vinegar
1 c. sugar

• Beat whites until frothy. Add salt and vinegar: continue beating until whites stand in stiff peaks.
• Add sugar, 1 tblsp. at a time. Beat well after each addition.
• Spoon into a well buttered and floured 9″ glass pie pan. Build up sides inside rim, using a spoon or pastry tube for a ruffled edge. Keep well inside rim; meringue will spread over rim during baking.
• Bake in very slow oven (275°) 45 minutes. Turn off heat. Let shell remain in oven 30 minutes. Remove and let cool out of draft.

Apricot Filling:

2 tblsp. water
1 tsp. unflavored gelatin
4 egg yolks
½ tsp. lemon rind
5 tblsp. lemon juice
⅔ c. sugar
1 c. dried apricots, cooked and puréed
1 c. heavy cream, whipped
⅓ c. slivered, toasted almonds

• Measure 2 tblsp. water into a small bowl. Sprinkle gelatin over surface and let stand until softened.
• Combine egg yolks, lemon rind and juice. Beat well. Add sugar; beat.
• Pour into the top of double boiler. Place over boiling water. Cook until very thick (about 7 minutes), stirring constantly. Add softened gelatin and stir until dissolved. Add puréed apricots; cool.
• Whip cream; fold into apricot mixture. Fill meringue shell. Chill overnight. Sprinkle top with almonds.

LEMON MERINGUE PIE

A miracle of luscious eating

1¼ c. sugar
3 tblsp. flour
3 tblsp. cornstarch
⅛ tsp. salt
2 c. boiling water
3 egg yolks
2 tblsp. grated lemon rind
⅓ c. strained lemon juice
1 tblsp. butter or margarine
1 (9″) baked pie shell
3 egg whites
6 tblsp. sugar

• Combine 1¼ c. sugar, flour, cornstarch and salt in top of double boiler; gradually stir in water. Cook until mixture thickens (about 10 minutes).
• Beat yolks; add rind, juice and butter. Add cooked mixture slowly; return to double boiler. Cook about 5 minutes longer, stirring constantly. Cool slightly; pour into baked pie shell.
• Make meringue by beating egg whites until stiff; add 6 tblsp. sugar gradually, beating until mixture is stiff and glossy. Pile lightly over cooled filling, spreading completely to edge of pastry. Bake in slow oven (325°) 20 to 25 minutes, or until lightly browned.

Lemon Snow Pie: Fold the meringue into the hot lemon filling. Cool slightly and pour into baked pastry shell. Chill.

Quick Lemon Pie: Prepare packaged lemon pudding pie filling mix as directed on package. While this filling is hot, add 1 tblsp. each butter and lemon rind.

Lime Meringue Pie: Substitute fresh lime juice and rind for lemon. Tint delicate green with food color, if desired.

Ice Cream Pies

Ice Cream Shell: Line 8″ pie pan with 1 pt. vanilla or favorite ice cream flavor. For a more generous "crust" use 1½ pts. Cut ice cream in ½″ slices; lay on bottom of pan to cover. Cut remaining slices in half; arrange around pan to make rim. Fill spots with ice cream where needed. With tip of spoon, smooth "crust." Freeze until firm before adding the filling.

SWEET 'N TART LEMON PIE

An ice cream pie everyone praises

3 eggs
½ c. sugar
¼ tsp. salt
¼ c. lemon juice
1 c. heavy cream
1 frozen vanilla ice cream shell

• Beat together 1 whole egg and 2 yolks. Add sugar, salt and lemon juice. Cook over low heat, stirring constantly until thick. Cool.
• Beat egg whites until stiff; then whip cream (no need to wash beaters). Fold cream into lemon mixture. Next, fold in whites. Pour into ice cream shell. Freeze.

SPICY PUMPKIN PIE

Use butter almond or butter pecan ice cream to make shell

1 c. cooked or canned pumpkin
1 c. sugar
¼ tsp. salt
¼ tsp. ginger
1 tsp. cinnamon
¼ tsp. nutmeg
1 c. heavy cream
1 frozen ice cream shell

• Mix together pumpkin, sugar, salt and spices. Cook over low heat 3 minutes. Cool.
• Whip cream; fold into pumpkin mixture. Pour into ice cream shell. Freeze.

BUTTERSCOTCH PECAN PIE

Pudding and ice cream duet

¼ c. brown sugar
1 (4 oz.) pkg. butterscotch pudding or pie filling mix
1 tsp. vanilla
2 c. heavy cream
½ c. chopped pecans
2 frozen ice cream shells

• Add sugar to pudding mix. Prepare as directed on package. Cool; then add vanilla.
• Whip cream. Add nuts to butterscotch mixture. Fold in whipped cream. Pour into 2 shells. Freeze.

Variation: Omit nuts and use butter pecan ice cream shell.

CRANBERRY NUT PIE

A make-ahead dessert that surprises everyone—different

2 c. fresh or frozen cranberries
1 c. sugar
1 c. heavy cream
½ c. chopped nuts
1 frozen vanilla ice cream shell

• Put cranberries through food chopper, using fine blade. (Grind your cranberries frozen—less juicy.) Add sugar; let stand overnight.
• Whip cream. Mix cranberries and nuts. Fold in whipped cream. Pour into ice cream shell. Freeze.

CHOCOLATE PEPPERMINT PIE

Perfect flavor combination

1 tblsp. cocoa
½ c. sugar
1 (4 oz.) pkg. chocolate pudding mix
1 tsp. vanilla
2 c. heavy cream
2 frozen ice cream shells

• Combine cocoa and sugar. Add to pudding mix and prepare as directed on package. Cool; add vanilla.
• Whip cream, and fold into chocolate mixture. Pour into peppermint stick ice cream shells. Freeze.

STRAWBERRY VANILLA PIE

Strawberries and ice cream—good team

1 (10 oz.) pkg. frozen strawberries, sliced (use fresh strawberries in season)
2 c. heavy cream
¼ c. confectioners sugar
½ tsp. vanilla
Red food color
2 frozen vanilla ice cream shells

• Partially thaw berries.
• Whip cream; add sugar, vanilla and food color. Fold in strawberries. Pour into ice cream shells. Freeze.

Party-Special Meringues

Meringue shells, with almost any filling, are a wonderfully delicious dessert—fair and feathery light, tender inside, yet lightly crisp on the outside. Make them white or a soft pastel color. Your success is assured with our recipe and a very slow oven to keep them from browning even the slightest.

You'll need an electric mixer for the long beating, unless you have some helpers with strong arms.

Bake the meringue shells the day ahead of your party, and prepare your filling. You can use any fresh, canned or frozen fruit or combinations in interesting colors—like raspberries in white or pink shells, peaches in pale green. Or use sherbet or ice cream, like vanilla ice cream with frozen blueberry topping in a pink shell. Try, too, a custard filling like our thick Lemon Custard Pudding, with shaved sweet chocolate topping in pale green shells.

The size you make the shells depends on the way you'll use them. If they're for dessert and coffee for a party, make them about 4½″ in diameter as suggested in the recipe. Since they're very sweet, you'll make them smaller for dessert with a meal—from 2″ to 3″.

If you're making the shells in quantity and have a number 12 or 16 ice cream scoop, you can speed up the shaping this way: Scoop out a meringue on the paper, then reverse the scoop and use the rounded side to make the hole in the mound of meringue. The shells are removed more easily from the baking sheet if it's covered with unglazed paper.

Strawberry Parfait Ring Berries and cream in glamorous new dress. Try other summer fruits in frozen cream ring. Recipe on page 18, first chapter.

Luscious Chocolate Torte Guests taste, then ask for the recipe. You will find this Refrigerator Cake, page 296, in Dishes to Make Ahead.

Molded Garden Salad Marinate vegetables in salad dressing for zip, then set in gelatin. Wilt-proof; make it ahead. Recipe, page 47, in Chapter 3.

Barbecued Chicken Nothing like it when fixed outdoors over coals. Food tastes better mixed with fresh air. Recipe, page 42, in Chapter 3.

PASTEL MERINGUE SHELLS

A memorable dessert—low baking temperature assures beautiful, pale tints

6 egg whites
1 tsp. cream of tartar
2 c. sifted sugar
2 tsp. vinegar
1 tsp. vanilla
About 30 drops food color

• Combine egg whites and cream of tartar in large mixer bowl. Beat at high speed until soft peaks form.

• Gradually add sugar, while beating; then beat in vinegar and vanilla. Beat about 12 minutes longer, until stiff peaks bend only slightly.

• For pastel shells, add food color now—enough to get desired tint, beating to blend evenly.

• For each meringue, pile 2 large rounded tblsp. of mixture in a solid high heap on 4½" circles of unglazed paper on baking sheet.

• With rounded side of spoon, make a hole in top by pushing down quickly and lightly to round out a good-sized well. Dip spoon often in hot water to prevent sticking and to shape smooth shells.

• Bake in very low oven (150°) 1 hour. Turn off heat but leave shells in oven until completely cooled. (Low temperature is secret of clear tint.)

• If you prefer hard shells, bake in very low oven (150°) 3 hours, then turn off heat but leave in oven until cooled.

• To remove paper, peel gently from shells. Makes 6 large meringues.

LEMON CUSTARD PUDDING

This is a delicious meringue filling

1 tsp. unflavored gelatin
¼ c. cold water
3 eggs yolks, beaten
1 c. light cream
¾ c. sugar
¼ tsp. salt
¼ c. lemon juice
1 tblsp. grated lemon rind

• Soften gelatin in water.

• Blend egg yolks and cream in top of double boiler. Stir in remaining ingredients.

• Cook over boiling water, stirring constantly, until mixture coats spoon slightly, about 6 minutes (175°).

• Add softened gelatin; stir to dissolve. Cool.

• Pour into pint jar to chill and store. Makes 2 cups.

CHOCOLATE MERINGUES

Dainty cookies to serve with ice cream

4 egg whites
⅛ tsp. salt
¼ tsp. cream of tartar
1 c. sugar
2 c. corn flakes, crushed
1 tsp. vanilla
¾ c. semi-sweet chocolate pieces

• Beat eggs until foamy; sprinkle on salt and cream of tartar and beat to make stiff meringue. Gradually spinkle in sugar and beat to make stiff meringue.

• Fold in corn flakes, vanilla and chocolate pieces.

• Drop from teaspoon 2" apart onto greased baking sheet. Bake in moderate oven (350°) about 15 to 18 minutes, or until firm to touch. Cool briefly in pan before removing to rack. Makes 3½ to 4 dozen.

Variation: Add 1¼ tsp. almond extract and 1 c. chopped almonds or 1 c. chopped walnuts.

ORANGE TAPIOCA A LA MODE

A dessert gay as sunshine

2 eggs, separated
6 tblsp. sugar
2 c. milk
3 tblsp. quick-cooking tapioca
¼ tsp. salt
1 tblsp. grated orange rind
1 tblsp. lemon juice

• Beat egg whites until foamy. Add 3 tblsp. sugar gradually. Beat to soft peaks.
• Beat yolks slightly. Add milk, 3 tblsp. sugar, tapioca, salt and rind. Bring to boil over low heat, stirring constantly.
• Remove from heat. Add juice. Slowly add a little hot mixture to egg whites; mix well. Quickly stir in remaining mixture. Chill. Makes 6 to 8 servings.

Topping: Trim with canned mandarin or fresh orange sections and flaked coconut. Top with orange sherbet.

STEAMED DATE PUDDING

Spring this on your gourmet guests—it will win them over

½ c. melted shortening
1 c. brown sugar, firmly packed
2 eggs, well beaten
1½ c. dates, pitted and chopped
1½ c. sifted flour
½ tsp. salt
1 tsp. baking soda
1 tsp. grated lemon rind
½ c. chopped black walnuts
Hard Sauce

• Combine shortening, brown sugar and eggs; stir in dates.
• Sift together dry ingredients. Fold into egg mixture with lemon rind and nuts. (If pudding seems dry, add 1 to 2 tblsp. milk.) Fill 8 greased individual molds ⅔ full.
• Steam on rack (with 1" hot water) in covered kettle 1 hour, or in pressure pan as directed by manufacturer.
• Serve warm with Fluffy Hard Sauce. Makes 8 to 10 servings.

Variation: Bake in well greased 7" tube pan or 1 qt. shallow mold. (Pudding is delicate and doesn't steam well in deep mold.) Seal snugly with foil.

FLUFFY HARD SAUCE

The rich crown good puddings deserve

½ c. butter or margarine
2 c. sifted confectioners sugar
1 egg yolk, beaten
1 tsp. vanilla
1 egg white, beaten stiff

• Cream butter; blend in sugar. Add egg yolk and vanilla; beat well.
• Fold egg whites into creamed mixture. Serve at room temperature. Makes 1⅔ cups.

FROZEN FRUIT CAKE

A Farm Journal 5-star recipe

1 c. heavy cream or evaporated milk
2 c. milk
½ c. sugar
¼ c. flour
¼ tsp. salt
2 eggs, beaten
1 tsp. vanilla
1 c. white raisins
2 c. cake crumbs—white cake, vanilla wafers or macaroons
½ c. candied red cherries, halved
¼ c. chopped candied green fruit—cherries, citron or mild ginger
1 c. broken pecans

• Chill cream for whipping.
• Scald milk in top of double boiler.
• Mix together sugar, flour and salt; add to milk all at once. Cook over hot water about 3 minutes, until smooth and medium thick, stirring constantly.
• Pour cooked mixture over beaten eggs; return to double boiler. Cook until thick, about 3 minutes, stirring constantly. Add vanilla. Cool.

• Stir raisins, crumbs, chopped fruits and nuts into mixture (reserve a few whole red and green fruits and nuts).
• Whip chilled cream and fold into mixture. Pour into 1½ qt. loaf pan, bottom greased and lined with waxed paper on which fruits and nuts have been arranged. Freeze overnight. Will keep in freezer about two weeks. Makes 8 servings.

BLUEBERRY BETTY

Your spoon never treated you to a better blueberry dish

4 c. (½") bread cubes
¾ c. melted butter or margarine
¼ c. sugar
1 tsp. cinnamon
2 c. fresh or frozen blueberries
2 tblsp. lemon juice
½ c. brown sugar

• Toss bread cubes with butter, sugar and cinnamon.
• Sprinkle berries with lemon juice and brown sugar. Alternate layers of bread cubes with fruit mixture, spreading evenly in 7½ ×12" baking dish.
• Bake in moderate oven (350°) 20 to 30 minutes, until bubbly. Makes 6 servings. May be served warm or cold, plain or topped with cream or whipped cream.

Favorites In Our Chocolate Collection

CHOCOLATE ANGEL PIE

A happy meal ending

Meringue Crust:

3 egg whites
⅛ tsp. salt
¼ tsp. cream of tartar
½ tsp. vanilla
¾ c. sugar
⅓ c. chopped pecans or walnuts

• Combine egg whites, salt, cream of tartar and vanilla. Beat stiff. Add sugar gradually, beating until very stiff and sugar is dissolved.
• Spread in well greased 9" pie pan. Build up sides. (Use cake decorator for fancy edge.)
• Sprinkle bottom with nuts.
• Bake in very slow oven (275°) 1 hour. Cool, fill with Chocolate Filling.

Chocolate Filling: Melt ¾ c. semi-sweet chocolate pieces in top of double boiler over boiling water. Add ¼ c. hot water, 1 tsp. vanilla and ⅛ tsp. salt. Stir until completely smooth. Cool. Fold in 1 c. heavy cream, whipped. Fill shell. Chill 4 hours or overnight. Serve with layer of whipped cream spread over top.

CHOCOLATE CHIP TORTE

Chocolate fans adore this dessert

1¾ c. sifted flour
2 tblsp. cocoa
½ tsp. salt
1 tsp. baking soda
1 c. boiling water
1 c. finely cut dates
1 c. shortening
1 c. sugar
2 eggs, beaten
1 tsp. vanilla
1 (6 oz.) pkg. semi-sweet chocolate pieces
¾ c. chopped nuts
Whipped cream

• Sift together flour, cocoa, salt and soda.
• Pour boiling water over dates.
• Cream shortening and sugar. Add eggs and vanilla. Beat thoroughly.
• Stir dates and water. Add alternately with flour mixture, mixing until just smooth after each addition.
• Spread in greased 13×9" pan.
• Sprinkle top with chocolate and nuts.
• Bake in moderate oven (350°) 45 minutes. Serve warm or cold.
• Cut in squares; top with spoonful of whipped cream. Makes 12 servings.

CHOCOLATE LOAF CAKE

Another chocolate delight

1½ c. sifted cake flour
1¼ c. sugar
½ c. cocoa
1¼ tsp. baking soda
1 tsp. salt
⅔ c. shortening
1 c. buttermilk or thick sour milk
1 tsp. vanilla
2 eggs, unbeaten

• Sift dry ingredients into mixing bowl; cut in shortening.
• Add milk and vanilla; beat 200 strokes (2 minutes by hand or low speed of mixer). Add eggs; beat 2 minutes more.
• Bake in greased and floured 9×5×3" pan in moderate oven (350°) 45 to 60 minutes.
• Remove from pan; cool and frost with Butterscotch Chocolate Frosting.

Butterscotch Chocolate Frosting: In saucepan combine 3 (1 oz.) squares unsweetened chocolate, ¼ c. butter or margarine, ½ c. light cream, ⅔ c. brown sugar, packed and ¼ tsp. salt. Bring to boil, stirring constantly; cook until chocolate is melted. Remove from heat; add vanilla and enough confectioners sugar for good spreading consistency (about 3 c.). Spread over sides and top of cake.

Variation: For sour milk, substitute sweet milk with ¼ tsp. cream of tartar or 1 tblsp. lemon juice or vinegar added.

SALTED PEANUT COOKIES

A Farm Journal 5-star recipe

2 eggs, beaten
2 c. brown sugar, firmly packed
1½ c. butter or margarine, melted
1½ c. salted peanuts, chopped
2½ c. sifted flour
1 tsp. baking soda
1 tsp. baking powder
½ tsp. salt
3 c. rolled oats
1 c. corn flakes

• Beat eggs; add sugar and mix well. Stir in butter, then peanuts and mix.
• Sift together flour, soda, baking powder and salt. Combine with rolled oats and corn flakes. Combine with egg mixture and stir well to mix.
• Drop tablespoonfuls of dough on greased baking sheet. Bake in hot oven (400°) 8 to 10 minutes. Makes 6 dozen.

Note: The good cook who sent us this recipe drops the dough from a teaspoon for dainty tea- or coffee-time treats, a tablespoon for family-size cookies. With a glass of milk they make what children vote the perfect snack.

CHOCOLATE MINT PIE

Chocolate and peppermint flavors go together like strawberries and cream

10 to 12 thin chocolate wafers
1 (4 oz.) pkg. vanilla pudding mix
2 c. milk
¼ c. semi-sweet chocolate pieces
½ tsp. peppermint extract

• Line bottom of 9" pie pan with cookies. Line sides with cookies cut in half, rounded side up.
• Add milk to pudding mix and cook as directed on package.
• Spoon 2 tblsp. of pudding over semi-sweet chocolate pieces. Let stand about 5 minutes to soften. Add peppermint extract; blend well.
• Pour remaining pudding into cookie-lined pie pan.
• Drop chocolate-mint mixture on top of filling, one spoonful at a time; swirl with tip of spoon.
• Chill about an hour. Makes 6 servings.

Punch—Hot or Cold

Hostesses like to serve icy cold or steaming hot fruit and tomato juice drinks to their guests. All these are worth sipping—we've served them successfully many times when entertaining in our Countryside Kitchens.

CRANBERRY SPIKE

As tasty as it is colorful

1 pt. cranberry juice cocktail
1 (12 oz.) can apricot nectar
2 tblsp. lemon juice

• Combine chilled juices. Ice, and serve. Makes 1 quart.

RASPBERRY FLOAT

A pretty party punch that sparkles

3 (3 oz.) pkgs. raspberry flavor gelatin
4 c. boiling water
1½ c. sugar
4 c. cold water
½ c. lime juice
2¼ c. orange juice
1¼ c. lemon juice
1 qt. ginger ale
2 (10 oz.) pkgs. frozen raspberries

• Dissolve gelatin in boiling water; add sugar, cold water and juices; cool, but do not chill or gelatin will congeal. (If you let it congeal, heat just enough to bring back to liquid state.)
• When time to serve, pour punch into punch bowl. Add ginger ale and frozen raspberries. Stir until raspberries break apart and are partially thawed. Makes about 4 quarts.

MULLED APRICOT NECTAR

Heat this spicy treat after guests arrive—they'll enjoy its aroma and taste

1 (46 oz.) can apricot nectar
½ lemon, sliced
2 (2½") sticks cinnamon
15 whole cloves
8 whole allspice berries

• Combine all ingredients in heavy saucepan and bring to boiling point. Simmer gently 5 minutes.
• Remove from heat; cover; allow to stand 30 minutes.
• Strain. If you wish, sweeten to taste with honey or sugar. Heat before serving. Makes about 5 cups.
Good idea: Pass a plate of fudge.

SPICED TOMATO JUICE

Hostess success tip: Serve this hot cheery drink and delight your friends

1 (46 oz.) can tomato juice
6 tblsp. brown sugar
6 whole cloves
2 (2½") sticks cinnamon
½ lemon, sliced

• Combine all ingredients in heavy saucepan. Bring to boil; simmer 5 minutes. Strain and heat before serving. Makes about 5 cups.

Good idea: Serve with a grilled cheese sandwich.

Pretty Desserts

This quartet of dessert recipes can prove to you, that there's nothing like a luscious dessert to make a woman famous as a good cook.

ORANGE PEKOE TEA ICE CREAM

You need an ice cream freezer to make this delightful dessert

2½ c. milk, scalded
6 whole cloves
1 tblsp. grated orange rind
2 tblsp. orange pekoe tea
1 envelope unflavored gelatin
⅓ c. cold water
¼ tsp. salt
¾ c. sugar
4 egg yolks, slightly beaten
¾ c. honey
4 egg whites, stiffly beaten
3 c. light cream

• Scald milk with cloves and orange rind. Add tea; let stand 5 to 8 minutes over hot water.
• Soften gelatin in water.
• Strain milk; return to double boiler top. Add salt, sugar and egg yolks, which have been mixed with some hot milk. Cook, stirring constantly, until thickened.
• Remove from heat, add softened gelatin; blend thoroughly. Add honey.
• When cold, fold in egg whites and cream. Freeze. Makes 1 gallon.

GOLDEN GLOW ICE CREAM

Well worth getting out the ice cream freezer—the best use for egg yolks left after baking an angel cake

¼ c. grated orange rind
2 c. milk
1 c. sugar
1 c. light corn syrup
½ tsp. salt
8 egg yolks, beaten
2 c. light cream
4 c. fresh orange juice

• Place orange rind in small cheesecloth bag. Scald with milk in top of double boiler.
• Add sugar, syrup and salt to egg yolks, which have been mixed with some hot milk.
• Cook, stirring constantly, until mixture coats spoon; cool.
• Stir in cream and orange juice. Freeze. Makes 1 gallon.

STRAWBERRY PARFAIT RING

A Farm Journal 5-star recipe

1 c. sugar
⅓ c. boiling water
Red food color (optional)
4 egg whites
1 tsp. vanilla
⅛ tsp. salt
2 c. heavy cream, whipped
Strawberries (about 1½ qts.)
Flaked or shredded coconut
1 c. heavy cream

• Cook sugar with water until syrup spins a thread (235°). Add a few drops of color if you wish a pink mold.
• Beat egg whites until stiff; gradually add hot syrup; continue beating until cool and light. Add vanilla and salt.
• Fold in the whipped cream; pour into a 2 qt. ring mold and freeze.
• At serving time unmold and fill center with berries. Sprinkle a fluff of coconut on top. If ring is not tinted, use coconut tinted pink. Border the ring with puffs of

whipped cream, one for each serving. Makes 12 to 16 servings.

Whipped Cream Garnish: Whip 1 c. heavy cream until fairly stiff. Drop from spoon onto cookie sheet or flat pan to make little mounds, and freeze. Garnish each puff with a whole strawberry just before serving.

Individual Strawberry Parfait Rings: Freeze parfait mixture in individual angel food pans or ring molds. To serve, turn out on dessert plates and fill centers with fresh or frozen strawberries. (Other berries or sliced peaches may be used.) Calorie conscious cooks may wish to omit the whipped cream garnish.

STRAWBERRY SNOWBALLS

½ gal. vanilla ice cream
1½ c. (3½ oz. can) flaked coconut
2 (1 lb.) pkgs. frozen whole strawberries

• Using small scoop, make balls of ice cream. Set each ball as shaped on tray in freezer.

• Spread coconut on large sheet of waxed paper. Roll ice cream balls in coconut to coat lightly. Return to freezer. When firm, package and keep in freezer.

• To serve, partly thaw strawberries in a large shallow serving dish. Top with snowballs; garnish each with a berry. Makes 10 to 12 servings.

Tempting Party Confections

ALMOND ACORNS

¼ c. semi-sweet chocolate pieces
⅔ c. blanched almonds, toasted
1 (2½ oz.) jar chocolate sprinkles

• Place chocolate pieces in pan over hot water. Let stand until soft, then stir to smooth paste.

• Toast nuts—spread blanched almonds in shallow pan; heat in moderate oven (350°) about 20 minutes. Or deep-fat fry at 265° about 1 minute until light brown.

• Dip one end of each almond into melted chocolate, then into chocolate sprinkles. Place on waxed paper until firm. Makes about 5 dozen.

PEAR PINWHEELS

Compliment catchers

¾ lb. dried pears
⅓ c. chopped dates
2 tblsp. honey
2 tblsp. chopped Brazil nuts, pecans or walnuts

• Pour boiling water over pears. Let stand 5 minutes, until softened. Drain; remove excess moisture with paper toweling. Pears should not be mushy, but soft and pliable.

• Arrange half of pears, skin side down, as rectangle on waxed paper. Overlap edges slightly so there are no spaces between pears. Cover with waxed paper and, with rolling pin, flatten into one smooth sheet. Repeat with remaining pears.

• Combine dates (should be moist and soft) and honey. Blend smooth; add nuts, and mix well.

• Spread half of mixture on each pear sheet. Roll, jelly roll fashion, into a log. Smooth down any rough spots with knife or small spatula. If surface seems too moist, let stand overnight at room temperature.

• Cut each log into 16 pieces. Makes 32 pinwheels.

APRICOT STICKS

Golden confection no one can resist

20 large dried apricot halves
½ c. flaked or shredded coconut
¼ c. candied pineapple, chopped fine
Sugar

• Wash apricots. Cover with boiling water; let stand 5 minutes, or until softened. Drain; dry on paper toweling.

• Combine coconut and pineapple; Mix well.

• Flatten each apricot half, skin side down. Spread portion of coconut-pineapple mixture over surface. Roll, jelly roll fashion.

• Place on tray to dry at room temperature.

• Roll in sugar. Store in loosely covered container at room temperature. Makes 20 apricot candies.

ALMOND FRUIT ROLL

¾ c. blanched almonds, toasted
½ c. preserved citron
¼ c. candied orange peel
⅓ c. candied cherries
1 c. sifted confectioners sugar
2 tblsp. soft butter

• Grind almonds, using food chopper with medium blade. Reserve ¼ c. for use later.

• Grind citron, orange peel and cherries. Combine with almonds. Add sugar and nuts; mix thoroughly.

• Divide mixture into fourths; form each into a log about 1½″ thick and 5″ long.

• Spinkle remaining nuts on sheet of waxed paper. Roll logs in nuts, completely covering outside surface. Wrap in waxed paper and chill. Slice each roll in 10 pieces. Makes 40 candies.

PRUNE CRYSTAL BALLS

Holiday tempters

1¾ c. sugar
2 c. water
2 thin slices of lemon
2 c. dried prunes
Salted peanuts or walnuts or Brazil nuts
2 tsp. grated orange rind

• Combine 1½ c. sugar, water and lemon slices in saucean. Place over medium heat; bring to boil.

• Add prunes, and boil slowly, uncovered, 45 minutes. Cool; drain well. With sharp paring knife, slit prunes open and carefully remove pits.

• Fill centers with two or three salted peanuts, a walnut half or a piece of Brazil nut. (For variation, stuff a miniature marshmallow into prune with nuts.)

• Blend orange rind with remaining sugar. Roll stuffed prunes in mixture. Makes about 3 dozen.

ORANGE WALNUTS

1½ c. sugar
½ c. orange juice
Few drops yellow food color (optional)
1 tsp. grated orange rind
½ tsp. vanilla
3 c. walnut halves

• Combine sugar and orange juice in saucepan. Cook to soft ball stage (240° on candy thermometer). Add a little food color to tint a delicate orange.

• Remove from heat, add orange rind, vanilla and walnut halves. Stir until syrup begins to look cloudy. Before it hardens, drop by spoonfuls on waxed paper. Separate nuts. Makes about 1 pound.

Salad Specials

Salad luncheons are a first choice with women—they're colorful and simplify meal planning. With a beverage and hot rolls, you often can dispense with dessert. We also include our cranberry salad because so many men say it's tops in turkey and chicken dinners.

CRANBERRY SALAD

Lettuce never framed a tastier salad

4 c. cranberries
½ c. water
3 c. sugar
1 (6 oz.) or 2 (3 oz.) pkgs. lemon flavor gelatin
1 c. boiling water
2 c. diced celery
1 c. chopped black walnuts
Crisp lettuce or salad greens

• Combine cranberries and water in saucepan; simmer until skins burst.
• Add sugar. Cook 3 minutes more.
• Combine gelatin and boiling water; stir to dissolve gelatin. Chill until syrupy.
• Fold in cranberries, celery and nuts. Pour into 2 qt. mold or 8 individual molds. Chill until firm.
• Unmold on lettuce or other greens. Serve with fluffy fruit dressing. Makes 8 servings.

GREEN GAGE PLUM SALAD

Your guests will taste and then ask for a pencil and paper to copy the recipe

1 (1 lb. 4 oz.) can green gage plums
1 (3 oz.) pkg. lemon flavor gelatin
Juice of 1 lemon
½ tsp. salt
¾ c. slivered toasted almonds
Crisp lettuce cups
Salad dressing

• Drain juice from plums; add water to make 2 c. liquid. Heat to boiling, and pour over gelatin. Add lemon juice and salt; stir to dissolve. Cool until thickened.
• Pour 2 tblsp. gelatin into 6 baking cups or individual molds. Chill until firm.
• Chill remaining gelatin until syrupy.
• Pit and chop plums. Fold with almonds into gelatin. Spoon over clear gelatin in molds. Chill until firm.
• Serve in lettuce cups with dressing. Makes 6 servings.

KRIS KRINGLE WREATH SALAD

Layers 1 and 2:

1 tblsp. unflavored gelatin
½ c. cold water
¾ c. hot water
½ tsp. salt
1 tblsp. lemon juice
Green pepper
Pimiento
1 (8 oz.) carton creamed cottage cheese

Layer 3:

4 c. tomato juice
1 bay leaf
1 tblsp. chopped onion
½ tsp. celery salt
Dash cayenne pepper
2 tblsp. unflavored gelatin
½ c. cold water
1 tsp. Worcestershire sauce
1 tsp. lemon juice
Crisp salad greens

• Soften gelatin in cold water; add hot water and salt. Stir to dissolve gelatin. Add lemon juice. Pour 3 tblsp. in 8″ ring mold; chill until firm. Arrange holly leaf pattern cut from green pepper with small pimiento rounds for berries over gelatin. Add 3 or 4 tblsp. liquid gelatin. Chill.

• Mix remaining gelatin with cottage cheese. Pour over first layer.

• For 3rd layer, combine tomato juice, bay leaf, onion, salt and pepper; simmer 15 minutes. Remove bay leaf.

• Soften gelatin in cold water.

• Add Worcestershire, lemon juice and gelatin to hot tomato mixture. Cool.

• Pour over cottage cheese layer; chill. Unmold; garnish with greens. Makes 8 to 10 servings.

FRUIT SALAD PLATE

A fruit plate for your luncheon party—serve with hot rolls

1 head lettuce
1 bunch escarole
3 oranges, peeled
3 grapefruit, peeled
2 doz. cooked prunes
1 (1 lb. 2 oz.) can Queen Ann cherries or dark sweet cherries
1 (1 lb. 14 oz.) can peach halves
2 red apples
Orange or grapefruit juice
2 (8 oz.) cartons cottage cheese
1 pt. fresh or frozen whole strawberries
Lime-Pineapple sherbet
Apple-Honey Dressing

• Wash and crisp greens. Section oranges and grapefruit (remove membrane). Pit prunes. Drain canned fruit. Slice and core apples; cover with orange or grapefruit juice to avoid darkening.

• Place greens on salad plates with mound of cottage cheese in center of each. Top with peach half, cut side up. Arrange other fruits around cottage cheese.

• Just before serving, fill peach half with Lime-Pineapple Sherbet, and serve with Apple-Honey Dressing (recipes follow). Makes 6 salads.

APPLE-HONEY DRESSING

1/3 c. sugar
1/4 tsp. dry mustard
1/2 tsp. paprika
1/4 tsp. salt
1/2 c. smooth applesauce
1/4 c. strained honey
3 tblsp. lemon juice
1 tblsp. vinegar
1/4 tsp. grated lemon rind
1 tsp. celery seed
1/2 c. oil

• Combine all ingredients except oil in bowl. Mix well. Add oil slowly, beating thoroughly. Chill. Shake or beat well before serving. Makes 1½ cups.

LIME-PINEAPPLE SHERBET

Cool and colorful atop fruits

1 c. sugar
2 c. water
1 (3 oz.) pkg. lime flavor gelatin
1 (6 oz.) can frozen limeade concentrate
1 tblsp. lemon juice
1 (9 oz.) can crushed pineapple
Few drops green food color
1½ c. milk

• Mix sugar and water in saucepan; bring to boil. Remove from heat; add gelatin. Stir until it dissolves.

• Add limeade concentrate, lemon juice, pineapple, food color and milk. Mix together. Pour into refrigerator tray; freeze firm.

• Remove to mixer bowl, break into pieces. Beat until light and fluffy. Fill trays and freeze. Makes 2 quarts. (This can be made ahead and frozen. Beat light and fluffy the day it is to be eaten.)

Waffle Surprises

When guests arrive and you have no exciting dessert, bake waffles at the table. These recipes are off-beat ones—Paired off with coffee, they ably pinch-hit for hot bread.

SPONGE CAKE WAFFLES

Bake at the table and serve for dessert

- **5 eggs, separated**
- **1 c. sugar**
- **1 c. sifted cake flour**
- **1 tsp. baking powder**
- **½ tsp. salt**
- **1½ c. chopped dates**
- **½ c. chopped nuts**
- **½ c. oil**
- **½ tsp. lemon rind**

• Beat egg yolks until light. Add sugar gradually; beat after each addition.
• Sift dry ingredients together. Add dates, nuts, yolks, oil, lemon rind. Mix well.
• Beat egg whites until stiff. Fold into batter.
• Pour 1 tblsp. batter on each section of moderately hot waffle iron. Bake 4 minutes. Makes 4 servings.

PUMPKIN NUT WAFFLES

Spread with butter, pour on maple syrup

- **2 c. sifted cake flour**
- **4 tsp. baking powder**
- **1 tsp. salt**
- **¾ tsp. cinnamon**
- **¼ tsp. nutmeg**
- **3 eggs, separated**
- **1¾ c. milk**
- **½ c. melted shortening**
- **½ c. canned pumpkin**
- **¾ c. chopped pecans**

• Sift together dry ingredients.
• Beat egg yolks. Combine with milk, shortening and pumpkin. Add to dry ingredients.
• Beat egg whites stiff. Fold into batter. Pour onto hot waffle iron. Sprinkle with 3 tblsp. nuts. Makes four 9" waffles.

CHOCOLATE NUT WAFFLES

Almost like a brownie

- **1½ c. sifted flour**
- **2 tsp. baking powder**
- **½ tsp. salt**
- **1 c. sugar**
- **2 eggs, separated**
- **¾ c. milk**
- **½ c. oil**
- **4 squares chocolate, melted**
- **½ c. chopped nuts**
- **1 tsp. vanilla**

• Sift dry ingredients together.
• Beat egg yolks. Combine with milk and oil. Add chocolate. Pour liquid into dry ingredients. Add nuts and vanilla.
• Beat egg whites until stiff. Fold into batter.
• Pour onto moderately hot waffle iron. Bake 3 minutes. Makes 4 servings.

GINGERBREAD WAFFLES

Fragrant dessert tempters

- **2 c. sifted flour**
- **1 tsp. salt**
- **1¼ tsp. baking soda**
- **2½ tsp. ginger**
- **1¼ tsp. cinnamon**
- **¼ tsp. cloves**
- **1 c. dark molasses**
- **½ c. sour milk**
- **1 egg, slightly beaten**
- **⅓ c. oil**
- **1 egg white, stiffly beaten**

• Sift dry ingredients together.
• Combine molasses, milk and beaten egg. Add to dry ingredients, then add oil. Mix well. Fold in beaten egg white.
• Pour onto a moderately hot waffle iron. Bake 3 minutes. Serve with vanilla ice cream. Makes 5 to 6 servings.

Main Dishes

These recipes are the kind every woman needs to have down pat, to welcome guests at mealtime.

POTATO-TUNA BAKE

Couldn't be easier—no peeling, cleaning, measuring or pot watching, and no waste

2 (7 oz.) cans tuna, chunk style
3 (2¼ oz.) cans shoestring potatoes
1 (14½ oz.) can evaporated milk
1 (10½ oz.) can cream of mushroom soup
1 (3 oz.) can mushroom pieces
1 (4 oz.) can chopped pimientos

• Dump all ingredients into a greased 2 qt. casserole and mix.
• Bake in moderate oven (375°) about 45 minutes. Makes 6 to 8 servings.

Variation: Substitute 1 (1 lb.) can salmon for the tuna.

To complete the menu have a buttered green vegetable, like peas, fruit salad, cookies and milk to drink. For a company meal, change the salad to lettuce dressed with sour cream, sugar and vinegar, mixed. Omit cookies; make biscuit-type shortcake and fix strawberries while main dish bakes. (Shortcake bakes while you eat first course.)

MACARONI-MEAT BALL SOUFFLE

A fluffy, delicate casserole that satisfies big appetites—wins praise

2 c. elbow macaroni (7 to 8 oz. pkg.)
2 c. milk, scalded
3 tblsp. butter or margarine
1 c. grated or shredded sharp process cheese
1 tblsp. minced onion
½ tsp. salt
⅛ tsp. pepper
3 eggs, separated
3 c. lightly packed soft bread crumbs

• Cook macaroni as directed on package, using 8 c. boiling water and 1 tblsp. salt. Cook until macaroni is tender. Drain.
• Combine milk, butter, cheese, onion, salt and pepper. Stir to melt cheese.
• Beat whites until stiff but not dry. Then beat yolks thoroughly. Add gradually to hot milk, stirring constantly. Add bread crumbs. Mix well. Remove from heat. Fold into egg whites.
• Fill bottom of well greased 2 qt. casserole with half of macaroni. Pour in half of milk-egg sauce. Add half of meat balls. (Recipe follows.)
• Add remaining macaroni and sauce. Arrange remaining meat balls over top.
• Place casserole in shallow pan. Set on lower rack in oven. Add 1" boiling water to pan. Bake in moderate oven (375°) 50 to 60 minutes, until knife comes out clean. Makes 6 to 8 servings.

COMPANY MEAT BALLS

Just the crown for puffed-up, browned macaroni casserole

½ lb. ground beef
½ lb. ground lean pork
1 egg, slightly beaten
½ c. fine day-old bread crumbs
⅓ c. milk
1 tsp. salt
⅛ tsp. white pepper
2 tsp. minced onion
2 tblsp. fat or oil

• Combine all ingredients except fat. Mix thoroughly. Shape into 12 to 14 balls, about 1½" in diameter.

• Heat fat in skillet over medium heat. Lightly brown meat balls. Cook 20 to 30 minutes; remove from pan.

2

Dishes to Tote

If you wish to rate as one of the neighborhood's best cooks, read on! Use these recipes for covered-dish suppers and you'll soon be recognized as one of those rare, gifted women with a flair for food. (Grandmother spoke of such talented cooks as women born with silver spoons in their hands.)

To garner a reputation as a cook, always carry attractive, tasty food to covered-dish suppers. Remember that when you unpack it at the church, Grange, Farm Bureau, Extension club or other supper, you set it out for everyone—it's your exhibit.

Fix show-off food—something unusual enough to attract attention and add a touch of glamor. See that it's sturdy enough to hold up during travel—utensils designed for dishes that travel, such as covered cake and pie pans, help protect foods. Most of all, strive to make your tote-dishes taste extra good. Soon folks will watch eagerly for what you bring and their turn to sample it. Then they'll start asking you in advance to bring one of your specialties. That's when you've arrived!

This chapter contains recipes for tote-dishes that have built enviable reputations for good cooks—a big black walnut cake, a hickory nut cake, golden orange-carrot cookies, tawny pumpkin and toasty pecan pies and party ham loaf, to single out a few. Other chapters have more recipes for dishes that will win praise at these cooperative meals for which country life is famous. You don't need a crystal ball to tell you this kind of social gathering is on the up-grade. It divides the work and cost between the kitchens and pocketbooks of friends and neighbors. And there's more enjoyment in a wonderful meal when everyone helps fix it.

Look in this cookbook for recipes contributed by farm women—the bright-with-color, molded fruit salads, beauty queens of covered-dish suppers; relishes that spark up menus; the pies, cakes, breads, vegetable combinations and meat dishes that are good carriers. They will be spectacular at group meals.

Main Dishes

SAVORY SAUSAGE RICE

Enthusiastic reports on this dish come from members of Farm Journal's Family Test Group who tried it in their kitchens

2 lbs. bulk sausage
1 c. finely chopped green pepper
¾ c. chopped onion
2½ c. coarsely chopped celery
2 (2⅛ oz.) pkgs. chicken noodle soup mix
4½ c. boiling water
1 c. uncooked rice
½ tsp. salt
¼ c. melted butter or margarine
1 c. blanched almonds, slivered (optional)

• Brown sausage in large skillet; pour off excess fat. Add green pepper, onion and 1 c. celery; sauté.
• Combine soup mix and boiling water in large saucepan; stir in rice. Cover and simmer 20 minutes, or until tender. Add sausage mixture and salt; stir well.
• Pour into greased baking dish, about 12×8×2". Sprinkle remaining celery over top; drizzle with melted butter. Bake in moderate oven (375°) 20 minutes. Makes 10 servings. If almonds are used, sauté all celery with green pepper and onion. Mix most of almonds with other ingredients; save a few to sprinkle on top. Omit melted butter.

BEEF LOAF

Take scalloped potatoes along and everyone will be happy

2 lbs. ground beef
1 medium onion, sliced
2 eggs, unbeaten
1½ tsp. dry mustard
1 tsp. chili powder
1½ c. stewed tomatoes
2 slices wheat bread, broken into pieces
2 tsp. salt
¼ tsp. pepper
4 strips bacon

• Combine all ingredients except bacon. Pack into 8×4" loaf pan. Place bacon strips across top. Bake in moderate oven (350°) 1 hour. Makes 8 to 10 servings.

POTATO-CHEESE SCALLOP

You won't go wrong on this if there are men at the table

2 tblsp. butter or margarine
1 medium onion, thinly sliced
6 medium potatoes (about 2 lbs.)
1 c. grated sharp process cheese
2 tblsp. flour
2 tsp. salt
⅛ tsp. pepper
2½ c. milk
¼ c. finely crushed cracker crumbs or potato chips

• Melt butter in skillet; sauté onion slices until lightly browned.
• Peel and slice potatoes; put layer in bottom of greased 2 qt. baking dish. Add ¼ of onion slices; sprinkle with ¼ c. cheese, ½ tblsp. flour, salt and pepper. Repeat layers. Pour milk over top.
• Sprinkle with crumbs. Cover and bake in moderate oven (350°) 1 hour. Remove cover for last 15 minutes of baking time. Makes 6 servings.

PARTY HAM LOAF

Jelly-brushed loaf glistens

5 c. ground cooked ham
⅔ c. minced onion
1 c. rolled oats
½ tsp. pepper
1 tsp. Worcestershire sauce
¼ tsp. ground cloves
2 eggs, slightly beaten
⅓ c. milk
¼ c. currant jelly
1 tblsp. prepared horse-radish

• Combine ham, onion, oats, seasonings, eggs and milk; mix thoroughly. Shape like a ham in shallow baking pan; score top in diamond designs.
• Bake in moderate oven (375°) 45 minutes. Remove; brush top with melted jelly and horse-radish mixed. Trim with pineapple and maraschino cherries if desired. Makes 8 servings.

MUSTARD HAM LOAF

Fancy it up with spiced crab apples when you take it to a party

1½ lbs. ground smoked ham
½ lb. ground fresh pork
1 c. milk
1 c. bread cubes (2 slices)
1 tblsp. dry mustard
½ c. brown sugar
¼ c. vinegar
2 tblsp. water

• Combine meat, milk and bread cubes. Mix lightly; form into loaf; place in shallow baking pan.
• Combine remaining ingredients for sauce; pour over meat.
• Bake in moderate oven (375°) 1½ hours, basting often with sauce in pan. Garnish with spiced crab apples. Makes 8 to 10 servings.

STUFFED TOMATOES

Tasty meat loaf mixture baked in red-ripe tomatoes

8 large firm tomatoes
3 tblsp. oil
½ c. minced onion
2 cloves garlic, chopped
¾ lb. ground pork shoulder
¼ lb. ground veal
1½ tsp. salt
¼ tsp. pepper
2 tblsp. chopped parsley
8 small mushrooms

• Wash tomatoes; slice off rounded bottom and scoop out pulp.
• Pour oil into 9×12″ baking pan. Add onion, garlic and scooped out tomato pulp; heat in moderate oven (375°) 6 to 7 minutes.
• Pour mixture into bowl, add meat and seasonings. Mix well.
• Stuff tomatoes lightly with meat mixture; return to oiled pan.
• Bake in moderate oven (375°) 25 to 30 minutes. Remove from oven, top each with tomato slice (removed to scoop out tomato) and a mushroom; secure with toothpick. Bake 5 minutes longer. Makes 8 servings.

SPANISH LIMAS

Hearty vegetable bake—tomato-cheese flavored

1 medium onion, chopped
1 green pepper, chopped
2 tblsp. butter or margarine
1 c. cooked or canned tomatoes
1 tsp. Worcestershire sauce
1 tsp. salt
¼ tsp. pepper
⅛ tsp. cayenne
2 c. cooked frozen or canned lima beans
1½ c. grated process cheese

• Fry onion and pepper slowly in butter until golden. Add tomatoes; simmer 10 minutes. Add seasonings and well-drained beans; combine.
• Alternate layers of bean mixture and cheese in greased 1 qt. casserole.
• Bake in moderate oven (350°) 30 minutes. Makes 6 servings.

HAM-NOODLE CASSEROLE

You may wish to take two of these casseroles to the Farm Bureau supper

1 (8 oz.) pkg. noodles
1½ c. chopped cooked ham
1 c. grated sharp process cheese
1 (10½ oz.) can condensed cream of chicken soup
½ c. milk
½ tsp. curry powder
2 tblsp. butter or margarine

• Cook noodles as directed on package; drain.
• Combine ham and ¾ c. cheese; alternate layers of noodles and ham in greased 1 qt. baking dish.
• Mix soup, milk and curry; pour over noodles. Sprinkle top with remaining cheese; dot with butter.
• Bake in moderate oven (375°) 20 to 30 minutes. Makes 6 servings.

CHEESE-HAM CASSEROLE

It carries well—tastes good!

1 (5 oz.) pkg. narrow noodles
2 c. cooked ham, cubed or ground
2 c. (½ lb.) grated process cheese
½ c. diced green pepper
1 c. fresh or 1 (4 oz.) can sliced mushrooms
1 (10½ oz.) can condensed tomato soup
1 soup can water

• Cook noodles as directed on package; drain well.
• Combine ham, cheese, green pepper and mushrooms.
• Alternate layers of noodles and ham mixture in greased 3 qt. casserole. Dilute soup with water; pour over layers in casserole.
• Bake in moderate oven (350°) 1 hour. Makes 6 servings.

TURKEY-OYSTER CASSEROLE

Why not ask someone to bring cranberry salad or relish?

½ c. butter or margarine
¼ c. flour
2 c. milk
½ tsp. salt
⅛ tsp. pepper
¼ tsp. dry mustard
2 c. diced cooked turkey
1 c. ground cooked ham
1 pt. oysters, preheated in juice
3 c. mashed potatoes
Paprika

• Melt butter; stir in flour; blend.
• Add milk, salt, pepper and mustard. Cook over low heat, stirring constantly, until smooth and thickened.
• Add remaining ingredients. Pour into greased 1½ qt. casserole. Arrange mashed potatoes around edge of casserole; sprinkle with paprika.
• Bake in moderate oven (350°) 30 minutes. Makes 6 to 8 servings. Serve with tossed salad for a good family supper.

BAKED CHICKEN LEGS

The drumstick gang will gather 'round this children's dream come true

12 chicken legs
2 eggs, beaten
1½ c. cracker crumbs
1 tblsp. salt
½ tsp. pepper
¾ tsp. monosodium glutamate
½ c. butter or margarine

• Dip chicken pieces in egg, then in cracker crumbs. Sprinkle with salt, pepper and monosodium glutamate.
• Place chicken in casserole; dot with butter. Cover; place on rack in roaster.
• Bake in moderate oven (350°) 45 to 60 minutes, or until tender. Makes 8 servings.

CHOPS BAKED-IN-SOUP

No watching—a dish you'll be proud to share with friends

6 rib chops, veal or pork
1 tsp. salt
¼ tsp. pepper
2 tblsp. butter or margarine
⅓ c. finely chopped onions
4 c. thinly sliced potatoes
1 (10½ oz.) can condensed cream of mushroom soup
1¼ c. milk

• Rub chops with salt and pepper.

• Melt butter in skillet; add onions and chops; brown lightly on both sides.

• Put sliced potatoes in buttered 2 qt. baking dish. Arrange chops over potatoes.

• Add soup and milk to onions in skillet. Blend until smooth. Pour over chops. Cover. Bake in moderate oven (350°) 30 minutes. Uncover; continue baking for 30 to 40 minutes, until potatoes are done. Makes 6 servings.

BROCCOLI AU GRATIN

2 (10 oz.) pkgs. frozen cut broccoli
2 (10½ oz.) cans condensed cream of chicken soup
½ c. buttered toasted bread crumbs
½ c. grated sharp cheese

• Cook broccoli as directed on package; drain. Bring soup to boil; add broccoli.

• Place in casserole. Sprinkle with crumbs and cheese. Serve hot. Makes 6 servings.

Cranberry Relishes

Take your pick of the three cranberry relishes when making the salad. Or tote them without molding.

CRANBERRY RELISH SALAD

2 (3 oz.) pkgs. fruit flavor gelatin
2 c. cranberry relish

• Follow directions on package to make gelatin. Cool; when mixture begins to thicken, fold in cranberry relish.

• Pour into molds; chill until firm. To serve, unmold and decorate with fresh cranberries and parsley sprigs. Pass mayonnaise or salad dressing. Makes 8 servings.

CRANBERRY-PINEAPPLE RELISH

4 c. (1 lb.) fresh cranberries
1 c. crushed pineapple, drained
1 tsp. lemon juice
1 c. sugar

• Wash and remove stems from cranberries. Put through food chopper.

• Add pineapple, lemon juice and sugar; mix well. Chill. Makes 2 pints.

CRANBERRY-ORANGE RELISH

4 c. (1 lb.) fresh cranberries
2 oranges, quartered
2 c. sugar

• Wash and remove stems from cranberries. Remove seeds from oranges.

• Put cranberries and oranges through food chopper. Add sugar and mix well. Chill. Makes 2 pints.

CRANBERRY-APPLE RELISH

4 c. (1 lb.) fresh cranberries
2 apples, quartered and cored
⅓ lemon, with peel
2 c. sugar

• Wash and stem cranberries.

• Put cranberries, apples and lemon through food chopper. Add sugar and mix well. Chill. Makes 2 pints.

MEAT BALLS IN TOMATO SAUCE

If several people bring this, no one will go home hungry or unhappy

Sauce:

2 tblsp. olive oil
1 clove garlic, minced
¾ c. chopped onion
2 (10 oz.) cans tomato purée—2½ cups
1 tsp. salt
⅛ tsp. pepper
1 bay leaf
2 tsp. sugar

• Heat oil in saucepan. Add garlic and onion; cook over low heat until golden brown.

• Add tomato purée and seasonings. Bring to boil; reduce heat; simmer 45 minutes. While sauce cooks, prepare meat balls.

Meat Balls:

3 slices white bread
⅓ c. milk
1 lb. ground beef
2 eggs, unbeaten
1 tsp. salt
⅛ tsp. pepper
1 clove garlic, minced
2 tblsp. chopped parsley
2 tblsp. shortening

• Break bread into mixing bowl. Add milk and let stand about 5 minutes, or until milk is absorbed.

• Add meat, eggs, seasonings, garlic and parsley. Mix until blended.

• Shape into 12 medium balls.

• Melt shortening in skillet; add meat and brown well.

• Add sauce; simmer with meat balls for 45 minutes more. Serve with ½ pound (8 oz.) spaghetti, cooked. Makes 6 servings.

BEEF PILAU

Satisfies the hungriest

1 lb. round or chuck steak
2 tblsp. butter or margarine
1 large onion, finely chopped
1 tsp. salt
1 c. packaged quick-cooking rice
1 (1 lb. 4 oz.) can tomatoes
1 (1 lb. 4 oz.) can red kidney beans
1 (10½ oz.) can beef consommé
1 tsp. chili powder
¼ tsp. oregano
1 tsp. salt

• Cut meat into 1″ cubes; heat butter in skillet. Add onion, salt and meat; brown.

• Fill 2 qt. casserole with: layer of meat, then rice, tomatoes and beans. Repeat.

• Combine consommé, chili powder, oregano and salt. Pour into casserole.

• Bake, uncovered, in moderate oven (350°) 1 hour. If casserole is shallow, add a little water as needed to keep mixture moist. Makes 4 to 6 servings.

CHILI CON CARNE

Hot corn bread and cool pineapple salad will help make this meal memorable

2 tblsp. shortening
½ c. chopped onion
1 or 2 cloves garlic, minced
1 lb. ground beef
1 tblsp. chili powder
½ tsp. salt
¼ tsp. cayenne pepper
⅛ tsp. black pepper
2 (10½ oz.) cans condensed tomato soup
1 (1 lb.) can red kidney beans (2 c.)

• Melt shortening in skillet; add onion, garlic and beef. Brown slightly.

• Add seasonings, soup and kidney beans; bring to boil. Cover; simmer slowly 30 minutes. Stir occasionally to prevent sticking (may cool, chill and reheat at serving time).

• Serve hot with crisp crackers and relishes. Makes 6 servings.

BEET PERFECTION SALAD

Zippy in flavor and colorful enough to brighten any meal—especially good with pork or chicken

2 (1 tblsp.) envelopes unflavored gelatin
½ c. cold water
1½ c. hot beet juice or boiling water
1 c. cider vinegar
Juice of 1 lemon
1 tblsp. prepared horse-radish
½ c. sugar
1 tsp. salt
2 c. finely shredded cabbage
2 c. coarsely shredded or diced cooked beets

• Soften gelatin in cold water; add hot liquid to dissolve. Stir in vinegar, lemon juice, horse-radish, sugar and salt. Chill until thick and syrupy.
• Fold in cabbage and beets. Pour into 1½ qt. mold or 8 individual molds. Makes 8 servings.

MOLDED FRUIT SALAD

A golden salad bouquet

1 (3 oz.) pkg. lemon flavor gelatin
1 (3 oz.) pkg. orange flavor gelatin
4 c. hot water
1 (1 lb.) can sliced cling peaches
1 (1 lb.) can pear halves
3 bananas
1 bunch water cress

• Dissolve lemon gelatin in 2 c. water as directed on package. Dissolve orange gelatin the same way in separate bowl. Chill lemon gelatin to syrupy stage. Set bowl in big pan of iced water to speed job.
• Drain peaches and pears. Lightly oil 7 c. mold. Set in pan of iced water. Add ¼ c. lemon gelatin. Tilt and turn mold to make thin coating of gelatin to anchor peach slices. Place 5 slices, or more if needed, around edge of mold for a pretty crown. Add a little gelatin to anchor.
• Add 1 sliced banana to half of lemon gelatin. Spoon into mold. Cool until firm (takes only a few minutes).
• Dice remaining peaches into rest of gelatin. Make another layer. Chill.
• Meanwhile, cool orange gelatin to syrupy stage. Add 2 sliced bananas. Pour about ⅓ over molded layers. Line sides of mold with well-drained pear halves, letting ends rest on firm layer. Fill mold. Chill until firm.
• To unmold, run tip of knife around edge of gelatin to loosen. Dip mold in warm (not hot) water a few seconds. Invert on serving tray. Garnish with fresh water cress or lettuce. Serve with Tangy Fruit Dressing. Makes 8 to 10 servings.

Tangy Fruit Dressing: Combine ⅓ c. sugar, 1 tblsp. flour, ½ tsp. salt and ¾ tsp. ginger in top of double boiler. Beat 1 egg yolk; add ¾ c. pineapple juice, 2 tblsp. lemon juice. Mix with dry ingredients. Cook over boiling water, stirring constantly, until thick, about 3 minutes. Cool. Blend in ¼ c. mayonnaise or salad dressing and ½ c. heavy cream, whipped.

ELISABETH'S FRUIT SALAD

Multiply this recipe by three, or have three club members bring it

1 (3 oz.) pkg. lemon flavor gelatin
2 c. water
1 tblsp. lemon juice
1 c. cooked dried prunes
½ c. cooked dried apricots
1 (3 oz.) pkg. cream cheese
¼ c. chopped walnuts

• Dissolve gelatin in 1 c. hot water. Add 1 c. cold water and lemon juice. Chill until syrupy.
• Pit cooked prunes. Cut prunes and apricots in small pieces.
• Whip cream cheese (at room temperature) until smooth.
• Whip thickened gelatin until frothy. Mix in cream cheese until smooth.
• Fold in prunes, apricots and nuts.
• Pour into 8×8" pan or 6 individual molds. Chill; serve on crisp lettuce leaves. Makes 6 servings.

RICE-BEAN SALAD

The excellence of this take-along salad was a nice surprise in our Test Kitchens

1 c. cooked rice
1 (1 lb.) can kidney beans, drained
2 hard-cooked eggs, chopped
½ c. sweet pickles, chopped
¼ c. chopped onion
¼ c. chopped celery
¼ c. chopped green pepper
½ tsp. salt
¼ tsp. pepper
⅓ c. mayonnaise or salad dressing
Crisp lettuce or other greens

• Combine ingredients in mixing bowl. Chill in refrigerator. Serve on crisp greens. Makes 6 to 8 servings.

Note: For the best flavor combine ingredients while rice is hot.

CHILI WITH TOMATOES

A slow-cooked favorite made hearty with red Mexican beans

1 pt. red Mexican beans
4 strips bacon
2 medium onions, chopped
1 green pepper, chopped
1 lb. ground beef
3½ tsp. salt
1 (1 lb. 4 oz.) can tomatoes
1 (1 lb. 4 oz.) can tomato juice
1 tblsp. chili powder

• Cover beans with water and soak overnight. Drain.
• Fry bacon until crisp. Remove from skillet. Add chopped onions and pepper; brown lightly.
• Add ground beef. Break into pieces with fork; sprinkle with 1 tsp. salt. Brown well.
• Combine beans, meat and remaining ingredients. Cover and simmer until beans are tender, about 3 hours. May cook in slow oven (300°). Makes 2 quarts.

ASPARAGUS CASSEROLE

Here's the answer when it's your turn to bring a vegetable dish

1 (1 lb. 4 oz.) can asaragus spears
2 tblsp. butter or margarine
1 tblsp. flour
1 tsp. salt
¼ tsp. pepper
½ c. evaporated milk
½ c. fine cracker crumbs
2 hard-cooked eggs, chopped
½ c. (⅛ lb.) cheese, grated

• Drain asparagus, reserving liquid.
• Melt butter; blend in flour, salt and pepper.
• Add evaporated milk to asparagus liquid (enough to make 1½ c.). Stir into flour mixture. Blend until smooth. Cook 2 minutes.
• Spread asparagus in bottom of greased, shallow, 1½ qt. casserole. Reserve a few asparagus spears for top.
• Sprinkle half cracker crumbs over asparagus. Add eggs and half sauce. Sprinkle with remaining crumbs. Arrange rest of asparagus spears over top. Pour over remaining sauce. Sprinkle with grated cheese.
• Bake in moderate oven (350°) about 30 minutes, or until casserole is bubbly. Makes 6 to 8 servings.

GARLIC OLIVES

Almost fill a pint jar with drained, canned ripe olives. Add five garlic cloves, sliced, and two thin lemon slices. Pour on enough olive or salad oil to cover, put lid on jar and chill 1 to 2 days. Drain to serve (strain oil and use to make French dressing for tossed salads).

HONEY RYE BREAD

Guaranteed to please in any crowd—homemade breads always make a hit

¼ c. honey
4 tsp. salt
2 tblsp. shortening or oil
1 tblsp. caraway or anise seed (optional)
1½ c. milk, scalded
2 pkgs. granular or compressed yeast
1 c. water
3 c. light rye flour
3½ c. sifted flour (about)
Melted butter or margarine

• Add honey, salt, shortening and caraway seed to milk; cool to lukewarm.

• Soften granular yeast in warm (110°) water; or compressed yeast in lukewarm (85°) water.

• Combine yeast with milk mixture; add rye flour and 1 c. flour. Beat thoroughly. Add remaining flour to make stiff dough.

• Turn dough out on floured board, let rest 10 minutes. Knead until smooth and elastic.

• Place in well greased bowl, turn once to bring greased side up. Cover, and set in warm place (80° to 85°), to rise until doubled, about 40 minutes.

• Without punching down, turn out on lightly floured board; divide into 2 equal parts. Shape into loaves. Place in 2 greased 9×5×3" pans.

• Cover and let rise until doubled, about 30 minutes.

• Bake in moderate oven (375°) about 50 minutes. Turn out of pans on rack away from drafts. Brush tops with melted butter or margarine. Makes 2 loaves.

Take-Along Cheese Spread for Honey Rye Bread: Melt 1 lb. Cheddar-type process cheese, diced, and 1 (14½ oz.) can evaporated milk in top of double boiler. Cook, stirring constantly, until cheese melts. Remove from heat and season to taste with minced chives, pimiento or parsley or chopped olives, pickle relish, Worcestershire sauce or prepared mustard. Makes about 1½ cups.

OATMEAL BREAD

It takes the center of the stage at any group supper

2 c. rolled oats
⅓ c. molasses
2 tsp. salt
2 tblsp. shortening or oil
1 c. boiling water
2 pkgs. granular or compressed yeast
¼ c. water
1¼ c. milk, scalded
5 c. sifted flour (about)

• Put oats, molasses, salt and shortening into large bowl. Pour boiling water over mixture; cool 10 minutes.

• Soften granular yeast in warm water (110°); compressed yeast in lukewarm water (85°).

• Cool milk to lukewarm; add yeast and milk to oats mixture; then add 1½ c. flour; beat thoroughly. Add flour to make a stiff dough.

• Turn dough out onto floured board. Let rest 10 minutes. Knead until smooth and elastic.

• Place in well greased bowl, turn once to bring greased side up. Cover and set in warm place (80° to 85°) to rise until doubled, about 40 minutes.

• Without punching down, turn out on lightly floured board; divide into 2 equal parts. Shape into loaves. Place in 2 greased 9×5×3" pans.

• Cover, and let rise until doubled, about 30 minutes.

• Bake in moderate oven (375°) about 50 minutes. Turn out of pans onto cooling rack away from drafts. Makes 2 loaves.

WHOLE WHEAT BREAD

It's extra-special

¼ c. molasses
1 tblsp. salt
3 tblsp. shortening or oil
1½ c. milk, scalded
2 pkgs. granular or compressed yeast
¾ c. water
3 c. whole wheat flour (stir flour before measuring)
4 c. sifted flour (about)

• Add molasses, salt, shortening to milk; cool to lukewarm.
• Soften granular yeast in warm water (110°); compressed yeast in lukewarm water (85°).
• Combine yeast with milk mixture; add whole wheat flour. Beat thoroughly. Add enough flour to make stiff dough.
• Turn onto floured board; let rest 10 minutes. Knead until smooth and elastic.
• Place in well greased bowl, turn once to bring greased side up. Cover and set in warm place (80° to 85°) to rise until doubled, about 40 minutes.
• Without punching down, turn out on lightly floured board. Divide into 2 equal parts. Shape into loaves. Place in 2 greased 9×5×3″ pans. Cover and let rise until doubled, about 40 minutes.
• Bake in moderate oven (375°) about 50 minutes. Turn out of pans on rack away from drafts. Makes 2 loaves.

POPPYSEED ROLLS

Hot rolls—praiseworthy and they'll receive plenty of it!

2 pkgs. granular or compressed yeast
½ c. water
½ c. plus 1 tblsp. sugar
1 c. scalded milk
½ c. shortening
2 tsp. salt
3 eggs, beaten
6 c. sifted flour (about)
Milk
Poppyseeds

• Sprinkle yeast over warm (110°) water or crumble compressed over lukewarm (85°) water. Add 1 tblsp. sugar. Let stand 5 to 15 minutes.
• Combine 1 c. milk, remaining sugar, shortening and salt in large mixing bowl; stir to melt shortening. Cool to lukewarm.
• Stir in eggs and 2 c. flour; mix well. Add yeast and beat 4 to 5 minutes (by hand, or mixer at medium speed).
• Add 2 to 3 c. flour; beat until smooth. Turn out on lightly floured board and knead until smooth and elastic, adding more flour as necessary to make soft dough.
• Shape into round; place in large greased bowl; grease top. Let rise until doubled.
• Punch down; divide in half. Roll each into 9″ circle; cut each circle into 12 wedges. Roll up, starting at wide ends.
• Place on greased baking sheet. Brush with milk; sprinkle liberally with poppyseeds. Let rise until doubled.
• Bake in hot oven (400°) 10 minutes; reduce heat to moderate (375°), and bake about 15 minutes more. Makes 2 dozen.

MINCE-CRANBERRY PIE

For social functions during the holidays

1⅔ c. mincemeat
1 (7 oz.) can whole cranberry sauce (1 c.)
¼ c. honey
½ tsp. grated lemon rind
1 tsp. flour
⅛ tsp. salt
Pastry for 2-crust (9″) pie

• Combine mincemeat, cranberry sauce (canned or home cooked), honey and rind. Add flour and salt; mix. Fill unbaked pie shell. Moisten pastry rim with water.
• Roll out top crust; cut design (with lattice pie cutter if you have one). Adjust top over filling; seal and crimp edges.
• Bake in hot oven (400°) 35 minutes, until lightly browned.

Variation: You may use 1 pkg. mincemeat. Prepare according to directions.

CRANBERRY-RAISIN PIE

The dessert to tote to a chicken or turkey supper

1 c. water
1 tblsp. cornstarch
1¾ c. sugar
⅛ tsp. salt
1 tsp. vanilla
2 drops almond extract
2 c. fresh cranberries
1 c. seeded raisins
Pastry for 2-crust (9″) pie

• Combine water and cornstarch in heavy saucepan. Bring to boil, stirring constantly. Let cook until clear.
• Add sugar, salt and flavorings. Cool.
• Put cranberries through food chopper.
• Rinse raisins in cold water; drain. Put through food chopper. (Cold water rinse avoids sticking.)
•Add cranberries and raisins to cornstarch mixture.
• Pour into pastry-lined pie pan. Top with pastry strips, lattice fashion, or a solid-rolled crust.
• Bake in hot oven (425°) 10 minutes. Reduce to slow oven (325°); continue baking 25 to 30 minutes.

PRUNE PLUM PIE

The crunchy brown crumb top complements the tart fruit filling

3½ c. pitted prune plums
½ c. sugar
¼ c. flour
¼ tsp. salt
1 tblsp. lemon juice
2 tsp. melted butter or margarine
1 (9″) unbaked pie shell

Crump Topping:
¾ c. flour
½ c. sugar
⅓ c. butter or margarine

• Wash and dry plums. Split; remove pits; cut in quarters.
• Combine sugar, flour and salt; add to plums. Add lemon juice and butter. Mix lightly. Spoon into pastry shell. Sprinkle on Crumb Topping.
• Bake in hot oven (425°) 10 minutes. Reduce to moderate oven (350°) and bake until filling is tender, about 20 minutes.

Crumb Topping: Sift flour and sugar. Cut in butter to make fine crumbs.

TOASTY PECAN PIE

The best we ever ate

1 c. white corn syrup
½ c. light brown sugar, packed
3 eggs, unbeaten
1 tsp. vanilla
¼ tsp. salt
1 c. shelled pecans
Pastry for 1-crust (8″) pie

• Combine syrup, sugar, eggs, vanilla and salt. Mix well; add pecans.
• Pour into an unbaked 8″ pie shell. Bake in a moderate oven (350°) for 50 minutes or until done.

QUICK APRICOT CHIFFON PIE

Velvet-toned, yellow-orange dessert—pretty and delicious

1 (3 oz.) pkg. lemon chiffon pie filling
1 c. apricot nectar
⅛ tsp. almond extract
⅓ c. sugar
1 (9″) baked pie shell

• Dissolve filling in ½ c. apricot nectar, heated to boiling. Beat in remaining nectar and almond extract. Add sugar and beat until peaks form.
• Spoon into baked crust and swirl filling. Chill until set. Garnish with toasted coconut, if desired.

TAWNY PUMPKIN PIE

Creamy, smooth filling is spiced to perfection

1¼ c. cooked or canned pumpkin
¾ c. sugar
½ tsp. salt
¼ tsp. ground ginger
1 tsp. cinnamon
1 tsp. flour
2 eggs, slightly beaten
1 c. evaporated milk
2 tblsp. water
½ tsp. vanilla
1 unbaked (9″) pie shell
Sliced process cheese

• Combine pumpkin, sugar, salt, spices and flour in mixing bowl.
• Add eggs; mix well. Add evaporated milk, water and vanilla; mix.
• Pour into unbaked pie shell. Bake in hot oven (425°) 45 to 50 minutes or until knife inserted near center comes out clean.
• Decorate, if desired, with Cheese Acorns and Leaves: Cut oak leaves from process cheese slices with cutter (or make cardboard pattern and cut out cheese leaf with point of small knife). Draw "veins" in leaf with knife tip. For acorn caps, cut rounds of cheese 1″ across; dust with nutmeg. For acorns, form 1 tsp. of soft cheese into ball (or shape with melon ball scoop). Toothpick caps to acorns. Stick a whole clove in top for stem.

SOUR CREAM RAISIN PIE

Favorite of the husband of one of our Family Test Group members

1 c. raisins
½ c. sugar
1 tblsp. flour
1 tsp. cinnamon
½ tsp. nutmeg
¼ tsp. salt
1⅓ c. dairy sour cream
3 egg yolks, beaten
1 tblsp. melted butter or margarine
1 tsp. vanilla
Pastry for 1-crust (9″) pie

Meringue:
3 egg whites
6 tblsp. sugar

• Pour hot water over raisins; let stand 20 minutes. Drain.
• Combine raisins with sugar, flour, cinnamon, nutmeg and salt. Add remaining ingredients.
• Blend until smooth. Pour into pastry shell. Bake in hot oven (400°) 10 minutes. Reduce heat to slow (325°); bake 45 minutes. Cool; top with meringue.

Meringue: Beat 3 egg whites to soft peak stage. Slowly add 6 tblsp. sugar; beat until stiff peaks form. Spread on pie; brown in moderate oven (350°) 10 to 12 minutes.

BLACK WALNUT CAKE

Country-style cake—big and luscious

3½ c. sifted cake flour
5 tsp. baking powder
1 tsp. salt
1¼ c. shortening
1 tsp. almond extract
1 tsp. vanilla
1¾ c. sugar
4 egg yolks
1½ c. milk
4 egg whites
1¼ c. chopped black walnuts

• Sift together flour, baking powder and salt.
• Cream shortening; add flavorings. Gradually add 1½ c. sugar and cream the mixture until light and fluffy.
• Add yolks; beat. Alternately add flour mixture and milk, beating until smooth after each addition (ending with flour).
• Beat egg whites until frothy; add remaining ¼ c. sugar; beat until meringue is glossy, but not dry. Lightly fold meringue and walnuts into batter. Pour into two well greased 9″ layer pans.

• Bake in moderate oven (350°) 45 minutes. Cool layers 15 minutes. Put together with chocolate filling made with 1 pkg. chocolate pudding mix (follow directions on box for making the filling). Frost with Sea Foam Frosting.

Sea Foam Frosting:

2 egg whites
1½ c. brown sugar
1 tblsp. light corn syrup
¼ c. cold water
¼ tsp. salt
1 tsp. vanilla

• Place all ingredients, except vanilla, in top of double boiler; mix thoroughly. Cook over rapidly boiling water, beating constantly until peaks form (about 7 minutes). Remove from heat; add vanilla.
• Beat until of spreading consistency. Spread over top and sides of cake. Makes enough to frost two 9″ layers.

PRUNE SPICE CAKE

A wonderful sugar 'n spice cake

1 c. boiling water
1 c. uncooked prunes, pitted and cut-up
2 c. sifted flour
1½ c. sugar
1 tsp. salt
1¼ tsp. baking soda
1 tsp. each cinnamon, nutmeg, cloves
½ c. oil
3 eggs, unbeaten
1 c. chopped nuts

• Pour boiling water over prunes; let stand 2 hours.
• Sift dry ingredients into large mixing bowl. Add prune mixture, oil, eggs and nuts. Blend thoroughly (about 1 minute). Beat 2 minutes at medium speed on mixer or 300 strokes by hand.
• Pour into a greased and floured 13× 9½×2″ pan. Sprinkle batter with Streusel Topping.
Bake in moderate oven (350°) 45 to 50 minutes. Cut in squares, serve warm. Or bake batter in paper-lined muffin pans, 20 to 25 minutes. Omit Streusel Topping if you wish, and frost. Makes 12 cupcakes. Or bake in 2 round 9″ cake pans 35 to 40 minutes. Delicious when cut in wedges and served hot with caramel sauce or vanilla ice cream.

Streusel Topping: Mix ½ c. sugar, 2 tblsp. flour and 2 tblsp. soft butter or margarine until crumbly.

POTATO CHOCOLATE CAKE

Stay-fresh cake—a favorite at Western ranch tables

½ c. milk
3 squares unsweetened chocolate
1 c. shortening
1¾ c. sugar
1 c. hot mashed potatoes
4 eggs, separated
2 c. sifted cake flour
1 tblsp. baking powder
⅛ tsp. salt
1 tsp. vanilla
¼ c. sugar

• Heat milk slowly in saucepan. Add chocolate, stir to melt. Cool.
• Cream shortening and sugar until light and fluffy.
• Combine chocolate mixture with potatoes. Add to creamed mixture. Beat in egg yolks.
• Sift together flour, baking powder and salt; stir into batter. Add vanilla.
• Beat egg whites until stiff, adding the ¼ c. sugar gradually. Fold into batter. Pour into 3 greased waxed paper-lined 8″ layer pans.
• Bake in moderate oven (350°) 30 minutes. Cool and frost as desired.

PRUNE CAKE

It's loaded with spicy-fruity flavors—a moist cake that came to us from a member of our Family Test Group

2½ c. sifted cake flour
1 tsp. baking soda
1 tsp. cinnamon
1 tsp. cloves
½ tsp. allspice
1 tsp. nutmeg
¾ tsp. baking powder
½ tsp. salt
½ c. shortening
1½ c. sugar
2 eggs
1 c. cooked, pitted, chopped prunes
½ tsp. lemon extract
1 c. thick sour milk

• Sift together flour, soda, spices, baking powder and salt.
• Cream shortening, add sugar gradually; cream until light and fluffy.
• Add eggs, one at a time; beat thoroughly after each addition. Stir in prunes.
• Add lemon extract to milk.
• Add dry ingredients and milk alternately to batter, mixing well.
• Pour into two greased and floured 8" layer pans. Bake in moderate oven (350°) about 40 minutes.
• Cool and frost with Sea Foam Frosting (recipe in this chapter).

DEVILS FOOD CAKE

Take this cake to the church supper and your reputation as a good cook will go up

2 c. sifted cake flour
1 tsp. baking soda
¾ tsp. salt
1 c. granulated sugar
½ c. brown sugar, firmly packed
½ c. vegetable shortening
⅔ c. buttermilk or thick sour milk
1 tsp. vanilla
2 eggs, unbeaten
3 squares unsweetened chocolate
½ c. boiling water

• Sift together flour, soda, salt and sugar into mixing bowl. Add brown sugar, shortening, ½ c. buttermilk, vanilla and eggs. Beat for 2 minutes at medium speed on electric mixer or by hand.
• Combine chocolate and boiling water; stir until smooth.
• Add remaining milk and chocolate mixture. Beat 1 minute more. Turn batter into 2 greased and floured 9" layer pans. Bake in moderate oven (350°) about 25 minutes. Let stand 5 minutes. Turn out; cool. Frost with Creamy Chocolate Icing.

Creamy Chocolate Icing: Combine 2 tblsp. water and ¼ c. sugar in saucepan. Boil 1 minute. Melt 2 squares unsweetened chocolate. Let cool. Meanwhile, beat 1 egg. Add 2⅓ c. sifted confectioners sugar; add hot sugar mixture, and mix well. Add ½ c. butter or vegetable shortening, 1 tsp. vanilla and cooled chocolate. Beat until creamy.

HICKORY NUT CAKE

For best flavor, cover this cake and let stand a day before serving

½ c. butter or shortening
1½ c. sugar
1 tsp. vanilla
2 c. sifted cake flour
2 tsp. baking powder
¼ tsp. salt
¾ c. milk
1 c. finely chopped hickory nuts
4 egg whites, stiffly beaten

• Cream butter, sugar and vanilla together until fluffy.
• Sift flour, baking powder and salt together; add alternately with milk to creamed mixture. Beat until smooth.
• Fold in nuts and egg whites.
• Pour into two greased 8×8×2" pans.
• Bake in moderate oven (350°) 35 minutes.
• Cool cake. Just before serving you may put layers together and frost with sweetened whipped cream. Sprinkle chopped hickory nuts over top.

Sundae Sauces

If ice cream is on the menu, tuck some homemade toppings in your basket. They'll make a hit.

Chocolate: Combine, in top of double boiler, 2 squares unsweetened chocolate and 1¼ c. light cream. Cook over boiling water until smooth. Stir occasionally. Combine ¾ c. sugar, 3 tblsp. flour and ¼ tsp. salt. Add enough hot mixture to make smooth paste. Combine paste with mixture in double boiler. Cook until smooth and slightly thick (about 10 minutes). Remove from heat; add 1 tblsp. butter or margarine and 1 tsp. vanilla. Serve hot or cold. Makes 2 cups.

Butterscotch: Combine 1 c. firmly packed brown sugar, ⅓ c. dark corn syrup, ¼ c. water and ¼ c. butter or margarine. Bring to a boil and cook, stirring occasionally, to soft ball stage (236°)—takes about 4 minutes. Remove from heat. Let cool slightly; add ⅓ c. light cream or evaporated milk, ⅛ tsp. salt and ½ tsp. vanilla. Beat well. Serve warm or cold. Makes 1 cup.

MINTED WALNUTS

Double the recipe or plan for two women to bring these—they're a nibbler's delight at a tea or reception

1 c. sugar
½ c. water
¼ c. light corn syrup
⅛ tsp. salt
6 marshmallows, cut up
3 drops oil of peppermint
2½ c. walnut halves

• Combine sugar, water, syrup and salt in saucepan. Bring to boil; cook until mixture reaches 230°, or just before the soft ball stage. Add marshmallows; stir to melt.
• Add oil of peppermint, then walnuts. Stir until mixture starts to lose its glossiness and hardens slightly.
• Quickly turn out on plain paper; separate into individual pieces. Cool. Makes 28 to 36 pieces.

ENGLISH TOFFEE

Homemade candy always is a welcome gift to take when you go visiting

1 c. sugar
1 c. butter or margarine
3 tblsp. water
1 tsp. vanilla
1 (4½ oz.) milk chocolate bar
½ c. finely chopped pecans

• Combine sugar, butter and water in heavy saucepan. Cook to 300°, or hard crack stage, stirring constantly.
• Add vanilla. Pour into buttered 9×9×1½" pan. Cool 5 minutes.
• Break chocolate bar in pieces; sprinkle over top. Spread as it melts. Sprinkle with nuts, pressing them lightly into chocolate. Cool; break into pieces. Makes 24 to 36 pieces.

MARSHMALLOW POPCORN BALLS

1 c. popcorn
1 tsp. salt
¼ c. butter or margarine
½ lb. marshmallows

• Pop corn; sprinkle with salt.
• Melt butter in skillet. Cut marshmallows in quarters. Alternate layers of popcorn and marshmallows in skillet.
• Cover; heat slowly until marshmallows are partially melted. Mix well; form into balls. Makes 9 (2") popcorn balls.

DATE-PECAN CANDY ROLL

Confections like this placed on the table stretch a slim dessert

2 c. sugar
½ c. light cream
⅓ c. dark corn syrup
2 tblsp. butter or margarine
½ lb. dates, cut in pieces
4 c. pecans, chopped

• Combine sugar, cream, syrup and butter in saucepan. Boil until reaches 234° to 238°, or a drop in cold water forms soft ball.
• Remove from heat; add dates. Beat until it cools and thickens.
• Add pecans; turn mixture out on damp towel. Roll into log. Cool; cut into 6 pieces. Re-roll each piece into a log, about 1" in diameter. Chill. Cut logs into ¼" slices.

CHEESE BONBONS

Wonderful with coffee or tea—a welcome change from sweet accompaniments

¾ c. shortening (part butter)
1½ c. shredded sharp cheese
¼ c. grated Parmesan cheese
1½ c. sifted flour
1 tsp. salt
1 tsp. paprika
Small pecan halves

• Cream shortening until light and fluffy; add cheese.
• Sift together dry ingredients; add to creamed mixture and mix well.
• Form dough into small balls about 1" in diameter; put on baking sheet about 1" apart. Place pecan half on each. Bake in moderate oven (350°) 15 minutes. Makes about 6 dozen.

RAISIN-PEANUT FUDGE

Extra-special—make a batch

4 c. sugar
1½ c. milk
2 tblsp. corn syrup
1 c. chopped raisins
½ c. peanut butter
1½ tsp. vanilla

• Combine sugar, milk and syrup in heavy saucepan. Cook until a little tested in cold water forms a soft ball, about 235°.
• Remove from heat. Add raisins, peanut butter and vanilla. Set aside until warm. Beat until creamy.
• Pour into small square pan 8" square, which has been well buttered. Cool. Cut into squares. Makes about 2 pounds.

Variation: Here's another interesting flavor change for this recipe. Omit raisins; add 1 c. chopped peanuts or dates to candy.

3

Eating Outdoors

Outdoor eating has become one of America's favorite pastimes. Old-time picnics in the grove, and later in the park, are giving way to meals served on the porch or in the back yard under a tree—wherever you find the nearest breeze. There's no basket to pack, no long hours of cooking; yet the way food disappears means it tastes extra-good mixed with fresh air. You don't have to call the kids to outdoor supper more than once, nor coax them to eat their vegetables and drink their milk.

Frequently one dish is cooked on a grill over embers—usually it's meat or chicken. Hamburgers and hot dogs have their innings, too, and of course men will settle any time for thick steak, broiled, tender and juicy with rich brown crust. The directions in this chapter for cooking steak over coals or in the kitchen's broiler oven come from a man who practices what he preaches, to the satisfaction of his friends.

Corn-on-the-cob, roasted in its husks until the tips of the kernels are a light taffy color (see our recipe), or lifted steaming from a kettle of hot water, is perfect outdoor eating if there's plenty of butter. As one of our good farm cooks says: Never do folks appear happier than when they are working down golden rows of hot corn lavishly spread with butter and sprinkled with salt and pepper. Only other requirements are time and more roasting ears! This chapter contains such barbecue specialties as crusty French bread you can bake ahead and freeze.

Some farm women feed their heat-weary men outdoors in the evening, where they relax on the grass and catch the breeze. They get hungrier and hungrier as they sniff the ham, chicken or steak sizzling on the outdoor grill nearby. Our directions for such a supper come from an Illinois farm woman who says they work like a man-charmer. There's delicious variety in these recipes.

Chicken Barbecue Supper

Take a lazy, summer evening, the family and a few friends and toss in the smoky aroma of chicken sizzling over charcoal as it turns a rich, golden brown—that's a recipe for happy times. All the food in this menu is kitchen-made except the chicken. Why don't you bring out a big, full-to-the-top cookie jar? That's an invitation to several helpings. Of course, there will be plenty of milk and coffee.

Menu

Charcoal-Broiled Chicken
Picnic Potato Salad   Sliced Tomatoes
Watermelon Pickles
French Bread
Butter-Pecan Ice Cream   Bar Cookies
Hot Coffee   Milk
Lemonade Cooler

CHARCOAL-BROILED CHICKEN

4 broilers (not over 2½ lbs. each, ready-to-cook weight)
Golden Ember Sauce

• Split chickens in half lengthwise.

• Brush generously on both sides with Golden Ember Sauce (recipe follows). Let flavors penetrate for several hours or overnight. (Store in refrigerator.)

• Place on grill, hollow side down, over coals white with ash (intense heat must have subsided). Cook for 20 to 25 minutes; brush with sauce and turn. Cook 20 or more minutes until chicken is tender. Another method is to brush with sauce often and turn chicken every ten minutes. The exact time depends on size of the broiler and amount of heat. To test for doneness, grasp end of leg. If leg joint moves easily, meat is done. Too hot a fire will give a charred coating before the chicken is done. Each half should serve one adult or two children.

Golden Ember Sauce: combine ¾ c. oil, ¼ c. melted butter or margarine, ¼ c. lemon juice, 1 tblsp. prepared mustard, 2 tblsp. brown sugar, 1 tblsp. salt, 1 tsp. paprika, ¼ tsp. pepper, 2 tsp. grated onion, 2 cloves garlic cut in half, ½ tsp. Worcestershire sauce, ¼ tsp. Tabasco sauce and ¼ c. ketchup in a jar or bottle. Shake thoroughly. Let stand several hours before using. Stir well before brushing on chicken.

LEMONADE COOLER

2 envelopes lemon-lime flavor summer drink powder
1⅓ c. sugar
2 qts. water
3 (6 oz.) cans lemonade concentrate
2 oranges or limes, sliced

• Combine summer drink powder, sugar and water. Stir until sugar is dissolved.

• Pour into ice cube trays. Freeze. Add water to lemonade concentrate according to directions on can.

• Place 2 or 3 green cubes in tall glasses or jumbo paper cups. Fill with lemonade. Garnish with a slice of orange or lime. Makes 3 quarts.

PICNIC POTATO SALAD

- **6 c. cubed cooked potatoes**
- **1 lb. cooked green beans**
- **¾ c. mayonnaise or salad dressing**
- **¼ c. French dressing**
- **1 tsp. prepared mustard**
- **½ tsp. salt**
- **¼ tsp. pepper**
- **4 hard-cooked eggs, sliced**
- **1 c. sliced radishes**
- **1 c. diced celery**
- **¼ c. chopped sweet pickle**
- **¼ c. minced onion**

• Cook unpeeled potatoes until just done. Cool. Peel and cube.

• Cut beans in short lengths. Cook in boiling salted water until tender.

• Blend mayonnaise, French dressing, mustard, salt and pepper in large bowl.

• Add cool potatoes, green beans, eggs (leave a few slices for garnish), radishes, celery, sweet pickle and onion. Toss lightly. Chill. Makes 3 quarts.

Feed the Men on the Lawn

An Illinois farm woman gave us this menu and the recipes for an outdoor meal that pleases her working men. She frequently fixes this type of supper for crews of corn shellers, hay balers and combiners when they work late in the evening. The men relax in the cool outdoors and no one needs to coax them to eat or help themselves to big pitchers of iced tea or lemonade. A portable grill for every six men takes care of the outdoor cooking.

To simplify the preparation, she keeps part of the meal on hand in the freezer and fixes the salad and relishes early—they stay crisp in the refrigerator. She cooks some of the food in the kitchen, but most of it on the outdoor grill.

FROM FREEZER

Lemonade Concentrate
Bread
Cherry Pie

FROM REFRIGERATOR

Cottage Coleslaw
Relish Tray
Milk

COOKED ON GRILL

Honeyed Ham Slices
Baked Potato Slices
Hot French Bread with Herb Butter

FROM KITCHEN RANGE

Cherry Pie au Gratin
Coffee

HONEYED HAM SLICES

Menfolks say it's mouth-watering to watch ham sizzling on a grill

6 slices pre-cooked lean ham, about ½" thick
¾ c. Honey Glaze (recipe follows)

• When coals are white with ashes, place heavy-duty metal foil on top of grill. Lay ham slices on foil; broil on one side, about 20 minutes.

• Turn ham; grill about 10 minutes. Brush generously with glaze and broil until ham looks shiny. Makes 6 to 8 servings.

Honey Glaze: Combine ½ c. honey, ½ c. brown sugar, 2 tblsp. flour and enough pineapple juice (about 2 tblsp.), orange juice or apricot nectar to make smooth paste. Makes about 1 cup.

Variation: Mustard Glaze— Combine ½ c. brown sugar, 2 tblsp. flour and 1 tsp. dry mustard. Rub into both sides of ham slices before grilling.

BAKED POTATO SLICES

Unwrap the foil packages—the potato slices are finger food

8 medium to large baking potatoes
½ c. soft butter or margarine
Salt or seasoned salt

• Scrub potatoes well; dry. Cut into ¾" crosswise slices. Brush cut surfaces with soft butter; sprinkle with salt (about 1 tsp. for each potato).

• Put potatoes back together and wrap each tightly in a square of heavy-duty foil. Broil over coals about 1 hour or until soft. Unwrap and eat with fingers or forks. Makes 6 to 8 servings.

COTTAGE COLESLAW

A salad men like; it's a good-for-you, tasty dish

½ c. cottage cheese
½ c. mayonnaise or salad dressing
3 tblsp. vinegar or lemon juice
1½ tsp. onion juice
¾ tsp. salt
½ tsp. pepper
1 tsp. caraway seed (optional)
6 c. finely shredded cabbage
2 c. diced cored apples
½ c. chopped green pepper (optional)

• Combine cottage cheese and mayonnaise. Add vinegar, onion juice, seasonings and caraway seed.

• Combine dressing with cabbage, apples and green pepper.

• Place in large bowl lined with cabbage leaves. Garnish with cottage cheese and green pepper. Chill thoroughly. Makes 8 to 10 servings.

CHERRY PIE AU GRATIN

Pie fresh from bakery to freezer then to oven—an easy way to fix this dessert

1½ c. grated or shredded sharp cheese
2 (7") cherry pies

• Sprinkle cheese over top of pies. Heat in moderate oven (350°) 10 minutes, or until cheese melts. Serve at once. Makes 8 to 10 servings.

Variation: Your own apple or favorite berry pie also may be served this way.

French Bread Dress-Ups

The men go for French bread, wrapped in foil and heated on a grill over coals. See our outdoor cook's Seasoned Butters in this chapter and try the recipe that follows.

HERB BUTTER

½ c. soft butter or margarine
½ tsp. salt
¼ tsp. paprika
¼ tsp. dried savory or 2 tsp. chopped parsley
½ tsp. dried thyme
Few grains red pepper
1 (13 to 16 oz.) loaf French or Vienna bread

• Cream butter with salt, paprika, savory or parsley, thyme and red pepper.
• Cut bread diagonally, almost through to bottom crust, in 12 equal slices. Spread Herb Butter between slices. Wrap loaf snugly in foil. Place on grill over hot coals, turning frequently; heat about 20 to 25 minutes. Or heat in hot oven (400°) about 15 minutes. Makes 6 servings.

Variation: Omit paprika, herbs and red pepper, and add 3 tblsp. minced onion.

Three Easy Picnic Meals

These three menus prove that you don't need fancy food when you eat outdoors. You get the meat and chicken ready in the morning to cook later. It's a good idea to slice and butter the bread for quick warming. And if it rains at mealtime, cook the same food in the broiler and eat in the house.

Menu 1—Kabobs make it different

Lamb Kabobs
Corn on the Cob
Potato Salad
Pickles Celery
Fresh Fruit
Milk Coffee

LAMB KABOBS

1½ lbs. lamb shoulder
⅔ c. oil
½ c. lemon juice
2 tsp. salt
¼ tsp. pepper
¼ c. ketchup
1 clove garlic, cut in half
2 onions, sliced
½ lb. mushrooms

• Cut lamb into 1″ cubes.
• Combine remaining ingredients except mushrooms; pour over lamb.
• Let stand at least 1 hour (or overnight in refrigerator).
• Alternate lamb and mushrooms on metal skewers (about 6 skewers). Allow space between pieces for thorough cooking.
• Broil, 3″ from source of heat, about 15 minutes. Turn to brown evenly.
• Arrange tomato wedges, cooked small onions and green pepper sections on additional skewers. Cook these the last 5 or 10 minutes. Turn to brown. Makes 6 servings.

Corn: Serve roasting ears hot from the kettle and keep them coming. They disappear fast.

Menu 2—Extra Easy

Special Frankfurters
Potato Chips Deviled Eggs
Cookies
Iced Tea Milk

SPECIAL FRANKFURTERS

1 lb. frankfurters
2 tblsp. prepared mustard
3 large dill pickles, cut into strips
8 slices bacon

• Slit frankfurters lengthwise.
• Spread with mustard; insert pickle.
• Wrap frankfurters spiral fashion with bacon slice; fasten with toothpick.
• Broil until bacon is crisp.
• Remove toothpicks before serving. Makes 6 servings.

Menu 3—Best of all!

Barbecued Chicken Special
Hot Garlic Bread
Sweet 'n Sour Green Beans
Tomato Slices
Watermelon
Milk Coffee

BARBECUED CHICKEN SPECIAL

3 broilers
½ tsp. salt
¼ c. oil
½ c. lemon juice
2 tblsp. chopped onion
½ tsp. black pepper
¼ tsp. paprika

• Wipe broilers with clean damp cloth.
• Mix remaining ingredients.
• Spoon this sauce inside and outside of chickens; let stand for 30 minutes.
• Place chickens on spit.
• Brush with sauce, turning so chickens brown evenly (if you don't have revolving type broiler or spit).
• Cook about 1 hour—until leg pulls away easily. Makes 6 servings.

SWEET 'N SOUR GREEN BEANS

2 (1 lb. 4 oz.) cans green beans
4 slices bacon, diced
1 small onion, sliced
¼ c. vinegar
¼ c. water
1 tsp. sugar

• Cook green beans (or heat canned beans). Drain; keep hot.
• Fry bacon and onion, stir in vinegar, water and sugar. Bring to boil.
• Pour over hot beans. Garnish with onion slices. Makes 6 to 8 servings.

Serve big cuts of thumping-ripe, cold melon. Slice man-size hunks of garlic bread and have plenty of coffee—some hot, some iced. Folks like to sip until the stars come out.

CHOCO-MARSHMALLOW COOKIES

Chocolate cookies topped with marshmallows and then frosting

1¾ c. sifted cake flour
½ tsp. salt
½ tsp. baking soda
½ c. cocoa
½ c. shortening
1 c. sugar
1 egg
1 tsp. vanilla
¼ c. milk
18 marshmallows, cut in halves
½ c. pecans

• Sift together flour, salt, soda and cocoa.
• Cream shortening and sugar; add egg, vanilla and milk, beating well. Add dry ingredients and mix. Drop by teaspoons onto greased baking sheet.
• Bake in moderate oven (350°) 8 minutes (don't overbake). Remove from oven and press ½ marshmallow, cut side down, on top each cookie. Bake 2 minutes longer. Cool; top with Cocoa Frosting, then with a pecan half. Makes 3 dozen.

Cocoa Frosting: Combine 2 c. sifted confectioners sugar, 5 tblsp. cocoa and ⅛ tsp. salt. Add 3 tblsp. soft butter or margarine and 4 to 5 tblsp. light cream.

Summer Porch Supper

One of the best ways to beat summer heat is to eat supper on the porch or in the yard under a canopy of leaves. This menu is right for such pleasant occasions, whether you're just the family or are joined by friends. It's easy to fix. The star performer is the mixed vegetable salad molded in gelatin. You make it ahead—also the deviled eggs. The only last-minute hot foods are the beans and muffins. We cooked green and lima beans separately, then combined and seasoned them, when we made this supper in our Countryside Kitchens. Two vegetables frequently taste better than one. We served wedges of cheese, but if you want to include meat in the menu, cold cuts will fill the bill.

Menu

Garden Salad Loaf
Assorted Cheese Deviled Eggs
Buttered Beans
Hot Corn Muffins
Cookies
Milk Iced Tea

GARDEN SALAD LOAF

Cool and beautiful—shimmering gelatin holds fresh garden vegetables

2 green peppers, cut in small strips
4 chopped green onions (include tops)
20 radishes, thinly sliced
2 medium carrots, thinly sliced
4 small tomatoes, cut in thin wedges
¾ c. French dressing
2 envelopes unflavored gelatin
¼ c. sugar
1 tsp. salt
2⅔ c. very hot water
½ c. vinegar
2 tblsp. lemon juice
2 c. shredded chicory or lettuce
1 c. coarsely torn spinach or shredded cabbage
¼ c. minced parsley

• Combine first 5 vegetables and marinate in French dressing (15 minutes or more).
• Combine gelatin, sugar and salt; add hot water and stir to dissolve ingredients. Add vinegar and lemon juice. Chill until gelatin thickens.
• Drain vegetables well. Fold marinated vegetables and crisp greens into gelatin mixture. (Chicory, spinach and parsley do not wilt easily, but you may use lettuce or shredded cabbage, too.) Pour into oiled loaf pan, about 8½×4½×3″; chill until firm.
• Unmold on platter. Makes 10 to 12 servings.

Fancy Touches: For a design of vegetables on top of mold when you turn it out, pour about ½ c. dissolved gelatin mixture into loaf pan and let set. On this arrange an interesting pattern with radish slices, green pepper and tomato strips. Spoon a little of gelatin mixture over vegetables to "anchor" them; let set before adding vegetable-gelatin mixture. A border of tomato wedges may be arranged around outer edge of mold for color.

Variation: Omit unflavored gelatin and sugar; substitute 2 (3 oz.) pkgs. lemon flavor gelatin and 3½ c. very hot water. Follow same procedure.

Food Tastes Better Outdoors

One of the members of Farm Journal's Family Test Group in Connecticut told us about the outdoor fireplace her family built near the pond on their farm. She passed along her three-point philosophy for a cook-out—don't fuss or hurry, enjoy cooking as well as eating and fix your family's favorites, each cooked to perfection. Some of her family's best-liked recipes follow:

BROILED BEEF PATTIES

Open a bun and slip in the burger—it's time to eat

1 tsp. salt
1/8 tsp. pepper
2 tsp. prepared mustard
1 small onion, chopped
1 tblsp. chopped parsley
1½ lbs. ground beef

• Add salt, pepper, mustard, onion and parsley to beef. Form into 6 patties.
• Brown on top of grill at medium heat, 15 to 20 minutes. Makes 6 servings.

BARBECUED SPARERIBS

Sweet and sour and—mighty good

3 sides spareribs
Salt
Pepper
1¼ c. French dressing
¾ c. chili sauce
3 tblsp. brown sugar
1 large onion, sliced
2 lemons, thinly sliced
1 to 2 tblsp. Worcestershire sauce

• Crack bones of spareribs. Sprinkle salt and pepper over ribs.
• Combine remaining ingredients for barbecue sauce; cook 10 minutes. Cool.
• Put ribs in bowl, pour sauce over ribs; chill several hours or overnight.
• Put ribs on skewer spit. Strain barbecue sauce and brush on ribs. Baste several times during baking. Barbecue according to rotisserie manufacturer's directions. Ribs may also be baked over outdoor grill for about 1½ hours, basting frequently with barbecue sauce. Makes 6 servings.

CHICKEN BUNDLES

Meal to cook in a package

2 fryer chickens, cut in quarters
8 slices peeled sweet potato
8 slices canned pineapple, drained
8 slices green pepper, cleaned
½ c. butter or margarine
2 tsp. salt
½ tsp. pepper
Heavy-duty aluminum foil

• For each serving, place individual portions of chicken, skin side down, in center of piece of foil large enough to cover and seal chicken.
• Top with slice of sweet potato, pineapple, pepper and 1 tblsp. butter, ¼ tsp. salt and dash of pepper.
• Bring foil up over food; seal edges with double fold seal to make airtight package.
• Place on grill over medium heat; cook about 50 minutes, turning once or twice. Unwrap and serve hot. Makes 8 servings.

LIMA BEAN BARBECUE

2 c. dried lima beans (or 4 c. cooked or canned)
2 tsp. salt
1 lb. pork sausage links
½ c. onions, chopped
1 c. ketchup
¼ c. liquid from cooked beans
1 tblsp. prepared horse-radish
1 tsp. Worcestershire sauce

• Cover dried beans with 5 c. water. Boil 2 minutes and then soak 1 hour, or overnight (cooking before soaking helps soften the skin which covers beans).
• Add salt and boil gently until tender—about 45 minutes for small lima beans, about 1 hour for large. Drain.
• Fry sausage until brown.
• Mix all ingredients except sausage.
• Place half of bean mixture in 1½ qt. casserole. Cover with ½ the sausages. Add remaining bean mixture. Garnish top with rest of sausages.
• Bake in hot oven (400°) 15 minutes. Makes 6 servings.

SOME-MORES

Longtime children's delight—but grown-ups also like them

Graham crackers
Thin sweet chocolate
Hot toasted marshmallow

• Arrange thin sweet chocolate on graham cracker, put hot toasted marshmallow on chocolate, then cover with another graham cracker. Press two crackers together. The hot marshmallow melts the chocolate to form a delicious dessert sandwich.

BAKED POTATOES

• Select medium-size baking potatoes. Wrap them in double thickness of foil. Place directly on top of the coals. Turn the potatoes over several times; pierce with fork through foil to tell when done. Serve hot with foil-roasted corn.

CORN ON THE COB

• Remove silk from corn by turning back husks. Replace inner husks. Place corn on grill, turn often. Roast about 15 minutes. Serve with plenty of butter, salt and pepper.
• If desired, corn can be husked. Spread corn with butter, sprinkle with salt. Wrap in foil. Place over hot coals about 10 or 15 minutes; turn several times.

DESSERT FROM FREEZER

• Prepare and freeze your favorite ice cream in paper dessert cups for easy serving. Or put a spoonful or two of Sundae Sauce in bottom of cups before adding ice cream. Pleasant surprise! For company, how about dasher-style ice cream served straight from the freezer?

FOIL FISH FRY

• Shape a large shallow pan from heavy-duty aluminum foil by turning up edges and mitering corners. Place on grill over medium hot fire. Add butter, margarine or other fat to the pan. Clean fish and roll in seasoned flour (equal parts cornmeal and flour give a very crisp coating). Fry golden brown, turning once or twice.

Hot Garlic Bread for Barbecues

If you bake French bread and store a loaf or two in the freezer, you have the favorite loaf to butter up and heat when a barbecue supper is scheduled. This recipe was developed in our Countryside Kitchens and has been praised by our readers who like crusty bread. Different Seasoned Butters offer variety, but garlic flavor ranks at the top in popularity.

FRENCH BREAD

Golden, long loaves with crackly-crisp crust—the result is worth your time

1 tblsp. shortening
1 tblsp. salt
2 tsp. sugar
2 c. water
1 pkg. granular yeast or compressed yeast
6 c. sifted flour (about)
Cornmeal

• Put shortening, salt and sugar into large mixing bowl. Add 1 c. boiling water; cool to lukewarm by adding 1 c. cold water. Sprinkle granular yeast over ¼ c. warm (110°) water or crumble compressed yeast into ¼ c. lukewarm (85°) water. Subtract this amount of water from liquid in recipe.

• Add flour in thirds; mix thoroughly—until dough begins to leave sides of bowl. Turn out on lightly floured board and knead until dough is smooth, elastic and does not stick to board. Add more flour if needed.

• Place in greased bowl, turning once to bring greased side up. Cover and let rise in warm place (85° to 90°) until doubled, about 1½ hours.

• Punch down and let rise again until almost double, about 1 hour.

• Turn out on lightly floured board and divide in half. Roll each half into 15×12" rectangle. Wind up tightly toward you, beginning with wide side. Seal edges by pinching together. Place rolls diagonally on greased baking sheets lightly sprinkled with cornmeal. Let rise until doubled, about 1 hour.

• Brush tops with cold water. Cut with scissors or knife to make 1 or 2 lengthwise or several diagonal ¼" cuts across tops of loaves.

• Set pan of boiling water in oven. Bake in hot oven (400°) 15 minutes; remove from oven and brush again with water. Reduce temperature to 350° and bake 35 to 40 minutes or until golden brown. Brush the third time with cold water and bake 2 to 3 minutes longer. Makes 2 loaves.

WAYS TO SERVE FRENCH BREAD

Slice on the bias, cutting almost, but not quite through loaf. The bottom crust holds slices together. Pull slices apart just enough to spread on butter or margarine, or better still, seasoned butter. Garlic butter is a universal favorite but it gets real competition from some of the Seasoned Butters that follow. Put the slices back together and wrap loaf loosely in foil. Heat in hot oven (400°) 15 to 20 minutes. Serve hot loaf on tray or plate or in long basket and let everyone break off his helping.

Or cut loaf in halves lengthwise, toast cut surface on grill and spread with butter. Break apart to serve. Another way to fix French bread is to cut loaf in 1" slices, spread with garlic butter, sprinkle with grated Parmesan or other hard cheese, spread on baking sheet and heat in hot oven (400°) 3 to 5 minutes.

SEASONED BUTTERS

• Soften ½ c. butter or margarine by creaming in mixing bowl. (Makes enough to spread one loaf French bread.) Add and mix well:
• Onion-Parsley: 4 tblsp. each minced onion and parsley.
• Chili-Ketchup: ½ tsp. chili powder, 2 tblsp. ketchup and 2 crushed garlic cloves. (Garlic press may be used.)
• Mustard: 2 tblsp. prepared mustard.
• Garlic: Crush 3 or 4 peeled garlic cloves. Add to butter or margarine. Let stand at room temperature an hour or two, stirring occasionally.
• Curry: ½ tsp. curry powder.
• Smoke: ½ tsp. smoke salt.
• Blue Cheese: ¼ c. crumbled blue or Roquefort cheese.
• Swiss Cheese: ½ c. coarsely shredded Swiss cheese.
• Sage: ½ tsp. powdered dry sage.
• Thyme: ½ tsp. powdered dried thyme.
• Sage and Thyme: ¼ tsp. each.

NEW HAM SANDWICH

• Cut French loaf in horizontal halves and spread on lower half this mixture: 1 (3 oz.) pkg. softened cream cheese mixed with ½ tsp. garlic salt, 2 tblsp. horse-radish and one (4½ oz.) can deviled ham. Press top on loaf, slice on bias almost to bottom crust, spread Mustard Butter on slices, wrap in foil and heat in hot oven.

Man, What a Steak!

It's thick, charcoal-broiled, juicy and tender—the surface is rich brown and crusty. These directions for cooking such a steak come from a West Texas man, whose hobby is cooking. He tells how to broil steak indoors and out. Either way, his technique proves: Nothing tastes better than steak. He rates as a champion cook in cattlemen's circles. It's easy to understand why.

BROILED SIRLOIN

The monarch of all broiled steaks is a top quality giant sirloin, 3″ to 3½″ thick. Build a fire of hickory wood and charcoal bricquets out under the grill and let it die down to embers before you fix this steak:

OUTDOOR BROILED STEAK

• Salt and pepper the meat on both sides; also sprinkle on a little monosodium glutamate. Sear steak on grill over embers, until it is brown on both sides. Now let it cook until done; allow about 1½ hours for medium steak. (If at any time the fire blazes up from fat dripping into the embers, remove meat until fire dies down to embers.) Serve on a big platter with Butter Sauce.

BUTTER SAUCE

• Melt 1½ sticks butter or margarine with ½ c. Worcestershire sauce and simmer 15 minutes. Slice broiled steak slantwise at an angle and pour sauce over it.

SPICY MARINADE

Among Southwestern steak wranglers there is a group that might be called the Marinaders, or the soak and broil school. Here's one of their favorite marinades:

Steak Sauce Supreme:

¼ c. vinegar
¼ c. oil
2 tblsp. minced onion
½ tsp. each salt and dry mustard
Dash each of mace, nutmeg and cloves
½ clove garlic, crushed

• Mix together all ingredients. Marinate T-bones or sirloins in sauce for an hour or two before broiling. Spoon the sauce on meat as it broils.

BARBECUE FAVORITE

Members of the Barbecue Brigade use sauces of widely varying pedigrees—some tame, some wild and hot, others just so-so. Here's a recipe that strikes a happy medium for any type of steak or roast:

TEXAS SPECIAL SAUCE

¾ c. ketchup
½ c. oil
½ c. vinegar
2 tblsp. garlic vinegar
1 tblsp. tarragon vinegar
½ c. water
1 tblsp. Worcestershire sauce
1 small onion, minced
2 tsp. brown sugar
½ tsp. salt
½ tsp. each: celery salt, garlic salt, mustard seed, celery seed and ground cloves
1 tsp. each: chili powder and oregano
1 small crushed bay leaf

• Place all liquids in heavy saucepan; set over medium heat and stir well.
• Mix dry ingredients in mixing bowl, add to liquid and stir until well blended. Reduce heat and simmer gently 25 minutes, stirring occasionally to prevent sticking. Remove from heat. Use as sauce to marinate and baste meats while broiling. Makes 2½ cups.

STEAK GO-WITHS

Except for thick and hefty French fried spuds, most Southwesterners go light on vegetables as sideliners for broiled steak. In fact, that type of fodder will seldom be missed at all, but there'll usually be a bowl of green salad in easy reach. And garlic bread!

SALAD BOWL

He-man tossed salad

2 tblsp. sesame seed
1 head lettuce or endive
6 tblsp. grated Roman cheese
3 tblsp. Parmesan cheese
1 green pepper, cut in strips
1 bunch radishes, sliced
Italian style dressing

• Toast sesame seed in heavy skillet until medium brown, or spread in pan and toast in moderate oven (375°) 8 to 10 minutes.
• Break or tear lettuce or endive in small pieces. Place in salad bowl and add cheese, pepper and radishes. Sprinkle sesame seed over salad in bowl and toss with Italian style or French dressing. Makes 4 to 5 servings.

Variation: Use summer lettuce and endive combined with sliced radishes and green pepper.

Time Table for Broiling

(For Filet Mignon, Porterhouse, T-Bone, Club, Rib, Small Sirloin—Steaks cold, Broiler preheated)

Thickness	*Approximate Minutes Per Side*
1 inch	5 minutes (rare)
	6 minutes (medium)
	7 to 8 minutes (well done)
1½ inches	9 minutes (rare)
	10 minutes (medium)
	12 to 13 minutes (well done)
2 inches	16 minutes (rare)
	18 minutes (medium)
	20 to 21 minutes (well done)

Large Sirloin Steaks

1 inch	10 minutes (rare)
	12 minutes (medium)
	14 minutes (well done)
1½ inches	12 minutes (rare)
	14 minutes (medium)
	16 minutes (well done)

KITCHEN-BROILED STEAK

Use 2″ T-bones or sirloins of heavy, aged beef. At least 2 hours before broiling, rub steaks on both sides with lemon juice and charcoal salt; dust with paprika. Broil (see Time Table), basting with melted butter or margarine, to which garlic has been added to taste.

Easy Variation: Use sirloin steaks 1½″ to 2″ thick. Rub both sides with cut cloves of garlic and salt and pepper. Broil (see Time Table). Or follow tips from barbecue chefs.

Barbecue Chefs Suggest: Finger test for doneness. Outdoor barbecue chefs judge doneness of broiled steak with a finger. Rare steak is bouncy, the firmer the steak the more well-done it is, or to quote a rare steak fan: "Well-done steak is about as resilient as shoe leather."

JUMBO HAMBURGERS

Double-thick and doubly good

2 lbs. ground beef
Ketchup
1 onion, thinly sliced
Smoke flavor cheese
Salt
Pepper
Butter or margarine
5 hamburger buns

• Divide beef into 10 equal portions, with ⅓ c. measure (if beef is lean, grind 4 oz. suet with it). Place between sheets of waxed paper and flatten to form patties about ½″ thick, 4″ across.

• Spread 5 patties with ketchup leaving ½″ around edge for sealing. Season with salt and pepper and top each patty with onion and slice of cheese roll. Top with other beef patties and seal edges well. (This is important to prevent leaking.)

• Spread both sides of patties lightly with soft butter or margarine or grease the grill. Season top of hamburgers with salt and pepper, place on grill over embers and broil about 10 minutes; turn and broil 10 minutes longer, or until beef is cooked the way you prefer. Slip hamburgers into split and toasted buns. Makes 5 servings.

Variations: Substitute prepared mustard for ketchup, pickle relish for onion. Or substitute ½″ cubes sharp process American cheese for smoke flavor cheese.

COOK-OUT SUPPER

Shish kabobs take the leading role in this delightful meal. If you can't find skewers, try your hardware store.

For each skewer, buy a 24″ length of steel wire (5/32″) and a wooden file handle. Insert the wire in the handle; tap firmly. Sharpen the business end of the wire with heavy file or whetstone. Dip the handles into red enamel paint to make your skewers look festive. You'll be glad to have them on hand for other picnics.

MENU

Beef Shish Kabobs
Super Potato Salad
Corn on the Cob
French Bread
Carrot Sticks Scallions
Chocolate Cake
Orangeade Coffee Milk

BEEF SHISH KABOBS

Beef—sirloin steak cut about 1½″ thick. Allow ⅓ to ½ lb. per person counting bone and fat weight, or about ¼ lb. per person trimmed. Cut meat into large cubes.

Mushrooms—not required but they're a wonderful flavor addition. Allow one or two per person (one pound is enough for 8 to 10 people).

Onions—one medium size, whole onion per person. Par-boil about 15 minutes in boiling water (add 1 tsp. salt per quart of water). Drain well. Or cut large Spanish onions into ½″ slices, to be grilled raw.

Tomatoes—medium to small, 1 per person. Wash and remove stem ends. Grill these whole; or if tomatoes are large, cut in halves or quarters.

Skewers—rubbed with paper toweling dipped in oil, or with pieces of fat from meat.

Spear cubes of steak, mushrooms and onions alternately on skewers, and take turns at the seasonings. Brush beef with Garlic Dressing (recipe follows), or season with salt and pepper; brush mushrooms and onions with melted butter or margarine. Then hold kabobs over fire, turning until done just right. Place tomato chunks on end of skewer for the last 5 or 10 minutes cooking time. Rest point of skewer on plate and push off grilled food with fork.

Garlic Dressing For Beef: Chop fine 4 cloves of garlic. Add 1 tblsp. salt. Continue chopping until garlic and salt are a pulpy mass. Add 2 tblsp. lemon juice, 2 tsp. Worcestershire sauce and ¼ c. oil. Blend well. Brush over skewered steak cubes just before broiling.

TRICKS OF OUTDOOR COOKS

Coffee, Swedish Style: Bring 2 qts. water to boil. Combine 1 c. regular grind coffee with ¼ c. cold water and 1 egg, beaten. Pour boiling water over coffee mixture; cover and let stand 12 to 15 minutes in warm spot on grill, but do not let boil. Makes 8 servings.

Fancy Frankfurters: Split frankfurters lengthwise, but not quite through. Spoon ketchup into cavities and add thin slices of cheese. Wrap slice of bacon around each frankfurter; fasten with toothpick. Grill over embers, turning to cook bacon. Serve in long buns.

Popcorn: Pop corn, sprinkle with salt or garlic salt and drench with melted butter or margarine. Pass at once with tomato juice as remainder of meal cooks over grill.

Cinnamon Rolls: Cut rolls in halves, spread cut surface with butter or margarine and toast in heavy skillet. Serve with coffee.

4

Cooking for a Crowd

If you hesitate to serve as chairman of the food committee for the church, school or club supper, this chapter is made to order for you. Or if you are "on the committee" and want to make a good contribution, check our king-size meals and big-scale refreshments.

You'll turn to this chapter when you help your husband put on a barbecue, or when the children make arrangements for a county-wide 4-H Club gathering. And we'll be surprised if you don't use some of the suggestions for family anniversaries and wedding receptions.

Much of the gaiety of country social life centers around the church, Grange or Farm Bureau supper and similar gatherings. They are special occasions and the food needs to rise to them—match the festivities. Eye appeal is almost as important as taste. The recipes must give high yields for there is no substitute for ample food. And frequently budget considerations are trying when you want to come out even or make money.

To indicate the variety: There are directions for making an authentic Southern Brunswick stew if you can get squirrels, and one with chicken if you can't. There is a South-of-the-Border chili supper. And there is how-to information for beef and chicken barbecues.

We include two glamorous wedding cake recipes for the most important social event in a girl's life. They were developed in our Test Kitchens but have won praise at sweet-music-and candle-light receptions in many homes.

Nothing surpasses a smooth-running, attractive, good-tasting meal, or luscious evening refreshments, to encourage neighborliness. And men and women working together on these social gatherings form friendships that rate as one of the best things of life.

Almost all neighborhoods can boast of one or two talented women who are clever managers and who, with a band of willing workers, excel in putting out meals for a crowd. Many of them are Farm Journal's readers and some of these champion cooks have shared their experiences with us. We pass their successes on to you in this chapter of menus and quantity recipes.

When Wedding Bells Ring

Letters from brides-to-be and their mothers start pouring in to Farm Journal's Food Department about the time the first crocus pokes up its head. The steady flow continues until June when it tapers off. In just about every letter we find this question: "Won't you please rush me a recipe for a beautiful wedding cake that's not too difficult to make?"

In answer to these requests we developed two prize bridal cake recipes—one a big glamorous one with yellow roses for the church wedding, and the other a smaller dainty cake with pastel-pink trim for the simple home wedding.

If you are not an experienced hand with a cake decorator, make your frosting designs on waxed paper before you attempt to put them on the cake. It's surprising how practice brings improvement. Or perhaps you can call on the champion cake baker in your community to help you. Almost every neighborhood has at least one woman clever at cake decorating.

FORMAL WEDDING CAKE

Bake three oblong cakes and three 9-inch-square cakes for this beauty

3 c. sifted cake flour *
4 tsp. baking powder
1½ tsp. salt
5 egg whites
6 tblsp. sugar
⅔ c. vegetable shortening
1⅔ c. sugar
1⅓ c. milk
1½ tsp. vanilla
¼ tsp. almond extract

*Use 3 c. and 2 tblsp. flour in batter when baking cake in one large pan.

• Sift together flour, baking powder and salt twice.

• Beat eggs until foamy. Add the 6 tblsp. of sugar, 1 tblsp. at a time, beating until mixture stands in soft peaks.

• Cream shortening; add sugar gradually. Cream until light and fluffy.

• Add flour, alternately with milk, a small amount at a time, beating after each addition until smooth. Add egg whites and flavorings; beat thoroughly (about 1 minute).

• Grease or line pans with waxed paper. Batter fills 2 square 9" pans or one large pan (about 13×9½×3").

• Bake in moderate oven (350°). Cakes in square pans take 30 to 40 minutes, in oblong pans, 35 to 50 minutes.

• Cool cakes on racks 10 minutes. Loosen from sides of pan, turn out and remove paper. Turn right side up to cool. To keep from drying, cover or wrap as soon as cooled. Make recipe 5 times; assemble cake. Makes about 100 servings.

• You will have one and one-half 9" square cakes left over to sample. To make cake to serve 40 you will have one-half 9" cake left over for a sampler. You can make the Formal Cake and the small edition with packaged white cake mix. Layers will not be so thick unless you add more batter—enough to fill the pans ½ to ⅔ full.

Frosting The Cake:

When cake is assembled, frost top and sides of whole cake. Start at top and work toward bottom layers. As each tier is finished, smooth it with spatula or glaze (see Frosting Facts which follow). When cake is frosted, work down—decorating top tier first, bottom tier last. Spread a layer of frosting over surface of board. (We used an 18″ square of white Masonite, with a piece of waxed paper 12× 13″ in the center when we made this cake.) Put trim around cake and edge of board.

Cutting The Cake:

The small top tier is removed for the bride. (She may wish to wrap and freeze it to serve on her first anniversary.) Cut each layer of the middle tier into 16 square pieces (a total of 32). Cut each of the larger layers of the bottom tier into 36 pieces (a total of 72).

ORNAMENTAL FROSTING

Make this recipe twice to frost the glamorous Formal Cake

- **½ c. butter or margarine**
- **½ tsp. salt**
- **12 c. confectioners sugar, sifted**
- **5 egg whites, unbeaten**
- **½ c. light cream**
- **2 tsp. vanilla**

• Cream butter; add salt. Gradually add about 1 c. sugar, blending after each addition.
• Add remaining sugar alternately—with eggs first, then with cream, until of right consistency to spread. Beat smooth after each addition. Add vanilla; blend. (While frosting cake, keep bowl of frosting covered with damp cloth to prevent crust that makes roughness, clogs decorating tube.) Makes 6 cups.

To Assemble Formal Cake:

• Use one and a half large oblong cakes for each of two bottom layers. Place one cake, top side down, on waxed paper. Cut another oblong cake in half, lengthwise; frost cut side. Push it, top side down, against long side of whole cake to complete bottom layer. Center it on board. Frost top; add second layer in same manner.
• Spread frosting on the bottom of a 9″ square cake. Place frosted side down, on the two bottom layers, centering it. Frost top of square cake; add another 9″ square.
• Cut third 9″ layer in four equal squares. Put two of them together with frosting for the top tier.

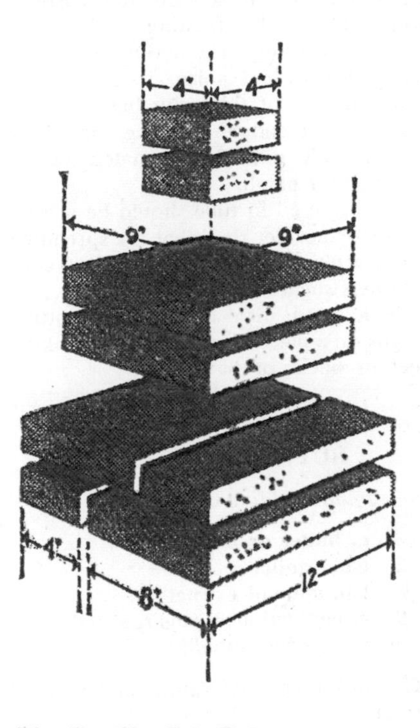

Tips For The Cake Baker:

• Before you start making the cake, check pan sizes and supplies needed. Use pliable spatulas to spread frosting; a short (4″) blade is best for sides of cake. You can make your own decorating bag from heavy waxed or parchment paper, but for inexperienced cake makers, it's easier with a cake decorating set.
• Make certain you have freezer space or other proper storage if you bake cake a day ahead. You can give it a thin glaze the day before you frost and decorate it to save time.

Frosting Facts:

• Sift confectioners sugar before using it. Tiny lumps clog tube and keep it from making clear-cut designs.
• Uncolored margarine may be used instead of butter, to give a pure white frosting.
• Apply thin glaze to cake before frosting, to anchor crumbs. Make glaze by adding hot water to some of the frosting, about 1 tblsp. to 1 c. frosting.
• To tint frosting, mix about ¼ tsp. of food color with 1 tblsp. frosting. Add small amounts of this color base to your frosting. Tint enough frosting for whole cake, as it's difficult to match colors with another batch.
• Frosting used in tube should be a little thicker or heavier than that for spreading with spatula. Just add a little sifted confectioners sugar.
• It's a good idea to practice putting designs on a piece of waxed paper, baking sheet or backs of pans.

BUTTER FROSTING

For a small wedding cake

¼ c. butter or margarine
2 tsp. vanilla
½ tsp. almond extract
9 c. confectioners sugar, sifted
½ to ¾ c. warm milk

• Cream butter. Add vanilla and almond extract.
• Add sugar and milk alternately, beating thoroughly after each addition. Add only enough milk for a good spreading consistency. Makes about 4½ cups.

INFORMAL WEDDING CAKE

Dainty pink frosting trim adds charm

2¾ c. sifted cake flour
4 tsp. baking powder
1 tsp. salt
1¾ c. sugar
⅔ c. vegetable shortening
1¼ c. milk
4 egg whites, unbeaten
2 tsp. vanilla
½ tsp. almond extract

• Grease or line bottoms of cake pans with waxed paper. (We used a 4-tier cake pan set. Pans measure approximately 9″, 7″, 5″ and 3″ in diameter.
• Sift flour; measure; add baking powder, salt and sugar, and sift into bowl.
• Add shortening and 1 c. of the milk. Mix at low speed until flour is dampened. Beat 2 minutes at low speed of the electric mixer or 300 strokes by hand.
• Add eggs, remaining milk and flavorings; beat one minute or 150 strokes by hand. Pour into pans, filling ½ to ⅔ full. It takes about half the batter to fill the 9″ and the 3″ pans, remaining batter to fill the 7″ and the 5″ pans.
• Bake in moderate oven (350°) about 20 minutes for 2 small cakes, 30 minutes for larger cakes. Cool cakes on racks 5 minutes. Loosen from sides of pan, turn out on rack, remove paper. Turn right side up to cool. Makes 20 servings.

Note: You may use two (17–20 oz.) packages white cake mix. The first package will fill the two large pans. Half the batter from second package will fill two small pans. (Make single layer or cupcakes from remaining batter for pre-wedding sampling.)

Base For Informal Cake:

• Place 12″ silver paper doily in center of your serving plate. Put a few dabs of frosting under center of doily and at various spots to hold it on plate.

Frosting The Cake:

• Use 1 recipe of Ornamental Frosting or 1 recipe of Butter Frosting. These are generous amounts. Coat all layers with a thin glaze (see Frosting Facts).

• It will take about 3 c. frosting to cover all the layers. Tint remaining frosting.

• Place 4 strips of waxed paper under edges of bottom cake layer. Then frost sides and top of layer. Paper will keep doily free of any drips. Remove waxed paper when frosting is completed.

• Add second tier and frost; repeat with remaining two tiers. Dip small spatula in hot water to smooth sides and top ready for decorations. Tint 2 c. frosting a delicate pink using red food color.

• As a finishing touch, outline a fluffy design of the pastel pink frosting around rim of the serving plate. Arrange the flowers just before serving.

Cutting The Cake:

• Cut top tier in half. Cut remaining layers in pie-shaped pieces. Makes about 20 servings.

CHAMPION ANGEL FOOD CAKE

You bake the batter in ring molds for zephyr-light Twin Wedding cakes

1¼ c. sifted cake flour
1¾ c. sifted sugar
1½ c. egg whites (10 to 11)
1½ tsp. cream of tartar
¼ tsp. salt
1 tsp. vanilla

• Sift together flour and ¾ c. sugar twice.

• Beat egg whites with rotary beater (electric or hand) until foamy; add cream of tartar, salt and vanilla; continue beating to soft peak stage.

• Beat in remaining 1 c. sugar a tablespoon at a time. Be careful not to overbeat! Beat only about one turn of bowl after each addition (5 turns of rotary beater); gently scrape sides.

• Add flour-sugar mixture in 3 or 4 parts, gently folding in with wire whisk, using about 12 strokes each time. Pour into large 10×14″ or two 10½×2½″ tube pans. Cut through batter with spatula to remove large air bubbles.

• Bake in moderate oven (375°) 40 to 50 minutes. Invert pan; cool about 1 hour before removing cake.

For top results: Take care not to overbeat egg whites. It's best to use eggs at room temperature rather than from the refrigerator. Whites should stand in soft peaks so that the tips drop over when beater is lifted. If you use your mixer, the cake will be less trouble to make.

TWIN WEDDING RING CAKES

Two cakes filled with ice cream are twice as pretty as one

• Bake Champion Angel Food Cake in 2 aluminum ring pans 10½″ across and 2½″ deep. Frost with 7-Minute Frosting and place on cake tray.

• At serving time, fill cake centers with strawberry ice cream. Round, half-gallon cartons of ice cream are about the same size as center of cake. Cut through cartons crosswise to obtain an ice cream circle for each cake. Cut cardboard away, and slip ice cream into center of cake. Cut in wedges to serve. Two cakes make 25 servings.

7-MINUTE FROSTING

The dress-up for Twin Wedding Ring Cakes

2 egg whites, unbeaten
1½ c. sugar
⅛ tsp. salt
⅓ c. water
1 tblsp. light corn syrup
1 tsp. vanilla

• Combine all ingredients in top of double boiler; beat with rotary beater 1 minute.

• Place over boiling water and beat about 7 minutes, stopping a few times to clean beater and sides of pan with scraper.

• Remove from boiling water when frosting stands in glossy peaks (has more body than a meringue). Continue beating until frosting is cool and thick enough to hold firm swirls. Makes enough frosting for two 8 or 9″ layers or 1 tube cake.

Silver or Golden Wedding-Anniversary Receptions

All you have to do to adapt this menu to two styles of entertaining: Mold the salads in gelatin for the buffet—for the reception spread them on baked cut-out pastry or fill Puff Shells. Omit asparagus (or broccoli) from reception menu.

ANNIVERSARY BUFFET MEAL

Molded Ham Chicken or Tuna Salad
Asparagus or Broccoli with Mock Hollandaise
Hot Buttered Rolls
Crisp Relishes Pickles Olives
Twin Wedding Ring Cakes
Coffee

PUFF SHELLS

Finger food that everyone enjoys

1 c. sifted flour
½ tsp. salt
½ c. shortening
1 c. hot water
4 eggs

• Sift together flour and salt.
• Bring shortening and hot water to boil in saucepan. Add dry ingredients all at once, stirring constantly. Continue cooking until mixture leaves sides of pan and follows spoon around sides of pan, about 15 minutes.
• Remove from heat; let cool a minute.
• Add eggs, one at a time; beat vigorously after each addition until mixture is smooth again.
• Drop from teaspoon, 1½" apart, on lightly greased baking sheet.
• Bake in very hot oven (450°) 10 minutes, then reduce heat to moderate (350°) and bake 15 minutes longer.
• Cool; cut open and fill with Ham, tuna or Chicken-Pineapple Salad. Makes 48.

MOLDED HAM, CHICKEN [OR TUNA]

Pretty on the buffet when served on crisp lettuce

2 (3 oz.) pkgs. lemon flavor gelatin
4 c. hot water
2 tblsp. lemon juice or vinegar
4 c. Ham, Chicken or tuna Salad

• Dissolve gelatin in hot water; add lemon juice. Chill until thick and syrupy.
• Stir in Ham, Chicken or your favorite tuna salad. Pour into two 9×4×1½" pans. Chill until firm enough to slice. Makes 25 servings.

HAM SALAD

A genuine favorite

2 c. ground cooked ham (about ½ lb.)
3 stalks celery
1 large dill pickle
¼ tsp. onion juice
½ c. mayonnaise or salad dressing
¼ tsp. dry mustard
½ tsp. salt
1 tblsp. lemon juice

• Put ham, celery and pickle through coarse blade of food chopper. Add remaining ingredients and mix together.
• Spread on rich pie pastry that has been rolled out and cut with cookie cutters. Bake in hot oven (425°) until brown. Makes 4 cups, enough for 5 dozen small pastries. Or use salad to fill Puff Shells.

Lovely Bride's Cake you can make and decorate, page 56. We help you plan right size for your reception. Smaller round cake, page 58.

Easiest Way to Serve Ham to a crowd: Slice pre-cooked ham, tie together, glaze and bake. To serve, cut the string! Recipe, page 309, is in Chapter 20.

Cinnamon Leaf Ring The weathervane's C stands for Central USA, where wonderful breads are popular with coffee. Recipe, page 317, is in Chapter 21.

It's a Choice of Cherry or lemon or apple when the coffee break comes in the evening—you'll find many excellent pie recipes in this book.

CHICKEN-PINEAPPLE SALAD

Chicken and pineapple make a special treat—raisins and nuts enhance it

½ c. crushed pineapple, drained
¼ c. white raisins
¼ c. blanched almonds
2½ c. coarsely ground cooked chicken
2 tblsp. mayonnaise or salad dressing
1 tsp. salt

• Chop pineapple, raisins and almonds; add chicken, mayonnaise and salt; mix well. Makes 4 cups.

ASPARAGUS WITH MOCK HOLLANDAISE

Attractive yellow and green combination for the buffet

1 c. mayonnaise or salad dressing
1 c. light cream
2 (12 oz.) pkgs. frozen asparagus (or broccoli), cooked

• Blend together mayonnaise and cream. Heat in double boiler.
• Pour over hot cooked asparagus and serve. Makes 2 cups.

How to Serve a Crowd Like Clockwork

Church women who serve this country-good turkey dinner, have told us it's a money-maker, that they please everyone who eats this home-cooked meal. The cooks make good use of portable electric roasters—a roaster roundup is about the first step in mobilizing for a church supper. But the turkey may be cooked in regular ovens if more convenient.

GOOD CHURCH-SUPPER MENU

Fruit Cocktail Crackers
Roast "Golden Breast" Turkey
Dressing Gravy
Fluffed Potatoes Creamed Peas
Butterhorn Rolls
Cranberry Sauce Relish Plate
Ice Cream with Chocolate Sauce
Homemade Cookies
Coffee Milk

ROAST TURKEY

(in electric roaster)

• Set electric roaster temperature control at moderate (350°).

• Wash turkey in cold water; pat dry. Sprinkle with salt, inside and out.

• Rub skin thoroughly with shortening; place bird on rack in insert pan of electric roaster.

• For an 18 to 20 lb. turkey allow 15 to 18 minutes roasting time per pound. Allow about 5 minutes less per pound if the turkey is not stuffed.

• About 15 to 30 minutes before roasting time ends, test turkey for doneness. Move drumstick up and down—the leg should give readily or break. Or press fleshy part of drumstick; the meat should feel very soft. Never pierce skin with a fork.

• Allow approximately ½ lb. ready-to-cook turkey per serving.

Turkey Giblets and Necks: Cook ahead. To hasten the job, cook in pressure saucepan at 10 lbs. pressure, 65 minutes, with salt, pepper, cloves, bay leaves, onions, carrots and celery stalks added for seasoning. Strain. Chill broth and meat overnight. Put giblets and neck meat through food chopper (use in the Baked Dressing).

To Make Gravy: While turkeys keep warm in electric roasters, pour drippings (fat and juices) from roasting pans. Let fat rise; skim off. Measure ½ c. of the fat back into a large, shallow pan. Add 2 c. flour; blend thoroughly. Place pan over low heat and cook slowly until mixture bubbles, stirring constantly with spoon or wire whisk. Gradually add 4 qts. liquid (dripping juices, broth from cooked giblets and milk), stirring constantly. Simmer until gravy is thick and smooth, about 5 minutes. Add 1 tblsp. salt and 1 tsp. pepper. Use ¼ c. gravy for each serving. Makes about 50 servings.

BAKED DRESSING

Bake it in pans instead of in turkeys!

½ c. butter or margarine
½ c. turkey fat
¼ c. chopped onion
2 c. chopped celery
5 loaves of bread, day old
2 tblsp. salt
1 tsp. pepper
1 tsp. seasoned salt
2½ to 3 qts. liquid (use all broth or broth and milk)
3 eggs, beaten
Ground giblets

• Melt butter and turkey fat (from giblet broth) in skillet. Add onion and celery; sauté 10 minutes.

• Cube bread. Add seasonings, cooked onion, celery and fat.

• Add liquid, eggs and giblets. Mix lightly.

• Pile lightly into large, greased rectangular pans. Bake in moderate oven (350°) 30 to 50 minutes, depending on quantity. Makes 50 servings.

Dinners for Daughters to Give Mothers

Mother-Daughter dinners are popular especially in the spring around Mother's Day. The food for these memorable meals must taste wonderful, of course, but also have color and appeal for feminine eyes. The following menu meets these requirements, but is planned so that with a dessert change the dinner will be suitable for men guests.

MOTHER-DAUGHTER DINNER

Pineapple-Cranberry Cocktail
Roast Loin of Pork   Rosy Apples
New Potatoes in Jackets
Vegetable Ribbon Salad
Robin's Nest Dessert
Milk   Coffee

PINEAPPLE-CRANBERRY COCKTAIL

Makes the table bloom with color

1 (6 lb. 8 oz.) can pineapple juice
2 (1 qt.) bottles cranberry juice cocktail

• Blend juices. Serve iced in small glasses. Makes 50 servings.

ROAST LOIN OF PORK

It glistens with a tasty apple glaze

4 (6 lb.) pork loin roasts

• Have meat cut almost free from backbone of roasts.
• Place, fat side up, on racks in shallow roasting pans.
• Roast, uncovered, in moderate oven (350°), allowing 30 minutes per pound. Allow 3 hours for 6 lb. roast.
• Spoon Pink Applesauce Glaze over roasts just before serving.

PINK APPLESAUCE GLAZE

2 (1 lb. 4 oz.) cans thick applesauce (5 c.)
2½ c. sugar
Few drops red food color

• Combine applesauce, sugar and food color (or substitute red cinnamon candies).
• Cook until sauce gets a shiny, translucent look, about 20 minutes, stirring frequently. Makes glaze for 4 (6 lbs.) pork roasts.

NEW POTATOES

Tiny potatoes need not be scraped

20 lbs. new red-skinned potatoes

• Wash potatoes well; cook until tender in boiling salted water (1½ gal. water and 6 tblsp. (3 oz.) salt). Drain.
• Serve with 1 lb. melted butter or margarine to which chopped chives or parsley has been added.

Variation: Peel and cook uniform small potatoes. Pour over a mixture of lemon juice and butter; then roll in minced parsley. Or toss with hot peas, then heat in light cream. Sprinkle with paprika.

ROSY SPRING APPLES

Pretty garnish for plates

24 firm, medium apples
Juice of 1 lemon
6 c. sugar
3 c. water
Few drops red food color

• Wash apples. Slice each into 4 or 5 rounds. Immerse slices in cold water, mixed with lemon juice or ascorbic acid powder.
• Make syrup of sugar, water and food color; simmer until sugar is dissolved, then boil 5 minutes.
• Simmer apple slices in sugar syrup until pink and glazed (about 5 minutes). Drain on waxed paper. Makes 50 servings (2 slices each).

VEGETABLE RIBBON SALAD

Brilliant and colorful

9 (3 oz.) pkgs. lemon flavor gelatin
2 qts. boiling water
1¾ qts. cold water
⅔ c. vinegar
2 tblsp. salt
1½ qts. finely chopped cabbage
1½ qts. grated carrots
1½ qts. raw spinach, finely chopped
3 tblsp. finely cut green onions
Crisp lettuce

• Dissolve gelatin in boiling water; add cold water, vinegar and salt. Divide into three parts. Chill until slightly thickened.
• Add cabbage to first part of gelatin. Turn into six loaf pans, 4×9×2½" to depth of 1". Chill until firm.
• Add carrots to second part of thickened gelatin; pour over firm cabbage layers. Chill until firm.
• Add spinach and onion to remaining gelatin; pour over carrot layers. Chill until firm.
• Unmold; cut each loaf into 8 slices. Serve on crisp lettuce. Makes 48 servings.

ROBIN'S NESTS

Picture-pretty dessert

Chocolate Coconut Nests:

1 (8 oz.) pkg. semi-sweet chocolate
9 (3½ oz.) cans moist flaked or shredded coconut
2 gals. pale green ice cream, such as mint or lime sherbet

• Melt chocolate in top of double boiler.
• Place coconut in bowl. Pour chocolate gradually over coconut, mixing well and tossing lightly so all coconut has even chocolate coating. Form small amounts into "nests" and place on trays or baking sheets covered with waxed paper, plastic film or aluminum foil. Place in refrigerator or cool place to harden. Makes 50 "nests."
• At serving time, place 1 scoop ice cream on each nest. Makes 50 servings.

Variation: Instead of mint ice cream or sherbet, use vanilla ice cream tinted pale green with a little food color.

BUTTERHORN ROLLS

Homemade rolls piping hot are one of the stars of this feast

5 c. milk
½ c. sugar
4 tblsp. salt
1¾ c. shortening
3 pkgs. compressed or granular yeast
1 c. water
4¾ lbs. sifted flour (19 c.)
Melted butter or margarine

• Scald milk; add sugar, salt and shortening. Let cool.
• Crumble compressed yeast into lukewarm water (85°); sprinkle granular yeast over warm water (110°). Stir into milk mixture.
• Add flour and mix thoroughly, kneading in the last portion.
• Place dough in well greased bowl. Turn over once to bring greased side up. Cover and set in warm place (80° to 85°) to rise until doubled.
• Turn out on lightly floured board. Knead until smooth and elastic. Return to bowl; let rise again until doubled.
• Divide into 4 portions. Turn out on lightly floured surface; roll to ¼" thickness. Cut into 3" triangles. Brush with butter. Roll each triangle to the center, starting with wide side. Brush again with butter.
• Place rolls on greased baking sheets. Let rise until doubled.
• Bake in hot oven (400°) 15 to 25 minutes, or until lightly browned. Makes 120 rolls, or 50 servings.

MOTHER-DAUGHTER DINNER

Market order for 50:

1 (6 lb. 8 oz.) can pineapple juice, or 2 (1 qt. 14 oz.) cans
2 qts. cranberry juice cocktail
4 (6 lb.) pork loin roasts (have meat cut almost free from backbone)
2 (1 lb. 4 oz.) cans applesauce
5 lbs. granulated sugar
1 lb. sugar cubes
1 bottle red food color (or 1 lb. red cinnamon candies)
24 firm, unbruised, medium apples
20 lbs. new potatoes (red-skinned)
1 lb. butter or margarine
1 bunch chives or parsley
9 (3 oz.) pkgs. lemon flavor gelatin
½ pt. white vinegar
1 (1 lb. 10 oz.) pkg. salt
1 (1½ lb.) head firm green cabbage
1½ lbs. carrots (about 14 medium carrots)
3 lbs. spinach
1 small bunch green onions
2 heads lettuce
2 gallons green ice cream or sherbet
9 (3½ oz.) cans flaked or shredded coconut
1 (8 oz.) pkg. semi-sweet chocolate pieces
13 qts. milk
4 oz. instant coffee (makes 36 c.)
1½ qts. light cream

How to Put on a Community Harvest Supper

Along about first-frost time, lights go on week nights in churches as members gather in church basements or "parlors" for a truly American style of Thanksgiving, a neighborhood supper.

SOUTHERN-STYLE BARBECUE

Numbers tell you how many women it takes to fix the food

Fruit Juice—1
Southern Barbecued Chicken—4
(3 to cut up and fry; 1 to make sauce)
Virginia Spoon Bread—1
Frozen Buttered Peas Tangy Diced Beets*—1
Relish Tray (sweet pickles, relish, radishes, carrot strips, jelly)—1
Homemade Parkerhouse Rolls**—2
Butter—1
Cake (donated)—1 and Ice Cream—1
Coffee—1

* Cooked with grated rind and juice from 6 oranges.
* * If short of help and time, buy bakery rolls.

SOUTHERN BARBECUED CHICKEN

Truly delicious and so easy to fix

8 to 10 roasting chickens (about 40 lbs.)
2 lbs. sifted flour
5 tblsp. salt
1 tblsp. pepper
3 lbs. shortening

• Cut chicken into serving pieces. Wash well and pat dry. Put giblets to stew in 1 qt. salted water. (You'll use this broth in barbecue sauce.)
• Put flour, salt and pepper into paper bag. Shake chicken in flour, a few pieces at a time.
• Sauté chicken pieces until golden brown on both sides in hot shortening in heavy skillets. Arrange pieces in open roasting pans. Add giblets. Pour barbecue sauce over chicken.
• Bake in moderate oven (350°) 1½ hours, basting frequently. (No harm to bake chicken a little longer—flavor actually improves.) Makes 50 servings.

BARBECUE SAUCE

The magic that gives the chicken a tangy taste and rich, appealing color

2 lbs. onions
1 pt. oil
½ c. flour
1 c. prepared mustard
2½ tblsp. salt
2 tsp. pepper
¾ c. brown sugar
1 qt. vinegar
1 qt. chicken broth
2 (14 oz.) bottles ketchup
2 (1 lb. 13 oz.) cans tomato purée
1 c. Worcestershire sauce

• Chop onions; sauté lightly in oil in heavy skillet.
• Combine flour, mustard, salt, pepper and sugar. Stir into onions. Add remaining ingredients; heat to boiling, stirring constantly.
• Simmer 15 minutes to blend flavors. Makes enough sauce for 50 servings.

Big Community Barbecues

Barbecues are a man's best chance to shine as a chef. Complete directions follow for serving a hungry crowd in this traditional western way, with pit-style cooking.

First dig your pit. Dig it deep, the size depending on the amount of meat you plan to barbecue. Here are some helpful figures: Make the pit 3½′ deep and 3′ wide for the large crowds; same depth, 1½′ wide by 3′ long for small groups. You can cook as little as 10 pounds of beef in it, enough for about 25 people. A trench, same depth, 3′ wide and 10′ long, will handle about 400 pounds of meat. For a general rule, allow about 3′ of length for each 100 pounds. For more than 800 pounds of meat, it's better to dig a second trench.

Clay in the soil helps hold the sides of a temporary pit. For a permanent one, wall up the sides with fire brick or concrete blocks, and fit with a sheet-metal cover.

Use dry, hard wood to make a 15″–18″ bed of coals. Green wood takes longer to burn. Soft wood won't hold long enough. Hard wood about 4″ across will burn down to coals in 3–4 hours.

Throw out any half-burned chunks, and keep just the coals. Have plenty of wood on hand at the start—at least 1½ tons for a 10′ pit.

An iron rod with a hook on the end is handy for fire tending.

You'll need dry sand. If it's wet, you'll have too much smoke and no fire. So, while making coals, put the sand on a piece of sheet iron over part of the pit and dry it.

Beef is most often barbecued, but you can cook pork, lamb and chickens equally well this way. Allow a half-pound of best-quality, properly-aged boneless beef for a generous serving per person.

Bone the meat first—it takes less room in the pit and is easier to carve and serve. Tie the boned cuts into uniform rolls of not less than 4″ nor more than 8″ across. You may place pieces of fat in each roll to give extra flavor and juiciness. Season with salt and pepper, then wrap in cheesecloth, muslin or a double layer of stockinette. Cover with clean burlap. The forequarter has just the right amount of fat with lean to make it juicy. Divide the shoulder or chuck into an inside and outside roll, cut along the shoulder blade and arm bone. Bone and roll the rib and plate (navel end).

The hindquarter breaks down into excellent boned cuts. Divide the loin into the sirloin end and the short loin. In boning the sirloin end, cut it into two pieces and roll. Strip the tenderloin out of the short loin and roll with the boned short loin. Divide with round into the inside, outside and sirloin tip. Cut the inside and outside pieces into two rolls each. Bone the rump and trim off some of the excess fat.

Place the meat in the pit 10–12 hours before time to serve. For a noon meal, you'd start the fire after supper the previous evening. Allow 3–4 hours for it to burn down to coals. Level coals with a rake, and cover all with a 1″–1½″ layer of the dry sand.

Working quickly, place the bundles of meat on the sand, leaving a little space between the bundles. Cover the pit at once with sheet iron or tight-fitting boards resting on pipe, steel posts or rods.

Throw 10″–12″ of dirt on the cover to prevent loss of heat. If steam leaks develop, plug them with mud.

If there's danger of rain, put a temporary cover of some kind over the pit, and dig a trench around it for drainage. Now you can go off and sleep, if you want to—there's nothing more to do! The meat will be done in about 12 hours, but you can't overcook it, for the coals will die down after a time anyhow.

When ready to serve, uncover the pit and remove the meat bundles with a clean pitchfork. Take off the coverings. Have one man ready to slice the meat as fast as two can serve it. Work fast.

Your barbecue sauce should be hot and ready to pour over the sliced hot meat just before it is served.

A standby menu is served in this order from long tables: two barbecued sandwiches (meat on buns) for each person, potato chips, relishes, lettuce or cabbage salad, ice cream and cake. Serve coffee, sugar and cream at a separate table, and use paper plates, cups, spoons and forks.

Whether you serve 25 or 500, you'll need an orderly system to keep the lines moving fast so that everybody is served hot meat. Place your foods, buffet style, on long tables. Station your helpers at each food along the tables, to fill plates completely before they're handed to the guests. With four long tables and additional ones for slicing meat and reserve food, plus two meat slicers, you can serve 600 people in 28 minutes at such a barbecue!

BARBECUE SAUCE

Ingredients	For 25	For 100
Ketchup	2 c.	6 (14 oz.) bottles
Worcestershire sauce	½ c.	3 (5 oz.) bottles
Prepared mustard	¼ c.	1 (6 or 7 oz.) jar
Prepared barbecue sauce	½ c.	3 (7 oz.) bottles

• Combine ingredients and mix well.

• Barbecue sauce should be hot and ready to pour over sliced hot meat just before serving.

• You can add other ingredients to the sauce to suit your taste—horse-radish, brown sugar, red pepper, salt or an oil.

• Lemon juice or vinegar will clean out bottles or measuring cups, and dilute the sauce to desired thickness.

BANANA DEVIL'S FOOD CAKE

An extra-tasty chocolate cake—big recipe that is a good barbecue end-up

3 c. sifted cake flour
2 tsp. baking powder
¾ tsp. baking soda
1½ tsp. salt
¾ c. shortening
2¼ c. brown sugar
1¼ c. buttermilk or thick sour milk
3 eggs
½ c. mashed banana
3 (1 oz.) squares unsweetened chocolate
1½ tsp. vanilla

• Sift together flour, baking powder, soda and salt.

• Cream shortening, sugar and ¼ c. buttermilk. Add eggs, one at a time, beating well after each addition. Blend in banana. Add melted chocolate.

• Combine remaining 1 c. buttermilk and vanilla. Add dry ingredients alternately with milk to creamed mixture; beat well.

• Pour into 3 greased 8" pans. Bake in moderate oven (350°) 45 minutes. Cool on racks, then frost with 7-Minute Frosting. Decorate with banana slices just before serving. Makes 18 servings.

One-Dish Family or Community Meals

You are certain to be in the South when you find this tempting and famous stew, but there's no reason why it can't be made in other areas. If squirrels are scarce or your hunters have no time to go after them, chicken makes a good substitute. The Brunswick Stew goes by different names. Squirrel Stew is one, and in some Carolina communities, it is called Squirrel Muddle.

For a large crowd the stew is cooked outdoors over coals in a big iron kettle. A Southern woman confides: "Brunswick Stew is the perfect way to serve a lot of people without a lot of fuss." Usually the leftover stew, if there is any, is sold to people in the crowd to take home and freeze. Then when an occasion demands something special for a family dinner, the stew is ready to reheat while the corn bread bakes.

BRUNSWICK STEW

It makes a one-dish meal for the entire neighborhood

About 70 squirrels, cut up
2 large stewing chickens, cut up
6 gals. water
2½ lbs. salt pork, chopped
2½ gals. butter beans (lima beans)
3½ gals. cubed potatoes
4 gals. peeled tomatoes, chopped
1 gal. cubed carrots
2½ gals. freshly cut corn
1 gal. shredded cabbage (optional)
1 pod red pepper, chopped
¾ c. black pepper
1¾ c. salt
1 lb. sugar

• Clean, dress and cut up squirrels and chickens. If your folks are not ardent squirrel hunters, increase the number of chickens. If you use all chickens, this recipe will take about 24 stewing chickens.

• Bring 4 gals. of the water to a boil in a 30-gallon iron kettle. Add meat. Cook, stirring frequently, until meat starts to come off the bone. (Take out pieces of bone before serving to small children.) Add remainder of water, as needed.

• Chop salt pork, fry out and add pork and drippings to boiling mixture. Add beans, potatoes, tomatoes, carrots and corn in order as each is prepared. Continue cooking and stirring until vegetables are tender.

• Add cabbage and seasonings, and cook, stirring, 1 hour, until stew is thick and flavors well blended. Remove kettle from the coals to serving area by hooking the handle over a heavy pole, several helpers carrying each end. Makes 15 gallons.

The stew may be served in heavy paper bowls (the kind used for ground meat). Folks usually stand up to eat it at big community suppers or other affairs—the bowls of stew and paper cups of iced tea rest on high, temporary tables which are simply wide boards nailed to waist-high poles. You will get big squares of crusty corn bread as long as it holds out. There's ice cream too, if you can still eat!

BRUNSWICK STEW

This is the recipe for your own kitchen—chicken takes the meat role

1 (6 to 8 lb.) chicken
1 lb. salt pork, sliced thin or chopped
2 qts. freshly cut corn
5 qts. tomatoes, peeled and sliced
1 qt. diced potatoes
2 qts. butter beans
2 medium onions, chopped
¼ tsp. ground red pepper or 1 medium pepper pod
Salt and pepper to taste

• Cut up chicken. Cover with water in heavy kettle; cook until meat falls away from bone, adding more water if necessary.
• Add salt pork. Add vegetables and seasonings. Simmer slowly until tender, and mixture is thick and well blended. Remove pepper pod, if used. Serve hot. Makes 15 to 20 servings. Freezes well.

VIRGINIA SPOON BREAD

Serve with Brunswick stew and serve with spoon

6 c. white cornmeal
4 qts. milk
2 doz. eggs
½ c. butter or margarine
3 tblsp. salt

• Put cornmeal into large kettle; add milk. Mix thoroughly and cook over medium heat until mixture thickens, stirring constantly. Remove from heat.
• Separate eggs. Beat whites until stiff; then yolks until thick and lemon-colored.
• Add yolks to cornmeal mixture; add butter and salt. Blend well; then fold in egg whites.
• Pour into 4 ungreased 9×13×2¼" pans. Bake in moderate oven (350°) 45 to 55 minutes. Makes 50 servings.

"Welcome Neighbor" Casseroles

Casseroles are friendly dishes. How frequently one hot-from-the-oven, carefully wrapped in newspapers to retain the heat, is sent as the first welcome to the new neighbor down the road on moving day—or to the family with illness in its ranks. Each of the three following recipes makes two family-size dishes. The busy cook fixes one for her family's dinner; at the same time she makes the gift for a neighbor.

FRENCH HUNTER'S DINNER

Hearty and extra-good

1 (8 oz.) pkg. spaghetti
1 qt. canned, drained whole kernel corn (or frozen)
2 (12 oz.) pkgs. frozen lima beans
1 c. chili sauce
2 lbs. bacon
2 lbs. cooked ham

• Cook spaghetti in boiling salted water, as directed on package, until tender. Drain.
• Mix together spaghetti, corn, lima beans and chili sauce.
• Dice bacon and ham; brown slowly in skillet. Drain. Add to vegetables, and pour into two buttered 2 qt. casseroles.
• Bake in moderate oven (350°) 30 minutes, or until sauce is thick. Makes 12 servings.

FRIDAY CASSEROLE

You can't miss with tuna, macaroni and cheese in the same dish

2 (8 oz.) pkgs. macaroni
3 (7 oz.) cans tuna, drained and flaked
2 c. canned, drained whole kernel corn
2 c. canned, drained peas or baby lima beans
2 c. cubed Cheddar (sharp) cheese
1 qt. milk, heated
4 tsp. salt
½ tsp. pepper
½ c. dry bread crumbs
2 tblsp. butter or margarine

• Cook macaroni in boiling salted water, as directed on package, until tender. Drain. Put in 2 greased 2 qt. casseroles.

• Add tuna, corn and peas.

• Melt cheese in milk; add seasonings. Pour over macaroni and fish-vegetable layer, mixing slightly. Sprinkle bread crumbs over top; dot with butter.

• Bake in moderate oven (375°) 20 minutes, or until browned. Makes 12 servings.

SCALLOPED CHICKEN

Serve with jellied cranberry sauce from a can on the cupboard shelf

4 c. cooked chicken, cut in large pieces
1 c. diced celery
1 c. soft bread crumbs
2 tblsp. minced parsley
2 c. chicken broth
4 eggs, slightly beaten
2 tsp. salt
½ c. milk

• Grease two 9″ baking dishes.

• Alternate layers of chicken with celery, bread crumbs and parsley.

• Measure chicken broth into bowl; add eggs, salt and milk, and pour over chicken. Set dishes in pan of hot water.

• Bake in moderate oven (350°) 1 hour, or until knife inserted in center comes out clean. Makes 8 to 12 servings.

CHILI DINNER MENU

Chili Con Carne
Chef's Salad
Hot Whole Wheat and White Rolls
Butter
Banana Split with Marshmallow Sauce
Coffee

CHILI CON CARNE

8 c. dry kidney beans (4 lbs.)
4 c. chopped onions
2 c. shortening or drippings
2 cloves garlic, crushed (optional)
20 lbs. ground beef
4 lbs. ground fresh pork
12 qts. cooked or canned tomatoes
5 tblsp. chili powder
⅔ c. salt
1 tsp. pepper
½ c. sugar

• Wash beans and soak overnight in water to cover. Drain, but do not season. Cover with freshly drawn water and simmer until tender. Or use 2 (6 lbs. 12 oz.) cans kidney beans.

• Brown onion slighty in hot shortening in heavy skillets; add garlic. Add ground beef and pork and cook until browned, stirring occasionally with fork to break up meat.

• Add cooked, drained kidney beans. Stir in tomatoes, chili powder, salt, pepper and sugar. Simmer 1½ hours, to blend flavors. Makes 50 servings (1 to 1½ cups each).

Note: If chili needs to be thinned, add 8 beef bouillon cubes dissolved in 2 qts. boiling water.

Variation: If you'd like to make this into an Italian Spaghetti Supper, leave beans out of Chili Con Carne and serve it over spaghetti:

18 qts. water
9 tblsp. salt
6 lbs. thin spaghetti

• Bring water to boil; add salt. Gradually add spaghetti; cook uncovered, stirring occasionally, until tender. Drain in colander; rinse.
• Makes 50 servings (about 1 cup each).

Note: If kettles won't hold 18 qts. water, cook 2 lbs. spaghetti at a time in 6 qts. boiling water, using 3 tblsp. salt for each 2 lbs. spaghetti.

CHEF'S SALAD

This mixed vegetable salad sets off the chili supper

12 hard-cooked eggs
10 heads lettuce
3 c. (½lb.) water cress or parsley
4 lbs. tomatoes
¼ c. chopped onions
2 c. cubed process cheese
3 green peppers, chopped
2 tblsp. salt
2 tblsp. paprika
2½ c. vinegar
½ c. olive or salad oil (or use 3 c. French dressing instead of vinegar and oil)

• Peel and chop eggs.
• Wash, drain and tear lettuce coarsely into bite-size chunks. Coarsely chop water cress; cut tomatoes into wedges. Combine these with onion, cheese and green peppers; toss lightly. Chill.
• Just before serving, combine salt, paprika, vinegar and oil; drizzle over salad, tossing lightly. Makes 50 servings (about 1 cup per person).

BANANA SPLIT

A dessert as American as Fourth of July

30 ripe bananas
2 gals. strawberry ice cream (or other flavor)
Marshmallow Sauce (recipe follows)
1 lb. chopped nuts

• Peel bananas and slice into 50 sauce dishes. Top each with scoop (No. 9 dipper) of ice cream.
• Spoon on sundae sauce; sprinkle with nuts. Makes 50 servings.

MARSHMALLOW SAUCE

Fluffy dessert topper for banana splits

1 lb. marshmallows or miniatures
2 lbs. sugar
2 c. water
1 c. egg whites, unbeaten (about 10)
1 tblsp. vanilla

• Cut marshmallows into quarters.
• Combine sugar and water; stir to dissolve. Boil to make thin syrup, 228° on candy thermometer.
• Add marshmallows; cook until melted and smooth, stirring constantly.
• Beat egg whites until stiff; slowly add syrup to whites, beating constantly until mixture is fluffy and well blended.
• Blend in vanilla. Makes sauce for 50 banana splits or sundaes.

Punch Bowl Favorites

The rhubarb in your garden gives our Good Luck Punch a lovely pink color and refreshing taste. One of our teenage readers who gave a graduation party with purple iris for the decoration, successfully substituted grape juice for the rhubarb. To make punch that packs some punch, add ginger ale or sparkling water just before serving.

Wreathe the punch bowl with ivy from the yard for a festive effect and float garden blossoms on orange or lemon slices. You can fasten a daisy, rosebud or freesia to the citrus "boat" by pulling the stem through the center. If you coat flowers with paraffin before floating them they will not wilt so fast. Freezing maraschino cherries or mint leaves in the ice cubes also provides a gala touch.

Another hostess trick is to make rainbow-hued ice cubes for lemonade or orange drinks. Just add a few drops of food color to the water for the different ice cube trays. When the cubes are frozen, put them in the punch cups, one color in each cup, just before pouring.

GOOD LUCK PUNCH

Pretty and pink for a party

1 qt. rhubarb (about 2 doz. stalks)
Water to cover
3 c. sugar
2 c. water
Juice of 6 lemons
1 c. pineapple juice
Rhubarb juice
1 qt. ginger ale

• Cut rhubarb in 1" pieces; add water to cover. Cook until soft, about 10 minutes. Drain through cheesecloth bag or sugar sack. Measure—should be 3 qts. juice.

• Dissolve sugar in 2 c. water; cook 10 minutes to make a syrup.

• Add lemon juice and the pineapple and rhubarb juice. Pour over chunk of ice in punch bowl.

• Just before serving, add ginger ale. Makes 1 gallon punch (24 servings).

HOT SPICY PUNCH

Especially refreshing for cold weather entertaining

½ c. tea leaves
4 sticks cinnamon
6 whole cloves
2 qts. boiling water
½ c. sugar
1 c. lemon juice
1 c. orange juice
1 qt. pineapple juice
2 c. cranberry juice cocktail
2 qts. cider (full-flavored, sweet cider)
2 qts. ginger ale

• Tie together in cheesecloth (or put in large metal tea bag) tea leaves, stick cinnamon and cloves.

• Submerge in boiling water; then remove from heat and steep 10 minutes. Remove bag.

• Add sugar, fruit juices and cider. Heat just to boiling, stirring.

• Pour ginger ale into 2 gal. punch bowl; then pour in hot tea. (A metal spoon in punch bowl will keep hot liquid from breaking it.)

FRUIT PUNCH

Makes a hit at any party

1 (6 oz.) can frozen orange juice
2 (6 oz.) cans frozen limeade
1 (6 oz.) can frozen lemonade
1 (1 lb. 14 oz.) can pineapple juice
1 pt. cranberry juice cocktail
2 to 4 c. cold water
2 qts. ginger ale, chilled
1 qt. plain soda water, chilled
Fruit; mint for garnish

• Empty frozen juices, pineapple and cranberry juice and water into large container or bowl. Thaw; stir well.
• Pour mixture into punch bowl. Add ice cubes. Just before serving, gently pour in ginger ale and soda water. Top with Fruit Ice Ring and sprigs of mint or other fruit garnish. Makes 30 servings.

Fruit Ice Ring: Use any combination of lime, lemon or orange slices. Arrange in a pattern in the bottom of the 8″ ring mold. Add water to cover fruit. Freeze. To unmold, loosen ring by dipping bottom of mold into warm water. Float on top of punch; garnish with mint leaves and, if available, fresh strawberry slices.

Big-Crowd Cakes and Candy

YELLOW LARD CAKE

1¼ c. lard
2½ c. milk
2½ tsp. vanilla
5½ c. sifted cake flour
2½ tblsp. baking powder
3⅛ c. sugar
2½ tsp. salt
5 eggs, unbeaten

• Put lard in mixing bowl; add 5 tblsp. milk and vanilla. Beat 2 minutes on mixer at medium speed, or until light and fluffy.
• Sift together flour, baking powder, sugar and salt. Add to lard mixture with ⅔ of remaining milk. Beat until smooth with mixer at medium speed, about 4 minutes.
• Add remaining milk and eggs. Beat until smooth, about 3 minutes.
• Pour into greased and floured 12½ ×18″ pan. Bake in moderate oven (350°) 35 to 40 minutes. Makes 54 (2″) squares.
• Cool and frost with Mocha Frosting.

MOCHA FROSTING

Coffee and chocolate flavors blend perfectly in this

1 c. strong coffee
¼ c. butter or margarine
¾ c. sifted cocoa
¾ tsp. salt
2 lbs. sifted confectioners sugar
1 tsp. vanilla

• Put coffee and butter in saucepan and heat to boiling.
• Add cocoa and mix well; add remaining ingredients and mix until smooth. (Add more sugar if necessary for frosting to hold shape.) Makes about 4 cups frosting, to cover top of yellow cake.

NEVER-FAIL FUDGE

We call it Merry Christmas candy because we have so many holiday requests for this big recipe

⅓ c. butter
4½ c. sugar
1 can (14½ oz.) evaporated milk
1 c. marshmallow cream
1 (13 oz.) bar sweet chocolate, grated
2 (12 oz.) pkgs. semi-sweet chocolate pieces
2 tsp. vanilla
2 c. walnuts, coarsely chopped

• Combine butter, sugar and milk. Boil 5½ minutes. Remove from heat and add remaining ingredients, except nuts. Beat until well mixed. Add nuts.
• Spoon into buttered pan. Cool until firm. Then cut. Makes 5 pounds.

Easy Main Dishes to Freeze

PORK SAVORY

Watch the meat-and-potato men and boys "fall to" when this casserole appears

3 lbs. lean pork, cut in 1" pieces
1½ tsp. salt
½ tsp. pepper
1 tblsp. fat or oil
3 c. water
2½ c. sliced carrots
1 c. sifted flour
3 c. dairy sour cream
3½ c. diced potatoes
1 tblsp. finely chopped onion
1½ c. green lima beans

• Sprinkle pork with 1½ tsp. salt and pepper.
• Brown in fat or oil. Add water, cover, and simmer until meat is tender.
• Cook carrots in a little water until almost tender.
• Combine flour and sour cream; beat until smooth.
• Add vegetables and salt, blend well. Combine with meat and broth. Makes 25 portions, ¾ cup each.

To Serve Immediately:
Bake covered in moderate oven (375°) 1 hour. Remove cover and continue baking 30 minutes, to brown top.

To Freeze:
Bake covered in moderate oven (375°) 1 hour. Cool quickly. Pack in freezer containers, seal and freeze immediately.

To Prepare Food For Serving:
Bake uncovered in hot oven (400°) until food is heated through, about 45 minutes for pints; 1 hour for quarts. Or reheat in saucepan over low heat, or in top of double boiler.

Menu Suggestion:
Serve with a tossed green salad, spiced crab apples and a fruit dessert.

BEANS AND SAUSAGE, MEXICAN STYLE

Big and little cowboys rave about this lusty Southwestern main dish

1½ qts. (2½ lbs.) dry kidney beans
4½ qts. boiling water
1 qt. chopped onions
1¼ c. chopped green pepper
1 tblsp. minced garlic
4 lbs. bulk pork sausage
2 tblsp. salt
2 tblsp. chili powder
2 qts. canned tomatoes
1 qt. bean liquor
½ c. flour

• Add beans to boiling water, boil 2 minutes. Remove from heat and soak in hot water 1 hour. (Or, if more convenient, soak overnight after 2-minute boil.) Cook the beans in soaking liquid about 1 hour (slightly underdone). Drain, save liquid.
• Combine onion, green pepper, garlic and sausage. Cook until sausage is light brown, breaking it with fork as it cooks.
• Add beans, salt, chili powder, tomatoes, bean liquor and flour. Blend well.
• Simmer until thickened, about 30 minutes, stirring frequently. Makes 25 portions, 1 cup each.

To Serve Immediately:
• Simmer until beans are tender. Spoon over mounds of fluffy rice.

To Freeze:
• Cool mixture quickly. Pack in freezer containers, seal and freeze immediately.

To Prepare Food For Serving:
• Add small amount of water and reheat in saucepan over low heat, stirring frequently. Or heat in top of double boiler. Or bake in hot oven (400°) until food is heated through, about 45 minutes for pints; 1 hour for quarts.

5

The Coffee Break

Styles come and go as do the seasons, but the coffee hour remains part of the pattern of farm life. It's the best excuse to pause briefly between breakfast and noon to relax—for people whose working day starts early to change their pace.

In winter when the men work nearby in the barnyard and feedlot more than in fields and pastures, they often are chilled and hungry by this time. No wonder the warmth of a cheerful kitchen and thoughts of full-bodied coffee and go-withs draw them to the house both morning and mid-afternoon. And in summer they frequently have coffee or iced tea from a vacuum jug, plus sandwiches and cookies, in the field.

Indeed, coffee time is family time, and everyone on hand gathers around the kitchen table to sip and eat and to exchange news of the weather . . . the new calf—how the hog market opened. And if someone drives into the yard, you invite him to join in.

When the coffee break started in this country, the setting was the pioneer home. Home-baking was routine—cookies and breads shared the spotlight with cakes and pies. Now that food freezers frequently replace cookie jars and bread boxes in many farm kitchens, baking fits into the busy woman's work schedule whenever time is available. To bring out and quickly warm frozen cookies and breads is little trouble.

Coffee time also is the busy woman's best friend. Have you discovered how much more your committee members accomplish over coffee or tea cups? Or how easy it is to entertain the new neighbor or visitor in the community? The party will move to the dining room, but the two-piece menu still holds.

Our readers tell us cookies and breads are the backbone of their coffee breaks, that their families—especially the men—prefer them. The recipes in this chapter are for coffee go-withs that are favorites of farm families. You will find coffee partners that are not too fancy. And you will spot other good ones throughout this cookbook in the chapter on cookies, for instance.

STICKIES

Pass paper napkins with this easy version of Philadelphia's Sticky Buns

⅓ c. butter or margarine
½ c. dark corn syrup
¼ c. chopped walnuts
1 pkg. refrigerator biscuits

• Preheat oven to 400°.
• Divide butter evenly in the bottoms of 10 cup muffin pan. Set in oven just long enough to melt butter.
• Remove from oven; pour corn syrup and nuts in each cup.
• Cut biscuits into thirds; roll each in syrup mixture. Put 3 pieces in each cup. Bake about 15 minutes.
• Let stand a few minutes, turn out of pan. Serve at once. Makes 10.

BISCUIT STICKS

All buttered up, ready to eat. Watch out, they're hot—that means delicious

¼ c. butter or margarine
1 (8 oz.) pkg. refrigerator biscuits
Poppy or celery seeds

• Preheat oven to 450°.
• Melt butter, pour half of it into an 8×8×2" pan.
• Shape biscuits into strips 8" long, rolling between hands and twisting; place in pan. Pour over remaining butter. Sprinkle with your choice of seeds. Bake 8 to 10 minutes.
• After removing from oven, allow to stand in pan about 2 minutes to absorb butter. Serve at once. Makes 10.

FRENCH TOAST

Looks so inviting—tastes wonderful

2 eggs, beaten
⅔ c. milk
¼ tsp. salt
8 to 10 slices day-old bread
Shortening

• Combine eggs, milk and salt.
• Dip both sides of bread slices in egg mixture quickly—do not soak. Brown lightly in shortening on hot griddle or skillet. Makes 4 to 6 servings.

French Toast in Oven or Broiler: Add 2 tblsp. sugar and 2 tblsp. melted fat to above egg-milk mixture; then dip bread. Bake in very hot oven (450°) 10 minutes per side, or broil 3" from source of heat, 4 minutes per side.

Waffle Iron French Toast: Make same recipe changes. Place dipped bread in pre-heated waffle iron. Toast is done when steam quits hissing from waffle iron.

Deep-Fat-Fried French Toast: Add 2 tblsp. sugar to egg-milk mixture. Dip bread and fry, several slices at a time in deep hot fat (380°). Turn once, drain on paper towels.

CHOCOLATE PEANUT CLUSTERS

Candy or cookie? They're luscious by either name and simple to make

⅓ c. sifted flour
⅔ c. sugar
½ tsp. salt
⅓ c. shortening
1 egg, unbeaten
2 (1 oz.) squares unsweetened chocolate, melted
2 tsp. corn syrup
1 tsp. vanilla
2½ c. shelled peanuts

• Sift flour, sugar and salt into bowl. Add shortening, egg, chocolate, corn syrup and vanilla; mix well. Add nuts.
• Drop teaspoonfuls of dough 1" apart, on greased baking sheet. Bake in moderate oven (350°) 8 minutes.
• Cool cookies before removing to wire rack—they're very tender when hot! Makes 3 dozen.

Variation: Use only 1½ c. nuts; add 1 c. raisins or use 1½ c. chopped walnuts and 1 c. chopped dates.

PEANUT DAINTIES

Tasty treat to keep on hand to serve on a minute's notice

1 lb. loaf, regular slice, white bread
½ c. peanut butter
3 tblsp. oil

• Trim crusts from slices of white bread; cut each into 4 strips.
• Spread strips of bread on baking sheet. Put crusts in a shallow pan. Cover with towel. Let stand overnight.
• Next day heat bread strips in slow oven (250°) until completely dried out. Bread ends should not curl—pieces should stay flat.
• Toast crusts; crush or use electric blender to make fine crumbs.
• Blend together peanut butter and oil. Dip bread strips into mixture; then roll in crumbs until completely coated.
• Store in tightly covered tins. Good served with hot coffee or tea. Makes 4½ dozen.

GRILLED SNACKS

Fix several helpings for the children—grownups, too

33 square graham crackers
½ c. peanut butter
⅓ c. miniature marshmallows

• Spread crackers with peanut butter; scatter marshmallows on top.
• Place low under broiler to heat and brown lightly. Serve at once.

Variation: Substitute 12 lightly toasted bun halves for graham crackers; use ¼ c. more peanut butter.

CHOCOLATE STICKS

Delightful served warm

• Make up chocolate cake batter from directions on package of mix.
• Spoon into greased corn-stick pans.
• Bake in moderate oven (350°) 18 to 20 minutes. Makes about 21.

Variation: Add 1 tblsp. instant coffee to 1 pkg. chocolate cake mix. Follow package directions for mixing and baking. Bake batter in greased 9" square pan. Frost this Mocha Cake when cool with Orange Frosting.

Orange Frosting: Blend 1 (3 oz.) pkg. cream cheese (room temperature) with 1 tblsp. shredded orange rind, 2 tsp. orange juice and 2 tsp. lemon juice. Blend in 3 c. sifted confectioners sugar. Spread on top and sides of cake; garnish with walnut or pecan halves. Makes 9 to 12 servings.

WHOLE WHEAT CUPCAKES

Just right for dessert or as a snack between meals with coffee, tea or milk

⅔ c. brown sugar, firmly packed
½ c. shortening
½ c. light molasses
2 eggs, unbeaten
2 c. sifted whole wheat flour
1 tsp. salt
1½ tsp. baking powder
½ tsp. baking soda
½ tsp. cinnamon
¼ tsp. nutmeg
1 c. grated, unpared apples
⅔ c. chopped nuts

• Gradually add sugar to shortening and cream well; stir in molasses. Add eggs, separately, beating after each.
• Sift together dry ingredients. Add to creamed mixture, alternately with apples. Blend in nuts. Fill greased muffin pans ⅔ full.
• Bake in moderate oven (375°) 20 minutes. Frost, if desired. Makes 24.

CINNAMON PECAN ROLLS

Nut-dotted, cinnamon rolls—gooey and truly luscious eating

1 c. milk, scalded
1 pkg. granular or compressed yeast
6 tblsp. shortening
6 tblsp. butter or margarine
¾ c. sugar
1 tsp. salt
2 egg yolks or 1 egg, beaten
3 c. sifted flour (about)
Melted butter or margarine
½ c. brown sugar, packed
2 tsp. cinnamon
1½ c. pecans

Caramel syrup:
1 c. corn syrup
1 c. brown sugar, firmly packed

• Cool milk to warm (110°); sprinkle granular yeast over top. (Or cool to lukewarm (85°), and crumble compressed yeast over top.)
• Cream shortening and 2 tblsp. butter; add ¼ c. sugar and salt; cream together until light and fluffy. Add yolks, yeast-milk mixture and enough flour to make soft dough. Knead until smooth and elastic on lightly floured cloth or board. Place in greased bowl; cover; let rise until doubled.
• Divide in half; roll into 2 rectangles, 9×18″, about ¼″ thick. Brush with butter.
• Mix together remaining ½ c. sugar, ½ c. brown sugar and cinnamon; sprinkle each piece of dough with half of mixture. Roll like jelly roll, cut into 1″ slices. Drop, cut side down, in greased muffin pans containing about 1 tblsp. caramel syrup and 4 to 5 pecans, rounded side down in syrup. Let rise.
• Bake in hot oven (400°) 12 to 15 minutes. Remove from oven, flip over pans at once. Remove rolls, pecan side up, onto large tray. Let pans stand over rolls a minute, so syrup drains onto them. Makes 3 dozen.

To make syrup: Mix together corn syrup, brown sugar and ¼ c. butter; heat slowly or in top of double boiler.

JAM TWISTS

For the Christmas coffee party

2 c. sifted flour
1 tblsp. baking powder
1 tsp. salt
4 tblsp. shortening
⅔ c. milk
Jam

• Combine flour, baking powder and salt; cut in shortening; then stir in milk.
• Turn dough on floured board and knead ½ minute. Roll to ¼″ thickness.
• Shape like ribbon candy by cutting dough into strips 3″ long and 1″ wide. Spread jam on half the strips, top with remaining strips; twist. Bake in moderate oven (375°) 20 to 25 minutes. Makes 16.

BLUEBERRY BUCKLE

Company special that wins enthusiastic approval from everybody

½ c. shortening
1 c. sugar
1 egg, beaten
2½ c. sifted flour
2½ tsp. baking powder
¼ tsp. salt
½ c. milk
2 tsp. lemon juice
2 c. blueberries (fresh or frozen)
½ tsp. cinnamon
¼ c. butter or margarine

• Cream shortening and ½ c. sugar; add egg; beat until light.
• Sift together 2 c. flour, baking powder and salt; add to creamed mixture alternately with milk. Spread in greased 9×9″ or 7½×12″ pan.
• Toss lemon juice with berries; sprinkle over batter.
• Make crumb topping of remaining ½ c. flour, ½ c. sugar and other ingredients; cover berries.
• Bake in moderate oven (350°) 1 hour, or until done. Serve warm. Makes 9 to 12 servings.

DUTCH PLUM CAKE

This fruity pudding cake also may be used for dessert. Serve it warm; top it with whipped cream or ice cream

1⅛ c. sugar
¼ c. flour
¼ c. butter or margarine
1½ c. sifted flour
2 tsp. baking powder
½ tsp. salt
½ tsp. grated lemon rind
¼ c. shortening
1 egg, beaten
⅓ c. milk
1 tblsp. melted butter or margarine
12 to 16 ripe prune plums
1 tblsp. lemon juice
Sweetened whipped cream

• Mix together ¾ c. sugar and ¼ c. flour. Cut in butter to make fine crumbs; set aside.

• Measure 1½ c. flour; sift with baking powder, salt and 6 tblsp. sugar. Add lemon rind; cut in shortening with pastry blender until mixture resembles coarse meal.

• Add egg and milk; stir to just moisten dry ingredients. Spread dough evenly in 8×8" greased pan. Brush with butter.

• Wash and dry ripe prune plums. Cut in half and remove pits. Press four rows of halves, skin side down, on dough; let overlap a little. Leave some space between rows. Number will depend on size of plums.

• Sprinkle with lemon juice; then with sugar-flour-butter mixture.

• Bake in moderate oven (375°) 45 minutes. Serve warm. Makes 6 servings.

Variations: Substitute 4 apples, peeled and sliced, or 6 peaches, peeled and pitted, for plums.

INDIVIDUAL PIZZAS

Spur-of-the-moment pizzas to serve hot from the oven

• Bake 1 pkg. refrigerator biscuits according to package directions. Cool and split each in half.
• Spread with tomato paste; sprinkle lightly with oregano. Top with thin slice of Mozzarella or natural sharp cheese. Sprinkle on a few drops of oil; then shake on grated Parmesan cheese.
• Bake in very hot oven (450°) 6 to 8 minutes. Dot each with piece of anchovy. Serve hot, whole or cut in half. Makes 20 pizzas.

ORANGE DATE BREAD

A good freezer. For sandwiches, use cream cheese as filling

2 c. sifted flour
1 tblsp. baking powder
½ tsp. salt
½ c. sugar
1 c. chopped dates
½ c. boiling water
½ c. orange juice
1 tsp. grated orange rind
1 egg, slightly beaten
3 tblsp. melted fat or oil
½ c. chopped pecans or other nuts

• Sift together flour, baking powder, salt and sugar.
• Chop dates, add water and let stand.
• Combine orange juice, rind, egg and fat.
• Add date mixture and nuts.
• Pour into dry ingredients. Stir to just moisten dry ingredients.
• Turn into greased 8×4" pan.
• Bake in moderate oven (350°) 1 hour. Test center of bread. If tester comes out clean, loaf is done.
• Let stand in pan 10 minutes; then turn out of pan to cool.

PRUNE PINWHEELS

Serve these whirligigs hot from the oven

2 c. sifted flour
2 tsp. baking powder
½ tsp. salt
2 tblsp. sugar
⅓ c. shortening
⅔ c. milk
2 tblsp. soft butter or margarine
¼ c. brown sugar
½ tsp. cinnamon
¼ c. raisins, chopped
¾ c. cooked, pitted prunes

• Sift flour, baking powder, salt and sugar.
• Add shortening; cut with blender or two knives until resembles coarse meal.
• Add all milk; stir just to blend.
• Knead lightly on slightly floured surface to smooth dough. Roll ¼" thick into rectangle about 8×12"; spread with butter.
• Combine brown sugar, cinnamon, raisins and prunes; spread on dough.
• Roll as jelly roll; cut into 8 slices.
• Fit slices, cut side down, into well greased medium-size muffin pans. Brush with milk.
• Bake in hot oven (400°) 15 to 20 minutes. Makes 8.

BRAN BREAD

It's full of fruit and nuts

1½ c. boiling water
1 c. chopped dates
2¼ c. sifted flour
1 tsp. baking soda
1½ tsp. baking powder
1 tsp. salt
½ tsp. cinnamon
½ c. quick-cooking rolled oats
1 c. whole bran cereal
½ c. chopped pecans or walnuts
2 c. light brown sugar
3 tblsp. melted shortening or oil
1 egg, beaten

• Pour water over dates; cool slightly.

• Sift flour with soda, baking powder, salt and cinnamon. Add oats, bran cereal and nuts.

• Add brown sugar, shortening and egg to date mixture. Stir well.

• Add dry ingredients. Stir to just blend thoroughly; do not beat.

• Pour into greased 9×5×3" loaf pan. Bake in moderate oven (350°) 60 to 80 minutes, or until done.

• Let stand 10 minutes. Turn out to cool on rack. Makes 1 loaf.

MARMALADE COFFEE CAKE

You'll want to share this coconut-crowned quick bread with friends

¼ c. shortening
½ c. sugar
1 egg, beaten
1 tblsp. grated orange rind
1¾ c. sifted flour
2 tsp. baking powder
½ tsp. salt
½ c. milk
3 tblsp. melted butter or margarine
1 c. flaked or shredded coconut
¾ c. orange marmalade
1 tblsp. sugar

• Cream shortening; add sugar and mix well. Add egg and orange rind.

• Sift together dry ingredients; add alternately with milk to creamed mixture. Beat after each addition.

• Spread dough in greased 9" square pan. Brush top with 1 tblsp. butter.

• Blend coconut with marmalade; add remaining butter. Drop by spoonfuls on dough; spread evenly over top; sprinkle with sugar.

• Bake in moderate oven (375°) 25 to 30 minutes. With glass pan, bake at 350°. Makes 9 to 12 servings.

APRICOT BISCUIT RING

Best when served warm

¾ c. drained, cooked dried apricots
¼ c. crushed pineapple, drained
4 tblsp. sugar
2½ c. prepared biscuit mix
¼ c. chopped nuts
¾ c. milk
2 tblsp. soft butter or margarine

• Combine apricots, pineapple and 2 tblsp. sugar.
• Combine biscuit mix, remaining 2 tblsp. sugar and nuts in mixing bowl.
• Add milk; moisten thoroughly with fork.
• Knead lightly on floured board or cloth.
• Roll out ¼″ thick, to make 8×14″ rectangle.
• Spread with butter, then with fruit mixture.
• Roll up, jelly roll fashion, along long side.
• Seal edge and side together; put sealed side down. Cut into ½″ slices.
• Overlap slices about halfway in well greased 8″ ring mold, or overlap slices to form ring on well greased baking sheet.
• Bake in moderate oven (375°) 20 to 30 minutes.
• Remove from pan to cooling rack. Makes 10 servings.

PINEAPPLE COFFEE CAKE

For everyone who takes a morning coffee break

1½ c. sifted flour
⅓ c. sugar
2 tsp. baking powder
¾ tsp. salt
1 egg, beaten
¼ c. melted shortening
½ c. pineapple juice (may be drained from crushed pineapple)

Pineapple Topping:

¼ c. sugar
1 tsp. cinnamon
1 tblsp. butter or margarine
⅓ c. crushed pineapple, drained

• Sift together flour, sugar, baking powder and salt.
• Combine egg, shortening and pineapple juice.
• Mix liquid and dry ingredients; beat until smooth.
• Spread in greased 9″ pie pan. Sprinkle with pineapple topping mixture.
• Bake in moderate oven (350°) 35 minutes or just until cake shrinks from sides of pan.
• Cool slightly, about 10 minutes, before serving. Makes 6 to 9 servings.

CARAWAY BREAD

All you need is butter, and tea or coffee to enjoy this

¼ c. shortening
¾ c. sugar
1 egg, beaten
1⅔ c. sifted flour
2½ tsp. baking powder
¼ tsp. salt
1 tblsp. caraway seeds
¾ c. milk
1 tsp. vanilla

• Cream shortening and sugar; add egg. Beat until light and fluffy.
• Sift together flour, baking powder and salt. Add seeds.
• Combine milk and vanilla. Add dry ingredients and milk alternately to creamed mixture. Pour into greased 9×5×3″ pan.
• Bake in moderate oven (350°) 1 hour. Cool before slicing. Makes 18 to 24 slices.

CINNAMON BREAD

Faintly warm, this fragrant coffee cake welcomes friends to your table

- **¼ c. shortening**
- **¾ c. sugar**
- **2 eggs, beaten**
- **2 c. sifted flour**
- **¾ tsp. salt**
- **1 tblsp. baking powder**
- **1½ tsp. cinnamon**
- **1 c. milk**

Topping:

- **1½ tsp. cinnamon**
- **½ c. sugar**
- **2 tsp. melted butter or margarine**

• Cream shortening and sugar well; add eggs. Beat until light and fluffy.

• Sift together flour, salt, baking powder and cinnamon. Add alternately with milk to creamed mixture.

• Pour into greased 9×9×1½" pan. Sprinkle top with mixture of topping ingredients.

• Bake in moderate oven (375°) 45 minutes, just until it shrinks from sides of pan. Cool 10 minutes before cutting—cuts more easily. Makes 9 servings.

RAISED DOUGHNUTS

Most folks like them warm and sugared

- **¾ c. milk**
- **⅓ c. sugar**
- **1 tsp. salt**
- **1 pkg. granular or compressed yeast**
- **¼ c. water**
- **4¼ c. sifted flour**
- **1 tsp. nutmeg**
- **⅓ c. soft shortening**
- **2 eggs**

• Scald milk. Add sugar and salt. Cool to lukewarm.

• Sprinkle yeast over warm (110°) water; or crumble compressed yeast into lukewarm (85°) water. Stir until dissolved. Add milk mixture, 2 c. flour and nutmeg. Beat well. Stir in shortening, then eggs.

• Add remaining flour, kneading in last portion on lightly floured surface.

• Place in greased bowl, turning once to grease top. Let rise in warm place until doubled.

• Turn out on lightly floured board. Roll dough ⅓" thick; cut.

• Remove trimmings and form into ball. When doubled, roll out and cut.

• Let cut doughnuts rise until very light (30 to 40 minutes). Leave uncovered so crust will form. Pick up on floured wide spatula and ease into deep hot fat (375°). Fry until golden brown, turning once. Drain. Makes 2 dozen.

Sugared Doughnuts: While doughnuts are still warm, dip into bowl of granulated sugar or mixture of sugar and cinnamon (½ c. sugar to ½ tsp. cinnamon). Or, when doughnuts have cooled, shake in bag containing confectioners sugar.

Glazed Doughnuts: Mix 1½ c. sifted confectioners sugar with enough boiling water to make thin glaze (about 3 tblsp.). Dip slightly cooled doughnuts into warm glaze. Cool on cake rack with piece of waxed paper underneath.

Raised Orange Doughnuts: Proceed as for raised doughnuts. In place of milk use ½ c. orange juice plus ¼ c. boiling water. Use 2 tblsp. finely grated orange rind for nutmeg.

MASHED POTATO DOUGHNUTS

A Cornhusker cook contributed this Nebraska favorite

- **¼ c. melted butter or margarine**
- **1½ c. sugar**
- **1 c. seasoned, hot mashed potatoes**
- **2 eggs, beaten**
- **4 c. sifted flour**
- **5 tsp. baking powder**
- **1 tsp. salt**
- **1 tsp. nutmeg**
- **½ c. milk**
- **Confectioners sugar**

• Cream together butter and sugar. Blend in mashed potatoes, then eggs.
• Sift dry ingredients together twice. Add to first mixture alternately with milk. Chill dough 2 hours.
• Use doughnut gun, or roll out ½" thick on lightly floured surface; cut with doughnut cutter.
• Fry in deep hot fat (360°) about 1 minute on each side. Fry 1 layer at a time and turn once. Drain on unglazed paper. Sprinkle with confectioners sugar while warm. Makes 3 dozen.

COCOA DOUGHNUT BALLS

Perfect with coffee

2 eggs, well beaten
⅔ c. sugar
2 tblsp. melted butter or margarine
1 c. milk
1 tsp. almond extract
3¼ c. sifted flour
2 tblsp. cocoa
1 tblsp. baking powder
¼ tsp. salt
Fat for deep frying
Confectioners sugar

• Combine eggs, sugar, butter, milk and almond extract; mix to blend.
• Sift together dry ingredients; slowly add to egg mixture. Beat until smooth.
• Heat fat to 370° (browns 1" bread cube in 1 minute).
• Dip balls of dough with spoon; slide into hot fat. Turn frequently to brown on all sides.
• Drain on paper toweling. Roll in confectioners sugar. Makes 3 to 4 dozen.

CHILDREN'S SNACKS

Orange-Banana Drink: Combine 1 mashed banana with 1 c. orange juice; beat to blend. Makes 1 glass.

Hot Tomato Juice: Heat 2 c. tomato juice, add 2 beef bouillon cubes and stir to dissolve. Serve in cups or mugs.

Dried-Fruit Lollipops: Stick soft, pitted prunes, stuffed with peanut butter, marshmallows, apricots or figs on skewers.

POTATO PUFF BUNS

Set out the butter and jelly, bring on the pot of coffee and these hot buns

1 pkg. granular or compressed yeast
½ c. warm water
1 c. milk, scalded
⅔ c. shortening
½ c. sugar
1½ tsp. salt
2 eggs, well beaten
1 c. mashed potatoes
6 c. sifted flour
1 tblsp. melted butter

• Crumble granular yeast over warm (110°) water or compressed yeast over lukewarm (85°) water.
• Scald milk, then cool to lukewarm.
• Cream shortening, sugar and salt; blend in eggs and mashed potatoes.
• Add yeast mixture to milk and stir into creamed mixture. Add flour to make soft dough. Turn onto floured board and knead thoroughly.
• Place in large greased bowl; cover to let rise in warm place until doubled (about 2 hours). Punch down, and knead again. Brush with butter.
• Cover tightly; place in refrigerator until ready to bake. (Will keep overnight but place in a very large bowl and cover tightly as dough rises in refrigerator.)
• About 2½ hours before baking time, pinch off dough and form into small rolls of desired shape. Place 2" apart on greased baking sheet. Cover, let rise in warm place until doubled, about 2 hours.
• Bake in hot oven (400°) 15 to 20 minutes or until lightly browned. Makes 2½ dozen.

DATE STREUSEL COFFEE CAKE

A foolproof, easy-does-it recipe for a hot bread that's a wonder

3 tblsp. sugar
2 tblsp. oil or melted shortening
1 egg, slightly beaten
¾ c. milk
2 c. prepared biscuit mix
1 (14 oz.) pkg. date bar mix

• Blend together sugar, oil, egg and milk. Stir in biscuit mix until thoroughly moistened.
• Make date filling and crumb mixture from date mix package directions.
• Spread ⅔ of biscuit dough in greased 9″ round or square baking dish. Cover with date filling mixture; sprinkle about ⅓ of crumb mixture over date filling. Add remaining coffee cake dough, spreading evenly as possible over crumbs. Sprinkle remaining crumb mixture on top.
• Bake in moderate oven (375°) 25 to 30 minutes, or until crumbs are lightly browned. Cool slightly before serving. Makes 8 to 10 servings.

CRANBERRY COFFEE CAKE

Crimson top is decorative, especially for the holidays

2¾ c. sifted flour
1 tblsp. baking powder
¾ tsp. salt
1 c. sugar
⅓ c. shortening
1 egg, beaten
½ c. milk
2 c. cranberries, coarsely ground
3 tblsp. cold butter or margarine

• Sift together 2 c. flour, baking powder, salt and ½ c. sugar. Cut in shortening until fine as meal.
• Mix egg and milk; add all at once to flour mixture, stirring until well blended. Spread evenly in greased 8″ layer pan; cover with raw berries.
• Mix remaining flour and sugar; cut in butter until mixture resembles coarse meal. Sprinkle over cranberries.
• Bake in hot oven (400°) 30 minutes. Makes 6 servings. This cake is delicious even when cold, but is best served warm.

THIRST-QUENCHER

A hot-weather treat to send to the men in the field—made with canned cider and fruit juice

1 (32 oz.) can or bottle apple cider
1 (18 oz.) can grapefruit juice
1 (18 oz.) can orange juice
Iced water
Sugar to taste

• Pour cider, grapefruit juice and orange juice in 10 qt. pail. Fill with iced water. Add sugar sparingly. Makes 10 quarts.

HALF-AND-HALF COOLER

Quick refreshment for a hot afternoon—in the house or out in the field

1 (6 oz.) can limeade concentrate
4 cans cold water
1 qt. cold ginger ale
1 lemon or lime, thinly sliced

• Combine concentrate with water according to can directions. When ready to serve, add ginger ale and lemon. Makes 8 (8 oz.) servings.

Variation: Use any flavor frozen or canned juice instead of limeade. Combine with equal amount chilled ginger ale.

Tutti-Frutti Punch: Add water as directed on cans to 1 (6 oz.) can frozen orange concentrate and 1 (5 or 6 oz.) can frozen lemonade concentrate.
• Combine with 1 (12 oz.) can apricot nectar and 1 (No. 2) can (about 2¼ c.) pineapple juice. Chill. Serve iced. Makes about 3 quarts.

6

The Cookie Jar

If you had a dollar for every batch of cookies baked last year in farm kitchens across country, you'd be rich. Of all types of baking, cookie making is most popular. For good reasons: Once the cookies are baked and put away, you can serve them on a split-second's notice. No fussing or cutting either—just arrange them on a plate and bring them to the table.

Many cookies are good keepers, too, although you may have to hide them or lock them in the freezer! And they come in "portions" which can be multiplied easily. Little children manage them well—there are fewer crumbs to sweep up than with cake. And cookies encourage milk drinking, for cookies and milk are like peaches and cream—great friends. Farm Journal readers tell us their husbands and youngsters are the lovable incentives that turn them into cookie-baking women.

Today's good cooks frequently do two jobs at a time. Getting a meal and baking cookies are two chores that combine well.

There is almost no end to variety in cookies. In the roundup of Farm Journal's recipes through the years, even the Food Department was amazed at the size of the collection. As we culled, there were constant comments like this: We *must* include the Lemon Coconut Squares—so many readers have asked us for the recipe . . . please keep all the molasses cookies—they're so good. This chapter is Farm Journal's big cookie jar.

Part of the joy of baking comes from trying different recipes to find out which ones your family and friends most enjoy. Such an adventure is the best way to build a collection of your own. We believe many of the recipes in this chapter will win a permanent place among your favorites.

Cookie Bars and Squares

ALMOND BARS

Confection or cookie? It's a skip-the-oven treat

¾ c. blanched almonds
¼ c. candied cherries
¼ c. toasted flaked or shredded coconut
1 tblsp. butter or margarine
1½ tblsp. honey
¼ tsp. almond extract
4 oz. sweet chocolate

• Grind almonds and cherries together. Add coconut.
• Cream butter, honey and almond extract together; add almond mixture; mix well.
• Shape into large rectangle on waxed paper.
• Melt chocolate; spread over top; chill until firm. Cut into 2×2½" bars. Makes 18 to 20 bars.

APPLE FUDGE SQUARES

Chocolate, applesauce and pecans blend flavors with good results

2 (1 oz.) squares unsweetened chocolate
½ c. shortening
1 c. sugar
2 eggs, well beaten
⅔ c. applesauce
1 tsp. vanilla
1 c. sifted flour
½ tsp. baking powder
¼ tsp. baking soda
¼ tsp. salt
½ c. chopped pecans

• Melt together chocolate and shortening. Blend in sugar, eggs, applesauce and vanilla.
• Sift together flour, baking powder, soda and salt; stir into chocolate mixture. Stir in nuts. Spread in greased 8×8×2" pan. Bake in moderate oven (350°) 35 to 40 minutes. Makes 16 (2") squares.

CHINESE CHEWS

Marvelous tasting

1 c. sugar
¾ c. sifted flour
1 tsp. baking powder
¼ tsp. salt
1 c. chopped pitted dates
1 c. chopped nuts
2 eggs, beaten

• Sift sugar, flour, baking powder and salt into bowl. Stir in dates and nuts.
• Add eggs; mix thoroughly. Spread in greased 15½×10½×1" pan. Bake in moderate oven (375°) about 20 minutes.
• Cut into squares while warm. Roll in confectioners sugar. Makes about 6 dozen.

NUT BARS

Chewy cookie with crackly top—perfect partner for baked apples

¾ c. sifted flour
¼ tsp. salt
¼ tsp. baking soda
2 c. brown sugar, lightly packed
2 eggs, unbeaten
1 c. walnuts, coarsely chopped

• Sift together flour, salt and soda. Add sugar and eggs, mix well; then beat quickly until fluffy. Add nuts.
• Bake in greased 9×9×1½" pan in moderate oven (350°) 30 minutes. Cool; cut. Makes 32 (1×2") bars.

SPICY APPLE BARS

Wonderful apple cookies from the Pacific Northwest

½ c. shortening
1 c. sugar
2 eggs, beaten
1 c. sifted flour
1 tsp. baking powder
½ tsp. baking soda
½ tsp. salt
1 tblsp. cocoa
1 tsp. cinnamon
½ tsp. nutmeg
¼ tsp. cloves
1 c. rolled oats
1½ c. diced peeled apples
½ c. walnuts, coarsely chopped
Confectioners sugar

• Cream shortening and sugar until light and fluffy; beat in eggs, singly.
• Sift together dry ingredients; add to creamed mixture. Stir in remaining ingredients.
• Spread into greased 11×16×1″ or 9×13″ pan. Bake in moderate oven (375°) about 25 minutes. Cool slightly; cut into bars or squares. Sprinkle with confectioners sugar. Makes 36 (2½× 1¼″) bars or 48 (2″) squares. You can bake the batter in a smaller pan and serve warm as pudding with hard sauce or lemon sauce.

BRAZIL NUT BARS

A new cookie with a rich, nutty flavor

2 c. sifted flour
2 tsp. baking powder
¾ tsp. salt
½ tsp. cinnamon
½ c. vegetable shortening
⅓ c. butter or margarine
1 c. light brown sugar, firmly packed
2 eggs, beaten
1 tsp. vanilla
1 c. Brazil nuts, thinly sliced or chopped
1 egg white

• Sift together flour, baking powder, salt and cinnamon.

• Cream shortening, butter and sugar until light and fluffy. Add eggs and vanilla; beat until light.

• Add flour mixture and half of nuts.

• Spread in greased shallow pan, 15× 10″ or two 8×8×2″ pans.

• Beat egg white slightly. Brush over dough. Sprinkle with remaining nuts.

• Bake in moderate oven (350°) 20 to 30 minutes. Cut into bars 1×2″. Cool on rack. Makes 6 dozen.

FROSTED MOLASSES CREAMS

Coffee and molasses flavors go together like crackers and cheese—one improves the other

½ c. shortening
½ c. sugar
1 egg, beaten
½ c. molasses
⅓ c. strong, hot coffee
1½ c. sifted flour
1½ tsp. baking powder
¾ tsp. salt
¼ tsp. baking soda
1 tsp. cinnamon
½ tsp. cloves

• Cream shortening and sugar; blend in egg, molasses and coffee.

• Sift together remaining ingredients; add to creamed mixture; blend well. Pour into greased, lined 9×13″ pan.

• Bake in moderate oven (350°) 25 minutes. While warm, frost with Confectioners Sugar Frosting. Cool; cut in squares. Makes 1½ dozen.

Confectioners Sugar Frosting: Cream ¼ c. butter or margarine with 2 c. confectioners sugar; add about 2 tblsp. coffee; mix until smooth enough to spread.

DREAM BARS

Two-layer cookies with chocolate, nuts and coconut on top

½ c. butter
1¾ c. brown sugar, packed
1¼ c. sifted flour
1½ squares unsweetened chocolate
2 eggs, beaten
1 tsp. vanilla
¼ tsp. salt
½ tsp. baking powder
½ c. chopped nuts
1 c. flaked or shredded coconut

• Blend butter, ¼ c. sugar and 1 c. flour; pat in bottom of 9×12″ pan; bake in moderate oven (350°) 15 minutes.
• Melt chocolate; cool. Combine eggs, vanilla, remaining 1½ c. brown sugar and salt; mix thoroughly.
• Sift together remaining ¼ c. flour and baking powder; add to egg mixture. Add chocolate, nuts and coconut.
• Remove pan from oven; pour batter on top. Bake 30 minutes longer. Makes 24 (2″) squares.

CHOCOLATE WALNUT COOKIES

Country kitchen favorite, rich with the taste of chocolate and black walnuts

1 c. sugar
2 eggs, well beaten
2 squares unsweetened chocolate
½ c. butter or margarine
1 c. sifted flour
1 tsp. baking powder
¼ tsp. salt
1 c. black walnuts, finely chopped
1 tsp. vanilla
Sifted confectioners sugar

• Gradually add sugar to eggs. Melt chocolate with butter; stir into eggs.
• Sift together flour, baking powder and salt. Add to first mixture with nuts and vanilla.
• Bake in greased 10½×15½″ pan in moderate oven (350°) 12 to 15 minutes. Cool slightly; dust with confectioners sugar. Cool completely; cut in diamonds, triangles, or bars. Makes about 7 dozen (1¾″).

TOFFEE COOKIE SQUARES

Like candy—good

½ c. butter or margarine
½ c. shortening
1 c. brown sugar, firmly packed
1 egg yolk, unbeaten
1 tsp. vanilla
½ tsp. salt
2 c. sifted flour
1 (6 oz.) pkg. semi-sweet chocolate pieces
½ c. chopped nuts

• Cream together butter, shortening, brown sugar and egg yolk. Stir in vanilla, salt and flour.
• Pat mixture into 15½×10½×1″ pan.
• Bake in slow oven (325°) 15 to 20 minutes.
• Melt chocolate; spread over warm baked mixture. Sprinkle with chopped nuts; cut into squares. Makes 3 dozen.

DATE-NUT BARS

You'll want to try these when you have a holiday cookie-baking bee

1 c. confectioners sugar
1 tblsp. fat or oil
2 eggs, beaten
¼ c. cake flour
¼ tsp. salt
½ tsp. baking powder
¾ c. chopped nuts
1 c. chopped dates
1 tsp. vanilla

• Add sugar and melted fat to eggs; blend well.
• Add sifted dry ingredients. Add nuts, dates and vanilla.
• Pour into greased 9×9″ pan. Bake in slow oven (325°) 25 minutes. Cut in bars; roll in confectioners sugar. Makes 1½ dozen.

Ball Cookies

ALMOND BUTTER BALLS

Snowballs are right for a tea party

1 c. butter or margarine
¼ c. confectioners sugar
1 tsp. vanilla
⅛ tsp. almond extract
2 c. sifted flour
1 c. chopped almonds
Confectioners sugar

• Cream butter and sugar until light and fluffy; add flavorings.
• Stir in flour and almonds; blend well.
• Form dough into tiny balls; place on ungreased baking sheet. Bake in moderate oven (350°) about 20 minutes.
• Roll cookies in confectioners sugar while warm. Makes 6 dozen.

BRAZILIAN LACE COOKIES

Lacy edges give these cookies a festive look—nice for a party

¼ c. soft butter or margarine
1½ c. brown sugar, firmly packed
2 tblsp. water
1 c. sifted flour
1 tsp. cinnamon
1 c. chopped Brazil nuts

• Cream butter; add sugar gradually and cream until light and fluffy. Blend in water.
• Sift flour and cinnamon; add nuts. Combine mixtures.
• Shape dough in small balls, about 1″. Place 2″ apart on greased baking sheet.
• Bake in slow oven (325°) about 15 minutes.
• Remove from oven; let stand about 30 seconds before lifting from sheet with wide spatula. (If cookies get too crisp to come off smoothly, return to oven and heat about a minute to resoften.) Makes about 5 dozen.

SPICY MOLASSES BALLS

Brown sugar adds to the sweet goodness of molasses

¾ c. shortening
1 c. brown sugar
1 egg, unbeaten
¼ c. molasses
2½ c. sifted flour
¼ tsp. salt
2 tsp. baking soda
1 tsp. cinnamon
1 tsp. ginger
½ tsp. cloves
Sugar

• Cream shortening and sugar; blend in egg and molasses.
• Sift together remaining ingredients; stir into creamed mixture; mix well. Shape into ¾″ balls; dip tops in sugar. Place on greased baking sheet.
• Bake in moderate oven (350°) 12 to 15 minutes. Makes about 4 dozen.

MOLASSES BUTTERBALLS

Hide these cookies if you want to have some left for supper

1 c. butter or margarine
¼ c. molasses
2 c. sifted flour
½ tsp. salt
2 c. walnuts, chopped fine

• Cream butter; add molasses.
• Sift flour and salt; stir in nuts.
• Add flour mixture to creamed mixture; blend well. Shape dough into small balls, about 1″ in diameter.
• Place on greased baking sheet; bake in moderate oven (350°) 25 minutes, or until lightly browned. Roll in confectioners sugar while warm. Makes 4 dozen.

MOLASSES-GINGER COOKIES

Good freezers. Try serving them as a side-kick to canned pears

3 c. sifted flour
1 c. nonfat dry milk
1½ tsp. salt
2 tsp. baking soda
1 tsp. cinnamon
½ tsp. ginger
¼ tsp. cloves
1 c. shortening
1½ c. molasses
¼ c. sugar
1 egg, unbeaten

• Sift together flour, dry milk, salt, soda and spices.
• Cream together shortening, molasses and sugar.
• Add egg, mix well; add dry ingredients, mix well. Chill.
• Shape into 1¼" balls, or drop from teaspoon onto greased baking sheet.
• Bake in moderate oven (375°) 10 to 15 minutes, until done. Makes about 8 dozen (2").

CRACKLE-TOP GINGER COOKIES

Their dark tops glisten with sugar

1 c. shortening
2 c. brown sugar, firmly packed
1 egg, well beaten
1 c. molasses
4 c. sifted flour
½ tsp. salt
2 tsp. baking soda
2 tsp. ginger
1 tsp. vanilla
1 tsp. lemon extract
Sugar

• Cream shortening; gradually add brown sugar. Blend in egg and molasses; beat until light and fluffy.
• Sift together dry ingredients; gradually blend into creamed mixture. (Dough should be soft but not sticky, or tops won't crackle.)
• Add vanilla and lemon extract. Chill until can be handled with light dusting of flour on hands and board (about 4 hours).
• Shape into balls about 1½" in diameter. Place on greased baking sheet. (Do not flatten.)
• Bake in moderate oven (350°) 12 to 15 minutes, or until brown. Sprinkle with sugar, then remove from baking sheet with pancake turner. Makes about 30 (large).

GINGERSNAPS

They look like brown flowers with creamy white centers

¾ c. shortening
1 c. brown sugar, firmly packed
¼ c. light molasses
1 egg, beaten
2¼ c. sifted flour
1 tsp. ginger
1 tsp. cinnamon
½ tsp. cloves
2 tsp. baking soda
¼ tsp. salt
25 blanched almonds

• Cream shortening and sugar; add molasses and egg; blend well.
• Sift dry ingredients; add to creamed mixture; mix well.
• Roll into balls (about 1½" in diameter); place 2½" apart on greased baking sheet. Flatten slightly; press almond in each.
• Bake in moderate oven (350°) 12 to 15 minutes. Makes 25 (large).

DATE AND NUT MACAROONS

⅔ c. sweetened condensed milk
1 c. flaked or shredded coconut
1 c. chopped nuts
1 c. chopped, pitted dates
1 tsp. vanilla

• Mix together all ingredients. Shape into balls and place on greased baking sheet, about 1" apart.
• Bake in moderate oven (350°) 10 to 12 minutes, until golden brown. Makes about 2 dozen.

CINNAMON FAVORITES

Dainty enough for a tea party—fine with ice cream

½ c. butter or margarine
1 c. sugar
1 egg, unbeaten
1 tsp. vanilla
1¼ c. sifted flour
1 tsp. baking powder
¼ tsp. salt
½ c. finely chopped nuts
1 tblsp. cinnamon
1 tblsp. sugar

• Cream butter and sugar. Add egg and vanilla; beat well (with electric mixer 2 minutes at medium speed).
• Sift together flour, baking powder and salt; add to creamed mixture; chill.
• Mix nuts, cinnamon and 1 tblsp. sugar.
• Mold dough into walnut-size balls; roll each in nut mixture.
• Place balls 2½″ apart on greased baking sheet. Bake in moderate oven (350°) 12 to 15 minutes. Makes about 20.

COOKIE BONBONS

Pecans inside and pecans on top—everyone raves about them

2 c. sifted flour
¼ c. sugar
½ tsp. salt
1 c. butter or margarine
2 tsp. vanilla
2½ c. finely chopped pecans
Nut halves (optional)
Confectioners sugar

• Sift flour, sugar and salt into mixing bowl. Blend in butter and vanilla with pastry blender. Add 2 c. nuts.
• Shape half the dough into ½″ balls. Roll in remaining nuts; or flatten balls and press a nut half in top of each. Bake in moderate oven (350°) 15 to 20 minutes.
• Roll remaining dough into logs; bake. Roll in confectioners sugar. Makes 4 dozen.

RAISIN-SOUR CREAM COOKIES

Please pass the coffee, too

1 c. shortening
1 c. sugar
2 eggs, beaten
2 tblsp. sour cream
½ tsp. salt
1 tsp. baking soda
1 tsp. cinnamon
1 tsp. nutmeg
1 tsp. allspice
3½ c. sifted flour
¾ c. raisins, chopped and floured

• Cream shortening and sugar; add eggs and sour cream.
• Sift together dry ingredients; stir into creamed mixture; blend well; add raisins. Chill.
• Shape into small balls; press flat with fork or sugared glass on greased baking sheet. Bake in moderate oven (375°) about 12 minutes. Makes 5 dozen.

SUPER-DUPER CHOCOLATE COOKIES

So you like chocolate, nuts and confectioners sugar? Here's your cookie

½ c. shortening
4 squares unsweetened chocolate
2 c. sugar
2 tsp. vanilla
4 eggs, unbeaten
2 c. flour
2 tsp. baking powder
⅛ tsp. salt
½ c. chopped nuts
Confectioners sugar

• Melt shortening and chocolate; add sugar and vanilla; mix well. Add eggs, singly, beating after each.
• Sift together flour, baking powder and salt. Add to chocolate mixture with nuts; mix well.
• Chill dough several hours.
• Form into small balls; roll in confectioners sugar. Bake in moderate oven (350°) 12 to 15 minutes. Makes about 6 dozen.

CRISSCROSS COOKIES

A winner because it has that wonderful lemon—brown sugar taste

4 c. sifted flour
1½ tsp. baking soda
2 tsp. cream of tartar
1 tsp. salt
1⅓ c. shortening
2½ c. brown sugar, firmly packed
1½ tsp. vanilla
1 tsp. lemon extract
3 eggs, beaten

• Sift together flour, soda, cream of tartar and salt.
• Cream shortening; add sugar gradually. Add vanilla, lemon and eggs; beat until light and fluffy.
• Add flour; mix until smooth; chill several hours.
• Roll level tablespoons of dough into balls size of small walnut.
• Place on greased baking sheet. Press lightly with tines of fork, making crisscross pattern.
• Bake in moderate oven (375°) 8 to 10 minutes. Makes 8 dozen.

CHOCOLATE MACAROONS

A chewy chocolate success

½ c. vegetable shortening
4 squares unsweetened chocolate
2 c. sifted flour
2 tsp. baking powder
½ tsp. salt
2 c. sugar
4 eggs, unbeaten
2 tsp. vanilla
Confectioners sugar

• Melt together shortening and chocolate.
• Sift together flour, baking powder and salt.
• Add sugar to chocolate, stirring until smooth. Add eggs singly, beating well after each; add vanilla.
• Add flour mixture; blend thoroughly.
• Chill dough 2 to 3 hours.
• Dip out rounded teaspoons of dough; form into small balls. Roll each in confectioners sugar.
• Bake in moderate oven (375°) about 10 minutes. (Do not overbake. Cookies should be soft when taken from oven.) Cool on rack. Makes 5 to 6 dozen.

PECAN DROPS

Cherry-decorated and rich

1 c. soft butter or margarine (half vegetable shortening may be used)
½ tsp. salt
½ c. sifted confectioners sugar
1 tblsp. vanilla
2 c. sifted flour
1 c. finely chopped pecans
Candied cherries

• Blend together butter, salt, sugar and vanilla. Add flour and pecans; mix well; chill.
• Shape into small balls; place on baking sheet. Press small hole in center of each ball with finger tip; insert piece of cherry in each. Bake in moderate oven (350°) about 15 minutes. Makes 5 dozen.

BUTTERSCOTCH DROPS

Soft and chewy

1 c. shortening
2 c. brown sugar, packed
2 eggs
½ c. buttermilk or water
3½ c. flour
1 tsp. baking soda
1 tsp. salt

• Mix shortening, sugar and eggs. Stir in buttermilk. Sift together flour, soda and salt, and add to mixture. Chill.
• Drop by teaspoonfuls on lightly greased baking sheet. Bake in hot oven (400°) until set (almost no imprint when touched with finger), 8 to 10 minutes. Makes 6 dozen (2½″) cookies.

Drop Cookies

CHOCOLATE HERMITS

Top with a chocolate confectioners sugar frosting—a decorative curl for dainty, tea-size cookies, a generous covering for the man-size cookies

1⅓ c. sifted flour
2 tsp. baking powder
½ tsp. salt
1 tsp. cinnamon
½ c. shortening
1 c. sugar
1 egg, well beaten
3 squares unsweetened chocolate, melted
1 tsp. vanilla
⅓ c. milk
1 c. raisins, chopped
1 c. nuts, chopped

• Sift together flour, baking powder, salt and cinnamon.
• Cream shortening; add sugar gradually; cream until fluffy.
• Add egg to creamed mixture with chocolate; blend well.
• Add vanilla and milk.
• Stir in dry ingredients, raisins and nuts.
• Mix well; chill 30 minutes.
• Drop by spoonfuls on greased baking sheet. Bake in moderate oven (350°) 15 minutes. Makes 2 dozen.

CHRISTMAS DROP COOKIES

Gay with holiday color, but festive any time in the year

1 lb. dates
½ c. chopped walnuts
½ c. chopped maraschino cherries
1 c. sugar
1 tsp. vanilla
3 egg whites, stiffly beaten
1 c. sifted flour

• Chop dates, nuts and cherries. Add sugar and vanilla; add egg whites to fruit mixture alternately with flour. (If mixture is dry, add a little cherry juice.)
• Drop by teaspoon on greased baking sheet. Top with pieces of cherries.
• Bake in moderate oven (350°) about 20 minutes, until lightly browned. Store in tightly covered container. (They keep indefinitely, and are better with aging.) Makes 4 dozen.

RAISIN-CARROT COOKIES

These are good keepers

1 c. sifted flour
¼ c. nonfat dry milk
¼ tsp. baking soda
1 tsp. baking powder
¼ tsp. nutmeg
¼ tsp. cinnamon
½ tsp. salt
⅓ c. shortening
⅓ c. brown sugar
½ c. molasses
1 egg, beaten
1 c. shredded carrots (or sweet potato)
1 tsp. grated lemon rind
½ c. ground or finely chopped raisins
1¾ c. quick-cooking rolled oats

• Sift together flour, dry milk, soda, baking powder and seasonings.
• Cream together shortening, sugar and molasses; add egg, then dry ingredients; stir until well blended.
• Add carrots, lemon rind, raisins and oats; mix well. (If dough is too stiff, add a few drops of milk.) Chill.
• Drop by teaspoonfuls onto lightly greased baking sheet. Bake in hot oven (400°) 10 to 12 minutes, until lightly browned. Cool on rack. Makes 5 dozen (2″) or medium size.

CORN FLAKE COOKIES

An unusual coconut delicacy

2 c. sifted flour
1 tsp. baking soda
½ tsp. salt
½ tsp. baking powder
1¼ c. shortening
1 c. white sugar
1 c. brown sugar, firmly packed
2 eggs, well beaten
1 tsp. vanilla
2 c. flaked or shredded coconut
2 c. corn flakes

• Sift together flour, soda, salt and baking powder.
• Cream shortening; add sugars gradually; beat until light. Add eggs and vanilla.
• Combine dry ingredients and creamed mixture; add coconut and corn flakes.
• Drop small teaspoonfuls on greased baking sheet, 1½" apart.
• Bake in moderate oven (350°) 8 to 10 minutes, or until delicately browned. Makes 8 dozen.

ORANGE COOKIES

Easy drop cookie with wonderful flavor

⅔ c. shortening
1 c. sugar
2 eggs, slightly beaten
1 tblsp. grated orange rind
2¼ c. sifted flour
½ tsp. salt
½ tsp. baking soda
½ c. orange juice
½ c. nuts, chopped

• Cream together shortening and sugar.
• Combine eggs, creamed mixture, rind.
• Sift together flour, salt, baking soda.
• Add dry ingredients to creamed mixture alternately with orange juice; mix until well blended. Add nuts.
• Drop tablespoonfuls onto greased baking sheet.
• Bake in moderate oven (375°) 10 minutes, or until golden brown. Makes 3 dozen.

FRUITY GUMDROP COOKIES

Apples, gumdrops and raisins add up to a taste sensation

2 c. sifted flour
½ tsp. salt
2 tsp. baking powder
½ tsp. cinnamon
½ c. shortening
½ c. sugar
1 egg, beaten
¾ c. thick applesauce
1 c. gumdrops, cut in small pieces
1 c. raisins

• Sift together flour, salt, baking powder and cinnamon.

• Cream shortening and sugar; add egg and applesauce; mix well.

• Add flour mixture; stir until well blended; stir in gumdrops and raisins.

• Drop teaspoonfuls onto lightly greased baking sheet. Bake in hot oven (400°) 10 to 15 minutes, until lightly browned. Transfer to cooling rack. Makes 4 dozen (2") or medium size.

Variations: Use drained, crushed pineapple or canned peaches, drained and mashed, instead of applesauce. Rolled oats may be substituted for gumdrops.

PEANUT MOLASSES COOKIES

Prunes and peanut butter join forces to make these cookies delicious

1 c. sifted flour
½ tsp. salt
1 tsp. baking powder
¼ tsp. baking soda
¼ c. shortening
¼ c. brown sugar
½ c. molasses
½ c. crunchy peanut butter

½ tsp. vanilla
1 egg, unbeaten
2 tblsp. milk
1 c. chopped, uncooked prunes

• Sift together flour, salt, baking powder and soda.

• Cream together shortening, sugar, molasses, peanut butter and vanilla.

• Add egg and milk; mix well. Add dry ingredients; stir until well blended.

• Add chopped prunes.

• Drop by spoonfuls on lightly greased baking sheet. Bake in moderate oven (375°) 10 to 15 minutes, or until done.

• Transfer to cooling rack. Store in tightly covered container. Makes 5 dozen (2").

HOLIDAY FRUITCAKE COOKIES

Glamor cookies with gay red and green topknots—rich with fruits and nuts

4 c. sifted flour
1 tsp. baking soda
1 tsp. salt
1 c. shortening
2 c. brown sugar, packed
2 eggs, beaten
⅔ c. thick sour milk or buttermilk
1 c. chopped pecans
1 c. candied cherries, cut in quarters
2 c. dates, cut up
2 (4 oz.) cans candied fruits and peels (1 c.)
Red or green candied cherries for top (optional)

• Sift together flour, soda and salt.

• Cream shortening; add sugar and eggs; beat until light and fluffy.

• Add sour milk and flour; then fold in nuts, cherries, dates and candied fruit.

• Chill dough.

• Drop teaspoonfuls about 2" apart, on lightly greased baking sheet.

• Top each with cherry half.

• Bake in moderate oven (375°) 8 to 10 minutes. Makes 8 dozen.

BROWN SUGAR COOKIES

Our favorite butterscotch cookies

⅔ c. butter or margarine
1½ c. brown sugar, firmly packed
2 eggs, unbeaten
1 tsp. vanilla
1 tblsp. vinegar
1 c. evaporated milk
2½ c. sifted flour
1 tsp. baking soda
½ tsp. baking powder
½ tsp. salt
1 c. chopped walnuts
Brown Butter Frosting (recipe follows)
Walnut halves

• Cream butter and brown sugar until light. Add eggs; beat well.

• Add vanilla and vinegar to milk.

• Sift dry ingredients and add alternately with milk to creamed mixture. Fold in walnuts.

• Drop by tablespoonfuls about 2" apart on greased baking sheet. Bake in moderate oven (350°) until delicately browned, about 15 minutes, or until firm to touch. Cool on cake rack. Frost with Brown Butter Frosting and garnish with nut halves. Makes about 4 dozen (2½").

Brown Butter Frosting:

½ c. butter or margarine
3 c. sifted confectioners sugar
¼ c. boiling water

• Melt butter over medium heat until light golden brown. Add sugar, then water. Beat until frosting holds its shape.

• Spread and swirl about 2 teaspoons frosting on each cookie. Makes about 2½ cups.

CRISP MOLASSES COOKIES

Precious Memory: Grandmother frosted the tops of these very thin cookies with pink icing for Christmas

3 c. sifted flour
1 tsp. salt
1 tsp. baking soda
2 tsp. cinnamon
2 tsp. ginger
⅓ c. sugar
¾ c. shortening
1⅓ c. molasses

• Sift together dry ingredients; cut in shortening.
• Heat molasses; add to flour mixture. Chill until stiff enough to roll (3 hours or overnight). Roll very thin, about 1/16", on lightly floured board. Cut with cookie cutter (leaves, butterflies, gingerbread men or other shapes). Decorate with nuts, colored sugar or orange rind.
• Bake on lightly greased baking sheets in hot oven (400°) 7 to 8 minutes, or until lightly browned. Makes 6 dozen.
• To make drop cookies, do not chill dough. After mixing, drop from teaspoon onto lightly greased baking sheet. Flatten with bottom of glass; bake as for rolled cookies.

ORANGE-CARROT COOKIES

Cheerful as a Kansas sunflower—kind to the budget

1 c. shortening
¾ c. sugar
1 c. cooked mashed carrots
1 egg, unbeaten
1 tsp. vanilla
2 c. sifted flour
2 tsp. baking powder
½ tsp. salt

• Cream shortening and sugar until fluffy. Add carrots, egg and vanilla; mix well.
• Sift together flour, baking powder and salt; add to carrot mixture; mix well. Drop batter by teaspoonfuls on greased baking sheet.
• Bake in moderate oven (350°) about 20 minutes. Makes 5 dozen. While warm, frost with Golden Glow Frosting.

Golden Glow Frosting: Combine juice of ½ orange; grated rind of 1 orange, 1 tblsp. butter or margarine and 1 c. sifted confectioners sugar.

OATMEAL MOLASSES COOKIES

Thin, crisp cookies with lacy edges

¾ c. flour
½ c. sugar
2 tsp. baking powder
½ tsp. salt
2 tsp. baking soda
1 tsp. cinnamon
½ tsp. nutmeg
½ tsp. cloves
2½ c. quick-cooking rolled oats
1 c. raisins
⅔ c. melted shortening
1 egg, beaten
¾ c. molasses
1 tblsp. milk

• Sift together dry ingredients.
• Combine oats and raisins; sift flour mixture over top.
• Combine in bowl shortening, egg, molasses and milk. Pour over dry ingredients; mix well. Drop by teaspoonfuls on greased baking sheet. Bake in moderate oven (350°) 8 to 12 minutes. Makes 3 dozen.

BROWN SUGAR DROPS

1 c. soft shortening
2 c. brown sugar, firmly packed
2 eggs
½ c. buttermilk or thick sour milk
3½ c. sifted flour
1 tsp. baking soda
1 tsp. salt

• Mix well shortening, sugar and eggs; stir in buttermilk. Combine with sifted dry ingredients. Chill dough.
• Drop spoonfuls on greased baking sheet about 2" apart. Bake in hot oven (400°) 8 to 10 minutes. Makes about 5 dozen.

Rolled Cookies

GINGER COOKIES

A big recipe to make when you wish to put cookies in the freezer

5½ c. sifted flour
1 tblsp. baking soda
2 tsp. baking powder
1 tsp. salt
¾ tsp. ginger
1 tsp. cinnamon
1 c. shortening
1 c. sugar
1 egg, beaten
½ tsp. vanilla
1 c. dark molasses
½ c. strong coffee

• Sift together flour, soda, baking powder, salt, ginger and cinnamon.
• Cream shortening; add sugar gradually; beat until light; add egg and vanilla.
• Add molasses and coffee, then sifted dry ingredients; mix well; chill.
• Roll out on lightly floured board ¼″ thick; cut with round 2″ cutter.
• Bake on greased baking sheet in hot oven (400°) 8 to 10 minutes. Makes 12 dozen.

MOLASSES COOKIES

Cutouts—as varied as the shape of your cookie cutters

1 c. sugar
1 c. shortening
1 c. light molasses
1 tblsp. vinegar
6 c. sifted flour
½ tsp. salt
1 tsp. baking soda
½ tsp. baking powder
1 tsp. ginger
1 tsp. cinnamon
2 eggs, beaten

• Combine sugar, shortening, molasses and vinegar in saucepan; bring to boil; cook 2 minutes. Cool.
• Sift together flour, salt, soda, baking powder and spices.
• Add eggs to cooled molasses mixture. Add dry ingredients; mix well. Chill.
• Roll out on lightly floured board, about ⅛″ to ¼″ thick. Cut; put on greased baking sheet.
• Bake in moderate oven (375°) 8 to 10 minutes or until done. Makes about 12 dozen (2½″) cookies.

SUGAR COOKIES

Sugar-topped, old-fashioned cookies—men say: "Make them bigger"

1 c. shortening
1 c. sugar
1 c. dairy sour cream
3 egg yolks, beaten
1 tsp. vanilla
3 c. sifted flour
1 tsp. salt
1 tsp. baking powder
½ tsp. baking soda

• Cream shortening and sugar thoroughly; add sour cream, egg yolks and vanilla.
• Sift together dry ingredients; add to creamed mixture, blending well; chill.
• Shape into balls, working with small portions at a time, keeping remaining dough chilled.
• Roll out ⅛″ thick on lightly floured surface. Cut with floured 2½″ cutter; sprinkle cutouts with sugar.
• Bake on greased baking sheet in moderate oven (375°) about 15 minutes. Makes 6 dozen.

MINCEMEAT CHEESE COOKIES

For the Christmas cookie jar

½ c. butter or margarine
¼ lb. (1 c.) cheese, grated
1 c. sifted flour
1 (9 oz.) pkg. mincemeat
½ c. water

• Cream butter; add cheese (at room temperature); cream together until well blended.
• Stir in flour; mix well; chill.
• Roll out ⅛" thick on lightly floured board; cut with floured 2" cookie cutter. Put half of circles on greased baking sheet 1" apart.
• Cook mincemeat and water until slightly thickened. When cool, put 1 tsp. of mixture in center of cookies on baking sheet. Top each with another circle of dough; press edges together with fork tines. Prick top cookie in several places.
• Bake in moderate oven (350°) 15 minutes, or until delicately browned. Makes 30.

ALMOND MOONS

Dainty crescents—from a California farm kitchen

2¾ c. sifted flour
1½ tsp. baking powder
¼ tsp. salt
¾ c. butter or margarine
1½ c. sugar
½ tsp. almond extract
2 eggs, beaten
½ c. ground unblanched almonds

• Sift together flour, baking powder and salt.
• Cream butter and sugar until light and fluffy. Add almond flavor and eggs; beat well.
• Put almonds through food chopper.
• Add flour and almonds. Chill dough.
• Roll dough about ⅛" thick. Cut with crescent-shaped cutter.
• Bake in moderate oven (350°) 8 to 10 minutes. Makes about 10 dozen.

Refrigerator Cookies

BLACK WALNUT COOKIES

A cousin of the old-fashioned Pennsylvania Dutch slapjacks

6 c. sifted flour
1 tsp. salt
½ tsp. baking soda
1 tsp. cream of tartar
1¾ c. butter or margarine
2¼ c. brown sugar, firmly packed
½ c. sugar
2 eggs, beaten
2 tsp. vanilla
1½ c. black walnut meats
1½ c. flaked or shredded coconut

• Sift together flour, salt, soda and cream of tartar.
• Cream butter, add sugars gradually. Beat until fluffy. Add eggs and vanilla.
• Grind nuts and coconut together in food chopper using medium blade or use blender. Add to creamed mixture; add flour mixture. Blend well. Chill.
• Shape into 4 rolls about 2" in diameter. Wrap in waxed paper or foil. Chill.
• Cut rolls into ⅛" slices; place on ungreased baking sheet.
• Bake in moderate oven (350°) 10 to 12 minutes. Makes 8 to 9 dozen.

LEMON COOKIES

A tea time delicacy

1 c. butter or margarine
½ c. sugar
1 egg, beaten
2 c. sifted flour
½ tsp. baking powder
⅛ tsp. salt
1 tblsp. lemon juice
½ tsp. grated lemon rind

• Cream together butter and sugar; add egg; mix well.

• Sift together flour, baking powder and salt; combine with sugar mixture. Add lemon juice and rind.
• Form into rolls; wrap in waxed paper or pack into frozen-juice cans; chill.
• Slice very thin. Bake on greased baking sheet in moderate oven (375°) 8 to 10 minutes. Makes 5 to 6 dozen.

OATMEAL REFRIGERATOR COOKIES

Bake at serving time—nothing is better than cookies warm from the oven

1½ c. sifted flour
1 tsp. baking soda
1½ tsp. salt
1 c. shortening
1 c. white sugar
1 c. brown sugar, firmly packed
2 eggs, well beaten
1 tsp. vanilla
3 c. quick-cooking rolled oats

• Sift together flour, soda and salt.
• Cream shortening; add sugars gradually; beat until light; add eggs and vanilla.
• Combine dry ingredients and creamed mixture; blend thoroughly. Add oats.
• Pack into frozen-fruit-juice cans. Chill thoroughly. Detach bottom of can; use to push dough out to slice. (Or shape dough into rolls 2″ across.)
• Cut into thin slices; bake on ungreased baking sheet in hot oven (400°) 6 to 8 minutes. Makes 6 dozen.

REFRIGERATOR COOKIES

To bake on the spur of the moment

3½ c. sifted flour
1 tsp. salt
1 tsp. cinnamon
1 tsp. baking soda
1 c. shortening (half butter)
2 c. brown sugar
2 eggs, well beaten
2 tblsp. warm water
1 tsp. vanilla
1 c. chopped nuts

• Sift together flour, salt, cinnamon, soda.
• Cream shortening; add sugar gradually; beat until light. Add eggs, water and vanilla; mix well.
• Combine dry ingredients and creamed mixture; blend well. Add nuts.
• Pack dough into clean, frozen-fruit-juice cans. Chill thoroughly—overnight for best results. Detach bottom of tin; use to push dough out to slice.
• Bake on ungreased baking sheet in hot oven (400°) 10 to 12 minutes. Makes 6 dozen.

Fancy Spritz Cookies

This is one of the most delightful cookies borrowed from Scandinavia where butter is the favored shortening. You can shape Spritz in tiny trees, flowers, the traditional S or in other fancy forms.

SPRITZ COOKIES

Dainty and rich—to serve on a winter night with hot fruit punch or coffee

2¼ c. sifted flour
½ tsp. baking powder
¼ tsp. salt
1 c. shortening (part butter)
¾ c. sugar
1 egg or 3 egg yolks, beaten
1 tsp. almond extract

• Sift together flour, baking powder and salt.
• Cream shortening; add sugar gradually; beat until light; add egg and almond extract.
• Add dry ingredients; work with hands if it seems crumbly.
• Force dough through cookie press onto ungreased baking sheet. Bake in hot oven (400°) 7 to 10 minutes until set but not brown. Makes 6 dozen.

These Cookies Travel Well

A California boysenberry grower's wife makes these cookies for her son away at school. She says they are good travelers—he says they are good tasters.

BROWNIES

More like candy than cake

1 c. sugar
2 eggs
2 squares unsweetened chocolate
½ c. butter or margarine
½ c. flour
1 tsp. vanilla
½ c. chopped walnuts

Frosting:

1 c. sugar
1 egg, beaten
2 tblsp. light cream
2 squares unsweetened chocolate
2 tblsp. butter or margarine
1 tsp. vanilla

• Add sugar to eggs; beat. Melt chocolate and butter; add to egg mixture. Blend in flour; add vanilla and nuts. Spread in greased 8×8×2" pan.
• Bake in moderate oven (350°) 25 to 35 minutes; cool.
• Combine frosting ingredients. Bring to boil, stirring constantly. Remove from heat; stir until of spreading consistency. Spread over cooled brownies. Cut in 2" squares. Makes 16.

FRUIT BARS

Cookie-jar raiders' dreams come true

2 c. seedless raisins
1½ c. glazed fruit, chopped
1 c. chopped walnuts
½ c. fruit juice (orange or pineapple)
2 tsp. vanilla
1 c. butter or margarine
2 c. sugar (or 1 c. brown and 1 c. white)
2 eggs, beaten
4½ c. sifted flour
2 tsp. cinnamon
2 tsp. baking powder
1 tsp. baking soda

• Rinse raisins in hot water, drain; dry on towel.
• Combine raisins, glazed fruit, nuts, fruit juice and vanilla; let stand.
• Cream butter, sugar and eggs. Add sifted dry ingredients in thirds; mix until smooth. Add fruit; blend well. Let stand 1½ hours in refrigerator (or overnight). Spread in greased 11×16×1" pan.
• Bake in hot oven (400°) 15 to 20 minutes, until lightly browned. When cool, cut into bars, 1½×3". Makes about 5 dozen.

LEMON-COCONUT SQUARES

A Farm Journal 5-star cookie

1½ c. sifted flour
½ c. brown sugar
½ c. butter or margarine

Filling:

2 eggs, beaten
1 c. brown sugar, firmly packed
1½ c. flaked or shredded coconut
1 c. chopped nuts
2 tblsp. flour
½ tsp. baking powder
¼ tsp. salt
½ tsp. vanilla

Frosting:

1 c. confectioners sugar
1 tblsp. melted butter or margarine
Juice of 1 lemon

• Mix together 1½ c. flour, ½ c. sugar and butter; pat down well in buttered pan (9×13"). Bake in very slow oven (275°) 10 minutes.

Filling: Combine eggs, sugar, coconut, nuts, flour, baking powder, salt and vanilla. Spread on top of baked mixture. Bake 20 minutes in moderate oven (350°).
• While warm, spread with frosting: combine confectioners sugar, melted butter and lemon juice. Cut in squares. Makes about 24 (2") squares.

7

Meats

Farm women carry platters to the table for just about every meal they serve. Meat takes the spotlight three times a day in their homes, for that's country custom and many farmers think they haven't had a square meal without it. Breakfast brings crisp bacon ribbons, ham slices dappled with brown, or expertly seasoned sausage cakes—and eggs. Dinner, still served at noon as a rule, features such favorites as roasts and steaks, with satiny smooth gravy. Supper platter specials are countless—ground beef in dozens of dress-ups has its share of champions.

The recipes in this Farm Journal meat collection are among the world's finest. We include beef, pork, lamb and veal recipes. But the great American hot dogs show up, too; so do directions for making tempters out of liver and tongue. More than half the recipes are worthy of highlighting company meals.

You'll find in this chapter the route to perfect roast beef, to pork roast shiny with apricot glaze. Roast lamb with mint, as prepared by good cooks in New England and the West, where it rates as a superb delicacy, is so rewarding that we predict our recipe will spread it to other areas. We also present elegant baked and glazed ham for gala meals, especially Christmas and Easter.

Our Food Department holds that a meat thermometer is the only accurate way to gauge the split-second degree of doneness that tailors a roast to family taste. All our recipes recognize the cardinal rule to successful meat: low-temperature cooking.

Because roasting meat properly keeps in the flavorful juices, gravy lovers sometimes think they are short-changed. They like the rich color and taste that juices browned in the pan give. Our Food Department offers an easy way to soothe their feelings—a recipe for superlative gravy without browned drippings.

Dozens of recipes in this chapter had their origin in farm and ranch kitchens of this great meat-eating country of ours. We are confident you'll find among them many new and some old friends that will please you and your meat-and-potato men.

Beef at Its Best

All choice country collections of meat recipes start with roast beef. In most farm kitchens salt and pepper are the only seasonings added, but garlic is coming up in popularity. Some good cooks slice an onion and, with toothpicks, pin it on the ends and over the top of the meat. They discard the onion when the roast is cooked, but it leaves a faint flavor in the meat and brown gravy.

STANDING RIB ROAST

No. 1 on the favorite-meat list

6 to 8 lb. standing rib roast
1 clove garlic (optional)

• Preheat oven to 325°. Stand roast, fat side up, in shallow open pan. Insert meat thermometer into center of thickest part. Do not let point touch bone. Insert peeled, cut garlic between two ribs or rub surface of meat with cut garlic. (Always roast 2 ribs or more.)

• Roast uncovered until meat thermometer reaches temperature for doneness desired: 140° for rare; 160° medium; 170° well done. (Approximate time for 6 lb.: rare—2¼ hours; medium—2½ hours; well done—3⅓ hours. For 8 lbs.: rare—3 hours; medium—3½ hours; well done—4½ hours.) Remove roast to hot platter.

Variation: For a new, tangy barbecue-type flavor combine ⅓ c. each vinegar, lemon juice and oil. Add ½ tsp. soy sauce, salt and pepper to taste. Mix well. Pour half over rib roast just before it goes into oven. When this has been absorbed, add remaining sauce and baste from pan every 30 minutes until done.

How to Make Gravy

Roasting meat at the correct low temperature, 325°, results in a roasting pan almost free of browned meat extractives—flavor so necessary for making good gravy.

Country women, with their meat-potato-and-gravy husbands, have found a way out: Brown the flour in some of the fat from the roast. Then for flavor add canned meat broth instead of water for the liquid. Canned beef broth goes into gravy made with roast beef or lamb, and chicken broth for veal and pork.

Here's how to do it. Remove roast to hot platter. Pour fat from roaster and add broth to pan. Let stand a few minutes and scrape loose any browned particles. Measure 4 tblsp. of the fat into heavy skillet. Add 4 tblsp. flour and cook, stirring, until quite brown. Add 2 c. broth and cook, stirring until thickened. Season with salt and pepper. Makes about 2 cups.

BRAISED POT ROAST

Fork-tender meat with lots of rich brown gravy

2 tblsp. flour
2 tsp. salt
¼ tsp. pepper
3 to 4 lbs. beef roast, cut 2" thick (blade or arm pot roast)
2 tblsp. fat or oil
1 medium onion, sliced
3 peppercorns (whole black peppers)
1 small bay leaf
1 c. water

• Combine flour, salt and pepper; rub mixture into surface of meat.
• Heat fat in electric skillet or Dutch oven over surface heat. Brown meat well on one side; add onion, pepper and bay leaf. Turn meat; brown other side.
• Place meat on flat, low rack. Add water; cover; cook slowly 2 hours. Add water as needed to keep ½ to 1" in pan. Makes 6 to 8 servings.

ROLLED POT ROAST

A bouquet of favorite vegetables cooks around the roast

4 to 5 lbs. rolled chuck or rolled rump beef roast
1 clove garlic, cut
2 tsp. salt
3 tblsp. flour
2 tblsp. fat or oil
1 c. water
6 medium potatoes, peeled
6 to 8 carrots, cleaned
6 medium onions, peeled

• Rub meat with cut garlic; sprinkle with salt; rub in flour.
• Heat fat in deep heavy pan or fryer. Brown beef on all sides (15 to 20 minutes). Place meat on low, flat rack.
• Add about 1 c. water. Keep ½ to 1" water in kettle. Cover tightly.
• Simmer over low heat or bake in moderate oven (350°) about 1 hour per pound or until meat and vegetables are tender. (Add vegetables 1 hour before roast is done.) Allow ⅓ lb. per serving. Makes 8 to 10 servings.

To Make Gravy: Remove meat to hot platter. Add 2 to 3 c. water, depending on size of roast. Use 3 to 6 tblsp. flour mixed with cold water to make thin, smooth paste. Stir slowly into hot broth. Cook 5 minutes, until thickened. Season.

SAVORY POT ROAST

Raisins are the surprise ingredient

2 onions, sliced
1 clove garlic, minced
2 tblsp. fat
4 lbs. blade or round bone chuck roast
1 tblsp. salt
¼ tsp. pepper
2 large bay leaves
½ c. raisins
1 c. water

• Brown onions and garlic lightly in hot fat in heavy skillet or Dutch oven.
• Add meat; brown slowly on all sides, about 20 minutes. Add remaining ingredients; cover tightly, and simmer slowly until tender, about 3 hours.
• Remove meat to warm platter. Discard bay leaves.

For Gravy: Measure liquid. To each cup broth, add 2 tblsp. flour blended with ¼ c. water. Cook until thickened. Serve gravy with meat. Makes 6 to 8 servings.

POT ROAST SEASONINGS

Curry: Mix 1 tblsp. curry powder and 1 tsp. sugar with ½ c. water. Stir into broth around pot roast.

Chili Sauce: About ¾ hour before pot roast is done, add 2 medium onions, sliced, 1¼ c. chili sauce and ½ c. chopped dill pickles to broth. Don't thicken broth for gravy—skim off fat.

SWISS STEAK

Spicy chili sauce substitutes for tomatoes ordinarily used

6 tblsp. flour
2 tsp. salt
¼ tsp. pepper
2 lbs. round steak, cut 1" thick
4 medium onions
6 tblsp. shortening
½ c. chopped celery
1 clove garlic, minced
¾ c. chili sauce
¾ c. water
1 green pepper (optional)

• Combine flour, salt and pepper; rub into both sides of steak, or pound in with meat mallet. Cut into 8 portions.
• Peel and slice onions. Preheat skillet; add half of shortening, then onions; brown lightly. Remove from skillet.
• Add remaining shortening. Brown steak on both sides. Reduce heat.
• Add celery, garlic, chili sauce and water. Cover; simmer 1 hour.
• Cut green pepper into slices. Add pepper and onions to meat. Continue cooking 30 minutes or until meat is tender. Makes 8 servings.

STEAK WITH TOMATO SAUCE

Have you forgotten how good this steak tastes—how easy it is to fix?

2 lbs. bottom round, chuck or rump steak, cut 1" to 1½" thick
1½ tsp. salt
⅓ c. flour
¼ c. fat or oil
1 large onion, sliced
1 (8 oz.) can tomato sauce
1 (4 oz.) can mushrooms (stems and pieces)

• Cut meat in half or in serving size pieces. Season with salt; rub with part of flour. Pound remaining flour into meat with meat mallet or edge of heavy plate. Continue to turn, flour and pound until all flour is used.
• Heat fat in skillet; add meat; brown well on both sides. Add onion rings during browning.
• Pour tomato sauce, ½ can water and mushrooms over meat. Cover; bake in moderate oven (350°) 2 hours or until tender. Makes 6 to 8 servings.

CIDER STEW

Proof there's something new in beef stews —something extra-tasty

3 large onions, sliced
3 tblsp. drippings
2 lbs. beef (neck or shank), cut in chunks
3 tblsp. flour
2 tsp. salt
¼ tsp. pepper
¼ tsp. thyme
1 c. cider
1 tblsp. ketchup
3 large potatoes, peeled
4 medium carrots, cleaned

• Brown onions in hot drippings; push aside and brown meat.
• Combine flour, salt, pepper and thyme; add gradually to meat. Stir in cider and ketchup.
• Cover and cook slowly until meat is almost tender, about 2 hours. (If you're pressure-stewing, use 15 pounds pressure for 18 minutes.)
• Cut potatoes and carrots into quarters; add to meat; simmer 30 minutes longer (5 minutes under pressure).
• Remove meat and vegetables to platter, and thicken drippings for gravy. Makes 6 servings.

BROWN STEW

Brown the meat "slow and deep" to achieve top flavor

3 tblsp. fat
1 clove garlic, cut in half
2 lbs. beef chuck, cut in 1½" cubes
2 tsp. salt

¼ tsp. pepper
1 tsp. Worcestershire sauce
1 tsp. lemon juice
1 small bay leaf
4 c. hot water
3 medium potatoes, cut in halves
4 carrots, cut in thirds
1 c. celery (in 1" pieces)
1 c. cooked lima beans
1 c. cooked peas
¼ c. flour
½ c. water

• Heat fat in Dutch oven, deep stew pan or large fryer. Add garlic and meat. Brown meat on all sides in hot fat.
• Add salt, pepper, Worcestershire sauce, lemon juice, bay leaf and 2 c. water. Cover. Simmer 2 hours; stir occasionally.
• Remove bay leaf. Add 2 c. water, potatoes, carrots and celery. Continue cooking 30 minutes or until vegetables are done. Add beans and peas.
• Blend together until smooth ¼ c. flour and ½ c. water. Stir into liquid to thicken. Makes 8 servings.

CHILI DUMPLING STEW

A Texas dandy—verdict of several ranchers in the Lone Star State

1 (1 lb. 4 oz.) can red kidney beans
2½ c. cubed raw potatoes
1 tblsp. salt
½ tsp. pepper
4 c. water
1 tblsp. shortening
½ c. chopped onion
1 lb. ground beef
2 tsp. chili powder
1 (10½ oz.) can condensed tomato soup

• Combine kidney beans (do not drain) with potatoes, 2 tsp. salt, pepper and water in 5 qt. saucepan; bring to a boil.
• While mixture boils, heat shortening in skillet. Sauté onion until tender; add beef, chili powder and 1 tsp. salt; cook until meat is well browned.
• Add meat and tomato soup; stir well; simmer 1 hour. Return to boil, and add Egg Dumplings.

Egg Dumplings: Sift together 2 c. flour, 4 tsp. baking powder and ½ tsp. salt; mix 1 beaten egg, and ¾ c. milk; stir into flour. Drop by spoonful onto boiling stew. Cover tightly; steam (without lifting lid) until done, 12 to 15 minutes. Add 1 c. dairy sour cream just before serving. Makes 12 servings.

LEMON BAKED BEEFSTEAK

Barbecue flavor with tantalizing aroma as it cooks

3 lbs. chuck steak
2 tblsp. softened butter or margarine
2 tsp. salt
¼ tsp. pepper
1 large lemon, sliced
2 medium onions, sliced
1 c. ketchup
1 tblsp. Worcestershire sauce
¼ c. water

• Wipe steak with damp cloth; place in large baking dish. Rub with softened butter. Season; cover with lemon and onion slices.
• Combine ketchup, Worcestershire sauce and water, and pour over steak. Cover tightly so meat will steam tender. (Aluminum foil makes a snug-fitting lid.) Bake in moderate oven (350°) 2 hours, or until tender. Makes 6 servings.

Mixed Herbs: Combine equal amounts fresh minced chives, parsley and thyme. Sprinkle on steaks.

Tips From Good Cooks: Borrow a trick from the French: tie a sprig each of thyme, parsley with a piece of carrot, a stalk of celery and a sprig of basil. Add to stew at start of cooking; remove to serve.

SHORT RIBS

A Farm Journal 5-star recipe

4 lbs. short ribs
1 tblsp. salt
1 qt. water
¼ tsp. pepper
1 small bay leaf
6 carrots, cut in 1½" pieces
2 c. small onions, peeled

• Brown meat on all sides in own fat; pour off excess. Add seasonings; cover with water. Simmer, covered, until tender, about 2 hours.
• Add carrots and onions the last 20 minutes.
• Thicken broth by adding mixture of 2 tblsp. flour and ¼ c. water for each cup of broth. Cook, stirring, until thick. Makes 6 to 8 servings.

Potato Dumplings:

2 c. riced potatoes
2 tblsp. flour
1 egg, beaten
½ tsp. salt
⅛ tsp. nutmeg
⅛ tsp. black pepper
2 tblsp. chopped parsley

• Combine all ingredients, except parsley; mix thoroughly.
• Drop dumplings on top of stew. Cover and steam 6 to 8 minutes.
• Sprinkle parsley on top of dumplings before serving. Makes 6 to 8 servings.

BARBECUED SHORT RIBS

Subtle blending of seasonings does big things for ribs—favorite with ranchers

3 lbs. short ribs
1 c. tomato sauce, purée or ketchup
1 c. water
¼ c. vinegar
1 tblsp. sugar
1 tblsp. prepared horse-radish
1 tblsp. prepared mustard
1 tsp. salt
¼ tsp. pepper
2 onions, chopped fine
2 tblsp. chopped parsley

• Wipe meat with damp cloth; place in deep bowl.
• Combine remaining ingredients; pour over short ribs. Let stand in refrigerator at least 4 hours (overnight, for best flavor).
• Place in Dutch oven or shallow baking pan. Cover (use foil if pan is coverless) and cook until tender, about 3 hours. Add more water as needed.
• Put meat in serving dish. Skim excess fat off sauce; then spoon sauce over ribs. Makes 6 servings.

Dutch Oven Dinner: An hour before end of cooking time, peel 12 medium-size whole onions and put alongside meat. Cut circle of aluminum foil, using lid for pattern, and fit into pan on top of meat. Put 6 scrubbed, medium potatoes on top of foil (out of barbecue sauce). Cover and continue cooking. Meat, onions and potatoes should be cooked in 1 hour. Makes 6 servings.

MEAT LOAF

Ribbons of bacon on top baste this loaf with fine flavor

2 lbs. ground beef
1 medium onion, sliced
2 eggs, unbeaten
1½ tsp. dry mustard
1 tsp. chili powder
1½ c. stewed tomatoes
2 slices bread, broken into pieces
2 tsp. salt
¼ tsp. pepper
4 strips bacon

• Combine all ingredients except bacon. Pack into 9×5×3" loaf pan. Place bacon strips across the top.
• Bake in preheated electric roaster or in moderate oven (350°) 1½ hours. Makes 8 to 10 servings.

TWIN MEAT LOAVES

Two loaves for a take-it-easy big meal

2 eggs, beaten
¾ c. milk
1½ c. bread crumbs
2 tsp. salt
¼ tsp. pepper
1 tsp. Worcestershire sauce
½ c. chopped onion
1 c. chopped carrot
2 lbs. ground beef

• Combine ingredients; mix well.
• Pack into two 7½×4×2" pans.
• Bake in moderate oven (350°) about 1 hour. Makes 10 to 12 servings.

SAVORY MEAT LOAF

Full of old-fashioned flavors

1 c. milk
1 tsp. savory
½ tsp. thyme
2 tblsp. minced parsley
3 c. soft bread cubes
1 tblsp. prepared mustard
2¼ tsp. salt
2 eggs
2 lbs. ground beef

• Combine all ingredients, except meat.
• Add meat and mix well; shape into loaf in shallow pan, or pack into 8½×4½" pan.
• Bake in moderate oven (350°) 1 hour. Makes 6 to 8 servings.
• Good served with buttered carrots and small whole potatoes.

WAYS WITH MEAT LOAVES

Cheese: Place layer of meat loaf made from 2 lbs. meat mixture in loaf pan, gently press down and place 2 slices process cheese on top. Repeat until ½ lb. cheese is used. Have cheese slices on top. Bake as usual.

Meat Loaf Ring: Spread ½ c. ketchup in ring mold. Turn meat mixture into mold and bake.

Quick Meat Loaf: Shape meat loaf mixture in oval-shaped mounds; place in greased baking pan. Bake—cuts cooking time in half.

ROLLED STUFFED FLANK STEAK

It will give the family a happy surprise for supper

1 flank steak (1½ to 2 lbs.)
1 tsp. salt
⅛ tsp. pepper
1 tblsp. prepared mustard
1½ c. day-old bread, cut in ½" cubes
1 tsp. poultry seasoning
1 medium onion, chopped
½ c. chopped celery
¼ c. melted shortening or oil
2 tblsp. flour
1 c. water or beef broth
Fat for frying

• Have steak scored (or do it yourself by crisscrossing shallow diamond-shaped cuts on both sides of meat to tenderize).
• Sprinkle both sides with salt and pepper; spread mustard over top.
• Toss bread, poultry seasoning, onion and celery with shortening.
• Spoon mixture evenly over top of steak. Roll up, beginning with narrow end; fasten with skewers, and lace with string, if necessary. Sprinkle with flour.
• Brown well on all sides in hot fat in Dutch oven over medium heat.
• Add water. Cover tightly; cook over low heat 1½ hours, or until tender. Or cover and bake in moderate oven (350°) 2 hours. Remove meat; make gravy. Makes 6 to 8 servings.

STUFFED MEAT ROLL

Just as delicious as it is thrifty

1½ lbs. ground beef
½ lb. ground fresh pork
1 tsp. salt
¼ tsp. pepper
1 (10½ oz.) can condensed tomato soup
¼ c. chopped onion
3 tblsp. butter or margarine
1 egg, beaten
3 c. bread cubes (6 slices)
¼ tsp. salt
⅛ tsp. pepper
¼ tsp. thyme or sage

• Combine meats, salt, pepper and soup.
• Turn onto waxed paper; pat into 14×9″ rectangle.
• Cook onion in butter; add to egg with remaining ingredients; mix.
• Spread over meat; roll lengthwise.
• Bake in shallow pan in moderate oven (350°) 1 hour. Garnish with spiced crab apples. Makes 6 to 8 servings.

NORWEGIAN MEAT PIE

Meat crust holds delightful filling

4 eggs
½ c. milk
1½ c. bread cubes
¾ lb. ground beef
1½ tsp. Worcestershire sauce
½ tsp. lemon juice
1 tblsp. chopped onion
1 tsp. salt
¼ lb. sliced bacon (about 5 strips)
¼ lb. sharp process cheese
½ c. chopped celery
2 c. milk
½ tsp. salt
½ tsp. celery salt
½ tsp. garlic salt

• Beat 1 egg with milk; add bread cubes; let stand about 5 minutes. Add beef, Worcestershire sauce, lemon juice, onion and salt; mix well.
• Line bottom and sides of 9″ or 10″ pie pan with mixture.
• Fry bacon until crisp; crumble, and sprinkle over meat in pan.
• Shred or cube cheese; sprinkle cheese and celery over top.
• Beat remaining 3 eggs slightly; add milk and seasonings. Pour gently into meat shell. Bake in hot oven (400°) 15 minutes. Reduce heat to moderate (350°) and bake 30 minutes, or until custard tests done. Makes 6 servings.

BEEF PIE SUPREME

Dip the spoon deep into the stew—it's a great dish

1½ lbs. beef for stew (boneless shoulder or chuck)
¼ c. flour
1 tsp. salt
⅛ tsp. pepper
3 tblsp. fat
1 c. water
1 c. canned tomatoes
2 tsp. Worcestershire sauce
6 carrots
12 small onions, peeled
3 c. mashed potatoes
⅓ c. process cheese spread
Melted butter or margarine

• Cut meat into 1½″ cubes.
• Mix flour, salt and pepper; roll meat in mixture to coat all sides.
• Brown meat well in hot fat; add water, tomatoes and Worcestershire sauce.
• Peel carrots; cut into 1″ crosswise slices. Peel onions; add to meat.
• Cover tightly. Simmer 2 hours. Stir occasionally to avoid sticking.
• Pour into greased 2 qt. casserole.
• With mixer blend together mashed potatoes and cheese spread. Drop by spoonfuls around rim of casserole. Brush with melted butter. Bake until bubbly hot in moderate oven (375°), about 30 minutes. Makes 6 to 8 servings.

Pork Chops With Carrots Simple, time-saving main dish, page 118, especially in electric skillet. One of many excellent meat dishes in Chapter 7.

Molded Beef Ring Meat set in gelatin and waiting in the refrigerator brings peace of mind when company's coming. Recipe, page 289, is in Chapter 19.

More Potato Variety One of our good potato salads in Chapter 9 (p. 146). Below, French Fries you can start (and freeze), finish at the last minute (p. 151).

Serve Potatoes With Variety In Chapter 9 you'll find recipes for Puffed-Up Potatoes, page 151, Cheese-Topped Potatoes, page 145 (both pictured).

SOONER MEAT BALLS

Exciting meal-in-a-dish

1 lb. ground beef (not too lean)
¼ tsp. celery seed
½ tsp. Worcestershire sauce
½ c. fine dry bread crumbs
¼ c. milk
2½ tsp. salt
¼ c. fat
2 c. tomato juice
1 c. water
2 c. green lima beans (fresh, canned or frozen)
½ c. uncooked rice
½ c. chopped onion
¼ c. chopped green pepper. .
⅛ tsp. pepper

• Combine the first five ingredients, with 1½ tsp. salt. Shape mixture into 12 balls.
• Brown meat balls on all sides in hot fat.
• Combine tomato juice, water, limas, rice, onion and green pepper. Add 1 tsp. salt and pepper; pour over meat balls.
• Cover; simmer about 30 minutes, or until rice is tender. Stir occasionally to prevent sticking. Makes 6 to 8 servings.

SAVORY MEAT BALLS

They're especially seasoned to pep up lazy appetites

1 (1 lb. 13 oz.) can tomatoes
2 tsp. chili powder
2 tsp. dry mustard
1¼ tsp. salt
¼ tsp. allspice
½ tsp. celery seed
1 tsp. Worcestershire sauce
2 tsp. prepared horse-radish
1 tsp. brown sugar
1 egg, beaten
1 c. milk
1 c. dry bread crumbs
1 tblsp. grated onion
½ tsp. pepper
1 lb. ground beef
2 tblsp. shortening

• Put undrained tomatoes through sieve into heavy 4 qt. saucepan. Add seasonings and sugar; mix well. Bring to boil; then simmer 20 minutes.
• Combine egg, milk, bread crumbs, and onion; let stand 5 minutes. Add ground beef. Shape into 1" balls. Makes 4 to 5 dozen.
• Melt shortening in skillet; add meat balls; cook until lightly browned. Add to tomato mixture.
• Simmer very gently 30 minutes. Serve with cooked spaghetti, macaroni or rice. Makes 6 to 8 servings.

MEAT PUFFS

Hamburger in new dress—what a dish!

2 tblsp. fat
2 medium onions, thinly sliced
6 slices bread
1 c. milk
2 eggs, unbeaten
½ c. finely chopped green pepper
1 tsp. seasoned salt
1 lb. ground beef
9 thin onion slices

• Melt fat in skillet; add onions; sauté until golden brown.
• Crumble bread into mixing bowl; add milk; let stand until bread is moist. Add eggs; mix well. Add onion, green pepper and salt; add meat; mix well.
• Pile mixture lightly into greased 2½" muffin pans. Top each with thin onion slice. Bake in hot oven (425°) until nicely browned, about 30 minutes. Makes 9 puffs.

HAMBURGER IDEAS

Potato Burgers: To 1 lb. ground beef add 1 c. crushed potato chips. Cook patties as usual.

Bean Burgers: To ¾ lb. ground beef add 1 c. drained and mashed, canned kidney beans. Cook patties in small amount of bacon drippings.

Cheese Bean Burgers: Lay process cheese slices on top of hamburgers the last few minutes of cooking. Serve topped with spoonful of hot baked beans in buttered bun halves.

MIXY-BURGERS

Measure in a few seasonings to make these hamburgers bring out praises

1 tblsp. shortening
½ c. chopped onion
¼ c. chopped green pepper
¼ c. chopped celery
1 lb. ground beef
¼ c. Cheddar cheese, diced
1 (8 oz.) can tomato sauce
1 tblsp. vinegar
1 tblsp. sugar
1½ tsp. Worcestershire sauce
⅛ tsp. pepper
1 tsp. salt
4 or 5 toasted hamburger buns, split in half

• Melt shortening in top of chafing dish or heavy skillet directly over heat.
• Add onion, green pepper and celery; cook until lightly browned.
• Add beef; stir with fork or spoon while meat browns.
• Add remaining ingredients. Simmer 10 minutes, stirring occasionally.
• To serve, spoon onto warm buns. Eat with fork. Makes 8 to 10 servings.

EASY-BURGERS

Plain good eating

2 eggs
1 tsp. salt
⅛ tsp. pepper
1 tblsp. flour
1 tblsp. finely chopped onion
1 lb. ground beef
¼ c. milk or cream

• Beat together eggs, seasonings and flour until smooth.
• Stir in onion, beef and milk; mix well.
• Drop 12 spoonfuls into hot fat in skillet; flatten to make small patties.
• Fry 2 to 3 minutes; turn and fry on other side. Serve between slices of buttered bread or in toasted buns. Makes about 12 thin patties.

CHEESE-STUFFED HAMBURGERS

Bite in—it's hamburger glorified

2 lbs. ground beef
1 tsp. salt
⅛ tsp. pepper
6 slices Cheddar or blue cheese

• Shape ground beef into roll, about 3" in diameter. Seal in plastic film; put in freezer.
• Cut roll of beef into 12 slices, ½" thick. Sprinkle with salt and pepper; lay slices of cheese on half of them. Top with remaining slices of beef, pinching sides together.
• Fry or broil, about 10 minutes per side. Makes 6 servings.
• You may also serve plain—slice roll in ½" slices and broil 10 minutes each side.

HAMBURGER DELIGHT

A "fix-and-forget" dish

¼ lb. thin spaghetti
4 tblsp. oil or melted fat
1 small green pepper, chopped
1 small onion, chopped
½ c. canned whole kernel corn
¼ c. grated process cheese
¼ lb. ground beef
1 (8 oz.) can tomato sauce
1 tsp. salt

• Cook spaghetti as directed on package; drain. Combine with all other ingredients.
• Pour into greased 1 qt. casserole.
• Bake in moderate oven (350°) 1 hour. Makes 4 servings.

TONGUE WITH SPICY SAUCE

Here's a tasty dish with pickup, if you like tongue

2 tblsp. fat or oil
1 small onion, minced
1 c. diced celery

1 (8 oz.) can tomato sauce
½ c. water
½ tsp. salt
1 tsp. Worcestershire sauce
⅛ tsp. pepper
Dash ground cloves
1 tblsp. vinegar
1 (6 oz.) can beef tongue

• Heat fat in saucepan. Add onion and celery; sauté until golden.
• Add remaining ingredients except the tongue; simmer 15 minutes.
• Cut tongue into ½" cubes; add to cooked sauce; heat through.
• Serve over cooked spaghetti, noodles or potatoes. Makes 4 servings.

LIVERBURGERS

Almost everyone goes for liver fixed this way with potatoes

1 lb. liver
2 c. diced raw potatoes
1 c. chopped onions
1½ tsp. salt
⅛ tsp. pepper
2 tblsp. fat

Gravy:

3 tblsp. tomato paste
1 tblsp. flour
1½ c. milk
½ c. cream
1 tsp. salt
⅛ tsp. pepper

• Put liver, potatoes and onions through meat grinder twice. Add seasonings.
• Drop liver mixture by spoonfuls onto hot fat in skillet. Fry quickly. Remove burgers from pan.
• For gravy, blend tomato paste and flour into drippings in pan. Add milk, cream and seasonings. Bring to boil, stirring constantly.
• Add liverburgers; simmer, covered, 15 minutes. Makes 8 servings.

LIVER LYONNAISE

We're in favor of this new way to fix liver

1 lb. sliced liver
3 tblsp. flour
2 tsp. salt
¼ tsp. pepper
3 tblsp. fat
3½ c. cubed potatoes
1 c. thinly sliced onions
1 (10½ oz.) can condensed cream of celery soup
½ c. milk

• Cut liver into 1½" cubes.
• Blend flour and half the salt and pepper. Roll liver in flour mixture. Brown on all sides in hot fat in heavy skillet; remove liver from pan.
• Fry potatoes and onion in remaining fat until lightly browned and potatoes are tender.
• Alternate liver and potato-onion mixture in 1½ qt. baking dish. Combine soup, milk, salt and pepper and pour over top.
• Cover; bake in moderate oven (375°) 40 minutes. Makes 6 servings.

LIVER PUFFS

1½ lbs. liver
3 onions, peeled
1 egg
1 c. cracker crumbs
1 tsp. salt
1 c. hot water

• Simmer liver in water until firm, then grind it with onions.
• Add remaining ingredients. Blend; shape into 6 patties and pan-fry in hot bacon fat until brown on both sides.

VEAL LOAF

Invitingly hot in cool weather and temptingly cold and frosty in summer

1½ lb. ground veal
¼ lb. ground lean pork
¼ tsp. garlic salt
½ c. finely chopped onion
2 c. bread cubes (4 slices)
¼ c. shredded Cheddar cheese
2 tsp. salt
½ tsp. pepper
2 eggs, beaten
¾ c. milk

• Combine all ingredients thoroughly.
• Pack into 9½×5¼×2¾" pan.
• Bake in moderate oven (375°) 1¼ hours. Makes 8 servings.

For "frosting" on cold loaf: Soak 1 envelope unflavored gelatin in 3 tblsp. cold water; dissolve over hot water. Add slowly to 1 c. mayonnaise and 2 tblsp. mustard dressing. Spread; chill. Garnish with stuffed olive slices.

VEAL PLATTER

Good hot or cold. Sweet potatoes are a fine accompaniment

2 lbs. onions, peeled
3 lbs. veal, cubed
2 eggs, slightly beaten
2 tblsp. water
⅔ c. fine, dry bread crumbs
⅓ c. cornmeal
2 tsp. salt
⅛ tsp. pepper
¼ c. hot fat
1 c. juice from spiced peaches
Spiced peaches

• Cook onions in boiling salted water, uncovered, until tender, about 20 minutes.
• Place veal cubes on 12 skewers.
• Combine eggs and water.
• Mix bread crumbs, cornmeal, salt and pepper.
• Dip meat into crumbs, then into egg, again in crumbs. Brown on all sides in hot fat in heavy skillet. Add juice from peaches.
• Drain; add cooked onions. Cook, covered, until meat is tender, about 30 minutes. Just before serving, add spiced peaches, heat through. Makes 8 servings.

GRILLED FRANKWICHES

Serve with potato salad on summery days—hot potato soup when weather is cold

12 slices bread
2 c. ground frankfurters
1 c. chopped walnuts
2 tblsp. prepared mustard
1 c. mayonnaise or salad dressing

• Toast bread on one side.
• Combine remaining ingredients. Spread on untoasted side of bread.
• Broil about 2 minutes or until edges brown. Cut sandwiches in halves and serve hot. Makes 6 servings.

SAVORY MACARONI AND FRANKFURTERS

You won't have to coax the family to eat this popular mixture

1 (12 oz.) can frankfurters
3 tblsp. fat or oil
3 tblsp. flour
1 tsp. salt
⅛ tsp. dry mustard
Dash of powdered sage
Dash of curry powder
⅛ tsp. chili powder
1 small bay leaf
1 (1 lb. 13 oz.) can tomatoes
1 (8 oz.) pkg. macaroni, cooked

• Cut frankfurters into 1" pieces.
• Heat fat; add frankfurters; brown lightly.
• Add flour and seasonings; blend with fat and frankfurters in pan.
• Force tomatoes through coarse sieve; add pulp to ingredients in pan. Bring to boil, stirring constantly. Reduce heat; continue to cook until thickened.
• Serve over hot, drained macaroni. Makes 6 servings.

Frankfurter Broiler Meal

MENU

Chilled Tomato Juice
Frankfurters Toasted Buns
Savory Cooked Carrots Buttered Corn
Head Lettuce Salad
Canned Pears Chocolate Sauce
Beverage

Here is a broiler meal that requires no more than 15 minutes last minute preparation. Early in the day, put the tomato juice, canned pears and chocolate sauce to chill in the refrigerator. Sometime during the day, cook the young carrots whole.

BROILER FOODS FOR 4 SERVINGS

1 (1 lb. 4 oz.) can whole kernel corn
8 frankfurters
Soy sauce
8 frankfurter buns
Small pre-cooked carrots (8 or 10)
Lemon juice
Butter or margarine

To broil the dinner:

• Drain corn; empty into pan under broiler rack, or onto large piece of foil; turn up edges of foil; sprinkle with salt and pepper; dot with butter or margarine.
• Place pan under heat to preheat (1 or 2 minutes); arrange food on broiler rack.
• Score frankfurters, making 2 or 3 shallow diagonal cuts in one side of each. Place on broiler rack. Brush with soy sauce.
• Place cooked carrots beside frankfurters. Brush with lemon juice; then with melted butter or margarine.
• Put rack over corn. Broil 5 minutes.
• Turn frankfurters and carrots.
• Place split buns on rack with them. Broil about 2 minutes, or until lightly toasted. Brush with melted butter. Serve a frankfurter between two halves.

CORNED BEEF CASSEROLE

Quick main dish for a busy day

¼ c. butter or margarine
¼ c. flour
2½ c. milk
2 tsp. salt
⅛ tsp. pepper
1 tblsp. prepared horse-radish
1 tsp. prepared mustard
1 (8 oz.) pkg. noodles, cooked
1 (12 oz.) can corned beef
1 (16 oz.) can peas, drained
1 tblsp. chopped pimiento

• Melt butter; add flour and stir until smooth. Gradually add milk and cook until thickened, stirring constantly.
• Add seasonings.
• Add half of sauce to drained noodles.
• Line bottom and sides of greased 2 qt. casserole with noodle mixture.
• To remaining sauce add cubed corned beef and peas. Fill center of casserole; sprinkle with chopped pimiento.
• Bake in moderate oven (350°) 20 minutes. Makes 6 to 8 servings.

HEARTY HE-MAN SNACKS

Eggs with Corned Beef Hash: Pat contents of 1 (12 oz.) can corned beef hash into small skillet. With back of spoon make 2 hollows in hash. Cook over low heat about 15 minutes. Break an egg into each hollow. Cover; cook 5 minutes or until eggs are cooked. Serve hot with ketchup and buttered toast or crusty bread.

Variation: Pat canned corned beef hash into pie pan. Bake in moderate oven (350°) about 20 minutes. Loosen edges of hash, cut into 4 pie-shaped pieces. Serve topped with creamed peas or potatoes.

Frankfurter Flapjacks: Cut frankfurters in penny-size slices. Add to pancake batter and bake like any other griddlecakes.

BEANS AND SAUSAGE

Supper on the spur of the moment

1 (1 lb. 10 oz.) can baked beans
1 small onion, chopped
¼ c. ketchup
1 tsp. prepared mustard
½ tsp. salt
½ tsp. monosodium glutamate
⅛ tsp. pepper
2 (4 oz.) cans Vienna sausages, drained

• Empty baked beans into a greased 1½ qt. casserole. Add onion. Combine ketchup, mustard and seasonings. Add to beans. Stir gently.

• Arrange sausages on beans. Bake in moderate oven (350°) 45 minutes. Makes 6 servings.

Beefburger Broiler Meal

MENU

Beefburger Special
Tomato with Parmesan Cheese
Green Beans
Shoestring Potatoes
Whole Wheat Bread
Chilled Cantaloupe or Watermelon
Beverage

This may become your Sunday night special, it's so easy to prepare. The meat, potatoes and other vegetables all go in the broiler. For the meat, combine: 1 lb. ground beef with 1 tsp. salt, ⅛ tsp. pepper, ½ c. soft bread crumbs, ¼ c. milk, 1 tblsp. minced onion. Shape mixture into 6 patties about ¾" thick. Wrap loosely in waxed paper; keep refrigerated until ready to broil. Wash and store tomatoes.

BROILER FOODS FOR 4 SERVINGS

1 (1 lb. 4 oz.) can cut green beans
Beefburgers
4 to 6 tomatoes
2 (2¼ oz.) cans shoestring style potatoes
Parmesan cheese

To broil the dinner:

• Drain green beans; place in pan under broiler rack or on large piece of foil; turn up edges of foil. Sprinkle with salt and pepper and dot with butter or margarine.

• Place burgers on broiler rack, over green beans. Broil 8 minutes (well done). Season with salt and pepper, and turn.

• Cut stem ends off unpeeled tomatoes, score tops; place on rack beside beefburgers; brush with melted butter or margarine. Broil 5 minutes.

• Empty shoestring potatoes on piece of foil with edges turned up to prevent spilling. Place on broiler rack.

• Top tomatoes with Parmesan cheese.

• Broil all food 1 or 2 minutes, to heat potatoes.

LIMA-SAUSAGE CASSEROLE

Quick, easy and satisfying

2 (10 oz.) pkgs. frozen lima beans
2 (4 oz.) cans Vienna sausages
1 (10½ oz.) can condensed tomato soup, undiluted

• Fill 6 individual casseroles or a 2 qt. casserole with lima beans. Top each with sausages. Spoon tomato soup over top.

• Bake, covered, in moderate oven (350°) 20 minutes.

How to Roast Pork

• Select roast, either loin or rib. Have your meat man loosen backbone from ribs for easy carving.
• Season with salt and pepper; place in roasting pan, fat side up.
• Roast uncovered in slow oven (325°) allowing 35 to 40 minutes per pound, or until meat thermometer registers 185°. Do not add water. Remove backbone before placing on platter. To carve, cut down between the ribs.

ROAST PORK WITH SPICY APRICOT GLAZE

Fat top is just brown enough, white meat is lean and tender

1 loin, rib or shoulder pork roast
Salt
Pepper
Whole cloves
1 c. dried apricots
2 c. water
½ c. brown sugar
1 tblsp. cornstarch
Cooked green beans

• Score roast by cutting through fat with knife to form squares. Rub with salt and pepper; stick with cloves. Place on rack in open roasting pan, fat side up. With meat thermometer, insert so bulb reaches the center of thickest part of meat. Roast in moderate oven (350°) 35 minutes per pound, about 3 hours for 5 lb. roast; or 185° on meat thermometer.
• Simmer apricots, without soaking, in water until tender; pour off juice (should be 1 cup).
• Half an hour before end of roasting time, combine brown sugar, cornstarch and half the apricot juice; spoon over meat. Baste frequently with mixture and drippings until pork has beautiful golden glaze. Put roast on platter. Circle with green beans and apricots. Season beans with ¼ c. drippings and remaining apricot juice.

HONEY-GLAZED BAKED HAM

King of the platter—this ham has made many a good cook's reputation

Whole or half ham
Cloves
Prepared mustard
¾ c. brown sugar
3 tblsp. honey

• Place ham, fat side up, on rack in shallow baking pan. Bake in slow oven (325°) uncovered and no water added, according to the timetable that follows.
• Remove from oven 30 minutes before it is baked. Pour off drippings. Remove all skin. With a sharp knife score fat into diamond shapes. Cut about ¼ inch deep. Stick a clove in the middle of each diamond.
• To glaze ham: Spread the whole surface with prepared mustard. Cover generously with brown sugar. Drizzle on honey. Return to a moderate oven (375°) and bake the remaining half hour. Serve hot, or chill and slice. Garnish with parsley.

Variation: Use Honey-Cherry Glaze instead of honey. Combine 1 c. clear strained honey, 2 tblsp. cherry juice drained from maraschino or canned cherries and 1 tsp. dry mustard. Add the last 30 minutes of cooking, basting every 10 minutes with some of the mixture.

Plan on the following amounts for a serving: uncooked ham with bone in, ¾ pound; uncooked boneless ham, ⅓ pound; cooked boneless ham, ¼ pound.

SWEET GLAZES FOR HAM

Spread any of the following glazes over hot fat-scored (diamond-cut) baked ham instead of honey glazes (above). Then bake in a hot oven (400°) until surface forms a glistening brown glaze.

• 2 c. maple syrup.
• 2 c. barbecue sauce.
• 2 c. ginger ale
• ½ c. orange, peach or apricot marmalade.
• 1 c. cranberry or currant jelly.

BAKED HAM TIMETABLE

Oven temperature 325°. Cooking time is for hams that have been refrigerated.

Type of ham	Wt. in lbs.	Hours
Uncooked ham	6 to 9	2½–3
(Cook-before-	9 to 12	3–3½
eating)	12 to 15	3½–4
	15 to 18	4–4½
Whole Cooked	6 to 9	1½–2
or	9 to 12	2–2½
Boned & Rolled	12 to 15	2½–3
(Ready-to-eat)	15 to 18	3–3½
Canned Hams	6 to 8	2–2½
	8 to 13	2½–3

If you use meat thermometer: Ham is done when internal temperature registers 160° for cook-before-eating type; 130° for ready-to-eat type.

HAM SLICE

Two-story treat with mincemeat in between the slices

2 slices ham, cut 1" thick
1½ c. prepared mincemeat
½ c. pineapple juice

• Place one ham slice in shallow baking pan. Spread mincemeat over ham; cover with second ham slice. Pour pineapple juice over top.
• Bake in moderate oven (350°) about 1 hour, basting frequently.
• Thicken remaining liquid for spicy gravy. Makes 6 servings.

HAM LOAF

Juicy, flavorful, brown-topped

2 lbs. ground smoked ham
1 lb. ground veal
2 c. soft bread cubes
¼ c. chopped onion
¼ c. chopped green pepper
½ tsp. salt
⅛ tsp. black pepper
⅛ tsp. ground cloves
½ tsp. Worcestershire sauce
1 (10½ oz.) can condensed cream of celery soup
2 eggs, beaten

• Mix ingredients; pack into 9×4" loaf pan.
• Bake in moderate oven (350°) 1¼ hours. Makes 8 servings.

Harvest Supper

Serve this with lima beans baked in cream, baked potatoes (or quick-cooking rice), and for dessert—Bing Cherry Mold.

HARVEST HAM BALLS

A duet of crusty ham balls and golden peaches

1 egg, beaten
½ c. soft bread crumbs
½ c. milk
1 tblsp. brown sugar
⅛ tsp. ground cloves
1 lb. ground cooked ham
8 canned peach halves, drained
Green celery tops or parsley

• Combine egg, crumbs, milk, sugar, cloves and ham; shape into 8 balls.
• Place peach halves, hollow sides up, in greased shallow baking dish. Nest a ham ball in each peach half. Bake in moderate oven (350°) 25 minutes.
• Garnish with celery. Makes 8 servings.

SPICY HAM SLICE

Something different, something good

1½" thick slice pre-cooked ham
2 tblsp. prepared mustard
3 tblsp. finely chopped onion
1 c. ketchup
½ tsp. anise seed
5 triangles American cheese
Onion rings

• Place ham in shallow baking dish.
• Spread with mustard; sprinkle with onion. Bake in hot oven (400°) 15 minutes.
• Remove from oven; pour ketchup over ham; sprinkle with anise seed.
• Arrange cheese triangles over the top.
• Bake 10 minutes longer, or until cheese melts. Serve with onion rings. Makes 4 servings.

HAM TAMALE PIE

Complete menu with tossed salad and fruit dessert

1 slice (1 lb.) ready-to-eat ham or 2½ c. cubed baked ham
3 tblsp. melted fat or oil
¾ c. chopped onion
1 clove garlic, minced
1½ tsp. chili powder
2 tblsp. flour
1 green pepper
2 c. tomato juice
1 (4 oz.) can mushroom stems and pieces
2 c. cooked lima beans (fresh, frozen or canned)
1 pkg. corn muffin mix
½ c. milk
1 egg, beaten

• Cut ham into 1" cubes.
• Heat fat in large skillet. Add onion and garlic. Cook 5 minutes. Add the cubed ham. Sprinkle with chili powder and flour. Continue to cook over moderate heat 10 minutes. Stir occasionally.
• Cut pepper into eighths; add to ham along with tomato juice, mushrooms with liquid and lima beans. Bring to boil; reduce heat, cook 2 to 3 minutes, stirring constantly.
• Pour hot mixture into greased 2 qt. casserole. (A shallow one allows more space for topping.) Place in moderate oven (375°) while mixing topping.
• Blend corn muffin mix with milk and egg. Spoon over hot ham mixture (in a wide crisscross pattern, if you wish).
• Bake 25 minutes, or until topping is golden brown.
• If meat and vegetable mixture is made ahead and chilled in refrigerator, heat it in oven until bubbly hot before adding topping. Makes 6 to 8 servings.

MENU

Ham-Vegetable Scallop
Cole Slaw
Hot Rolls
Apple Pie with Cheese
Coffee Milk

HAM-VEGETABLE SCALLOP

Good main dish around which to build—see menu above

1 (10½ oz.) can condensed cream of mushroom soup
½ c. milk
⅓ c. finely chopped onion
2 c. diced potatoes
1 c. sliced carrots
1 (10 oz.) pkg. frozen lima beans, thawed
1½ c. cooked ham, cut in strips
½ c. buttered soft bread crumbs
Parsley

• Mix soup and milk; heat to boiling, stirring; add vegetables alternately with ham to fill greased 1½ qt. casserole. Sprinkle bread crumbs over top. Make cup-shaped hole in center; line with thin ham slices. Border with ham strips.
• Bake in moderate oven (350°) 1 hour. Tuck crisp sprigs of parsley into ham "cup" before serving. Makes 6 servings.

HAM-MACARONI ROLL-UPS

Ham glamorizes macaroni and cheese

½ (8 oz.) pkg. whole macaroni
2 cloves garlic
6 to 8 thin slices cooked ham
½ lb. sharp process cheese
⅓ c. milk
½ tsp. dry mustard
½ tsp. Worcestershire sauce

• Cook unbroken macaroni in boiling salted water with garlic. Drain and divide into 3 or 4 portions. Cut each in half; wrap with ham slices; fasten with toothpicks.
• Bake in shallow pan in slow oven (300°) 10 to 15 minutes. Serve hot with cheese sauce.
• To make sauce, melt cheese in milk; stir until smooth; add mustard and Worcestershire. Makes 6 to 8 servings.

Variation: If you wish, wrap asparagus spears in ham instead of macaroni.

CREOLE PORK CHOPS

Brown chops right after breakfast; fix and bake casserole at dinner time

4 loin or center cut pork chops 1½" thick
Salt and pepper
1 tblsp. fat or oil
⅓ c. ketchup
½ c. water
½ tsp. salt
½ tsp. celery seed
3 tblsp. cider vinegar
¼ tsp. ginger
1 tsp. sugar
1 tsp. flour

• Sprinkle chops lightly wth salt and pepper. Brown on both sides in fat in a heavy skillet. Remove chops to casserole or baking dish.
• Combine remaining ingredients; pour over chops.
• Bake uncovered in slow oven (325°) 1½ hours. Turn chops after first hour of baking. Makes 4 servings.

NIPPY PORK CHOP PLATTER

Mustard gives chops the tang

6 lean pork chops, ¾" thick
Prepared mustard
¼ c. flour
1 tsp. salt
¼ tsp. pepper
2 tblsp. melted fat
1 (10½ oz.) can condensed chicken rice soup

• Spread pork chops with thin coating of mustard.
• Combine flour, salt and pepper in paper bag; shake chops in bag to coat with flour, then brown in melted fat in heavy skillet.
• Place chops in baking dish; cover with soup. Cover; bake in moderate oven (350°) 40 minutes. Makes 6 servings.

Scalloped Tomatoes and Corn are a good accompaniment for these Pork Chops. Combine in casserole: Canned tomatoes, whole kernel corn, chopped onion, strips of green pepper and seasonings; top with crumbs. Bake in moderate oven (350°) 40 minutes. A relish tray of pickles and carrot sticks with sherbet for dessert completes the meal.

STUFFED PORK CHOPS

Pockets in thick chops hold savory bread stuffing

4 double pork chops with slit for pocket
3 tblsp. butter or margarine
2 tblsp. chopped onion
1 c. chopped celery
½ tsp. poultry seasoning
2 c. soft bread crumbs
1 green pepper, cut in ½" slices
6 carrots, peeled and sliced ½" thick
1½ c. water

• Melt butter; add onion, celery and seasoning. Cook until soft and tender.
• Toss with bread crumbs. Fill chops with mixture, fastening with toothpicks.
• Brown chops in heavy or electric

skillet, set as manufacturer directs for chops.
• Add ½ c. water; cover and cook according to directions for chops, until well done and tender. Add vegetables and remaining 1 c. water; cook 10 to 15 minutes more. Makes 4 servings.

SAVORY PORK ROLLS

Pork rolled around well-seasoned stuffing —"pork birds," the children call them

6 pork shoulder steaks
1 tsp. salt
¼ tsp. pepper
1 egg, beaten
¼ c. milk
2 c. cubed soft bread (day old)
¼ c. chopped onion
½ lb. ground beef
1 tsp. prepared mustard
¼ tsp. poultry seasoning
½ tsp. salt
2 tblsp. flour
1 tblsp. fat or oil
½ c. water

• Trim fat and remove any bone from steaks. Pound with mallet or meat hammer to flatten. Season with salt and pepper.
• Combine egg, milk and bread cubes; add onion, ground beef, mustard, poultry seasoning and salt; mix well.
• Spoon stuffing on pork pieces. Roll up, jelly-roll fashion; fasten with wooden picks or string.
• Dust with flour; brown lightly in hot fat in skillet. Remove meat to 1½ qt. casserole.
• Pour off fat in skillet. Add water to brown drippings. Stir; pour over meat rolls in casserole; cover. Bake in moderate oven (350°) 1 hour.
• Serve with mushroom sauce made by combining 1 (10½ oz.) can condensed cream of mushroom soup and ½ c. milk; simmer 2 minutes. Makes 6 servings.

SPARERIBS WITH ORANGE STUFFING

Good meat juices and oranges flavor the stuffing

2 (1½ lb.) pieces spareribs
2 tsp. salt
¼ tsp. pepper
1½ c. dry or toasted bread cubes
2 tblsp. melted butter or margarine
¼ c. hot water
⅓ c. chopped whole orange
1 tsp. grated orange rind
1 c. diced celery
1 egg, beaten
¼ tsp. salt
Dash pepper
⅛ tsp. poultry seasoning

• Rub spareribs with salt and pepper. Place 1 piece in baking pan, fat side down.
• Toss remaining ingredients together lightly; pat stuffing firmly over ribs.
• Place second piece of meat over stuffing, fat side up; skewer or tie two pieces together. Brown in very hot oven (450°) ½ hour; reduce heat to moderate (350°) and bake 1 hour longer. Cut between each two ribs to serve. Makes 6 to 8 servings.

BAKED SPARERIBS

2 sets spareribs
Salt (about 2 tsp.)
Pepper
½ c. tomato juice
1 onion, sliced

• Cut ribs into 3-rib portions. Brown over low heat in heavy skillet, turning to brown evenly. Add remaining ingredients. Cover.
• Bake in moderate oven (350°), 1½ to 2 hours. Add more tomato juice if needed. Makes 5 to 6 servings.
• Serve with scalloped potatoes, corn bread, pineapple salad and cookies.

BARBECUED SPARERIBS

On the peppy side

2½ to 3 lbs. spareribs
2 tsp. salt
¼ tsp. pepper
⅓ c. onion, chopped
1 (8 oz.) can tomato sauce
2 tblsp. chili sauce
2 tsp. vinegar
½ tsp. Worcestershire sauce
Dash of Tabasco

• Break rib bones for serving. Wipe clean with damp paper towel; sprinkle with salt and pepper.
• Cut ribs into 2 or 3 rib serving pieces. Place in shallow baking pan; cover with aluminum foil.
• Bake in hot oven (400°) 45 minutes. Drain off excess fat.
• Meanwhile, combine remaining ingredients; pour over spareribs. Continue baking uncovered about 45 minutes more, or until very tender. Turn meat once. Makes 6 servings.

SPARERIBS WITH PINEAPPLE

Neat balance of tangy-sweet fruit and colorful tomato

4 lbs. spareribs
Pineapple juice
1½ tsp. salt
½ tsp. pepper
1 (8 oz.) can tomato sauce
1 (1 lb. 4 oz.) can crushed pineapple, drained

• Marinate ribs 2 to 3 hours in juice drained from crushed pineapple; rub with salt and pepper; cut in serving portions.
• Bake on rack in broiler pan in moderate oven (350°) 1 hour. Remove ribs and rack from broiler pan; pour off fat; place ribs in pan.
• Combine tomato sauce with drained pineapple; cover ribs with part of mixture. Bake 30 minutes. Turn ribs, cover with remainder of sauce mixture. Bake 30 minutes longer. Makes 6 servings.

SKILLET SUPPER

Have this on a cold day, with corn muffins and apple salad

1 lb. bulk sausage
1 large onion, chopped
1 medium green pepper, chopped
1 (1 lb. 4 oz.) can tomatoes
½ c. water or tomato juice
2 c. uncooked elbow macaroni
1 tsp. salt
2 tblsp. sugar
2 tsp. chili powder
2 c. dairy sour cream

• Brown sausage in heavy skillet, breaking meat apart with a fork. Pour fat off as collects (important).
• Stir in remaining ingredients, except sour cream.
• Bring to boil; cover pan. Simmer, stirring often to prevent sticking. Cook until macaroni is tender (20 to 25 minutes).
• Blend in sour cream; reheat just to boiling. Makes 6 servings.

SWEET-SOUR PORK

Here's a Chinese dish that will make a meal outstanding

3½ lbs. pork shoulder
½ tsp. salt
1 tblsp. fat or oil
¾ c. water
1½ c. undrained pineapple chunks
½ c. drained pineapple juice
¾ c. water
3 tblsp. brown sugar
¼ tsp. ground ginger
3 tblsp. cornstarch
¼ c. cider vinegar
2 tblsp. soy sauce
1 green pepper
1 medium onion
Hot fluffy rice

• Trim off excess fat; remove bones to make 1½ lbs. lean pork. Cut lean meat into ½" slices. Cut slices into strips 2" long. Sprinkle with salt. Brown in fat in

skillet. Add water. Cover; simmer 1 hour.
• Drain pineapple. Combine ½ c. pineapple juice and ¾ c. water. Add brown sugar, ginger, cornstarch, vinegar and soy sauce. Pour over meat. Cook until slightly thickened.
• Cut green pepper into strips, lengthwise; the onion into thin crosswise slices. Add to meat. Add 1 c. pineapple chunks. Bring to boil. Cook for 5 minutes. Serve with rice. Makes 4 servings.

30-MINUTE CHOP SUEY

Quick main dish—a winner

1½ lbs. ground pork
2 tblsp. butter or margarine
3 c. chopped onions
3 c. chopped celery
¾ c. chopped celery tops
2 (4 oz.) cans sliced mushrooms, undrained
2 green peppers, chopped
3 bouillon cubes
3 c. hot water
½ c. flour
1 tblsp. soy sauce (optional)

• Brown pork in butter in large skillet. Add onions, celery, celery tops, mushrooms and green peppers.
• Dissolve bouillon cubes in hot water; add to pork mixture. Cook over low heat until meat is well done, about 15 minutes. (Vegetables should still be crisp.)
• Stir in flour, blend with small amount of water. Stir until mixture is thickened; add soy sauce. Makes 6 servings.

SAUSAGE CRUMBLES

Try this savory topping on cream soups, or on hot, cooked vegetables

½ lb. bulk pork sausage
3 tblsp. minced onion
2 tblsp. chopped parsley (optional)

• Brown sausage lightly in skillet; drain off all but about 1 tblsp. drippings; add onion and parsley.
• Toss together lightly; drain on absorbent paper. Sprinkle on soups or cooked vegetables. Makes about 1 cup.

Variation: Try Sausage Crumbles on baked potatoes (white, sweets or yams): Cut cross in tops of potatoes, squeeze sides gently to split open; add butter or sour cream and top with sausage.

SAUSAGE FRIZZLES

Tasty garnish—sausage "pennies"

Shape bulk pork sausage into a roll about 1" in diameter. Wrap as for refrigerator cookies and freeze. To use: Remove from freezer, slice thin and cook slowly to brown lightly. Drain and serve over cooked foods, such as vegetables.

SAUSAGE LOAF

A new meat loaf—good with sweet potatoes and coleslaw

1 lb. ground beef
1 lb. bulk pork sausage
1 (10½ oz.) can split pea or black bean soup
2 eggs, unbeaten

• Combine ingredients and pack into 9 ×5×3" loaf pan. Bake in moderate oven (375°) 75 minutes. Makes 8 to 10 servings.

CRUSTY SAUSAGE CAKES

1 lb. bulk pork sausage
2 eggs, slightly beaten
1 c. crushed corn flakes
1 tsp. fat

• Shape sausage into 8 patties, ½" thick. Dip into egg, then roll in corn flakes. Pan-fry slowly in fat in heavy skillet to cook thoroughly. Turn to brown well on both sides. Serve with tart jelly or applesauce. Makes 4 to 6 servings.

Good Ways with Lamb

ROAST LEG OF LAMB

• Buy 7 to 8 lb. leg of lamb. Leave on the fell (thin parchment-like covering or skin which helps leg keep its shape and keeps meat moist and juicy while baking).
• Wipe meat with damp cloth or paper towel; rub surface with cut clove of garlic or an onion (optional). To add flavor to drippings, drop a few onion slices in pan during last half hour of roasting.
• Place roast on rack, skin side up, in shallow pan; sprinkle with salt and pepper.
• Roast in slow oven (325°) 3½ to 4 hours, or about 30 minutes per pound. Do not cover or add water.
• If you use a meat thermometer, insert it into roast so that bulb reaches center of meatiest section. It should not touch bone or fat. The thermometer registers 175° for medium well, 180° for well done.
• When roast is done, remove from pan; keep hot while making gravy. Makes 6 to 8 servings.

Brown Gravy:

• Drain fat and brown drippings from pan.
• Put ¼ c. fat back in pan; blend in ¼ c. flour; let bubble over low heat.
• Remove from heat. Pour rest of fat off brown drippings; add drippings and 2 c. cold water to browned flour paste.
• Return to heat; cook until thick and smooth, stirring constantly. Season to taste with salt and pepper. Makes about 2 cups gravy.

LAMB SHOULDER CUSHION ROAST WITH STUFFING

Stuffing is unusual—adds flavor to meat

3 to 4 lbs. square cut shoulder of lamb
2 tblsp. chopped onion
½ c. chopped celery
2 tblsp. butter or margarine
1 tsp. salt
¼ tsp. ginger
2 tblsp. brown sugar
1 tblsp. dried mint (or 2 tblsp. chopped fresh mint)
2 c. chopped apples, unpeeled
1 c. (¼") bread cubes
¼ c. milk

• Have bones removed from roast to form a pocket.
• Sauté onion and celery in butter. Add remaining ingredients; toss together lightly.
• Fill lamb cavity with stuffing; skewer or sew edges together.
• Place, fat side up, on rack in shallow, uncovered pan. Roast in slow oven (325°) about 2½ hours. Makes 6 to 8 servings.

LAMB CHOP MARINADE

You may wish to double this recipe

4 lamb chops (loin or rib, 1" thick)
¼ c. oil
1 tblsp. lemon juice
1 tsp. salt
½ tsp. pepper
1 small bay leaf
1 tsp. chopped parsley
1 clove garlic
1 small onion, sliced

• Place chops flat in glass baking dish or pan.
• Combine oil, lemon juice, salt, pepper, bay leaf and parsley.
• Mash garlic or put through press; add with onion to marinade.
• Pour marinade over chops; chill at least three hours. Turn once or twice.
• Place on oiled broiler rack so meat is 3 to 4" from source of heat. Turn indicator to half-way mark. Broil 12 minutes. Makes 4 servings.

WYOMING LAMB KABOBS

Cook indoors in broiler or outdoors on grill

1½ lbs. lamb shoulder
¾ c. French dressing
1 clove garlic
½ lb. button mushrooms (optional)
4 slices bacon
1 tsp. salt
¼ tsp. pepper

• Cut lamb into 1″ cubes
• Pour French dressing over meat; add cut clove of garlic unless dressing already contains garlic. Let stand at least 1 hour or overnight in refrigerator.
• Cut bacon into 1″ pieces.
• Alternate lamb, bacon and mushrooms on metal skewers. Allow space between for thorough cooking. Season with salt and pepper.
• Broil 3″ from source of heat, about 15 minutes. Turn to broil evenly. Makes 6 servings.

Variations: Alternate cubes of lamb with canned pineapple chunks and 1″ pieces of bacon on skewers. Brush with melted butter and broil as above. Or, use small, whole cooked potatoes instead of the pineapple.

Lamb Seasoned with Mint

Lamb patties, broiled, run a close second to choice lamb chops in many homes. The two recipes show different quick ways to capture the mint flavor.

LAMB PATTIES

For a hurry-up meal

1½ lbs. ground lamb
1 tsp. salt
½ tsp. dried mint
6 slices bacon
Cooked peas and corn (fresh, frozen or canned)
6 peach halves
Brown sugar

• Combine lamb with seasonings. Divide into 6 patties; wrap bacon slice around each; fasten with toothpick.
• Place peas and corn in bottom of broiler pan. Place lamb patties on broiler rack, 2″ from heat.
• When browned on one side, turn. About 10 minutes before lamb is done (broiling time 5 to 8 minutes per side), place peach halves sprinkled with brown sugar on rack with patties. Makes 6 servings.

BROILED LAMB PATTIES

Sauce makes this a company dish

• Buy 1 lb. ground lamb; form into patties about 1″ thick. (Or buy four ready-to-broil patties.) Wrap slice of bacon around patties to retain shape.
• Arrange patties on greased broiler rack, allowing 2″ between top of patties and source of heat.
• Broil on one side until browned, about 10 minutes. Season, turn and brown other side, 6 to 8 minutes. Serve piping hot with Mint Sauce.

Mint Sauce: Combine ½ c. mint-flavor jelly, 2 tsp. grated lemon rind and 2 tblsp. lemon juice in top of double boiler. Heat over boiling water. Beat until smooth. Makes 3 to 4 servings.

Substitution: Instead of Mint Sauce, brush hot lamb patties when broiled with Lemon-Butter Topping. To make, blend 2 tblsp. butter or margarine, 1 tblsp. lemon juice and a dash of chili powder or garlic salt. Sprinkle with chopped parsley and serve at once. For a golden garnish broil drained canned pineapple slices or peach halves, brushed with corn syrup or honey, 10 minutes with the patties.

PERUVIAN LAMB STEW

Let's give thanks to South America for this savory stew

2 lbs. lamb shoulder, boned and cut in 2" pieces
Boiling broth
Juice of 1 lemon
1/8 tsp. allspice
1/2 tsp. black pepper
3 tblsp. fat
2 tblsp. minced onion
1 clove garlic, crushed
3/4 tsp. salt
1 qt. cooked, seasoned lima beans (fresh, frozen or canned)

• Prepare broth from bones and trimmings.
• Place meat in heavy pan with lemon juice, onion, garlic and seasonings (except salt); let stand about 2 hours in this marinade.
• Remove meat, reserving marinade mixture. Drain; brown well in hot fat in heavy skillet.
• Place meat in stew pot; add marinade, then boiling broth to cover 3/4 of meat.
• Cover pot; bake in very slow oven (275°) until tender, adding salt at end of first hour.
• When meat is done, remove from broth; skim off all fat. Add limas; simmer on top of range about 15 minutes. If gravy is not thick enough, blend 1 tblsp. fat with 1½ tblsp. flour; stir into gravy. Makes 2 quarts.

BIG IRISH LAMB STEW

You'll want to cook this some cool day when you're house-bound

3 lbs. lamb shoulder, boned and cut in 2" pieces
1 qt. cold water
1 sliced medium onion
1 celery top
1/2 (10½ oz.) can consommé
1 small clove garlic, crushed
1 tsp. brown sugar
1 sprig parsley
1/8 tsp. thyme
1 bay leaf
1/4 tsp. black pepper
2 finely shredded peeled raw potatoes
Boiling broth to cover
12 small whole onions, parboiled
6 potatoes, cut to walnut-size pieces
1 tblsp. salt
2 c. cooked peas (fresh, canned or frozen)

• Trim bones and skin from meat.
• Place all trimmings but skin in heavy saucepan with water, onion and celery. Simmer slowly until all flavor is drawn from trimmings and bones, about ½ hour if bones are small. Strain; reserve liquid for stew, adding consommé.
• Brown cut-up meat in heavy skillet with fat. Place in stew pot; add all seasonings, except salt, including sugar. Add shredded potatoes and broth.
• Cook slowly, uncovered, to reduce broth, about 1½ hours. (Liquid will be slightly thickened and shredded potatoes entirely dissolved.)
• Add onions, potatoes and salt; cook 30 minutes. Serve in tureen with circle of peas around edge. Makes 3 quarts.

LITTLE IRISH LAMB STEW

Have hot biscuits with this masterpiece

2 tblsp. flour
1 tsp. salt
1/8 tsp. pepper
1½ lbs. lamb, cut into 2" pieces (shank, shoulder, breast or neck)
2 tblsp. fat
1/4 tsp. dill seeds
3 c. water
8 small onions
3 carrots, cut in 1" slices
2 potatoes, peeled and cubed
1/2 c. light cream
1 tblsp. flour

• Mix flour, salt and pepper; roll meat in mixture; brown in hot fat. Add dill and water. Cover; simmer 1½ hours.
• Add onions, carrots and potatoes.

Cover; cook 25 minutes, or until vegetables are tender.
• Combine cream and flour, stirring until smooth; blend into meat mixture; cook until thickened, stirring to avoid lumping. Makes 4 servings.

CHINESE MUTTON STEW

Thrifty—a little on the exotic side, but very appetizing

2 c. cold cooked mutton, chopped
¼ c. butter or margarine
1 c. fresh or frozen peas
1 c. broth or diluted consommé
1 small clove garlic, crushed
1 minced onion
½ head lettuce, chopped
1 tsp. salt
¼ tsp. black pepper
¼ tsp. ground ginger
½ tsp. sugar
Hot fluffy rice

• Blend ingredients except rice together in saucepan; simmer 1 hour.
• Serve on fluffy cooked rice. To serve, make individual nests of rice, then fill with stew mixture. Makes 4 cups.

LAMB SHANKS IN TOMATO SAUCE

A dish for kings—men like it

6 lamb shanks
2 tsp. seasoned salt
1 tblsp. shortening
1 (10½ oz.) can condensed tomato soup
½ can water
1 tblsp. vinegar
2 tblsp. soy sauce
2 tsp. Worcestershire sauce
2 tblsp. flour
½ c. water
Fluffy hot rice

• Wipe shanks with damp paper towel; remove excess fat; sprinkle with salt.
• Brown meat in hot fat in heavy skillet or Dutch oven.
• Combine remaining ingredients except flour and water; pour over browned shanks.
• Cover snugly; cook over low heat 1½ hours or until very tender.
• Skim off excess fat.
• Combine flour and water; add to sauce. Cook until slightly thickened.
• Serve with rice. Makes 6 servings.

LAMB CURRY

Spoon it over hot, fluffy rice, fall to and enjoy good eating

2 lbs. boned lean lamb breast or shoulder
1 tsp. curry powder
1½ tsp. salt
⅛ tsp. pepper
⅛ tsp. ginger
¼ c. flour
3 tblsp. fat
1 c. hot water
1 medium onion, sliced
1 sprig parsley
1 red apple, diced
1 c. milk
3 c. hot cooked rice

• Wipe meat with damp paper towel; remove excess fat. Cut into small pieces.
• Combine curry, salt, pepper, ginger and 1 tblsp. flour; sprinkle over meat. Brown meat in hot fat over moderate heat (about 20 minutes).
• Add water, onion and parsley.
• Cover; cook over low heat 45 minutes or until meat is tender. Add apple.
• Blend remaining flour with milk; add slowly to meat, stirring constantly. Cook three minutes or until thickened.
• Serve with rice. Makes 6 servings.

Good Menu: Lamb Curry, Rice, Tossed Green Salad, Crusty Rolls, Peach Chutney, Fruit Cup, Tea, Milk.

LAMB 'N SAUSAGE ROLL

Lamb and sausage are friends—they complement each other

3 lbs. boned breast of lamb
Salt
Pepper
½ lb. bulk pork sausage
2 tblsp. fat
½ c. ketchup
¾ c. water
½ c. chopped onion

• Rub lamb with salt and pepper. Spread with sausage meat. Roll lengthwise; tie or fasten with skewers.
• Brown in fat in heavy skillet.
• Combine ketchup and remaining ingredients; pour sauce over lamb. Cover; simmer about 1½ hours or until lamb is tender and sausage cooked through. (Add more water during cooking as needed.) Skim off fat. Slice; serve with sauce. Makes 4 generous servings.

LAMB CHOPS

The jelly gravy makes this platter a treat to remember and to repeat

6 lamb shoulder chops (½″)
1 tblsp. fat
3 tblsp. flour
¾ tsp. salt
⅛ tsp. pepper
1½ c. water
3 tblsp. currant jelly

• Heat fat in heavy skillet. Brown chops, reduce heat and cook until done. Remove them from skillet and keep hot while making gravy. Makes 5 to 6 servings.

Jelly Gravy: If there are more than 4 tblsp. of fat in skillet, drain off surplus. Add flour and stir, loosening brown bits. Cook and stir until flour browns. Add salt, pepper, water and cook, stirring, until gravy is smooth. Add jelly and stir until it melts and blends in the gravy. Serve hot with chops.

DRIED BEEF WITH EGGS

Scrambled eggs in a new dress

1 (4 oz.) pkg. dried beef
Water
3 tblsp. butter or margarine
8 eggs
½ c. milk

• Pour boiling water over dried beef. Drain. Melt butter in skillet. Cut dried beef in small pieces with scissors and fry for a minute in the butter.
• Beat eggs and milk slightly. Pour over beef. Stir gently while cooking. Serve at once while still moist. Makes 6 servings.

Other Dried Beef Specials

DRIED BEEF SANDWICHES

They're grilled until bubbly and hot

½ c. shredded dried beef
1 (5 oz.) jar pimiento cheese spread
⅓ c. pickle relish
⅓ c. mayonnaise or salad dressing
6 slices buttered bread

• Combine beef, cheese, relish and mayonnaise and spread equal portions on bread slices.
• Broil until bubbly and hot. Makes 6 servings.

Dried Beef Sprinkles: Shape cream cheese in small balls (about 1″ in diameter). Roll in finely shredded dried beef. Place on toothpicks and pass with crackers.

Different Deviled Eggs: Slice 8 hard-cooked eggs in lengthwise halves. Scoop out yolk and mash; add juice of ½ lemon, ¼ tsp. dry mustard, ½ tsp. salt, 3 tblsp. salad dressing and ½ c. finely shredded dried beef. Combine well and fill each egg white with mixture. Garnish with minced parsley and a paprika sprinkle.

8

Chicken and Other Poultry

You can't miss on a chicken dinner when you're having company or celebrating a special occasion. Skim the pages of this chapter and you'll be convinced there's almost no end to the truly delicious ways to fix chicken. Three of our recipes display five stars, and that means we've singled them out as extra-special. One of them owes its intriguing, subtle overtones to packaged dry salad mix, garlic flavored. The second is a fabulous sour cream and paprika dish with Old World background appreciated in our country kitchens. The third is a superior chicken pie.

We give you broiled chicken—several recipes for it. Cook it outdoors over embers or in the broiler oven of your range. Either way you'll come out with glistening, golden brown results. And if you select fairly small broilers, you can give everyone a half chicken—no family quarrels over light and dark meat. Country hospitality always has honored the custom of giving everyone, especially guests, a choice of light or dark meat. Some women place the light meat on one side of the baking dish, the dark or the other, when making chicken pie. It's amusing to watch guests when asked, "Light or dark?"—they wonder how you can tell which kind the serving spoon will bring up when it breaks through the tender, crisp crust.

As for our chicken pie that boasts five bright stars, it's superb—all chicken, gravy and pastry. You'll also find in this chapter turkey, duck and goose recipes that suggest holiday feasts.

Enjoy reading the recipes that follow and picking out the ones to try first. Don't overlook the chicken salads, the cold and the hot, with fruit and without. Farm Journal is particularly proud of all these poultry dishes. We believe you'll use most of them—that you'll live up to the saying around our Countryside Kitchens: We can't print too many good chicken recipes to please homemakers.

CRUSTY FRIED CHICKEN

New way to fix fork-tender chicken—moist within and brown outside. A Farm Journal 5-star recipe

3 (3 lb.) ready-to-cook frying chickens (use breasts, thighs and legs)
2 pkgs. dry salad dressing mix, garlic flavor
3 tblsp. flour
2 tsp. salt
¼ c. lemon juice
2 tblsp. soft butter or margarine
1½ c. prepared pancake mix
1 c. milk
Fat or oil for frying

• Wipe chicken pieces (use damp paper toweling).
• Combine salad dressing mix, flour and salt in small bowl. Add lemon juice and butter; mix to a smooth paste.
• Brush all sides of chicken pieces with paste. Stack in bowl; cover. Store in refrigerator overnight.
• About 1½ hours before supper, place ¼ to ½" of fat in bottom of large skillet or Dutch oven; heat.
• Dip chicken parts in milk, then in dry pancake mix. Coat well. Dust off excess. Lightly brown in hot fat. Turn with tongs—not fork.
• Place browned chicken one layer deep, in shallow baking pan. Spoon about half the rest of dipping milk over pieces.
• Cover with lid or aluminum foil. Bake in moderate oven (375°) 30 minutes.
• Remove lid. Baste with remaining milk. Cook uncovered 20 to 30 minutes, or until tender. Makes 8 servings.

CRISP BAKED CHICKEN

Once your friends taste this, the recipe will be in demand

1 (2½ to 3 lb.) chicken, cut into serving pieces
3 tblsp. melted fat
2 tsp. salt
¼ tsp. pepper
3 c. corn flakes

• Rub chicken with 1 tblsp. fat, salt and pepper.
• Crush corn flakes into fine crumbs. Roll chicken in crumbs until well coated.
• Place in greased, shallow baking pan and sprinkle with remaining fat. Bake in very hot oven (450°) 10 to 15 minutes, or until browned; reduce to slow oven (325°) and bake 30 minutes longer, or until tender. Makes 4 to 6 servings.

PAN FRIED CHICKEN

Can't miss with perfect fried chicken

2 (2 to 3 lb.) fryers, cut in serving pieces
6 tblsp. flour
1½ tsp. salt
1 tsp. paprika
⅛ tsp. black pepper
Oil or melted fat
2 tblsp. water

• Toss chicken pieces (except neck, giblets and liver) in paper bag containing flour, salt, paprika and pepper.
• Heat oil (about ½") in heavy skillet. Add chicken and brown lightly on all sides, about 20 minutes. Reduce heat; add water. Cover tightly and cook slowly until tender, about 20 to 30 minutes. Turn pieces for even browning.
• Uncover last 5 to 10 minutes to recrisp skin. Add cooked giblets, neck and uncooked liver last 15 minutes.

To make gravy: Remove and save fat. Measure back into pan 3 tblsp. fat; add 3 tblsp. flour. Blend thoroughly. Add 2 c. liquid—milk, giblet broth or water. Season to taste. Simmer 5 minutes. Makes 4 servings.

Oven Fried Chicken: Season broilers with garlic, salt and pepper, sprinkle lightly with flour. Place in single layer in pan. Pour over ½ c. melted butter or margarine for each broiler. Cover tightly and bake in moderate oven (350°) 30 minutes. Remove cover and complete cooking—about 30 more minutes.

GLAZED BROILED CHICKEN

Once the family gets a whiff of what's cooking, appetites for supper will soar

3 (1½ to 3 lb.) broiler-fryer chickens
Fruit Barbecue Sauce (recipe follows), heated

• Split chicken in halves, lengthwise. Place in large bowl, skin side down. Pour Fruit Barbecue Sauce over chicken and rotate pieces in it to coat completely. Cover bowl and marinate in refrigerator overnight or for several hours. Turn the chicken occasionally.
• Remove chicken from sauce. Place, skin side down, in broiler pan without rack, or in large shallow pan. Brush top of chicken with hot sauce.
• Broil according to range directions. Chickens should be 7" to 9" from heat and will take 20 to 30 minutes for each side to brown completely. If broiler does not allow this distance, reduce heat to about 350°. After 10 minutes, chicken should begin to brown on one side. If it browns faster, reduce heat. Sauce browns quickly, so watch chickens carefully. Cover with foil if skin is completely brown before chicken is cooked thoroughly.
• Baste with remaining hot sauce every 10 minutes. Turn when top side is brown.
• Chicken is done when drumstick twists easily out of thigh joint, about 40 to 60 minutes, according to weight. Serve with any remaining sauce. Makes 6 to 10 servings, depending on size of chickens.

FRUIT BARBECUE SAUCE

The secret of the chicken's tangy taste and its inviting glossy, browned look

1 (6 oz.) can frozen pineapple-grapefruit juice concentrate
1 tsp. salt
¼ tsp. ginger
3 tblsp. lemon juice
6 tblsp. butter or margarine

• Thaw juice concentrate and combine with salt, ginger and lemon juice. Heat to boiling.
• Before basting chicken, reheat glaze with butter. Makes 1⅓ cups.

To cook chicken with Fruit Barbecue Sauce in oven, prepare and marinate as for broiling. Place chicken, skin side down, on rack in shallow pan. Line bottom of pan with foil to catch drippings. Baste chickens with hot sauce.
• Bake in hot oven (400°). After about 30 minutes, turn chicken; baste with hot sauce. Bake 30 minutes more or until done. If chicken browns too fast, cover with foil.

To broil on outdoor grill, prepare and marinate chicken as for cooking in range broiler. Wait until charcoal in grill has burned to white in daylight; if still red, heat will be too intense. Place chicken on grill, skin side up. Baste with hot sauce. Broil 10 minutes, baste again and turn. Repeat basting and turning every 10 minutes until done, about 30 to 40 minutes. If heat gets too intense, sprinkle water on coals.

SAUCE VARIATIONS

Deviled Chicken: Brush chicken with blend of 1 tblsp. dry mustard and ¾ c. prepared mustard; cover and refrigerate for several hours or overnight. Baste while cooking with this mixture: ¾ c. melted butter or margarine, ¼ tsp. salt, 1½ tsp. onion salt, ½ tsp. pepper, ½ tsp. celery salt and 1½ tsp. dry mustard.

Herb Chicken: Melt ⅓ c. butter or margarine; add ½ tsp. dried marjoram, ½ tsp. dried thyme, ⅛ tsp. pepper, ¼ c. snipped fresh parsley and 2 tblsp. minced onion. Heat slowly 5 minutes. Add 1 tblsp. lemon juice, 1 chicken bouillon cube and ¾ c. water. Heat to dissolve bouillon cube. Pour over chicken and marinate several hours. Reheat and use to baste chicken during broiling. Makes 1½ cups.

PAPRIKA CHICKEN

A Farm Journal 5-star recipe

2 (2¼ lb.) ready-to-cook fryers, cut up
⅓ c. flour
¾ tsp. salt
1 tblsp. paprika
⅛ tsp. pepper
⅓ c. fat
½ c. chopped onion
2 to 3 chicken bouillon cubes
2½ to 3 c. hot water
1 c. dairy sour cream

• Thoroughly coat pieces of chicken with mixture of flour, salt, paprika and pepper. Dust any remaining over pieces in pan.
• Brown chicken in fat in heavy skillet, about 15 minutes. Add onion.
• Dissolve bouillon cubes in hot water; add ½ c. to chicken in pan. (Add more as needed.) Cover and simmer over low heat 30 to 40 minutes, or until tender. Remove to serving platter.
• Add remaining bouillon and sour cream (add ½ c. more sour cream for extra lusciousness) to pan drippings. Stir well; heat. Makes 6 to 8 servings.

Fried Chicken Creole Style: Coat chicken pieces with flour mixture and brown in fat as for Paprika Chicken. Add 1½ c. sliced onion, 1 tsp. salt, ¾ tsp. celery seed, 1 green pepper, cut into strips, 2½ to 3 c. tomato juice and 2 tsp. Worcestershire sauce. Cover tightly and cook over moderate heat 25 minutes, or until tender. Makes 6 to 8 servings.

SMOTHERED CHICKEN

Popular with the whole family—the chicken is so tender

2 (2½ lb.) fryer chickens
1 c. flour
1 tblsp. salt
⅛ tsp. pepper
Fat for frying
3½ c. milk

• Clean chicken; cut in pieces.
• Combine flour, salt and pepper. Roll chicken in flour mixture; coat each piece thoroughly.
• Heat fat until hot, but not smoking. Brown floured chicken pieces well. Remove from pan.
• Pour off all but about 4 tblsp. fat. Stir in ¼ c. remaining seasoned flour, then add milk. Heat to boiling, stirring constantly.
• Return chicken to pan. Cover tightly; simmer 1½ hours or until tender. Stir occasionally.
• Add more salt and pepper, if needed. Makes 6 to 8 servings.

BROILED CHICKEN

Golden on the outside—moist within

Use chickens 1½ to 2½ lbs. ready-to-cook weight. Split in halves lengthwise—with backbone and neck removed; cut again crosswise to serve quarters. (Precook neck and giblets, except liver, in salted water about an hour.)

Steps in Broiling:
• Sprinkle both sides of chicken with salt and pepper.
• Place pieces, skin side down, in bottom of well-oiled broiler pan.
• Brush with melted butter or margarine.
• Broil slowly; regulate heat, or adjust pan, so browning begins in 10 minutes.
• Turn every 15 minutes. Brush with melted butter or margarine each time.
• Add giblets (including uncooked liver) and neck last 15 minutes.
• Broil until nicely browned and tender —40 to 50 minutes.

For Flavor Changes: Sprinkle with onion seasoned salt, savory or basil. Or add lemon juice to melted butter (1 tblsp. per chicken). Marinate in sharp French dressing 1 to 3 hours before broiling.
• Or before broiling, rub chicken well with cut lemon, brush with melted butter and sprinkle lightly with granulated sugar. Or borrow a Southern trick and soak chicken in buttermilk several hours before broiling or frying.

TEXAS BARBECUED CHICKEN

You fix it in a skillet

1 ready-to-cook fryer, 3 to 3½ lbs.
¾ c. flour
1 tblsp. salt
1 tsp. paprika
3 tblsp. butter or margarine

• Shake chicken pieces in paper bag with flour and seasonings.

• Melt butter in skillet. Add chicken; fry until golden brown. Turn pieces with tongs.

• Add sauce (see recipe below). Use ½ cup to each pound of chicken. Cook slowly for 40 to 45 minutes. Turn pieces frequently. Serve on platter with sauce. Makes 4 servings.

Barbecue Sauce: Combine in saucepan, 1 tsp. salt, ¼ tsp. pepper, 1 tsp. paprika, 1 tblsp. sugar, ½ minced clove garlic, ½ c. chopped onion, ½ c. water and 1 c. ketchup. Heat to boiling; simmer, uncovered, 20 minutes. Remove from heat, add ¼ c. lemon juice and 2 tblsp. butter. Mix well. Makes 2½ cups sauce.

BARBECUE FRIED CHICKEN

Chicken and tomatoes star in this skillet treat

1 (4 lb.) chicken or 2 (2½ lb.) broilers
1 c. flour
Fat for frying
¾ c. water
2 tblsp. vinegar
1 tsp. prepared mustard
1 tblsp. brown sugar
2 tsp. Worcestershire sauce
1 tblsp. chopped onion
2 c. canned tomatoes
1½ tsp. salt
½ tsp. pepper
¼ tsp. chopped garlic

• Wash chicken; pat dry with paper toweling. Cut into serving pieces.

• Flour, coating each piece thoroughly. Fry chicken until golden brown.

• Blend together small amount of water with 2 tblsp. flour. Add remaining ¾ c. water. Mix well with remaining ingredients.

• Drain excess fat from chicken. Pour sauce over chicken, cover; simmer 1 hour, or until tender. Takes less time for broilers. Makes 4 servings.

DEVILED CHICKEN

Lively sauce does something wonderful to chicken

3 broilers, cut in halves
Salt
⅓ c. butter or margarine
1 tsp. prepared mustard
Salt and pepper
½ tsp. paprika
1 tsp. vinegar
Dash Tabasco sauce
½ c. bread crumbs

• Rub chicken with salt. Place, skin side up, on greased broiler rack 5″ from source of heat; broil 10 minutes. If chicken browns too quickly, place farther from heat. Turn and broil 10 minutes on other side.

• Put chicken in drip pan, skin side up.

• Cream together butter, mustard, salt, pepper, paprika, vinegar and Tabasco sauce. Pour over chicken. Sprinkle with bread crumbs.

• Cover pan with baking sheet or large lid; bake in moderate oven (350°) 20 minutes, or until chicken does not look pink when cut at joint. Makes 6 servings.

Chicken Pie—Superb Gift

The good New England cook who sent us this recipe for chicken pie bakes a few of them every year just after Thanksgiving Day. She stores them in her freezer. During the week-before-Christmas bustle, she delivers the pies, her Christmas gifts, to lucky friends. The pie rated exceptionally high in taste tests made in our Countryside Kitchens.

MAINE CHICKEN PIE

All chicken and gravy under crisp, flaky pastry—men like its meatiness

1 (5 lb.) whole stewing chicken
1½ qts. water
2 tsp. salt
1 small onion
1 carrot
1 stalk celery
¾ tsp. monosodium glutamate
3½ c. chicken broth
½ c. sifted flour
½ tsp. onion salt
½ tsp. celery salt
Few grains pepper
2 or 3 drops yellow food color
Pastry

• Place chicken in large kettle and add next six ingredients, using ½ tsp. monosodium glutamate, and 1 tsp. salt. Simmer, covered, until tender, 3 to 3½ hours.
• Remove bird to rack. Strip meat from bones, removing in large pieces. Refrigerate when cool.
• Combine flour, onion salt, celery salt, pepper, 1 tsp. salt and ¼ tsp. monosodium glutamate with ½ c. chicken broth. Mix until smooth.
• Heat 3 c. chicken broth to boiling. Add flour mixture, beating with a wire whip to prevent lumping.
• Cook over medium heat, stirring constantly until mixture is smooth and thickened. Add food coloring if desired.
• Add chicken and blend well.
• Line 9" deep-dish pie pan with pastry. Fill with chicken mixture. Cover with pastry. Seal well and flute edges.
• Make several slits for steam to escape around edge of top crust.
• Bake in hot oven (400°) 45 minutes or until browned. Makes 6 to 8 servings.
• When pie is cool, wrap and freeze.
• Remaining broth may be frozen or used to make gravy to serve with pie.

CHICKEN LOAF

Sour cream and herbs add subtle, new flavors to this favorite

1 (4 to 5 lb.) chicken, cut up
1½ c. soft bread crumbs
2 eggs, beaten
⅛ tsp. rosemary
Pinch of marjoram
Salt and pepper
Few grains nutmeg
2 stalks celery, diced
1 c. dairy sour cream
2 tblsp. chicken broth (optional)

• Cook chicken in boiling, salted water until tender, or pressure cook. Remove meat from bones and cut up.
• Combine chicken with remaining ingredients; toss lightly.
• Pour into greased loaf pan (8½ × 4½ × 2½"). Bake in pan of hot water in moderate oven (350°) 50 minutes—until knife inserted in center comes out clean. Unmold and slice. Makes 6 servings.

CHICKEN SUPPER DISH

1 (3½ to 4 lb.) stewing chicken, cut up
3 hard-cooked eggs, sliced
1 (6 oz.) can sliced mushrooms, drained
2 tblsp. flour
1 c. chicken broth
1 c. light cream
1 tsp. salt
⅛ tsp. pepper

• Simmer chicken in water and seasonings until fork-tender, about 3 to 4 hours. Cut meat from bones. Chill meat and broth separately.

• In greased 1½ qt. casserole, arrange alternate layers of chicken, egg and mushrooms by thirds, until all is used.
• Mix flour with ¼ c. broth until smooth. Heat remaining broth with cream; stir in flour mixture and seasonings. Cook until smooth and thickened; pour into casserole.
• Bake uncovered in moderate oven (350°) about 35 minutes. Makes 6 to 8 servings.

CHICKEN DUMPLINGS

This dish gives you old-time flavor with modern cooking

2 c. sifted flour
½ tsp. salt
1 tblsp. baking powder
1 egg, well beaten
1 tblsp. melted shortening
½ c. milk
¼ c. softened butter or margarine
½ c. chopped celery leaves
¼ tsp. poultry seasoning
2 (10½ oz.) cans condensed cream of chicken soup

• Sift together flour, salt and baking powder.
• Combine egg, shortening and milk; stir into dry ingredients, just to moisten. (Or use prepared biscuit mix.)
• Roll ¼" thick; spread with butter. Sprinkle with celery leaves and poultry seasoning. Roll up, pinching edge to seal. Slice ½" thick.
• Put chicken soup in pan with tight-fitting lid. Add 1 soup-can water; heat but do not boil; drop in dumplings; steam without lifting lid for 15 minutes. Makes 6 servings.

CHICKEN GUMBO

A hearty, main-dish soup to eat at once, to can or freeze

3 lbs. cooked chicken, boned
1 lb. smoked ham
2 c. chopped onion
1 green pepper, chopped
4 c. cooked or canned tomatoes
2 (1 lb. 4 oz.) cans sliced okra
1 bay leaf
1 to 2 qts. chicken broth

• Cut chicken meat and ham into small pieces. Add vegetables, bay leaf and broth.
• Simmer 15 minutes. Taste and add seasonings. Remove bay leaf; pour hot mixture into hot, sterilized pint jars. Seal. Process in pressure canner 65 minutes at 10 lbs. pressure. Process quarts 75 minutes at 10 lbs. pressure. Makes 12 pints.

To freeze: Cool; put into containers and quick-freeze.

CHICKEN TAMALE PIE

Good Southwestern cooks add 1 to 3 teaspoons chili powder

2 c. cornmeal
1 c. boiling water
2 tsp. salt
1 (5 lb.) stewing chicken
2 tblsp. chicken fat
3 medium onions, sliced
2 c. chicken broth
1 c. tomato purée or ketchup
¼ tsp. cayenne
¼ tsp. pepper
¼ tsp. dry mustard
4 tsp. Worcestershire sauce
1 tsp. sugar
1 bay leaf

• Cook cornmeal in boiling, salted water to make thick mush. Cool. Line sides and bottom of 6 individual baking dishes, or a greased 2 qt. casserole.
• Cut up chicken and cook in salted water to cover, until tender.
• Melt chicken fat; add onions and cook until soft and yellow. Stir in chicken broth and tomato purée.
• Mix seasonings together in a cup, add to tomato sauce. Cook 20 minutes to blend flavors.
• Remove chicken from bones; add to tomato sauce. Spoon into baking dishes; bake in hot oven (400°) 20 minutes, or until cornmeal crust browns. Makes 6 to 8 servings.

CHICKEN SUPREME

You can substitute cooked asparagus for the broccoli

1 (5 lb.) chicken
2 lbs. broccoli or 3 pkgs. frozen
½ c. grated Parmesan cheese

• Simmer chicken until tender in boiling salted water, or pressure cook. Cool quickly in broth. Remove meat from bones in large pieces; slice.
• Cook broccoli in salted water until tender; place on oven platter. Sprinkle with ¼ c. cheese. Arrange chicken slices on broccoli. Spoon Mock Hollandaise Sauce or Easy Hollandaise Sauce over top. Sprinkle with ¼ c. cheese.
• Broil, 5" from source of heat until sauce browns. Makes 6 servings.

Mock Hollandaise Sauce: Blend ½ c. mayonnaise or salad dressing, ½ c. heavy cream and 2 tblsp. lemon juice.

Easy Hollandaise Sauce: Cream thoroughly ½ c. butter or margarine; gradually beat in 3 egg yolks, 1½ tblsp. lemon juice, ½ tsp. salt, dash paprika and few grains cayenne; blend well. Slowly stir in ¼ c. boiling water. Place in top of double boiler. Cook over 1½" boiling water (so water doesn't touch top part of double boiler) 5 minutes, stirring constantly. Remove from heat; beat 1 minute.

FRENCHED CHICKEN SANDWICH

The best reason to hope there will be leftover chicken

1 egg, beaten
2 tblsp. milk
4 slices bread, day old
8 slices cooked chicken
1 (10½ oz.) can condensed cream of chicken soup

• Blend together egg and milk.
• Cut bread slices diagonally. Dip in milk-egg mixture. Brown lightly on both sides in small amount of hot fat in heavy skillet. Arrange in baking pan.
• Cover with chicken. Pour on soup. Bake in moderate oven (375°) 20 minutes. Makes 4 servings.

CHICKEN SANDWICH FILLING

You also can make it with tuna

1¼ c. cooked, chopped chicken or tuna
¼ c. chopped pickle
1 tsp. Worcestershire sauce
⅓ c. undiluted cream of chicken soup
¼ tsp. celery salt

• Mix together all ingredients. Makes enough filling for 6 sandwiches.

CHICKEN WITH DUMPLINGS

Pass tart cranberry jelly or peach pickles after they've helped themselves to chicken and dumplings

1 qt. water
2 tsp. salt
2 carrots, sliced
1 onion, sliced
1 stalk celery, including leaves
4 to 5 lb. stewing chicken, cut into pieces
⅓ c. flour
1¾ c. milk
2 c. biscuit mix
½ c. chopped parsley

• Heat water in saucepan. Add salt, carrots, onion and celery; add chicken. Cover; simmer (do not boil) 3 to 4 hours or until meat is tender.
• Remove cooked chicken from broth and keep hot. Strain; measure. Add water to make 3 cups broth. Return to saucepan.
• Combine flour and 1 cup milk. Shake in covered jar or beat to blend thoroughly. Add flour mixture slowly to hot broth, stirring constantly, about 5 minutes.
• Make dumplings 20 minutes before serving.

Dumplings: Combine biscuit mix and parsley; stir in ¾ c. milk until flour is dampened.

• Drop from a spoon onto chicken pieces (not into liquid) in boiling stew. Cook, uncovered, over low heat 10 minutes; cover, cook 10 minutes longer. Makes 8 servings.

CHICKEN-ALMOND CASSEROLE

Expertly seasoned

5 lb. stewing chicken, cut up
2 celery stalks
2 carrots, cut up
1 medium onion, sliced
2 tsp. salt
½ tsp. pepper
8 c. boiling water
2 c. cooked rice
1 (4 oz.) can sliced mushrooms
¼ c. chopped pimiento
1 c. blanched, slivered almonds
4 tblsp. butter, margarine or chicken fat
2 tblsp. flour
¼ tsp. marjoram
¼ tsp. thyme
½ c. fine dry bread crumbs

• Simmer chicken until tender with celery, carrots, onion, salt and pepper in boiling water. Simmer, do not boil.

• Remove chicken from bone in large pieces. Save broth.

• Combine rice, chicken, mushrooms, pimiento and ¾ c. almonds.

• Melt 2 tblsp. butter; blend in flour and 2 c. chicken broth. Cook until smooth and thick, stirring constantly.

• Add marjoram, thyme and more salt if necessary. Stir into chicken mixture.

• Turn into 11×7½×1½" baking dish; sprinkle with bread crumbs and remaining almonds. Dot with 2 tblsp. butter.

• Bake in moderate oven (350°) 1 hour. Serve with gravy made from remaining chicken broth. Makes 8 servings.

CHICKEN TETRAZZINI

Chicken and rice dish to serve guests at home or to carry to a covered-dish supper

1 qt. water
2 tsp. salt
4 to 5 lb. stewing chicken, cut into pieces
1¾ c. chicken broth
1 (2 to 4 oz.) can sliced mushrooms
2 tblsp. flour
½ tsp. garlic salt
⅛ tsp. pepper
½ c. cream
1 c. grated Cheddar cheese
4 c. cooked rice
1 tblsp. chopped parsley
4 strips bacon, cooked and crumbled
¼ c. cracker crumbs
¼ tsp. poultry seasoning

• Heat water in saucepan, add salt and chicken; cover. Simmer (do not boil) 3 to 4 hours or until the thigh meat is tender. Take meat from bones and cut into chunks.

• Heat chicken broth with juice from mushrooms. Blend flour, garlic salt, pepper and cream. Stir into broth; cook, stirring constantly until thickened. Remove from heat.

• Stir in cheese. Combine rice, chicken, mushrooms and chopped parsley in another container.

• Alternate layers of chicken-rice mixture and sauce in buttered 3 qt. casserole. Top with combination of bacon, crumbs and seasoning. Bake in very hot oven (450°) 30 minutes. Makes 10 servings.

These go well with Chicken Casseroles: Pickled peaches, jellied cranberry sauce, olives (green, pimiento stuffed or ripe), pineapple slices topped with coleslaw or whole apricots, pickles (dill, sour, sweet), celery (cheese-stuffed), carrots (sticks or curls), currant jelly, cucumber slices and pickled crab apples.

CHICKEN CASSEROLE

Try this when you have leftover chicken. It pleases

1 c. elbow macaroni
½ c. diced celery
¾ c. chicken broth
1 (10½ oz.) can condensed cream of celery soup
1 (3 or 4 oz.) can mushrooms
2 c. cut-up chicken or turkey
½ c. minced parsley
½ tsp. Worcestershire sauce
¾ c. soft bread cubes
2 tblsp. butter or margarine

• Cook macaroni according to directions on package. Drain.
• Cook celery in chicken broth (or use a chicken-flavored bouillon cube plus ¾ c. water) for 5 minutes.
• Combine cooked macaroni, celery, broth, celery soup, mushrooms, chicken (or turkey), parsley and Worcestershire sauce. Add salt if needed.
• Pour into greased 2 qt. casserole.
• Sprinkle with bread cubes; dot with butter. Bake in moderate oven (350°) 30 to 40 minutes. Makes 8 servings.

CHICKEN CRUNCH CASSEROLE

Just the hot dish to serve with cranberry sauce or molded salad

2½ c. diced cooked chicken
1 (10½ oz.) can condensed cream of mushroom soup
1 c. rich milk
½ tsp. salt
3 c. crushed potato chips
4 tblsp. shredded sharp cheese
Paprika

• Combine chicken, soup, milk and salt. Heat to boiling.
• Spread 1½ c. potato chips on bottom of greased 2 qt. casserole. Pour in chicken mixture. Cover with remaining chips; sprinkle cheese and paprika over top.
• Bake in moderate oven (350°) 25 to 30 minutes. Makes 6 servings.

Variation: Substitute cooked turkey for chicken.

CHICKEN WITH DRESSING

Baked chicken with dressing that's easy to serve—no bones

1 (3 to 4 lb.) chicken, cut up
1 stalk celery
1 onion, sliced
1 tblsp. salt
3 to 4 peppercorns
1½ qts. dry bread cubes
½ tsp. sage
⅛ tsp. pepper
½ tsp. salt
¼ c. minced onion
⅓ c. butter or drippings

• Simmer chicken, celery, onion, salt and peppercorns in water to almost cover. When chicken is tender (about 2 hours) remove from bones in good-size pieces. Arrange in 2 qt. casserole.
• Combine bread cubes, sage, pepper and salt. Brown onion in butter; add to bread mixture. Spread over chicken.

Gravy:

½ c. fat (from broth)
¾ c. flour
4 c. chicken broth
1½ tsp. salt
⅛ tsp. pepper
4 egg yolks, well beaten

• Melt fat in heavy skillet; add flour with seasonings; stir until smooth. Blend in chicken broth; cook until thick and smooth, stirring constantly.
• Mix a little hot gravy with yolks; pour into remaining gravy. Cook over medium heat about 3 minutes, stirring constantly. Pour over chicken and dressing.
• Bake in moderate oven (375°) 35 minutes or until custard gravy is set and golden brown on top. Makes 8 servings.

Make-at-Home Club Sandwiches: Spread slices of toast with butter. Add layer of sliced cooked chicken. Top with another slice of toast. Add strips of crisp bacon, slices of tomato and lettuce. Cover with slice of toast. Skewer together with toothpicks; cut into quarters.

CHICKEN IN CRUMB BASKETS

Company specialty of a Kansas farm woman, member of Farm Journal's Family Test Group

Crumb Baskets:

- **5 c. soft bread crumbs**
- **¼ c. minced onion**
- **1 tsp. celery salt**
- **⅛ tsp. pepper**
- **½ c. butter or margarine, melted**

• Combine bread crumbs with onion, seasonings and butter.
• Line 6 greased individual casseroles with crumb mixture. Press into place.
• Bake in moderate oven (375°) 15 minutes, or until crumbs are brown.

Chicken Filling:

- **⅓ c. butter or margarine**
- **⅓ c. flour**
- **½ c. light cream**
- **1½ c. chicken broth**
- **½ tsp. salt**
- **⅛ tsp. pepper**
- **1 tsp. Worcestershire sauce**
- **1 c. cooked or canned peas**
- **3 c. cooked chicken, chopped**

• Melt butter, blend in flour. Add cream, chicken broth and seasonings.
• Cook until thickened, stirring constantly. Add peas and chicken. Serve in Crumb Baskets. Makes 6 servings.

CREAMED CHICKEN

Peas and pimiento make this colorful

- **2 c. cooked, cubed chicken**
- **1 c. cooked peas, drained**
- **½ tsp. salt**
- **⅛ tsp. pepper**
- **1 tsp. grated onion**
- **2 tblsp. chopped pimiento**
- **1 (10½ oz.) can condensed cream of celery, chicken or mushroom soup**

• Combine all ingredients except soup. Let stand in refrigerator about 1 hour.
• Pour soup, undiluted, in top pan of chafing dish or double boiler.
• Add chicken mixture; blend together. Cover; heat; serve piping hot on toast. Makes 6 servings.

UPSIDE-DOWN CHICKEN DINNER

Makes a satisfying meal

- **2 (2 to 3 lb.) fryers**
- **½ c. flour**
- **2 tsp. salt**
- **1 tsp. paprika**
- **3 tblsp. shortening**
- **¼ c. water**
- **½ c. currant jelly**

• Cut chicken into serving pieces. (For a prettier platter, leave thigh and drumstick in one piece; remove bony ribs from breasts and split down the center.)
• Combine flour, salt and paprika in paper bag. Shake chicken in bag to coat.
• Melt shortening in heavy skillet; fry chicken until golden brown. Add water; steam chicken, covered, until tender and no liquid remains, about 15 minutes.
• Arrange chicken attractively in skillet; spoon jelly over it. Cover with Short Biscuit Dough.

Short Biscuit Dough:

- **2 c. sifted flour**
- **2 tsp. baking powder**
- **¾ tsp. salt**
- **⅓ c. butter or margarine**
- **⅓ c. shortening**
- **1 egg yolk**
- **½ c. hot water**

• Sift together flour, baking powder and salt. Combine remaining ingredients; mix with fork until fat is size of small peas. Stir into dry ingredients. Blend well and knead on lightly floured surface. Pat out circle of dough ½″ thick, and fit over chicken in skillet. Bake in moderate oven (375°) 35 minutes. To serve, turn out on platter and cut through biscuit around each piece of chicken. Lift onto plates. Makes 6 servings.

Four Chicken Salads

COMPANY CHICKEN SALAD

Gorgeous two-way salad—serve it piled in lettuce cups, or mold with gelatin

2½ c. cooked chicken, diced
1 c. fine-cut celery
1 c. small seedless grapes
1 c. shredded nuts (walnuts, Brazil nuts, etc.)
1 tsp. minced onion (or ½ tsp. onion juice)
1 tsp. salt
1 c. mayonnaise or salad dressing
½ c. heavy cream, whipped
Crisp lettuce or other greens
Pimiento-stuffed or ripe olives
Sweet pickle gherkins

• Combine first 8 ingredients; chill. Serve on greens, garnished with thin slices of chicken, olives and/or pickles. Parsley helps, too. Makes 8 servings.

FRUITED CHICKEN SALAD

Exciting when garnished with red-ripe strawberries

2 c. cooked chicken, cut in cubes
1 orange, peeled and sectioned
½ c. grapes, halved and seeded
½ c. toasted almonds or pecans
2 medium bananas, peeled and sliced
1 c. mayonnaise or salad dressing

• Put chicken (preferably white meat) in bowl; add other ingredients, tossing lightly. Chill.

• Serve on crisp greens; garnish with whole strawberries (if in season). Or serve on pineapple slices with perky sprigs of water cress or Bibb lettuce. Makes 6 to 8 servings.

HOT CHICKEN SALAD

Marvelous texture contrast—moist chicken mixture and crunchy, brown potato chips

2 c. cooked chicken, cut in large pieces
2 c. chopped celery
⅓ c. chopped green pepper
3 tblsp. pimiento, cut in small strips
2 tblsp. minced onion
1 tsp. salt
2 tblsp. lemon juice
½ c. mayonnaise or salad dressing
⅓ c. shredded sharp or Swiss cheese
3 c. coarsely broken potato chips

• Blend together ingredients except cheese and potato chips. Drop into greased 1½ qt. baking dish. Sprinkle cheese, then potato chips over top. Bake in moderate oven (350°) 25 to 30 minutes, until melted cheese is delicately browned and bubbly. Makes 6 to 8 servings.

CHICKEN AND RICE SALAD

Pretty ripe tomato cups hold this curry-flavored chicken and rice salad

1½ c. cooked cubed chicken
1½ c. cooked rice
⅓ c. diced onion
⅓ c. chopped green pepper
1½ c. chopped celery
1 tblsp. vinegar
2 tblsp. oil
1 tsp. curry powder
¾ c. salad dressing or mayonnaise
6 tomato "cups"
Crisp salad greens

• Toss together lightly in bowl all ingredients except salad dressing, tomatoes and greens. Cover; chill 3 to 4 hours.

• Just before serving blend in salad dressing. Serve in scooped out tomatoes, sprinkled inside with salt, on salad greens. Makes 6 servings.

Turkey Cookery

TURKEY DINNER MENU

Turkey and Gravy
Celery Stuffing
Sweet Potato Casserole
Buttered Peas
Creamed Onions
Relish Tray
Jellied Cranberry Mold
Dinner Rolls
Date Pudding with Fluffy Hard Sauce
Coffee Milk

ROAST TURKEY

• Prepare stuffing (allow ¾ c. for each pound of ready-to-cook turkey). Stuff bird just before roasting.
• Lightly stuff neck cavity; skewer skin to back. Shape wings "akimbo" style; bring wing tips onto the back.
• Place turkey, breast down, in deep bowl. Rub cavity with salt. Spoon in stuffing. Shake to settle stuffing, but do not pack.
• Lace cord around skewers to close opening. Tie drumsticks securely to tail.
• Rub skin thoroughly with shortening.
• Place bird on rack in shallow pan. If V-rack is used, place turkey breast down. If bird is too heavy to handle and turn, roast with breast up.
• Lay fat-moistened cheesecloth (three thicknesses), large enough to drape down sides, over top of bird.
• Roast in slow oven (325°).

ROASTING CHART FOR WHOLE TURKEYS

Ready-to-cook weight	Temp.	Roasting Time
4 to 8 lbs.	325°	3 to 4 hrs.
8 to 12 lbs.	325°	4 to 4½ hrs.
12 to 16 lbs.	325°	4½ to 5 hrs.

Allow approximately ½ pound ready-to-cook turkey per serving.

• If turkey begins roasting with breast down, turn breast up for the last hour. When bird is about two-thirds done, according to chart, cut cord holding drumstick ends to tail.
• About 15 to 30 minutes before roasting time ends, test turkey for doneness. Move drumsticks up and down—the leg should give readily. Do not pierce skin with fork!
• Start roasting bird to allow 30 to 40 minutes leeway before dinner, if turkey takes longer then estimated. Allows time to make gravy, and permits turkey to absorb juices.
• Cook giblets in seasoned water. Use broth in stuffing and gravy.

CELERY STUFFING

7 c. dry bread crumbs
1 c. chopped onion
2 c. finely chopped celery
2 tsp. salt
½ tsp. pepper
1½ tsp. sage
½ tsp. poultry seasoning
⅔ c. melted butter or margarine
1⅓ c. milk
1¼ c. turkey broth
2 eggs, slightly beaten

• Combine bread crumbs, onion, celery and seasonings.
• Add melted butter, milk, broth and eggs. Toss lightly to blend.
• Stuff loosely into cavities of bird. Makes 6½ cups stuffing—enough for 12 lb. ready-to-cook turkey.

Crumbly Bread Stuffing: Heat 1⅛ c. butter or margarine in deep kettle; sauté ¾ c. minced onions until soft and tender. Combine with 4½ qts. day-old bread crumbs, ¼ c. diced celery, 1½ tsp. poultry seasoning, ½ c. snipped parsley (optional), ¼ tsp. pepper and 2¼ tsp. salt. Heat well without browning, stirring frequently. Makes enough to stuff neck and body cavity of 10 lb. ready-to-cook turkey.

TURKEY GRAVY

• Remove turkey from roasting pan. Pour drippings—fat and meat juices—into pint measuring cup. Skim off fat.
• Return 3 tblsp. fat and 3 tblsp. flour to roasting pan; blend thoroughly.
• Cook slowly, stirring over low heat to brown fat and flour slightly.
• Add water, milk or giblet broth to meat juices to make 2 c. liquid. Add fat and flour.
• Cook, stirring constantly, until smooth and thickened. Simmer about 5 minutes. Season. Makes 2 cups.

TURKEY-CRANBERRY SALAD

Ruby-topped salad is festive and flavorful —a luncheon special

Turkey Layer:

2 envelopes unflavored gelatin
½ c. cold water
1½ c. turkey broth
1 tblsp. lemon juice
Salt to taste
¾ c. mayonnaise or salad dressing
1½ c. finely diced turkey
½ c. finely diced celery

Cranberry Layer:

1 (1 lb.) can jellied cranberry sauce
1 tblsp. lemon juice
Dash of salt
1 envelope unflavored gelatin
¼ c. cold water
½ c. boiling water

• Soften gelatin in cold water. Heat 1 c. broth or chicken bouillon (made from 2 cubes and 1½ c. boiling water); add gelatin, stir until dissolved. Add remaining broth, lemon juice and salt. Cool.
• Blend a little gelatin mixture into mayonnaise until smooth; add remaining gelatin mixture. Chill until syrupy. Fold in turkey and celery. Pour into oiled 1½ qt. oblong baking dish. Chill until set.
• Mash cranberry sauce with fork. Add lemon juice and salt.
• Soften gelatin in cold water. Add to boiling water; stir until dissolved. Add cranberry sauce; blend well.
• When turkey layer is set, pour over cranberry mixture (for extra smoothness, sieve cranberry mixture before molding). Chill several hours until cranberry layer is set.
• To serve, cut in squares and place on crisp greens. With tiny cookie cutter, or knife, cut design in center of each square. Remove cutout; fill hole with mayonnaise. Makes 6 (3") squares.

TURKEY SURPRISE

For a change, spoon over waffles, fried noodles or biscuits instead of rice

4 tblsp. shortening
½ clove garlic, chopped fine
4 tblsp. flour
2 c. turkey broth
1 tblsp. soy sauce
3 c. diced cooked turkey
Hot cooked rice

• Melt shortening; add garlic and sauté slightly. Stir in flour and cook until bubbly, stirring constantly. Add broth or chicken bouillon (2 bouillon cubes in 2 cups boiling water), soy sauce, turkey and seasonings, if desired.
• Cook until thickened and thoroughly heated, about 20 minutes. Serve with hot cooked rice. Makes 6 servings.

TURKEY TETRAZZINI

Fine for company—with green salad, crusty rolls and a fruit dessert

1 (10½ oz.) can condensed cream of mushroom soup
1 (10½ oz.) can condensed cream of chicken soup
1 c. turkey broth
2 c. grated process cheese
6 c. cooked spaghetti (12 oz. uncooked)
4 c. boned turkey, diced
½ c. mushrooms or toasted almonds (optional)
½ c. grated Parmesan cheese
Dash paprika

• Blend soups and broth (part milk may be used). Stir in process cheese; mix with spaghetti, turkey and mushrooms. Turn into greased shallow baking dish, about 7½×12". Sprinkle top with cheese and paprika.
• Bake in moderate oven (350°) until bubbly and browned, about 30 minutes. Makes 8 to 10 servings.

TURKEY DIVAN

Your family will like broccoli fixed this interesting way

12 large slices cooked turkey
2 (10 oz.) pkgs. frozen broccoli or asparagus, cooked and drained
1 (10½ oz.) can condensed cream of chicken soup
¾ c. shredded sharp cheese

• Arrange sliced turkey on bottom of greased shallow baking dish, about 7×11"; cover with layer of broccoli. Pour on soup. Sprinkle top with cheese.
• Bake in moderate oven (375°) 20 to 25 minutes or until lightly browned. Makes 6 servings.

Variation: Blend 1 c. mayonnaise with 1 beaten egg white; substitute for soup.

Festive Goose

If goose is first choice for the Christmas platter, here are your recipes. The bird browns beautifully and the dressing is out-of-this-world in taste. One secret of the good cook, who gave us these recipes, is to take off some of the fat early in the baking process. A festive start for the goose dinner is chilled fruit juice—apple and cranberry, half and half.

STEAM-BAKED GOOSE

1 (10 to 12 lb.) goose
1 tblsp. salt
12 c. bread stuffing (recipe follows)
2 tblsp. melted fat
2 c. hot water
¼ tsp. black pepper
1 small onion, minced
1 clove garlic, mashed
½ c. coarsely ground green pepper
1 (10½ oz.) can condensed cream of mushroom soup

• Rub 1 tsp. salt inside body cavity of goose. Stuff cavity and neck with bread stuffing. Skewer and lace skin openings with string. Tie legs and wings close to body. Brush goose with melted fat. Place in bottom of roaster pan, breast side up.
• Add water—more as needed during cooking period. Add remaining salt, pepper, onion, garlic and green pepper to water. Bake, covered, in slow oven (300°) 2 hours.
• Remove from oven. Carefully skim off all goose fat from broth. Add mushroom soup; return goose to oven. Bake uncovered 2 hours longer, basting frequently with savory broth. Remove bird to serving platter and make gravy in roasting pan.

DELICIOUS BREAD STUFFING

8 c. dry bread crumbs
2 eggs, beaten
2 c. coarsely ground carrots
2 small onions, coarsely ground
1 (10½ oz.) can condensed cream of mushroom soup
½ lb. bulk pork sausage
½ lb. round steak, finely ground
Goose heart, liver and gizzard, ground together
1 tsp. sage
½ tsp. sweet marjoram
⅛ tsp. cinnamon
⅛ tsp. nutmeg
2 tsp. salt

• Blend all ingredients thoroughly in large kettle or mixing bowl. Stuff goose cavity and neck. Makes 12 cups stuffing or enough for a 10 to 12 lb. goose.

ROAST DUCK

Orange stuffing brings out the best duck flavor

1 (4 to 5 lb.) ready-to-cook duck
Seasonings
Stuffing

• Clean duck, also removing "down"; wrap loosely. Keep chilled until roasting time. (If do not plan to use within 2 days, wrap and freeze.)

• Rub body cavity lightly with salt, seasoned salt, caraway or celery seeds or any desired seasoning. May roast unstuffed if you wish.

• For flavor stuff with thick onion slices, dried prunes, rice, cored and quartered thick apple slices, sauerkraut, celery tops or some combination, as apple, celery and onion (discard these after roasting). Or stuff with Bread or Orange Stuffing.

• Place duck on rack in shallow roasting pan. Roast in slow oven (325°) 1 to 1½ hours, until tender. To test doneness, grasp end of leg. If thigh moves easily or drumstick meat is very soft when pressed between fingers, bird is cooked. Skin should be crisp.

• Do not baste or prick skin during baking—meat juices could then drain off, leaving meat dry and of grayish color. Pour off fat (while clear) during roasting.

• Use brown drippings and small amount of fat for gravy. Makes about 4 servings, allowing 1¼ lbs. dressed weight per serving.

ORANGE STUFFING

2 c. chopped celery
1 c. boiling water
¼ c. chopped green pepper (optional)
⅓ c. chopped onion
⅓ to ½ c. butter or shortening
2 c. peeled, diced oranges with juice
2 tsp. grated orange rind
¾ tsp. poultry seasoning
1 tsp. salt
¼ tsp. pepper
7 to 8 c. lightly packed soft bread crumbs

• Simmer celery in water until tender, about 10 to 15 minutes. Drain.

• Sauté green pepper and onion in butter until tender, but not brown.

• Combine oranges, seasonings and crumbs; add cooked vegetables (celery and onion) and toss together lightly. Makes enough to stuff one 5 lb. duck.

FRIED DUCKLING

1 (3 to 4 lb.) duckling
1 c. flour
2 tsp. salt
¼ tsp. pepper
2 tsp. paprika
¼ c. butter or margarine
Shortening
1 c. water

• Shake pieces of duckling, 2 or 3 at a time, in paper bag with dry ingredients to coat thoroughly.

• Heat butter and enough shortening in skillet to make ¼" layer. Place duckling in hot fat skin side down. Brown and turn. Add water and cover tightly.

• Reduce heat and cook slowly or bake in moderate oven (350°) about 1 hour. Uncover and continue to cook about 30 minutes until duckling pieces have crisp crusts. Makes 4 to 6 servings.

Serving Suggestion: Cut duck lengthwise with kitchen scissors (or poultry scissors) and sharp knife, then crosswise. Arrange stuffing in center of large platter, the duck quarters around it.

9

Potatoes

Farmers love potatoes. And for good reason—country cooks set such wonderful potato and meat dishes before them. This chapter features both important potato families, the whites and sweets. The kind you prefer indicates on which side of the Mason-Dixon line you live, although most Americans enjoy both.

The whites, or Irish potatoes, are good mixers. Country cooks use them in everything—breads, cakes, salads, soups and main dishes. But the every-day-of-the-year role of these tubers is to escort meat, fish or poultry, and eggs.

Wide experience with potatoes explains much of the farm woman's success in cooking them. She is not scared off by talk of how fattening they are. Haven't nutrition classes in the Home Demonstration club given her assurance that a medium spud has only about as many calories (100) as an orange or apple?

The country cook learns what to do about potato flaws. If potatoes darken during cooking (too much rain at the harvest season), she adds a little vinegar or lemon juice to the cooking water. That green tinge is sunburn—makes potatoes bitter. Overly sweet potatoes have been stored in a too cold place—several days of room temperature convert the sugars back to starch.

Every household has its first choice of color and degree of moistness or dryness in sweet potatoes. But all informed women value this vegetable for its vitamin A and the variety of dishes it makes—pies, puddings, biscuits, cookies and combinations with fruits. Sweet potatoes have an affinity for fruits, especially oranges, lemons, pineapple and apples. They take to touches of spice, nuts, brown sugar, maple and cane syrups, coconut and marshmallows. They're famed ham, pork and chicken go-withs. And candied sweets are one of this country's great dishes, of course.

Sweet potatoes don't keep well immediately after harvesting, before they're cured. Then farm women cook and freeze them for quick use later on—they're good freezers.

SKILLET CREAMED POTATOES

Spuds in bubbling hot sour cream—with pimiento for a Spanish accent

6 medium-size potatoes, boiled
2 c. dairy sour cream
3 tblsp. finely chopped onion
2 tblsp. finely chopped pimiento stuffed olives
1 tsp. salt
½ tsp. pepper
½ tsp. paprika
1 tblsp. chopped parsley

• Dice cold boiled potatoes.
• Pour cream into skillet; add potatoes. Heat slowly over medium heat until cream bubbles over potatoes. Add onion and olives.
• When potatoes are thoroughly heated, add salt and pepper. Serve at once, garnished with paprika and parsley. Makes 6 servings.

Variation: Substitute chopped pimiento for olives. And if you like more pronounced flavor, use ½ clove garlic, chopped, instead of onion.

SKILLET-SCALLOPED POTATOES

They're luscious with cream and cheese—another fast-fix potato dish

6 medium-size potatoes
4 tblsp. shortening or bacon drippings
1 medium onion, chopped
1 tsp. salt
¼ tsp. pepper
4 tblsp. light cream
⅓ c. process sharp cheese spread

• Peel potatoes; slice thinly.
• Heat shortening in large skillet. Add potatoes, onion and seasonings. Fry potatoes slowly over low heat until golden brown, turning frequently.
• Pour on cream; add cheese, stirring gently to mix. Cover; cook slowly 10 minutes, or until potatoes are tender. Makes 6 servings.

LYONNAISE POTATOES

Pretty-as-a-picture potatoes–golden brown flecked with red and green

¼ c. shortening or oil
4 c. raw potatoes, peeled and cut in ½″ cubes
1 small onion, chopped fine
1 tsp. salt
4 pimientos, chopped
2 tblsp. minced parsley

• Heat shortening in skillet over high heat. Add potatoes, onion and salt. Cook until potatoes are almost tender.
• Add pimiento and parsley. Mix carefully. Cook until potatoes are golden brown. Serve at once. Makes 4 servings.

HURRY-UP POTATOES

They cook in 6 minutes alongside the meat—sesame seed adds a new flavor

4 medium-size potatoes
2 tblsp. melted shortening or oil
1½ tsp. salt
4 tsp. sesame seed

• Wash and peel potatoes. Cut crosswise in ⅛″ thick slices.
• Brush broiler rack with a little shortening or oil and arrange potatoes on rack. Brush their tops with remaining shortening or oil. Sprinkle with salt and sesame seed.
• Broil until tender and golden brown, about 6 minutes. Serve at once. Makes 6 servings. (Place potato slices on rack around meat for last 6 minutes of cooking when broiling steaks, hamburgers or chops.)

Grated Potatoes, Panbroiled: Scrub and grate 4 medium-size potatoes. Spread in well greased heavy skillet to depth of about ¼″. Cook over medium to slow heat until browned on bottom. Flip over and repeat. Season. Serve hot. Makes about 4 to 5 servings.

CHEESE-TOPPED POTATOES

Perfect baked potatoes to serve with hamburgers or steak

6 baking potatoes
Salt
½ c. melted butter or margarine
6 slices American cheese
Parsley

• Scrub potatoes well. Cut diagonally, with skins on, in 1½″ slices. Place in greased baking dish.
• Sprinkle with salt; brush with butter. Bake uncovered in hot oven (400°) 40 minutes. Remove from oven.
• Top with cheese slices. Return to oven about 5 minutes or until cheese is melted. Garnish with sprigs of parsley. Makes 6 servings.

COUNTRY FRIED POTATOES

A favorite since pioneer days, this continues to rate high

⅓ c. lard
6 c. sliced, peeled potatoes, ¼″ thick
1 c. sliced onions
2 tsp. salt
¼ tsp. pepper
Chopped parsley (optional)

• Heat lard in heavy skillet (bacon drippings or other fat or oil may be used). Arrange in skillet a layer of potatoes, then one of onions; repeat.
• Sprinkle with salt and pepper. Sauté, covered, over low heat, about 15 minutes. Uncover; increase heat slightly and sauté 10 minutes longer, or until potatoes are crisp and brown on underside. Do not stir.
• Sprinkle with parsley. Fold in half like an omelet and serve on a hot platter. Makes 4 to 6 servings.

Variation: Omit onion and use shredded instead of thinly sliced potatoes.

BEEF POTATO ROLL

On the tricky side, but a company special that folks like

2 lbs. ground beef
2 tsp. salt
⅛ tsp. pepper
1 tblsp. Worcestershire sauce
1 onion, chopped
1 egg, slightly beaten
3 slices crisp bacon, crumbled
3 c. hot mashed potatoes (about 6 to 9 potatoes)

• Combine in bowl all ingredients, except potatoes.
• Place meat on waxed paper and pat into rectangle ⅓″ thick. Mound the mashed potatoes down the center of meat. Bring up edges of waxed paper to wrap meat around potato roll; press meat edges together.
• Place in shallow pan, remove paper. Bake in moderate oven (350°) 1 hour. Serve with chili sauce. Makes 6 to 8 servings.

BAKED STUFFED POTATOES

Keep these potatoes on the half-shell in the freezer to reheat quickly

6 medium-size baking potatoes
½ c. warm cream or milk
3 tblsp. butter
Salt and pepper to taste
½ c. grated cheese (optional)

• Scrub potatoes well.
• Bake in hot oven (400°) until done—45 to 60 minutes.
• Cut crisscross gash on potato top, scoop out potato and mash. Add cream, butter and seasonings.
• Refill potato shells, sprinkle each with grated cheese, if desired. Heat thoroughly in moderate oven (350°) or wrap and freeze.
• To serve frozen spuds, remove from wrapping. Place in baking pan; heat in moderate oven (350°) 20 minutes.

Country New Potatoes

Potatoes that come directly from garden to kitchen have a flavor of their own. They are especially good in salads. This French recipe also is excellent.

PROVINCIAL POTATOES

Inspired by the French who highly regard small potatoes fresh-from-the-earth

3 lbs. new potatoes
¼ c. butter or margarine
1 tsp. grated lemon rind
1 tblsp. lemon juice
2 tblsp. chopped chives
¼ tsp. salt
Dash of pepper

• Wash potatoes. Steam, with skins on, in colander over boiling water until tender.
• To make sauce, melt butter. Add remaining ingredients. Pass sauce to pour over each serving of potatoes. (It is equally good over baked potatoes.) Makes 6 servings.

SWEEPSTAKES POTATO SALAD

It's glamorous with radish-pineapples, egg water lilies and crisp greens

4 c. cold boiled potatoes, diced
¾ c. sliced green onions
⅓ c. radish slices
3 hard-cooked eggs, cubed
½ c. mayonnaise or salad dressing
¾ c. dairy sour cream
2½ tblsp. herb vinegar
1½ tsp. salt
¾ tsp. celery seed

• Combine potatoes, onions, radishes and hard-cooked eggs.
• Blend remaining ingredients; mix lightly with potato mixture. Chill.
• Serve in salad bowl lined with endive or leaf lettuce, and garnish with hard-cooked eggs (we cut them with an egg slicer) and radish-pineapples (tuck 1" lengths of sliced green onion tops in holes cut in radishes.) Makes 6 servings.

EIGHT VARIATIONS

Carrot: Add 1 c. shredded carrots to vegetables before mixing with dressing.

Cucumber: Add 1 c. diced cucumber to vegetables before adding dressing.

Celery: Omit celery seed; add 1 c. chopped celery to vegetables.

Green Pepper-Onion: Substitute ¼ c. chopped onion and ⅓ c. chopped green pepper for green onions.

Ham: Add 1 c. chopped ham or luncheon meat before adding dressing.

Bacon: Add 8 strips of bacon, crumbled, before adding dressing.

Shrimp: Add 1 c. (5 oz. can) cooked shrimp to vegetables.

Sharp Cheese: Add 1 c. sharp cheese, cubed, to salad before final mixing.

MASHED POTATO SALAD

Serve it hot or cold

4 c. mashed hot potatoes (unseasoned)
⅓ c. mayonnaise or salad dressing
1 tblsp. vinegar
1 tsp. salt
1½ tblsp. chopped green pepper
1½ tblsp. finely chopped pimiento
¾ c. finely chopped celery
¾ c. finely chopped green onion

• Toss ingredients together. Serve hot or cold. Makes 6 servings.

Quick Scalloped Potatoes: In ½ c. boiling water in covered saucepan, cook 4 c. diced, peeled potatoes, 1 c. minced onions, 2 tsp. salt 10 minutes. Uncover; simmer, stirring occasionally, until water is almost evaporated. Add ½ c. each light cream and grated cheese. Heat. Makes about 6 servings.

SAVORY POTATOES

Hearty and different. It's the tomatoes and peppy seasoning that do the trick

4 slices bacon
4 c. raw potatoes, sliced thin
1 onion, sliced
2 c. cooked tomatoes
1½ tsp. salt
¼ tsp. pepper
½ tsp. prepared mustard
½ tsp. celery salt

• Pan-fry bacon in heavy skillet until crisp, and drain on paper toweling.
• Add potatoes and onion to bacon drippings and cook about 10 minutes. Turn gently with a spatula to distribute fat.
• Add remaining ingredients and simmer until potatoes are tender and tomato juice thickens, about 20 minutes.
• Crumble bacon over top. Serve hot. Makes 4 to 6 servings.

BROWNED POTATO LOAF

Perfect to serve with baked ham

4 tblsp. butter or margarine
4 tblsp. flour
1⅓ c. rich milk
Salt
Pepper
7 medium-size cold boiled potatoes
1½ tblsp. minced parsley
Melted butter or margarine
½ to ¾ c. grated cheese

• Make thick white sauce of butter, flour and milk. Season with salt and pepper.
• Dice or slice potatoes into sauce and combine. Add parsley; cook 5 minutes longer (makes a stiff mixture).
• Place in well greased oblong pan (9×5×3") and press down firmly. Chill several hours or overnight.
• About half an hour before serving, remove from pan to oven-proof platter or pan. Sprinkle with grated cheese.
• Bake in moderate oven (375°) until hot and nicely browned. Garnish with parsley or other vegetables. Serve very hot. Makes 6 servings.

Company Creamed Potatoes: Melt ¼ c. butter or margarine in heavy skillet; add 6 c. diced cold boiled potatoes; season with salt and pepper. Stir lightly. Gradually drizzle on about ⅔ c. light cream. Heat slowly until potatoes absorb cream, but do not brown. Serve piping hot. Makes 6 servings.

BEEF-POTATO POT PIE

Borrowed from a country kitchen where Pennsylvania Dutch cooking is an art

2 lbs. stewing beef
¼ c. flour
2 tsp. salt
2 tblsp. shortening
1 c. water
3 medium onions, quartered
1 c. mashed potatoes
½ tsp. marjoram
3 carrots, cut in strips
1 c. fresh or frozen peas
1 c. chopped celery, cut in 1" pieces
Pastry or biscuit dough made from 1 c. flour
Melted butter or margarine

• Cut beef in 2" cubes. Combine flour and salt in paper bag; add beef cubes and shake until thoroughly coated.

• Heat shortening in Dutch oven or other heavy kettle. Add beef and brown.

• Slowly add water and onions. Cover and cook 1 hour, adding more water if necessary.

• Add potatoes and marjoram. Cover and simmer 1 hour. (The mashed potatoes will thicken stew so no other thickening is necessary.)

• About 15 minutes before stew is done, add carrots, peas and celery. Pour into greased 2 qt. casserole. Top with rolled pie dough or rolled or dropped biscuit dough. Brush with melted butter.

• Bake in very hot oven (450°) 15 minutes. Makes 8 servings.

MEAT-POTATO HASH

Call your meat-and-potato man to supper, confident of pleasing him

6 medium-size potatoes, peeled
1 medium-size onion, peeled
2 c. cubed, cooked meat
3 strips bacon, cut in pieces
1 tsp. salt
1/8 tsp. pepper
1/2 c. water
1/2 c. gravy (or use a bouillon cube plus 1/2 c. water)

• Put potatoes, onion and meat through food chopper using medium blade.
• Preheat electric skillet; set temperature control at medium heat or heat a heavy skillet.
• Fry bacon until lightly browned. Add chopped ingredients and seasonings. Cook until well browned on bottom. Turn browned portion to top.
• Add water and gravy; reduce temperature control or heat to low. Cover and simmer 1 hour. Makes 6 servings.

POTATO PANCAKES

Serve with cane or maple-blended syrup for breakfast, with meat for dinner

3 egg yolks, beaten
2 tsp. salt
1 tblsp. sugar
3 c. milk
1 tblsp. melted fat
2 1/2 c. sifted flour
3 c. grated raw potatoes
3 egg whites, stiffly beaten

• Combine well-beaten egg yolks, salt, sugar, milk and fat. Gradually stir in flour, beating to blend well.
• Stir in grated potatoes (for best flavor, peel and grate potatoes just before adding). Fold in egg whites.
• Bake at once on greased, hot griddle. Allow 1 rounded tablespoonful batter for each cake. Bake 3 minutes on each side, turning once. Makes 2 dozen pancakes.

Variation: Finely chopped onions may be put on top of batter on griddle, if you are serving the potatoes with meat.

POTATO WAFFLES

Good eating with topper of creamed meat or fish, or cheese sauce

1 c. sifted flour
2 tsp. baking powder
1 tsp. salt
2 eggs, beaten
1 c. milk
5 tblsp. melted fat
1 1/2 c. cooked, mashed potatoes
1/4 c. minced onion

• Sift together flour, baking powder and salt.
• Combine eggs, milk, fat, potatoes and onion. Add to dry ingredients and beat with rotary beater 30 seconds.
• Allow 3/4 c. batter for each waffle. Bake in hot waffle iron until steaming stops, 3 to 4 minutes. Makes 4 (4 section) waffles.

TUNA POTATO PUFFS

Complete supper with buttered peas, stewed tomatoes and hot biscuits

1 (7 oz.) can tuna
1 1/2 c. mashed potatoes
2 egg yolks, beaten
1/2 tsp. salt
Pepper to taste
1 tblsp. onion
2 egg whites, stiffly beaten

• Drain and flake tuna; mix with potatoes. Stir in egg yolks.
• Add salt, pepper and onion; fold in egg whites. Put mixture in 6 greased custard cups. Bake in moderate oven (350°) 30 minutes. Makes 6 servings.

POTATO-EGG SCRAPPLE

Thank the Pennsylvania Dutch for this hearty dish

2 tblsp. shortening or oil
1 medium-size onion
2 tblsp. chopped green pepper
½ tsp. salt
¼ tsp. pepper
3 medium potatoes, diced
1 diced tomato
4 eggs, separated

• Heat shortening in skillet over low heat. Add chopped onion and green pepper; sauté until tender.
• Add salt, pepper and potatoes; cook covered until potatoes are tender, about 20 minutes. Stir in tomato.
• Beat egg yolks until lemon colored. Beat whites until stiff, but not dry. Fold in yolks; then fold into potato mixture.
• Bake covered in moderate oven (350°) until eggs are firm and top slightly brown, about 20 minutes. Makes 4 servings.

CREAM OF POTATO SOUP

Irresistible on a cold day, when your men have been outdoors all forenoon

4 large stalks celery and leaves
2 medium onions
1½ c. water
2 chicken bouillon cubes
1½ c. mashed potatoes
1 tblsp. butter
2 c. milk
Dash of paprika
Chopped chives or parsley garnish

• Chop celery and onions; add water and simmer 30 minutes. Strain through sieve (should be about 1 cup).
• Stir in bouillon cubes. While hot pour over potatoes, stirring until they dissolve. Rub through strainer to make sure no lumps remain.
• Add butter, milk and paprika and heat. Serve with chopped chives or parsley. Makes 4 to 6 servings.

BROWN POTATO SOUP

It's the browned crumbs that add oomph

2½ c. diced, peeled potatoes
4 c. water
1 tblsp. salt
¼ tsp. pepper
¼ tsp. onion salt
¼ tsp. celery salt
4 c. milk
2 tblsp. butter or margarine
¾ c. flour

• Cook potatoes until tender in 2 c. water. While cooking, add salt, pepper, onion and celery salts.
• Drain. Add milk and remaining 2 c. water to the drained, seasoned potato water. Heat to boiling; simmer.
• While liquid simmers, cut fat into flour until mixture looks like crumbs. Brown these in small heavy skillet, stirring constantly. Stir browned crumbs into hot liquid; cook about 5 minutes, stirring.
• Add potatoes, and heat about 5 minutes more. Serve hot. Makes 6 to 8 servings.

POTATO-CHEESE SOUP

A different potato soup—delicious

4 medium potatoes, peeled
1 medium onion, sliced
4 c. boiling water
⅓ c. diced summer sausage
½ tsp. thyme
½ tsp. marjoram
1½ tsp. salt
Pepper
2 tblsp. butter or margarine
½ c. grated sharp cheese
1 tblsp. grated Parmesan cheese (optional)

• Cut potatoes in half. Cook with onion slices in 2 c. water, until tender. Do not drain.
• Mash potatoes. Add sausage, thyme, marjoram, salt, pepper, butter, sharp cheese and remaining boiling water. Simmer 10 minutes.
• Add grated cheese just before serving. Makes 6 servings.

Oyster Stew with Potatoes

The Maryland farm woman who gave us this unusual recipe buys two or three bushels of oysters at a time. The entire family helps her shuck them—they open the shells with oyster knives, scrape out the oysters and rinse them quickly in cold water. One bushel yields 2 or 3 quarts. But even if you live far from oyster farming country and buy your oysters without shells, ready to use, you'll want to try this stew. It makes a delightful supper dish. And who can improve on the accompaniment the originator of the dish suggested—crisp coleslaw?

"STRETCHER" OYSTER STEW

A new kind of oyster stew—potatoes make it hearty enough for the hungriest

2 c. finely diced potatoes
1 c. water
2 tsp. salt
1 pt. oysters, drained and cut coarsely or chopped
1 pt. oyster liquor (add milk to make 1 pt.)
⅓ c. butter or margarine
1 c. cream or top milk
⅛ tsp. pepper
¼ tsp. paprika

• Cook potatoes in water with salt added until almost soft, about 10 minutes. Add oysters and liquor and bring just to a boil. Remove from heat at once.
• Add butter, cream and seasoning. Cover and let stand about 15 minutes before serving. Makes 5 to 6 servings.

POTATO-SALMON CHOWDER

A hearty meal-in-a bowl—serve with cabbage salad and crackers

6 medium potatoes, peeled and cut into ½" cubes (4 c.)
1 c. sliced carrots
1 tblsp. salt
3 c. water
1 (10 oz.) pkg. frozen peas
⅓ c. butter or margarine
⅓ c. chopped onion
¼ c. flour
5 c. milk
1 lb. can salmon, pink or red
1 c. thinly sliced celery
½ tsp. Worcestershire sauce

• Cook the potatoes and carrots in a covered saucepan in salted water until just tender.

• Add frozen peas. Bring to boil. Cook 1 minute.

• Remove from heat. Do not drain.

• Melt butter in a skillet. Add onions and cook until lightly browned. Add the flour, stir until smooth. Cook 1 minute. Add half the milk, stirring constantly. Cook over low heat until mixture boils and thickens.

• Remove skin and the bone from the salmon. Flake the fish and add, with the fish liquid, to the vegetables.

• Add hot white sauce, celery, Worcestershire sauce and remaining milk to the vegetables and salmon. Heat thoroughly. Serve at once. Makes 3 quarts or 12 generous servings.

Garnish For Potato Soups: Just before serving add crumbled crisp bacon, chopped parsley or chives, grated cheese, dabs of butter sprinkled with paprika, chopped hard-cooked eggs or croutons. To make croutons cut slices of day-old bread in ¼" cubes and brown in hot bacon fat or butter.

Mashed Potato Balls: Make 3 c. hot mashed potatoes. Add 3 eggs, 1 tsp. baking powder, ½ tsp. salt and dash of paprika. Beat together well and drop teaspoonfuls into deep hot fat. Cook until puffs are brown; drain on paper toweling. Serve hot or reheat in hot oven (425°). Garnish with parsley.

Perennial Favorite—Fried Potatoes

In the Great Plains kitchens fried potatoes are the dish good cooks serve with steaks and hamburgers. The first recipe comes from France—the four that follow are from cattle ranches on the prairies.

PUFFED-UP POTATOES

Two-step fried potatoes—one of many wonderful French importations

8 large potatoes
Shortening or oil
Salt

• Peel potatoes; cut in even ⅛" slices. Soak 4 minutes in ice water; pat dry on paper toweling.
• Heat shortening or oil in deep kettle to 300°. Cook a few slices at a time at this temperature until light brown and half-done, about 10 minutes. Remove from kettle; drain on paper toweling on racks.
• After frying all potatoes at 300°, heat shortening to 400°. Add more shortening, if needed.
• Finish frying potatoes, a few at a time, turning constantly. (They will puff quickly.) Drain on paper toweling. Keep hot in oven while frying the rest. Sprinkle with salt; serve at once. Makes 6 to 8 servings.

FRENCH FRIED POTATOES

In our Countryside Kitchens we like this two-step, or blanch-and-brown method

6 medium potatoes, peeled
Cold water
Fat for frying
Salt and pepper

• Cut potatoes lengthwise, then crosswise into ⅜" strips. Rinse in cold water; dry thoroughly between towels.

Step 1:

• Fry small amounts in deep, hot fat (360°) about 5 minutes, until tender but not brown. Drain on paper toweling; repeat with remaining batches.
• Cool to room temperature. Brown before serving. Or package and freeze.

Step 2:

• Arrange partly cooked potatoes on baking sheet; put in extremely hot oven (500°) 10 minutes, or until brown, turning once.
• Or, fry about half of potatoes in deep, hot fat (390°) about 1½ minutes, or until crisp and brown; drain on toweling. Fry rest of batch.
• Quickly season to taste. Serve immediately. Makes 6 servings.

HASH-BROWNED POTATOES

For a delightful flavor change substitute sour cream for light cream

3 c. potatoes, cooked and cubed (about 4 potatoes)
¼ c. minced onion
¼ c. minced parsley or spinach
3 tblsp. flour
1½ tsp. salt
½ tsp. pepper
¼ c. light cream
3 tblsp. bacon drippings

• Combine potatoes with onion, parsley, flour, salt and pepper; toss lightly to mix well. Stir in cream.
• Heat 2 tblsp. drippings in heavy 8" skillet. Spread potato mixture in skillet, packing down with spatula. Brown over medium heat until bottom is crusty, 10 to 15 minutes. (Shake pan constantly from side to side to prevent sticking.) Lift to hot platter, browned side up. Scrape and wipe pan free of crumbs with paper towel.
• Heat 1 tblsp. drippings in skillet. Slide potato "pancake" back into skillet, browned side up. Brown 5 to 10 minutes, shaking constantly, and firming edges with spatula. Turn onto hot platter; cut in wedges to serve. Makes 6 servings.

POTATO SUNFLOWERS

Shaggy shreds make the potato petals of this country favorite

4 medium-size potatoes
4 tblsp. melted shortening or oil
Salt and pepper
Garlic salt

- Coarsely shred peeled potatoes.
- Heat shortening in heavy skillet. Drop rounded tablespoons of potatoes in fat. Spread a little, keeping the cakes thin. Fry until golden brown on both sides, about 5 minutes.
- Drain on paper toweling; sprinkle with salt, pepper and garlic salt. Serve at once. Makes 6 servings.

OVEN-FRIED POTATOES

No fuss to fix these crisp, brown potato slices that are mealy inside

4 medium potatoes, peeled
3 tblsp. melted fat
1 tsp. salt
⅜ tsp. pepper
⅜ tsp. paprika

- Cut potatoes crosswise in ⅜" slices. Brush with melted fat.
- Bake in hot oven (425°), basting frequently with fat or oil until tender and golden brown on both sides.
- Sprinkle with salt, pepper and paprika, and serve immediately. Makes 5 servings.

Sweet Potatoes and Yams

Southern women speak of potatoes, and Irish potatoes. To them, potatoes are what northern people call sweet potatoes or yams. And what wonderful dishes southern cooks make with them! Among the memorable ones are potato balls—seasoned mashed sweet potatoes shaped into golf ball size around raisins, nuts, pineapple chunks or marshmallows, then rolled in corn flakes. These golden beauties are prepared and refrigerated or frozen in large quantity before the Christmas holidays to bring out and heat quickly. A Tennessee woman told Farm Journal's Food Department she likes to add a few chopped black walnuts to the mashed sweet potatoes when making the holiday balls. You may like to try this variation with the recipe that follows:

SWEET POTATO BALLS

Golden balls with sweet centers

3 c. cooked yams or sweet potatoes
¼ c. butter
¾ c. brown sugar
2 tblsp. milk
¼ tsp. salt
½ tsp. grated lemon rind
8 marshmallows
½ c. crushed corn flakes

- Mash sweet potatoes. Add butter, sugar, milk, salt and lemon rind.
- With tablespoons scoop up about ¼ c. of mixture. Center with marshmallow. Cover with more potato. Shape in balls.
- Roll each ball in crushed corn flakes.
- Place in buttered baking dish.
- Cover with aluminum foil. Freeze.
- When ready to serve, bake until marshmallows begin to ooze, about 20 minutes. Makes 8 balls.

SWEET POTATO CASSEROLE

Sweet potatoes in a tutti-frutti holiday dress, and so good with turkey!

3 tblsp. butter or margarine
¾ tsp. salt
¼ c. orange juice
3 c. cooked, mashed sweet potatoes
1 (9 oz.) can crushed pineapple, drained (1 c.)
1 tblsp. butter or margarine
6 marshmallows, cut in halves

• Add 3 tblsp. butter, salt and orange juice to sweet potatoes; beat until light. Fold in pineapple.

• Spoon potatoes into 1 qt. casserole; dot with 1 tblsp. butter. Put marshmallows on top.

• Bake in moderate oven (350°) until marshmallows are puffed and browned. Makes 6 servings.

SWEET POTATO CHIPS

You'll bask in the compliments these crispies bring when served with salads

Sweet potatoes or yams
Shortening for frying

• Cover whole sweet potatoes with cold water. Quickly bring water to a temperature between 175° and 190°; keep water at this heat 30 minutes.

• Rinse potatoes in cold water. Peel, and slice paper-thin.

• Preheat fat. Deepfry chips at 300° until edges begin to brown—2½ to 3 minutes for yams, 5 minutes for sweet. (Notice difference in time.)

• Drain; sprinkle with salt or a little confectioners sugar. Spread on paper towels to cool. Pack in air-tight containers.

SWEET POTATO SOUFFLE

Just right for hungry people

1 lb. bulk pork sausage
3 c. cooked sweet potatoes or yams
¼ c. brown sugar
1 tsp. salt
⅛ tsp. pepper
¼ tsp. nutmeg
2 tblsp. butter or margarine
1 egg
1 c. crushed pineapple

• Break sausage into pieces; brown over low heat in heavy skillet. Drain off fat.

• Combine remaining ingredients in large bowl; beat with rotary beater until fluffy. Stir in crisp sausage.

• Drop in mounds on greased baking sheet. Bake in moderate oven (375°) 25 minutes. Makes 6 servings.

YAM CHOPS

Faint orange and lemon flavors are delightful in this sweet potato-pork dish

8 thick pork chops
2 tblsp. cornstarch
½ c. brown sugar, firmly packed
½ tsp. salt
1 c. orange juice
1 c. lemon juice
2 tblsp. grated orange rind
8 medium yams, cooked

• Brown chops on both sides in skillet; transfer to baking dish. Cover; bake in moderate oven (350°) 1 hour.

• Mix cornstarch, sugar and salt. Add to drippings in the skillet. Gradually add fruit juices and rind. Stir over medium heat until sauce boils and thickens.

• Place one yam on each chop. Pour sauce over the chops.

• Continue baking; uncovered, 30 minutes, basting frequently. Makes 8 servings.

YAM FRUIT SALAD

Honey and lemon juice in the dressing spark this unusual salad

3 medium yams, cooked, or 1 (17 oz.) can yams
2 firm bananas
2 red apples
2 c. seedless grapes
1 c. mayonnaise or salad dressing
1 tblsp. honey
1 tblsp. lemon juice

• Peel and cube the yams, or drain canned yams and cube.
• Slice the bananas, dice unpeeled apples, and add grapes; toss together lightly.
• Combine mayonnaise, honey and lemon juice for dressing.
• Serve on crisp cabbage leaves or lettuce with the honey dressing. Makes 4 to 6 servings.

YAM FLOWERETTES

Pretty vegetable combination that tastes wonderful—try it with pork

6 large onions, cooked
2 c. mashed yams, cooked or canned
2 tblsp. evaporated milk, undiluted
1 tblsp. butter or margarine
½ tsp. salt
Dash pepper
Dash paprika
Butter

• Remove centers from onions; spread "petals" to enlarge onion cavity. Fill with yams mixed with milk, 1 tblsp. butter, salt and pepper.
• Place onion centers on top; sprinkle with paprika. Dot with butter.
• Bake in buttered baking dish in hot oven (400°) about 20 minutes; add a little boiling water to prevent sticking. Makes 6 servings.

To Complete Menu: Serve Yam Flowerettes with pork roast or fresh ham, a buttered green vegetable, relishes, hot muffins and pineapple upside-down cake.

BROILED HAM AND YAMS

In one fell swoop you cook the dinner—it's broiled

3 c. cooked whole kernel corn and green beans, mixed
¼ c. honey
2 tsp. grated orange rind
1½ lb. slice ham, cut 1" thick
6 yams, cooked or baked with skins on
Butter

• Season corn and beans; spread out in broiler pan.
• Mix honey and orange rind; brush one side of ham, using half of this glaze.
• Put ham, glazed side up, on broiler rack, and place over corn and beans.
• Slice tops from cooked yams; ruffle with fork tines. Season and dot with butter.
• Set broiler pan 4" from heat, broil about 10 minutes.
• Add yams when ham slice is turned.
• Turn ham slice, brush with remaining glaze, broil 7 minutes longer. Makes 6 servings.

FLUFFY YAMS WITH PRUNES

Dash of orange rind adds delightful flavor to orange-colored yams

8 prunes
5 lbs. yams
¼ c. butter or margarine
½ c. heavy cream
1 egg
1 tsp. salt
1 tblsp. grated orange rind

• Cook prunes until tender; remove pits.
• Peel yams (to retain bright color). Cook in salted water until tender, 30 to 40 minutes. Mash thoroughly.
• Add butter, cream, egg, salt and orange rind; beat very fluffy. Fold in pitted prunes, saving some to garnish top.

• Pile in greased casserole. Bake in moderate oven (350°) 20 to 30 minutes, until heated through. Makes 8 to 10 servings.

Variation: Omit prunes. Alternate mashed sweet potatoes with drained, canned cling peach halves in shallow baking pan. Bake in moderate oven (350°) to heat through.

FILET MIGNYAM

Bacon does something to yams—something good

4 or 5 medium yams
12 slices bacon

• Bake, boil or steam yams tender in their skins; peel.
• Cut potatoes in rounds about 1½" thick. Wrap each in slice of bacon, securing ends with toothpicks.
• Bake in shallow pan in very hot oven (450°) 10 to 15 minutes or until bacon is well done.
• Serve with sautéed mushrooms or fried apple rings. Makes 6 to 8 servings.

SWEET POTATO PIE

Makes you grateful to Southern kitchens, origin of this dessert

1½ c. mashed, cooked sweet potatoes
½ c. sugar
½ tsp. salt
½ tsp. nutmeg
1 tsp. cinnamon
¼ tsp. cloves
2 eggs, well beaten
½ tsp. vanilla
¼ c. butter
1 c. milk
1 (9") unbaked pastry shell

• Combine sweet potatoes, sugar, salt, nutmeg, cinnamon, cloves, eggs and vanilla.
• Melt butter in milk. Gradually pour into potato mixture, stirring. Beat gently with rotary beater until well blended and smooth.
• Turn into pastry-lined pie pan, with edges of pastry fluted. Bake in very hot oven (450°) 10 minutes; reduce heat to moderate (350°) and bake 45 minutes, or until silver knife comes out clean.

YAM PUDDING

A dessert favorite in country where magnolias bloom

½ c. sugar
½ c. unsulphured molasses
⅓ c. butter, melted
1 tsp. nutmeg
1 tsp. cinnamon
½ tsp. salt
3 eggs, beaten
1½ c. milk
4 c. peeled and grated raw yams

• Combine sugar, molasses, butter, spices and salt. Add eggs and milk.
• Stir in yams, mixing thoroughly.
• Pour into greased 1½ qt. casserole. Bake in moderate oven (350°) 1½ hours. Serve warm or cold with cream. Makes 6 servings.

SWEET POTATO DRESS-UPS

No measurements are required. Just enjoy seasoning this favorite vegetable to your family's taste

Fluffy Sweets: Fold a little whipped cream into the mashed potatoes and season with salt and a touch of nutmeg or cinnamon.

Spicy Sweets: Add juice of pickled peaches or apples to mashed sweet potatoes.

Fruited Sweets: Fold drained crushed pineapple or orange juice and grated orange rind into the mashed potatoes.

Surprise Sweets: Scrub sweet potatoes and bake in a moderately hot oven (375° to 400°) until tender, about 45 minutes. Cut cross in top of each potato and press down on the four corners. Insert a pat of butter and 1 tablespoon orange marmalade in each potato.

LOUISIANA YAM MUFFINS

- **1¾ c. sifted flour**
- **2 tblsp. brown sugar**
- **1 tblsp. baking powder**
- **1 tsp. salt**
- **½ c. coarsely chopped walnuts**
- **2 eggs, beaten**
- **¾ c. milk**
- **1¼ c. mashed cooked yams (fresh or canned)**
- **¼ c. melted butter or margarine**
- **Cinnamon**
- **Sugar**

• Sift together flour, brown sugar, baking powder and salt. Add walnuts; mix well.

• Combine eggs, milk, yams and butter; mix well.

• Add yam mixture to dry ingredients. Mix only until just moist.

• Fill greased 2″ muffin pans ⅔ full. Sprinkle lightly with cinnamon and sugar.

• Bake in hot oven (425°) about 35 minutes, until done. Makes 18 muffins.

YAMS WITH LEMON SLICES

Extra-tasty—tangy lemon brings out the yam's finest flavors

- **6 large yams, peeled and sliced ¼″ thick**
- **3 tblsp. melted butter or margarine**
- **Juice and grated rind of 1 lemon**
- **½ tsp. salt**
- **½ lemon, sliced thin**

• Cook yam slices until almost tender. Drain. Brown in hot butter. Arrange slices in greased 1½ qt. baking dish.

• Combine lemon juice, rind and salt; pour over yams.

• Tuck lemon slices between yams.

• Bake in moderate oven (350°) 15 to 20 minutes. Makes 6 servings.

CORNED BEEF WITH CHEESE YAMS

- **4 c. cooked corned beef**
- **2 c. soft bread crumbs**
- **⅓ c. chopped onion**
- **2 eggs, slightly beaten**
- **1½ c. milk**
- **2 tsp. prepared horse-radish**
- **1½ tsp. dry mustard**
- **2 c. grated or shredded sharp process cheese**
- **6 medium yams, cooked and peeled (fresh or canned)**
- **Paprika**

• Chop corned beef very fine or grind with medium blade of food chopper.

• Mix together corned beef, bread crumbs, onion, eggs, 1 c. milk, horse-radish and mustard. Spread evenly in greased 8″ ring mold.

• Bake in moderate oven (375°) about 1 hour, or until firm.

• Meanwhile, combine remaining ½ c. milk and cheese in saucepan or top of double boiler. Cook over low heat to melt cheese, stirring constantly.

• Cut yams in half lengthwise; add to cheese sauce. Heat thoroughly.

• To serve, unmold corned beef onto heated platter. Fill center with yam mixture. Sprinkle with paprika. Makes 6 to 8 servings.

SCALLOPED SWEET POTATOES AND APPLES

- **8 medium-size sweet potatoes, cooked**
- **4 medium-size apples, cored and cut in rings**
- **½ c. brown sugar, firmly packed**
- **½ c. pecans, halves or cut**
- **1 tsp. salt**
- **½ tsp. mace**
- **2 tblsp. butter or margarine**

• Peel sweet potatoes and cut in lengthwise slices about ½″ thick. Arrange layers of potato slices, apples, brown sugar, pecans and seasoning in greased 2 qt. casserole. Cover and bake in moderate oven (350°) 50 minutes. Makes 6 servings.

10

Eggs

Women who are recognized as the best cooks in their neighborhoods depend on a bountiful supply of eggs to keep their laurels. Before enterprising poultrymen stepped up seasonal production to year-around, hens started to cackle louder in March, as a salute to spring. Then egg cookery went into high gear, a farm kitchen custom that continues to this day. Egg dishes never are enjoyed more than in jonquil and tulip time. Lent encourages their frequent appearance, followed by bright-colored Easter eggs that delight the children.

But eggs are a staple food, and farm kitchens use them every day of the year. Short-order cooks rely on them when the need for a quick meal comes up with almost no notice. They are proud to deliver a platter of carefully fried eggs with ham or bacon, or eggs baked atop corned beef hash from a hurriedly opened can.

If a perfect omelet, puffed up like a pale cloud tinged on the outside with burnished-gold is the badge of a good cook, country kitchens are rich in talent. Even a swift glance at the omelet recipes in this chapter shows there is one for every mood. All of them are flawless. So are the failproof recipes for soufflés included in this chapter.

Do try the custards—the egg and milk concoctions that enjoy prestige on both sides of the Atlantic. Our recipes come off the farm, but they would make a Parisian chef bow. After all, egg cookery has its roots in the country, and there the skill, largely compounded of fresh eggs and low-temperature cooking, flourishes.

We give you recipes for sponge cakes in tall glory, masterpieces in any collection of rural egg dishes. So are deviled and stuffed eggs that go to picnics just as they did in Grandmother's day, but today they show up at barbecues, too.

But why enumerate all the virtues of our egg recipes—turn the pages and take your pick.

EGGS BENEDICT

Serve with a green vegetable to complete the main course

6 thin small ham slices
6 eggs
3 hamburger buns, split

• Score fat edges of ham slices. Place on broiler rack, 3" from heat. Broil 3 minutes; turn.
• Poach eggs; keep warm.
• Place bun halves on broiler. Broil until light golden, but broil ham 3 minutes longer.
• Place ham on buns. Top with poached eggs. Pour Hollandaise Sauce over all. Makes 6 servings.

HOLLANDAISE SAUCE

Smooth sailing with such an easy recipe

½ c. butter or margarine
3 egg yolks
1½ tblsp. lemon juice
⅛ tsp. salt
Dash paprika
Few grains cayenne papper
¼ c. boiling water

• Cream butter until fluffy. Beat in egg yolks, lemon juice and seasonings. Blend well. Gradually blend in boiling water.
• Place mixture in top of double boiler. Cook over boiling water 5 minutes, stirring constantly. (Do not boil vigorously as water should not touch top pan of double boiler.)
• Remove from heat. Beat 1 minute. Makes 1 cup.

POACHED EGGS IN HASH

Just the dish for lunch when unexpected guests arrive

1 tblsp. shortening or oil
¼ c. chopped onion
2 (1 lb.) cans corned beef hash
6 eggs
Salt
Pepper

• Heat shortening in 9" or 10" heavy skillet. Add onion; cook 2 minutes. Add hash, breaking it up with spoon. Cook over medium heat, 6 minutes, stirring occasionally.
• Reduce heat to low; pat hash level in pan and make 6 deep hollows with back of spoon. Drop an egg into each hollow; season with salt and pepper.
• Cover skillet tightly. Cook 5 minutes or until set.
• Divide into 6 portions. With wide spatula or pancake turner, carefully lift out each portion to serving plate. Serve with ketchup or chili sauce, if desired. Makes 6 servings.

Scrambled Eggs

The secret of tender, scrambled eggs is to cook them over low heat and only until they are cooked throughout, but still are glossy and moist. Using water for liquid instead of milk increases tenderness, but you lose the milk's nutritional value. If you like the mottled yellow-and-white appearance, don't beat the eggs—just stir them with a fork.

Here are a few ways we vary scrambled eggs in Countryside Kitchens:

• Sprinkle grated Swiss cheese and buttered bread crumbs over the cooked eggs and brown 1 minute under the broiler.
• Add a little grated onion when the cooking eggs start to thicken.
• Add flaked pieces of dried beef, or crumbled, cooked bacon, a bit of finely chopped green pepper, a well drained and chopped fresh tomato or a 2 or 4 oz. can mushroom stems and pieces.
• When in an adventurous mood use ¾ c. orange juice or dairy sour cream for the liquid.
• For a gourmet's touch, fold in a little chopped dill or chives just before serving.

PERFECT SCRAMBLED EGGS

Top results guaranteed every time

1 tsp. salt
1/8 tsp. pepper
8 eggs
1/2 c. milk or light cream
3 tblsp. butter, margarine or bacon drippings

• Break eggs into bowl and stir with fork. Mix in milk or cream, salt and pepper.
• Melt butter in heavy skillet over medium heat, add egg mixture and reduce heat to low. (You may scramble eggs in double boiler. Takes less watching, but more time for cooking.)
• When eggs begin to set at bottom and sides, push them back with pancake turner to allow the uncooked eggs to flow to the bottom of the pan. Repeat until the eggs are just cooked through. Remove from skillet at once. Serve on warm platter. Makes 4 to 6 servings.

EGGS IN BUTTERCUPS

A new way to serve fluffy scrambled eggs

12 slices fresh bread
Melted butter or margarine
8 eggs
2 tsp. salt
1 tsp. pepper
1/4 c. heavy cream
Crisp-fried bacon bits

• Trim crusts from bread, save crusts for crumbs to be used later. Press slices into muffin pans, brush with butter. Bake in hot oven (400°) 20 minutes.
• Beat eggs until fluffy; add salt, pepper, cream and bacon.
• Pour into greased skillet or double boiler. Cook over low heat until set, lifting occasionally with spatula to let uncooked portion run underneath.
• Spoon into toast cups. Serve immediately. Makes 6 servings.

PUFFY OMELET

Failure-proof—adding the sauce makes the omelet sturdier

1/4 c. butter or margarine
3 1/2 tblsp. flour
1 tsp. salt
1 c. milk
4 eggs, separated
2 tblsp. shortening
Creamed Shrimp (recipe follows)
Chopped parsley

• Melt butter in small saucepan over low heat. Blend in flour and salt; cook 1 minute, stirring constantly.
• Remove from heat; gradually stir in milk; return to heat. Cook, stirring constantly, until white sauce is thick and smooth. Cool.
• Beat egg whites until stiff enough to hold firm peaks. Then beat the yolks.
• Blend egg yolks into white sauce. Then fold in beaten egg whites.
• Heat shortening over low heat in a 10" skillet. Pour in the omelet mixture. Cover with a close fitting lid.
• Cook over low heat 15 to 20 minutes, or until a light brown crust is formed on bottom and top is firm.
• Loosen the omelet from the sides of skillet and cut through the center down to crust in bottom. Tilt pan; fold one half over the other. Slide onto platter.
• Unfold and pour Creamed Shrimp over one half of omelet. Fold other half over the sauce. Sprinkle with chopped parsley. Serve immediately with Creamed Shrimp, Chicken Sauce with Peas, Shrimp Creole Sauce or Asparagus-Mushroom Sauce. Makes 4 servings.

Extra-Special Omelet: Just before folding omelet, spread lower half with 1/3 c. grated sharp cheese, 3 slices crisp bacon, crumbled, 1 tsp. chopped chives or parsley or 1/2 c. hot chopped, cooked chicken. Serve with Creamed Shrimp or Asparagus-Mushroom Sauce.

CREAMED SHRIMP

2 tblsp. butter or margarine
2 tblsp. flour
½ tsp. salt
Dash of pepper
1¼ c. milk
1 tsp. grated onion
1½ c. cooked and cleaned shrimp, fresh, canned or frozen

• Blend together in a small saucepan over low heat butter or margarine, flour, salt and pepper. Cook for 1 minute. Remove from heat; add milk and onion. Cook over low heat, stirring constantly, until thick and smooth. Add shrimp. Cook long enough to heat through.

CHICKEN SAUCE WITH PEAS

You can stir up this sauce while the omelet cooks

¼ c. water
¼ tsp. salt
1 c. fresh or frozen peas
1 (10½ oz.) can condensed cream of chicken soup

• Heat water and salt to boiling. Add peas, cook covered until tender, about 7 minutes.
• Heat undiluted soup, stir until smooth. Add peas. Pour inside and over Puffy Omelet.

SHRIMP CREOLE SAUCE

It's a good idea to fix this before you start the omelet

2 tblsp. butter or margarine
¼ c. chopped onion
¼ c. chopped green pepper
1 (10½ oz.) can condensed tomato soup
¼ tsp. salt
Dash of pepper
1 tsp. sugar
1 (5 oz.) can shrimp, drained

• Melt butter in saucepan, add onion and pepper. Cook until pepper is soft.
• Stir in undiluted soup, salt, pepper and sugar. Simmer until thick, about 45 minutes.
• Just before serving, add cleaned shrimp; heat. Pour inside and over Puffy Omelet. Makes about 1½ cups.

ASPARAGUS-MUSHROOM SAUCE

Spring comes to the table the year around with this tasty trimming on omelets

12 to 15 stalks fresh or frozen asparagus
¾ c. boiling water
1 (10½ oz.) can condensed cream of mushroom soup

• Cook asparagus covered in boiling water until tender, about 15 minutes. Place about 3 cooked stalks on one omelet half; fold omelet over.
• Heat undiluted soup, stir until smooth. Pour over Puffy Omelet and remaining asparagus. Makes about 1⅓ cups.
• You can fix this sauce while the omelet puffs up and browns.

WAFFLE OMELET

The waffle iron is the short-order cook—it bakes your omelet at the table

4 tblsp. flour
4 tblsp. hot water
4 eggs, separated
½ tsp. salt
⅛ tsp. pepper
2 tblsp. melted butter or margarine

• Make a paste of flour and hot water.
• Beat egg yolks until thick. Add flour paste, seasonings and melted butter to yolks. Mix well.
• Beat egg whites stiff; fold into batter.
• Bake 3 minutes in a moderately hot waffle iron. Spread with jelly and roll. Cut to make 4 servings.

OMELET PANCAKES

Best invitation to early breakfast

¾ c. sifted flour
1 tsp. salt
¼ tsp. pepper
¾ c. milk
6 large eggs, beaten

• Combine flour, salt and pepper in mixing bowl. Stir in milk slowly and beat to form a smooth batter.
• Stir in beaten eggs, blend well.
• Pour ½ cup of batter on very hot, greased 10" griddle; spread batter to edges.
• Cook about 20 seconds until browned. Turn, brown on other side.
• Remove to warm plate. Spread with cooked bulk sausage, cranberry sauce, jam or cinnamon and sugar. Roll up if you wish.
• Keep warm in oven while cooking remaining pancakes. Makes 6 pancakes.

HASTY OMELET

A delicious way to salvage bread crumbs

3 eggs, slightly beaten
2 c. milk
1 tsp. salt
⅛ tsp. pepper
3 c. coarse day-old bread crumbs

• Blend together beaten eggs, milk, salt and pepper. Stir in bread crumbs lightly. Turn into greased heavy skillet.
• Cover tightly. Cook slowly over low heat until set and lightly browned.
• Cut in serving size pieces, turn and brown on other side. Serve immediately, plain or with tomato or cheese sauce. Makes 4 to 6 servings.

SPECIAL DEVILED EGGS

Every good cook has her pet way of making stuffed or deviled eggs, but everyone agrees that appearance has much to do with their appeal. We find in our Countryside Kitchens that putting the mashed and seasoned yolks through a pastry bag with a large star tube gives the eggs a professional look. And it's quicker to stuff the egg whites that way than with a spoon. Running the cooked yolks through a food mill assures satiny smoothness.

For a welcome surprise put a small cube of ham or cheese or tiny olive in the whites before adding the filling. Another favorite of Farm Journal's Food Staff is to fix hard-cooked yolks by seasoning with 3 tblsp. soft butter (for 6 yolks), 2 tblsp. mayonnaise, salt and pepper.

Tasty hot supper dish: Arrange deviled eggs in a shallow baking dish and spread a coverlet of 1 (10½ oz.) can each tomato and cream of mushroom soup, mixed, over them. Heat in a slow oven (325°) 20 minutes or until bubbly hot. For a change, lay cooked broccoli in bottom of baking dish, then add the eggs and mushroom soup.

EGGS IN A BASKET

The eggs are poached in milk and shredded wheat makes the basket

6 shredded wheat biscuits
2 c. milk
2 tblsp. butter or margarine
6 eggs

• Halve shredded wheat biscuits lengthwise. Warm in slow oven (300°).
• Heat milk to simmering in skillet; add butter. Poach eggs in milk mixture.
• Spoon eggs and milk mixture on top of warmed shredded wheat biscuits. Season with salt and pepper. Makes 6 servings.

To round out the supper menu: Serve sausages, pickled beets, and peach or cherry cobbler. This easy-to-fix dish can be prepared by the junior cooks when they start to share in mealtime preparation. For variety, dissolve 1 to 2 tsp. sugar in the milk before poaching the eggs. This dish is recommended as nourishing for little shut-ins, too.

DEVILED EGGS

Yellow and white beauties

6 hard-cooked eggs
¼ c. mayonnaise or salad dressing
1 tblsp. grated horse-radish
1 tblsp. chopped dill pickle
1 tblsp. chopped parsley
½ tsp. salt
¼ tsp. dry mustard
½ tsp. paprika

• Halve eggs lengthwise. Mash yolks, add remaining ingredients. Blend well.
• Fill white halves with mixture. Makes 6 servings.

CURRIED EGG CANAPE

These open-face sandwiches never go begging

2 hard-cooked eggs
1 tblsp. mayonnaise or salad dressing
¼ tsp. salt
¼ tsp. curry powder
Bread
Butter
Carrot and olive garnish

• Chop eggs fine. Add mayonnaise, salt and curry powder. Makes about ½ cup spread.
• Cut bread into desired shapes. Butter lightly. Spread with egg mixture.
• Decorate with carrot wedges and a green olive slice; put ripe olive slices on others.

CAMP-STYLE EGGS AND CORN

Cook it in the kitchen or outdoors on the grill

½ lb. bulk pork sausage
1 (16 to 17 oz.) can cream style corn
6 eggs

• Brown sausage in skillet; pour off fat. Add corn.
• Beat eggs. Add to corn-sausage mixture, and cook as for scrambled eggs. Makes 6 servings.

Variation: Substitute ¼ lb. bacon, chopped, for the sausage. Or, use ¼ lb. shredded cooked ham for the meat. Sauté in 3 to 4 tblsp. fat or drippings before adding eggs. Vary the color and flavor by adding ¼ c. minced onion or scallions and 3 tblsp. finely chopped green pepper.

CREAMED EGGS WITH CHEESE

Frankfurters and toast triangles make this an interesting egg dish

12 hard-cooked eggs
⅓ c. butter or margarine
½ c. flour
1 c. light cream
2½ c. milk (about)
½ lb. sharp process cheese, cut up
1 tsp. salt
Dash of pepper
12 frankfurters
8 slices white bread
2 tblsp. chopped parsley

• Chop yolks and whites of 2 eggs, separately, for garnish.
• Quarter remaining eggs.
• Melt butter, blend in flour. Add cream slowly; cook, stirring constantly. Add milk to make a smooth, rather thin sauce. Stir in cheese, salt and pepper.
• Cover pan and simmer, without stirring, over low heat until cheese melts—10 to 15 minutes.
• Stir to blend and add quartered eggs. Bring sauce to a boil. (If sauce gets too thick, add a little more milk.)
• Split frankfurters, and cut in halves; fry or broil until crisp and brown.
• Toast bread slices. Cut into triangles.
• Pour creamed eggs onto hot serving platter. Garnish with rows of chopped egg yolks, egg white and parsley. Poke frankfurters part way into egg mixture around the edge of dish, alternately with toast triangles. Makes 8 servings.

EGGS A LA SUISSE

Downright good eating

1 c. grated sharp cheese
6 eggs
Salt and pepper
½ c. light cream

• Sprinkle half of cheese in greased shallow baking dish. Break each egg into small cup; slide on top of cheese, being careful not to break yolks. Season.
• Pour cream over eggs and sprinkle remaining cheese on top.
• Bake in moderate oven (350°) 15 minutes. Makes 6 servings.

EGGS IN SPANISH SAUCE

Serve this, and your reputation as a cook will go up several notches

2 c. canned tomatoes
½ small onion, sliced
½ bay leaf
3 cloves
1 tsp. sugar
¾ tsp. salt
2 tblsp. butter or margarine
2 tblsp. flour
3 c. cooked rice (1 c. uncooked)
6 eggs
3 tblsp. grated cheese
½ c. buttered crumbs

• Simmer tomatoes, onion, spices, sugar and salt 10 minutes. Strain.
• Melt butter and blend in flour. Add tomato mixture; cook until thickened, stirring constantly.
• Spread rice in greased shallow 2½ qt. casserole, making six hollows in it with tablespoon. Break an egg into each nest.
• Carefully pour sauce over all. Sprinkle with cheese and crumbs.
• Bake in moderate oven (350°) 20 minutes, or until eggs are firm. Makes 6 servings.

OVEN-COOKED EGGS

Baked eggs are easy to fix and often they provide a meal change. To please the children split thick hamburger buns in halves; hollow out each half. Spread with butter or margarine and drop an egg in each hollow. Season with salt and bake in a slow oven (325°) about 15 minutes, or until the eggs are partly set. Top each bun half with a slice of tomato and cheese and broil until cheese starts to brown. Eggs in toast rings may be grilled or baked.

EGG PLATTER

You cook these eggs in the oven

⅔ c. uncooked rice
⅓ c. melted butter or margarine
1½ c. cooked peas (fresh, frozen or canned)
½ c. grated process cheese
6 eggs

• Cook rice according to package directions. Combine with butter, peas and half the cheese.
• Spoon into greased oven platter or shallow casserole. With back of spoon, makes 6 small hollows in rice mixture. Break an egg into each. Sprinkle with remaining cheese.
• Bake in moderate oven (350°) until eggs are set, about 20 minutes. Makes 6 servings.

To complete this supper: Have a tossed green or tomato salad, hot biscuits or buttered toast and banana slices molded in cherry flavor gelatin crowned with almond-flavored whipped cream, slightly sweetened. Cookies, too, if you have a supply in the freezer or cookie jar.

EGGS IN TOAST RINGS

Serve for supper with sausage or ham and coleslaw

12 slices bread
Butter
12 eggs
Salt
Pepper

• Cut centers from bread slices with small biscuit cutter. Toast rims on one side on grill. Butter untoasted side, turn.
• Break an egg into each toast ring, season with salt and pepper. Cook until eggs are set, 12 to 15 minutes.

Variation: Instead of grilling, bake on greased baking sheet in moderate oven (350°) 15 to 20 minutes, or until eggs are set. Bread need not be toasted before baking eggs this way. Makes 10 to 12 servings.

SALMON FONDUE

A Friday call to supper

1 (1 lb.) can salmon, pink or red
3 tblsp. chopped onion
⅛ tsp. pepper
2 tsp. lemon juice
2 tblsp. melted butter or margarine
8 slices day-old bread
3 eggs
1¾ c. milk
¼ tsp. salt

• Drain salmon, save liquid to add later. Remove skin and bones. Break into pieces.
• Add onion, pepper, lemon juice and butter.
• Trim crusts from bread. Arrange four slices in shallow 8" square baking dish or casserole. Cover with salmon.
• Place remaining slices on top.
• Beat eggs; add milk, salt and salmon liquid.
• Pour over contents of casserole and let stand 30 minutes or longer. Bake in moderate oven (350°) 40 to 50 minutes, or until puffed and brown. Makes 6 servings.

Try this main dish with French fried potatoes, coleslaw, and hard rolls, split, toasted and buttered. For dessert, cherry pie or strawberry ice cream sundae.

SAUSAGE-FLOWER CASSEROLES

Men's favorite: Potatoes, sausage and eggs baked together

3 lbs. bulk pork sausage
10 to 12 medium potatoes (about 4 lbs.)
1 c. hot milk
½ c. butter or margarine
8 eggs
Salt and pepper
Parsley (optional)

• Form sausage into 24 (3") patties. Put in large shallow baking pan. Bake in hot oven (400°) about 15 to 20 minutes, turning once. Heat individual casserole dishes in oven.
• Peel, cook and mash potatoes; add milk and butter, beat until light.
• Reduce oven to 350°; remove sausage and casseroles. Pour 1 tsp. sausage drippings into each casserole; add potatoes. Make indentation on top of potatoes with spoon. Slip an egg into each; sprinkle with salt and pepper.
• Place sausage patty halves around edge of casserole. Bake to set egg, about 15 to 20 minutes. Sprinkle with parsley. Serve immediately. Makes 8 servings.

Variation: For raw potatoes substitute 1 (7 oz.) pkg. instant mashed potatoes.

There are many occasions when this main dish is just right. The meat may be varied—crisp bacon, little Vienna sausages, cooked ham or corned beef are suggestions. Vary the flavor also with a sprinkling of fresh herbs or seasoned salts. Occasionally bake it in a large skillet and serve in pie-shaped wedges.

HARVEST SANDWICH SPECIAL

An extra-quick main dish for supper or lunch on a cool day

1½ c. process cheese cubes
½ c. light cream
6 slices process cheese
6 slices toast
6 (½″) tomato slices
6 poached eggs
6 slices cooked bacon

• Put cheese cubes and cream in saucepan over low heat, stirring constantly to blend. Keep hot.
• Lay thin cheese slices on toast and broil to brown lightly. Top with tomato and then with hot egg. Pour on cheese sauce; add bacon. Serve at once. Makes 6 servings.

Favorite Desserts Made with Eggs

WHITE WONDER CAKE

Lemon filling and frosting make this cake a beauty queen

½ c. shortening
1⅓ c. sugar
1 tsp. vanilla
2¼ c. sifted cake flour
2½ tsp. baking powder
½ tsp. salt
1 c. milk
4 egg whites

• Cream shortening. Add sugar and vanilla; beat until fluffy.
• Sift flour, baking powder and salt.
• Add dry ingredients to creamed mixture alternately with milk. Blend until smooth after each addition.
• Beat egg whites until stiff enough to form peaks. Fold into batter.
• Pour batter into 2 well greased 8″ cake pans. Bake in moderate oven (375°) about 25 minutes. Cool.
• Put layers together with Lemon Filling and frost with Lemon Cream Frosting.

Lemon Filling:

3 tblsp. cornstarch
1 c. sugar
⅛ tsp. salt
2 egg yolks, slightly beaten
1 c. cold water
¼ c. lemon juice
1 tblsp. butter or margarine
1 tsp. grated lemon rind

• Combine cornstarch, sugar and salt.
• Stir together egg yolks, water and lemon juice. Add to dry ingredients.
• Cook until thick, stirring constantly.
• Remove from heat; add butter and lemon rind. Cool.
• Spread over bottom cake layer; top with other layer. Frost cake with Lemon Cream Frosting.

Lemon Cream Frosting:

½ c. butter or margarine
2½ c. sifted confectioners sugar
1 tblsp. cream
1 egg yolk
1 tblsp. lemon juice
Few drops yellow food color

• Cream butter. Blend in all other ingredients. Beat until smooth. (If mixture seems too stiff to spread easily, add a few drops of hot water.)

Variation: Frost top and sides of cake with Creole Frosting instead of Lemon Cream Frosting. Cream ¼ c. butter or margarine with 2 c. sifted confectioners sugar. Stir in 2 egg yolks, beaten. Add 1 tblsp. lemon juice and 3 tblsp. mashed banana.

SUNSHINE LAYER CAKE

Lovely yellow Easter cake

5 egg whites
1/8 tsp. cream of tartar
1/4 tsp. salt
1 tsp. vanilla
1 c. sugar
3 egg yolks
2 tblsp. orange juice or water
1 tsp. lemon juice
1 c. sifted cake flour

• To egg whites in mixing bowl, add cream of tartar, salt and vanilla. Beat with rotary beater or wire whisk until they stand in moist peaks.
• Add ½ c. sugar, a little at a time, folding in well after each addition.
• In separate bowl, beat egg yolks with orange and lemon juice. Beat in remaining ½ c. sugar until mixture is thick and lemon colored.
• Fold yolks into whites. Sift in flour gradually; fold lightly to mix well. Pour batter in 2 ungreased 8″ layer pans.
• Bake in slow oven (325°) 25 minutes. Invert pans on rack to cool, about 45 minutes. Remove cakes with spatula.

Sunshine Ice Cream Cake: Place 8″ layer of cake on a serving plate. Pack ice cream firmly into chilled 8″ layer pan. (You can freeze ice cream in advance.) Turn ice cream out quickly onto cake and top with second cake layer. Freeze or serve at once. To serve, cut in wedges and pass a pitcher of Fluffy Orange Sauce.

FLUFFY ORANGE SAUCE

As springlike and cheerful as a bed of jonquils

Juice and grated rind of 1 orange
2 egg yolks, beaten
½ c. corn syrup or sugar
1 c. heavy whipped cream

• Combine orange juice and rind, egg yolks and syrup in top of double boiler. Cook 5 minutes, stirring constantly, until slightly thickened. Cool.
• Just before serving, fold in whipped cream. Makes 2½ cups.

CHOCOLATE ANGEL FOOD CAKE

A generous wedge, a cup of coffee—your party is planned

¾ c. sifted cake flour
¼ c. cocoa
¼ tsp. salt
1¼ c. egg whites (10 to 12 eggs)
1 tsp. cream of tartar
1¼ c. sifted sugar
1 tsp. vanilla

• Sift flour and cocoa together 4 times.
• Add salt to egg whites. Beat until frothy. Add cream of tartar. Beat until stiff enough to form peaks.
• Fold sugar into whites, ¼ c. at a time. Add vanilla.
• Fold flour mixture into whites, 2 tblsp. at a time.
• Pour batter into ungreased 10″ angel food pan. Bake in moderate oven (375°) 1 hour.
• Invert pan and let cake cool in pan about 1 hour before taking it out to be frosted. Remove any loose cake crumbs, so frosting will go on smoothly. Frost with Orange Frosting.

Orange Frosting:

1 (3 oz.) pkg. cream cheese
1 tblsp. orange juice
2½ c. sifted confectioners sugar
½ tsp. grated orange rind

• Blend cream cheese and orange juice.
• Add the sugar gradually, blending well.
• Add orange rind; blend again. Makes enough frosting for one 10″ tube cake.

YELLOW ANGEL CAKE

Try 7-Minute or Chocolate Frosting on this cake

6 eggs (about), separated (you need ½ c. yolks, ¾ c. whites)
½ c. cold water
1⅓ c. sugar
½ tsp. vanilla
½ tsp. orange extract
½ tsp. almond extract
1½ c. sifted cake flour
¼ tsp. salt
¾ tsp. cream of tartar

• Beat egg yolks until very thick and lemon colored. Add water. Beat until thick. Add sugar gradually, beating constantly—about 10 minutes with electric mixer at highest speed.
• Fold in flavorings.
• Sift flour and salt together at least 3 times.
• Carefully fold into egg yolk mixture.
• Beat egg whites until foamy. Add cream of tartar. Beat until stiff enough to form peaks. Fold into batter.
• Pour into ungreased 10″ angel food pan.
• Bake in moderate oven (350°) about 1 hour. Invert and let cool in the pan about 1 hour. Frost as desired.

CUSTARD PIE

Velvety custard in tender-crisp pastry

2½ c. milk
½ c. sugar
1 tsp. vanilla
½ tsp. almond extract (optional)
¼ tsp. salt
4 eggs, slightly beaten
1 (9″) unbaked pie shell

• Scald milk; add sugar, flavorings and salt; mix together. Stir slowly into beaten eggs.
• Pour into unbaked pie shell; bake in hot oven (400°) 20 to 25 minutes.

QUICK AND EASY LEMON PIE

The filling requires no cooking

1 (8″) baked pastry shell
½ c. lemon juice (fresh, frozen or bottled)
1 tsp. grated lemon rind
1 (15 oz.) can sweetened condensed milk
2 eggs, separated
¼ tsp. cream of tartar
4 tblsp. sugar

• Combine lemon juice and rind. Blend in condensed milk. Beat egg yolks slightly; blend into mixture. Pour into cooled pastry shell.
• Beat egg whites until foamy; add cream of tartar. Add sugar, 1 tblsp. at a time, beating in well after each. Continue beating until very stiff peaks form. Pile lightly on pie filling.
• Brown in moderate oven (350°) about 10 minutes. Makes 6 servings.

LEMON SNOW

Drifts of dessert that suggest cold snow—a good summer meal ending

2 envelopes unflavored gelatin
½ c. cold water
1½ c. sugar
¼ tsp. salt
2 c. hot water
½ c. lemon juice
2 tsp. grated lemon rind
2 egg whites, beaten stiff

• Soften gelatin in cold water. Add sugar, salt and hot water; stir until gelatin is dissolved.
• Blend in lemon juice and rind. Chill until quite thick.
• Beat with whisk until frothy. Add egg whites; continue beating until well blended.
• Turn into mold that has been rinsed with cold water. Chill. When firm, unmold and serve with Rich Custard Sauce. Makes about 8 servings.

BLACK CHERRY CHIFFON PIE

A zephyr-light filling with the luscious cherry taste

2 (1 lb.) cans pitted black cherries
1 tblsp. unflavored gelatin
4 eggs, separated
½ c. sugar
¼ tsp. salt
1 tsp. lemon juice
1 (9″) baked pastry or crumb crust
Toasted almonds to garnish

• Drain and chop cherries; reserve juice. Soften gelatin in ¼ c. cherry juice.
• Beat together egg yolks, sugar, salt, lemon juice and ½ c. cherry juice. Stir over boiling water until thick.
• Fold in gelatin and cherries. Chill until thick and syrupy.
• Beat egg whites; fold into cherry mixture. Pour into crust. Chill until firm, about 3 hours.
• Serve garnished with toasted almonds. Makes 6 to 8 servings.

MERINGUE SHELLS

Party-perfect dessert if filled with ice cream, or berries topped with whipped cream

4 egg whites
½ tsp. salt
1 tsp. cream of tartar
1 c. sugar

• Beat egg whites until foamy. Add salt and cream of tartar. Add sugar, 1 tblsp. at a time, beating well after each addition. Beat until stiff peaks form.
• Shape meringues on heavy wrapping paper (ungreased) on baking sheet. Hollow out centers with back of teaspoon which has been dipped in warm water.
• Bake in very slow oven (250°) 60 to 70 minutes, or until dry. (Use an oven thermometer if your oven has no regulator.) Makes 12 medium size shells.

Serving suggestions: Try peppermint stick ice cream in the Meringue Shells and serve with chocolate sauce. Or, fill shells with ice cream or sherbet in three pastel colors of your choice, as raspberry and orange sherbet and vanilla ice cream.

STRAWBERRY MERINGUE CAKE

Guests will toss bouquets to you

Cake:

2¼ c. sifted cake flour
1 c. sugar
1 tblsp. baking powder
1 tsp. salt
½ c. oil
5 egg yolks, unbeaten
¾ c. cold water
2 tsp. vanilla
2 tsp. grated lemon rind
8 egg whites
½ tsp. cream of tartar
½ c. sugar

Meringue:

4 egg whites
½ tsp. salt
1 tsp. cream of tartar
1 c. sugar
Sweetened strawberries (fresh or frozen)

• Sift together into mixing bowl the cake flour, 1 c. sugar, baking powder and salt. Make a well in dry ingredients and add oil, egg yolks, water, vanilla and lemon rind. Beat with spoon until smooth.
• Combine egg whites and cream of tartar in large mixing bowl; whip until foamy. Add ½ c. sugar, 1 tblsp. at a time; beat until mixture forms stiff peaks.
• Gradually fold egg yolk mixture into whipped whites until just blended.
• Line 2 (8″) square cake pans with waxed paper. Pour batter into pans. Bake in moderate oven (350°) 40 to 45 minutes. Remove from pan. Cool; place on 2 baking sheets.
• Make meringue by beating together the egg whites, salt and cream of tartar until foamy. Add sugar, 1 tblsp. at a time. Continue beating 10 to 15 minutes, or until meringue forms stiff peaks. Spread over cakes.

• Place cakes in hot oven (425°) 4 to 4½ minutes—just long enough to brown peaks, if you like a soft meringue. Or, if you prefer a crisp meringue, place in a slow oven (250°) 60 to 70 minutes, or until dry.
• To serve, cut into squares and spoon strawberries over the top. Makes 16 servings.

SCHAUM TORTE

Foam cake makes a party dessert you can fix a day early

Meringue Shell:

4 egg whites
½ tsp. cream of tartar
1 c. sugar

• Beat egg whites until frothy. Add cream of tartar. Continue beating until stiff enough to hold a peak.
• Add sugar gradually, beating well after each addition. Mixture should be stiff and glossy.
• Spread on well greased and floured 9″ pie pan.
• Bake in very slow oven (275°) 1 hour. Turn off heat; leave pie in oven until cool.
• Remove from pan immediately, and make Lemon Filling.

Lemon Filling:

4 egg yolks
½ c. sugar
3 tblsp. lemon juice
2 tsp. grated lemon rind
1 c. heavy cream, whipped

• Beat egg yolks in top of double boiler until thick and lemon colored. Beat in sugar gradually. Blend in lemon juice and rind.
• Cook over hot water 5 to 8 minutes, stirring constantly.
• Spread ½ of cream over cold shell.
• Cover with cold lemon custard.
• Top with remaining whipped cream.
• Chill 24 hours in refrigerator. Makes 6 servings.

Variation: Omit Lemon Filling. Use sweetened whipped cream and strawberries or sliced peaches instead.

FESTIVE RICE PUDDING

Try this treat when it's harvest time in the cranberry bogs

3 c. cooked rice
1 qt. milk
3 eggs, slightly beaten
¾ c. sugar
1 tsp. salt
3 tblsp. melted butter or margarine
2 tblsp. cinnamon
Whole cooked cranberries
2 c. cranberry sauce

• Heat cooked rice and milk in top of double boiler.
• Combine eggs, sugar, salt and butter.
• Pour rice and milk into greased 2½ qt. baking dish. Slowly pour egg mixture over top and mix well.
• Bake in moderate oven (350°) 40 minutes. Spoon rice into serving dish.
• Decorate top with crisscross lines of cinnamon, placing a whole cooked cranberry in each square.
• To serve, ladle a generous spoonful of cranberry sauce over each serving. Makes 8 to 10 servings.

Variations: For a spring version, substitute chilled rhubarb sauce for cranberries. Cut rhubarb in 1″ pieces, add 1 c. sugar to 4 c. rhubarb and pour ½″ water into saucepan. Cover and simmer until tender. Or use 3 parts rhubarb to 1 c. strawberries, cooking as for rhubarb sauce. When in a hurry, try grape juice poured over rice pudding. Whipped cream may be used as garnish.

PERFECT SOFT CUSTARD

Smooth and creamy, with a hundred glamorous uses

3 egg yolks
2 tblsp. sugar
⅛ tsp. salt
1 c. milk
½ tsp. vanilla

• Combine egg yolks, sugar and salt in top of double boiler. Beat just enough to blend together. Stir in milk, mixing well.

• Cook over gently simmering water about 10 to 15 minutes, stirring constantly, until temperature reaches 174° or until mixture coats metal spoon smoothly.

• Remove from heat; stir in vanilla. Strain and cool. Makes about 1 cup. For 1 or 2 qts.: Use scalded milk with same ingredients for each cup. Add (scalded) milk slowly to beaten egg mixture, stirring while adding. Place over water; cook.

PERFECT BAKED CUSTARD

So tender and delicate it quivers like jelly—tastes best when frosty cold

6 eggs
½ to ¾ c. sugar
½ tsp. salt
4 c. hot milk
2 tsp. vanilla

• Combine eggs, sugar and salt in mixing bowl. Beat just enough to blend together. Add hot milk slowly and mix well. Stir in vanilla. Strain.

• Pour into 1½ qt. shallow baking pan, 1½ qt. deep casserole or into 8 individual custard cups. (Use cold rather than hot milk to make individual custards.) Place in a pan of hot water.

• Bake in slow oven (325°) until inserted knife comes out clean—shallow baking pan, 45 minutes; deep casserole, 60 minutes; individual custards, 30 minutes. Cool. Makes 6 to 8 servings.

RICH CUSTARD SAUCE

2 c. milk
2 egg yolks and 2 whole eggs, or 5 egg yolks
¼ c. sugar
⅛ tsp. salt
½ tsp. vanilla
¼ c. cream, light or heavy

• Scald milk in top of double boiler.

• Beat eggs slightly; add sugar and salt. Slowly stir in hot milk.

• Return to double boiler and cook, stirring constantly until mixture coats a metal spoon (4 to 5 minutes).

• Remove from heat immediately and place in a pan of cold water. Add vanilla and cream. Stir until slightly cooled. Chill. Makes 2½ cups.

• Overcooking will make sauce curdle, so watch it carefully. If it curdles, beat smooth with rotary beater.

Fruit Custard: Make Rich Custard Sauce and chill. Pour over cut-up fresh fruit, bananas, peaches, strawberries, orange sections, small green seedless grapes or seeded halves of Tokay grapes, in individual dessert dishes.

11

Butter and Cream

Most country cooks follow this motto: Use butter and cream with a free hand. It's a secret kitchen weapon—a quick and sure way to cooking success. The distinctive flavor of these two dairy products is what counts. Adding them to a dish provides the extra-special touch as truly as do drops of vanilla or almond extract, and slivers of lemon or orange rind. Or as one reader wrote, when sending Farm Journal's Food Department a top-ranking cake recipe: "The wonderful, rich taste comes from the butter and cream." These two ingredients have helped win many a blue ribbon at country fairs.

Butter-and-cream cooks got off to a head start when every farm had its own cows. Fondness for these dishes passes from one generation to the next and continues to thrive in the face of all the calorie chatter. And while less of these two dairy products may enter mixing bowls and ovens today, enough is used by the best cooks to supply the delicate richness so highly prized everywhere. Knowing how much to use is a fine point in cooking—the recipes in this chapter will be your tried-and-true guide.

Sour cream climbs to greater popularity every year. Once thrifty farm women regarded it as something to salvage after a hot day or a thunder storm, when refrigeration was not widespread. But even then many of them won their cooking spurs with such marvels as sour cream cookies, cake, hot biscuits, pancakes and candies. They knew what a superb dressing the cream made for garden stuff—for tender lettuce leaves in spring, and cool cucumber slices in summer.

The recipes in this chapter are only a few of the excellent ones in this book that butter and cream glorify. Several masterpieces wound up in Company Specials. Indeed, you'll find them on many pages throughout the book, for butter and cream complement most foods—apples, potatoes, chicken, fish and game. You'll even find, in this chapter, directions for making fresh, country-sweet butter in your electric mixer.

Butter Makes These Special

JEWELED POUND CAKE

Bright bits of candied fruits give a festive new look to the traditional cake. Takes a pound of butter, but worth it

¼ c. candied cherries
¼ c. candied orange peel
¼ c. citron
¼ c. candied pineapple
6 tblsp. light corn syrup
1 lb. butter
1¼ c. sugar
2 tsp. vanilla
½ tsp. salt
10 eggs, separated
4 c. sifted cake flour
1¼ c. sugar

• Chop fruits. Grease three 9¼×5¼×2¾" loaf pans. Pour 2 tblsp. syrup into bottom of each pan and sprinkle an equal quantity of fruits into each pan.
• For cake batter, cream butter until fluffy. Add sugar, vanilla and salt gradually, while beating. Continue beating with electric mixer until mixture is light and fluffy and no sugar particles remain (about 5 to 7 minutes). If beating by hand, cream until very light and fluffy.
• Beat egg yolks until light and lemon-colored; combine with creamed mixture. Blend in flour.
• Beat egg whites until soft peaks form. Gradually add remaining 1¼ c. sugar, beating constantly. Continue beating until whites stand in stiff peaks.
• Fold meringue into cake batter; blend well, but do not beat. Pour into prepared loaf pans over fruit.
• Bake in slow oven (325°) 80 minutes for metal pans—10 minutes less for glass pans. Turn out of pans; cool upside down. Makes 3 loaves.

Cake Dress-ups: Keep this cake in the freezer to slice and serve to drop-in guests. Cut in squares and top with whipped cream and fruit—berries, sliced peaches and bananas, or strawberries, fresh or frozen. Or serve it with ice cream and a sundae sauce. For a change, pour pudding sauce, orange or lemon, over the cake just before serving.

BUTTER SPONGE CAKE

As cheerful as sunshine and mighty good

11 egg yolks
2 c. sifted sugar
1 c. milk, scalded
1 tsp. vanilla
2¼ c. sifted cake flour
2 tsp. baking powder
½ c. butter, melted

• Beat egg yolks and sugar until light-colored and fluffy. Add milk and vanilla.
• Sift flour and baking powder. Add to batter.
• Fold in butter.
• Bake in 2 greased 8×8" pans in moderate oven (350°) 30 to 40 minutes. If you wish, put layers together and cover with Fluffy Frosting.

Fluffy Frosting:

1 c. sugar
4 egg whites
1 tblsp. corn syrup
⅛ tsp. cream of tartar

• Mix all ingredients in top of double boiler. Set over hot water and stir constantly until mixture becomes very hot. Pour into mixing bowl and beat by hand or with electric mixer until it stands in peaks.

Chocolate Trim: With a razor blade remove thin shavings from back of chocolate bar, barely heated. The shavings will curl. Scatter them on top of cake frosted white for an appealing garnish.

RIBBON CAKE

An elegant cake—fruited layers ribboned with creamy white frosting

1 c. butter
2½ c. sugar
4 eggs
4 c. sifted cake flour
1 tblsp. baking powder
1 c. milk
½ c. raisins
1 c. currants, dried
1 c. finely cut citron
1 tblsp. molasses
1 tsp. cinnamon
1 tsp. ground cloves
1 tsp. nutmeg

• Cream butter and sugar. Beat in eggs.
• Sift flour with baking powder; add alternately with milk to creamed mixture, beating until well blended.
• Pour 2⅔ c. batter into 1 greased and floured 9" layer pan. Add remaining ingredients to rest of batter. Pour into 2 greased and floured 9" layer pans.
• Bake in moderate oven (350°) about 35 minutes. Cool and frost with Butter Frosting.

Butter Frosting:

¾ c. soft butter
5 c. sifted confectioners sugar
¼ c. light cream
½ tsp. lemon extract

• Blend butter and sugar together. Stir in cream and lemon extract.

WHIPPED CREAM CAKE

A glamorous dessert belle

2 c. sifted cake flour
1 c. sugar
1 tblsp. baking powder
½ tsp. salt
½ pt. (1 c.) heavy cream
1 tsp. vanilla
2 eggs

• Lightly grease two 8" round layer cake pans, then line bottoms with waxed paper and lightly grease.
• Sift flour, sugar, baking powder and salt together twice. Pour cream and vanilla into a deep 1 qt. bowl; beat cream with electric mixer or rotary beater until just stiff, about 1½ minutes.
• Add unbeaten eggs and beat just until blended. Add flour mixture and beat. If an electric mixer is used, beat at low speed to blend batter. Turn into pans.
• Bake in moderate oven (350°) until top of cake springs back when lightly touched with finger, 25 to 30 minutes.
• Cool cake in pans. Set on cake rack about 10 to 15 minutes. Remove from pans; take off waxed paper. Turn cake right-side up on rack, finish cooling and frost with your favorite chocolate frosting or Coffee Butter Frosting.

Coffee Butter Frosting:

⅓ c. butter
3 c. confectioners sugar
1½ tsp. instant coffee
3 tblsp. light cream

• Cream butter. Sift sugar and coffee together. Add gradually to butter, creaming until light and fluffy.
• Add cream as frosting becomes thick. Makes enough to frost top and sides of two 8" layers.

Variations: Omit coffee and cream and instead use orange or lemon juice and 2 tsp. grated rind. Or add ⅓ c. drained crushed pineapple or ¼ c. crushed fresh or frozen strawberries. For a chocolate frosting, stir 3 (1 oz.) squares chocolate, melted, into the creamed butter and sugar. Or lightly brown the butter in heavy skillet over medium heat; blend with the sugar. Or substitute 3 tblsp. mashed banana and lemon juice for the coffee and cream.

For Special Occasions: Homemade Mixer-Butter

Remember how Grandmother used to churn butter? And how wonderful hot, brown-topped biscuits, cornbreads and delicate light rolls tasted with little golden pools of it melting on them? Few country cooks now have time to make butter. But there are the once-in-a-blue moon occasions when the homemade kind adds a charm that makes everyone sit up and take notice. Table conversation revolves around it and if handled carefully, the butter tastes good enough to deserve the spotlight.

When cream is available and important guests are coming, butter making frequently returns briefly to the good cook's kitchen. The children no longer count strokes and take turns lifting the churn's dasher up through the cream and pushing it down again. The electric mixer handles the job. The work is in the precise preparation of the cream which so greatly affects the quality of the end product.

The directions for making country-fresh butter that follow came to Farm Journal from an Iowa farm woman. We have used them successfully in our Countryside Kitchens and think you will have good luck with them when you wish to try your hand with an old country culinary art.

HOW TO MAKE BUTTER

Collect 1 to 1½ qts. heavy cream from separator (or buy it at the store, in which case omit pasteurizing step). Pasteurize it in an electric pasteurizer or by the flash method (heat it until it begins to rise in the pan, remove from the heat, let the cream settle and repeat two more times). Cool the cream by setting the pan in cold water. Pour into a glass jar, cover and store several days in the refrigerator. Cream must be at least 24 hours old to churn well. Use cream with at least 30 per cent butter fat. (You can buy heavy cream at most markets.)

Ripen the cream by letting it stand at room temperature from 4 to 6 hours. It will thicken and become mildly sour. This procedure helps give the butter a mild, good taste.

Cool cream again in refrigerator.

Pour cream into larger bowl of the electric mixer. Use no more than 1½ qts. cream to prevent spattering. Add a few drops of butter color if desired. Beat at high speed until flecks of butter begin to form. Then turn to low speed until butter separates from milk. Watch to keep the spattering to a minimum. Push down the sides of the bowl with spatula as cream whips.

Pour off the buttermilk.

Add cold water, about as much as there was buttermilk. Let beater run at lowest speed. Pour off the water and repeat.

Add a scant tablespoon of salt. Let beater mix it into butter. Remove beaters, scrape off butter with spatula and work out water with a spatula by pressing butter against side of bowl. Be sure to work out all the water.

Mold butter in a butter press or empty it into a container with tightly fitting lid. Store in refrigerator or in freezer for longer periods of time.

One quart cream makes about 1 pound butter, although it depends on how heavy the cream is.

FLAVORED BUTTER SPREADS

Spread on crisp crackers for a snack

• Use ¼ c. butter as a base for preparing any of the following spreads. Cream or whip butter, add ingredients as indicated and mix thoroughly. Store in tightly covered jar in refrigerator.

Cheese Butter: Add 1 to 3 tblsp. Blue, Roquefort or Parmesan cheese rubbed through a sieve. Season to taste.

Garlic Butter: Crush 1 to 2 cloves of garlic with ½ tsp. salt, few grains black pepper, ¼ tsp. Worcestershire sauce and a drop of Tabasco sauce (sauces may be omitted).

Honey Butter: Add ¼ c. honey and blend.

Nut Butter: Add 2 to 4 tblsp. finely chopped pecans, hazel nuts or almonds. Season with salt.

Olive Butter: Add 2 tblsp. finely chopped green or stuffed olives and a few drops of onion juice.

Parsley or Chives Butter: Add 1 to 2 tblsp. chopped parsley or chives.

Heavy Cream—The Country Touch

STRAWBERRY BAVARIAN CREAM

Everybody's favorite—combination of strawberries and cream

1 (3 oz.) pkg. strawberry flavor gelatin
2 c. hot water
1 c. heavy cream, whipped
1 pt. strawberries, sliced

• Combine gelatin and hot water according to package directions. Chill until syrupy.
• Fold in whipped cream and strawberries. Turn into sherbet or parfait glasses or chill in 1 qt. mold until set. Makes 6 servings.

Variation: Raspberries or other fruit may be substituted for strawberries.

CHEESE-PINEAPPLE SALAD

Cranberry cutouts sparkle like rubies

1 envelope unflavored gelatin
¼ c. cold water
¾ c. sugar
½ c. pineapple syrup
1 c. crushed pineapple, drained
1 c. grated cheese
1 c. heavy cream, whipped
1 (7 oz.) can jellied cranberry sauce, thinly sliced

• Soften gelatin in cold water.
• Dissolve sugar in pineapple syrup over low heat; add softened gelatin and stir until dissolved. Chill until syrupy.
• Fold in pineapple, cheese and whipped cream. Chill in 1½ qt. mold until firm. Garnish with fancy shapes cut from canned cranberry sauce slices. Makes 6 to 8 servings.

RICE DELIGHT

Serve with thin crisp cookies

1 c. cooked rice (⅓ c. uncooked)
1 c. drained, cubed pineapple or apricots
12 diced marshmallows or ½ (6¼ oz.) pkg. miniature marshmallows
½ c. heavy cream

• Combine rice, fruit, and marshmallows.
• Whip cream; fold into rice mixture. Chill in sherbet glasses. Makes 6 servings.

OVERNIGHT SALAD

Twenty-four-hour salad is another old-fashioned name for this ever popular salad-dessert

2 eggs
¼ c. white vinegar
¼ c. sugar
2 tblsp. butter
1 c. heavy cream, whipped
1 (1 lb. 4 oz.) can pineapple tidbits, drained
2 c. seedless grapes, halved
2 oranges, peeled and diced
2 c. quartered or miniature marshmallows

• Beat eggs in top of double boiler. Add vinegar, sugar and butter. Cook over boiling water, stirring constantly, until thick. Cool.
• Fold in whipped cream, fruits and marshmallows. Chill 24 hours. Serve in lettuce cups. Makes 8 to 10 servings.

Variation: Substitute for grapes: 1 (1 lb. 1 oz.) can Royal Anne cherries, drained, pitted and halved.

YULETIDE SALAD

Good during the holidays and at all other seasons—especially if chicken is on the platter

1 (3 oz.) pkg. lemon flavor gelatin
2 c. boiling water
2 tblsp. white vinegar
2 tblsp. sugar
1 c. crushed pineapple, drained
1 c. grated cheese
1 c. heavy cream, whipped

• Dissolve gelatin in boiling water. Add vinegar and sugar. Chill until syrupy.
• Fold in pineapple, cheese and whipped cream. Pour into individual bell-shaped molds or use 1 qt. mold. Chill until thoroughly set. Unmold on curly endive or other greens. Makes 6 to 8 servings.

SWISS STRAWBERRY RICE

Heavenly rice is an appropriate name for this homespun country dessert

1 c. uncooked rice
3 c. milk
½ c. sugar
½ tsp. salt
2 eggs, beaten
½ c. heavy cream
1 tsp. almond extract
1 (10 oz.) pkg. frozen sliced strawberries

• Cook rice in milk in top of double boiler until tender, stirring occasionally, about 1 hour. Add sugar and salt.
• Add a little hot mixture gradually to beaten eggs. Stir into remaining hot mixture. Blend well; cool.
• Whip cream; add almond extract; fold into rice. Chill. Serve with strawberries partly thawed. Makes 6 servings.

RICE SUPREME

Snowy white with bright-red cherry crown

½ c. rice
1½ qts. boiling water
1 qt. milk
¾ c. sugar
1 tsp. salt
1 tblsp. butter
3 envelopes unflavored gelatin
½ c. cold water
1 pt. heavy cream
2 tblsp. vanilla

• Pour rice into boiling water. Boil briskly 2 minutes. Drain, rinse with cold water.
• Return to pan. Add 2 c. milk, 1 tblsp. sugar, and salt. Bring to boil; add butter. Cover, simmer 20 minutes—do not stir.
• Pour into bowl. Add remaining milk and sugar. Cool.
• Soften gelatin in cold water 5 minutes. Heat slowly until gelatin dissolves. Add to rice. Chill until thick enough that kernels don't sink.
• Whip cream, adding vanilla gradually, as you whip. Fold into rice.

• Pour into oiled, 2 qt. mold. Cover with foil. Chill overnight. Makes 8 to 10 servings. Serve with Cherry Sauce.

Cherry Sauce:

3 c. pitted sour cherries
1¼ c. water
1 tblsp. lemon juice
⅔ c. sugar
2 tblsp. cornstarch
2 tblsp. butter

• Bring cherries, 1 c. water, lemon juice and sugar to a boil.
• Blend together cornstarch and remaining ¼ c. water. Stir into sauce.
• Cook, stirring until thick and clear, 2 to 3 minutes. Remove from heat, add butter. (Sauce should be tart, but a little more sugar may be added if desired.)
• Chill before serving. Makes about 5 cups.

VICHYSSOISE

Dip in your spoon and taste—you'll want to give thanks to the French chef in New York who invented this cold soup

¼ c. unsalted butter
4 leeks, chopped
1 onion, minced
1 qt. chicken broth
Sprig of parsley
Stalk of celery
Salt and pepper to taste
Few grains nutmeg
Few drops Worcestershire sauce
2 potatoes
1 c. heavy cream
Chives to garnish

• Melt butter over low heat. Add leeks and onion; cook slowly until tender, but not brown.
• Add chicken broth, parsley, celery, salt, pepper, nutmeg and Worcestershire sauce. Add peeled potatoes, sliced thin. Cook until potatoes are tender.
• Put through fine sieve into china or glass bowl. Stir in heavy cream; chill.
• Serve cold, sprinkled lightly with chopped chives. Makes 6 to 8 servings.

PEAS WITH CREAM

A company special that has its start in a country garden

2 tblsp. butter
2 small onions
1 heart of lettuce
Few sprigs parsley
6 c. shelled peas
1 tsp. salt
Boiling water
½ c. light cream

• Melt butter in large saucepan. Add whole onions. Tie lettuce heart and parsley with clean string. Add with peas, salt and about 1" boiling water in bottom of pan.
• Start cooking over high heat. After 10 minutes, reduce heat and cook, tightly covered, until peas are tender—about 10 minutes. Remove onions, lettuce and parsley.
• Drain peas, reserving ¼ c. of the cooking liquid. Add liquid to cream and pour over peas. Serve very hot. Makes 8 to 10 servings.

VEGETABLES IN CREAM

Tomatoes: Sauté thick tomato slices in batter until browned on both sides. Remove to hot serving dish. Stir ½ c. light cream into drippings and let simmer over low heat until brown. Serve over hot tomatoes.

Lima Beans: To 2 c. hot cooked lima beans add 2 tblsp. chopped onion, 2 tblsp. butter, ½ c. dairy sour cream, salt and pepper to season.

Carrots: Combine 1 egg yolk with 1 c. light cream, add 2 tblsp. butter, ½ tsp. sugar. Heat until mixture thickens. Add 2 c. cooked carrot slices.

Turnips: Mash and season with salt. Fold in whipped cream. Add a dash of nutmeg.

CHICKEN AND SWEET CREAM BISCUITS

A Sunday special—bring guests home from church to enjoy it

1 (5 lb.) stewing hen
2 tsp. salt
1 celery stalk
5 carrots, cut in big pieces
1 medium-size onion, quartered
¼ c. chicken fat
¾ c. flour
2 c. chicken broth
2 c. light cream
2 egg yolks, beaten
Parsley

• Cut chicken in serving-size pieces; place in kettle. Add water to cover. Add salt, celery, carrots and onion. Simmer, covered, until tender, about 3 hours.
• Drain broth from chicken. Skim fat from broth, saving ¼ c. fat for gravy. Strain broth; save carrots. Measure 2 c. broth for gravy. Pour remaining broth back into kettle with chicken to keep hot.
• Measure chicken fat into saucepan; blend in flour. Gradually add broth and cream. Cook until thick and smooth—stirring constantly. Add a small amount to egg yolks; then add yolk mixture to gravy. Cook 2 minutes more.
• Place hot chicken and carrots in serving dish or soup tureen; pour in gravy. Sprinkle with parsley and top with baked Sweet Cream Biscuits. Makes 10 to 12 servings.

Sweet Cream Biscuits:

4 c. sifted flour
1 tsp. salt
2 tblsp. baking powder
1½ c. heavy cream
4 tblsp. water

• Sift dry ingredients together. Stir in cream with fork just until all flour is moistened; add water if necessary.
• Knead on lightly floured surface, about 10 times. Roll ¾″ thick; cut with small floured cutter or juice glass.
• Bake on ungreased baking sheet in very hot oven (450°) 12 minutes or until golden brown. Makes 36 small biscuits.

SWEET-SOUR CABBAGE SLAW

No one has invented a coleslaw to surpass this one

3 c. finely shredded cabbage
1 tblsp. grated onion
½ tsp. celery salt
1 tblsp. sugar
1 tblsp. vinegar
¼ tsp. salt
⅛ tsp. cayenne pepper
½ c. heavy cream, whipped or thick sour cream

• Combine cabbage, onion and celery salt.
• Blend together sugar, vinegar, salt, pepper and cream. Pour over cabbage and toss. Makes 6 to 8 servings.

CREAMY FRUIT DRESSING

Just right for fruit salads

⅔ c. sugar
2 tblsp. flour
2 tblsp. oil
1 c. pineapple juice
2 eggs
Juice of 1 lemon
Juice of 1 orange
1 c. heavy cream, whipped

• Combine sugar, flour, oil and pineapple juice in top of double boiler. Cook over boiling water until thick, stirring constantly.
• Beat eggs slightly. Slowly stir in lemon and orange juice. Gradually add half of hot mixture, while stirring.
• Slowly stir egg mixture into remaining hot mixture in double boiler. Stir constantly for 3 minutes over hot, not boiling, water. Remove from heat; cool.
• Fold whipped cream into cooled mixture. Makes 3 cups.

WALNUT CREAM PIE

Rich and satisfying, this is a pie that calls for coffee

¾ c. butter
1½ c. sugar
2 eggs
¼ c. light cream
1½ tsp. cloves
½ c. raisins
1½ c. walnuts, broken
2 tblsp. flour
2 tsp. vanilla
1 (9″) unbaked pie shell
1 c. heavy cream, whipped

• Cream butter and sugar together. Beat in eggs, one at a time. Blend in light cream slowly. Add cloves.
• Dredge raisins and nuts in flour. Add to creamed mixture with vanilla. Spoon into pie shell.
• Bake in hot oven (450°) 10 minutes. Reduce temperature to moderate (350°); bake 40 minutes longer. Cool. Serve topped with whipped cream. Makes 8 servings.

REFRIGERATOR PIE

Stunning black and white dessert

Crust:

5 oz. plain chocolate cookies
¼ c. melted butter

Filling:

1 c. milk
½ lb. marshmallows (32)
¼ tsp. salt
1 c. heavy cream, whipped
1 tsp. vanilla

• Crush cookies to make 1½ to 2 c. crumbs. Reserve 3 tblsp. for topping.
• Add butter to crumbs; mix well. Press into 9″ pie pan.
• Scald milk in large saucepan. Add marshmallows and salt, melt. Cool until mixture begins to thicken.
• Fold in whipped cream and vanilla. Pour into cookie crust. Sprinkle top with remaining cookie crumbs. Chill 2 to 3 hours, or until set. Makes 6 servings.

SATIN SAUCE

Wonderful on cooked celery, broccoli or zucchini

3 egg yolks, beaten
⅔ c. light cream
½ tsp. salt
⅛ tsp. nutmeg
Dash cayenne pepper
1 tblsp. lemon juice
3 tblsp. soft butter or margarine

• Combine all ingredients, except butter, in top of double boiler. Cook, stirring, over moderate heat until mixture thickens. Remove from heat.
• Blend in butter. Serve at once. Makes 1 cup.

WHIPPED CREAM TOPPINGS

Nothing gives an angel cake glamor so quickly as a crown of whipped cream. Whipped cream also makes wonderful cake fillings.

Pineapple Frosting:

2 tsp. gelatin
1 tblsp. water
1 c. drained crushed pineapple
1 c. heavy cream
2 tblsp. confectioners sugar
Green food color

• Soften gelatin in water and dissolve over hot water. Stir into pineapple. Chill. When partially set fold in cream, whipped, with sugar added. Tint a delicate green.

Variation: Use 1 c. mashed apricot pulp, sweetened, instead of pineapple. For an attractive cake use this for filling and cover top and sides with Pineapple Frosting.

Sour Cream Gives a Special Flavor

Sour cream with berries or fruit winds up many successful country meals. One favorite starts with 1 c. brown sugar blended with 2 c. sour cream. Slice 8 fresh peaches, peeled, and alternate in a glass bowl with the sour cream-sugar mixture. End with the cream. Chill until very cold. Frozen peaches may be substituted for the fresh fruit.

CHICKEN LIVERS DE LUXE

If you like chicken livers you will prize this way of fixing them

1½ c. thick sour cream
1 tblsp. minced onion
½ tsp. salt
4 tblsp. butter
1 lb. (about 15) chicken livers
¼ tsp. pepper
6 slices bread

• Beat cream until light and fluffy. Add onion and ½ tsp. salt.
• Melt butter in skillet over low heat. Brown livers in butter; add salt and pepper.
• Toast bread; cut each slice diagonally in 4 triangles.
• Place about ½ c. sour cream mixture on each plate. Arrange toast points and hot livers in cream. Makes 6 servings.

PORK CHOPS CONTINENTAL

A German inspiration, with ardent friends across the USA

6 thick pork chops
1 tblsp. salt
¼ tsp. pepper
½ tsp. paprika
2 tblsp. chopped onion
1 qt. sauerkraut
1 c. hot water
1 c. thick sour cream
1 c. buttered dry bread crumbs

• Brown chops in their own fat in heavy skillet over medium heat. Season with salt, pepper and paprika.

• Place 3 chops on bottom of greased 3 qt. casserole. Cover with onion and half the sauerkraut. Add other 3 chops. Top with remaining sauerkraut.

• Add hot water to drippings in pan for broth. Pour broth and sour cream over all. Cover.

• Bake in moderate oven (350°) 1¼ hours. Uncover; sprinkle with crumbs; bake 15 minutes longer to brown crumbs. Makes 6 servings.

FISH WITH SOUR CREAM

Almost everyone votes approval when fish teams with sour cream

6 fish fillets
½ c. sifted flour
2 tsp. salt
¼ tsp. pepper
1 tblsp. butter
1½ c. thick sour milk
¾ c. thick sour cream
1 c. buttered bread crumbs
Few sprigs parsley

• Coat each fillet with mixture of flour, salt and pepper. Arrange in one layer in shallow greased baking dish 12×8×2", containing melted butter. Pour milk over fish.

• Bake in moderate oven (350°) 45 minutes until fish is tender and almost all the milk has been absorbed. Cover with sour cream; top with crumbs.

• Bake in hot oven (450°) 10 minutes longer until crumbs are browned. Garnish with parsley. Makes 6 servings.

Dozens of Ways to Serve and use cheese appear throughout our Cookbook. Recipe for Cheese Ball center, page 196, in Chapter 12, also cheese dips.

Watching Your Diet? Cottage cheese combines with fresh fruits for a nutritious salad, page 198—dressing is frozen fruit juice concentrate.

Baked Tomatoes Stuffed with Corn Perfect garden combination, page 247, to serve with broiled chicken. All recipes in Chapter 15 start in the garden.

For a Touch-up for Vegetables and meats you can't beat fresh herbs. Try our Onion Pie with Herbs—recipe, page 241, in the Garden Chapter.

SOUR CREAM RASPBERRY PIE

You'll call it a red letter day when you taste this pie

1½ c. thin sour cream
2 egg yolks, beaten
½ c. sifted flour
¼ tsp. cloves
½ tsp. cinnamon
¼ tsp. nutmeg
1 tsp. baking soda
¾ c. sugar
2 c. fresh, firm raspberries
2 tblsp. butter
1½ tblsp. lemon juice
1 (8") baked pie shell
2 egg whites
4 tblsp. sugar
½ tsp. vanilla
⅛ tsp. salt

• Heat cream in top of double boiler over hot water. Combine egg yolks, flour, spices and the ¾ c. sugar in bowl. Slowly stir a little of the hot cream into egg mixture; add to remaining cream in double boiler. Cook until thick, stirring constantly—about 10 minutes.
• Stir in raspberries and butter, cook 5 minutes longer. Cool. Add lemon juice. Pour into pie shell.
• Beat egg whites until foamy. Add sugar, a tablespoon at a time, beating well after each addition. Continue beating until very stiff. Add vanilla and salt. Spread over pie filling.
• Bake in slow oven (325°) 20 minutes, or until meringue is lightly browned.

GREEN BEANS IN SOUR CREAM

Baked green beans de luxe

2 lbs. green beans, cooked or 1 (1 lb. 13 oz.) can
1 onion, sliced
2 tblsp. finely cut parsley
2 tblsp. butter
1 tsp. salt
¼ tsp. pepper
2 tsp. grated lemon rind
2 tblsp. flour
1 c. thick sour cream
1 c. buttered bread crumbs

• Put cooked beans in greased 2 qt. casserole.
• Sauté onion and parsley in butter until lightly browned. Add salt, pepper, lemon rind, flour and sour cream. Heat just until hot.
• Spoon cream mixture over beans. Top with crumbs. Bake in moderate oven (350°) 20 minutes. Makes 6 servings.

SOUR CREAM BEETS

A first-class beet dish

15 small peeled beets
2 tblsp. butter
2 tblsp. sugar
1 tsp. salt
¼ tsp. pepper
½ c. water
1 tblsp. flour
1 c. thick sour cream

• Put peeled beets through coarse food chopper or chop with large knife. (There should be 1 qt. chopped beets.)
• Melt butter in saucepan; stir in beets, sugar, salt, pepper and water. Bring to boil and cook gently until beets are tender, about 12 minutes.
• Blend flour into sour cream and fold into beet mixture. Serve immediately. Makes 4 to 6 servings.

SOUR CREAM DRESSINGS

They are quick to make and give salads delightful flavor. There is no end to the variations.

Chives: Add ½ c. dairy sour cream to ½ c. mayonnaise and fold in 2 tblsp. minced chives. Serve on sliced cucumbers or tomatoes, lettuce or mixed chopped vegetables.

Celery: To ½ c. dairy sour cream add ½ tsp. celery seed, ¼ c. minced onion, 1 tblsp. vinegar and ¾ tsp. salt. Use on vegetables.

Jelly: Add ¼ c. beaten tart jelly (like currant) and ⅛ tsp. salt to ½ c. sour cream. Serve over fruits.

HORSE-RADISH CREAM SAUCE

Tops when baked ham is on the platter

1 c. thick sour cream
2 tblsp. lemon juice
½ c. prepared horse-radish
½ tsp. salt
⅛ tsp. pepper

• Whip cream until stiff. Combine horse-radish, salt, pepper, lemon juice.
• Fold into whipped cream. Makes 2 cups.

SAUERBRATEN

They'll want seconds of the flavorful sour cream gravy

4 lbs. beef (chuck, rump or rolled roast)
2 tsp. salt
1 onion, sliced
3 bay leaves
1 tsp. whole black peppers
2 c. cider vinegar
2 c. water
¼ c. sugar
2 tblsp. shortening or oil

Sour Cream Gravy:

Liquid from meat
¼ c. sugar
¼ c. seedless raisins
4 to 6 crumbled gingersnaps
1 c. thick sour cream

• Rub meat with salt. Put in crock or large bowl with onion, bay leaves and peppers.
• Heat vinegar and water together. Stir in sugar and pour over meat.
• Cover and refrigerate 3 or 4 days, turning meat once each day.
• Remove meat from liquid; save liquid for basting. Pat meat dry with paper toweling. Brown on all sides in hot shortening in covered roaster or Dutch oven.
• Add 1 c. of the marinating liquid. Cover and cook in slow oven (300°) 3 hours or until tender. Add more marinating liquid, if necessary.
• Remove meat, slice for serving, and keep hot while you make Sour Cream Gravy—gravy curdles if it stands.
• To make gravy, strain liquid left from cooking meat; skim off fat. Melt sugar in skillet. Stir in strained liquid gradually.
• Add raisins and gingersnaps. Cook until thick and smooth while stirring. Blend in sour cream. Continue cooking just long enough to heat cream. Serve immediately over meat. Makes 8 servings.

GRAPE-CREAM SHERBET

Cool, refreshing, smooth-as-velvet

1 c. thick sour cream
1 c. milk
1½ c. sugar
1 egg, well beaten
1 c. grape juice
¼ c. lemon juice

• Combine all ingredients in bowl. Beat until sugar is dissolved.
• Pour into 2 refrigerator trays and freeze nearly firm.
• Turn mixture into chilled bowl. Beat with chilled rotary or electric beater until fluffy-smooth, but not melted.
• Return to trays and freeze firm. Makes 6 servings.

SURPRISE PUDDING

A dream dessert everyone raves over

2 tblsp. shortening
⅓ c. sugar
½ tsp. vanilla
1 egg, beaten
1 c. sifted flour
1½ tsp. baking powder
¼ tsp. salt
⅓ c. milk
¾ c. sour cream
¾ c. brown sugar

• Cream together shortening and sugar. Add vanilla and egg; beat until light and fluffy.
• Sift together flour, baking powder and

salt. Add alternately to creamed mixture with milk.

• Put in each of 6 greased custard cups, 2 tblsp. sour cream and 2 tblsp. brown sugar. Top with batter. Bake in moderate oven (350°) 30 minutes.

• To serve, turn upside down in sauce dishes and top with whipped cream. Makes 6 servings.

WINTER SALAD BOWL

The sour cream dressing makes this salad distinctive

2 c. shredded cabbage
6 c. diced, cooked beets
1 c. cooked, diced green beans
½ c. French dressing
1 tsp. mayonnaise
½ c. thick sour cream
1 tsp. chopped chives
½ tsp. salt
Pepper
Paprika
1 hard-cooked egg

• Combine cabbage, beets and beans in salad bowl.

• Mix together French dressing, mayonnaise, sour cream, chives, salt, pepper and paprika. Chop hard-cooked egg and press through sieve. Stir into dressing.

• Pour dressing over vegetables; toss. Makes 6 servings.

SOUR CREAM GINGER SQUARES

Some call them ginger cookies—they're good by any name

1 c. butter
½ c. sugar
1 tsp. ginger
1 tsp. cinnamon
1 egg, beaten
1 c. light molasses
½ c. thick sour cream
3½ c. sifted cake flour
2 tsp. baking soda
¾ tsp. salt

• Cream butter with sugar and spices.

• Combine beaten egg, molasses and sour cream.

• Sift together flour, soda and salt. Add alternately with molasses mixture to creamed butter and sugar.

• Spread in greased shallow baking pan, 15½ × 10½ × 1". Bake in moderate oven (350°) 20 minutes.

• Cool in pan. Frost with Sour Cream Frosting (page 3) or confectioners sugar frosting. Cut in squares. Makes about 3 dozen (2") squares.

SOUR CREAM FILLING

You may add 1 c. raisins before cooking, ⅔ c. chopped nuts before spreading

4 egg yolks, or 2 whole eggs
⅔ c. sugar
⅛ tsp. salt
1 c. thick sour cream
½ tsp. vanilla

• Beat egg yolks until thick and lemon-colored; gradually add sugar, beating constantly. Add salt and sour cream.

• Cook over boiling water until thickened, stirring constantly, about 15 minutes.

• Cool; add vanilla. Makes filling for two 8" or 9" cake layers.

SOUR CREAM CAKE

Sift together 1½ c. flour, 1 tsp. baking powder, ½ tsp. salt. Beat until thick 3 eggs and gradually beat in 1 c. sugar. Alternately add dry ingredients and 1 c. sour heavy cream (whipping) with 1½ tsp. vanilla added. Pour batter into greased 9" square pan. Bake in moderate oven (350°) 35 to 40 minutes. Frost with Peanut Frosting.

Peanut Frosting: Stir together until creamy and of spreading consistency ¼ c. chunk-style peanut butter, 3 c. sifted confectioners sugar, ¼ to ⅓ c. milk.

BEST-EVER CHEESE CAKE

Just the dessert to serve with coffee when friends come in for the evening

2 c. fine zwieback crumbs
2 tblsp. sugar
¼ c. butter or margarine
2 (8 oz.) pkgs. cream cheese
½ c. sugar
2 tblsp. flour
¼ tsp. salt
1½ tsp. grated lemon rind
4 tsp. lemon juice
½ tsp. vanilla
4 eggs, separated
1 c. light cream
1 c. thick sour cream
1 tblsp. sugar
1 tsp. vanilla

• Mix together crumbs and 2 tblsp. sugar. Cut in butter with pastry blender.

• Reserve ½ c. mixture for top decoration. Press remainder on bottom and 1½" up side of 9" spring-form pan. Bake in slow oven (325°) 5 minutes. Cool.

• Soften cheese to room temperature. Add ½ c. sugar, flour and salt. Stir in lemon rind, juice and ½ tsp. vanilla.

• Add yolks, one at a time; beat well after each addition. Beat in light cream.

• Beat egg whites until stiff. Fold into cheese mixture. Pour into the crumb-lined pan.

• Bake in slow oven (325°) 1 hour, or until center is set.

• Combine sour cream, 1 tblsp. sugar and 1 tsp. vanilla. Spread evenly over top of cheese cake (careful not to work in air bubbles).

• Return cake to oven 5 to 8 minutes—topping should be warm and slightly firm. Remove from oven and cool in pan 1 to 1½ hours.

• Remove rim of pan. Use remaining crumbs to garnish top with appropriate design. Makes 8 to 10 servings (or 12 small ones). Cheese cake tastes best the day it's baked.

If you don't have a spring-form pan use a round 9" layer cake pan. For extra height, fit a 22" length of 12" foil across bottom of pan; fold long ends back to build up sides at least 1". To complete extra height around rim, cut a 6" length of foil in two; fit pieces along "short" sides and fold above rim. When cake is baked, you can lift it out by edges of long foil sheet.

Variation: Substitute ½ c. toasted sesame seeds for same amount of zwieback crumbs. To toast seeds, spread in a large shallow baking pan. Place in moderate oven (375°) 12 to 15 minutes or until well browned.

12

Milk and Cheese

When you or your little helpers pour cold milk into glasses polished until they shine, it's a signal supper is ready. Drinking milk is one of those firmly established customs taken for granted in most farm homes. And using milk abundantly as an ingredient is basic in country cooking.

This chapter contains many recipes for delightful rich-in-milk dishes. There are more scattered through other chapters, however, for milk gets into the finest cakes, pies, ice creams and other marvelous desserts. It imparts its goodness to breads and no one will deny that its claim on custards is as legitimate as that of eggs. Indeed one of the virtues of milk, like its near relative, cheese, is its compatability with other foods.

The cheese family is big. But this chapter highlights the two real favorites—Cheddar (often called American cheese) and cottage cheese. Swiss cheese is a runner-up. But all the cooked dishes in this chapter are fixed with Cheddar unless otherwise specified.

Cheese and milk are great enhancers. Finger through the pages that follow, and you will find a galaxy of recipes for cottage cheese salads and pies that have a habit of carrying off honors in meals. There are milk drinks, frosty-cold, soups that steam in bowls and scalloped potatoes that men vote for. And many main dishes star in this recipe collection—reminders that milk and cheese are protein foods capable of standing up, at least in some meals, to the competition of a platter of meat.

A recipe for pancakes from a thin-with-milk batter in Swedish style suggests that you get out the griddle. We've robbed the Eggs chapter of one recipe—a custard that makes its own tasty caramel sauce while it chills, after baking. There are a host of treats made with the canned milks—evaporated and sweetened condensed, and nonfat milk powder.

Most of the recipes in this chapter are the hearty kind, health and energy builders. Mothers rely on them for help in making young America strong. But best of all, they make downright good eating.

Milk in Soup Bowls

For crunchy tastiness, scatter a few small potato chips, or coarsely crumbled large ones, on top just before serving.

VELVETY CHEESE SOUP

Peas and pimiento add flashes of color

¼ c. butter
¼ c. minced onion
¼ c. flour
1 tsp. salt
4 c. milk
1 c. (¼ lb.) grated process cheese
½ c. cooked green peas
¼ c. diced pimiento

• Melt butter in saucepan.
• Add onion; cook until clear.
• Remove from heat. Blend in flour, salt and milk.
• Cook until thick, stirring constantly.
• Add cheese, stirring until it melts.
• Add green peas and diced pimiento. Makes 6 servings.

WATER CRESS SOUP

A spring song in the soup bowl

2 (10½ oz.) cans condensed cream of chicken soup
2 soup cans milk
½ c. chopped water cress
2 hard-cooked eggs, sliced

• Empty soup into saucepan. Add milk; heat as directed on can.

• Wash water cress. Save sprigs for garnish. Chop (about ¼ bunch) very fine. Add to hot soup just before serving.

• Pour into soup bowls. Top each serving with egg slice and sprig of water cress. Makes 6 servings.

VEGETABLE OYSTER STEW

What could be better for supper on a cold, blustery evening?

2 medium carrots, scraped and grated
½ c. diced celery
¼ c. butter or margarine
1 qt. milk
1 qt. oysters
Salt
Pepper (freshly ground best)
Paprika
Minced parsley

• Sauté carrots and celery in butter until soft and tender (not brown). Add milk and bring to boil.
• Cook oysters in own liquor until edges curl (about 5 minutes).
• Combine oyster and vegetable mixtures. Season to taste with salt, pepper and paprika. Garnish with parsley.
• Serve immediately—curdles if left standing. Makes 8 servings.

Variation: Tiny parboiled onions may be added with milk and vegetables.

CORN CHOWDER

Cool chowder before serving if there's time—reheating improves its flavor

¼ lb. salt pork, diced
3 medium-size onions, chopped
3 or 4 potatoes, peeled and diced
½ c. water
4 c. corn, cut from cob
1 qt. milk
2 tsp. salt
⅛ tsp. pepper

• Fry pork until almost crisp; add onions and cook until golden brown—this gives a definite tang to the chowder.
• Add potatoes and water; simmer 5 minutes. Add corn and cook 5 minutes more, or until tender.
• Stir in milk, salt and pepper. Heat slowly until chowder is piping hot. Makes 6 to 8 servings.

Milk in Hot Breads

SKILLET CORN BREAD

Hot corn bread too soft to cut—you serve it with a spoon

1 c. milk
1 c. cornmeal
1½ tsp. baking soda
1½ tsp. salt
4 eggs, beaten
3 c. milk
2 tblsp. bacon drippings

• Scald milk; add cornmeal. Cook over boiling water to consistency of mush.
• Add baking soda, salt and eggs. Stir in milk and drippings which have been melted in heavy iron skillet.
• Pour batter into hot skillet. Bake in moderate oven (350°) 40 minutes. Spoon out and rush to table. See that gravy or butter is passed with it. Makes 8 servings.

BUTTERMILK BRAN MUFFINS

Hot breads liven up meals, and these muffins have the delightful flavor that only buttermilk gives

1 c. sifted flour
2 tsp. baking powder
1 tsp. salt
½ tsp. baking soda
3 c. bran cereal
⅓ c. shortening
½ c. sugar
1 egg
1 c. buttermilk

• Measure and sift dry ingredients together. Add bran and mix well.
• Cream shortening and sugar. Add egg and beat till light and fluffy.
• Add dry ingredients to the creamed mixture alternately with buttermilk. Stir only enough to mix. Fill greased muffin tins ⅔ full.
• Bake in hot oven (400°) 20 minutes. Makes 12 large muffins.

SWEDISH-STYLE PANCAKES

Wonderful for a supper dessert or with bacon as the main dish for breakfast

1 c. flour
1 tblsp. sugar
½ tsp. salt
3 eggs, unbeaten
3 c. milk

• Sift together in large bowl the flour, sugar and salt.
• Beat eggs just enough to blend yolks and whites. Stir in milk. Add mixture gradually to dry ingredients, stirring to mix well. Let stand 2 hours. (This lets batter thicken so that the cakes will hold their shape on the griddle.)
• Heat griddle until drop of water will dance on the surface; brush with butter or shortening. Beat batter again; spoon onto griddle 2 tablespoonfuls for each cake. Brown on both sides.
• Spread with Currant Sauce; wind up like a jelly roll and sprinkle with confectioners sugar. Keep warm in oven until all pancakes are baked. Makes about 24 small pancakes.

Note: You need not roll these pancakes. Serve them swimming in melted butter and maple syrup instead of the sauce.

Currant Sauce:

¾ c. sugar
½ c. boiling water
2 c. stemmed currants
2 tblsp. cornstarch
¼ c. cold water

• Add sugar to boiling water; simmer 5 minutes to make syrup. Add currants; simmer until berries heat through.
• Make a paste of cornstarch and water; add small amount of hot currant mixture, then stir into mixture in pan. Cook, stirring until thick and clear, about 10 minutes.

QUICK RAISED CORN BREAD

One of Grandmother's best loaves—try it for sandwiches or extra-special toast

1 c. thick sour milk
2 pkgs. granular yeast
3 tblsp. sugar
1 c. cornmeal
½ c. whole wheat flour
1½ tsp. salt
¼ c. dry nonfat milk
½ c. wheat germ
2 eggs, beaten
3 tblsp. bacon drippings

• Scald milk and add sugar. Dissolve yeast in warm, not hot, milk (110° to 115°).
• Sift together cornmeal, whole wheat flour, salt, dry milk. Stir in wheat germ.
• Add eggs and drippings to yeast-milk mixture. Add dry ingredients, stirring well. Pour into greased 8×8×2" pan. Bake immediately in moderate oven (350°) 30 minutes.
• When the top crust of a quick bread browns before the center has finished rising, it may crack. Avoid by letting batter stand 20 minutes for partial rising before baking. Then bake loaf at 375° instead of the usual 350°.

Vegetable Scallops

This is a favorite way to serve vegetables, and one which generally brings requests for "seconds." Substitute any cooked or canned vegetable for the cabbage in this recipe—spinach, green beans, or onions.

SCALLOPED CABBAGE

Special, because the cabbage heats briefly in rich cheese sauce

3 c. cooked shredded cabbage
3 tblsp. butter or margarine
3 tblsp. flour
½ tsp. salt
⅛ tsp. pepper
1½ c. milk
¾ c. cheese, grated
Buttered bread crumbs

• While cabbage is cooking (cook 7 to 8 minutes in boiling water to cover), prepare white sauce: melt butter; add flour and seasonings, blend thoroughly. Stir in milk gradually, cook until thickened.
• When cabbage is tender, drain well.
• Alternate layers of cabbage, grated cheese and warm white sauce in greased casserole. Top with buttered crumbs; bake in moderate oven (350°) 20 minutes, or until crumbs are delicately browned. Makes 6 servings.

SCALLOPED POTATOES

Dried beef is the surprise in this old-time favorite

8 medium potatoes (about 2 lbs.)
2 tblsp. minced onion
¼ lb. dried beef
2 tblsp. butter
2 tblsp. flour
4 c. milk
Pepper
1 c. soda cracker crumbs

• Peel potatoes, slice thin.
• Lightly brown onion and dried beef in melted butter. Blend in flour. Add milk gradually. Cook until thick and smooth, stirring constantly.
• Place potatoes in thick layer in large, buttered casserole. Sprinkle with pepper. Alternate layers of creamed dried beef and cracker crumbs, ending with crumbs. Bake in moderate oven (350°) 1 hour. Makes 6 servings.

Scalloped Potatoes and Ham: Cut ¾ lb. ham into ½" cubes; brown lightly in hot fat in skillet. Peel and slice 6 to 8 medium potatoes. Heat 2 c. milk to boiling; add ham and potatoes and again heat to boiling. Add 1 tsp. salt and ⅛ tsp. pepper. Put in greased 2 qt. casserole. Bake in slow oven (325°) 30 to 45 minutes, until potatoes are tender. Makes 6 servings.

Milk Shakes

BANANA MILK SHAKE

Children's Choice, mothers call this

2 c. milk
2 ripe bananas
2 tblsp. sugar or molasses

• Combine all ingredients in blender. Mix at high speed for 1 minute. Mixture should be smooth and foamy.
• Pour into glasses. Serve immediately.
• For a tasty variation use 2 tblsp. chocolate syrup in place of the sugar or molasses. Makes 3 servings.

Note: You can mash bananas, add the other ingredients and blend them in the electric mixer instead of the blender.

PEPPERMINT MILK SHAKES

Pretty, pink, rich—the tastiest way to salvage broken Christmas candy canes

½ c. crushed peppermint candy
2 c. milk
1½ pts. vanilla ice cream

• Add candy to milk and beat to blend (electric blender works best).
• Add ice cream and beat until smooth. Serve at once. Makes 6 (6 oz.) glasses.

PINEAPPLE MILK SHAKE

A drink that will pinch-hit for dessert if passed with chocolate cookies

1 c. milk
½ c. crushed pineapple, undrained
1 tsp. sugar
1 tblsp. lemon juice

• Combine all ingredients in blender. Mix at high speed for 1 minute. Mixture should be smooth and foamy.
• Pour into serving glasses. For a thicker drink add a small scoop of ice cream during mixing. Makes 1 large serving.

Note: Reconstituted nonfat dry milk may be used.

CHOCOLATE MALTED MILK

Just the drink for folks who are a little underweight

½ c. malted milk powder
3 c. whole milk
4 egg yolks, beaten
¾ c. chocolate syrup
1½ tblsp. sugar
4 egg whites, stiffly beaten
Crushed ice
Nutmeg

• Mix malted powder with ¼ c. milk to form a smooth paste. Stir in beaten egg yolks. Add remaining milk and chocolate syrup.
• Add sugar to beaten egg whites. Add half of whites to chocolate mixture; beat with rotary beater, or shake until foamy. Pour over finely crushed ice in tall glasses.
• Pile remaining egg white meringue on top of each glass. Sprinkle with nutmeg. Makes 4 to 6 servings.

STRAWBERRY MILK SHAKE

½ (10 oz.) pkg. frozen strawberries or 1 pt. cleaned fresh strawberries and ¼ c. sugar
1½ c. cold milk
½ pt. vanilla ice cream

• Blend well. Makes 2 large glasses.

Variations: Add ¼ c. plain malted milk or use raspberries in place of strawberries.

FRESH PEACH SHAKE

1 c. diced fresh peaches
1 to 2 tblsp. sugar
2 tblsp. lemon juice
1 c. cold milk
½ pt. vanilla ice cream

• Mix well until thick and fluffy. Makes 2 large glasses.

Desserts Made with Milk

LIME DESSERT TREAT

Cool, pale green filling between crunchy brown crumbs—truly refreshing

1½ c. crushed, sugar-frosted cereal
¼ c. regular dry milk powder
⅓ c. butter or margarine
2 (15 oz.) cans sweetened condensed milk
1 c. lime juice (about 4 large limes)
2 tsp. grated lemon rind
4 egg yolks, slightly beaten
Green food color
Strawberries (optional)

• Blend together cereal crumbs and dry milk; toss with melted butter. Put aside ¼ c. of mix; then press remaining crumb mixture into 8×8×2" pan to make bottom layer.
• Combine sweetened condensed milk, lime juice, lemon rind and egg yolks; beat until mixture thickens. Use a few drops of color to tint a delicate green.
• Pour into pan over crumbs; sprinkle remaining crumbs over top. Chill 24 hours before cutting in squares and serving. Garnish with fresh strawberries. Makes 8 servings.
• If you desire, place dessert in freezer a few hours to stiffen; then thaw slightly before serving.

ORANGE MARMALADE BAVARIAN

A good company luncheon dessert to make a day early

4½ c. milk
6 egg yolks, slightly beaten
¼ c. sugar
½ tsp. salt
2 tblsp. unflavored gelatin
1 c. orange marmalade
2 tsp. vanilla
½ tsp. almond extract
1 tblsp. butter
1 c. (3½ oz. can) flaked coconut
Orange sections
Shredded orange rind

• Reconstitute instant or regular dry milk by package directions. Scald 4 c. of this reconstituted milk.
• Mix egg yolks, sugar and salt in top of double boiler. Add scalded milk, place over boiling water. Cook, stirring constantly, until mixture coats spoon.
• Soften gelatin in remaining ½ c. cold milk; dissolve in hot custard mixture. Chill until partly thickened.
• Blend in marmalade and flavorings with mixer or blender. Pour into 3 pt. mold or individual molds. Chill 24 hours before serving. At serving time, unmold and garnish. Makes 10 servings.

Garnish: Melt butter, add coconut and sauté until golden brown; cool. Surround mold with coconut and stud with orange sections arranged in groups of three. Sprinkle orange rind on top.

CARAMEL CUSTARD

Dessert magician—the custard makes its own luscious sauce

⅓ c. sugar
⅓ c. water
4 eggs
¼ tsp. salt
¼ c. granulated sugar
2¼ c. milk
1 tsp. vanilla

• Combine sugar and water in small saucepan over moderate heat; cook without stirring about 6 to 8 minutes or until mixture has become a light brown caramel syrup; remove from heat.
• Quickly pour equal portions of caramel into 6 (6 oz.) custard cups, rotating cups to coat; cool until firm.

• Beat eggs with salt until they begin to froth; add 1/4 c. sugar, milk (reconstituted dry milk may be used), and vanilla; stir to dissolve sugar; strain.
• Pour egg-milk mixture over caramel, filling cups 3/4 full. Place cups in baking pan filled with about 1" hot water.
• Bake in slow oven (325°) about 35 minutes, or until center is set and tip of knife inserted comes out clean.
• Remove from oven; lift cups from water; cool. Chill 6 to 8 hours or overnight to allow sauce to form on bottom.
• To serve, unmold, turning custard upside down onto serving plate. Caramel forms a sauce. Makes 6 servings.

LEMON-APRICOT ICE CREAM

A wonderful year-around dessert for special occasions

2 (5 1/3 oz.) cans evaporated milk
1 pkg. lemon flavor instant pudding
1 (13 oz.) can evaporated milk
3 (7 3/4 oz.) jars strained apricot-apple baby food
1/4 c. light corn syrup
1 tblsp. lemon juice
2 tsp. grated lemon rind
1 (6 oz.) can frozen lemonade concentrate, thawed

• Empty each small can of milk into a separate freezing tray. Chill until fine crystals form around edges. (If milk freezes more, thaw until there are only a few ice crystals.)
• Prepare pudding according to package directions using only the 13 oz. can of evaporated milk for liquid.
• When pudding is set, add 1/2 cup of it to apricot-apple pulp and corn syrup.
• Turn milk from one freezing tray into chilled bowl; (chill beater) whip quickly until very stiff. Add lemon juice and blend. (If whipped milk begins to fall, return to freezing tray and re-chill.)
• Fold into apricot mixture. (You may add food color. For apricot: 1/2 tsp. red color and 1 tsp. yellow, mixed.) Pour into two loaf pans about 10 1/4×3 5/8×2 5/8". Freeze while fixing second layer.
• Add lemon rind and lemonade concentrate to remaining pudding mixture.
• Whip milk from second tray. Fold into lemon mixture. Pour over apricot layers in pans. Freeze until firm. Slice to serve. Makes 2 1/2 quarts.

Lemon Fluff Variation: Prepare pudding as for lemon layer in Lemon-Apricot Ice Cream, using all the pudding, from 1 to 2 tsp. grated lemon rind, the lemonade concentrate and 1 small can milk, whipped. Makes 12 servings.

CHERRY CUSTARD SHORTBREAD

The famous red, tart cherries in a new kind of dessert pie

1 1/4 c. sifted flour
6 tblsp. sugar
1/2 c. butter or margarine
1 pkg. vanilla pudding mix
2 c. milk
2 1/2 c. fresh or frozen pitted sour red cherries, or 1 (1 lb. 4 oz.) can cherries, drained
1/2 c. drained cherry juice
2 tblsp. cornstarch
1 c. heavy cream, whipped

• Combine flour and 2 tblsp. sugar. Cut in butter until mixture resembles cornmeal.
• Line a 10×6×1 1/2" greased baking dish with mixture.
• Bake in hot oven (400°) 25 minutes. Cool.
• Prepare pudding with milk according to package directions. Cool.
• Cook fresh or frozen cherries in 1 c. water 10 minutes. Drain and reserve 1/2 c. juice.
• Combine cherries, cherry juice, cornstarch and sugar. Stir and cook until slightly thickened. Cool.
• Pour pudding into baked crust; top with cherry mixture. Serve with whipped cream. Makes 6 servings.

Dishes Enhanced with Cheese

The cheese story divides into four parts. That's because there are four basic types of cheese—the very hard, the firm, the semi-soft and the soft. The very hard cheeses are commonly used for grating—one of these which you'll find often in this cookbook is Parmesan.

In the firm cheese branch of the family the Cheddars are famous, with mild or sharp flavors, depending on their cure. Cheddar holds its flavor through heating—that's one of the reasons it's the favorite in cooking. Gouda, and Swiss, the "cheese with eyes," also belong in the firm group.

Some of the best known semi-soft cheeses are those with a blue mold, like the Roquefort of France and blue cheese of Denmark and the United States. Gorgonzola of Italian ancestry and Stilton, as British as John Bull, are other examples.

Soft cheeses divide into two families: the ripened dessert cheese like Camembert; and the unripened cottage, pot and cream cheeses, and the Ricotta and Mozzarella used in so many popular American-Italian dishes.

Knowledge of the cheese families helps in buying the kind suited to the use you expect to make of it. If men are better shoppers for cheese than women, as it sometimes is claimed, it's because they let their noses tell them what to buy. But taste is as important as smell and selecting the cheese best adapted to the way you wish to use it also matters greatly.

Main Dishes and Accompaniments

CHEESE AND NOODLE RING

Attractive for buffet suppers. For larger crowds, multiply recipe, bake in shallow pans, serve in squares

3 tblsp. chopped onion
3 tblsp. diced pimiento
¾ tblsp. butter or margarine
1 egg, slightly beaten
1 c. milk, scalded
1 c. grated cheese
1 tsp. salt
⅛ tsp. pepper
1½ c. cooked noodles (¾ c. uncooked)
1 c. soft bread crumbs

• Cook onion and pimiento in melted butter until onion is tender (do not brown).

• Combine egg, milk, cheese, salt and pepper.

• Mix noodles and bread crumbs with cheese mixture. (Prepare crumbs in electric blender if you have one.) Pour into greased ring mold or loaf pan. Set in pan of warm water and bake in moderate oven (350°) 1 hour.

• Unmold and serve with creamed chicken, fish or vegetables. Makes 6 servings.

CHEESE SOUFFLE

It's tall and light—extra good

1½ c. milk
¼ c. butter or margarine
¼ c. flour
1 tsp. salt
⅛ tsp. pepper
½ lb. sharp process cheese, shredded
6 eggs, separated

• Heat but do not scald milk.
• Melt butter in saucepan; stir in flour, milk and seasonings; cook, stirring, until smooth and thickened. Blend in cheese.
• Beat egg yolks; blend with a little cheese sauce; slowly stir into remaining cheese sauce.
• Beat egg whites until stiff but not dry. Slowly fold in cheese sauce, blending completely. Pour into ungreased 2 qt. casserole.
• Bake uncovered in slow oven (300°) about 1¼ hr. Do not open oven while baking! Serve at once. Makes 6 servings.

CHEESE FONDUE

Add buttered peas or spinach, crusty bread, crisp celery, and baked apples to the menu

8 slices day-old white bread
2 tblsp. butter or margarine
½ lb. Cheddar cheese, shredded
4 eggs, slightly beaten
2½ c. milk
½ tsp. Worcestershire sauce
½ tsp. dry mustard
1 tsp. salt

• Make four sandwiches from bread and butter. Cut into quarters or cubes.
• Place two of the cut sandwiches in the bottom of a buttered 1½ qt. casserole. Sprinkle with half the cheese. Repeat, using remaining bread and cheese.
• Combine eggs, milk and remaining ingredients; pour over layers in casserole. Refrigerate 1 hour.
• Bake in slow oven (300°) 1 hour and 15 minutes. Serve immediately.
• For convenience, mix ahead; refrigerate and bake just before serving. Makes 6 servings.

COTTAGE CHEESE SALMON LOAF

To round out the supper have green peas or asparagus and hot biscuits

Cheese Layer:

1 envelope unflavored gelatin
½ c. milk
1 tsp. chopped onion
½ tsp. salt
3 c. cottage cheese
1 cucumber
Pimiento

• Soften gelatin in half of the milk. Heat remaining milk until hot. Add gelatin; stir until dissolved.
• Add onion, salt and cottage cheese.
• Lightly oil 1½ qt. loaf pan. Arrange pattern of unpeeled cucumber slices and pimiento pieces on bottom of pan. Cover with cottage cheese mixture. Chill. Top with Salmon Layer.

Salmon Layer:

1 envelope unflavored gelatin
¼ c. cold water
1 tblsp. lemon juice
¾ c. mayonnaise or salad dressing
1 c. finely chopped celery
2 tblsp. chopped sweet pickle or pickle relish
1 (1 lb.) can salmon

• Soften gelatin in cold water. Heat over boiling water until gelatin dissolves. Add lemon juice. Cool slightly.
• Combine gelatin and mayonnaise. Add celery and sweet pickle.
• Add liquid from salmon. Remove skin and bones from salmon. Flake and add to mayonnaise mixture. Pour over cheese layer. Chill until firm.
• Unmold on platter. Makes 10 servings.
• Serve with dressing made by combining equal amounts of finely diced cucumber and mayonnaise. Takes about 1 c. of each.

CHEESE STRATA

Either a mixed fruit or tossed green salad makes a good companion

12 slices bread
½ lb. cheese (2 c.), grated
4 eggs, beaten
2½ c. milk
¾ tsp. salt
⅛ tsp. pepper
¼ tsp. mustard

• Arrange bread and cheese in alternate layers in greased baking dish (bread on bottom and top layers).
• Combine eggs, milk and seasonings. Pour over bread and cheese. Chill in refrigerator 1 hour.
• Bake in moderate oven (350°) 1 hour or until no particles adhere to a silver knife when inserted. Makes 6 to 8 servings.

TUNA MACARONI-AND-CHEESE

Just the main dish to serve when your club meets for lunch

2 (8 oz.) pkgs. macaroni
3 (7 oz.) cans tuna, drained and flaked
2 c. cooked (fresh, frozen or canned) whole kernel corn, drained
2 c. cooked (fresh, frozen or canned) peas or baby lima beans, drained
2 c. cubed Cheddar cheese
1 qt. milk
4 tsp. salt
½ tsp. pepper
½ c. dry bread crumbs
2 tblsp. butter

• Cook macaroni in boiling salted water; drain. Place in two buttered 2 qt. casseroles. Add tuna, corn and peas.
• Melt cheese in milk. Add salt and pepper. Pour over macaroni, mixing slightly.
• Top with bread crumbs; dot with butter. Bake in moderate oven (375°) 20 minutes. Makes 12 servings.

TOMATO-CHEESE RAREBIT

Good main dish for hurry-up suppers. Tomato flavor is the new addition

2 tblsp. butter or margarine
¼ c. chopped onion
1 (10½ oz.) can condensed tomato soup
2 c. (½ lb.) cheese, grated
1 egg, slightly beaten
Salt and pepper to taste
Paprika to taste

• Melt butter; add onion, cook until tender. Add soup.
• When heated, add cheese; cook, stirring until cheese melts. Add egg and seasonings. Cook, stirring constantly until mixture thickens. Serve immediately on toast or crackers. Makes 4 servings.

NEW POTATOES AU GRATIN

Perfect with fried chicken or ham loaf

2 tblsp. butter or margarine
2 tblsp. flour
2 c. milk
1 tsp. salt
⅛ tsp. pepper
1 c. grated American cheese
12 to 15 small new potatoes, peeled and cooked

• Melt butter in saucepan. Add flour, stir until blended. Add milk gradually; stir until thickened. Season with salt and pepper.
• Stir ¾ c. of the grated cheese into white sauce.
• Place potatoes in baking dish. Pour heated sauce over the potatoes. Sprinkle with remaining cheese. Bake in hot oven (400°) until bubbly hot and freckled with brown, about 15 minutes. Makes 8 to 10 servings.

CORN AND BEANS WITH CHEESE

Serve with ham and a citrus salad

2 c. green beans (fresh, frozen or canned)
1 (12 oz.) can whole kernel corn
6 tblsp. process cheese spread
1 tblsp. cream
¼ tsp. salt
Dash of pepper

• Cook and drain green beans. Drain and add corn. Simmer until hot.
• Add cheese spread, cream, salt and pepper. Stir until cheese mixture is blended in. Makes 4 servings.

DOUBLE CHEESE BISCUITS

A luncheon party special when served hot with a big, chilled fruit salad

Filling:

1½ c. grated sharp cheese
¼ c. chopped ripe or pimiento-stuffed green olives
2 tsp. grated onion
¼ tsp. celery seed
1 tsp. prepared mustard
Few drops Worcestershire sauce
½ tsp. salt
⅛ tsp. pepper

Cheese Biscuits:

1½ c. grated cheese
3 c. prepared biscuit mix
1 c. milk
4 tblsp. melted butter or margarine

• Mix cheese, olives, onion, celery seed, mustard, Worcestershire sauce, salt and pepper.
• To make biscuits, cut cheese into biscuit mix. Add milk, stirring well with fork. Knead gently 10 times. Roll out ⅛" thick; cut in 3" circles.
• Place about 1 tblsp. filling on one circle; top with second one. Repeat with remaining circles. Place on baking sheet; brush tops with melted butter.
• Bake in very hot oven (450°) 12 to 15 minutes. Makes 15 sandwiches.

BACON AND CHEESE SAUCE

Delicious dress-up for cooked vegetables

2 slices bacon, diced
2 tblsp. bacon fat
2 tblsp. flour
1 c. milk
¼ tsp. salt
Few grains pepper
¾ c. cheese, grated

• Fry bacon until crisp; remove from skillet.
• Measure bacon fat into double boiler. Add flour, stir until blended. Stir milk in gradually and cook until thickened. Add seasonings.
• Cool sauce slightly and add cheese all at once, stirring vigorously. (If necessary, reheat in double boiler until cheese is melted.)
• Add the bacon and pour immediately over hot cooked cauliflower, onions, broccoli, green beans or other vegetable. Makes 4 to 6 servings.

CREAM CHEESE AND CLAM DIP

A snack folks rave about

2 (3 oz.) pkgs. cream cheese
1 (7½ oz.) can minced clams
2 drops Tabasco sauce
¼ tsp. salt
Dash of pepper
1 tsp. minced onion
1 tsp. lemon juice

• Soften cream cheese. Drain clams and add 2 tblsp. clam juice to cheese. Blend until smooth.
• Add minced clams, Tabasco sauce, seasonings, onion and lemon juice. Mix well. Chill; serve with chips or crackers. Makes 1⅓ cups.

Cheese Balls: Combine 1 (8 oz.) pkg. cream cheese, whipped, with ½ c. chopped nuts and 8 small pickled onions, chopped. Roll into balls. Use to garnish green salad.

CHEESE CRACKERS

Watch the nibblers reach for these crispies

1½ c. sifted flour
½ tsp. salt
1 tblsp. chopped chives
½ c. butter or margarine
½ lb. sharp process cheese, grated (2 c.)

• Sift flour; measure. Add salt and chives.
• Cream together butter and cheese.
• Add flour mixture. Mix well.
• Roll into 1" balls; place on baking sheet. Flatten to about ¼" thickness (bottom of glass tumbler good for this). Prick top with a fork.
• Bake in moderate oven (350°) for 12 to 15 minutes. Makes 5 dozen crisp crackers.

BLUE CHEESE BALL

Place 1 (8 oz.) pkg. cream cheese in mixing bowl. Let come to room temperature. Add 6 oz. blue cheese, ½ tsp. vinegar, ½ tsp. prepared mustard and ⅛ tsp. Worcestershire sauce. Cream or beat until smooth. Chill; form into a ball. Roll in ¼ c. chopped salted peanuts or other nuts. Refrigerate. Serve as a spread for crackers. Let everyone slice off his own serving. Makes 1½ cups.

Another attractive way to mold the cheese mixture is in a small roll as for refrigerator cookies. Wrap in foil, waxed paper or plastic film. Chill. If you make the roll the right size, the slices will fit top of crackers.

Or pass a wooden tray of fragrant cheese and assorted crackers for dessert or evening refreshments. Lay individual servings of cheese of different kinds and crackers on tray. Bring in pot of bubbling hot coffee. And watch the men's enthusiasm!

Easy Blue Cheese Snacks: Spread blue cheese on thin apple slices that have been dipped in lemon juice. Put together sandwich-style.

Cheese Sandwiches

CIRCLE SANDWICHES

The ketchup touches the sandwich filling with color and flavor

1 (3 oz.) pkg. cream cheese
2 tblsp. soft butter or margarine
3 tblsp. ketchup
½ tsp. salt
½ tsp. prepared mustard
2 tblsp. finely chopped chives
6 sweet pickles, chopped
Dark or light bread

• Have cream cheese at room temperature. Add butter, ketchup, salt and mustard. Blend; add chives and pickles.
• Cut rounds of bread with a 3" cookie cutter. Cut a small round from center of half the bread rounds.
• Spread whole slices with butter or margarine. Spread with a tablespoon of filling. Top with remaining slices. Makes 12 sandwiches.

CHEESE BARBECUE SANDWICHES

Your big and little cowboys will go for these sandwiches

2 eggs, hard-cooked
1 green pepper
1 small onion
6 green olives
1½ c. grated American cheese
3 tblsp. ketchup
½ tsp. Worcestershire sauce
3 hamburger buns

• Chop fine: eggs, green pepper, onion and olives. Mix with cheese, ketchup and Worcestershire sauce.
• Cut buns in halves; spread with cheese mixture. Toast in moderate oven (350°) to melt cheese. Makes 3 sandwiches.

Note: Open packaged process cheese carefully so unused portion can be rewrapped and stored in refrigerator.

BROILED SANDWICHES

Heat the soup and cut carrot sticks while the sandwiches broil—luncheon will be ready on time

- **1 (12 oz.) can spiced luncheon meat**
- **½ lb. process cheese**
- **1 small onion, sliced**
- **½ green pepper**
- **1 small pickle**
- **3 tblsp. ketchup**
- **2 tblsp. milk**
- **6 hamburger buns**

• Put meat, cheese, onion, green pepper and pickle through food chopper. Add ketchup and milk, mix well.

• Split buns crosswise. Spread each half with ¼ c. meat mixture.

• Place on broiler rack about 4 inches from heat. Broil until edges toast to light brown and cheese melts, 3 to 4 minutes. Makes 6 servings.

CHEESE-TUNA SURPRISE

It's fun to unwrap and eat this tasty fix-ahead sandwich

- **1 c. (¼ lb.) sharp cheese**
- **1 (7 oz.) can tuna, flaked**
- **2 tblsp. chopped onion**
- **2 tblsp. chopped sweet pickles**
- **3 hard-cooked eggs, chopped**
- **2 tblsp. diced green pepper**
- **2 tblsp. chopped stuffed olives**
- **½ c. mayonnaise or salad dressing**
- **6 hot dog buns**

• Combine cheese (cubed), tuna, onion, pickles, eggs, green pepper, olives and mayonnaise. Spread on buns cut in halves lengthwise.

• Place sandwiches on baking sheet. Heat in very slow oven (250°) 30 minutes. Or wrap in foil and refrigerate a few hours if you wish to make them early. Heat and serve in foil. Makes 6 servings.

Variation: Heap Cheese-Tuna mixture on thick tomato slices instead of buns. Bake as above for a hot salad.

HARVEST CHEESE SANDWICH

An extra-quick main dish for supper or lunch on a cool day

- **1½ c. process cheese cubes**
- **½ c. light cream**
- **6 slices process cheese**
- **6 slices toast**
- **6 (½") tomato slices**
- **6 poached eggs**
- **6 slices cooked bacon**

• Put cheese cubes and cream in saucepan over low heat, stirring constantly to blend. Keep hot.

• Lay thin cheese slices on toast and broil to brown lightly.

• Top with tomato and then with hot egg. Pour on cheese sauce; add bacon. Serve at once. Makes 6 servings.

BOLOGNA-CHEESE SANDWICHES

Two layers of this savory filling in every sandwich

- **½ lb. bologna**
- **½ lb. process pimiento cheese**
- **1 small onion**
- **⅛ green pepper (optional)**
- **6 small sweet pickles**
- **½ tsp. salt**
- **6 tblsp. salad dressing or mayonnaise**
- **1 tsp. prepared mustard**
- **Dark or light bread**
- **Fresh garden lettuce**

• Grind bologna, cheese, onion, green pepper and pickles into a bowl.

• Add salt, salad dressing and mustard. Makes 2½ cups.

• For each sandwich, butter lightly 3 slices bread. Spread two with about ¼ c. filling. Stack together with buttered slice in middle. Insert lettuce. Makes enough filling for 10 triple sandwiches.

Note: Other types of favorite ready-to-serve sausages may be substituted for bologna. Or a leftover roast will combine very well with this filling mixture.

LUNCHEON SALAD SPECIAL

Few serve-yourself salads equal this one for the summer company buffet or supper on the porch. It also makes a fine main-dish luncheon for a women's group, especially if there are calorie watchers among them. Colorful, tangy frozen fruit concentrates make the dressing for the melons, fruits and cottage cheese—a fascinating contrast to the snowy-white, mild-flavored cottage cheese. Fresh melons share honors with both canned and frozen fruits, which are ready-to-go when you start to fix the salad. And to save time, quickly cut melons into wedges instead of shaping into the usual time-consuming balls. It's a beauty!

COTTAGE CHEESE AND FRUIT SALAD

Picture-pretty summer salad

1 ripe honeydew melon
2 to 3 round slices watermelon
1 (1 lb. 14 oz.) can peach halves
1 (1 lb. 14 oz.) can pineapple slices
1 pt. fresh or frozen strawberries
2 (6 oz.) cans frozen pink lemonade concentrate
3 to 4 (16 oz.) pkgs. large curd creamed cottage cheese
Salad greens
1 (6 oz.) can frozen grape juice concentrate
1 (6 oz.) can frozen orange and grapefruit concentrate

• Cut honeydew lengthwise into 8 sections. Lay in serving bowl, petal fashion.
• Cut each watermelon slice into small, fan-shaped wedges.
• Arrange watermelon, peaches and pineapple alternately in bowl using honeydew sections as dividers. Add strawberries. Pour can of partly thawed pink lemonade concentrate over fruit and melon. Set in refrigerator to chill.
• Empty cottage cheese into a bowl. Arrange crisp salad greens in third bowl.
• Pour thawed pink lemonade from second can into cruet or small pitcher. Repeat with grape juice and orange and grapefruit juice.
• Remove fruit from refrigerator.
• Set fruit, cottage cheese, salad greens and cruets containing fruit concentrates on table. Let each person help himself to greens, a big spoonful of cottage cheese, his choice of fruit and pour a little of the juice concentrates over the cheese as a dressing. (You may lightly mix juice into cheese if desired. Suggestions: orange and grapefruit concentrate with peaches, pink lemonade with melon, grape with pineapple.) Makes 8 to 12 servings.

Cheese Pies

Just as fruit and cottage cheese guarantee salad success they also pair off in glamorous make-ahead pies. It pays to take time to put the cheese through a food mill or sieve to insure a smooth filling for pie. The trio of cottage cheese-fruit pies that follow prompt folks to praise country-good meals. They are a godsend to the busy hostess for they help her avoid last-minute rush.

REFRIGERATOR CHEESE PIE

A no-bake pie—rich and delicious

2 envelopes unflavored gelatin
½ c. cold water
2 egg yolks, beaten
½ c. sugar
½ c. milk
1 tsp. salt
2 c. cottage cheese
1 tsp. grated lemon rind
2 tblsp. lemon juice
1 tsp. vanilla
2 egg whites, beaten
1 c. whipped cream
1 (9") crumb crust

• Soften gelatin in ½ c. cold water.
• Combine egg yolks, sugar, milk and

salt. Cook over boiling water until thick and smooth, stirring constantly.
• Stir in gelatin. Chill until thick.
• Beat until smooth cottage cheese, lemon rind, juice and vanilla. Blend into custard mixture. Fold in egg whites and whipped cream.
• Pour into crumb crust. Chill 3 hours. Makes 8 to 10 servings.

CRANBERRY CHEESE PIE

We found this recipe in a Cape Cod country kitchen

½ c. finely crushed corn flakes
1 tblsp. brown sugar
2 tblsp. melted butter or margarine
1 envelope unflavored gelatin
¼ c. cold water
1¾ c. milk
2 eggs, separated
⅓ c. brown sugar
⅛ tsp. salt
1 pkg. lemon pudding or pie filling
1 (8 oz.) carton creamed cottage cheese, sieved

• Mix corn flakes, brown sugar and butter. Spread evenly on bottom and sides of buttered 9" pie pan. Press firmly into place.
• Soften gelatin in cold water.
• Combine milk and egg yolks in saucepan; beat until well blended. Add sugar, salt and lemon pudding. Mix well. Cook over medium heat, stirring, until mixture comes to a boil and is thickened (about 5 minutes). Remove from heat.
• Add gelatin; stir until thoroughly dissolved and mixture is smooth.
• Add sieved cheese.
• Beat egg whites until stiff. Fold into pudding and cheese mixture.
• Pour into crumb shell. Chill until set, about 4 hours. Top with Cranberry-Nut Glaze.

Cranberry-Nut Glaze: Combine 1½ c. cranberries and ½ c. water in saucepan. Cover, boil about 10 minutes. Add ½ c. sugar, ¼ c. brown sugar and a dash of salt; cook until sugar dissolves, about 4 minutes. Remove from heat; add ¼ c. chopped walnuts. Cool; then chill. Spoon over top.

Cherry Glaze: Mix 2½ tsp. cornstarch with 2 tblsp. sugar. Slowly stir in ½ c. liquid drained from canned pitted red sour cherries. Simmer until clear and thickened. Add 1 c. drained pitted cherries, 1 tsp. lemon juice, ¼ tsp. almond extract and a few drops red food color. Cool and spoon over cheese pie instead of Cranberry Glaze.

STRAWBERRY CHEESE PIE

A dish to repeat several times during the strawberry season

1 qt. strawberries
1 c. sugar
¼ c. water
¼ c. cornstarch
1 tblsp. butter
Dash of salt
1 tsp. lemon juice
Red food color
2 tblsp. light cream
1 (3 oz.) pkg. cream cheese
1 (9") baked pastry shell

• Sprinkle berries with sugar. Toss lightly; let stand about 2 hours.
• Drain all juice from berries. Add water to juice to make 1¼ c. liquid. Heat to boiling.
• Mix ¼ c. water with cornstarch. Add gradually to boiling liquid, stirring constantly. Cook until clear.
• Add butter, salt, lemon juice and a few drops red food color. Cool slightly.
• Add light cream to cream cheese; mix until smooth. Spread over bottom of baked pie shell.
• Add whole berries to cooked mixture. Pour into pie shell and chill well, at least 2 hours.
• For color contrast, decorate top of pie with softened cream cheese or whipped cream. Makes 6 servings.

HAM-EGG-CHEESE SANDWICHES

Let the teen-age youngsters fix them when their friends come over

3 hamburger buns, cut in halves
1 (4½ oz.) can deviled ham
3 eggs
¾ c. grated cheese

• Spread buns with deviled ham.
• Scramble eggs; put over ham-spread buns. Sprinkle with grated cheese. Toast in moderate oven (350°) to melt cheese. Makes 6 open-face sandwiches.

TOMATO-CHEESE SAUCE

A hot sandwich that rings the supper bell

1 (8 oz.) can tomato sauce (1 c.)
1 chopped onion
Parsley
1 tsp. salt
¼ tsp. pepper
1 tsp. paprika
½ lb. sausage or hamburger
6 slices American process cheese
6 hamburger buns

• Combine tomato sauce, onion, parsley, salt, pepper and paprika. Cook until thick, about 10 minutes.
• Brown sausage; break into small pieces with a fork.
• Spoon a tablespoonful of warm tomato sauce into each bun, then a spoonful of meat; top with a slice of cheese. Brown open buns in hot oven (400°) 8 to 10 minutes. Makes 6 servings.

CHEESE-DRIED BEEF FILLING

No one can guess what makes this sandwich filling so good

1 (3 oz.) pkg. cream cheese
1 tblsp. milk (optional)
½ c. shredded dried beef
1 tblsp. prepared horse-radish
1 tblsp. cooked salad dressing

• Cream cheese with milk. Add remaining ingredients. Makes ¾ cup.

Two Swiss Cheese Dishes

SWISS SOUFFLE

Some country cooks hold you should never cook mild, nut-sweet Swiss cheese; others rate it a top-notch ingredient

2 tblsp. butter or margarine
2 tblsp. flour
½ tsp. dry mustard
½ tsp. salt
⅛ tsp. pepper
1 c. milk
¼ lb. (1 c.) Swiss cheese, grated
4 eggs, separated

• Melt butter in small saucepan. Blend in flour, mustard, salt and pepper.
• Add milk gradually and cook until mixture thickens, stirring constantly. Simmer for 1 minute.
• Add cheese; stir until it melts.
• Beat egg whites until stiff but not dry. Then beat yolks until thick.
• Pour hot mixture into beaten yolks, stirring constantly. Fold in egg whites.
• Pour mixture slowly into top of 2 qt. double boiler. Cover; cook over gently boiling water 1 hour, or until knife inserted comes out clean. (Do not let water touch top pan of double boiler containing cheese mixture.)
• Serve at once. Makes 6 servings.

CHEESE PIE

This pie and Swiss cheese soufflé come from a famous Wisconsin cheese area

1½ c. grated Swiss cheese
1 tsp. minced onion
4 eggs
1 tsp. salt
1 c. heavy cream
Pastry for 8" pie shell

• Combine cheese, onion, eggs, salt and cream. Mix well. Pour into chilled, unbaked pie shell.
• Bake in hot oven (400°) 10 minutes. Reduce heat to slow (300°) and bake 40 minutes, or until knife comes out clean.

Creamy Cottage Cheese

Cottage cheese is wonderful in salads, with every kind of fruit, melon and crisp greens. Make a colorful, interesting salad this way: add fruit to your choice of flavored gelatin and chill until firm (try crushed pineapple in orange flavor gelatin). Cut into cubes. Surround mounds of cottage cheese with these colorful cubes and fresh dates or your choice of other fresh, canned or cooked dried fruits.

Plump cooked prunes, pitted, stuffed with cottage cheese and garnished with dots of pimiento or dabs of orange marmalade, make a tempting salad.

WOMEN'S LUNCHEON

Cheese-Pineapple Salad
Chicken Sandwiches
Pickles
Peach Sundae
Coffee

MOLDED CHEESE AND PINEAPPLE SALAD

Serve this two-toned salad on crisp greens and pass mayonnaise

1 (3 oz.) pkg. lemon flavor gelatin
1 c. boiling water
1 c. heavy cream, whipped
1½ c. cottage cheese
1 (3 oz.) pkg. lime flavor gelatin
1 c. boiling water
1 c. pineapple juice
1 c. crushed pineapple

• Dissolve lemon flavor gelatin in 1 c. boiling water. Chill until slightly thickened. Beat until light and fluffy.

• Fold in whipped cream. Add cottage cheese. Pour into 10 individual molds to partly fill them.

• Dissolve lime flavor gelatin in boiling water. Add pineapple juice. Chill until slightly thickened. Add pineapple.

• Pour onto lemon layer, filling molds. Chill until firm. Makes 8 to 10 servings.

FRUIT-COTTAGE CHEESE RING

Sparks up the meal with color and flavor

1 (1 lb.) can fruit cocktail
1 (3 oz.) pkg. lime flavor gelatin
1 c. hot water
¾ c. ginger ale
2 tblsp. lemon juice
2 c. creamed cottage cheese
2 tblsp. mayonnaise or salad dressing
¼ c. chopped pecans
Lettuce

• Drain fruit cocktail.

• Dissolve gelatin in hot water; add ginger ale. Divide into two equal parts. Add lemon juice and drained fruit to one part. Pour into 5 cup ring mold. Chill until firm.

• Blend together cottage cheese and mayonnaise. Add pecans and remaining gelatin. Pour over congealed fruit layer. Chill until firm.

• Makes 8 servings. Good with Minted Mayonnaise.

Minted Mayonnaise: Combine 2 tblsp. finely chopped mint leaves and 1 tsp. lemon juice. Mash leaves a little with tip of spoon to extract flavor. Add 1 tsp. grated lemon rind and 1 c. mayonnaise or mayonnaise-type salad dressing. Makes about 1 cup.

PINEAPPLE-CHEESE PIE

Fluffy filling in crisp pastry—a dessert to spring on company

¾ c. evaporated milk
1 c. drained, crushed pineapple
¼ c. sugar
½ tsp. salt
1 beaten egg
¼ c. lemon flavor gelatin
1 c. cream style cottage cheese, sieved
1 baked (9") pie shell

• Chill milk in bowl in refrigerator.

• Combine pineapple, sugar, salt and egg in heavy saucepan. Cook over low heat until thickened, stirring constantly. Remove from heat. Add gelatin; stir until dissolved.

• Beat milk until thick and fluffy. Fold in the fruit mixture. Then fold in cottage cheese. Chill 20 minutes.

• Turn into baked pie shell. Chill several hours, or overnight, before cutting. Makes 6 servings.

FLAVORFUL FRUIT VARIATIONS

Fruited Cheese Pie: In basic recipe (above), use only ½ c. drained, crushed pineapple, ⅓ c. sugar, and 2 tblsp. each strawberry flavor and lemon flavor gelatin. Fold 1 c. sliced fresh strawberries (or other berries) into fruit mixture before folding in cottage cheese. Garnish with strawberries, sliced lengthwise, and puffs of whipped cream.

Cherry Cheese Pie: Omit pineapple; substitute 1 c. drained red sour cherries, ½ c. sugar, 2 tblsp. cherry juice. Use 2 tblsp. each cherry and lemon flavor gelatin.

Heart-of-Gold Cheese Pie: Omit pineapple; substitute 1 c. chopped drained peaches or apricots (canned or dried-cooked), ⅓ c. sugar, ¼ c. orange flavor gelatin; flavor with ½ tsp. almond extract. Garnish with mint sprigs and fruit.

POINSETTIA CHEESECAKE

A welcome dessert for the holiday season—be sure to serve coffee with it

1¼ c. graham cracker crumbs (about 18 crackers)
¼ c. sugar
½ c. butter or margarine
1 c. cream style cottage cheese, sieved
2 (3 oz.) pkgs. cream cheese
2 eggs
½ c. sugar
1 tsp. vanilla
¼ tsp. salt
½ c. dairy sour cream
2 tblsp. sugar
½ tsp. vanilla
3 maraschino cherries, quartered
3 citron strips

• Combine crumbs and ¼ c. sugar.

• Melt butter; cool. Mix thoroughly with crumbs. Press mixture onto bottom and sides of a well greased 9" spring-form pan (or other round pan with deep sides). Bake in moderate oven (350°) 8 minutes. Cool.

• Blend until smooth cottage cheese, cream cheese, eggs, the ½ c. sugar, 1 tsp. vanilla and salt. Pour into crust. Bake in moderate oven (350°) about 18 minutes, or until set.

• Blend together cream, sugar and vanilla. Spread over top of cheesecake.

• Arrange cherries and citron, poinsettia fashion, over cream topping. Chill overnight. Makes 8 servings.

WHITE AND GOLD SANDWICHES

Spread slices of whole wheat bread with snowy cottage cheese. Top each open-face sandwich with drained, canned peach halves, dusted lightly with nutmeg. Serve with forks. For accompaniments have chicken or tuna salad and coffee or tea.

13

Apples

This chapter is chock-full of apple treats—the firsts from farm kitchens, where the red-cheeked fruit is a staple food, like potatoes, chicken, eggs and milk. No wonder FARM JOURNAL has collected so many superior recipes through the years!

Apple cookery is in season around the calendar. But when branches bend with fruit in autumn, apple time reaches its colorful, flavorful peak. Spicy fruit butter bubbles in ovens and glasses of clear amber jelly sparkle on cabinet counters. Juice flows from cider presses, and good farm cooks pour some of it into measuring cups for baking and cooking.

If you haven't tasted our old-fashioned Cider and Spice cake, a pleasant new experience in eating awaits you. And hot apple punch with its come-hither aroma is a hostess' dream. We like to tantalize guests in our Countryside Kitchens with its fragrance and then delight them with steaming cups of punch. Thick juicy pies and dumplings also are at their best in the fall.

Winter brings hearty apple pancakes and muffins, fried apples and sausage, lush pudding-desserts, and a horde of salads in which the unpeeled fruit flashes its bright red, yellow and green bits. And how would mincemeat taste without apples? Or cold weather meals with never a king-sized baked apple stuffed with raisins, nuts and spice or brown sugar and butter, swimming in cream?

Spring gives canned applesauce and apple slices a big rush, for blossom-laden trees promise more fruit on the way. Then applesauce cake reigns on the cake stands. It's always apple pie time, but in spring good cooks use a heavier hand with spices than in the prime harvest season.

Summer and its apple crop arrive almost before spring has lavished its lilacs. Then comes tart-sweet green apple pie, rival of all desserts and second to none. Scoops of ice cream top the faintly warm pieces of pie in a great American original—apple pie à la mode. Frequently slices of cheese accompany the glistening, sugar-topped apple pie wedges. No library has a more valuable gold mine of appealing recipes than country kitchens.

Pies and Cobblers

QUICK APPLE PIE

One of the tastiest apple pies that ever came brown and fragrant from the oven

5 to 6 tart cooking apples
1 c. sugar
1 tsp. cinnamon
⅛ tsp. salt
2 to 3 tblsp. water
2 tblsp. butter or margarine
½ pkg. prepared pie crust mix
Sugar

• Pare and core apples; dice or slice (need about 5 c.).
• Mix sugar, cinnamon and salt; sprinkle over apples; toss lightly.
• Put sugar-coated apples in 9″ pie pan; add water; dot with butter.
• Sprinkle pie crust mix over top of apples or cut chilled stick of mix into thin slices; cover apples. Sprinkle with sugar.
• Bake in moderate oven (350°) 45 minutes or until apples are tender. Serve plain, with whipped cream or ice cream. Makes 6 servings.

FAVORITE APPLE PIE

A pie that lives up to its name—plain or caramelized

6 large tart apples
Pastry for 2-crust (9″) pie
2 tblsp. flour
½ c. granulated sugar
½ c. brown sugar, firmly packed
¾ tsp. cinnamon
¼ tsp. nutmeg
⅛ tsp. ginger
⅛ tsp. salt
1 tblsp. lemon juice
3 tblsp. butter or margarine

• Peel and quarter apples into saucepan (cut each into about 4 slices). Add ¼ c. cold water; simmer until tender, about 5 minutes. Cool.
• Line 9″ pie pan with ½ pastry; fill with apples.
• Combine remaining ingredients, except butter; sprinkle over apples; dot with butter. Moisten edges of undercrust.
• Adjust top crust with 6 vents (cut like chevrons—1 in each piece); trim and seal edges.
• Bake in very hot oven (450°) 10 minutes; reduce heat to moderate (350°) and bake 45 minutes longer. Makes 6 servings.

Caramel Variation: Cover bottom pastry with ¼ c. melted butter or margarine; spread evenly with ½ c. brown sugar, then sprinkle with ½ c. pecans. Follow above recipe for apple pie, using only ¼ c. brown sugar. This makes a luscious caramelized apple pie.

DEEP-DISH APPLE PIE

For the apple pie men around your table

Filling:

9 to 12 apples (2½ qts. sliced)
1½ c. sugar
½ tsp. cinnamon
½ tsp. nutmeg
Dash of mace
¾ tsp. salt
3 tblsp. butter or margarine

Pastry:

1½ c. sifted flour
½ c. shortening
3 tblsp. cold milk
Cream

• Peel and slice apples to fill 12×8×2″ baking dish. Combine sugar, spices and ¼ tsp. salt; sprinkle over apples, mixing lightly. Dot with butter.

• Sift together flour and ½ tsp. salt; cut in shortening until pieces are size of small peas. Add milk by teaspoonfuls, tossing with fork until mixture is just dampened.

• Turn mixture onto square of waxed paper; gather up corners, pressing from outside to form compact ball. Roll out about ⅛″ thick between two sheets of waxed paper or on floured board; place over apples. Brush with cream; cut steam vents.

• Bake in very hot oven (450°) 15 minutes; reduce heat to moderate (350°) and bake 45 minutes longer. Makes 8 to 10 servings.

SOUR-CREAM APPLE PIE

Come on, sour cream fans—here's your apple pie

2 tblsp. flour
⅛ tsp. salt
¾ c. sugar
1 egg, unbeaten
1 c. dairy sour cream
1 tsp. vanilla
¼ tsp. nutmeg
2 c. diced apples
Pastry for 9″ pie shell

• Sift together flour, salt and sugar; add egg, cream, vanilla and nutmeg. Beat to smooth, thin batter. Stir in apples.

• Pour into pastry-lined pie pan. Bake in hot oven (400°) 15 minutes, then in moderate oven (350°) 30 minutes. Remove from oven; top with Spicy Topping.

Spicy Topping: Mix well ⅓ c. sugar, ⅓ c. flour, 1 tsp. cinnamon and ¼ c. butter or margarine. Sprinkle over pie. Return to hot oven (400°) 10 minutes to brown.

FROSTED APPLE-RAISIN PIE

Pastry for 2-crust (9″) pie
¾ c. sugar
2 tblsp. flour
⅛ tsp. salt
½ tsp. cinnamon
6 c. peeled, sliced tart apples
½ c. seedless raisins
2 tblsp. orange juice
3 tblsp. butter or margarine

• Divide pastry in 2 parts; roll out half to line 9″ pie pan.

• Combine sugar, flour, salt and cinnamon; mix with apples and raisins; place in pie pan. Sprinkle with orange juice; dot with butter.

• Cover with top crust; seal edges.

• Bake in hot oven (400°) 15 minutes; reduce heat to moderate (350°) and bake 40 minutes longer. Makes 6 servings.

Confectioners Sugar Frosting: Mix together 1 c. sugar, 3 tblsp. strained orange juice and 1 tsp. grated orange rind. Spread over hot pie.

TWO-FRUIT COBBLER

Red sour cherry purée makes this a rosy dessert to remember

1½ c. flour
1½ tsp. baking powder
1 tblsp. sugar
¼ tsp. salt
¼ c. shortening
1 egg, slightly beaten
¼ c. milk
1½ c. fruit purée
1 large apple, sliced
¼ c. sugar

• Sift together flour, baking powder, 1 tblsp. sugar and salt; cut in shortening.

• Combine egg and milk; add to flour mixture. Knead 30 seconds on floured board; pat to fit top of 8×8×2″ dish.

• Combine purée, apple and ¼ c. sugar. Turn into baking dish, cover with dough, bake in hot oven (400°) 25 to 30 minutes. Serve warm. Makes 6 to 8 servings.

Apple Breads and Cakes

Good cooks in Washington State, where apple trees frequently march right up to the front door, have a habit of adding finely chopped or grated raw apple to many baked foods. They like to stir ½ c. grated fruit into chocolate cake batter, for instance—keeps the cake moist longer. Both the sandwich breads that follow use uncooked apples. Spread generously with butter—delicious with coffee or tea.

APRICOT-APPLE RING

Inviting, with its golden crust

⅔ c. boiling water
1 c. chopped dried apricots
2 c. sifted flour
2½ tsp. baking powder
¼ tsp. baking soda
½ tsp. salt
½ tsp. cinnamon
Milk
½ c. shortening
¾ c. sugar
1 egg, beaten
1 c. finely diced, unpeeled apples
⅓ c. chopped pecans
Whole pecan halves

• Pour boiling water over apricots; let stand.

• Sift together flour, baking powder, soda, salt and cinnamon.

• Drain apricots. Add milk to apricot liquid to make ⅔ c. liquid.

• Cream shortening; add sugar gradually, then egg; mix thoroughly. Add dry ingredients alternately with liquid. Beat after each addition.

• Fold in apricots, apples and nuts.

• Spoon into well greased 9" ring mold; decorate with whole pecans.

• Bake in moderate oven (350°) 30 to 35 minutes. You may also bake batter in 9×5×3" loaf pan 50 to 55 minutes.

FRESH APPLE BREAD

Oranges and apples get together in this California loaf. Excellent for cheese sandwiches

2 c. sifted flour
1 tsp. baking powder
½ tsp. baking soda
½ tsp. salt
⅓ c. shortening
1 c. sugar
1 egg
⅓ c. orange juice
¾ c. raisins
¼ c. chopped nuts
1 c. finely chopped apples
1 tblsp. grated orange rind

• Sift together flour, baking powder, soda and salt.

• Cream shortening; add sugar gradually. Add egg; beat thoroughly.

• Add dry ingredients and orange juice alternately to creamed mixture; blend well after each addition. Add remaining ingredients; mix well.

• Pour into three well greased No. 2-tin cans. Bake in moderate oven (350°) 45 minutes. Makes 3 loaves.

Suggestion: Make open-face cheese sandwiches with this apple bread for a party. Garnish with slices of pimiento-stuffed olives.

APPLE NUT BREAD

A sandwich special from the heart of apple land—Washington State

½ c. butter or margarine
1 c. sugar
2 eggs, unbeaten
1 tsp. vanilla
1½ tblsp. dairy sour cream
2 c. sifted flour
1 tsp. baking powder
1 tsp. baking soda
½ tsp. salt
1 c. chopped nuts
1 c. chopped unpeeled apples

• Cut butter into sugar; add eggs, one at a time, mixing well after each addition. Blend in vanilla and sour cream.
• Sift together dry ingredients; add nuts. Combine with first mixture. Stir in apples. Pour into greased 9×5×3″ pan or 2 small loaf pans.
• Bake in slow oven (325°) about 1 hour. Makes 1 large or 2 small loaves.

APPLE GRIDDLE CAKES

Quick with the butter and syrup

2 c. sifted flour
5 tsp. baking powder
2 tsp. salt
3 tblsp. sugar
1 tsp. cinnamon
2 c. sweet milk
6 tblsp. melted shortening or oil
2 eggs, beaten
1 c. finely chopped unpeeled apples

• Sift together flour, baking powder, salt, sugar and cinnamon.

• Add milk, shortening and flour mixture to eggs; beat until smooth. Fold in apples.

• Heat griddle or heavy frying pan slowly until moderately hot. Test temperature by sprinkling a few drops of water on it—if they "dance," temperature is right. Or use electric griddle, following manufacturer's directions.

• Grease griddle very lightly before baking. Pour in about ¼ c. batter for each cake. Bake until top is bubbly and edges dry; turn and brown on other side.

• Makes 2½ dozen cakes 4″ to 5″ in diameter or one dozen 6″ to 7″ in diameter.

Sour Milk Griddle Cakes: Substitute 2¼ c. sour milk or buttermilk for sweet milk. For leavening use 1 tsp. baking soda and 1 tblsp. baking powder.

APPLE TREAT CAKE

1 c. sifted flour
1½ tsp. baking powder
½ tsp. salt
½ c. sugar
¼ c. shortening
1 egg, beaten
¼ c. milk
4 c. sliced, peeled cored tart apples
1 tsp. cinnamon
¼ tsp. nutmeg
3 tblsp. melted butter or margarine
⅓ c. currant jelly or apricot jam
1 tblsp. hot water

• Sift together flour, baking powder, salt and ¼ c. sugar. Cut in shortening until like coarse meal. Stir in combined egg and milk.

• Spread dough in greased 8×12×2″ baking dish. Arrange apples, slightly overlapping, in parallel rows on top. Sprinkle with mixture of cinnamon, nutmeg, remaining sugar and butter. Bake in hot oven (400°) 35 minutes, until apples are tender.

• Beat jelly with enough of the hot water to make syrup. Brush over cake.

• Serve warm, cut into squares, with soft custard or cream. Makes 6 to 8 servings.

APPLESAUCE FRUIT CAKE

One of Farm Journal's 5-star recipes—you'll use it over and over again

3 c. thick applesauce
1 c. shortening
2 c. sugar
1 lb. dates, pitted and chopped
1 lb. light or dark raisins
1 lb. nuts, coarsely chopped
¼ lb. candied cherries, quartered
¼ lb. candied pineapple, chopped
¼ lb. citron, finely chopped
4½ c. sifted flour
4 tsp. baking soda
1 tsp. nutmeg
2½ tsp. ground cinnamon
½ tsp. ground cloves
1 tsp. salt

• Boil applesauce, shortening and sugar together 5 minutes, stirring occasionally. Let stand until cool.

• Line four (1 lb.) coffee cans with waxed paper. (Or use any desired pans which together will hold 11 cups when filled ¾ full. Molds which can't be lined with waxed paper should be well greased and floured.)

• Mix fruit and nuts together in a 3 qt. mixing bowl. Sift together flour, soda and spices over fruit and nuts, mixing until each piece of fruit is coated.

• Stir in cooled applesauce mixture. Turn into greased or lined cans. Bake in a very slow oven (250°) about 2 hours, or until wooden pick inserted in center of cake comes out clean. When cakes are as brown as desired, cover with brown paper. Remove baked cakes from cans; cool on racks. Store in moisture-proof wrapping in a cold place, or freeze. (Cakes frozen in cans with tight lids need not be wrapped.)

• Let mellow at least 2 weeks before cutting. Before serving, bring to a boil ½ c. light corn syrup and ¼ c. water. Cool to lukewarm; pour over cold cakes for a shiny glaze. Decorate immediately with candied fruit and whole nuts. Makes 4 cakes.

CIDER AND SPICE CAKE

Grandmother called it October cake, but today folks call it good!

3 c. sifted cake flour
1 tblsp. baking powder
¾ tsp. salt
1 tsp. cinnamon
1 tsp. nutmeg
¼ tsp. ground cloves
¾ c. shortening
1½ c. brown sugar, firmly packed
3 eggs, beaten
1 tblsp. lemon juice
1 c. apple cider

• Sift together flour, baking powder, salt and spices.

• Cream shortening and sugar; add eggs; beat until thoroughly blended.

• Add lemon juice to cider. Add alternately with dry ingredients to creamed mixture, beating after each addition.

• Pour batter into 3 greased round 8" pans. Bake in moderate oven (350°) 25 to 30 minutes.

• Let stand 10 minutes; turn out to cool. Spread Cider Filling between layers; frost with Creamy Cider Icing.

Cider Filling: Combine ½ c. sugar, ¼ tsp. salt and 3 tblsp. cornstarch in saucepan. Add 1 c. cider; mix. Cook over low heat, stirring constantly, until thick and clear. Remove from heat. Add 2 tblsp. lemon juice and 2 tblsp. butter or margarine. Cool.

Creamy Cider Icing: Melt ½ c. butter or margarine in saucepan; blend in 3½ tblsp. flour and ¼ tsp. salt. Add ½ c. cider; stir well. Bring to boil; cook 1 minute, stirring constantly. Remove from heat. Add 3 c. sifted confectioners sugar and beat well. Add ½ c. finely chopped nuts.

Reminders for Exploring Cooks: Substitute cider for water when baking apples. Baste ham with cider as it bakes. You'll win compliments.

COMPANY APPLE CAKE

A good Swedish cook gave us this recipe that makes six servings. She brought it from her native country

½ c. butter or margarine
1 c. sifted confectioners sugar
2 eggs
1 c. sifted cake flour
1 tsp. baking powder
Grated rind of 1 lemon

• Cream together butter and sugar; add eggs, one at a time, beating well after each addition.

• Combine flour, baking powder and lemon rind; add to creamed mixture; blend well. Pour batter into greased 8" layer pan.

• Bake in moderate oven (350°) 25 to 30 minutes. Cool. Prepare Rosy Apples.

Rosy Apples:

1 c. sugar
2 c. water
Juice of 1 lemon
1 small cinnamon stick
Few drops red food color
5 to 6 cooking apples

• Combine in saucepan and cook slowly 10 minutes: sugar, water, lemon juice, cinnamon and food color.

• Peel, core and quarter apples. Simmer slowly in syrup until tender; cool. Arrange apples on cake. Top with meringue; bake in slow oven (300°) 20 to 30 minutes. Serve with chilled Vanilla Sauce.

Meringue: Beat 3 egg whites and ½ tsp. cream of tartar to form soft peaks. Gradually add 1 c. sifted confectioners sugar and ½ tsp. vanilla.

Vanilla Sauce: Beat 3 egg yolks; slowly add ⅔ c. sifted confectioners sugar and ½ tsp. vanilla. Fold in 1 c. heavy cream, whipped; chill.

APPLE LAYER CAKE

Perk up dinner with this dessert—tender cake and tart-sweet apples

1 c. butter or margarine
1½ c. sugar
3 egg yolks, beaten
1 tblsp. grated lemon rind
2 c. sifted flour
2 tsp. baking powder
½ tsp. salt
1 c. dry crumbs (bread or cracker)
4 large apples, peeled, cored and sliced
1 tblsp. cinnamon
¼ c. chopped pecans
¼ c. melted butter or margarine
3 egg whites
6 tblsp. sugar

• Cream butter and 1 c. sugar until fluffy; blend in yolks and rind.

• Sift together flour, baking powder and salt; add to creamed mixture; add crumbs.

• Blend together (with pastry blender, knives or finger tips), until like cornmeal.

• Divide in half; press one half smoothly over bottom of 8×12" dish.

• Spread apple slices evenly over crumb layer; sprinkle with mixture of ½ c. sugar, cinnamon, nuts and butter. Cover with remaining crumb mixture.

• Bake in moderate oven (350°) about 45 minutes.

• While baking, make meringue of egg whites and sugar; spread over top of cake. Brown in hot oven (425°) about 5 minutes. Makes 8 servings.

APPLESAUCE TRICKS

Tint delicate pink by adding red cinnamon candies or a few drops of red food color. Serve faintly warm in sherbet glasses and top with vanilla or butter pecan ice cream. Add pineapple juice instead of water when making applesauce.

NOBBY APPLE CAKE

The wife of a New England apple grower, Family Test Group member, invented this Farm Journal 5-star recipe

3 tblsp. butter or margarine
1 c. sugar
1 egg, beaten
½ tsp. cinnamon
½ tsp. nutmeg
½ tsp. salt
1 tsp. baking soda
1 c. sifted flour
3 c. diced apples
¼ c. chopped nuts
1 tsp. vanilla

• Cream butter and sugar; add eggs; mix well.
• Sift dry ingredients together. Add to creamed mixture. Stir in diced apples, nuts and vanilla.
• Pour into greased 8×8×2" pan. Bake in moderate oven (350°) 40 to 45 minutes. Serve hot or cold, with or without whipped cream or ice cream. Makes 8 to 9 servings.

Apple Salads

APPLE-CHEESE SALAD

You'll never find another picture-pretty salad that's more delicious

¼ c. small, red cinnamon candies
1 (3 oz.) pkg. cherry flavor gelatin
1 c. hot water
1½ c. sweetened applesauce (canned or homemade)
1 (8 oz.) pkg. cream cheese
½ c. nuts, chopped
½ c. finely cut celery
½ c. mayonnaise-type salad dressing

• Mix cinnamon candies and gelatin, pour on hot water; stir to dissolve. Stir in applesauce.
• Pour half of mixture in 8×8×2" pan. Chill.
• Blend together cream cheese (room temperature), nuts and celery; add salad dressing. Spread in layer over firm apple mixture. Pour on remaining apple mixture. Chill until firm, unmold; garnish with small bunches of sugared grapes. Makes 6 servings.

APPLE CHIP SALAD

A Hollowe'en delight—also rings the bell in winter meals

2 (3 oz.) pkgs. apple flavor gelatin
2 c. hot water
2 c. apple cider
2 c. diced, unpeeled apples
¾ c. coarsely broken nuts

• Empty gelatin into bowl. Add water; stir to dissolve; add cider.
• Chill until mixture thickens slightly.
• Fold in apples and nuts; pour into mold or 8×8×2" pan. Makes 8 servings.

APPLE-GRAPEFRUIT SALAD

You need apples with rosy cheeks to make this beauty

1 (3 oz.) pkg. lemon flavor gelatin
3½ c. boiling water
1 apple
1 (3 oz.) pkg. lime flavor gelatin
1 c. diced unpeeled apples
½ c. coarsely chopped nuts
1 (1 lb. 4 oz.) can grapefruit sections, well drained

• Dissolve lemon gelatin in 1½ c. water. Cool. Pour about ½ c. in 2 qt. mold; let set. Chill remaining lemon gelatin until syrupy.
• Core apple; cut into narrow wedges and arrange in pattern, skin side down, on gelatin in bottom of mold. Pour remaining lemon gelatin into mold; let set until firm.

• Dissolve lime gelatin in remaining 2 c. water; cool until syrupy. Add diced apples, nuts and grapefruit. Spoon over set layer in mold; chill until firm.
• Unmold on platter; surround with crisp salad greens; serve with mayonnaise. Makes 10 to 12 servings.

POINSETTIA SALAD

Red, cinnamon apples make the petals for a gorgeous holiday salad

6 medium apples
1½ c. water
1 c. sugar
6 very thin lemon slices
¼ c. red cinnamon candy
8 pineapple slices
1 hard-cooked egg yolk

• Peel and core apples; cut each into 8 lengthwise slices.
• Put water, sugar, lemon and cinnamon candies in saucepan; bring to boil. Add apples; simmer slowly in syrup until tender but firm, about 10 minutes. Chill in syrup until serving time.
• Place pineapple slices on individual salad plates. Arrange 6 drained apple slices on pineapple to form flower petals.
• Rub egg yolk through sieve; sprinkle a bit in center of apples. Add a few sprigs of greens for stem. Makes 8 servings.

SEPTEMBER APPLE SALAD

A surprise—apples and cucumbers pair off in a Farm Journal 5-star salad

2 c. diced unpeeled apples
2 c. diced peeled cucumbers
½ tsp. salt
¼ c. lemon juice
½ c. salad dressing
¼ c. chopped nuts (optional)
Lettuce

• Toss apples and cucumbers with salt; sprinkle with lemon juice. Mix in salad dressing and nuts. Serve chilled on lettuce. Makes 6 servings.

Apple Desserts, Puddings, Dumplings

VIRGINIA APPLE PUDDING

This Dixieland treat came to us from a friend in the Shenandoah Valley of Virginia, the heart of a famous apple country. You mix and bake the pudding in the same dish, tossing the apples on top of the batter. During baking the batter rises above the fruit forming a chewy, brown crust. Its texture contrasts most delightfully with the mellow flavor of the fruit. In our Countryside Kitchens, we served the pudding with different members of the cream family—plain pour cream, whipped cream and ice cream. We also enjoyed it with lemon sauce.

½ c. butter or margarine
1 c. sugar
1 c. sifted flour
2 tsp. baking powder
¼ tsp. salt
¼ tsp. cinnamon
1 c. milk
2 c. cooked or canned apple slices

• Melt butter in 2 qt. casserole.
• Combine next six ingredients to make batter; pour on butter. Drain apples; pile in center of batter.
• Bake in moderate oven (375°) until batter covers fruit and crust browns, 30 to 40 minutes. Makes 4 to 6 servings.

OLD-TIME APPLE DUMPLINGS

The tart-sweet sauce emphasizes the fruity flavor of the apples

2 c. sifted flour
2 tsp. baking powder
½ tsp. salt
½ c. shortening
⅔ c. milk
6 baking apples
⅓ c. sugar
¼ tsp. cinnamon
1 tblsp. butter or margarine
Milk

• Sift together flour, baking powder and salt; cut in shortening. Stir in milk; mix until soft dough is formed.

• Turn out; knead lightly. Roll ⅛"; cut into 6 squares.

• Core apples; peel; place 1 on each square. Combine sugar and cinnamon; sprinkle into center of each apple. Add ½ tsp. butter to each.

• Moisten edges of dough; press corners up over apples; brush with milk. Place in greased baking pan.

• Bake in moderate oven (350°) 30 minutes. Serve with Sweet-Sour Sauce. Makes 6 servings.

Sweet Sour Sauce:

2 c. water
⅓ c. vinegar
⅓ c. butter or margarine
⅓ c. flour
1 c. sugar
1 tsp. cinnamon
⅛ tsp. nutmeg

• Heat water, vinegar and butter together.

• Combine remaining ingredients; mix thoroughly. Stir into hot mixture; cook over low heat, stirring until thickened. Pour warm over apple dumplings. Makes about 2½ cups.

APPLE DUMPLINGS

Spicy, sweet-tart apples hide under crisp pastry jackets

3 tblsp. butter or margarine
¾ tsp. cinnamon
¾ tsp. allspice
¾ tsp. nutmeg
⅓ c. sifted brown sugar
Pastry based on 2 c. flour
8 medium apples, peeled and cored
3 tblsp. jelly
1½ c. boiling water
1½ c. sugar
3 tblsp. fruit juice (orange, lemon, pineapple, apricot, etc.)
Food color (optional)

• Make paste of butter, spices and brown sugar.

• Roll out pastry ⅛" thick; cut into eight (6") squares. Place apple in center of each; put jelly or orange marmalade in cavity, and spread spicy paste over each apple.

• Moisten edges of pastry; bring points together over apple; seal sides firmly. Roll leftover pastry; cut into "streamers" to lay across tops of dumplings.

• Place in large greased baking dish, about 11×15"; bake in moderate oven (375°) 30 minutes.

• While apples are baking, make syrup of water, sugar and fruit juice; simmer to dissolve sugar. Pour over apples; bake 10 to 20 minutes more, basting frequently, to give attractive glaze. A little color may be added to syrup. Serve warm with cream. Makes 8 servings.

APPLE-WALNUT CRISP

Nuts and apples—a natural twosome

1 egg, well beaten
1 c. diced apples
1 c. chopped nuts
⅔ c. sugar
2 tblsp. flour
1 tsp. baking powder

• Combine egg, apples and nuts.
• Sift together sugar, flour and baking powder. Combine with apple mixture; spread in greased round 8" layer pan.
• Bake in moderate oven (350°) 35 to 40 minutes. Makes 6 servings.

MINCEMEAT BROWN BETTY

Hearty, homespun favorite

2 c. coarse dry bread crumbs
4 apples, sliced in eighths
1 c. prepared mincemeat
½ c. sugar
¼ tsp. cinnamon
¼ tsp. salt
3 tblsp. lemon juice (1 lemon)
¼ c. water
2 tblsp. butter or margarine

• Put ⅓ of crumbs into bottom of buttered 1½ to 2 qt. casserole; cover with half of apples and half of mincemeat.
• Mix sugar, cinnamon and salt together; sprinkle half over mincemeat.
• Add layer of crumbs; then one of apples and mincemeat; sprinkle with remaining sugar mixture.
• Top with remaining crumbs; pour lemon juice and water over all; dot with butter.
• Cover; bake in moderate oven (350°) 20 minutes; uncover; bake 15 minutes longer. Serve hot or cold with plain or whipped cream. Makes 5 servings.

APPLE CAKE PIE

Cake or pie—good eating by any name

5 large apples, cored and thinly sliced
1 tsp. lemon juice
¾ c. sugar
¼ c. butter or margarine
1 egg, beaten
½ c. sifted flour
½ tsp. baking powder
⅛ tsp. salt

• Place apples in well greased 10" pie pan; sprinkle with lemon juice; cover with ¼ c. sugar.
• Cream together butter and remaining ½ c. sugar; add egg and mix.
• Sift together flour, baking powder and salt; mix with creamed mixture. Spread over fruit.
• Bake in moderate oven (350°) 45 minutes. Serve hot or cold, with thin custard sauce or whipped cream. Makes 8 servings.

Custard Sauce: Combine 3 beaten egg yolks, ¼ c. sugar and dash of salt. Stir in 2 c. scalded milk. Cook over hot water, stirring constantly, until mixture coats spoon. Add 1 tsp. vanilla. Chill. Makes about 2½ cups.

APPLE MYSTERY DESSERT

Everyone who eats it asks how to make it

2 c. graham cracker crumbs
½ c. melted butter or margarine
¼ c. sugar
3 egg yolks, well beaten
1 (15 oz.) can sweetened condensed milk
1 c. thick applesauce
⅓ c. lemon juice
1 tblsp. grated lemon rind
3 egg whites, beaten stiff

• Mix together crumbs, butter and sugar; reserve ½ c. mixture. Press remaining crumbs in bottom and on sides of 8×12" pan.
• Combine yolks, milk, applesauce, lemon juice and rind. Fold in egg whites. Pour into crumb crust. Top with remaining crumbs. Chill several hours or overnight. (May also freeze for later use.)
• Serve with whipped cream. Garnish with mint leaves if available. Makes 10 to 12 servings.

CIDER SHIMMY

Just the dessert for Sunday dinner during Indian Summer

2 envelopes unflavored gelatin
4 c. cider
½ c. sugar
1 c. chopped or sliced apples, or other fruit
2 egg whites

• Soak gelatin in ¼ c. cider.
• Bring 2 c. cider to boil and add to gelatin. Stir until dissolved. Add sugar and remaining cider. Chill until mixture is syrupy.
• Pour half of syrupy mixture into large or individual molds to cover bottom well. Arrange fruit in bottom as desired. Chill until fruit is set.
• Beat other half of congealed mixture until frothy. Fold in stiffly beaten egg whites. Pour over fruit mixture and chill.
• Unmold and serve with custard sauce made with egg yolks. Makes 8 servings.

BUTTERSCOTCH BAKED APPLES

Buttery, sweet sauce and apples—you couldn't ask for more

6 baking apples
⅓ c. light cream
⅓ c. dark corn syrup
⅓ c. chopped nuts

• Wash and core apples; place in greased shallow baking dish.
• Combine cream, corn syrup and nuts; use to fill centers of apples.
• Bake until tender in moderate oven (350°). Serve with Butterscotch Sauce.

Butterscotch Sauce: Combine 1 c. light cream, ⅓ c. dark corn syrup, 2 tblsp. butter or margarine and 1 tsp. vanilla. Cook over low heat until thickened (20 to 30 minutes), stirring occasionally. Serve warm. Makes 6 servings.

CARAMEL CANDY APPLES

Children adore the candy-coated fruit

12 medium red apples
12 wooden skewers or orange sticks
1 lb. light-colored caramels
¼ c. light cream

• Wash and dry apples; stick skewers in stem end.
• Put caramels and cream in top of double boiler; cook over hot water, stirring occasionally, until caramels melt. Plunge apples into syrup; twirl once or twice to coat evenly.
• Place in refrigerator on tray covered with waxed paper or foil. (Takes 2 hours to harden.) Makes 12 caramel-coated apples.

HOT APPLE PUNCH

A Farm Journal 5-star recipe

2¼ c. sugar
4 c. water
2 (2½") sticks cinnamon
8 whole allspice berries
10 whole cloves
1 whole piece ginger root (about size of quarter)
4 c. orange juice (fresh, canned or reconstituted frozen)
2 c. lemon juice or a 16 oz. bottle
2 qts. apple cider or juice

• Combine sugar and water and boil 5 minutes. Remove from heat; add spices. Let beverage stand, covered, 1 hour. Strain.
• Just before serving, combine syrup, fruit juices and cider; bring quickly to boiling. Remove from heat; serve at once. Makes 4½ quarts.

14

Special Sweetenings

Hot biscuits with amber honey, a stack of steaming pancakes drenched with maple or cane syrup, frosted Caramel Layer Cake, luxuriously rich Butterscotch Pie and a big cookie jar filled with crinkly sugar-topped molasses cookies—this is country cooking at its best. The pleasing sweetness of honey, maple and cane syrups, caramelized and brown sugars and molasses is only half the story, however. It's delightful flavor that makes these old-time dishes unforgettable.

Honey is the most widely used natural sweetener the world over. It's fragrance and flavor vary with the locality, depending largely on the flowers that attract the bees. When used as an ingredient in mixing bowls, it makes baked foods stay moist longer—elevates them to the make-ahead class.

Maple sugar and syrup are not nearly so plentiful nationally as honey, but they have a band of loyal admirers, especially in the Northeast. Our recipes come from New England and upstate New York farm kitchens. Cane syrup enjoys equal popularity in the South. In areas where maple sugar and syrup are unavailable or expensive, maple-blended syrups have prestige. In the Pacific Northwest and California a bottle of maple flavoring has an honored place next to vanilla on the cupboard shelf.

When appetites pall, it's time, good cooks say, to bring out a heavy skillet and melt or caramelize sugar. They add water to dissolve the light golden brown sugar to make syrup for flavoring candy, cake, cookies, ice cream, puddings and a myriad of desserts. Grandmother called them burnt-sugar dishes, but that's a misnomer, for scorching or burning spoils the flavor—it's what the careful cook strives to avoid.

Butterscotch recipes are scattered throughout this cookbook, and prove that when butter and brown sugar get together great things happen to a dish. The same goes for molasses—we give you only a sampling of recipes in this chapter—you'll find Boston Baked Beans, Indian Pudding, gingerbread and more molasses cookies elsewhere in this book. All these treats are from farm kitchens where they are relied on for good country eating.

Honeyed Triumphs

Country cooks revel in the use of honey. Every area has its favorite kind—sourwood in the southern Appalachians, tupelo in Florida, buckwheat in Pennsylvania, mesquite in the Southwest, orange in California. Baked foods containing honey have exquisite taste and stay fresh longer. No wonder the top-ranking natural sweet has stood the test of time—the ancients prized it highly.

One enjoyable farm use of honey is honey butter, made by creaming ¼ c. butter with 2 tblsp. honey and beating in ¼ c. heavy cream, until the mixture is fluffy and smooth as satin. It's a perfect topper for warm gingerbread, pancakes and toast.

HONEY-LEMON RHUBARB PIE

A Farm-Journal 5-star recipe

4 c. rhubarb, cut in ½" pieces
1¼ c. sugar
6 tblsp. flour
¼ tsp. salt
2 tsp. grated lemon rind
⅓ c. strained honey
4 to 5 drops red food color
Pastry for 2-crust (9") pie
2 tblsp. butter or margarine

• Combine rhubarb, sugar, flour, salt and rind; mix well. Blend in honey and food color. Let stand while making pastry.

• Line 9" pie pan with pastry. Fill with rhubarb mixture; dot with butter. Adjust top crust and seal edge. (For sparkling top, brush with milk and sprinkle with sugar.)

• Bake in very hot oven (450°) 10 minutes; reduce heat to moderate (350°) and bake 35 to 45 minutes more.

Variation: Use pastry for unbaked pie shell. Sprinkle filling top with crumbly crust, made by blending together ½ c. brown sugar, ⅓ c. flour, ¼ tsp. cinnamon; cut in ¼ c. butter or margarine. Cover top with foil until last 20 minutes.

FAVORITE HONEY BARS

Cookie jar raiders go for these chewy cookies—better double the recipe

½ c. shortening
½ c. sugar
½ c. honey
1 egg, well beaten
⅔ c. sifted flour
½ tsp. baking soda
½ tsp. baking powder
¼ tsp. salt
1 c. quick-cooking rolled oats
1 c. flaked coconut
1 tsp. vanilla
½ c. chopped nuts

• Cream shortening, sugar and honey until light and fluffy. Add egg and blend.

• Sift flour with soda, baking powder and salt; add to creamed mixture. Add oats, coconut, vanilla and nuts.

• Spread in greased 10½×15" pan; bake in moderate oven (350°) 20 to 25 minutes. When cool, cut into bars, about 1½×2½". Makes 36 bars.

Variation: Sprinkle confectioners sugar over tops of bars before serving.

HONEY-FILLED COFFEE CAKE

Breakfast bread with a sparkling top and rich filling—a Farm Journal 5-star recipe

2 pkgs. granular or compressed yeast
¼ c. lukewarm water
½ c. shortening
2 tsp. salt
¼ c. sugar
1 c. scalded milk
2 eggs, beaten
4½ c. sifted flour
Honey Filling

• Sprinkle granular yeast over warm (110°) water; or crumble compressed yeast over lukewarm (85°) water. Let stand until thoroughly dissolved (5 to 15 minutes).
• Combine shortening, salt and sugar in large bowl; add scalded milk. Stir until shortening is melted, then cool until lukewarm.
• Add eggs and yeast; mix well.
• Add flour gradually, beating thoroughly after each addition. Turn onto lightly floured board and knead to a smooth dough.
• Place in greased bowl and brush top of dough with melted shortening. Cover; let rise in warm place until light and doubled (about 1½ hours).
• Punch down and let rest 10 minutes. Turn out onto floured board. Divide dough in two, keeping one half covered with cloth.
• Roll out the other half into a rectangle, about 12×16″. Brush with melted butter and spread with half the Honey Filling. Roll like jelly roll; seal edges.
• Cut into 1″ slices; make bottom layer in 10″ greased tube pan, placing slices (cut side down) so they barely touch. Arrange remaining slices in layers, covering up the spaces—with no slice directly on top of another. (This gives an interesting swirl pattern when coffee cake is sliced.)
• Prepare remaining half of dough in same manner, placing slices on top in layers as before. Cover and let rise in warm place about 30 minutes or until doubled.
• Bake in moderate oven (350°) 45 to 60 minutes, or until sides and top are well browned. (If bread browns too soon, cover with foil the last half of baking.)
• Loosen bread from pan; turn out on rack to cool. If desired, pour over glaze made by simmering together until thick (about 5 minutes): ½ c. honey, ½ c. sugar, 1 tblsp. butter or margarine and 1 tblsp. coarsely grated orange rind. Pour glaze over bread.

Honey Filling: Combine ½ c. honey, ¼ c. sugar, grated rind of 1 orange or lemon, 1 tblsp. orange or lemon juice, 1 tsp. cinnamon, ⅓ c. raisins, cut fine, ⅓ c. nuts, chopped fine and 1 tblsp. melted butter or margarine.

HONEY WAFERS

Crisp, dainty, delicious

½ c. butter
½ c. honey
2 c. sifted flour
1 tsp. baking soda
½ tsp. cinnamon
¼ tsp. cloves
¼ tsp. allspice
¼ c. crushed bran flakes

• Cream together butter and honey.
• Sift together flour, baking soda, cinnamon, cloves and allspice. Mix with bran flakes.
• Combine dry ingredients with honey and butter. Chill 1 hour, or until firm enough to roll easily.
• Roll ⅛″ thick on lightly floured board. Cut with floured cookie cutter. Bake on greased baking sheet in moderate oven (350°) 8 to 10 minutes. Makes 3 dozen.

To Store Crisp Cookies: Pack them lightly in cookie jar or container with a loose-fitting cover. If they soften, heat in a slow oven (300°) about 5 minutes before serving. Or crisp in your electric skillet (steam vent open).

FRUITED HONEY CAKE

Cake baked in a long angel food pan slices like a charm—is handsome, too

3 c. seedless raisins
3 c. currants
1¼ c. (½ lb.) candied red cherries, quartered
1 c. chopped nuts (pecans, walnuts)
3 c. sifted flour
1½ tsp. salt
1½ tsp. baking soda
½ tsp. cinnamon
½ tsp. nutmeg
½ tsp. mace
½ tsp. allspice
1 c. shortening
1 c. honey
¼ c. brown sugar, firmly packed
6 eggs, beaten
½ c. fruit juice or canned fruit syrup
6 tblsp. vinegar

• Soften raisins and currants over boiling water; dry and cool on paper towels. Mix with cherries, nuts and ½ c. flour.
• Sift together 2½ c. flour, salt, soda and spices.
• Cream shortening with honey and brown sugar until fluffy. Beat in eggs.
• Combine fruit juice and vinegar; add alternately with dry ingredients, stirring well after each addition. Blend in fruit-nut mixture.
• Pour into greased 15½ × 14½ × 4½" pan lined with greased heavy brown paper. Bake in slow oven (300°) 2 to 2½ hours. Remove from pan; cool on rack. Freeze if desired. Makes about 5 pounds.

Variation: Batter may be baked in paper-lined 10" tube pan in slow oven (300°) about 3 hours instead of in loaf pan (grease paper lining).

For a Special Highlight: Brush top (after baking) with heated corn syrup. Decorate top with candied cherries, blanched almonds and slivers of green-tinted citron. Wrap tightly in airtight layers of waxed paper, foil or clear plastic wrap. Aging improves the flavor of this fruitcake.

CHOCOLATE-NUT DROPS

Favorite from recipe files of an Iowa honey producer's wife

½ c. butter or margarine
6 tblsp. brown sugar
6 tblsp. honey
1 egg, unbeaten
1¼ c. sifted flour
½ tsp. baking soda
½ tsp. salt
Few drops hot water
½ tsp. vanilla
1 (6 oz.) pkg. semi-sweet chocolate pieces
½ c. chopped walnuts

• Cream butter; gradually add sugar and honey, mixing well. Beat in egg.
• Sift together flour, soda and salt. Add to creamed mixture. Add water and mix to blend.
• Add vanilla, chocolate pieces and nuts. Drop from teaspoon onto greased baking sheet. Bake in moderate oven (375°) 10 to 12 minutes. Cool slightly before removing from sheet. Makes about 3 dozen.

BAKED HONEY CUSTARD

Flavor change for a favorite farm dessert

4 eggs
½ c. honey
2½ c. milk
½ tsp. salt
½ tsp. almond extract

• Beat eggs slightly with a fork. Add honey, milk, salt and almond extract. Strain.
• Pour into custard cups. Place in a pan and pour boiling water around cups to a depth of 2".
• Bake in moderate oven (350°) 40 to 50 minutes, or until center is firm.
• Remove from water to cool. Chill. Unmold, or serve in cups—plain or with a favorite sauce. Makes 6 servings.

HONEY CHEESE CAKE

The Sunday touch in this cake is honey

3 tblsp. butter
2 c. sieved cottage cheese
2 tblsp. sifted flour
1 tsp. salt
⅓ c. honey
3 tblsp. lemon juice
1 tsp. lemon rind
4 eggs, separated
⅓ c. sugar
⅔ c. milk

Crumb Base:

2 c. crushed graham cracker crumbs
½ c. butter, melted
1 tsp. cinnamon
⅓ c. honey

• Cream butter; blend in cottage cheese, flour and salt. Beat in honey, lemon juice and rind.
• Add egg yolks, one at a time, beating well after each addition.
• Beat egg whites until stiff. Slowly add sugar; beat until soft peaks form. Fold into cheese mixture. Blend in milk.
• Combine all ingredients for Crumb Base. Press all but ½ c. mixture firmly along bottom and sides of 11½×7½×1½″ pan.
• Pour in filling; sprinkle with remaining crumb mixture. Bake in moderate oven (350°) 1 hour. Chill for easier cutting. Makes 9 servings.

HONEY BUNS

Easy to change these to butterscotch or maple buns, if you're out of honey

¼ c. warm water
1 tsp. sugar
1 pkg. granular or compressed yeast
½ c. shortening
½ c. sugar
1 tsp. salt
3 c. sifted flour
¾ c. water
1 egg, well beaten
½ c. honey
½ c. chopped nuts

• Combine warm water and 1 tsp. sugar. Sprinkle granular yeast over warm (110°) mixture; or crumble compressed yeast over lukewarm (85°) mixture. Let stand 5 minutes.
• Cream shortening, ½ c. sugar and salt. Mix in 1 c. flour and ¾ c. water. Add to yeast mixture.
• Stir in 2 c. flour and egg; cover and refrigerate overnight.
• Grease muffin pans, enough for 24 buns. In each muffin cup put 1 tsp. each honey and nuts. Drop 1 tblsp. of dough in each muffin cup. Let rise in warm place until doubled.
• Bake in moderate oven (375°) 12 to 15 minutes. Serve bottoms up.

Variations: Substitute maple sugar or brown sugar for honey. With maple sugar use butternuts.

HONEY COCONUT ICE CREAM

Adapted from a tropical dessert recipe

1 c. honey
1 envelope unflavored gelatin
2 tblsp. cold water
¼ c. brown sugar
2 eggs
3 c. light cream
1 tsp. coconut extract
½ c. flaked or shredded coconut

• Heat honey (do not boil).
• Soften gelatin in water; add to honey along with sugar, eggs, cream and coconut extract. Beat about 2 minutes. Pour into refrigerator tray. Freeze until firm, but not hard.
• Turn mixture into chilled bowl. Beat until fluffy. Pour back into refrigerator tray and freeze until firm.
• Toast coconut; sprinkle over each serving. Makes 6 servings.

HONEY FRUIT CAKE

A California holiday cake brimful of fruits and nuts

PART I

½ c. dried prunes
1⅔ c. dried apricots
1½ c. chopped dried figs
1½ c. chopped dates
1½ c. seedless raisins
1½ c. currants
½ c. diced candied orange peel
½ c. diced candied lemon peel
2 c. honey

PART II

¼ c. sliced candied pineapple
¼ c. shaved preserved citron
½ c. sliced candied cherries
¾ c. chopped pecans
¾ c. chopped walnuts
3½ c. sifted flour
1 tsp. salt
2 tsp. baking powder
¼ tsp. cloves
¼ tsp. nutmeg
¼ tsp. allspice
¾ tsp. cinnamon
1 c. butter or margarine
3 eggs, beaten
½ c. fruit juice or coffee
Almonds

• Cook prunes and apricots separately. Cover each with water. Bring to a boil and simmer 3 minutes; drain. Chop softened fruit.

• Combine all ingredients in Part I. Stir well, cover, and let stand 1 week. Stir each day; at end of week add fruit and nuts in Part II, except almonds.

• Sift flour with salt, baking powder and spices.

• Cream butter; add fruit-nut mixture. Add eggs and fruit juice; beat well.

• Add flour mixture in four parts, beating after each addition.

• Line bottoms of 4 well greased 1 lb. coffee cans with two thicknesses of waxed paper. Divide batter, filling cans to about 1″ from top. Press almonds in top surface.

• Bake in very slow oven (250°) 2 hours. Place pan with 1″ water in it on rack below cakes while baking.

• Or bake cakes in 3 greased, paper-lined 8×4″ loaf pans about 2½ hours, or until cake tests done.

• Cool slightly; remove from pans and cool completely. Wrap in waxed paper or aluminum foil. Store in airtight container in a cool place.

HONEY LEMON LAYER CAKE

One taste and compliments start

½ c. shortening
1 c. honey
2 eggs
2 c. sifted cake flour
¾ tsp. baking soda
½ tsp. salt
¼ c. milk
2 tblsp. lemon juice

• Cream together shortening and honey.

• Add eggs, one at a time, beating well after each addition.

• Sift together flour, baking soda and salt.

• Sour milk with lemon juice. Add sifted dry ingredients alternately with sour milk to egg mixture.

• Pour into 2 greased 8″ layer cake pans. Bake in moderate oven (350°) 25 to 30 minutes. Frost with Honey Cream-Cheese Frosting.

Honey Cream-Cheese Frosting:

1 (3 oz.) pkg. cream cheese
1 tblsp. honey
2½ c. sifted confectioners sugar

• Blend cheese with honey. Gradually add sugar; beat until smooth.

HONEY ORANGE SAUCE

Serve on ice cream, waffles or pancakes

1 c. honey
¼ c. finely chopped orange peel
⅛ tsp. salt

• Combine all ingredients. Heat 5 minutes, but do not boil. Makes about 1 cup.

CAKE TOPPING

Broiled coconut-honey topper glamorizes any cake

2 tblsp. soft butter
⅔ c. flaked or shredded coconut
¼ c. honey
1 tsp. grated lemon rind
⅛ tsp. salt

• Spread top of cake with butter.
• Combine coconut, honey, lemon rind and salt, and blend well.
• Spread over cake.
• Broil just long enough to toast coconut lightly, 2 to 4 minutes.

HONEYED APPLES

Apples cook on top the range—come off glistening and tempting

6 to 8 medium-size cooking apples
⅔ c. raisins
⅔ c. honey
⅔ c. sugar
2 tsp. cinnamon
⅛ tsp. red food color

• Peel and core apples.
• Plump raisins in hot water.
• Blend together in saucepan honey, sugar, cinnamon and food color. Bring to boil and boil 10 minutes.
• Add apples and cook until tender but not soft, turning often so that they cook evenly. Lift apples onto platter.
• Spoon raisins into center of apples; pour syrup over apples. Serve with cream or ice cream. Makes 6 to 8 servings.

NO-COOK CANDY

A sweet for Junior Cooks to make

1 c. honey
1 c. dry milk powder
1 c. peanut butter
Chopped peanuts (optional)

• Mix ingredients together and shape in small balls. Roll in chopped nuts or chocolate sprinkles. Makes 36 balls, 1½" in diameter.

ROSE GERANIUM-HONEY JELLY

Just as tasty on hot biscuits and toast as Grandma's famous geranium jelly

2½ c. strained honey
¾ c. water
6 or 7 rose geranium leaves
½ bottle (3 oz.) fruit pectin
2 tblsp. lemon juice

• Combine honey, water and 2 or 3 rose geranium leaves; quickly bring to a boil.
• Add pectin, stirring constantly; bring to a full rolling boil.
• Add lemon juice and remove from heat. Remove leaves from mixture carefully. Place a fresh, clean leaf in each jar and quickly pour hot jelly into hot sterilized jars (the leaves rise to top). Seal. Makes 4 (8 oz.) jars.

Honey Salad Dressing: Mix 1 c. honey, 1 tblsp. salt, 1 tblsp. dry mustard, 1½ tblsp. paprika, ½ c. lemon juice, 1 c. vinegar and slowly add 2 c. oil, beating constantly. Extra good on grapefruit and orange salads and on orange and thin sweet onion slices. Makes about 4 cups.

Honey-Coconut Cake Topping: Combine ⅓ c. honey, ¼ c. melted butter, 1 c. flaked or shredded coconut. Spread on top of slice or other baked cake. Broil slowly until golden brown, about 5 minutes. Watch as frosting burns easily. Makes topping for a 9×9×2" cake.

COTTAGE CHEESE DRESSING

For fruit or melon salads, try this combination of honey and cottage cheese

½ c. cottage cheese, sieved
1 tblsp. honey
¼ c. orange juice
½ tsp. grated lemon rind
1 tblsp. lemon juice
½ tsp. salt
Dash of paprika

• Mix cottage cheese with honey and orange juice. Add remaining ingredients. Mix well. Chill before serving. Makes ¾ cup.

HONEY FRUIT SALAD DRESSING

A Montana rancher's wife invented this dressing that enhances fruits and melons

1 c. strained honey
1½ tblsp. flour
1 tsp. salt
1 tsp. dry mustard
1 tsp. celery seed
1¼ tsp. paprika
⅓ c. vinegar or lemon juice
1 c. oil

• Put honey in double boiler (if you like it less sweet use ¾ c. honey). Mix flour, salt, mustard, celery seed and paprika with vinegar until smooth. Add to honey and stir until thick and well cooked.

• Cool; then beat in oil gradually until well blended; keep refrigerated, will not sugar or separate. Drizzle over fruit you have selected and placed on crisp lettuce leaf.

Combinations of Fruit: Grapefruit sections, pineapple chunks, pear halves, peaches and maraschino cherries; Bing cherries, grapefruit, banana, orange; apricot, pear, grapefruit, tangerine; tomato wedge, cantaloupe, peaches.

Made with Butterscotch

Put brown sugar and butter together and you have butterscotch, a high in luscious eating. Calorie counters may shake their heads in dismay when they confront a wedge of butterscotch pie, but few Americans resist occasionally lifting their forks and enjoying this great dessert.

BUTTERSCOTCH MERINGUE PIE

Good to the last forkful—tender, crisp pastry with buttery, brown sugar filling

⅓ c. sifted flour
1 c. brown sugar
¼ tsp. salt
2 c. milk, scalded
3 egg yolks, beaten slightly
3 tblsp. butter or margarine
½ tsp. vanilla
1 (9″) baked pie shell

• Mix flour, sugar and salt; gradually add milk. Cook over moderate heat, stirring constantly, until mixture thickens and boils. Cook 2 minutes and remove from heat.

• Add small amount milk mixture to egg yolks, stir into remaining hot mixture; cook 1 minute, stirring constantly.

• Add butter and vanilla; cool slightly. Pour into pastry shell and cool.

• Top with meringue, bake in moderate oven (350°) 12 to 15 minutes.

Meringue: Beat 3 egg whites and ¼ tsp. salt until frothy; beat in 6 tblsp. sugar, 1 tblsp. at a time. Beat until meringue is stiff and glossy. Add ½ tsp. vanilla; beat only enough to blend.

Sugar Country Treats

When the Indians taught our New England forebears how to obtain sugar from maple trees, they started us on an adventure in good eating that continues to this day. Vermont is the foremost maple state, followed by New York and Ohio. But all New England and some other states produce maple sugar and syrup—their country kitchens are treasure-troves of intriguing recipes.

The universal use of maple syrup is as a companion to butter on pancakes and waffles. Some of the homespun ways with both the sugar and syrup are so simple you scarcely call them recipes—making cinnamon toast with maple sugar instead of granulated, and basting ham with maple syrup as it bakes. The maple recipes that follow are sugar country favorites.

MAPLE PIE TOPPING

At home on the Thanksgiving pumpkin pie

1 c. heavy cream
¼ c. maple syrup

• Whip cream until it stands in soft peaks. Drizzle syrup over top and carefully fold into cream. Serve on cold squash or pumpkin pie.

Variation: Substitute molasses for maple syrup.

MAPLE GINGERBREAD

Feast for the gods—warm squares of this gingerbread with bowls of applesauce

1 c. maple syrup
1 c. dairy sour cream
1 egg, well beaten
2⅓ c. sifted flour
1 tsp. baking soda
1½ tsp. ginger
½ tsp. salt
4 tblsp. melted butter or margarine

• Blend syrup with cream and egg.
• Sift dry ingredients and stir into syrup mixture. Add butter and beat thoroughly.
• Pour into an 8×12" baking pan, lined with greased brown paper. Bake in moderate oven (350°) 30 minutes. Makes 8 servings.

MAPLE UPSIDE-DOWN CAKE

An upstate New York dessert you'll never forget

3 tblsp. butter or margarine
1 c. maple sugar
1 c. pineapple chunks
3 eggs, separated
1 c. sugar
¼ c. milk
1 tsp. lemon extract
1 c. sifted flour
½ tsp. salt
1½ tsp. baking powder

• Melt butter in bottom of 8" round cake pan. Mix in maple sugar; arrange pineapple chunks to cover bottom of pan.
• Mix beaten egg yolks with sugar; add milk and extract, then dry ingredients sifted together.
• Fold in stiffly beaten egg whites; pour batter over pineapple. Bake in moderate oven (350°) about 45 minutes. Invert and serve cut in wedges, garnished with unflavored whipped cream. Makes 6 servings.

HEAVENLY RICE

Vermont's rice pudding has the name it deserves

1 c. heavy cream
3 c. cooked rice
Maple syrup

• Whip cream and fold into cooled rice. (Rice is seasoned with salt, but add no other seasonings.) Chill.
• Serve in dessert glasses with maple syrup as the sauce. Makes 6 servings.

Serve maple syrup over vanilla ice cream for a treat. It's also a tasty dress-up for plain baked custard.

Melted Sugar Desserts

Caramelizing granulated sugar in a heavy skillet is an old art—getting the right brown without scorching. But women everywhere know how to stir the sugar as it liquefies and watch carefully for the light golden brown hue. An old name for the sweet is burnt-sugar. Southern cooks long have considered burnt-sugar or caramel cake one of the world's best. A charming custom of the South is to serve the cake warm from the oven, unfrosted, and with vanilla ice cream. These recipes come from farm women, and all were awarded top rank when tested in our Countryside Kitchens.

CARAMELIZED SYRUP

The start for marvelous dishes

2 c. sugar
1 c. boiling water

• Pour sugar in heavy skillet that heats uniformly. Melt over low heat, stirring constantly with wooden spoon to prevent scorching (don't worry about the lumps—they'll melt away).
• When sugar becomes a clear, brown syrup, remove from heat. Stir in boiling water, slowly so that it doesn't spatter. Return to low heat, and stir until syrup is smooth again. Cool.
• Pour into clean pint jar, cover tightly, and store at room temperature. Keeps 6 to 8 weeks. Makes 1⅓ cups.

Note: Because there are so many flavorful uses for this syrup, you may prefer to double the recipe.

CARAMEL CAKE

The most famous burnt-sugar use

2¼ c. sifted cake flour
1 tblsp. baking powder
1 tsp. salt
1 c. sugar
1 c. milk
⅓ c. caramelized syrup
1 tsp. almond extract
½ c. shortening
2 eggs, unbeaten

• Sift into mixing bowl cake flour, baking powder, salt and sugar.
• Thoroughly blend milk, caramelized syrup and almond extract. Add ⅔ of this mixture to dry ingredients. Then add shortening. Beat about 2 minutes by hand or with mixer (use medium speed), until batter is well blended and glossy, scraping down sides of bowl frequently.
• Add the remaining liquid. Add the eggs. Beat 2 minutes more or until batter is very smooth.

• Pour into 2 greased 8″ layer cake pans lined with waxed paper. Bake in moderate oven (350°) 30 minutes. Frost with Caramel Cream Frosting.

Caramel Cream Frosting:

- **6 tblsp. soft butter or margarine**
- **1 egg yolk, beaten**
- **5 tblsp. caramelized syrup**
- **4 c. sifted confectioners sugar**
- **1 tsp. almond extract**
- **2 tblsp. cream**

• Cream together butter and egg yolk. Beat in alternately caramelized syrup and confectioners sugar. Add almond extract and cream.
• Beat until smooth and creamy enough to spread. Frosts 2 (8″) layers.

CARAMEL FLAVORED CUSTARD

A world-wide famous French dish that our good country cooks have adopted

- **3 c. milk, scalded**
- **⅓ c. caramelized syrup**
- **4 eggs, well beaten**
- **⅓ c. sugar**
- **½ tsp. salt**
- **1 tsp. vanilla**
- **1 tblsp. coarse pieces dry cake or cookies**

• Blend together milk and caramelized syrup.
• Combine eggs, sugar, salt and vanilla. Slowly stir liquid into egg mixture. Pour into 8 (6 oz.) custard cups.
• Break or crumble cake over top of each custard. Set custards in pan of hot water.
• Bake in moderate oven (350°) 40 minutes, or until knife inserted in center comes out clean. Cool before turning out. Makes 8 custards.

CARAMEL CUSTARD PIE

To avoid soggy crust, bake custard and crust separately

• Make custard from recipe above. Bake in buttered 10″ pie plate in moderate oven (350°) 40 minutes, or until knife inserted in center comes out clean. Cool.
• Meanwhile, prepare 10″ pie shell. Bake in hot oven (425°) 12 minutes.
• Loosen edges of custard carefully with spatula. Shake gently to loosen bottom. Slide custard from pie plate into cooled pie shell.

CARAMEL ALMOND SPONGE

Rich and luscious

- **½ c. blanched almonds**
- **1 envelope unflavored gelatin**
- **¼ c. cold water**
- **¾ c. milk**
- **1 c. caramelized syrup**
- **¼ c. sugar**
- **½ tsp. salt**
- **1 tsp. vanilla**
- **1 c. heavy cream**

• Cut almonds into slivers and toast.
• Soak gelatin in cold water.
• Scald milk; add syrup. Stir gelatin into mixture. Add sugar, salt and vanilla.
• Set bowl in pan of ice water; stir (to speed cooling) until it thickens.
• Whip cream. Fold into thickened gelatin mixture (only until you have marbleized effect).
• Chill in bowl until firm. Spoon (small portions because it's very rich) into sherbet glasses; sprinkle with almonds. Makes 8 to 10 servings.

CARAMEL SUNDAE SAUCE

Makes ice cream a royal dessert

- **¼ c. hot water**
- **½ c. caramelized syrup**
- **¼ c. chopped nuts**
- **¼ c. candied ginger, minced, or orange or lemon peel**

• Combine all ingredients. Chill. Serve over vanilla ice cream. Makes enough for 6 sundaes.

Dishes Benefiting from Molasses

CARROT RELISH

Gifts of the garden for winter pleasure

1 qt. white vinegar
1¼ c. light molasses
1 tblsp. celery seed
1 tblsp. mustard seed
3 tblsp. salt
3 c. coarsely ground onions
1½ qts. coarsely ground carrots
2 c. coarsely ground sweet red peppers
1 c. coarsely ground sweet green peppers
1½ c. coarsely ground cabbage

• Combine 3 c. vinegar, molasses, spices and salt in large kettle. Bring to boil. Boil rapidly 5 minutes.
• Add all vegetables to vinegar-molasses mixture. Cook briskly 20 minutes, stirring frequently.
• Add remaining 1 c. vinegar and cook 5 minutes longer. Pack in hot, sterilized jars. Seal. Makes 6 pints.

MOLASSES WHOLE WHEAT COOKIES

Raisins make these cookies special

½ c. nonfat dry milk
½ tsp. baking soda
2 tsp. baking powder
½ tsp. salt
⅓ c. shortening
¾ c. molasses
1 tsp. vanilla
2 eggs, beaten
1 c. plus 2 tblsp. whole wheat flour
½ c. raisins

• Sift together dry milk, soda, baking powder and salt.
• Cream together shortening, molasses, and vanilla; add eggs, blend well.
• Add sifted ingredients and wheat flour; stir until thoroughly mixed. Add raisins (whole, chopped or ground).
• Drop by teaspoonfuls on lightly greased baking sheet. Bake in moderate oven (350°) 10 to 12 minutes, until lightly browned. Makes 4 dozen (2″).

LARGE DARK FRUIT CAKE

To add to your collection of superlative fruit cakes

5 eggs, separated
½ c. molasses
¼ c. grape juice
1 c. butter or margarine
1 c. sugar
1⅓ c. raisins
½ lb. cut up candied pineapple
½ lb. whole candied cherries
1¼ c. chopped dates
¼ lb. chopped citron
¼ lb. chopped orange peel
¼ lb. chopped lemon peel
1¾ c. cut pecans
2 c. sifted flour
½ tsp. nutmeg
½ tsp. cloves
½ tsp. mace
1 tsp. cinnamon
1 tsp. baking soda

• Beat egg yolks; combine with molasses and grape juice.
• Cream butter and sugar. Add egg yolk mixture. Blend well.
• Combine fruit and nuts; mix with 1 c. flour.
• Warm in oven 5 minutes.
• Sift remaining flour with spices and soda.
• Beat egg whites until peaks form and fold into creamed mixture. Stir in fruits, nuts and dry ingredients.
• Bake in slow oven (300°) 2 hours in 9″ tube pan, bottom greased, then lined with brown paper, also well greased.
• Put on rack to cool. Wrap in foil. Store in cold place (it freezes well).

15

From the Garden

Garden-fresh vegetables are among the top joys of country eating and cooking. From the time the first delicate green asparagus stalks and strawberry-red rhubarb shoots announce Spring, until pumpkins end up in jolly jack-o'-lanterns and thick, spicy pies, there's an ever changing procession of succulent vegetables. During the rest of the year, good cooks strive to capture the same marvelous flavors in the dishes they fix from frozen and canned vegetables and the fresh ones they select from the food store's garden patch. Cooks wise in this art have contributed many of the recipes in this chapter. We believe you'll applaud their success.

You'll find recipes for vegetables cooked tender-crisp to retain their bright colors. And you'll note unusual seasoning like herbs from the garden, others from far-away places. Most of the dishes are glamorized but simplified—the kind that tempt the cook to fix them and the family to like them.

There are chives and dill with green beans, for example, saffron added to asparagus, sour cream and horse-radish with beets, peanuts teamed with cabbage, onion pie with caraway seed, peas with mushrooms, honey-sweetened rhubarb (yes, rhubarb's a vegetable!). If you consider these dishes somewhat unusual, or on the exotic side, look at our homespun ones—bean porridge and corn chowder for cold days, wilted garden lettuce, parsnip patties, yams with lemon slices and many other tried-and-true friends.

Our recipes that follow extend from A to Z—asparagus to zucchini. They challenge you to fix more beautifully cooked vegetables for your meals. Just follow the alphabet through this chapter.

SAFFRON ASPARAGUS

A new dress for tender asparagus stalks

40 tender asparagus tips
2 tblsp. soft butter or margarine
10 toast rounds
1 tsp. saffron
2 c. light cream, heated
2 tblsp. cold, firm butter or margarine

• Cook asparagus in small amount of salted water, tips upright, until just tender (about 15 minutes).
• Spread soft butter on edges of toast; then dot edges with bits of saffron.
• Arrange hot asparagus on saffron-tinged toast rounds in deep serving dish. Pour hot cream in center; drop firm butter in cream to melt at table. Makes 5 servings.

Plank Dinner

MAY MENU

Lamb Chops
Asparagus with Hollandaise Sauce
Fluffy Mashed Potatoes

For a May plank dinner, arrange lamb chops on plank, and oil the wood around them. (Plank should always be *completely* covered with food, or well oiled to avoid charring.) Put in moderate oven (375°) 10 minutes, to brown chops on one side.

Meanwhile, cook asparagus in small amount of boiling water, and pressure-cook potatoes for mashing, or use packaged instant mashed potatoes. (They'll be especially fluffy if you whip in the two egg whites left from the Hollandaise Sauce for the asparagus.) Turn the chops; border with asparagus and potatoes. Return the plank to the oven for 15 minutes while you make Hollandaise Sauce. (See recipe, Egg Chapter.)

KIDNEY BEANS AND ONIONS

Man, this is a dish for a cold day!

4 c. drained red kidney beans (cooked or canned)
1½ c. grated or shredded sharp cheese
6 medium or 12 small white onions, cooked
½ c. liquid drained from beans
2½ tsp. salt
¼ c. mild molasses
1½ tsp. dry mustard
⅛ tsp. pepper
1 tsp. Worcestershire sauce
2 tblsp. melted butter or margarine

• Put half of beans in 2 qt. casserole. Sprinkle with 1 c. cheese. Add remaining beans. Arrange onions over top. Sprinkle remaining cheese in center and over onions.
• Combine remaining ingredients. Pour half of mixture over beans. Bake in moderate oven (350°) 20 minutes. Spoon remaining liquid over top, and bake 5 minutes longer. Makes 6 servings.

BAKED LIMA BEANS

Sweet-sour flavor complements the beans

2 c. cooked, dried baby lima beans
¼ c. mild molasses
1 c. dairy sour cream
1 tblsp. minced onion
½ tsp. dry mustard
⅛ tsp. black pepper
1 tsp. salt
1 tsp. Worcestershire sauce
3 strips bacon

• Drain beans, saving ½ c. liquid. Combine with molasses, sour cream, onion, mustard, pepper, salt and Worcestershire sauce.
• Place beans in 3 qt. casserole. Add liquid. Arrange strips of bacon on top.
• Bake in slow oven (325°) 1 hour. Makes 8 servings.

Meals Made Easy Keep main dishes or their makings in the freezer. In Chapter 16 we tell how to use Frozen Beef Cubes, page 251, as a "starter."

Ice Cream's a Freezer Staple Tops many desserts like Orange Tapioca Pudding, page 14, Fruit-Filled Meringues, page 306, Applesauce Cake, page 5.

Stores are Full of Short Cuts to quick and easy cooking. Recipes for Hasty Rarebit, page 313, Chiii-Topped Toast, page 309, and Easy Pizzas, page 308.

Tempting Citrus Desserts Our Citrus Fruit Custard, page 297, was made ahead, then topped with meringue at serving time.

GREEN BEAN SOUP

One of summer's best garden gifts

1½ lb. ham bone with meat
15 whole allspice
8 to 10 sprigs parsley
4 sprigs summer savory (1 tsp. dried)
1 small onion, minced
1½ c. diced potatoes
2 c. cut green beans
½ c. light cream
1 tblsp. butter or margarine
2 tsp. salt

• Place ham bone in soup kettle with water to cover. Tie allspice, parsley and savory in small cheesecloth bag or put in tea ball; add to kettle. Simmer 2 hours, adding more water if needed.
• Add onion, potatoes and beans; cook until vegetables are tender, 20 to 30 minutes. Remove spice ball.
• Just before serving, blend in cream, butter and salt. Makes 8 to 10 servings.

GREEN BEANS WITH CHIVES

A favorite herb-accented recipe of ours

3 c. green beans (canned or frozen)
⅓ c. butter or margarine
½ c. slivered almonds
½ tsp. salt
1 tblsp. chopped chives

• Cook beans in small amount salted water until just tender.
• Melt butter in heavy skillet; add almonds, and toast lightly over moderate heat, shaking pan. Add salt and chives. Pour over beans. Serve hot. Makes 6 servings.

FRENCHED GREEN BEANS

You put them in the oven and forget about them as they thaw and cook

1 (10 oz.) pkg. frozen French-style green beans
2 tblsp. butter or margarine
¼ tsp. salt

• Place beans in 1 qt. baking dish. Dot with butter and sprinkle with salt.
• Cover; bake in moderate oven (350°) 30 minutes. Makes 4 servings.

BEAN PORRIDGE

Serve it piping hot on a blustery day

4 c. cooked or canned beans, puréed
2 c. stewed tomatoes (fresh or canned)
1 bay leaf
1 tblsp. chopped parsley
2 tblsp. chili sauce
1 c. sliced carrots
1 c. sliced celery
½ c. sliced onions
1 c. sliced potatoes
2 qts. water
2 tsp. salt

• Combine beans, tomatoes, bay leaf, parsley and chili sauce.
• Cook remaining vegetables until just tender.
• Combine bean-tomato mixture, vegetables, water and salt. Simmer 2 hours. Serve hot. Makes 8 servings.

GREEN BEANS WITH DILL

The dill lifts these beans out of the ordinary

3 tblsp. butter or margarine
⅔ c. chopped onion
1 c. water
½ c. chili sauce
½ tsp. dried dill
1½ tblsp. cornstarch
2 tblsp. water
3 c. cooked green beans

• Melt butter in saucepan; add onion. Sauté until soft and clear. Add water, chili sauce and dill.
• Blend together cornstarch and water; add smooth paste to onion mixture. Cook, stirring, until thickened.
• Combine sauce with beans. Makes 6 servings.

FLUFFY BEETS

Savory makes this dish outstanding

4 c. raw beets, peeled
2 tblsp. butter or margarine
1 tblsp. sugar
1 tsp. salt
½ c. water
1 tblsp. flour
1 c. dairy sour cream
1 tsp. dried savory

• Coarsely shred beets. Combine with butter, sugar, salt and water. Cook until beets are tender, about 10 minutes.
• Blend flour and sour cream. Add savory, and fold into beets. Heat through. Makes 6 servings.

SPICY BUTTERED BEETS

One way to cook beets: Wrap them in foil, bake in moderate oven (350°) 1 hour. Peel when cool

¼ c. sugar
¾ tsp. salt
½ tsp. cinnamon
¼ tsp. ground ginger
6 to 8 medium cooked beets, peeled and diced
¼ c. butter or margarine

• Combine sugar, salt, cinnamon and ginger. Sprinkle over beets; toss lightly to coat evenly. Scoop into greased ½ qt. baking dish. Dot with butter.
• Bake in moderate oven (350°) 20 minutes, or until beets are heated through. Makes 6 servings.

HORSE-RADISH BEETS

You'll want to double this flavorful recipe when there's company

2 tblsp. butter or margarine
2 tblsp. flour
½ tsp. salt
1 c. milk
3 tblsp. prepared horse-radish
3 c. cooked, diced beets

• Melt butter in saucepan. Stir in flour and salt.
• Add milk gradually. Cook, stirring, until thick and smooth. Add horse-radish; mix well.
• Pour sauce over hot beets. Serve immediately. Makes 4 to 6 servings.

BROCCOLI SOUFFLE

Borrowed from the French

3 tblsp. butter or margarine
3 tblsp. flour
1 c. milk
2 tblsp. finely chopped onion
1 c. shredded process cheese
3 egg yolks, slightly beaten
1 tblsp. marjoram
½ tsp. salt
¼ tsp. paprika
1½ c. cooked, chopped broccoli
3 egg whites, stiffly beaten
½ c. buttered cracker crumbs

• Melt butter in saucepan; blend in flour. Add milk and onion. Cook over moderate heat, stirring, until thickened.
• Remove from heat. Add cheese, egg yolks, marjoram, salt and paprika. Stir until cheese is melted; mix in broccoli.
• Fold in egg whites.
• Pour into greased 6×10" baking dish. Top with crumbs.
• Bake in moderate oven (350°) 45 minutes. Makes 6 servings.

Variation: Spinach or asparagus may be used instead of broccoli.

HOLIDAY BROCCOLI

2 (10 oz.) pkgs. frozen cut broccoli
1 or 2 chicken bouillon cubes
2 (10½ oz.) cans condensed cream of celery soup
½ c. grated sharp cheese
Strips of pimiento

• Cook broccoli with bouillon cubes and water until just tender. Heat soup to boiling; pour over broccoli. Garnish with cheese and pimiento. Serve at once. Makes 6 servings.

How to Cook Cabbage

Cook cabbage quickly and in only a little water. One way is called "panning"—steaming in a heavy covered skillet for a short time, adding meat drippings to water. Shredding the cabbage speeds up the cooking.

PANNED CABBAGE DE LUXE

Quick-cooked, it's at its peak

1 large onion, sliced
1 tblsp. fat
2 c. shredded cabbage
1 c. grated carrots
1 tsp. salt
⅛ tsp. pepper
1 c. boiling water

• Sauté onion in hot fat in heavy skillet until soft and clear. Add cabbage, carrots and seasonings.
• Pour water over vegetables. Cover, and simmer 12 minutes. Serve hot. Makes 6 servings.

CABBAGE CASSEROLE

Out-of-the-routine vegetable dish—children approve of the franks

3 c. shredded cabbage
3 red apples, cored
4 frankfurters, cut in chunks, or 1 lb. cooked ham, cut into cubes
Sweet-Sour Sauce (recipe follows)
Butter or margarine
½ c. cracker crumbs

• Steam cabbage in covered saucepan with small amount of water until tender-crisp. Drain if necessary.
• Slice apples evenly. Place in greased 1 qt. casserole with cabbage.
• Add frankfurters. Cover with Sweet-Sour Sauce. Dot with butter. Sprinkle with crumbs.
• Bake covered in moderate oven (350°) 30 minutes. Uncover; bake 15 minutes longer. Makes 6 servings.

Sweet-Sour Sauce:

2 tblsp. butter or margarine
¼ c. brown sugar
½ c. water
¼ c. vinegar
¾ tsp. salt
2 tblsp. cornstarch

• Melt butter in saucepan. Stir in sugar, ¼ c. water, vinegar and salt.
• Make a paste of cornstarch and remaining ¼ c. water. Add hot mixture, stirring until thick and clear.

CABBAGE WITH APPLES

A welcome variation from boiled and buttered cabbage

1 head cabbage
1 red apple, cored and sliced

Sauce:

½ c. dairy sour cream
1 tblsp. butter or margarine
½ tsp. salt
3 tblsp. lemon juice

• Cut cabbage into 6 wedges. Cook in small amount of boiling salted water 5 minutes.
• Add apple; cook about 3 minutes more, until tender. Drain. Serve with Sour Cream Sauce.

Sour Cream Sauce: Combine all ingredients. Heat through. Pour on cabbage. Serve hot. Makes 6 servings.

CABBAGE WITH CHEESE

Double this recipe if you like cabbage—it's excellent with pork

3 c. shredded cabbage
1 tsp. salt
½ c. boiling water
¼ c. light cream
½ c. grated process cheese

• Cook cabbage in boiling salted water until tender, about 6 to 9 minutes.
• Drain. Add cream and cheese. Place over low heat; stir until cheese melts and coats cabbage. Makes 4 servings.

CABBAGE-BACON CASSEROLE

Riches from the garden for your table

3 c. shredded cabbage
12 slices bacon
1½ c. fresh spinach leaves
Sweet-Sour Sauce (recipe in this chapter)
Butter or margarine
½ c. cracker crumbs

• Steam cabbage in covered saucepan with small amount of water until tender-crisp. Drain.
• Fry bacon until crisp. Drain on paper toweling. Crumble into greased 1½ qt. casserole with cabbage and spinach. Cover with Sweet-Sour Sauce. Dot with butter; sprinkle with crumbs.
• Bake, covered, in moderate oven (350°) 30 minutes. Uncover and bake 15 minutes longer. Makes 6 servings.

Variation: Substitute 1 (1 lb.) can red salmon, ½ c. chopped sweet pickles and 2 c. frozen peas, partly thawed, for the bacon and spinach. Substitute ¼ c. pickle juice for the Sweet-Sour Sauce.

TANGY BACON SAUCE

Try this in the fruit-shy winter months

4 slices bacon
2 tblsp. sugar
2 tblsp. flour
½ c. water
⅓ c. vinegar
⅛ tsp. pepper

• Fry bacon slowly until crisp. Drain slices on paper toweling.
• Blend sugar and flour into remaining bacon fat.
• Add water and vinegar; cook until thick, stirring frequently. Add pepper. Pour sauce over cooked cabbage just before serving. Garnish with bacon. Makes 6 servings.

STUFFED CABBAGE LEAVES

You also can bake your favorite meat loaf mixture in cabbage leaves

1 large head cabbage (about 1 lb.)
1½ tblsp. butter or margarine
¼ c. finely diced green pepper
¼ c. minced onion
¼ c. chopped celery
1½ c. cooked, seasoned rice
1 c. bulk pork sausage
½ tsp. salt
½ tsp. thyme
1 c. tomato juice
2½ c. water
1 small whole onion

• Remove heart from cabbage. Cover with boiling water; let stand until cabbage is wilted.
• Separate leaves, being careful not to break. Drain; dry on paper toweling.
• Melt butter in heavy skillet; sauté pepper, onion and celery 2 minutes. Add cooked rice and sausage to vegetables. Mix well; season.
• Put about ¼ c. mixture on each cabbage leaf (or overlap two smaller leaves). Roll with filling inside; fasten edges with toothpicks; place in greased baking dish. Add tomato juice, water and whole onion.
• Bake in moderate oven (350°) 1 hour. Remove rolls to heated platter, and thicken sauce for gravy. Makes 6 servings (12 small rolls).

TART SCALLOPED CABBAGE

Here's a tasty casserole, quick to fix

4 c. shredded cabbage
¼ c. boiling water
½ tsp. salt
2 eggs, slightly beaten
¼ tsp. salt
¼ c. vinegar
½ c. mayonnaise or salad dressing
1 c. coarsely crushed potato chips

• Parboil cabbage 2 to 3 minutes in boiling salted water; do not drain.
• Combine eggs, ¼ tsp. salt, vinegar and mayonnaise. Add cabbage (and any liquid).
• Pour into greased 1 qt. casserole. Sprinkle potato chips over top.
• Bake in moderate oven (350°) 25 minutes. Makes 4 servings.

SLAW WITH MUSTARD MOLD

A "chop-chop" salad of this kind goes best with a meat or main dish that has definite form: roast chicken, ham loaf or sliced corned beef. The mustard mold should be prepared a day ahead, or at least several hours before serving

Mold:

1 envelope unflavored gelatin
¼ c. cold water
¾ c. sugar
3 tblsp. dry mustard
¾ tsp. salt
1 c. vinegar (may be herb or wine type)
3 eggs, slightly beaten
½ c. heavy cream

Slaw:

6 c. shredded cabbage
½ c. chopped salted peanuts
¼ c. diced pimiento
¾ c. French dressing

• Soften gelatin in water.
• Combine sugar, mustard and salt in top of double boiler; add vinegar and eggs. Cook, stirring, over low heat until thickened. Do not boil.
• Remove from heat; add softened gelatin, stirring until dissolved. Chill until thickened.
• Whip cream; fold into gelatin mixture.
• Rinse 1 qt. mold with cold water; spoon in mustard gelatin. Chill until firm. Unmold on Cabbage Slaw.
• To make slaw; combine cabbage, peanuts, pimiento and dressing. Toss lightly. Makes 8 servings.

CABBAGE-TOMATO CASSEROLE

Serve with pork chops and corn bread

5 c. shredded cabbage
1 c. drained canned tomatoes
½ c. drained tomato juice
¼ c. chopped onion
½ c. medium cracker crumbs
1½ tsp. salt
⅛ tsp. pepper
½ c. grated or shredded process cheese

• Steam cabbage in covered saucepan with small amount of water until tender-crisp. Drain, if necessary.
• In greased 1 qt. casserole, arrange alternate layers of cabbage, tomatoes, onions and crumbs. Add juice; seasonings. Bake, covered, in moderate oven (350°) 30 minutes. Remove cover; bake 10 minutes more. Sprinkle cheese over top; then bake uncovered 5 minutes more, until cheese is melted and bubbly. Makes 6 servings.

BUTTERED CARROT STICKS

Bake this along with your oven dinner

6 medium carrots
¼ c. water
½ tsp. salt
2 tblsp. butter or margarine

• Peel carrots and quarter lengthwise. Place in 1 qt. casserole. Add water and salt. Bake in moderate oven (350°) 50 minutes.
• Serve buttered. Makes 6 servings.

CREAMY CARROTS

Mayonnaise is the surprise seasoning

8 medium carrots
½ c. boiling water
½ tsp. salt
3 tblsp. mayonnaise or salad dressing
2 tblsp. light cream

• Wash and scrape carrots. Cut into quarters, lengthwise.
• Put carrots, boiling water and salt in saucepan. Cover. Cook until tender but still a little firm, about 15 minutes. Drain.
• Blend mayonnaise and cream; pour over carrots, and mix lightly. Serve immediately. Makes 5 to 6 servings.

BAKED CAULIFLOWER

Oregano steps up the bland taste of this vegetable

1 head cauliflower, broken into flowerets
1½ c. drained, canned tomatoes
½ c. chopped onion
½ tsp. dried oregano
½ tsp. salt
⅛ tsp. pepper
¾ c. grated or shredded cheese
¾ c. coarse cracker crumbs

• Cook cauliflower 20 minutes, until just tender.
• In greased 2 qt. casserole combine tomatoes, onion, oregano, salt and pepper. Cover with cauliflower.
• Mix cheese and crumbs; sprinkle over cauliflower.
• Bake in hot oven (400°) 20 minutes. Makes 6 to 7 servings.

CAULIFLOWER SALAD

Try using crisp raw cauliflower flowerets in vegetable and fruit salads. You'll like this: Combine shredded raw cauliflower with orange and grapefruit sections and sliced bananas. Pour French dressing over; chill several hours.

TWO SAUCES FOR COOKED CAULIFLOWER

TOMATO CURRY SAUCE

1 small onion, diced
2 tblsp. fat
1 tblsp. curry powder
1 tblsp. cold water
¼ tsp. salt
1 c. tomato purée
¼ tsp. Worcestershire sauce
Few drops Tabasco sauce

• Cook onion in fat until lightly browned.
• Combine curry powder with water to form a paste; stir into sautéed onion. Add remaining ingredients.
• Simmer together about 10 minutes to blend flavors well. Pour over cooked cauliflower. Makes 1 cup.

BRAZIL NUT BUTTER

¼ c. butter or margarine
½ c. chopped Brazil nuts

• Melt 1 tblsp. butter over low heat. Add nuts. When brown, add remaining butter. Pour over cooked cauliflower. Makes ½ cup.

CORN CAKES

A fine partner for fried chicken

2 eggs, separated
1 c. cream style corn
½ tsp. salt
1 tblsp. soft butter or margarine
½ c. medium cracker crumbs
2 tblsp. flour
½ tsp. baking powder
2 tblsp. minced parsley
2 tblsp. melted fat or oil

• Beat egg whites until stiff; then beat yolks slightly.
• Add corn, salt and butter to yolks; mix.

• Mix crumbs, flour and baking powder. Add with parsley to corn mixture.
• Fold in egg whites.
• Heat fat in heavy skillet. Drop spoonfuls of mixture on hot fat; flatten slightly. Fry until golden brown on each side. Makes 12 to 14 cakes.

CORN PIE

Want to have fried chicken with this?

1¼ c. fine cracker crumbs
½ c. melted butter or margarine
2 tblsp. butter or margarine
1¼ c. milk
2 c. fresh raw corn (2 or 3 ears)
½ tsp. salt
2 tblsp. flour
½ tsp. onion salt (optional)
2 eggs, beaten

• Combine crumbs and melted butter. Reserve ½ c. for topping. Line 9" pie pan with remaining crumbs.
• Combine butter, 1 c. milk, corn and salt. Bring to boil. Reduce heat, and cook 3 minutes.
• Add flour to remaining ¼ c. milk; mix to smooth paste. Add slowly to hot milk-corn mixture, stirring constantly. Cook 2 to 3 minutes, or until thick.
• Cool slightly. Add onion salt. Add eggs slowly, stirring constantly.
• Pour into crumb-lined pan. Sprinkle remaining crumbs over top. Bake in hot oven (400°) 20 minutes. Makes 6 servings.

ROAST CORN

Farm families used to roast field corn in the husks on top of the cook stove, with a roaring fire to provide the necessary heat. Now they roast sweet corn in the broiler or oven of their heat-controlled ranges, or over coals on a grill in the back yard. Food for the gods.

BROILED CORN IN HUSKS

Choose corn in the milk stage for top flavor and tenderness

• Pick 12 ears of corn about 2 hours before mealtime.
• Remove thick outer husks.
• Turn back inner husks and remove silk, being careful not to detach husks from ear. Pull husks back around ears.
• Soak in ice water 1 hour.
• Pre-heat broiler. Shake excess water from corn. Arrange on rack, about 4 inches from heating unit.
• Broil 7 minutes on one side; turn with tongs or fork and continue broiling on all sides until corn is done—about 30 minutes. Or roast in a 400° oven.
• Serve right in husks, so that corn keeps steaming hot. Butter and salt, of course —some like pepper.

CORN WAFFLES

Serve creamed chicken on waffles and have fruit salad—it's a meal

2 c. sifted flour
2½ tsp. baking powder
½ tsp. salt
2 eggs, separated
1½ c. milk
½ c. melted shortening or oil
1 c. cream style corn

• Sift together flour, baking powder and salt.
• Beat egg yolks. Add milk, shortening and canned corn. Add all at once to dry ingredients, stirring just to moisten.
• Beat egg whites until stiff but not dry. Fold into corn batter.
• Bake on hot waffle iron as manufacturer directs until golden brown on both sides.
• Serve hot. Makes 4 large waffles.

CORN "OYSTERS"

When your family has had its fill of roasting ears, make up a batch of Corn Oysters—so named because a spoonful of the corn mixture puffs up like an oyster when it hits the hot griddle

6 ears select corn (fresh-picked or frozen-thawed)
3 egg yolks, well beaten
¼ c. flour
½ tsp. baking powder
¾ tsp. salt
¼ tsp. pepper
3 egg whites, stiffly beaten

• Slash down each row of kernels with a sharp knife, then cut from cob. (Easier than grating and just as effective for getting every bit of milky kernel.) Add egg yolks; blend.
• Sift together flour, baking powder, salt and pepper. Stir into corn-egg mixture; blend. Gently fold in egg whites.
• Drop by spoonfuls on hot, well greased griddle. Fry until nicely browned. Makes 4 servings.

CORN 'N PEAS WITH SAVORY

Why serve plain corn when you can fix this with only a little more effort?

3 tblsp. butter or margarine
¼ c. chopped onion
½ c. chopped celery
2 c. cooked peas
2 c. whole kernel corn, drained (fresh or canned)
2 tblsp. chopped parsley
½ tsp. dried summer savory
½ tsp. salt
⅛ tsp. pepper
½ c. dairy sour cream

• Combine butter, onion and celery in saucepan.
• Cook over low heat 3 to 4 minutes.
• Add remaining ingredients, except sour cream. Heat thoroughly.
• Just before serving add sour cream. Makes 6 servings.

PLATTER SUPPER

JULY MENU

Wieners on Corn with Tomato Sauce
Green Lima Beans Mashed Potatoes

Money-saving July platter: Cut corn from cob, and precook 3 minutes. Put in center of platter. Lay wieners on top and cover with tomato sauce (fresh-made or canned). Border with cooked green lima beans and mashed potatoes. Heat in hot oven (400°) 20 minutes.

BAKED EGGPLANT WITH HAM

Double this recipe for a wonderful supper main dish

1 lemon
1 c. water
1 large eggplant
¼ c. minced onion
1 c. cooked ham, diced
2 tblsp. butter or margarine
1 egg, beaten
¼ c. grated or shredded cheese
½ c. buttered bread crumbs

• Combine lemon juice with water.
• Peel eggplant. Dip in lemon water. Dice, and dip again. Rinse in cold water.
• Parboil diced eggplant about 10 minutes.
• Sauté onion and ham in butter; add eggplant and egg. Mix well. Put mixture in greased 1 qt. casserole. Combine cheese and crumbs; sprinkle over top.
• Bake in moderate oven (350°) 40 minutes. Makes 4 servings.

EGGPLANT CLAM BAKE

A bargain in good flavors

2 large eggplants
2 (7½ oz.) cans minced clams, drained
2 c. cracker crumbs
2 tblsp. melted butter or margarine

2 eggs, beaten
Salt and pepper
2 tblsp. milk (optional)
Butter or margarine

• Peel eggplant; cut in 1" thick slices. Let stand in water 20 minutes.
• Cook slices until soft (15 minutes); drain and mash. (Makes about 2 c.)
• Add clams, 1½ c. cracker crumbs, melted butter, egg, salt, pepper and milk, if mixture seems dry.
• Place in 2 qt. baking pan or individual casseroles. Cover with remaining crumbs. Dot with butter and bake in slow oven (325°) until brown. Makes 6 servings.

STUFFED EGGPLANT

Family won't eat egglant? Try them with this eggplant-ham casserole

1 eggplant
Salt
Paprika
Lemon juice
1 clove garlic, cut
1 c. chopped cooked ham
¼ c. soft bread crumbs
1 c. chopped tomatoes
1 tblsp. butter or margarine
¼ c. grated or shredded cheese

• Cut eggplant in lengthwise halves. Scoop out pulp, leaving ¾" shell. Sprinkle with salt, paprika and lemon juice. Rub outside with garlic.
• Cook pulp in boiling salted water until tender. Drain, and mash. Add ham, bread crumbs and tomatoes. Fill eggplant shells with mixture.
• Dot with butter, and sprinkle with cheese. Bake in moderate oven (375°) 30 minutes. Makes 4 servings.

EGGPLANT SOUFFLE

Puffs up and browns—very inviting

1 eggplant
Juice of 1 lemon
1 c. water
2 tblsp. butter or margarine
2 tblsp. flour
1 c. milk
¾ c. bread crumbs
½ c. grated cheese
1 tblsp. ketchup
1½ tblsp. grated onion
1½ tsp. salt
2 egg yolks, beaten
2 egg whites, stiffly beaten

• Peel eggplant; dip in mixture of lemon and water. Dice, and dip again.
• Cook with small amount of water 10 minutes, until just tender.
• Melt butter in top of double boiler. Blend in flour. Add milk.
• Cook 10 minutes until thick, stirring.
• Add diced cooked eggplant, crumbs, cheese, ketchup, onion and salt. Stir in egg yolks. Fold in egg whites.
• Pour into greased 1 qt. casserole.
• Bake in moderate oven (350°) 45 minutes. Makes 4 servings.

RUSSIAN EGGPLANT

Serve hot from the oven—good with ham

1 large eggplant
Juice of 1 lemon
1 c. water
2 onions, thinly sliced
3 tomatoes, sliced
2 tblsp. flour
2 tsp. salt
¼ tsp. pepper
1 c. dairy sour cream

• Peel eggplant; slice in ⅓" slices. Dip in mixture of lemon and water. Rinse in cold water.
• Cook in small amount of salted water until barely tender, 8 minutes. Drain.
• Alternate layers of eggplant, onion and tomatocs in greased 2 qt. casserole. Sprinkle with flour and seasonings. Spoon sour cream over top.
• Bake in moderate oven (350°) 45 minutes. Makes 6 servings.

EGGPLANT STEAKS

Include a tomato salad in the menu

1 eggplant
⅓ c. melted butter or margarine
½ c. fine, dry bread crumbs
1 tsp. salt
¼ tsp. pepper

Sauce:

1 c. process cheese (about ¼ lb.)
⅓ c. undiluted evaporated milk

• Peel eggplant; cut in slices ½" thick. Brush with butter.
• Combine crumbs and seasonings. Dip eggplant slices in mixture.
• Bake on greased baking sheet in very hot oven (450°) 8 minutes. Serve with cheese sauce.
• To make sauce, melt cheese in top of double boiler; add milk. Cook, stirring, until smooth. Pour over eggplant.
• Serve with crisp bacon slices. Makes 6 servings.

DELICATE GARDEN LETTUCE

Use crisp lettuce right from the garden

1 qt. leaf lettuce
1 clove garlic, cut in half
1 tblsp. lemon juice
3 tblsp. oil
1 tsp. salt

• Wash lettuce; chill.
• Rub wooden salad bowl with cut sides of garlic.
• Put lemon juice, oil and salt into bowl, and mix well. Add lettuce; whisk around in dressing, tossing lightly. Marinate about 30 minutes before serving. Makes 6 servings.

BACON 'N EGG SALAD BOWL

Delicious with fried chicken

3 or 4 hard-cooked eggs
½ lb. bacon (about 12 slices)
½ head cauliflower
3 or 4 green onions
1 head lettuce
Crisp toast
1 clove garlic, peeled
⅔ c. French dressing
Seasonings

• Peel, then chop eggs.
• Fry bacon until crisp; crumble coarsely.
• Break cauliflower into flowerets. Slice thin—should be about ¾ c.
• Chop onions. Tear lettuce into bite-size pieces.
• Make garlic croutons by rubbing both sides of toast with cut garlic; cut into cubes.
• Place croutons in salad bowl first, then add remaining vegetables. Chill.
• At serving, add French dressing and toss together lightly. Add any desired seasonings—freshly ground pepper, seasoning salt, herbs, etc. Makes 6 to 8 servings.

Green Salad

For the easiest kind of dressing: Cut a clove garlic (one per salad is enough) and rub it around a wooden salad bowl. Sprinkle a little coarse-ground black pepper and paprika over the greens; add a little vinegar; toss. Before serving, add salad oil or olive oil, and toss again.

How much vinegar and how much oil? It's up to you, but most people like about 3 parts oil to 1 part vinegar. Cider vinegar is all right for salads, but you may like the flavor of herb or wine vinegars better. (Herb vinegars like tarragon, are just cider vinegar with herbs added.)

To make cider vinegar more zippy, try this horse-radish version: Add 1 c. grated horse-radish, 2 tblsp. minced onion, 1 clove garlic and a pinch of red pepper to 1 qt. cider vinegar. Cover tightly; let stand 10 days in refrigerator. Strain through cheesecloth; store in bottle. It's hot!

DRESSINGS

French: Put into a bottle or jar 1 tsp. sugar; ½ tsp. each salt, dry mustard, paprika; 2 tblsp. each lemon juice and vinegar; ½ c. oil and a dash of red pepper. Cover with tight-fitting lid and shake hard before pouring over salads. Chill. Makes ¾ c.

Russian: Cook ½ c. sugar and 6 tblsp. water until syrup spins thread. Cool. Combine 2 tsp. each salt, paprika and celery seed; 2 tblsp. each vinegar, lemon juice and Worcestershire sauce with 2 c. oil and 2 tblsp. grated onion. Add syrup; beat well, then chill. Makes 4 cups.

Old-Fashioned Sour Cream: Mix in bowl ½ c. dairy sour cream, 1 tblsp. lemon juice, 1 tblsp. prepared mustard, 2 tblsp. sugar and ½ tsp. salt. Enough for 6 individual salads.

Chili Sauce: Mix together ¼ c. each mayonnaise or salad dressing and chili sauce. Chop, and add 1 hard-cooked egg and 1 sweet pickle. Thin with cream if necessary; pour over individual salads. For 6 to 8 salads.

Roquefort: Crumble 3 tblsp. Roquefort or blue cheese into 1 tblsp. oil. At serving time, add 1 tblsp. vinegar, ¼ c. mayonnaise or salad dressing and 2 tblsp. sweet or sour cream. Mix well; pour over individual servings of greens. Do not toss. Enough for 6 to 8 salads.

Thousand Island Dressing: Rub small bowl with half of clove garlic. Combine in bowl ½ c. mayonnaise or salad dressing; 2 tblsp. light cream; 2 tblsp. chili sauce; 2 tblsp. chopped green pepper; ½ c. coarsely diced hard-cooked egg; ½ tsp. salt and ½ tsp. paprika. Blend together well, stirring lightly. Refrigerate in covered container. Makes about 1¼ cups.

GREEN SALAD

Many men say you can't beat a green salad. This one proves their point

1 head lettuce
¼ lb. spinach, cleaned
1 large cucumber
1 c. chopped celery
1 clove garlic
6 small tomatoes
1 slice cheese, ¼" thick

• Wash crisp lettuce and spinach; then dry thoroughly. (You may add other greens.) Tear greens into bite-size pieces.
• Cut cucumber into thick slices, quartered.
• Toss greens, cucumber and celery together. Rub large bowl or individual wooden bowls with cut clove garlic.
• Fill with salad greens. Top each with thin wedges of tomatoes, flower fashion. Cut cheese into strips. Place in center of flowers. Serve with tangy or herb-type French dressing. Makes 6 to 8 salads.

HOLLAND HOT SALAD

A New York version of wilted lettuce

4 c. crisp leaf lettuce
⅛ lb. bacon or salt pork, finely cut
3 tblsp. cider vinegar
1 tsp. salt
2 tblsp. sugar
1 c. hot mashed potatoes
3 hard-cooked eggs, sliced
12 red radishes
12 green onions

• Chill lettuce in salad bowl.
• Slowly fry bacon in skillet until crisp. Drain, and crumble.
• Sprinkle over lettuce.
• Add vinegar, salt and sugar to bacon fat in skillet. Heat through. Pour over crisp lettuce and bacon, tossing lightly.
• Carefully fold in hot mashed potatoes and hard-cooked eggs. Garnish with crisp red radishes and scallions. Serve immediately. Makes 6 servings.

From the Herb Garden

Herbs are an important ally of good cooks. Many farm families grow parsley, chives, mint, sage and dill, but too few include these six. Try them in your garden and kitchen.

Savory: Its slender leaf has a piquant and pleasant flavor. Called the "bean herb," it blends naturally with the pea-bean-lentil family—fresh, canned or dried. Very good in vegetable dishes, scrambled eggs, meat balls, stews and gravies; in bread stuffings instead of sage. Peps up leftovers.

Oregano: The aromatic leaves from this beautiful bush do wonderful things to the flavor of tomatoes. Very good in spaghetti sauces, pizza, tomato or bean soup; good in appetizers, too. Nice in veal, lamb and pork dishes; a hint in sea food salads, and just a touch in white sauce. Good in pork sausage. Use a little in the cooking water for vegetables.

Marjoram: These grayish-green leaves are spicy and exceptionally sweet, somewhat like oregano, but not quite as strong. A versatile herb, it is good in practically everything. Try a pinch in your meat casserole, hash or meat pie. Rub a little in the cavity of your roasting chicken or turkey before you fill it with stuffing. Good in squash, especially.

Thyme: Most common variety is the Garden, or English. Found in herb blends, and is the soul of the French *bouquet garni.* An herb for all-around usage, it is a favorite of southern cooks. Blends well with pork or veal and is a stand-by for soups and stews. Good in fresh or canned vegetables, in croquettes, salads. A *must* in Manhattan clam chowder.

Tarragon: These dark green leaves have an unusual, intriguing flavor that is a bit astringent. Wonderful for marinades for fish and meats; or just sprinkle a bit on steak before you cook it. Very good in Hollandaise and tartar sauce. A favorite for fish and fish sauces—hot or cold. In fact, it is good in almost any type main course sauce. Also adds tang to egg dishes, aspics and does wonderful things for mushrooms.

Basil: The leaves of this annual have a peppery, clove-like scent and taste. The flavor blends with almost all foods. It, too, is a popular choice for tomato dishes. Very good in soup, especially turtle or green pea. A pinch in the cooking water adds flavor to boiled potatoes or spaghetti. Good with vegetables like cauliflower and cabbage, and in coleslaw and green salad. Gives a wonderful tang to egg dishes, meat balls and steak, pork and sausage.

RULES OF GOOD HERB COOKS

When you use herbs, keep these general rules in mind:

• One-fourth teaspoon dried herbs equals 1 teaspoon minced fresh herbs.
• Start by adding about 1/4 tsp. (dried) herbs for a recipe for four. It's easier to add more than to subtract!
• If cooking time is more than an hour, add herbs for just the last hour.

SAVORY DRESSING

Serve with garden-fresh vegetables—carrot sticks, celery, cauliflower flowerets

1/3 c. blue cheese, mashed
1 (8 oz.) pkg. cream cheese
1 clove garlic, minced or crushed (optional)
1 c. dairy sour cream
1 tsp. Worcestershire sauce
1 tsp. salt
2 tsp. lemon juice

• Blend blue cheese, cream cheese and garlic; stir in sour cream.

• Add remaining ingredients; blend well. Chill.
• Store in covered jar in cold place.
• Makes about 2 cups.

ONION PIE
(Zwiebel Kuchen)

A main-dish pie of German origin

Pastry for baked 10" shell:

1½ c. sifted flour
¾ tsp. salt
1½ tsp. caraway seeds
½ c. shortening
2 to 3 tblsp. water

Filling:

3 c. peeled onions, thinly sliced
3 tblsp. melted butter, margarine or fat
½ c. milk
1½ c. dairy sour cream
1 tsp. salt
2 eggs, well beaten
3 tblsp. flour
Bacon slices

• Combine flour, salt and caraway. Add shortening; cut into flour until mixture resembles small peas and coarse cornmeal.
• Stir water in lightly with fork; stir until mixture adheres and follows fork around bowl.
• Turn onto floured board; roll to ⅛" thickness. Fit into 10" pie pan.
• Bake in hot oven (425°) 10 minutes, or until lightly browned.

To make filling: Sauté onions in fat until lightly browned. Spoon into pastry shell.
• Add milk, 1¼ c. cream and salt to eggs.
• Blend flour with remaining ¼ c. cream. Combine with egg mixture; pour over onion mixture.
• Bake in slow oven (325°) 30 minutes, or until firm in center.
• Garnish with crisp bacon. Makes 8 servings.

CREAMED KALE AND ONIONS

Good with pork chops

1½ lbs. kale, cleaned
2 lbs. small white onions, peeled (about 12)
¼ c. shortening
3 tblsp. flour
1½ c. vegetable liquid or milk
Seasonings

• Cook kale in boiling salted water—enough to come halfway up—until tender, about 15 minutes.
• Cook onions in boiling salted water until tender, about 15 minutes.
• Drain and save vegetable liquid. Combine vegetables.
• Make white sauce of shortening, flour, milk and seasonings (salt, pepper, etc.). Pour over kale and onions. Serve hot. Makes 6 servings.

CREAMED ONIONS

Traditional vegetable for Thanksgiving, with pepped-up flavor

2 lbs. small white onions
2 tsp. salt
Boiling water
3 tblsp. butter or margarine
3 tblsp. flour
2 bouillon cubes
1½ c. milk
¼ c. chopped green pepper
2 tblsp. chopped pimiento

• Peel onions. Add salt and onions to boiling water. Cook slowly, uncovered, until tender, about 20 minutes.
• Meanwhile, melt butter in skillet. Blend in flour and bouillon cubes.
• Add milk. Cook over medium heat, stirring constantly, until mixture is smooth and thickened.
• Add well-drained onions to sauce. Keep mixture hot until ready to serve. Garnish with chopped green pepper and pimiento. Makes 6 servings.

ONIONS WITH SAVORY SAGE STUFFING

Put onions in muffin pans or custard cups to bake—they'll hold their shape

6 large onions, peeled
Favorite stuffing, based on 4 c. bread cubes

• Simmer onions until almost tender, about 10 minutes; drain, and hollow out, leaving ¾" shell.
• Chop pulp. Combine with your favorite stuffing recipe. Stuff onions.
• Bake in slow oven (325°) 30 minutes. If roasting meat, arrange onions around meat at close of cooking period. Makes 6 servings.

ONION PARSLEY SAUCE

Ladle over hot cooked vegetables to add flavor and eye appeal

2 tblsp. butter or margarine
1 small onion, chopped fine
1½ tblsp. flour
½ tsp. salt
⅛ tsp. pepper
1 tblsp. minced parsley
1 c. milk
1 egg yolk, beaten

• Melt butter. Sauté onion in butter until soft and clear. Remove from heat.
• Blend in flour, seasonings, parsley and milk. Cook until thickened, stirring.
• Blend egg yolk into sauce. Pour hot sauce over vegetables, as hot cooked peas, carrots or green beans. Makes 1 cup.

PARSNIP CASSEROLE

Ham and mushrooms glamorize parsnips, with marvelous results

3 c. mashed cooked parsnips
1 c. cubed cooked ham
1 c. canned mushrooms, drained
1 c. shredded sharp process cheese
½ c. crushed ready-to-eat cereal

• Season hot parsnips with salt, pepper, seasoned salt, etc.
• Combine ham, mushrooms and cheese.
• Alternate layers of parsnips and ham mixture in greased 2 qt. casserole. Sprinkle top with crumbs.
• Bake in moderate oven (350°) 25 minutes. Makes 6 servings.

Variation: Use 3 c. sliced cooked parsnips, ⅔ c. diced process cheese. Alternate layers of parsnips and cheese. Bake in moderate oven (350°) 30 minutes. Top with slices of crisp-cooked bacon. Makes 6 servings.

PARSNIP PATTIES

What could be better with roast beef? You'll want to double this one

6 medium parsnips, scrubbed
½ c. light cream
2 tblsp. flour
1½ tsp. salt
Pepper
Butter or fat

• Cook parsnips in boiling water until tender. Cool, peel and mash. (If parsnips have woody cores, cut in half lengthwise, and strip out the tough fibers.) Should make 2 c.
• Stir in cream, flour and seasonings; shape into 8 patties.
• Brown slowly in small amount butter for nice crisp crust. Makes 4 to 5 servings.

TOPSY-TURVY POTATO PIE

A pie made of your garden's gifts

7 medium potatoes, peeled and cooked
2 large carrots, scraped and just cooked
1¼ c. cooked shelled peas (or frozen)

• Mash and season hot potatoes. Should make 4 c.

• Slice hot carrots 1½″ thick, then cut these pieces into lengthwise ⅛″ slices. Arrange carrot slices "standing-up" around sides of greased 1½ qt. baking dish.
• Cover bottom of dish with peas; fill center with mashed potatoes. Place dish in pan of hot water.
• Bake in moderate oven (350°) 20 minutes. Flip pie upside down on heated serving plate (slips out easily if pan was well greased). Serve at once. Makes 6 servings.

CREAMED PEAS AND DEVILED HAM

Milk
1 (10½ oz.) can condensed cream of mushroom soup
1 (2¼ oz.) can deviled ham
2½ c. cooked fresh peas (or frozen or canned)

• Add enough milk to soup to make 2 c. Blend in ham; fold in drained peas; stir lightly. Heat.
• Serve over toast, waffles or baked potatoes. Makes 6 to 8 servings.

FRENCH PEAS

Garden peas in their Sunday best

2 tblsp. butter or margarine
1 tsp. rich brown prepared mustard
1 clove garlic, minced or crushed
2 c. shelled peas
4 medium mushrooms, sliced thin
1 tsp. salt
1 tblsp. water

• Melt butter in heavy skillet; blend in mustard.
• Add garlic, peas, mushrooms and salt; sprinkle with water. Cover pan tightly.
• Cook over medium heat 10 minutes, until peas are just tender, shaking pan occasionally. Serve immediately. Makes 6 servings.

COOKED PEAS IN POD

In our recipe the peas cook 1 hour; the Germans cook them even longer. The Orientals like pod-peas cooked slightly, to tender-crispness. Try both cooking times to find your family's preference

2 qts. edible-pod peas
2 tsp. salt
½ tsp. pepper
1 tblsp. butter or margarine
4 tblsp. heavy cream

• Wash pods through several waters. Remove stems.
• Simmer 1 hour in enough water to cover bottom of saucepan.
• Just before serving, add salt, pepper, butter and cream.
• To serve, pour cooking liquid over peapods. Makes 8 servings.

PEAS AND GREEN ONIONS

Perfection of flavors

2 lbs. fresh peas (about 2¼ c. shelled)
1 c. water
¼ tsp. salt
3 green onions
2 tblsp. butter or margarine
Salt
Pepper

• Shell fresh peas.
• Bring 1 c. water to boil. Add salt and peas. Cover, and cook about 10 minutes.
• Cut green onions crosswise into thin slices. Add to peas. Cook 1 minute. (There will be only a little liquid left.)
• Add butter. Season to taste with salt and pepper. Serve immediately. Makes 4 servings.

OVEN COOKED PEAS

Easy way to cook frozen vegetables

1 (10 oz.) pkg. frozen peas
½ tsp. salt
2 tblsp. butter or margarine

• Remove frozen peas from package and place in 1 qt. casserole.
• Sprinkle peas with salt; dot with butter. Cover with tight fitting lid.
• Bake in moderate oven (350°) 30 minutes. Makes 3 to 4 servings.

GREEN PEA MEDLEY

Imagine cheese, hard-cooked eggs, peas and green onions in the same dish!

4 tblsp. butter or margarine
4 tblsp. flour
½ tsp. salt
⅛ tsp. pepper
2 c. milk
1 (8 oz.) pkg. process cheese, shredded
3 c. hot, cooked seasoned peas
3 hard-cooked eggs, coarsely chopped
⅓ c. chopped onions (green or white)

• Make white sauce of melted butter, flour, seasonings and milk. Add ¾ of cheese; stir until melted.
• Put peas on platter; cover with cheese sauce. Sprinkle with eggs and onions, then with remaining cheese.
• Place under preheated broiler just long enough to melt cheese. Makes 8 servings.

RHUBARB CRUNCH

A delicious use for the garden's tender pink stalks

Crumb topping:

1 c. sifted flour
¾ c. uncooked rolled oats
1 c. brown sugar, firmly packed
½ c. melted butter or margarine
1 tsp. cinnamon

Fruit mixture:

4 c. diced rhubarb
1 c. sugar
2 tblsp. cornstarch
1 c. water
1 tsp. vanilla
Whipped cream (optional)

• Mix together crumb topping ingredients until crumbly. Press half of crumbs in greased 9″ layer pan.
• Cover with rhubarb.
• In small saucepan combine: sugar, cornstarch, water and vanilla. Cook, stirring, until thick and clear. Pour over rhubarb. Top with remaining crumbs.
• Bake in moderate oven (350°) 1 hour. Cut in squares, and serve warm, plain or with whipped cream. Makes 8 servings.

RHUBARB-ORANGE CREAM PIE

Rhubarb in orange custard fills the pastry—it puffs up while baking

Pastry for 9″ pie shell
3 eggs, separated
1¼ c. sugar
¼ c. soft butter or margarine
3 tblsp. frozen orange juice concentrate
¼ c. flour
¼ tsp. salt
2½ c. rhubarb, cut in ½″ pieces
⅓ c. chopped pecans

• Line 9″ pie pan with pastry; make high fluted rim.
• Beat egg whites until stiff; add ¼ c. sugar gradually, beating well after each addition.
• Add butter and juice concentrate to egg yolks; beat thoroughly. Add remaining 1 c. sugar, flour and salt; beat well.
• Add rhubarb to yolk mixture; stir well. Gently fold in meringue. Pour into pastry-lined pan; sprinkle with nuts.
• Bake on bottom rack in moderate oven (375°) 15 minutes. Reduce heat to slow (325°); bake 45 to 50 minutes more.

ROSY RHUBARB SWIRLS

Elegant eating

1½ c. sugar
½ c. cranberry juice cocktail
¼ c. water
3½ c. rhubarb, cut in ½" pieces
2 c. biscuit mix
½ tsp. nutmeg
1 tblsp. oil
⅓ to ½ c. milk
2 tblsp. soft butter or margarine

• Combine 1 c. sugar, cranberry juice and water in saucepan. Bring to boil; boil 1 minute.
• Put half of rhubarb in greased 8×8×2" pan.
• Combine biscuit mix, 2 tblsp. sugar and nutmeg. Add oil and milk to make soft dough; knead lightly on floured surface.
• Roll into 9" square. Spread with butter; sprinkle with remaining rhubarb and 4 tblsp. sugar. Roll as jelly roll; seal; cut into 9 slices.
• Place slices, cut side up, over rhubarb in pan. Pour over cranberry syrup; sprinkle with 2 tblsp. sugar.
• Bake in hot oven (425°) 25 to 30 minutes. Serve warm. Makes 9 servings.

RHUBARB AMBROSIA BETTY

Delightful as Maytime—pretty, too

5 c. rhubarb, cut in ½" pieces
1¾ c. sugar
1 tblsp. flour
¼ tsp. salt
1½ tsp. grated orange rind
Sections from 1 orange, cubed
4 c. bread cubes (½")
½ c. melted butter or margarine
½ c. flaked or shredded coconut

• Mix together rhubarb, sugar, flour, salt, ¾ tsp. orange rind and fruit. Add 2 c. bread cubes and ¼ c. butter; mix.
• Put into greased 8×8×2" pan.
• Combine remaining bread cubes, butter, orange rind and coconut. Sprinkle over top of rhubarb.
• Bake in moderate oven (375°) about 40 minutes, until browned. Serve warm. Makes 6 to 8 servings.

RUTABAGA-POTATO CASSEROLE

Complete the main course with pork sausage and buttered green beans

2 medium potatoes
2 medium rutabagas
½ c. flour
1 tsp. baking powder
1 tsp. salt
⅛ tsp. pepper
4 eggs, well beaten
¼ c. milk
¼ c. melted butter or drippings

• Peel potatoes and rutabagas; cover with cold water and let stand.
• Sift together flour, baking powder and seasonings.
• Blend half of dry ingredients with eggs. Stir in milk and butter; mix.
• Drain vegetables; grate fine or use blender.
• With wooden spoon, quickly mix remaining dry ingredients with vegetables. Work quickly to avoid dark potatoes!
• Place in greased 1 qt. casserole. Set in pan of hot water with level at least ⅔ up side of casserole.
• Bake in slow oven (325°) 1 hour. Makes 6 servings.

GRANDMA'S TURNIPS

• Combine 1½ c. hot, unseasoned mashed turnips, white or yellow, with 3 c. hot mashed potatoes. Season with salt, pepper and 6 tblsp. melted butter or margarine. Makes 5 servings.

Variation: Fold ⅔ c. grated process cheese into Grandma's Turnips just before serving.

SQUASH MEDLEY

Use little yellow, white and green squash and you'll have a charmer

8 squash

Filling:

1 large red or green pepper, chopped
3 medium to large ripe tomatoes, chopped
2 medium onions, chopped
3 slices bacon, chopped
1 (8 oz.) pkg. process cheese, shredded
1 tsp. salt
¼ tsp. pepper
Fine dry bread crumbs
Butter or margarine

• Parboil squash (zucchini take about 3 minutes; yellow crooknecks or small white pattypans, 5 minutes; and white scallops, 15 to 20, depending on size.)
• Cut zucchini, crooknecks and pattypans in half; cut top out of scallops. Scoop out seeds.
• To make filling, combine remaining ingredients except crumbs and butter. Mix well. Spoon into each squash.
• Top each with bread crumbs and dab of butter.
• Bake in hot oven (400°) 20 minutes. Makes 6 to 8 servings.

SQUASH WITH SAUSAGE

3 medium acorn squash
3 tblsp. melted butter or margarine
Salt and pepper
6 small onions, peeled
12 link sausages
Dash of paprika

• Cut squash in half, remove seeds. Brush edges and center with 1 tblsp. melted butter. Sprinkle with salt and pepper.
• Brush onions with butter. Place on baking sheet or shallow pan; cover with inverted squash halves.
• Bake in moderate oven (375°) 35 to 40 minutes, or until tender.
• Meanwhile, cook sausage according to directions on package.
• With fork, mash squash in shell. Place 2 sausage links in each squash half. Put onion in center. Brush with butter, sprinkle with paprika. Bake 10 minutes more. Makes 4 to 6 servings. (Wrap extra onions in aluminum foil; bake beside squash halves.)

POTATO "TOADS"

They puff up while baking—are crisp and brown on the outside; children call them "toads"

6 baking potatoes
Shortening
1 tsp. salt
1 (1" thick) ham slice

• Cut potatoes in thirds, lengthwise. Chill 1 hour in ice water.
• Roll potatoes in melted shortening. Arrange 1 layer deep around slice of ham on plank. Sprinkle with salt.
• Bake in moderate oven (375°) 20 minutes. Turn potatoes and ham, and bake 20 minutes more.
• Baste potatoes with ham drippings. Push to one side, and put cooked green beans on plank. Makes 6 servings.

TOMATO ASPIC

Basil and chives make it different and delicious

1 tsp. sweet basil
2 c. tomato juice
1 (3 oz.) pkg. lemon flavor gelatin
2 tblsp. chives or garlic vinegar
½ tsp. salt
Crisp salad greens
4 tsp. mayonnaise or salad dressing
Paprika

• Add basil to tomato juice; heat to boiling. Let stand 10 minutes, strain.
• Add gelatin, vinegar and salt; stir to dissolve.

• Pour into individual salad molds. Chill.
• Unmold. Serve on crisp salad greens. Top each with 1 tsp. mayonnaise, garnished with dash of paprika. Makes 4 servings.

TASTY TOMATO BAKE

Bacon flatters tomato flavor

2 strips bacon
2 c. soft bread cubes (3 slices bread)
¼ c. chopped green pepper
¼ c. chopped onion
6 medium tomatoes
1 tblsp. sugar
2 tblsp. flour
1 tsp. salt
⅛ tsp. pepper
Dash of sage
⅓ c. grated or shredded sharp process cheese

• Fry bacon. Remove strips and drain; leave about 3 tblsp. fat in skillet.
• Add bread cubes; toss. Add green pepper and onions; sauté lightly.
• Peel tomatoes; cut into cubes. Add to bread mixture.
• Combine sugar, flour, salt, pepper and sage. Sprinkle over tomatoes; toss lightly.
• Spoon mixture into greased 1½ qt. casserole.
• Crumble bacon over top, then cheese.
• Bake in moderate oven (350°) 20 to 30 minutes. Makes 4 servings.

CORN-STUFFED TOMATOES

Choose firm ripe tomatoes and tender yellow corn to serve with chicken

4 c. cooked corn, or 2 (1 lb.) cans whole kernel corn, drained
1 tsp. salt
¼ tsp. pepper
¼ c. melted butter or margarine
10 medium tomatoes

• Wash tomatoes, slice off tops, scoop out pulp. Combine pulp in bowl with remaining ingredients.
• Stuff tomatoes with mixture. Place in greased muffin cups. Bake in moderate oven (375°) about 20 minutes. Makes 10 servings.

BAKED DEVILED TOMATOES

4 large ripe tomatoes, cut in half
1 tsp. prepared mustard
1 tblsp. chopped chives or onion (green or white)
2 tblsp. chopped green pepper
2 tblsp. chopped celery
½ tsp. salt
⅓ c. melted butter or margarine

• Place tomatoes, cut side up, in greased baking dish. Spread tops with mustard.
• Combine chives, green pepper, celery and salt; sprinkle over tomatoes. Drizzle butter over top.
• Bake in hot oven (425°) 8 minutes. Makes 6 to 8 servings.

SAVORY BROILED TOMATOES

Bet you'll double this recipe

3 tblsp. melted butter or margarine
½ c. coarse cracker crumbs
2 tblsp. minced parsley
¼ tsp. thyme
½ tsp. salt
⅛ tsp. pepper
4 medium ripe tomatoes

• Combine butter, crumbs, parsley, thyme and seasonings; mix well.
• Cut stem end from tomatoes; cut in half crosswise. Spread crumb mixture on cut sides.
• Place on rack in preheated broiler, about 4" from heat. Broil until tomatoes are heated through and topping is lightly browned, 3 to 5 minutes. Serve immediately. Makes 4 servings.

BAKED TURNIPS WITH PEANUTS

A Dutch treat

3 c. sliced cooked turnips
1 medium onion, sliced
1 c. chopped peanuts
2 tblsp. butter
2 tsp. salt
½ tsp. paprika
Chopped parsley

• Arrange turnips, onion and peanuts in well greased baking dish. Dot with butter, add salt and paprika. Bake uncovered in moderate oven (350°) 15 minutes. Sprinkle with parsley. Makes 6 servings.

Variation: Substitute cooked rutabaga for turnips.

TURNIPS IN CHEESE SAUCE

If your family doesn't fancy turnips, try this

3 c. crisp, fresh turnips, peeled
¼ c. butter or margarine
¼ c. flour
1½ c. light cream
1 c. shredded process cheese
1 tblsp. minced chives

• Slice turnips; cook in boiling salted water 8 to 10 minutes. Drain; cover to keep hot.

• Melt butter in saucepan; stir in flour. Add cream; cook, stirring, until thickened. Add cheese, and stir until melted in.

• Add turnips to sauce. Sprinkle with chives. Makes 6 servings.

Note: New Englanders refer to yellow and white turnips, but in some areas the yellow ones are called rutabagas. White turnips are more delicate in flavor, but they may be used interchangeably.

TURNIP STEW

The Czechoslovakian way

3 tblsp. butter or margarine
3 c. diced cooked turnips
½ c. whole kernel corn (canned)
1 medium onion, chopped
1 medium apple, sliced
1 tsp. salt
¼ tsp. nutmeg
¼ c. dairy sour cream
1 tblsp. prepared horse-radish

• Melt butter, add turnips, corn, onion, apple and seasonings. Simmer until apple and onion are soft, about 15 minutes.

• Add sour cream, heat through; add horse-radish and serve. Makes 6 servings.

BAKED FILLED ZUCCHINI

An Italian dish with many Western friends

3 zucchini (1" to 2" thick)
Salt
Pepper
1 tblsp. butter or margarine
¼ c. chopped onion
½ c. chopped celery
1 c. ground beef or leftover cooked meat
1 slice bread, cubed
1 (8 oz.) can tomato sauce
¼ c. grated Parmesan cheese

• Cook zucchini in boiling salted water about 3 minutes. Cut in half, lengthwise. Scoop out pulp. Salt and pepper.

• Melt butter; add onion, celery and meat. Cook until lightly browned. Add bread cubes, scooped out pulp and tomato sauce. Stuff mixture in zucchini.

• Place in shallow baking pan. Sprinkle with cheese. Bake in moderate oven (375°) 30 minutes, until tender. Makes 6 servings.

16

Good Eating from the Freezer

Home food freezers have revolutionized country cooking. They've banished leftovers and complaints about having the same foods warmed up several times. Now meal remnants go into freezers to appear days or weeks later as something brand new—the first appearance is forgotten. So meals can have wider variety.

Even a big turkey is no problem after a holiday feast; leftover meat packaged and frozen appears in many pleasing dishes in the months that follow.

Freezers deserve the credit for millions of "make-ahead" cooks. One of the best recommendations for a recipe now is: You can make it ahead and freeze it. With the right food in the freezer, you can avoid the uneasy flurries just before mealtime, both for family and company dinners. And if you're a busy woman who sometimes arrives home when it's almost time to get dinner or supper, you find prepared foods in the freezer a real comfort—while they warm, you set the table and fix the remainder of the meal.

Most farm women have their pet dishes to freeze for fast-fix meals. Recipes for some of their favorites follow in this chapter. Our readers tell us that unexpected guests are more cordially welcomed because freezers simplify the problem of what to feed them. They find it's a great advantage to fix cakes, pies, breads, cookies and sandwiches (party- or lunch-size) ahead at their leisure and freeze them.

Women also say freezers cut down on the time they spend cooking, for frequently they fix enough for two meals instead of one. They rejoice that freezers have made ice cream available any day it's craved instead of a rare Sunday special. And as we mentioned elsewhere in this cookbook, the freezer is the cookie jar and bread box in thousands of homes. Even fruit jams are frozen these days . . . but turn the page in this chapter and you'll see how freezers help make clever cooks.

TWICE-BAKED ROLLS

A Farm Journal 5-star recipe

2 pkgs. granular or compressed yeast
1 c. water
1 tsp. sugar
5 tsp. salt
¼ c. sugar
2 c. scalded milk
10 c. sifted flour (about)
½ c. cooled, melted shortening

• Sprinkle granular yeast over warm (110°) water; or crumble compressed yeast over lukewarm (85°) water. Add 1 tsp. sugar.

• Combine salt and ¼ c. sugar in bowl; pour in milk. Stir to dissolve; cool to lukewarm, then add yeast mixture.

• Mix in 6 c. flour, then add shortening and about 4 more c. flour.

• Turn out on lightly floured board; knead until smooth and satiny.

• Put dough in greased bowl; grease top. Cover with clean, damp towel, redampen occasionally. Let double in bulk in warm place (85°). Punch down.

• Knead again on floured board; divide in four parts. Cover with damp towel; let rest 20 minutes. Shape 4 loaves or 4 to 6 dozen rolls (see variations).

• Let rise in warm place (85°) until ¾ as high as regular rolls or loaf. (Otherwise they fall when baked.)

• Bake pan rolls in slow oven (275°) 40 minutes; bread, 75 minutes. Let set 20 minutes in pans. Turn out, cool at room temperature.

• Wrap in freezer paper; freeze as long as 3 months.

• To serve; place rolls and bread on ungreased baking sheet, and brown in very hot oven (450°) 7 minutes.

Quick Butterhorn Rolls: Roll dough into a 10″ circle, ½″ thick. Brush with melted butter; cut, like pie, into 12 pieces. Roll up each piece from wide end. Lay on well greased baking sheet, with tip underneath.

Individual Butterfly Coffee Cakes: Roll dough into 6×10″ rectangle, ¼″ thick. Brush with melted butter; sprinkle with sugar and cinnamon. Roll like jelly roll; cut in 1″ slices. Place on well greased baking sheet. Pinch in with forefinger and thumb to form butterfly. Press a toy wooden clothespin in center to hold dough in butterfly shape. Bake; remove holder.

Cinnamon Bread: Shape dough in 6× 10″ rectangle, ½″ thick. Brush with melted butter. Mix ½ c. sugar and 2 tsp. cinnamon, and sprinkle over dough. Roll up like jelly roll; flatten ends with hand and turn under, pinching in place. Put in well-greased 5×9″ loaf pan.

INDIVIDUAL MEAT LOAVES

Easy to bake these individual loaves on a busy day

2 lbs. ground beef
1 c. dry bread (or cracker) crumbs
½ c. chopped onion
1 egg, beaten
½ c. milk
1 tsp. salt
¼ tsp. pepper
¼ c. ketchup

• Combine all ingredients and mix well.
• Shape into six individual loaves.
• Wrap in freezer paper; freeze.
• To serve, unwrap and place in baking dish. Bake in moderate oven (350°) 45 minutes. Makes 6 servings.

Stuffed Peppers: Fill uncooked green peppers, seeds removed, with above meat loaf mixture. Wrap or place in freezer containers and freeze. Bake without thawing in covered baking dish in moderate oven (350°) until tender.

SPAGHETTI MEAT SAUCE

Ready for a spaghetti supper whenever you want to have one

1 large onion, chopped
1 clove garlic, minced
¼ c. oil
1 lb. ground beef
2½ c. tomatoes, or 1 (1 lb.) can
1 (6 oz.) can tomato paste
1 c. water
1 tsp. salt
½ tsp. pepper
1 bay leaf

• Sauté onion and garlic in oil. Add meat and cook until browned.

• Add remaining ingredients; simmer slowly about 1 hour.

• Cool quickly; freeze in trays (with dividers). Transfer cubes to freezer container.

• To serve, heat as many cubes as needed over low heat. Spoon sauce over freshly cooked spaghetti. Sprinkle with grated cheese. Makes 6 servings.

Beef Dishes—Quick

Country women take advantage of a leisurely day (frequently a stormy one when they must be indoors) to cook large quantities of such things as beef, or tomato sauce, or a big turkey for freezing. Later they use these foods as the basis for many tempting dishes that have no earmarks of leftovers. We give you a recipe for freezing beef cubes, then four quick recipes using the frozen cubes. These recipes were tried and approved by members of Farm Journal's Family Test Group.

TENDER BROWN BEEF CUBES

4 tblsp. shortening
10 to 12 lbs. beef (cut as for stew)
Salt and pepper

• Heat shortening in 2 heavy skillets; brown beef on all sides in hot fat.
• Place beef in large heavy kettle; add seasonings and water to the depth of 1″.
• Cover; simmer until just tender, 1 to 2 hours. Cool; package meat in 1 quart, 4 pint and 4 half-pint containers (to fit recipes). Package broth separately. Freeze. Makes 4 to 5 quarts.

QUICK STEW

Make this with frozen beef cubes

2 (10 oz.) pkgs. frozen mixed vegetables
2 c. beef broth
5 tblsp. flour
3 c. frozen beef cubes
Salt and pepper
1 (7 oz.) pkg. instant mashed potatoes

• Cook vegetables as directed on package; drain.

• Heat 1½ c. broth; add flour blended with remaining ½ c. broth to make smooth paste. Heat, stirring frequently, until smooth and thickened.

• Add beef, vegetables, salt and pepper; simmer about 20 minutes.

• While stew simmers, prepare instant mashed potatoes by package directions. Serve stew piping hot with potatoes around edge. Makes 6 servings.

Variations: Omit potatoes and serve stew over quick-cooking rice, or top hot stew with packaged refrigerator biscuits; bake uncovered in hot oven (425°) 20 minutes.

HEARTY SHORTCAKE

A platter treat—hot biscuits and beef

3 c. frozen beef cubes
1 (10 oz.) pkg. frozen peas, cooked and drained
3 hard-cooked eggs, diced
1 onion, chopped
1 tblsp. prepared mustard
2 (10½ oz.) cans condensed cream of mushroom soup
½ c. beef broth or liquid drained from peas
3 c. biscuit mix

• Combine all ingredients except biscuit mix. Heat thoroughly, about 20 minutes.
• Make biscuits by package directions. (may add ¾ c. shredded cheese).
• Split hot biscuits in halves; top with beef mixture. Makes 6 servings of 2 (3") biscuits each.

DINNER BEEF PIE

Serve this plump meat pie hot from oven

2 tblsp. shortening
1½ c. chopped celery
1½ c. chopped onion
1½ c. chopped green pepper
3 c. frozen beef cubes
1 (10½ oz.) can tomato soup
2 tblsp. prepared mustard
¼ c. ketchup
¾ tsp. salt
Pastry for 2-crust (9") pie

• Heat shortening in skillet; add celery, onion and green pepper; sauté until soft. Stir in beef, soup and seasonings.
• Place meat mixture between two pastry crusts, slashing top to make steam vents. Bake in hot oven (425°) 40 to 50 minutes. Makes 6 servings.

Note: Green pepper may be omitted; then use 2¼ c. each celery and onion.

BEEF WITH SOUR CREAM

Quick, unusual and tasty

2 tblsp. shortening
2 medium onions, sliced thin
½ c. beef broth or water
3 c. frozen beef cubes
3 tblsp. shredded sharp cheese
½ tsp. salt
⅛ tsp. pepper
½ c. dairy sour cream

• Melt shortening in skillet. Add onions; sauté until soft and clear. Add broth, beef, cheese and seasonings. Cover; simmer gently to heat.
• Just before serving blend in sour cream. Makes 6 servings.

Frozen Tomato Sauce—Main Dish Starter

HOME-COOKED TOMATO SAUCE

Freeze this to have on hand to make the special dishes that follow

4 (1 lb. 12 oz.) or 8 (14 oz.) cans Italian-style peeled tomatoes
8 (6 oz.) cans tomato paste
1 qt. water
6 bay leaves
½ c. oil
4 cloves garlic
5 tsp. salt
½ tsp. pepper
¼ c. Parmesan cheese

• Combine all ingredients in 8 qt. kettle; bring to boil. Simmer uncovered over very low heat about 6½ hours, or until tomato pulp cooks down and flavors blend, stirring occasionally. Add more water, if necessary, to give sauce consistency of thick white sauce. Remove bay leaves. Divide into 1 qt. portions; cool.
• Freeze in glass loaf pans. When frozen, remove sauce from pans; wrap blocks

separately in heavy-duty foil or place in pliofilm bags; store in freezer. Makes 4 (1 qt.) blocks. For recipe amounts, cut blocks with frozen food saw or heavy knife.

TUNA-SPAGHETTI BAKE

Something new for covered-dish suppers

1 qt. block frozen tomato sauce
1 c. water
1 bouillon cube (beef or chicken)
1 (8 oz.) pkg. spaghetti
2 (7 oz.) cans tuna
2 slices (3½" square) sharp process cheese, quartered

• Heat tomato sauce and water with bouillon cube. Cook spaghetti by package directions; drain; return to kettle.
• Add tuna, coarsely broken, and tomato sauce; toss together. Place in greased 2½ qt. baking dish; top with cheese.
• Bake covered in moderate oven (375°) 10 minutes; uncover and bake 10 minutes longer. Makes 6 servings.

SKILLET BARBECUED FRANKS

Try this on corn bread or toasted buns

¾ block frozen tomato sauce (3 c.)
1 c. water
1 medium onion, finely chopped
½ tsp. salt
1 tsp. Worcestershire sauce
5 drops Tabasco sauce
1 lb. frankfurters

• In skillet, heat to boiling: tomato sauce, water, onion, and seasonings. Add frankfurters, split and cut in 1" lengths. Simmer uncovered 10 minutes. Makes 6 servings.

Note: Frankfurters are cooked when you buy them. They will keep two weeks or less in the freezer in original package. To store longer, rewrap in moisture-vapor-proof material.

GOULASH WITH NOODLES

An eye-catcher—spicy red sauce trickles down through hot, buttery egg noodles

¾ block frozen tomato sauce (3 c.)
3 onions, cut fine or minced
¾ tsp. salt
¼ tsp. pepper
4 c. beef cubes
1 (8 oz.) pkg. egg noodles
2 tblsp. butter or margarine
1 tblsp. caraway or poppy seeds

• Heat tomato sauce with onions and seasonings over medium heat to boiling. Stir in beef; simmer to heat.
• Cook noodles by package directions; drain. Toss with butter and seeds.
• Spread noodles on hot platter; pour meat mixture over them, leaving border of noodles. Serve hot. Makes 6 servings.

Variation: Omit frozen tomato sauce and use 3 (8 oz.) cans tomato sauce.

TAMALE PIE

Perfect accompaniments: Crisp green salad, cool pineapple or banana dessert

1 lb. ground beef
¾ block frozen tomato sauce (3 c.)
1 tsp. salt
4 tsp. chili powder
¼ tsp. garlic salt
1 qt. chilled cornmeal mush
Pitted ripe olives (optional)

• Brown beef in heavy skillet; drain off fat. Add tomato sauce and seasonings; heat thoroughly.
• Pour into 2 qt. oblong baking dish lined with thin (⅛") slices of mush; top with more mush slices. If desired, stud top with ripe olives.
• Bake in hot oven (425°) 25 to 30 minutes. Makes 6 servings.

Short Cut: Line baking dish with hot mush (following package directions for 3 c. cornmeal); reserve about ⅓ to spread over top of pie.

COMPANY CHICKEN

New color with frozen tomato sauce

2 (2½ to 3 lb.) frying chickens
½ c. shortening or oil
1⅓ c. chopped onion
1 qt. block frozen tomato sauce
2 tsp. salt
2 tsp. garlic salt
1 c. apple juice
4 tsp. lemon juice
2 c. water

• Brown chicken pieces in hot shortening in skillet. Pour off fat. Add onion and cook over low heat until golden.
• Add chopped or thawed tomato sauce and remaining ingredients. Bring to boil; cover. Simmer 35 to 45 minutes or until chicken is tender. Makes 6 servings.

BEEFEATERS' KIDNEY BEANS

A dish to satisfy ravenous appetites

½ lb. ground beef
½ qt. block frozen tomato sauce (2 c.)
½ c. water
2 (1 lb.) cans kidney beans
1 medium onion, chopped
1 tblsp. chili powder
¾ c. (¼ lb.) ½" cubes process cheese

• Brown ground beef in large saucepan. Add tomato sauce, water, liquid from beans, onion and chili powder.
• Bring to boil and simmer (covered) 10 minutes. Add beans; cover and simmer 10 to 15 minutes. Serve topped with cheese. Makes 6 servings.

Soups from Frozen Stock

SUPER SOUP STOCK

Wonderful to have stored in your freezer

10 lbs. soup bones
1 lb. soup meat chunks
2 tblsp. peppercorns
3 onions, quartered
6 cloves garlic

• Crack bones. Put into 7 qt. pressure canner, being careful not to fill above "full" mark. (If using 7 or 8 qt. pressure saucepan, use half this recipe.)
• Add soup meat, peppercorns, onions and garlic. Cover with cold water. (Stock will be highly concentrated, so it's best to add salt later, when you make soup.)
• Close pressure canner cover; bring up steam. Exhaust air, close valve when pressure reaches 15 pounds. Adjust heat to hold at 15 pounds. (Good idea to watch for about ½ hour to be sure pressure is maintained steadily.)
• Cook under pressure 4 to 8 hours. Remove from heat. Let pressure go down without opening petcock. Cool stock until it can be handled easily, and fat rises to top. Skim off fat.
• Pick out bones with kitchen tongs. Use perforated spoon to remove big bone fragments and chunks of fat and gristle; strain through cheesecloth, returning bits of lean meat to stock. Makes 8 quarts.

To Freeze: Dip cool stock into plastic freezer containers. (Pint size holds enough stock to make 6 or 8 servings of soup.) Cool completely; skim off any fat that forms; seal airtight. Freeze.

To Can: Pour cooled stock into clean pint or quart jars. Put on caps, screwing bands tight. Process in pressure canner, 40 minutes at 10 pounds.

Good Freezers: Some of the soups that freeze well are: Split pea, navy bean, black bean, cream of corn, asparagus purée, French onion and meat broth. Cool soup quickly by setting kettle in pan of cold water. To thaw, heat cream soups in double boiler, clear soups in saucepan. They will keep satisfactorily in the freezer for about six months.

BEAN AND FRANKFURTER SOUP

Made with frozen soup stock—you can't imagine how good it is

2 c. dried lima beans
4 c. water
2 c. thawed soup stock
1 onion, sliced thin
1 tblsp. salt
½ tsp. pepper
½ tsp. dry mustard
3 tblsp. vinegar
3 tblsp. Worcestershire sauce
2 tblsp. brown sugar
1 lb. frankfurters

• Soak beans overnight in water to cover.
• Place beans in large pan. Add water, stock, onion, salt, pepper and mustard. Simmer in tightly covered saucepan about 1½ hours, or until beans are soft. Mash beans or put through food mill.
• Return bean purée to saucepan. Add vinegar, Worcestershire sauce and sugar.
• Slice frankfurters; add to soup. Bring to boil; simmer 15 minutes. Makes 6 to 8 servings.

VEGETABLE CHOWDER

2 c. canned or raw corn
2 c. chopped celery
½ green pepper, cut in thin strips
1 onion, thinly sliced
1 c. cooked tomatoes
1 tblsp. salt
⅛ tsp. pepper
2 c. thawed soup stock
¼ c. butter or margarine
3 tblsp. flour
2 c. milk, scalded
½ c. grated cheese
½ c. chopped pimiento
¼ tsp. paprika

• Put corn, celery, green pepper, onion, tomatoes, salt and pepper in kettle. Add thawed soup stock, bring to boil and simmer 30 minutes.
• Melt butter and stir in flour; gradually add milk and cook 5 minutes, stirring constantly until smooth and thickened; add to vegetable mixture. Add remaining ingredients, stirring until cheese is melted. Makes 6 servings.

FRENCH ONION SOUP

Dress it up with a sprinkling of cheese

¼ c. butter or margarine
3 onions, sliced
Salt and pepper
4 c. water
2 c. thawed soup stock
1 tsp. Worcestershire sauce

• Melt butter in large pan; add onions. Fry in butter until soft and yellow. Season with salt and pepper.
• Add water, stock and Worcestershire sauce. Simmer slowly 45 minutes. Serve in bowls topped with circles of toast sprinkled with grated cheese. Makes 6 servings.

QUICK SOUPS

Use Frozen Soup Stock with canned or packaged soups

4 c. cold water
1 c. frozen soup stock
1 (10½ oz.) can soup, or 1 pkg. dehydrated soup mix

• Combine all ingredients; simmer gently until frozen stock melts and flavors blend. Makes 6 servings. If desired, two different commercial soups can be combined for new flavor treats, such as Black Bean and Onion; Tomato and Split Pea, or Vegetable Noodle; Mushroom and Onion. For 2 cans, increase water to 8 c. Makes 12 servings.

Frozen Sandwiches

Country women who pack lunches praise frozen sandwiches. They make them at slack times to have ready for quick use. These filling recipes make 6 sandwiches. They keep in the freezer 2 to 3 weeks in excellent condition—thaw in 3 hours. While fillings introduce pleasing variety, different breads also provide change. You also will find many recipes in this cookbook for interesting sandwich breads.

BEEF AND KETCHUP FILLING

1¼ c. cooked ground beef
½ tsp. salt
1 tsp. Worcestershire sauce
⅓ c. ketchup
1 tblsp. softened butter or margarine

• Mix together. Makes about 1⅓ cups.

CORNED BEEF, RELISH AND ONION FILLING

1 (12 oz.) can corned beef, chopped (1 c.)
½ c. cooked salad dressing
2 tblsp. pickle relish
1 tsp. finely chopped onion
½ tsp. celery salt

• Combine ingredients; mix well. Makes about 1¼ cups.

BAKED BEAN AND SALAMI FILLING

1 (1 lb.) can baked beans (2 c.)
1 c. salami, chopped fine (¼ lb.)
2 tblsp. chili sauce
2 tsp. prepared mustard

• Mix well. Makes about 2¾ cups.

SARDINE AND PIMIENTO FILLING

2 (3¼ oz.) cans sardines
¼ c. ketchup
1 tblsp. lemon juice
2 tblsp. chopped pimiento

• Combine ingredients; stir lightly. Makes about ¾ cup.
(Olives may be substituted for pimiento.)

CHICKEN AND PICKLE FILLING

1¼ c. cooked, chopped chicken or tuna, flaked
¼ c. chopped pickle
1 tsp. Worcestershire sauce
⅓ c. undiluted cream of chicken soup
¼ tsp. celery salt

• Combine ingredients. Makes about 1⅓ cups.

CREAM CHEESE-DRIED BEEF FILLING

1 (3 oz.) pkg. cream cheese
1 tblsp. milk (optional)
½ c. shredded dried beef
1 tblsp. prepared horse-radish
1 tblsp. cooked salad dressing

• Blend cheese and milk. Stir in remaining ingredients and mix well. Makes about ¾ cup.

Frozen Fruit Salads, Desserts

FROZEN FRUIT SALAD

You can make this salad-dessert two weeks or two months before the party

1 envelope unflavored gelatin
¼ c. maraschino cherry juice
1 c. diced apricots
1 c. diced pineapple
1 c. halved, seeded grapes
1 c. chopped maraschino cherries
3 tblsp. lemon juice
½ c. sugar
1 c. heavy cream
½ c. mayonnaise or salad dressing

• Soften gelatin in cherry juice in top of double boiler. Dissolve over boiling water. Add fruits, lemon juice and sugar. Chill until syrupy.
• Whip cream until light and fluffy. Stir in mayonnaise. Fold into fruit mixture with a wooden spoon, using an over-under motion.
• Spoon salad into molds. Use ½ pt. waxed freezer cartons with snap-on lids. They store easily in freezer.
• Unmold salads on lettuce leaves 2 hours before serving. Run a knife around each cup; press bottom to release salad. Chill until served. Makes 8 servings.

FROZEN SALADS IN ORANGE SHELLS

Good with baked ham, a green vegetable and hot rolls—nice for Sunday dinner

4 oranges
½ c. orange pulp
1½ c. canned fruit cocktail, drained
¼ c. chopped, blanched almonds
2 (3 oz.) pkgs. cream cheese
¼ c. mayonnaise or salad dressing
1 tblsp. vinegar
¼ tsp. prepared mustard
⅛ tsp. salt
½ c. heavy cream

• Cut oranges in half and scoop out. Dice the pulp.
• Combine orange pulp with fruit cocktail and almonds. Blend in cream cheese, mayonnaise, vinegar, mustard and salt. Mix together lightly.
• Whip cream; fold into fruit mixture. Heap salad in orange shells. Freeze. Wrap airtight in freezer paper if for later use.
• Let salads stand at room temperature a few minutes before serving. Garnish with small scoops of orange sherbet. Makes 8 servings.

PUMPKIN TARTS

1 tblsp. cornstarch
¾ c. sugar
½ tsp. cinnamon
¼ tsp. ginger
2 egg yolks, slightly beaten
1 c. milk
¾ c. cooked or canned pumpkin
2 egg whites, stiffly beaten
½ c. heavy cream, whipped
⅓ c. chopped pecans

• Mix cornstarch, sugar, cinnamon and ginger. Stir in egg yolks and milk. Cook over hot water in double boiler until thickened, stirring constantly. Add pumpkin. Freeze.
• Break into chunks: turn into bowl. Beat smooth with rotary beater (this extra beating adds air, makes a smoother ice cream).
• Fold in egg whites, whipped cream and nuts. Pour into 8 small tart shells. Freeze firm. Makes 8 servings.

Whole Wheat Tart Shells: Combine 2 c. unsifted whole wheat flour, 1 tsp. salt, ½ c. shortening, cutting in shortening until mixture resembles fine cornmeal. Stir in 6 tblsp. cold water; form into ball and chill. Roll out on lightly floured board. Bake in hot oven (425°) 12 minutes. Makes 8 (4") shells.

ICE CREAM LAYER CAKE

Use angel food, sponge or chiffon cake

1 qt. ice cream
2 c. heavy cream
1 tblsp. sugar
1 tsp. vanilla
1 can or box flaked or shredded coconut

• Cut cake lengthwise into three layers. Spread ice cream between layers.
• Place cake in freezer to harden.
• Whip cream; add sugar and vanilla; use to frost top and sides of cake. Cover with coconut; and return to freezer until whipped cream is hard. Wrap in freezer paper; freeze.
• To serve, slice without thawing. Serve at once. Makes 16 to 20 servings.

SNOW BALLS

Make them ahead for Christmas or birthdays and freeze

• Make large snow balls of vanilla ice cream using an ice cream scoop. Roll in flaked or shredded coconut. Press a hole in top if candle is to be used. Work quickly and put each ball in freezer when shaped. When frozen solid, dump into a plastic bag and return to freezer. To serve, decorate top of each ball with holly, a small lighted candle, or other appropriate garnish.

PINK PARTY ROLL

Pretty dessert for February holidays

3 c. heavy cream
1 c. cherry preserves
1/8 tsp. salt
1/4 tsp. almond extract
24 chocolate wafers
2 tblsp. whole cherry preserves
Red food color

• Whip 2 c. cream.
• Chop the 1 c. cherry preserves fine with vegetable chopper. Fold into whipped cream; season with salt and almond extract.
• Place heaping teaspoonful of whipped cream mixture on chocolate wafer; top with another wafer, sandwich fashion. Makes 3 stacks of 8 cookies each (easier to handle than one big stack).
• Lay cookie stacks on their sides on several thicknesses of waxed paper or freezer wrapping. Put stacks together with more cream to make long roll. Wrap tightly and freeze until firm, about 4 hours. Will keep in freezer about 2 weeks.
• To serve, whip 1 c. cream; fold in the 2 tblsp. whole cherry preserves. Add few drops food color to make a delicate pink.
• Unwrap frozen roll; frost with whipped cream. Cut diagonally in small slices—a very rich dessert! Serve at once. Makes 8 to 10 servings.

RASPBERRY ICE CREAM PIE

1 (9") baked pie shell
1½ c. raspberry jam
1 pt. vanilla ice cream

• Spread cooled pie shell with raspberry jam. (Use spatula to work jam well up sides of shell to form raspberry border.)
• Slightly soften ice cream at room temperature. Spoon into center of pie; swirl top with spatula. Freeze until firm. Makes 6 to 8 servings.

To store pie, freeze until solid, so it will be easy to handle. Then wrap and return to freezer. Let soften slightly at room temperature before serving.

Frozen Cakes—Extra Good Keepers

These layer cakes are exceptionally good freezers. You can freeze them in halves on cardboard or baking sheets; they'll stay fresh and moist.

3-WAY GOLD CAKE

A super-special cake

11 egg yolks
¼ tsp. salt
2 c. sugar
1 c. milk, scalded
2½ c. sifted cake flour
2 tsp. baking powder
1 tsp. lemon extract
1 tsp. vanilla
½ c. butter or margarine, melted

• Beat yolks with salt until thick. Gradually add sugar; beat until thick and puffy. Add hot milk; mix.
• Sift together flour and baking powder; add to egg mixture. Add flavorings and butter. Pour into greased 9×13×2" or 15½×10½×1" pan. Bake in moderate oven (350°) 35 to 40 minutes, or until cake tester inserted in center comes out clean. Remove from pan; cool, cut in thirds and wrap separately for freezer. **To Serve:** Frost one section a dainty pink and cut in small diamonds; split one, put together with mint jelly or raspberry jam and sprinkle top with confectioners sugar; cut last third in fingers to serve with fruit compote.

ORANGE CAKE

4 large oranges (1 c. juice)
½ c. milk
1 c. shortening
3 c. sugar
4 tblsp. grated orange rind
4 eggs, beaten
4 c. sifted cake flour
5 tsp. baking powder
1 tsp. baking soda
½ tsp. salt

• Squeeze juice from oranges. Add milk.
• Cream shortening. Gradually add sugar, orange rind and eggs.
• Sift together flour, baking powder, soda and salt. Add alternately with liquid to creamed mixture. Beat well.
• Pour into 3 greased 8×8×2" pans. Bake in moderate oven (350°) 45 minutes. Cool on racks. Frost 2 layers with Creamy Chocolate Frosting; freeze third layer for use later.

Creamy Chocolate Frosting:

2½ c. sugar
½ c. cocoa
1 c. light cream or evaporated milk
1 tsp. vanilla

• Mix sugar and cocoa in saucepan; add cream. Cook over moderate heat, stirring constantly, until it begins to boil. Boil about 3 minutes, or until a teaspoonful will form a soft ball in cold water.
• Add vanilla. Cool and beat until thick and creamy. Spread on cake.

BANANA LAYER CAKE

2 c. mashed bananas (4 or 5)
¼ c. milk
1 c. shortening
2 tsp. vanilla
2 c. sugar
4 eggs, unbeaten
4½ c. sifted cake flour
4 tsp. baking powder
1 tsp. salt

• Combine bananas and milk.
• Cream together shortening and vanilla; gradually add sugar, beating until light and fluffy.
• Add eggs, one at a time, beating well; mix until light and fluffy.
• Sift together flour, baking powder and salt. Add alternately with bananas and milk to creamed mixture, beating smooth after each addition.
• Pour into 3 greased 9" layer pans. Bake in moderate oven (350°) 30 to 35 minutes. Cool layers and freeze.

Freezing Special Fruits, Vegetables

Herbs: Wash but do not blanch (blanching destroys flavor). Package 1 or 2 sprigs of thyme, basil, mint, savory or other herbs in small cellophane bags; label. Freeze; keep in container in freezer. Ready for instant use.

Orange and Lemon Rind: Shred rind, package in ½ and 1 tsp. lots in small cellophane bags. Freeze.

Bananas: When fruit ripens faster than it can be used, put it through food mill, add lemon juice or anti-darkening agent and freeze. It comes in handy in making breads and cakes.

Green Peppers: Keep small quantities on hand for casseroles and salads. Wash, dry and seed peppers. Cut them in halves or fourths. Seal in cellophane bags. Pack several bags in a container.

Elderberries: Wash berries; remove from stem. Package to freeze (no sugar needed); seal airtight. Freeze. Use in elderberry-apple pie recipe. You can also substitute frozen, unsweetened rhubarb for the apples. Thaw the fruit only enough to mix with tapioca; bake pie longer—45 minutes instead of 20.

Persimmons: Select soft-ripe fruit (American or Oriental variety). Peel, cut into sections and sieve or put through food mill. To 1 qt. persimmon pulp add ⅛ tsp. ascorbic or other anti-darkening powder. Pack unsweetened into freezer containers. Seal airtight; freeze. Use in persimmon recipes elsewhere in our cookbook.

Currants (whole fruit): Rinse ripe currants in cold water; shake off water, then pick over berries directly into freezer cartons. Seal airtight. Freeze at once. These work up best into desserts that use mashed currants or juice, rather than whole fruit.

Currant Juice: Wash ripe currants well. Shake off water, stem enough currants to make 3 qts. Add 1 c. water; bring to boil and simmer, covered, 10 to 15 minutes. Strain; chill. Pour juice into freezer cartons; seal airtight; freeze. Use in jelly or punch.

PEACH PUREE

Salvage ripe, soft peaches by freezing them to make a delightful topping for ice cream and other desserts

• Divide peaches into two lots according to degree of bruising. Use ripest, softest fruit. Dip peaches in boiling water for 30 seconds, cool in running water and remove skins. Place in bowl of salted water (about 2½ tblsp. per gal.) while you trim and pit peaches.

• Mash fruit with a mesh-type potato masher. Four to five average-size peaches make 3 c. purée—to this quantity add ¼ tsp. powdered ascorbic acid (or other anti-darkening powder) to prevent discoloration. Add 1 pkg. powdered pectin; stir well to dissolve; let stand 15 minutes, stirring occasionally. Add 3 c. sugar and stir to dissolve.

• Remove peel, pits and bruised spots from less bruised fruit in same way. But instead of mashing, cut each peach in 12 slices and then run the knife around the center of the fruit to cut slices in halves.

• Fill pint-size glass or other freezer containers with equal parts peach purée and slices mixed together lightly. Seal and freeze.

17

Homemade Relishes

The aroma of country kitchens reaches its most delightful peak in pickle-making time, as kettles of vinegar, fruits, vegetables and spices simmer lazily and give promise of good eating the year around. While women no longer devote days on end to pickling and preserving, the best cooks can their specialties every year to add that fresh, country taste to their tables. Many of the recipes in this chapter are their treasured favorites.

We also include directions for assembling unseasonal relishes from staples on the grocer's shelf—mustard, ketchup and horse-radish. They are of real help to busy women who know there's nothing like a relish to give snap and flavor step-up to meals.

On the sweet side, there are recipes for jams, marmalades and a variety of fruity concoctions. Bluebarb Jam unites flavors that complement each other—blueberries and rhubarb. And the Grape Conserve is one of the tastiest ever spooned on a plate. If you remember Grandmother's luscious yellow tomato preserves, you'll be happy with our recipe, which uses either yellow or red tomatoes. Our Green Tomato Mincemeat is another tantalizing memory awakener—pies plump, juicy and spicy with this filling salvaged from the garden just before frost.

We're willing to predict the youngsters in the family will load their hamburgers and frankfurters with our Hot Dog Relish, and that everyone will reach more than once for the Corn Relish if it's served with pork or baked beans. If you make our dill pickles, you'll observe that guests munch happily on them. And we just know you'll be opening the watermelon pickles when there's a chicken dinner ready for serving.

All our relish recipes have ardent supporters, women who have used them successfully. Some of our friends report they can a few extra jars to sell at church bazaars, to give as presents and to tuck in basket when toting food to a covered dish supper.

Jams, Jellies, Preserves

1-MINUTE RED RASPBERRY JAM

Tastes like berries fresh from the patch—a Farm Journal 5-star recipe

3½ c. red raspberry purée (about 7 c. berries)
6½ c. sugar
1 (2½ oz.) pkg. powdered pectin
1 c. cold water

• Put ¾ ripe and ¼ slightly under-ripe berries through food mill. Add sugar and mix well.
• Put pectin and water in saucepan. Bring to boil over medium heat, stirring constantly. Boil hard 1 minute, stirring.
• Remove from heat; immediately add berry mixture. Stir about 5 minutes, or until sugar crystals are thoroughly dissolved and mixture begins to thicken.
• Pour immediately into freezer containers. Cover; let stand 24 hours in cool place, until completely jelled. Seal airtight; freeze. Makes about 3½ pints.

Variation: For Blackberry Jam, use 3½ c. blackberry purée (about 8 c. berries) and decrease sugar to 5½ c.

PLUM-RASPBERRY JAM

In short-grass Kansas country it's a top favorite

3 lbs. (5 c.) prune plums, ground
5 c. sugar
1 (10 oz.) pkg. frozen raspberries

• Put ripe, firm plums through food chopper using medium blade.
• Combine fruit and sugar in a 5 or 6 qt. pan. Add raspberries. Mix together.
• Bring to boil; reduce heat and simmer until thick, about 40 minutes. Stir occasionally. Pour into hot sterilized jars. Seal at once. Makes 8 half-pints.

BLUEBARB JAM

The union of blueberries and rhubarb is a miracle flavor-blend

3 c. finely cut rhubarb or 1 (12 to 16 oz.) pkg. frozen rhubarb, thawed
3 c. crushed blueberries
7 c. sugar
1 (6 oz.) bottle liquid fruit pectin

• If fresh rhubarb is used, simmer gently until tender. Combine with blueberries in large saucepan, add sugar; mix.
• Place over high heat; bring to full, rolling boil and boil hard 1 minute, stirring constantly. Remove from heat, add pectin. Stir and skim for 5 minutes. Ladle into hot sterilized glasses. Cover at once with thin layer paraffin. Makes about 9 half-pints.

GRAPE CONSERVE

Juicy purple grapes and oranges get together with raisins and nuts

6 c. Concord grapes
6 c. sugar
Juice of 2 oranges
½ c. water
½ tsp. salt
½ lb. seedless raisins
1 c. chopped walnuts

• Skin grapes (save skins). Cook pulp until seeds can be separated by forcing pulp through strainer.
• Combine grape pulp with sugar, orange juice, water, salt and grape skins. Bring to boil. Add raisins. Simmer 20 minutes, or until thick.
• Add nuts; cook a few minutes more. Pour into hot, sterilized jars. Seal at once. Makes about 5 pints.

PLUM CONSERVE

Adds exciting tartness to the meal

8 c. plums (2¾ lbs.)
¼ tsp. salt
4 c. sugar
2 c. light corn syrup
1 (3″) stick cinnamon
1 c. chopped, seedless raisins
1 large orange

• Pit and quarter plums. Add salt, sugar, corn syrup, cinnamon and raisins.

• Peel orange; cut away white membrane from peel and pulp. Cut peel and pulp in small pieces. Add to plums. Bring to boil, stirring occasionally.

• Reduce heat; simmer 1 hour, stirring occasionally, until mixture thickens to jelly-like consistency. Skim and cool 5 minutes.

• Cover nuts with boiling water. Soak 3 minutes. Drain and cover with cold water. Drain again; chop and add to plum mixture.

• Remove cinnamon. Pour into hot sterilized glasses. Seal at once. Makes 10 (6 oz.) glasses.

SPICED BLUEBERRY JAM

Spices pep up the berries

2 qts. blueberries
4½ c. sugar (2 lbs.)
1 tsp. cinnamon
1 tsp. allspice
1 (6 oz.) bottle liquid fruit pectin

• Crush berries. Add sugar and spices. Bring quickly to boil in large kettle, stirring constantly. Boil 2 minutes.

• Add pectin. Skim jam carefully. Pour into hot sterilized pint jars or jelly glasses. Seal at once. Makes 3 pints or 9 (6 oz.) glasses.

SOUR-CHERRY AND PINEAPPLE JAM

Picture-pretty and delectable

2 lbs. cherries
1 (1 lb. 4 oz.) can crushed pineapple
2 c. sugar (1 lb.)

• Pit cherries. Add pineapple; put through coarse blade of food grinder. Add sugar.

• Boil to 230° on candy thermometer, or until thick and clear. Pour into hot, sterilized glasses. Seal at once. Makes about 6 (6 oz.) glasses.

SPICED PEACH JAM

Ripe peach flavor makes it extra-good

4 c. (about 3 lbs.) ripe peaches, peeled, pitted and ground or chopped fine
¼ c. lemon juice
7½ c. sugar
1 tsp. cinnamon
½ tsp. cloves
½ tsp. allspice
½ (6 oz.) bottle liquid fruit pectin

• Combine peaches and lemon juice.

• Add sugar and spices; mix well. Place over high heat and bring to a full rolling boil; boil hard 1 minute, stirring constantly.

• Remove from heat; immediately stir in pectin. Skim off foam with metal spoon. Cool slightly; stir and skim by turns for 5 minutes. Ladle into hot sterilized jars and seal. Makes 6 half-pints.

• Let jam set about 2 weeks before using.

Note: Add Spiced Peach Jam to cream cheese for a delightful sandwich spread. Or serve as relish with cold meats, such as ham, or with chicken.

SPICED GRAPE JELLY

A de luxe jelly

3 lbs. Concord grapes
1 tsp. cloves
2 tsp. cinnamon
½ c. vinegar
8 c. sugar
½ c. liquid pectin

• Cook grapes with cloves, cinnamon and vinegar (vinegar takes the place of water, starts grapes "juicing").
• After juice forms, boil only 5 to 10 minutes—long boiling destroys pectin, color and flavor.
• Strain juice (use milk filter pad in a wire strainer). Should have 4½ c. juice. Combine with sugar.
• Heat, stirring, and boil rapidly to jelling stage, 219° to 221° on candy thermometer, or when two drops run together and sheet off a metal spoon.
• Add pectin. Boil hard 30 seconds; stir constantly. Skim; pour quickly into hot, sterilized glasses. Seal at once. Makes about 12 (6 oz.) glasses.

QUINCE GINGER

For extra-special company

6 lbs. ripe quince
4 lbs. sugar
2 c. water
1 tblsp. grated fresh ginger root
4 lemons, sliced thin

• Pare and core quince; cut into small pieces.
• Combine sugar and water; stir to dissolve. Boil 5 minutes. Add chopped quince, ginger root and lemon slices.
• Simmer 2 hours, until fruit is transparent and deep red in color. Pour into hot, sterilized glasses; seal at once. Makes 5 pints.

If fresh ginger root is unavailable, use a small piece of the dried root, but discard before sealing glasses.

TOMATO PRESERVES

Like the preserves Grandmother used to can—marvelous

5 lbs. firm, red or yellow tomatoes
5 lbs. sugar
1 lemon, sliced thin
Small piece ginger root, or 1 tsp. ground ginger

• Skin and cut up tomatoes. Add remaining ingredients.
• Simmer slowly until thick, stirring frequently, about 45 minutes. Remove ginger root, if used.
• Pour into hot sterilized glasses. Seal at once. Makes about 4 (6 oz.) glasses.

ORANGE-LEMON MARMALADE

A perfect dress-up for buttered toast

12 oranges
3 lemons
Water
Sugar

• First day, slice fruit very thin; measure. Add 2 c. water for each cup of fruit. Let stand.
• Second day, boil this mixture 30 minutes.
• Third day, cook in small quantities using 3 c. fruit and water to 2 c. sugar. Cook about 2 hours. Pour into hot sterilized glasses; seal. Makes 24 (6 oz.) glasses.

SOUR-CHERRY PRESERVES

Bright red and tasty—from the fruit almost everyone likes

1 lb. ripe, firm cherries
1 lb. sugar

• Pit cherries; add sugar. Boil to 240° on candy thermometer, or until syrup is thick.
• Seal in hot, sterilized pint jars. Makes about 2 pints.

LEMON-CARROT MARMALADE

As cheerful on the table as sunshine on a cold day

12 large carrots, grated (9 c.)
9 c. sugar
Juice of 3 lemons
Juice of 1 orange
⅛ tsp. salt

• Scrape carrots and grate coarsely; add sugar (use equal amounts carrots and sugar). Let stand overnight.
• Add fruit juice and salt. Bring to boiling, and simmer 2 hours. Stir often, and skim when necessary. Seal in hot, sterilized glasses. Makes about 11 (6 oz.) glasses.

Orange and lemon peel sliced very thin without any of the white membrane makes a nice addition.

AMBER GRAPE MARMALADE

A treasure for your cupboard—set it out for company

1⅓ c. Concord grapes
2⅔ c. Thompson seedless grapes
½ c. water
2 c. unsweetened applesauce
3½ c. sugar
2 tsp. grated lemon rind

• Slip skins off Concords; add pulp to seedless grapes; add water.
• Cook until soft, put through sieve or food mill. Sieve applesauce, add to mixture. Bring to boil, stirring frequently.
• Add sugar and lemon rind. Simmer until thick and jelly-like. (Two drops of mixture should run together and sheet from metal spoon.)
• Pour into hot sterilized glasses or jars. Seal immediately. Makes 2½ pints.

Ketchups, Chutneys, Relish Mixtures

GRAPE KETCHUP

Another relish that perks up meals

5 lbs. Concord grapes
½ c. water
5 c. sugar
2 c. white vinegar
1 tsp. salt
½ c. mixed pickling spices

• Cook grapes with water. Put through colander, sieve or food mill—should be 9 c. pulp. Stir in sugar, vinegar and salt.
• Tie spices in small cheesecloth bag; add to grape pulp. Cool slowly until thick, stirring occasionally. Remove spices.
• Pour into hot, sterilized jars or bottles; seal at once. Store in cool, *dark* place. Makes about 4 pints.

Good Idea: Mix ½ c. each French dressing and ketchup. Serve on lettuce wedges.

PEAR CHUTNEY

A special touch for a special occasion

8 lbs. ripe pears
2 white onions
1 clove garlic
1 c. white raisins
1 c. sugar
2 tblsp. salt
2 tblsp. ginger
2 tblsp. white mustard seed
1 hot red pepper pod (or chili pod), dried or fresh
1 qt. white vinegar

• Core and dice pears.
• Peel and chop onions and garlic.
• Place pears, onions and garlic in large canning kettle. Add remaining ingredients. Cook until clear and thick, stirring occasionally, about 4 hours. Pour into hot sterilized jars. Seal. Makes 5 pints.

GREEN APPLE CHUTNEY

Enhances the food it accompanies

6 lbs. green apples
2 lbs. onions
2 lbs. sugar
¼ c. salt
2 qts. white vinegar
1 clove garlic
2 tsp. whole cloves
2 tsp. whole allspice
2 pieces dried ginger root
2 (2½") sticks cinnamon

• Core and quarter apples. Peel and chop onions. Put apples and onions in large canning kettle.
• Add sugar, salt, vinegar and garlic.
• Put spices in tea ball or tie them in a cheesecloth bag; add to mixture. Simmer, uncovered, until thick, about 4 hours, stirring occasionally. Remove spices.
• Pour into hot, sterilized pint jars. Seal. Makes 7 pints.

PEACH CHUTNEY

Good with chicken and pork dinners

5 lbs. firm ripe peaches
½ lb. seeded raisins
½ lb. dates, chopped
2 c. vinegar
¼ c. lime juice (optional)
1 lemon
2 to 3 c. sugar
½ c. candied ginger, coarsely chopped
½ c. nuts, chopped (optional)

• Pare and cut peaches in small pieces. Add raisins, dates, vinegar and juice.
• Quarter lemon; remove seeds and slice very thin. Add to mixture. Cook until peaches are soft, stirring to prevent sticking. Add sugar.
• When mixture is thick, add ginger and nuts (1 tsp. powdered ginger also added at this stage gives wonderful flavor).
• Seal in hot sterilized jars. Makes 7 half pints.

GREEN TOMATO MINCEMEAT

If you have the time to make it, it will make you some marvelous pies

12 green tomatoes, coarsely ground
6 large pears, coarsely ground
9 large apples, coarsely ground
4½ c. seedless raisins
Rind of 3 oranges, coarsely ground
3 tblsp. grated lemon rind
1 c. cider vinegar
⅓ c. orange juice
⅓ c. lemon juice
3 c. light molasses
1 c. brown sugar
2 tblsp. cinnamon
1½ tsp. nutmeg
1½ tsp. ginger
1½ tsp. allspice
1½ tsp. ground cloves
1½ tsp. salt

• Place all ingredients, except spices, in large kettle. Bring to boil, and cook briskly until mixture starts to thicken, about 30 minutes.
• Add spices and cook 5 minutes longer. Pack in hot, sterilized jars. Seal. Makes 7 quarts.

GREEN TOMATO CHUTNEY

Team this treat with rice dishes of Oriental flavor

8 lbs. green tomatoes
¾ c. chopped onions
1 c. brown sugar
¼ c. salt
1 tblsp. peppercorns or ¼ tsp. pepper
¼ c. mixed pickling spices
½ clove garlic
3 c. white vinegar
1 lb. apples
¾ c. white raisins
¾ c. sugar

• Core and quarter tomatoes. Combine in large kettle with onions, brown sugar, salt, peppercorns, pickling spices, garlic and vinegar. Boil mixture 15 minutes.

• Put through colander or food mill (this strains out whole spices). Return to heat; simmer 4 hours, until thick and clear.

• Core and chop apples. Combine with raisins and sugar. Simmer until fruit is soft. Stir into tomato mixture, and pour into hot sterilized pint jars. Makes 4 pints.

CORN RELISH

Try this with baked beans, ham, hot rolls and apple pie—wonderful supper

12 ears corn
1 small head cabbage
4 medium onions, peeled
3 sweet red peppers, seeded
3 tblsp. salt
3 tblsp. flour
1 tsp. turmeric powder
2 c. sugar
1 tblsp. mustard
1 qt. vinegar

• Cook corn on cob just enough to "set" milk (about 3 minutes); cut from cob.

• Put cabbage, onions and peppers through food chopper, using coarse blade. Combine all vegetables.

• Blend salt, flour, turmeric, sugar and mustard; add vinegar gradually. Bring to boil and add vegetables.

• Simmer 25 to 30 minutes.

• Seal at once in hot sterilized jars. Makes about 8 pints.

CRANBERRY MARMALADE RELISH

Good served with ham—also try a spoonful spread over ham in a sandwich

2 lemons
4 c. (1 lb.) fresh cranberries
2 c. orange marmalade

• Quarter lemons and discard seeds. Put through food chopper, using coarse blade, with cranberries. Add marmalade. Mix well, and let stand a few hours and blend. Makes 1 quart.

HOT DOG RELISH

Spoon this over hamburgers, and be prepared to share the recipe

3 carrots, peeled
3 sweet red peppers, cored and seeded
2 qts. cucumbers
2 qts. green tomatoes, peeled
2 qts. onions, peeled
½ c. salt
1½ lbs. sugar
1½ c. vinegar
½ tsp. cayenne pepper
2 tblsp. mixed pickling spices

• Chop or grind vegetables; place in bowl. Sprinkle with salt and allow to stand overnight.

• Drain; add sugar, vinegar and cayenne pepper. Add spices (tied loosely in cheesecloth bag).

• Simmer 45 minutes. Pour at once into hot sterilized jars; seal. Makes about 6 pints.

MIXED BEET RELISH

Brings out the best in your meat dish

2 c. white vinegar
2 c. sugar
1 tblsp. salt
⅔ c. grated horse-radish
2 qts. cooked beets, diced
3 small onions, chopped
3 green peppers, diced

• Heat vinegar. Dissolve sugar and salt in it. Add horse-radish, and bring to boil. Add beets, onions and peppers; simmer about 20 minutes.

• Place in hot sterilized jars and seal. Makes 4 pints.

RELISH SANDWICH SPREAD

Favorite of Virginia homemakers

3 c. cider vinegar
2 c. brown sugar
3 tblsp. salt
18 green and red peppers, coarsely ground
6 green tomatoes, coarsely ground
6 onions, coarsely ground
6 peeled cucumbers, coarsely ground
6 tblsp. flour
3 tblsp. dry mustard
1½ c. butter or margarine

• Combine 2 c. vinegar, brown sugar and salt in large saucepan. Add ground vegetables; cook together 15 minutes.

• Make paste of flour, mustard and 1 c. vinegar; add to vegetables. Cook 15 minutes.

• While hot, blend in butter. Pack in hot, sterilized jars. Seal. Makes 10 pints.

Quick Relish Stir-Ups

TOMATO CREAM SAUCE

2 c. mayonnaise
1 c. ketchup
1 tblsp. lemon juice

• Combine ingredients in top of double boiler and heat thoroughly. Serve with salmon or other fish. Makes 3 cups.

ANCHOVY BUTTER SAUCE

• Mash 1 or 2 anchovy fillets with fork. Add to melted butter and pour over boiled or baked white fish or salmon just before serving.

DAD'S BEST RELISH

Serve it with meat or cheese dishes

3 large turnips, grated (about 5 c.)
1 medium onion, grated
1 tsp. salt
½ c. vinegar
2 tblsp. prepared horse-radish
3 to 4 tblsp. sugar
Dash cayenne pepper

• Combine turnips and onion.

• Mix together remaining ingredients. Pour over vegetable mixture. Chill. Makes about 5½ cups.

QUICK SEAFOOD SAUCE

¼ c. chili sauce
½ c. mayonnaise or salad dressing

• Blend ingredients. Makes ¾ cup.

QUICK TOMATO SAUCE

1 (10½ oz.) can condensed tomato soup
1 bay leaf
4 cloves
1⅓ c. mayonnaise or salad dressing
3 tblsp. finely chopped olives (ripe or green)

• Heat tomato soup with bay leaf and cloves; simmer 10 minutes. Strain.

• Combine mayonnaise and olives; fold into tomato mixture. Makes 2⅓ cups.

PICKLED HORSE-RADISH

1 c. finely ground horse-radish root (use finest blade of chopper)
1½ tsp. brown sugar
3 tblsp. vinegar
½ tsp. salt

• Combine ingredients, and let stand overnight before using. It will be hot, very hot, for several days, so go easy! Makes ¾ cup.

HORSE-RADISH SAUCE

¼ c. freshly ground horse-radish
2 tsp. prepared mustard
2 tsp. vinegar
1 tsp. salt
½ tsp. pepper
1 tsp. sugar
4 tblsp. light cream

• Blend ingredients thoroughly and heat through, but do not boil. To serve, pile into cooked beet cups and place around meat on platter. Makes ⅝ cup.

HORSE-RADISH JELLY

½ c. finely ground horse-radish
½ c. vinegar
3½ c. sugar
½ c. liquid pectin

• Combine horse-radish, sugar and vinegar, stirring to dissolve sugar. Bring to boil and add pectin, stirring constantly. Boil hard for ½ minute. Remove from heat, skim and pour at once into small jelly molds which have been rinsed in cold water. Unmold when firm. Makes 5 small molds.

FRANKFURTER RELISH

To serve with frankfurters, combine one part of ground horse-radish with four parts of cranberry sauce. Spread on frankfurters just before serving.

TOMATO HORSE-RADISH SAUCE

1 tblsp. horse-radish (powdered)
1 c. ketchup

• Blend ingredients. Makes 1 cup.

BEET RELISH

½ c. sugar
6 tblsp. vinegar
¼ c. prepared horse-radish
2½ c. cooked, diced beets

• Dissolve sugar in vinegar, add horse-radish. Pour over beets, cover and chill overnight. Makes 2½ cups.

CELERY IN CARROT RINGS

• Cut Pascal celery into 3" lengths.
• Cut large pieces in half lengthwise.
• Slit both ends at ⅛" intervals, but not all the way to center.
• Cut thick slices of carrot. Remove centers, leaving a ring.
• Push two celery pieces through carrot ring, until ring is around middle.
• Drop in ice water. Celery will fan out, held in place by rings.

KETCHUP SAUCE

¾ c. tomato ketchup
1 tblsp. horse-radish, freshly ground or prepared
Juice of 1 lemon
1 tblsp. chopped sour pickle
¼ c. finely minced celery

• Combine ingredients in order given. Makes 1¼ cups.

This is a delicious sauce to serve with fried smelts, crisply brown outside and white and tender within, or with finnan haddie, too. Pass sauce separately when fish is served.

Picture-Pretty Relishes: Pickled peach halves filled with cranberry sauce or whole pickled peaches rolled in celery leaves. Sliced jellied cranberry sauce around spiced apricots; and carrot curls with fringed celery or celery fans or green, ripe and stuffed olives.

Pickles Worth Your Effort

Some of the blue ribbon winners at county and state fairs are rather tedious to make. But if you remember Grandmother's pantry shelves, you know how these wonderful pickles lifted ordinary meals above the commonplace. The kind of pickles you make depends on your time. The two watermelon pickle recipes we give you, for example, offer a choice of 3 or 14 days in the making. Try the watermelon syrup, too—different!

WATERMELON PICKLES

These take a 3-day period to make

7 lbs. watermelon rind
Salt water (1/4 c. salt to 1 qt. water)
7 c. sugar
2 c. white vinegar
1/2 tsp. oil of cloves
1/2 tsp. oil of cinnamon
Red food color (optional)

• Use rind from firm, preferably underripe melon; trim off dark green skin and pink section. Cut into 1" cubes or circles with small biscuit cutter or inside of doughnut cutter.
• Soak about 2 hours in salt water to cover. Drain; rinse and cover with cold water.
• Bring to boil; cook until tender, but not soft (about 10 minutes); drain.
• Combine sugar, vinegar and spices; heat to boiling. Add color if desired. Pour over rind in large glass or pottery bowl; let stand overnight at room temperature, covered with waxed paper.
• In the morning drain off syrup; heat to boiling and pour back over rind. Let stand overnight.
• On third morning heat rind in syrup; seal in hot sterilized jars. Makes 8 pints.

Relish Tray: Arrange alternate rows of watermelon pickles, celery hearts and carrot sticks. Or, set sherbet glass of sparkling jelly in tray's center, with watermelon pickles on one side, celery hearts on other.

CLEAR WATERMELON PICKLES

Takes a 14-day period to make these, but you end up with superlative pickles

4 to 5 qts. watermelon rind
Boiling water
1 tblsp. salt
1 qt. cider vinegar
6 1/2 qts. sugar (26 c.)
28 whole cloves
14 cinnamon sticks

• Choose firm, fresh melon with thick white rind. Peel, and trim away all but faintest pink pulp. Cut rind into pieces: Cube, shamrock, heart or Christmas tree shapes.
• Cover rind with boiling water; add salt. Bring to boil and cook 10 minutes, or until cubes can be pierced easily with a fork (overcooking makes soft pickles).
• Drain well. Squeeze out extra liquid. Pack into crock or enameled kettle.
• Bring vinegar and 6 c. sugar to a boil; pour over rind. Let stand overnight.
• Each day, drain off syrup and bring just to boil, adding more sugar as follows: 1st day, 4 c.; 2nd day, 2 c.; 3rd day, 2 c.; 4th day, 2 c., and 5th to 14th day 1 c. daily.
• Skim if necessary; pour over pickles. (If you skip a day now and then, don't worry. The secret of crisp, clear pickles is in adding sugar gradually.)
• Pack pickles in hot sterilized pint jars. To each jar add 2 cloves and 1 stick cinnamon. Cover with syrup and seal. Makes 14 pints.

WATERMELON SYRUP

A special treat on waffles or pancakes

1 ripe watermelon
½ c. sugar

• Cut watermelon in half; scrape pulp from rind. Put pulp through food mill, strainer or colander.
• Measure 1 gal. watermelon purée into kettle. Add sugar, stirring until dissolved. Bring to boil; cook 25 minutes, skimming often. Continue cooking until mixture is thick and clear. (Takes hours, but worth it.) You end up with 1 pint.
• Pour hot into sterilized pint jar; seal at once.

5-DAY SWEET CHUNK PICKLES

First Day: Select 2 gals. fairly large firm cucumbers, not more than 2" in diameter. Cut into 1½" slices. Place in stone crock or enamel-lined kettle. Mix together 2 qts. cold water and 1 c. pickling salt; pour over chunks in crocks. Cover and weight it down. Let stand 24 hours in cool place.

Second Day: Drain brine from pickles, but do not rinse. Add 1 gal. boiling water. Let stand overnight.

Third Day: Drain water from pickles. Cover with diluted pickling solution—half white vinegar and half water. Let stand overnight.

Fourth Day: Drain diluted pickling solution from pickles. Make syrup of 2 qts. white vinegar, 3 c. sugar and 2 tblsp. mixed pickling spices. Pour over pickles to cover. Cool thoroughly before putting on weighted lid.

Fifth Day: Drain syrup from pickles. Add 3 c. sugar; bring to boil. Pack pickles in sterilized jars lined with grape leaves. Pour boiling syrup over pickles. Seal at once. Store in cool, dark place. Makes 5 pints.

SWEET-SOUR DILL CHUNKS

A best-liked New England pickle—it will win friends across country

Medium-size or dill-size cucumbers
Onion slices
2 celery stalks, quartered
8 heads fresh dill
4 c. sugar
½ c. salt
1 qt. vinegar
2 c. water

• Wash freshly picked cucumbers and cut in 1" chunks or in quarters—enough to fill 4 sterilized quart jars.
• To each jar add 3 or 4 slices onion, 2 pieces celery and 2 heads dill.
• Dissolve sugar and salt in vinegar and water; bring to boil. Pour, while still hot, over cucumbers in each jar to cover; seal at once. Store in cool place. For best flavor, do not use for 30 days. Makes 4 quarts.

Variation: Slice cucumbers ¼" thick. Just right to tuck in hamburgers.

DELICIOUS DILLS

No friends like the old, tried-and-true

Green grape leaves
Cucumbers, 4 to 5" long
8 heads and stems of dill
2 tsp. ground horse-radish
2 tsp. mustard seed
2 large onion slices (or 2 cloves garlic)
5 c. water
½ c. vinegar
⅓ c. salt

• Line bottoms of 2 qt. (or 4 pt.) jars with grape leaves. Halve cucumbers lengthwise, then use to fill jars. To each jar, add half of dill, horse-radish, mustard seed and onion slices.
• Boil water, vinegar and salt together. Pour hot over cucumbers in jars; seal at once. Do not open for at least 2 weeks so flavor has a chance to develop. Makes 2 quarts or 4 pints.

BREAD AND BUTTER PICKLES

A must in all worthy collections of pickle recipes

- **1 gal. firm, clean cucumbers**
- **8 small white onions**
- **2 green peppers**
- **2 red peppers**
- **½ c. salt**
- **1 qt. cracked ice**
- **5 c. sugar**
- **1½ tsp. turmeric**
- **½ tsp. ground cloves**
- **2 tsp. mustard seed**
- **1 tsp. celery seed**
- **5 c. white vinegar**

• Slice cucumbers, onions, green and red peppers in paper-thin rounds. Place in stone crock. Mix salt and ice. Pack around sliced vegetables.

• Cover crock with weighted lid; allow to stand 3 hours, then drain.

• Combine sugar, spices and vinegar. Pour over vegetables in large enamel or aluminum kettle. Bring to boil over low heat.

• Pour into hot sterilized jars, seal immediately. Makes 7 pints.

DILLY BEANS

Crisp green beans and dill combine into this prize winner

- **2 lbs. small tender green beans**
- **1 tsp. red pepper**
- **4 cloves garlic**
- **4 large heads of dill**
- **2 c. water**
- **¼ c. pickling salt**
- **2 c. white vinegar**

• Stem green beans, and pack uniformly in hot sterilized jars.

• To each pint add ¼ tsp. red pepper, 1 clove garlic and 1 head of dill.

• Heat together water, salt and vinegar. Bring to boil; pour over beans.

• Seal. Makes 4 pints.

DILLED OKRA PICKLES

Amazingly good

- **3 lbs. young okra, uncut**
- **Celery leaves**
- **Cloves garlic**
- **Large heads of dill and stems**
- **1 qt. water**
- **1 pt. white vinegar**
- **½ c. salt**

• Pack scrubbed okra into hot sterilized pint jars with a few celery leaves, clove of garlic and head of dill for each jar.

• Make brine of water, vinegar and salt; heat to boiling. Pour over okra. Seal. Let stand 3 to 4 weeks. Makes 6 pints.

SWEET DILLS

• Slice 6 large dill pickles ½" thick. Boil 2 c. sugar, 1 c. water and ½ c. vinegar to make thin syrup. Add the pickle slices and heat. Put in glass jars and let stand in cool place until clear.

PICKLED EGGS PENNSYLVANIA DUTCH STYLE

• Place whole, peeled hard-cooked eggs in glass jar. Cover with mixture of equal parts beet juice and vinegar. Add a little chopped onion and a few whole cloves. Cover and chill 2 or 3 days before using. Serve sliced on lettuce for salad or in sandwiches or whole in bowl as relish. The eggs are a red-purple on the outside, shading first to pink and then to yellow. A bowl of them at a barbecue supper always wins compliments.

18

From Stream and Field

Fish and game free for the taking from streams, fields and woods, are among the special events of farm dinner tables. Many farmers and their sons count fishing and hunting their favorite sports—the best way to have a good time. The boys grow up knowing how to get their fish and game and how to dress and clean it for cooking. Their mothers and sisters are equally skillful at handling prized quarry in the kitchen. No wonder—they have plenty of practice! They inherited many of their techniques, for fish and game were of great importance in pioneer days. They're still staples in thousands of country kitchens, sources for the recipes in this chapter.

Nothing has stretched seasons and variety for fish and game more than home food freezers, plus locker storage plants. When the fish or game is frozen and brought out on occasion, nobody has a chance to tire of it.

In Wyoming, families consider trout as traditional for the Christmas holidays as turkey and ham in the South. Usually this fish is frozen in blocks of ice and when cooked it has that fresh-from-a-cold-stream taste. And in venison country, women vouch for the supremacy of mincemeat and chili con carne made with the gamey meat.

When it comes to game, most farmers hold that as a partner, nothing surpasses red currant jelly or currant jelly mixed with horse-radish. Quince and grape jellies make satisfactory game accompaniments, too.

The recipes that follow reveal some of the ways farm cooks fix their fish and game. Piquant sauces make good partners for fish, and we give you some excellent recipes for them in this chapter.

You'll also find in this chapter, and throughout this cookbook, recipes that use canned and frozen fish. They are from kitchens that do not have access to gifts from streams, fields and woods.

Minnesota Fish Treats

These three recipes came to us from a woman who likes to fish and who excels in fish cookery.

DIFFERENT FRIED FISH

Fried fish with a flair

2 lbs. dressed fish (whole small fillets or steaks from larger fish)
1 egg
2 tblsp. water
1 c. prepared biscuit mix
3 tblsp. ketchup
½ c. shortening or oil

• Dip fish first in egg beaten with water, then in biscuit mix blended with ketchup.
• Fry slowly in heated shortening until golden brown on both sides. Serve with lemon and parsley. Makes 6 servings.

FISH PICKLE

Some folks call it sour fish

6 to 8 (about 1 lb.) whole small fish or pieces of larger fish
2 tblsp. oil
½ c. water
½ c. vinegar
2 tblsp. minced onion
1 tsp. mixed pickling spice or 1 bay leaf
½ green or red pepper, seeded and diced
1 tsp. salt
⅛ tsp. pepper

• Gently simmer fish in salted water until cooked, or use leftover, fried fish.
• Mix remaining ingredients together in a bowl. Add fish and gently turn in this mixture. Cover and let stand in refrigerator at least 24 hours before serving, turning fish occasionally.
• Serve cold, as a relish, or as a main dish. Makes about 2½ cups. Fish Pickle will keep in refrigerator 1 to 2 weeks.

FISH IN CREAM

Your husband will hurry home with his catch when he recalls how good this is

2 lbs. dressed fish
½ c. flour
1 tsp. salt
¼ tsp. pepper
¼ tsp. paprika
1 egg
1 tblsp. water
¼ c. shortening
2 medium onions, sliced
½ c. light cream
Parsley (optional)

• Dip fish in flour mixed with salt, pepper and paprika, then in egg beaten with water.
• Fry until brown on one side in heavy skillet containing heated shortening. Turn. Place onions on top of fish; cook until under side is brown. Drain fat.
• Pour cream over fish; cover and simmer until cream is absorbed. Makes 6 servings. Garnish with parsley.

Variation: After frying, carefully remove fish and onions from skillet; place in casserole. Add cream, cover and bake in hot oven (425°) 30 minutes.

BROILED FISH

Lime juice does wonders for fish flavor—mayonnaise top bubbles temptingly brown

Heavy-duty aluminum foil
2 large fish fillets
Juice of 2 limes
Mayonnaise or salad dressing
Paprika
Salt and pepper
Parsley

• Grease foil well. Place on baking sheet. Turn up edges of foil so juices will not run off.
• Place fillets on foil, skin side down. With a sharp knife, score fish in crisscross fashion. Squeeze lime juice over surface. Let stand 30 minutes before broiling.

• Preheat broiler. Spread surface of fish with mayonnaise. Place baking sheet 5" from broiler unit. Broil 5 minutes, until mayonnaise bubbles and is brown. Sprinkle with paprika and seasonings; garnish with parsley. Makes 4 servings.

BAKED TROUT

Men's favorite—they like the snappy cheese butter that goes with the fish

4 to 6 fresh water trout
Lemon juice

• Clean and rinse trout well in cold water. Dip in lemon juice.
• Place in greased pan and bake in hot oven (425°) 20 minutes, or until fish flakes easily.
• Place on warm platter and spread with Blue Devil Butter. Makes 4 to 6 servings.

Blue Devil Butter:

6 tblsp. softened butter or margarine
3 tblsp. blue cheese
1 tblsp. anchovy paste
½ tsp. dry mustard
1 tsp. white vinegar
1 tsp. lemon juice

• Combine butter, blue cheese and anchovy paste.
• Dissolve mustard in vinegar and lemon juice. Blend into butter mixture. Serve with Baked Trout. Makes about ½ cup.

BAKED FLOUNDER WITH BACON

Spicy, colorful with tomatoes—there's a hint of bacon in the flavor

4 slices bacon
2 lbs. flounder fillets
4 thin slices lemon
½ c. condensed tomato soup
½ c. water
2 bay leaves
Salt and pepper
1 large onion, sliced
Paprika

• Place fish on top of 2 slices bacon in greased baking dish. Cover with remaining bacon and lemon slices.
• Combine tomato soup and water. Add bay leaves, salt, pepper and sliced onion. Pour over fish.
• Bake in moderate oven (350°) 30 minutes.
• Place on heated serving platter. Strain sauce around fish. Sprinkle with paprika. Makes 4 to 6 servings.

BAKED BASS WITH BACON

You'll repeat it whenever there's bass

6 bass, cleaned
½ c. cornmeal
1½ tsp. salt
1½ tsp. paprika
6 bacon slices
3 tomatoes, peeled and cut in wedges

• Cut bass in serving size pieces.
• Mix together cornmeal, salt and paprika. Dip fish in cornmeal mixture. Place in greased baking dish. Top with bacon.
• Bake in hot oven (425°) 20 minutes. Remove from oven and arrange tomatoes around fish.
• Broil 5" from heat, about 6 minutes. Makes 6 servings.

GARNISHES FOR FRIED FISH

• Lemon, lime or orange slices sprinkled with minced pimiento, parsley or green pepper.
• Grapefruit sections dusted with paprika.
• Thick tomato slices topped with pickle relish or with thin lemon slices topped with slice of stuffed olives.
• Canned pineapple slices, drained, topped with little haystacks of coleslaw.
• Celery sticks or fans or cheese stuffed.
• Cucumber slices, fluted and sprinkled with tarragon vinegar.
• Pickled beet slices dotted with horse-radish sauce.

OVEN-FRIED FISH

Oven does the frying for you—fish comes out golden, sizzling, good

¼ lb. butter or margarine
8 fish fillets or pieces
1 egg, well beaten
1 c. fine bread crumbs
Salt and pepper

• Heat oven to moderate (375°).
• Place butter in baking dish and place in oven. Watch carefully while browning butter.
• Dip fish in beaten egg, then in crumbs. Coat well. Place each fillet in butter, turning to coat evenly. Season to taste.
• Bake 15 to 20 minutes. Makes 6 to 8 servings.

FILLETS SUPREME

Cream enhances the flavor

1 (1 lb.) pkg. frozen fillets (haddock, flounder or ocean perch), thawed
2 tblsp. butter or margarine
1 medium onion, sliced
1 (3 oz.) can sliced mushrooms
1 (8 oz.) can tomato sauce
3 sprigs parsley
¼ tsp. salt
⅛ tsp. pepper
1 egg yolk, unbeaten
½ c. heavy cream

• Thaw frozen fillets as directed on package.
• Melt butter in large skillet; add onion, mushrooms, tomato sauce and parsley.
• Separate fillets. Cut large fillets in half; place side by side on top of tomato mixture. Sprinkle with salt and pepper. Bring to boil. Cover tightly; reduce heat and simmer 10 to 12 minutes, until tender.
• Remove fillets to hot serving platter.
• Cook liquid in pan until reduced to about half. Add egg yolk to cream, and mix well. Add a little hot liquid to cream; turn into pan, stirring constantly. Bring just to boiling, but do not boil.
• Pour over fillets; garnish with lemon wedges and parsley. Makes 6 servings.

BAKED FISH AU GRATIN

1 (1 lb.) pkg. frozen fillets (cod, ocean perch, halibut or flounder)
2 tblsp. fine crackers crumbs
1 c. canned tomatoes
2 tblsp. chopped onion
¼ tsp. salt
⅛ tsp. black pepper
1 tblsp. butter or margarine
¼ c. Cheddar cheese, cut fine

• Thaw fillets as directed on package.
• Grease 1 qt. shallow baking dish. Sprinkle with cracker crumbs. Lay fillets on crumbs.
• Combine tomatoes, onion, salt and pepper; pour over fillets. Dot with butter and cheese.
• Bake in moderate oven (350°) 35 minutes, until fish "flakes" when pierced with fork. Makes 4 servings.

PAN FRIED FILLETS

Into the skillet and out in a jiffy

1 (1 lb.) pkg. frozen fillets (ocean perch, haddock or flounder)
¼ c. melted fat or oil
⅓ c. fine dry cracker or bread crumbs
½ tsp. salt
1 tsp. paprika
⅛ tsp. pepper
¼ c. milk

• Thaw fillets enough to separate.
• Heat fat in large skillet.
• Combine crumbs with salt, paprika and pepper.
• Dip fillets in milk, then in crumbs; fry in fat over moderate heat 8 to 10 minutes, turning to brown both sides.
• Serve with Cucumber or Egg Sauce. Makes 4 servings.

To make Cucumber Sauce: Combine ½ c. mayonnaise or salad dressing, ½ c. finely chopped fresh cucumber, ¼ tsp. salt, 1 tsp. vinegar, ¼ tsp. Worcestershire sauce and 1 tsp. grated onion.

To make Egg Sauce: Combine ½ c. mayonnaise or salad dressing, 1 hard-cooked egg, chopped, 2 tblsp. ketchup, 2 tsp. grated onion, ½ tsp. salt and dash of black pepper (freshly ground best).

MOLDED FISH

Gelatin gives the professional look

6 medium fresh water trout
2 chicken bouillon cubes
2 c. hot water
1 tblsp. lemon juice
1 envelope unflavored gelatin
¼ c. cold water
Lemon slices
Olives

• Simmer trout in chicken broth made by dissolving bouillon cubes in hot water and adding lemon juice. Remove fish to deep serving platter; let stand until cool.
• Soften gelatin in cold water. Add to hot broth in saucepan, and stir until dissolved. Chill until gelatin starts to thicken.
• Spoon half of gelatin mixture over fish; chill until firm.
• Garnish with lemon slices and olives; spoon over remaining gelatin; chill. Serve with Sour Cream Cucumber Sauce. Makes 4 to 6 servings.

Cucumber Sauce:

¾ c. dairy sour cream
¼ tsp. prepared mustard
½ tsp. salt
1 tsp. grated onion
Chopped parsley
½ c. chopped cucumber
Juice of ½ lemon

• Combine all ingredients; chill. Makes about ¾ cup.

TROUT AU BLEU

Sounds fancy but it's easy to fix and has an extra-special taste

6 fresh trout or bass, cleaned
½ c. mild vinegar
½ c. chicken broth
1 small bay leaf

• Trim fish and split down back.
• Combine in skillet vinegar and broth (make broth by dissolving 1 chicken bouillon cube in ½ c. hot water). Add bay leaf. Simmer 10 minutes.
• Add fish to broth; simmer 15 minutes, or until tender. Remove to platter and serve with Caper Sauce. Makes 6 servings.

Caper Sauce:

⅓ c. melted butter or margarine
Juice of ½ lemon
⅓ c. capers, drained

• Combine all ingredients. Serve warm.

LOUIS SAUCE

Exceptionally popular on the West Coast

1 c. mayonnaise
¼ c. ketchup
1 tsp. prepared horse-radish
1 tsp. Worcestershire sauce
Salt
Pepper

• Mix all the ingredients. Serve on broiled or fried fish, in fish salads or on seafood cocktails. Makes 1½ cups.

Sauces for Fish

A richly-colored and flavored sauce perks up fish. These recipes are easy.

MORNAY SAUCE

2 tblsp. butter or margarine
2 tblsp. flour
½ tsp. salt
½ tsp. prepared mustard
Dash of cayenne
1 c. milk
½ tsp. Worcestershire sauce
½ c. grated or shredded sharp process cheese
1 tblsp. lemon juice

• Melt butter; stir in flour, salt, mustard and cayenne.
• When well blended, add milk slowly, stirring constantly over low heat until mixture thickens and bubbles.
• Add Worcestershire sauce, cheese and lemon juice; heat to melt cheese. Makes 1½ cups.

MUSTARD BUTTER SAUCE

Pour this zippy sauce over boiled or broiled fish just before serving

¼ c. butter
1 tsp. prepared mustard
1 tsp. lemon juice

• Heat butter until light brown; stir in mustard and lemon.

JIFFY CHEESE SAUCE

¼ c. butter or margarine
½ c. minced onion
½ c. undiluted evaporated milk
2 dashes Tabasco sauce
½ lb. process sharp cheese, sliced

• Sauté onion in butter until slightly tender. Add remaining ingredients. Heat, stirring occasionally, until blended. Makes 2 cups.

SEAFOOD SAUCE

½ c. chili sauce
⅓ c. ketchup
⅓ c. prepared horse-radish
1½ tsp. Worcestershire sauce
¼ tsp. salt
2 tblsp. lemon juice
⅛ tsp. pepper
¼ c. minced celery

• Combine all ingredients. Place in jar, cover and chill before serving. If a milder sauce is preferred, substitute ¼ c. puréed canned tomatoes for half the chili sauce. Makes 1½ cups.

TOMATO-CHEESE SAUCE

1 (10½ oz.) can condensed tomato soup
1 c. grated or shredded cheese
¼ tsp. prepared mustard

• Heat all ingredients together until cheese melts. Nice on oven-fried or baked fish. Makes about 1½ cups.

FISH SOUP

An excellent way to cook the smallest of the catch

6 to 8 fish, cleaned
1 qt. water
5 parsley sprigs
2 small carrots, scraped
3 celery stalks
2 medium onions, peeled
2 lemon slices
1 tblsp. salt
3 peppercorns or ¼ tsp. black pepper
1 c. light cream
2 egg yolks, unbeaten
3 tblsp. parsley, dill or chives, chopped

• Combine in kettle; fish, water, parsley, carrots, celery, onions, lemon, salt and pepper. Simmer 1 to 2 hours. Strain stock.
• Beat cream and egg yolks in large bowl. Add parsley.
• Pour hot stock over cream-egg mixture, and serve at once. Makes 4 to 6 servings.

FISH CHOWDER

It hits the spot with Dad—especially if made with his catch

4 slices of bacon, cut in pieces or 1½" salt pork cube
2 lbs. fish fillet (haddock or cod, frozen or fresh)
1 large onion, thinly sliced
2 c. thinly sliced potatoes
2 c. scalded milk
1½ tsp. salt
Dash of pepper
1½ tblsp. butter or margarine

• Place bacon or salt pork in large heavy saucepan. Brown well; remove, leaving drippings.
• Cut fish fillets into 1" pieces.
• Place layers of potato, onion and fish in saucepan. Add 1½ c. water. Cover. Bring to a boil, reduce heat; simmer 10 to 15 minutes, until potatoes and fish are just cooked.
• Add milk, seasonings, butter and bacon. Keep warm over low heat. Makes 4 generous servings.

OYSTER PIE

Cranberry salad is a splendid accompaniment for this main dish

Pastry for 2-crust (9") pie
1½ pts. oysters (3 c.)
Milk plus cream
⅓ c. butter or margarine
⅓ c. flour
1 tblsp. minced parsley
1 tsp. salt
Pepper to taste

• Make pastry. Divide dough in 2 portions. Roll each to ⅛" thickness. Cut top, bottom and 4 strips for sides to fit 8× 8" baking dish. Transfer pastry to baking sheet. Prick well with fork.
• Bake in very hot oven (450°) until lightly browned, 8 to 10 minutes.
• Drain oysters; reserve liquor. Add enough milk and some cream to liquor to make 3½ c. liquid.
• Melt butter in saucepan. Stir in flour. Add liquid slowly; boil 2 or 3 minutes, stirring constantly.
• Add parsley, salt, pepper and oysters. Heat again just to the boiling point.
• Fit baked crust in bottom and sides. Just before serving add hot oyster filling. Place crust on top. Garnish with gay splashes of paprika, pimiento, and green pepper. Makes 6 servings.

SALMON-OYSTER PIES

Pastry for 2-crust (9") pie
¼ c. butter or margarine
¼ c. flour
1½ c. milk
1 tblsp. minced parsley
1 tblsp. lemon juice
1 pt. oysters
1 (7¾ oz.) can salmon

• Line 6 large custard cups or individual casseroles with pastry. Prick, crimp edges. Bake in hot oven (425°) 15 minutes, until browned.
• Melt butter; blend in flour, and stir in milk, ½ c. at a time. Add parsley and lemon juice.
• Cook oysters in their liquor until edges curl, about 3 minutes. Add salmon, flaked. Add both to white sauce. Heat through slowly.
• Pour into baked pastry shells. (Or serve oyster-salmon mixture over steamed rice.) Makes 6 servings.

Oven-Fried Oysters: Roll 24 large oysters in 1½ c. flour with 1¼ tsp. salt and ¼ tsp. pepper. Dip into 2 slightly beaten eggs; roll in fine bread crumbs. Sprinkle both sides with oil. Bake in large shallow pan in hot oven (400°) until brown, about 15 minutes. Serve with lemon wedges. Makes 5 to 6 servings.

Oyster Sandwiches: Use fried oysters, lettuce, thin tomato slices and crisp bacon between hot buttered toast slices.

SALMON LOAF

A supper loaf the family will like

1 (1 lb.) can salmon
¾ c. milk
¼ c. chopped green pepper
2 eggs, well beaten
1½ c. dry bread crumbs
2 tblsp. chopped onion
¼ c. melted butter or margarine

• Drain salmon, reserving liquid for sauce (see below). Flake; remove skin and bones. Add remaining ingredients; mix well. Spoon into greased 8×4" pan. Pack meat in tightly.
• Bake in moderate oven (350°) 50 minutes. Makes 6 servings. Serve with sauce.

Sauce: Melt 2 tblsp. butter or margarine. Add 2 tblsp. flour; blend well. Add ¾ c. milk and liquid from salmon; stir constantly. Cook until thick.

SALMON CASSEROLE

Quick main dish for lunch

½ c. cooked carrots
¼ c. cooked onions
1 (1 lb.) can salmon, cleaned
1 c. cooked macaroni
1 (10½ oz.) can condensed cream of celery soup
1 tsp. salt
⅛ tsp. pepper
2 tblsp. butter or margarine
½ c. bread crumbs
¼ lb. cheese, cut in strips

• Cook carrots and onions in small amount of salted water; drain.
• Break salmon into chunks; place in greased 2 qt. casserole; add carrots, onions and macaroni.
• Stir in soup, salt and pepper. Melt butter; toss with bread crumbs. Top with crumbs and cheese.
• Bake in moderate oven (375°) about 20 minutes. Makes 4 servings.
• Serve with stewed tomatoes, apple, celery and nut salad and fruit cobbler dessert.

MOLDED SALMON SALAD

Summer supper salad

2 envelopes unflavored gelatin
¼ c. cold water
3 tblsp. lemon juice
1 c. hot water
1 (1 lb.) can salmon, cleaned and flaked
¾ c. mayonnaise or salad dressing
1 c. diced celery
¼ c. chopped green pepper
1 tsp. minced onion
½ tsp. salt
⅛ tsp. pepper
Crisp lettuce leaves

• Soften gelatin in cold water and lemon juice.
• Dissolve in hot water; chill until thickened and syrupy.
• Fold in remaining ingredients. Pour into oiled 2 qt. mold. Chill until firm.
• Unmold on lettuce. Makes 6 servings.

TUNA FISH PIE

When your fisherman comes home without a catch, try this main dish

Pastry for 2-crust (9") pie
½ c. chopped celery
1 small onion, minced
2 tblsp. butter or shortening
3 tblsp. flour
2 c. milk
1 chicken bouillon cube
2 (7 oz.) cans tuna, flaked
½ c. diced cooked potatoes
2 hard-cooked eggs, chopped

• Line 9" pie pan with half of pastry; roll out top.
• Sauté celery and onion in butter until soft and clear. Blend in flour.
• Add milk, then bouillon cube; cook until thick and smooth, stirring constantly. Stir in tuna, potatoes and eggs. Turn into unbaked pastry shell.
• Cover with pastry; cut steam vents.
• Bake in very hot oven (450°) 10 minutes, then reduce heat to hot (400°), and bake 20 minutes more. Makes 6 servings.

Game Recipes from Hunters' Wives

PHEASANT DINNER MENU

Pheasant — Rice Stuffing
Broccoli-and-Onion Casserole
Green Salad — Oregano Dressing
Hot Rolls — Coffee

PHEASANT WITH RICE STUFFING

All hunters' wives will like this recipe

2 pheasants (about 2½ lbs. each)
1 tblsp. salt
1½ c. long grain rice
3 c. water
½ c. butter or margarine
1 c. finely chopped celery
3 tblsp. minced onion
½ c. fresh mushrooms, sliced (or canned and drained)
⅛ tsp. crushed sage
⅛ tsp. crushed thyme
⅛ tsp. crushed savory
Melted butter or margarine
6 bacon slices

• Rub 1 tsp. salt into cavity of each pheasant.
• Brown rice in dry frying pan. Transfer to saucepan; add water and 1 tsp. salt; cook until tender.
• Melt butter in frying pan. Add celery, onions and mushrooms, and cook 10 minutes. Add to rice along with herbs.
• Stuff birds lightly. (Extra stuffing may be baked in covered casserole last 30 minutes of roasting time.)
• Truss the birds, brush them with melted butter. Place strips of bacon across breasts.
• Roast in covered pan in moderate oven (350°) about 2 hours, or until tender. Baste frequently. (Roast pheasant is a lighter color than chicken or turkey, because it has less fat.) Makes 6 to 8 servings.

CASSEROLE OF CURRIED BROCCOLI AND ONIONS

Pronounced flavors hold their own with game

1 (10 oz.) pkg. frozen broccoli
3 tblsp. butter or margarine
3 tblsp. flour
½ tsp. curry powder
¼ tsp. paprika
Dash cayenne
1½ c. milk
½ c. grated or shredded sharp process cheese
1 (15½ oz.) can small whole onions (2 c. cooked)

• Cook broccoli as directed on package.
• Melt butter; add flour and seasonings. Blend. Add milk; cook, stirring constantly, until thickened. Add cheese; stir until melted.
• Drain onions; add to broccoli in greased 1½ qt. casserole.
• Pour sauce over vegetables. Bake in moderate oven (350°) 20 minutes. Makes 6 servings.

OREGANO SALAD DRESSING

Toss lettuce with this dressing for the pheasant or fish dinner

¾ c. vinegar
1 tblsp. salt
1 tblsp. sugar
1 tsp. oregano
2 tsp. black pepper
1½ tblsp. sweet basil
2 cloves garlic, split
¾ c. oil

• Marinate seasonings and garlic in vinegar 24 hours.
• Strain vinegar; add oil. Shake vigorously. Makes 1½ cups.

ROAST WILD DUCK WITH PRUNE-ORANGE STUFFING

2 wild ducks, singed and cleaned
Seasonings (salt, pepper, etc.)
Bacon slices or strips of salt pork

Stuffing:

2 c. day-old bread crumbs
¼ c. melted butter or margarine
¼ c. diced orange sections
¼ tsp. grated orange rind
¾ c. diced celery
1 c. cooked prunes, pitted and quartered
½ tsp. salt
⅛ tsp. pepper

• Cover ducks with cold water to which 2 tsp. baking soda has been added (1 tsp. per fowl). Simmer 1 hour; remove from water; drain. Rub inside and out with salt and pepper.
• Stuff cavity lightly and truss. Place on rack, breast side up, in shallow roasting pan. Lay 4 to 6 slices bacon or salt pork across each breast.
• Roast in moderate oven (350°), allowing 15 minutes per pound for young birds, 20 minutes for older, basting frequently with pan drippings until well done.
• For stuffing, toast bread lightly in butter in large skillet.
• Add oranges and rind, celery, prunes and seasonings; toss together lightly. Makes 6 to 8 servings.

Other stuffing suggestions: Add about ½ c. peanuts to your favorite bread stuffing; or sauerkraut makes an easy, delicious duck stuffing. If you do not care to stuff, place a stalk of celery, a small onion and an apple inside duck to add flavor during roasting.

ROAST WILD GOOSE

1 young wild goose (6 to 8 lbs. dressed)
Juice of 1 lemon
Seasonings (salt, pepper, etc.)
4 to 6 slices bacon
Melted fat or drippings

Stuffing:

¼ c. butter or margarine
¼ c. chopped onion
1 c. chopped tart apple
1 c. chopped dried apricots
3 c. soft bread crumbs (day-old bread)
½ tsp. salt
¼ tsp. pepper

• Rub cleaned goose inside and out with lemon juice and seasonings.
• For stuffing, melt butter in heavy skillet or saucepan. Sauté onion until soft and clear; mix in apple, apricots, crumbs, salt and pepper.
• Spoon stuffing lightly into cavity. Close opening with skewers and truss bird. Cover breast with bacon slices and cheesecloth soaked in melted fat.
• Place breast side up in roasting pan. Roast in slow oven (325°), allowing 20 to 25 minutes per pound, until tender. Baste frequently with fat or pan drippings.
• If age of goose is uncertain, pour 1 c. water into pan and cover last hour of cooking. Remove cheesecloth, skewers and string before serving. Makes about 6 servings.

How to Roast Venison

The best-eating venison is stripped of all fat which isn't edible. For roasts, keep meat from drying out by larding with salt pork or bacon before cooking.
• Ripen meat—hang at least 4 days to 2 weeks. If the deer is full grown, meat should be marinated.

To Marinate: Chop 1 onion, 1 carrot and stalk of celery. Make bouquet in cheesecloth of parsley, thyme, bay leaf and a few whole cloves. Cook 1 to 2 minutes in hot fat or oil, then add 1 c. vinegar. Bring to boil, and simmer about 20 minutes. Strain; then cool. Pour over venison.
• Let stand 12 to 24 hours in glass, earthenware or china container—not

metal. (Marinating tenderizes meat and takes away some of gaminess.)
• After marinating 24 hours, lard well with salt pork and a few pieces of garlic. Roast on rack in shallow pan in moderate oven (350°) allowing 30 minutes per pound, basting frequently with drippings. Serve with red currant jelly.

SCALLOPINE OF VENISON

2½ lbs. venison
Seasoned flour (with salt, pepper, paprika)
Fat for frying
2 medium onions, peeled and sliced
1 tsp. sugar
1 (4 oz.) can mushrooms
1¼ c. tomato purée
1¼ c. hot water

• Wipe meat with vinegar-soaked cloth—vinegar picks up hairs and clotted blood more easily.
• Cut meat into serving pieces and roll lightly in seasoned flour. Flatten slightly with edge of plate or meat pounder.
• Fry until golden brown on both sides in hot fat. Add onions after first turning.
• Place in greased casserole; add remaining ingredients. Bake in moderate oven (350°) about 2 hours, until tender. Makes 8 to 10 servings.

ONION-STUFFED RABBIT

Excellent way to cook squirrels, too

1 rabbit (about 2 lbs.)
1½ tsp. salt
⅛ tsp. pepper
1½ c. onion slices
3 bacon slices

• Rub salt and pepper inside rabbit.
• Stuff with onion slices. Truss.
• Lay strips of bacon over rabbit.
• Wrap in aluminum foil; place in shallow baking pan. Bake in moderate oven (350°) 1½ hours. Makes 4 servings.

ROAST RACCOON

It's fixed this way for an Illinois community's coon suppers

3 to 4 raccoons, 4 to 6 lbs. each
5 tblsp. salt
2 tsp. pepper
2 c. flour
1 c. shortening
8 medium onions, peeled
12 small bay leaves

• Skin, draw and clean raccoons soon after killing. Remove, without breaking, the brown bean-shaped kernels from under forelegs and each thigh.

• Cut into pieces. Reserve meaty backs and legs for baking. Cook bony pieces in water to make broth for gravy and dressing. Add small amount of seasonings. Simmer until meat is tender; strain, and use only the broth.

• Sprinkle back and leg pieces with salt and pepper. Then dredge with flour.

• Heat shortening in heavy skillet. Add meat; brown on all sides.

• Transfer pieces to roaster; add onions and bay leaves. Cover.

• Bake in moderate oven (350°) 2 hours, until tender.

• Make gravy by adding flour to drippings in pan. (Use 2 to 3 tblsp. for each cup of liquid or broth used.) Makes 24 servings.

• As meat is roasting, prepare stuffing of: 3 loaves day-old bread, crumbed; 2½ tsp. salt; 1 tsp. pepper; 2½ tsp. powdered sage; 4 beaten eggs; 1 (1½ oz.) pkg. dehydrated onion soup; 4 stalks chopped celery; ½ c. butter or margarine; and 4 c. coon broth. Bake in large shallow pan in moderate oven (350°) 30 minutes. Makes 24 servings.

Coleslaw to Serve With Fish and Game: Sprinkle 2½ c. finely shredded cabbage with 1 tsp. salt, moisten with mayonnaise and add ½ c. each cut up cucumber and green onions. Sprinkle with celery seed.

Pressure-Cooked Game

When a beaming hunter proudly dumps his limit of pheasants on the porch or unloads a ten-point buck from the car fender, his wife, if she's a smart game cook, checks up on the pressure cooker. She knows many a pheasant has roamed too much to be tenderized by dry heat and that, like beef, certain cuts of venison cannot be successfully broiled or roasted. Pressure cookers are mighty efficient in tenderizing game, as the following recipes from farm women prove.

WILD RABBIT WITH VEGETABLES

Simply delicious gravy

2 (3 to 4 lb.) rabbits
¼ c. flour
2 tsp. salt
2 tsp. curry powder
⅛ tsp. paprika
Fat for frying
8 potatoes, peeled
12 whole carrots, scraped
2 thick onion slices
1 c. hot water
1 bay leaf
1 c. dairy sour cream

- Skin, clean and cut up rabbits.
- Combine dry ingredients in paper or plastic bag; shake rabbit pieces in flour mixture.
- Brown meat lightly in hot fat in pressure pan.
- Add vegetables, then water and bay leaf.
- Cover, set control at 10, and cook for 18 to 20 minutes after control jiggles. Reduce pressure normally.
- Arrange rabbit and whole vegetables on heated platter.
- Thicken liquid for gravy by forcing remaining vegetables through sieve, food mill or blender. Stir in cream; simmer 5 minutes. Serve hot. Makes 8 servings.

STUFFED PHEASANT

They'll want second helpings

2 (3 to 4 lb.) pheasants
Salt
Bread stuffing
Fat for frying
1 c. water

- Clean, dress and salt inside pheasants.
- For each pound of pheasant, allow ½ c. favorite bread stuffing; stuff loosely. Sew or skewer openings together.
- Brown pheasants in hot fat in pressure pan. Add water.
- Cover, set control at 10, and cook 20 to 30 minutes (depending on age of birds) after control jiggles.
- Cool 5 minutes, then place pan under cold water to reduce pressure quickly. Makes 8 servings.

VENISON STEAKS

Fork tender, good eating

3 tblsp. flour
1½ tsp. salt
¼ tsp. marjoram
6 venison steaks, cut from the round
Fat for frying
1 small onion, peeled
4 medium carrots, scraped
½ c. diced celery and tops
1½ c. beef broth

- Mix flour, salt and marjoram; rub over meat. Brown steaks in hot fat in pressure pan.
- Add vegetables and broth; cover, and set control at 10. Cook 20 to 30 minutes after control jiggles.
- Cool normally 5 minutes, then place pan under cold water to reduce pressure quickly.
- Thicken liquid for gravy by rubbing vegetables through sieve, food mill or blender. Makes 6 servings.

19

Make-Ahead Dishes

Make-ahead dishes are miracle workers. Attractive and delicious, they are easy on the cook who fixes food at her convenience . . . in the morning before the summer sun has heated the kitchen . . . in the afternoon when the babies are napping.

Getting meals on time, for home folks or company, is one situation make-ahead dishes solve. Sometimes you can fix food a day early—we have a Sunday dinner that you get on Saturday. Or you can whip up salads and desserts in the afternoon for dinner the following day. The timing is up to you. Our collections of recipes will give you many suggestions.

We give top billing to tempting refrigerator dishes. There are dependable gelatin salads that display fruits and vegetables. There's a frozen fruit salad, and many refrigerator desserts, rich, satisfying and cool for meal endings. Or for a cheery welcome to neighbors who drop in for the evening, don't miss our refrigerator ice cream. More velvety ones you'll never find.

Do try our chiffon pies. They're as American as Valley Forge—the first ones were made in California. We have some beauties.

Our jellied meat, chicken and fish loaves have attracted much favorable attention—every summer new requests pour in asking for our beef mold that a Midwestern cattleman's wife originated. Pressed beef has an old-fashioned name, but don't be misled—it suits today's taste.

You'll note a sandwich loaf in this chapter, the kind you make in advance for parties. And is it good! There are those quick fruit and nut loaves that keep well. Make them a couple days early, and on the morning of the party, slice them, spread with butter or cream cheese and you have open-face sandwiches to serve with coffee or tea. They're a young homemaker's special. These smart hostesses have nothing left to do about refreshments when the church group arrives for the afternoon, besides make coffee or tea, pour it and pass sandwiches.

SUNDAY DINNER TO FIX SATURDAY

Molded Chicken Loaf
Sliced Tomatoes and
Green Pepper Ring Garnish
Tangy Mayonnaise
Scallions and Ripe Olives
Brown 'n Serve Rolls
Ice Cream and Chocolate Cake
Coffee Milk

MOLDED CHICKEN LOAF

2 envelopes unflavored gelatin
2½ c. chicken broth
4 c. diced cooked chicken (cooking instructions follow)
Salt and pepper to taste
2 tsp. lemon juice
2 tblsp. chopped parsley
¾ c. finely chopped celery
2 tblsp. chopped sweet pickle
¼ c. chopped pimiento
1 c. mayonnaise or salad dressing

• Soften gelatin in ½ c. chicken broth. Heat remaining broth. Add gelatin; stir until gelatin dissolves.

• Add the chicken. Add salt and pepper to taste. Cool until mixture starts to thicken. Then fold in remaining ingredients. Pour into a 2-quart loaf pan. Chill several hours.

• Unmold on platter. Garnish with tomato slices and green pepper rings. Makes 10 to 12 servings.

To cook chicken: Singe and wash a 4 to 5 lb. stewing fowl. Cut up; put pieces in a 6 qt. kettle. Add a small onion, a carrot, a branch of celery, a small bay leaf and 6 c. boiling water. Cover tightly; bring to a boil. Reduce heat and simmer about 3 hours or until meat is tender. Add 1 tblsp. salt after first hour of cooking. Cool to lukewarm. Remove chicken. Strain broth; skim off fat. Remove skin and bones of chicken. Cut meat into pieces.

SUNDAY SUPPER MENU

Tuna Mounds
Carrot Stick Garnish
Potato Chips
Buttered Green Beans
Whole Wheat Rolls
Sliced Bananas with Butterscotch Sauce
Iced Tea with Lemon Milk

TUNA MOUNDS

1 envelope unflavored gelatin
½ c. water
1 (10½ oz.) can condensed cream of asparagus soup
1 (7 oz.) can tuna, flaked
1 tblsp. lemon juice
¼ c. chopped radishes
⅓ c. diced celery
½ tsp. seasoned salt
¼ c. mayonnaise or salad dressing

• Soften gelatin in water.

• Put soup in saucepan; bring to boil. Add gelatin; stir until it is dissolved.

• Cool mixture until slightly thickened. Add tuna and remaining ingredients. Spoon into 4 custard cups (or a 3-cup mold). Chill until firm.

• Unmold; serve on lettuce leaves. Garnish with spoonful of mayonnaise and radish slices. Makes 4 servings.

SUNDAY NIGHT COMPANY SUPPER

Ham and Potato Salad Ring
Deviled Egg Garnish
Buttered Broccoli
French Bread
Cantaloupe and Fresh Fruit
Coffee Milk

HAM AND POTATO SALAD RING

New way to serve potato salad and ham

1 envelope unflavored gelatin
½ c. cold water
1 (8 oz.) can tomato sauce
1 (10 oz.) can chopped ham or pork
1 tblsp. prepared horse-radish
¼ c. chopped green pepper
4 c. cubed, cooked potatoes
¾ c. finely chopped celery
3 hard-cooked eggs, chopped
3 tblsp. chopped onion
2 tblsp. pickle relish
½ tsp. salt
1 c. mayonnaise or salad dressing

• Soften gelatin in cold water.
• Heat tomato sauce. Add softened gelatin; stir until gelatin dissolves.
• Dice ham. Add ham, horse-radish and green pepper to tomato mixture.
• Pour into a 9½" ring mold (6 cup) and chill until firm.
• Meanwhile make potato salad. Combine potatoes, celery, eggs, onion, pickle relish, salt and mayonnaise. Spoon into mold over layer of meat. Chill 2 or 3 hours, or until set.
• Unmold; garnish with greens or hard-cooked eggs. Place a bowl of mayonnaise in the center. Makes 8 servings.

SUMMER SUPPER MENU

Tomato Cocktail
Jellied Cucumber-Cabbage Mold
Hearty Corned Beef Salad Radish Roses
Toasted English Muffins
Chocolate Mint Pie
Milk Hot or Iced Coffee

TOMATO COCKTAIL

• Instead of plain tomato juice, chop peeled raw tomatoes fine; season with salt and freeze to a mush in refrigerator tray. Serve in chilled glasses (with spoons) as first course. May garnish with lemon slices.

CUCUMBER-CABBAGE MOLD

Just bring it cold and shimmering from the refrigerator at mealtime

2 (3 oz.) pkgs. lemon flavor gelatin
2 c. hot water
1¼ c. cold water
½ tsp. salt
2 tblsp. vinegar
1 large green cucumber
1½ c. finely shredded cabbage

• Dissolve gelatin in hot water.
• Add cold water, salt and vinegar.
• Pour ½ c. of mixture into 5-cup mold or loaf pan. Chill until firm.
• Cut 10 paper-thin slices from unpeeled cucumber. Overlap in a row on chilled gelatin.
• Spoon a little of liquid gelatin over slices; chill again.
• Chill rest of gelatin until it begins to congeal. Chop remaining cucumber. Add it and cabbage to gelatin.
• Mix; fill mold. Chill until firm.
• To unmold, hold mold in warm water a few seconds. Slip knife along one side to let in air. Unmold on platter.
• Garnish with crisp greens and radish roses. Makes 8 servings.

HEARTY CORNED BEEF SALAD

Also makes a good sandwich filling

1 c. mayonnaise or salad dressing
2 tblsp. prepared horse-radish
2 tblsp. sweet-pickle juice
1 (12 oz.) can corned beef
2 c. cooked peas (fresh or 1 pkg. frozen)
3 c. diced cooked potatoes
2 tblsp. chopped sweet pickles
Lettuce cups for 6

• Combine mayonnaise, horse-radish and pickle juice in a bowl.
• Dice corned beef. Mix with peas, potatoes and pickles.
• Add mayonnaise mixture. Toss to coat.
• Cover; chill in refrigerator.
• Fill lettuce cups. Makes 6 servings.

MINTED CHOCOLATE PIE

Caloric, but worth fasting for

1 envelope unflavored gelatin
¼ c. cold water
½ c. sugar
¼ tsp. salt
½ c. cocoa
¾ c. scalded milk
4 egg yolks, slightly beaten
4 egg whites, beaten stiff
½ tsp. peppermint extract
½ c. heavy cream
1 (9") vanilla cookie crumb crust

• Soften gelatin in cold water.
• Combine sugar, salt and cocoa. Slowly add scalded milk.
• Add egg yolks to cocoa mixture; cook over boiling water until thickened. Stir in gelatin. Chill until thick and syrupy.
• Blend egg whites and peppermint extract.
• Whip cream; blend with whites. Fold into chocolate mixture; pour into crumb crust. Chill until firm, about 3 hours. Serve with whipped cream.

Variation: To make Mocha Chiffon Pie, substitute ¾ c. coffee for milk; omit peppermint extract.

Build Meals Around These

HAM AND NOODLES

Fix casserole and refrigerate—bake just before serving

½ (8 oz.) pkg. broad noodles
1 small green pepper
1½ c. (¾ lb.) ground, smoked ham
1 egg, beaten
2 tblsp. melted butter or margarine
1 (1 lb. 4 oz.) can cream style corn
1½ c. corn flakes
¾ c. (4 oz.) diced, process cheese

• Cook noodles according to package directions.
• Cut six crosswise slices from narrow end of pepper. Reserve for garnish.
• Chop remaining pepper.
• Combine ham, egg and butter. Add noodles, chopped pepper, corn, corn flakes and cheese.
• Spoon into greased 1½ quart casserole.
• Bake in moderate (350°) oven 50 minutes. Garnish top with pepper rings. Makes 6 servings.

CHICKEN LOAF

With mushroom sauce—this is a hostess' dream

Chicken Loaf:

3 c. cooked chicken, chopped
1 c. cooked rice
2 c. soft bread crumbs
2 tsp. salt
2 c. chicken broth
4 eggs, beaten
¼ c. chopped pimiento

Mushroom Sauce:

¼ c. butter
1 c. fresh mushrooms, sliced, or 1 (4 oz.) can
¼ c. flour
½ tsp. salt
⅛ tsp. pepper
2 c. chicken broth
¼ c. cream
½ tsp. lemon juice
⅛ tsp. paprika
Chopped parsley

• Combine chicken with rice, crumbs, salt and broth. Add eggs; stir in pimiento.
• Pour into greased 9" baking dish. Bake in moderate oven (350°) 1 hour, or until firm. Cut in squares; serve with Mushroom Sauce. Makes 6 to 8 servings.
• To make sauce, melt butter; add and brown mushrooms. Stir in flour, salt and pepper. Add chicken broth and cream. Cook until thickened, stirring. Add lemon juice, paprika and parsley.

PRESSED BEEF

Horse-radish sauce supplies lively accent

4 lb. meaty beef shank with bone
2 qts. water
6 cloves
1 medium onion, sliced
1 stick cinnamon
2 tsp. salt
¼ tsp. pepper
1 tblsp. powdered sage
1 envelope unflavored gelatin
¼ c. cold water

• Cover meat with water; add onion and all seasonings, except sage; simmer until meat pulls from bone.
• Remove meat from broth; tear with forks until finely shredded.
• Add sage to liquid; cook down to 3 cups.
• Soften gelatin in cold water; add to broth.
• Chill broth until syrupy. Add meat.
• Pour into loaf pan; chill until firm. Makes 8 to 10 servings. Slice thin; serve with Fluffy Horse-radish Sauce.

Fluffy Horse-radish Sauce: Whip 1 c. heavy cream; stir in 2 tblsp. grated horse-radish, drained, ⅛ tsp. salt and 1 tsp. lemon juice. Chill ½ hour.

JELLIED BEEF MOLD

We've never tasted a better jellied meat loaf—a Farm Journal 5-star recipe

1½ lbs. boneless chuck beef
1 c. hot water
1 envelope unflavored gelatin
⅓ c. chopped celery
¼ c. chopped onion
¼ c. cubed dill pickles
1 (10½ oz.) can condensed beef consommé
½ tsp. salt
⅛ tsp. pepper
12 pimiento-stuffed olives
Strips of pimiento
Parsley
Olives

• Simmer beef in water until tender. Remove meat; put through food chopper using coarse blade. (There should be 2 c. ground beef.)
• Cool broth; soften gelatin in 2 tblsp. broth.
• Cook celery and onion in remainder of broth until tender, but still slightly firm, about 10 minutes. Drain, save broth. Mix celery, onion and pickles with meat.
• Add enough broth to consommé to make 2 c.; heat. Add softened gelatin; stir to dissolve. Pour thin layer of gelatin into 1½ qt. loaf pan; chill. To remainder of gelatin mixture add salt, pepper and beef.
• Arrange olive slices and pimiento strips in design over gelatin in pan. Spoon in beef mixture; chill.
• To serve, unmold on platter. Garnish with parsley and stuffed olives. Makes 8 servings.
• Double the recipe for a crowd.

MOLDED EGG SALAD

1 envelope unflavored gelatin
1 c. beef broth
½ tsp. salt
1 tsp. grated onion
1 tsp. Worcestershire sauce
¾ c. mayonnaise or salad dressing
5 hard-cooked eggs
1 c. diced celery
¼ c. chopped green pepper

• Soften gelatin in ¼ c. of the broth.
• Heat rest of broth to boiling point. Add softened gelatin and stir until gelatin is dissolved.
• Add salt, onion and Worcestershire sauce.
• Cool; gradually pour into mayonnaise, stirring, to blend smoothly.
• Reserve one egg to slice for garnish, and dice the rest.
• Add diced egg, celery and green pepper. Spoon into individual molds. Chill until firm.
• Unmold; serve with slice of egg on top. Makes 4 to 5 individual molds.

Sandwiches, Salads to Make Ahead

SANDWICH CAKE

It's the yellow cheese frosting that gives the sandwich a Halloween look

1 (8″) round loaf rye bread
6 c. chicken salad
3 to 4 (5 oz.) jars sharp process cheese spread
2 to 3 tblsp. milk

•Remove outside crust from fresh loaf rye (or white) bread. Cut crosswise into four equal slices.
• Put slices together like layer cake, using 2 c. of your favorite chicken salad mixture between each pair bread slices, 6 c. filling in all. (Other good fillings are: ham, chicken, egg, tuna, salmon and finely cut shrimp salads. Two or three kinds may be used for each "cake.")
• Frost as you would cake with cheese thinned with milk to good spreading consistency. Chill several hours. Makes 16 to 20 servings.

HAM PINWHEELS

Fancy enough for a party

½ lb. bologna
1 (2¼ oz.) can deviled ham
¼ c. pasteurized process cheese spread
1 loaf sandwich bread, unsliced
¼ c. soft butter or margarine
Stuffed olives

• Put bologna through food chopper using medium blade.
• Add deviled ham and cheese spread. Mix until well blended.
• Cut loaf of bread into lengthwise slices, a little less than ½″ thick. Remove crusts; spread each slice with butter. Then spread with ham mixture (about ¼ c. on each slice).
• Lay a row of olives across one end of bread slice. Roll like a jelly roll, keeping olives in center. (If bread cracks when rolled, surface is too dry. Then, place slice on a damp cloth or damp paper towels for a short while.)
• Wrap rolls in waxed paper or foil. Chill well before slicing. Cut each roll crosswise into 7 or 8 slices.

RIBBON SANDWICH LOAF

Sandwiches look like striped ribbon

1 loaf (14 oz. or 16 oz.) day-old bread, unsliced
Butter or margarine
½ lb. sharp process cheese, sliced
Egg-ham fillings (recipes follow)
3 (3 oz.) pkgs. cream cheese
⅓ c. light cream or top milk

• Remove crust from bread. With sharp knife cut lengthwise into 6 slices. Butter one side of each slice.
• On two slices, butter side up, place sliced cheese; spread two slices with Egg Filling; then one with Ham Filling.
• Stack slices, with Ham Filling in middle. Top with remaining bread slice. Press together firmly.
• Combine cream cheese (at room temperature) with cream. Beat until smooth and fluffy. Spread mixture over top and sides of loaf. Chill loaf several hours. Slice to serve.
• Decorate top with gay pimiento flowers and green pepper leaves.

Egg Filling: Combine 5 chopped hard-cooked eggs, 1 tblsp. chopped celery, 2 tsp. minced onion, ½ tsp. salt, ½ tsp. prepared mustard and 3 tblsp. mayonnaise.

Ham Filling: Combine ½ lb. ground cooked ham and contents of 1 (2¼ oz.) can deviled ham with 1 or 2 tblsp. mayonnaise.

GRAHAM PRUNE BREAD

One way to avoid out-of-breath hostessing. Just slice, pass butter and pour coffee

¾ c. prunes
1 c. sifted flour
½ tsp. baking powder
½ tsp. salt
¾ tsp. baking soda
⅔ c. unsifted graham flour
1 egg
⅔ c. sugar
⅓ c. prune juice
⅔ c. sour milk or buttermilk
2 tblsp. melted butter
½ c. chopped nuts

• Simmer prunes in water to cover. When tender, drain, saving liquid. Cut prunes in halves; remove pits.
• Sift together flour, baking powder, salt and soda. Mix in graham flour.
• Beat egg; blend in sugar.
• Combine prune juice and sour milk. Add to egg-sugar mixture alternately with dry ingredients. Stir in prunes. Add butter and nuts.
• Pour into greased 8½×4½×2½" loaf pan lined with waxed paper. Bake in moderate oven (350°) 1 hour, or until toothpick inserted in center comes out clean. Cool on wire rack.

FRUIT NUT BREAD

Apricots, dates and nuts make this extra-special

¾ c. dried apricots
1 c. sifted flour
2 tsp. baking powder
½ tsp. salt
1 c. whole wheat flour
½ c. brown sugar
½ c. chopped nuts
½ c. chopped dates
1 egg
1 c. milk
¼ c. shortening, melted and cooled

• Soak apricots in small amount cold water 1 hour.
• Sift together flour, baking powder and salt. Stir in whole wheat flour, sugar, nuts and dates.
• Chop apricots; add dry ingredients.
• Beat egg; blend in milk and shortening. Stir in dry ingredients. Pour into greased 8½×4½×2½" loaf pan. Bake in moderate oven (350°) 1 hour.

JELLIED CRANBERRY MOLD

Perfect to tote to the chicken supper or to serve at home

1 (3 oz.) pkg. orange flavor gelatin
1 (3 oz.) pkg. lemon flavor gelatin
2½ c. boiling water
2 c. fresh cranberry sauce (recipe follows) or 1 (16 oz.) can whole cranberries
¾ c. crushed pineapple, drained
½ c. chopped walnuts

• Dissolve orange and lemon gelatin in boiling water. Chill until syrupy.
• Break up cranberry sauce with fork; add pineapple and nuts; fold into gelatin. Chill until firm in 1½ qt. mold. Makes 12 servings.

To make fresh cranberry sauce: Boil 1 c. water and ¾ c. sugar for 5 minutes. Add 2 c. fresh cranberries; cook 5 minutes. Cool until set.

RHUBARB CELERY SALAD

Different and delicious

• Make lemon gelatin according to package directions. When gelatin is syrupy, stir in ½ c. cooked drained rhubarb sauce and ⅔ c. chopped celery.
• Chill until firm. Makes 6 servings. Serve with salad dressing.

MOLDED GRAPEFRUIT SALAD

Especially good with pork and chicken

1 c. boiling water
1 (3 oz.) pkg. lime flavor gelatin
1 c. grapefruit juice
1 c. grapefruit pieces
½ c. diced celery
1 c. cottage cheese
¼ tsp. ground ginger

• Dissolve lime flavor gelatin in boiling water. Add ginger and grapefruit juice. Chill until it starts to congeal.
• Add grapefruit pieces, celery and cottage cheese. Mix well.
• Pour into a 5- to 6-cup mold. Chill until firm. Unmold on crisp greens. Serve with mayonnaise. Makes 6 servings.

Citrus fruits combined in salads with berries, melons and other fruits—fresh (in season), canned, frozen or dried—deserve a good salad dressing. Two of our favorites:

AVOCADO SALAD DRESSING

It's a pretty green

1 avocado, ripe but firm
½ c. mayonnaise
1 tblsp. sugar
2 tblsp. lemon juice
½ c. orange juice
½ tsp. salt

• Peel avocado; halve and discard pit. Press avocado through sieve.
• Add remaining ingredients. Beat with rotary beater. Makes 1½ cups.

LIME-HONEY SALAD DRESSING

Lime and honey bring out the best in grapefruit

½ tsp. grated lime rind
⅓ c. lime juice
¼ c. strained honey
½ tsp. salt
½ tsp. paprika
½ tsp. prepared mustard
¾ c. oil

• Combine all ingredients in a bowl; beat thoroughly with a rotary beater.
• Store in a jar with a tight-fitting lid. Chill. Beat before serving.

FROZEN CHRISTMAS SALAD

Red and green cherries make it a Merry Christmas salad

1 (3 oz.) pkg. cream cheese
1 tblsp. mayonnaise or salad dressing
1 c. canned sweet cherries
½ c. cut up red maraschino cherries
¼ c. cut up green maraschino cherries
¼ c. cut up orange sections
1 c. crushed drained pineapple
1 c. chopped walnuts
1 c. heavy cream, whipped

• Soften cheese; blend with mayonnaise. Add cherries, remaining fruit and nuts.
• Fold whipped cream into mixture.
• Spoon in loaf pan; cover tightly; freeze.
• To serve, unmold and slice in cubes. Makes 10 to 12 servings.

FROZEN SALAD SUPREME

Luncheon salad for guests sent by a member of our Family Test Group

1 (1 lb. 4 oz.) can fruit cocktail
1 (9 oz.) can crushed pineapple
1 (1 lb. 4 oz.) can apricot halves
1 (3 oz.) pkg. lemon flavor gelatin
2 bananas, sliced
Juice of 1 lemon
1 tsp. lemon rind
¼ tsp. salt
½ c. heavy cream, whipped
½ c. mayonnaise or salad dressing

• Drain juice from fruits. Heat 2 c. and add to gelatin. Chill until syrupy.
• Combine drained fruits, bananas, lemon juice and rind; stir into gelatin.
• Add salt to whipped cream; blend in mayonnaise. Fold into gelatin.
• Pour into 2 refrigerator trays. Freeze at least 3 hours.
• Cut in small squares; press fork tines into squares and insert perky pieces of

lettuce. Serve in lettuce cups. Or, break salad with silver forks and heap into lettuce cups. Makes 8 servings.

GRAPEFRUIT-AVOCADO SALAD

You'll search a long time to find a more gorgeous fruit salad than this

- **1 (10 oz.) pkg. frozen, sliced strawberries**
- **6 grapefruit**
- **2 or 3 ripe avocados**
- **1 pt. fresh strawberries**
- **1 head lettuce**

• Thaw strawberries in package; drain.
• With sharp knife, peel membrane and skin from grapefruit. Remove sections from membrane. Add ¼ c. grapefruit juice and about ⅓ of sections to strawberry juice. Let marinate 6 to 8 hours, or overnight.
• Peel avocado. Cut into cubes, or scoop out balls with melon ball cutter. Drop into salted water (1 tblsp. salt to 1 qt. water) or in grapefruit or lemon juice to prevent discoloring. (May be fixed 2 or 3 hours early.)
• An hour or two before serving, drain fruits; arrange crisp lettuce leaves on individual dishes or on one large platter. Arrange drained fruits and fresh strawberries on platter. Refrigerate, covered with transparent plastic or waxed paper. Serve with Poppy Seed Dressing (recipe follows). Makes 8 servings.

Poppy Seed Salad Dressing:

- **1 c. sugar**
- **½ tsp. salt**
- **1 tsp. dry mustard**
- **1½ tsp. paprika**
- **½ c. vinegar**
- **1½ c. oil**
- **1 tsp. grated onion**
- **2 tblsp. poppy seed**

• Mix sugar, salt, dry mustard, paprika and vinegar together thoroughly.
• Add oil gradually, beating constantly.
• Add onion and poppy seed; shake to mix thoroughly. Makes 2½ cups.

CHEESE LIME SALAD

Brings out the best chicken flavors—also good with ham

- **1 (3 oz.) pkg. lime flavor gelatin**
- **2 c. boiling water**
- **1 (3 oz.) pkg. cream cheese**
- **1 tblsp. lemon juice**
- **1 cucumber**
- **4 slices canned pineapple**

• Dissolve gelatin in boiling water; add cream cheese and lemon juice and blend. Chill until slightly thickened.
• Chop cucumber and pineapple. Fold into gelatin mixture. Pour into 1½ quart mold. Chill firm. Makes 6 to 8 servings.

TUNA-ONION SALAD

Mainstay at lunch or supper. Serve with hot rolls

- **1 c. mayonnaise or salad dressing**
- **2 tblsp. lemon juice**
- **2 (6½ or 7 oz.) cans tuna**
- **12 green onions**
- **4 c. diced cooked potatoes**
- **½ c. chopped celery**
- **12 midget gherkins, sliced**
- **Fresh garden lettuce**
- **1 large carrot**

• Combine mayonnaise and lemon juice in mixing bowl. Drain oil from tuna into bowl; blend. Flake and add tuna.
• Cut 4 green onions into thin crosswise slices.
• Add cut onions, potatoes, celery and gherkins to tuna. Toss just enough to mix. Chill before serving.
• Serve on crisp lettuce leaves.
• For color, garnish with carrot rings strung on green onions. Makes 8 servings.

Make-Ahead Cake and Pie Desserts

STRAWBERRY ANGEL CAKE

Strawberries, ice cream and angel cake make this pretty pink and white dessert

1 (8") round angel food cake
2½ c. boiling water
2 (3 oz.) pkgs. strawberry flavor gelatin
1 (10 oz.) pkg. frozen sliced strawberries
⅛ tsp. salt
2 tsp. lemon juice
1 pt. vanilla ice cream
1 pt. fresh strawberries
½ pt. heavy cream or 1 (2 oz.) pkg. dessert topping mix

• Mold this dessert in the bowl in which you mix your ingredients. To find right size, turn cake upside down in bowl—it should fit loosely. (Try a 3 qt. size.)
• Measure boiling water into bowl; add gelatin. Stir to dissolve.
• Add frozen berries, salt and lemon juice. Break apart with fork or spoon as it thaws.
• Add ice cream; break apart. Stir, blending into mixture as it melts.
• In a matter of minutes the gelatin mixture will start to thicken. Push cake upside down, into middle of mixture. Lay a piece of waxed paper over top. Place small plate over cake; then put a light weight on plate. Chill. Remove weight when gelatin sets (about 15 minutes).
• To unmold, set bowl in hot water 2 or 3 minutes. Run spatula around side; invert on serving plate.
• Garnish entire mold with whipped cream or whipped dessert topping mix and fresh berries. Or cut into wedges and serve wedges on individual plates with whipped cream and fresh berries. Makes 10 to 12 servings.

Note: Use just enough weight to keep the cake immersed; overweighting will make it too compact.

AMBROSIA REFRIGERATOR DESSERT

Orange blossom pudding is one name for this luscious company dessert

2 envelopes unflavored gelatin
1½ c. orange juice
1 c. boiling water
¾ c. sugar
⅛ tsp. salt
1½ c. heavy cream, whipped
½ c. flaked or shredded coconut
1½ tsp. grated orange rind
1 c. peeled orange pieces, drained
12 lady fingers

• Soften gelatin in ½ c. orange juice. Add boiling water and sugar; stir to dissolve gelatin. Add remaining orange juice and salt; chill until thickened.
• Whip gelatin mixture until fluffy; blend with cream. Fold in fine-cut or flaked coconut, orange rind and pieces.
• Line bottom of 7" spring form pan with lengthwise lady finger halves. Cover with about ⅓ of orange-cream mixture.
• Stand 14 to 16 lady finger halves up along sides of pan, rounded side out, and touching bottom of pan. Add remaining orange filling.
• Chill several hours, or overnight. Serve with whipped cream or garnished with coconut and orange pieces. If lady fingers stand above filling, bend down for scalloped rim. Makes 7 to 8 servings.

STRAWBERRY REVEL

Strawberries-and-cream dessert

1 qt. strawberries
½ c. sugar
1 envelope unflavored gelatin
¼ c. water
1 tblsp. lemon juice
1 c. heavy cream, whipped
Lady fingers or pound cake

• Wash and hull berries; save some for garnish. Slice remainder. Sprinkle with sugar; toss lightly. Let stand.
• Soften gelatin in water.
• Drain juice from berries. Add gelatin. Heat to dissolve.
• Add sliced strawberries and lemon juice; cool until syrupy.
• Fold strawberry mixture into cream.
• Line a 1 qt. mold with lady fingers or 1" strips of pound cake. Fill with strawberry mixture. Chill.
• Unmold on serving dish. Garnish with extra berries. Makes 4 to 6 servings.

Substitution: Use 1 (10 oz.) pkg. frozen berries, thawed; omit sugar.

BLUEBERRY TREAT

Off the beaten path in blueberry desserts —rewarding taste adventure

1⅓ c. graham cracker or vanilla wafer crumbs
¼ c. sifted confectioners sugar
¼ c. melted butter or margarine
2 eggs, unbeaten
⅓ c. sugar
1 (8 oz.) pkg. softened cream cheese
¼ tsp. salt
2 c. fresh or frozen blueberries
½ c. sugar
2 tblsp. cornstarch
¼ tsp. salt
¾ c. water
¼ tsp. grated orange rind

• Mix together crumbs, confectioners sugar and butter; press in layer 8×8×2" pan.
• Beat eggs; add ⅓ c. sugar, cream cheese and salt; blend together. Pour over crumb crust; bake in moderate oven (375°) 20 minutes. Cool.
• Cover with 1 c. blueberries. Blend together ½ c. sugar, cornstarch, salt and water. Add remaining blueberries and rind. Cook over low heat until clear and thick, stirring constantly. Pour over berries. Chill before serving. May garnish with whipped cream. Makes 8 servings.

PEANUT BUTTER CHIFFON PIE

A friendly home agent in Georgia gave us this recipe—also an unforgettable sample to eat and enjoy

1 envelope unflavored gelatin
1 c. cold water
3 egg yolks, well beaten
½ c. sugar or light corn syrup
½ tsp. salt
½ c. smooth peanut butter
½ tsp. vanilla
3 egg whites, unbeaten
1 (9") baked crumb crust
½ c. heavy cream, whipped stiff (optional)
Peanut halves
Chocolate pieces

• Soften gelatin in ¼ c. water.
• Combine egg yolks, ¼ c. sugar, ¼ c. water and salt in top of double boiler; blend. Add gelatin.
• Place over boiling water; beat constantly with rotary beater until thick and fluffy (about 5 minutes). Cool.
• Place peanut butter in bowl; add remaining ½ c. water gradually; beat until smooth. Add vanilla to egg yolk mixture; blend. Chill until slightly thickened, but still syrupy (10 to 15 minutes).
• Beat egg whites until foamy; add remaining sugar gradually, beating until stiff. Fold into peanut butter mixture. Turn into crumb crust (you may use baked pastry shell). Chill until firm. Makes 6 servings.
• To serve, cover top with thin layer whipped cream if desired. (Cream is pretty but detracts from the peanut flavor.) Decorate with "daisies" of peanut halves and chocolate pieces for centers.

Crumb Crust: Mix 1⅓ c. fine graham cracker crumbs (they come in handy 13½ oz. bags—enough to make 3 pie crusts), ¼ c. sugar and 6 tblsp. soft butter or margarine until crumbly. Press mixture in even layer on bottom and sides of well greased 9" pie pan. Build up crust rim around edge of pan. Chill well.

LEMON CHIFFON PIE

Lemon fluff in crisp, spicy crust

1 envelope unflavored gelatin
¼ c. cold water
4 egg yolks, beaten
½ c. sugar
¼ tsp. salt
¼ c. lemon juice
¼ tsp. grated lemon rind
4 egg whites, beaten stiff
¼ c. sugar
1 (9″) crumb crust (p. 295)

• Soak gelatin in cold water.
• Combine egg yolks, sugar and salt. Add lemon juice and rind. Cook over boiling water, stirring constantly, until thick.
• Stir in gelatin. Chill until thick and syrupy.
• Beat egg whites and sugar. Fold into egg yolk mixture. Turn into crust. Chill until firm, about 3 hours. Serve with Frosted Grapes. To fix them, dip 1 lb. white or green grapes, broken into clusters, in 1 egg white, slightly beaten with 1 tblsp. water. Roll in sugar, spread on waxed paper. Chill in refrigerator at least 1 hour.

PEPPERMINT CHIFFON PIE

Chocolate crumb crust holds the candy-flecked filling

1 envelope unflavored gelatin
¼ c. cold water
¾ c. milk
½ c. sugar
¼ tsp. salt
1 c. crushed peppermint stick candy
4 egg yolks, slightly beaten
4 egg whites, beaten stiff
1 (9″) chocolate cookie crumb crust
Whipped cream

• Soak gelatin in cold water.
• Scald milk; stir in sugar, salt and peppermint candy.
• Add egg yolks to milk mixture; cook over boiling water until mixture coats spoon.
• Stir in gelatin; chill until thick and syrupy.
• Beat egg whites. Fold in custard. Pour into crumb crust. Chill until firm, about 3 hours. Serve with whipped cream.

REFRIGERATOR CAKE

End dinner the chocolate-cream way

2 (4 oz.) bars German's sweet chocolate
5 eggs, separated
1 tsp. vanilla
12 lady fingers (3 oz.)
1 c. heavy cream

• Melt chocolate in top of double boiler over boiling water.
• Beat egg yolks well; add vanilla and yolks to chocolate. Beat well.
• Beat egg whites until stiff; fold into chocolate mixture.
• Line a 1 qt. bowl or mold with waxed paper. Pour a little chocolate mixture into bottom of mold.
• Line sides of bowl with lady finger halves, pushing ends into filling to keep upright. Add layer of lady fingers; then remaining filling. Top with lady fingers.
• Refrigerate 12 to 24 hours. Unmold on serving dish. Remove paper. (For buffet serving, cut cake into pieces before adding whipped cream. Dip knife into hot water before cutting each slice.)
• Whip cream. Add frills with cake decorator or spread cream over dessert; sprinkle with grated chocolate. Makes 8 servings.

LEMON REFRIGERATOR CAKE

It has that delicate lemon taste

2 tblsp. butter or margarine
15 square graham crackers
½ c. melted butter or margarine
6 eggs, separated
¼ tsp. salt

½ c. lemon juice
Grated rind of 1 lemon
1 (15 oz.) can sweetened condensed milk
½ tsp. cream of tartar
½ c. sugar

• Cream 2 tblsp. butter; spread over sides and bottom of a 10″ spring mold or pie plate.
• Roll crackers fine; mix with ½ c. butter; pat into buttered pan to form crust.
• Beat egg yolks until thick and fluffy; add salt, lemon juice and rind. Slowly add condensed milk; beat until fluffy and well blended.
• Beat egg whites until foamy; add cream of tartar; beat until stiff.
• Gently fold ¼ of egg whites into lemon mixture. Pour into crust.
• Add sugar to remaining egg whites; beat to make meringue. Spread over top of cake. Bake in moderate oven (350°) 15 minutes. Chill overnight. Makes 8 servings.

LIME CHOCOLATE PIE

Crust:

1¼ c. chocolate cookie crumbs (about 20 cookies)
⅓ c. butter or margarine, melted

• Combine crumbs and butter. Press firmly into buttered 9″ pie pan.
• Chill until firm.

Filling:

1 (3 oz.) pkg. lime flavor gelatin
1 c. boiling water
¼ c. sugar
⅔ c. evaporated milk or 1 (5½ oz.) can
2 tblsp. lemon juice
2 tsp. grated lemon rind
Few drops green food color

• Combine gelatin and water; stir until dissolved. Add sugar. Chill until thickened and partly set.
• Chill evaporated milk in refrigerator tray until ice crystals form.
• Whip milk until stiff. Add lemon juice.
• Fold in gelatin mixture. Add rind and food color.
• Pour into crust. Chill about 4 hours, or until firm. Bring pie to room temperature (about 30 minutes) before cutting.

CITRUS FRUIT CUSTARD

Happy ending to any dinner—team with coconut cookies for guests

⅔ c. sugar
2 tblsp. cornstarch
2 egg yolks
1 egg white
1 pt. milk
1 tsp. butter
⅛ tsp. salt
2 tblsp. lime juice
2 oranges, sectioned

• Mix sugar and cornstarch thoroughly.
• Beat egg and egg yolk.
• Bring milk to a full boil in top of double boiler over direct heat.
• Place over rapidly boiling water.
• Stir in sugar-cornstarch mixture and beaten egg.
• Cook until thick. Remove from heat.
• Add butter, salt and lime juice. Cool.
• Place orange sections in serving dishes; spoon custard over them. Top with meringue.

Meringue:

1 egg white
2 tblsp. sugar

• Beat egg white until stiff but not dry. Continue beating, and slowly add sugar. Meringue will be glossy, and will hold its shape.

Refrigerator-Tray Ice Creams

RHUBARB ICE CREAM

Pink dainty that's tasty—try it with chocolate cake

2 c. cubed rhubarb
¾ c. sugar
2 egg yolks, beaten
1 c. heavy cream
1 tblsp. lemon juice
2 egg whites, unbeaten

• Combine rhubarb and ½ c. sugar. Cook in covered pan 15 minutes over low heat (do not add water); cool.
• Combine egg yolks, cream, lemon juice and rhubarb; mix well.
• Pour into refrigerator tray. Freeze until firm.
• Turn into bowl; break in chunks. Beat until fluffy, but not melted.
• Beat egg whites and ¼ c. sugar; fold into ice cream. Return to refrigerator tray. Freeze. Makes 6 servings.

COFFEE ICE CREAM

Try scoops of this on faintly warm gingerbread

1 rennet tablet
1 tblsp. cold water
2 c. light cream
½ c. sugar
2 tblsp. instant coffee

• Crush rennet tablet; dissolve in water.
• Pour cream into top of double boiler.
• Sift together sugar and coffee; stir into cream. Heat slowly to lukewarm. Add rennet; stir quickly a few seconds.
• Pour into refrigerator tray. Let stand at room temperature until set (about 10 minutes); then freeze firm.
• Turn into chilled bowl; break into chunks with wooden spoon; beat fluffy smooth with electric or rotary mixer. Return to cold tray; freeze firm. Makes 6 to 8 servings.

LEMON SHERBET

Mighty good on slices of angel food or yellow sponge cake

1 envelope unflavored gelatin
2½ c. milk
1 c. sugar
½ c. lemon juice
1 tsp. grated lemon rind
⅛ tsp. salt
2 egg whites

• Soak gelatin in ½ c. milk.
• Add sugar to remaining milk; scald.
• Dissolve gelatin mixture in scalded milk; cool.
• Add lemon juice very slowly; add rind.
• Freeze in refrigerator tray until mushy.
• Add salt to egg whites and beat. Beat in lemon mush.
• Return to refrigerator tray; freeze thoroughly, stirring occasionally. Makes 6 servings.

LEMON ICE CREAM

Serve in dessert dishes or drop spoonfuls on mixed fruit salads

2 eggs, unbeaten
⅛ tsp. salt
1 tsp. grated lemon rind
½ c. lemon juice
½ c. sugar
½ c. light corn syrup
1½ c. rich milk
1 c. heavy cream, whipped

• Beat eggs with salt and lemon rind; add lemon juice and sugar.
• Stir in corn syrup and milk. Pour into refrigerator freezing trays. Freeze until mushy, about 45 minutes.
• Remove from trays to chilled bowl. Beat smooth with fork or beater.
• Fold in whipped cream. Pour back into trays to freeze until firm. Makes 1 quart.

Variation: Substitute 1 c. sweetened condensed milk for sugar and corn syrup.

20

Quick and Easy Cooking

Many farm women tell us they are having to simplify their cooking. Some have jobs off the farm or help outdoors with farm work; others give time to community housekeeping. That's why we include this chapter, our Busy Woman's Cookbook in miniature. Even busy women don't want to let down their standards or forfeit their reputations as good cooks. They want their families and friends to find good solid eating and fine flavor on their tables.

The recipes that follow show how our Food Department meets this challenge. They are designed for the fast pace of living almost everyone faces today; they make liberal use of handy prepared and partly-prepared foods available. But every recipe has at least one imaginative touch—something to make the result of your mix, for instance, different from the one your neighbor down the road makes from the same kind of package.

If, as a farm woman, you have qualms about being loyal to the family business when you use packaged and canned products, consider that you're supporting a widening market for agricultural products. The flour in cake, biscuit, muffin and other mixes and the cans and packages of milk, potatoes, rice, meat and chicken, for example, are farm produced of course. In many instances convenient forms of merchandising actually increase the demand for what you grow. If you have a choice of no cake or a fine one made in a jiffy from a mix, why do without cake?

Women who prefer the traditional type of cooking that takes more time, will find plenty of recipes in this book. But we believe most up-to-date good cooks treasure both kinds of recipes—they use what we call short and long cookery methods. Almost everyone has extremely busy days when hurry-up meals are necessary and somewhat more leisurely ones when there is more time for cooking. So we give you both kinds of recipes.

We believe you will discover that you can spend less time in the kitchen than your mother did and still feed the family well, economically and happily. And you'll find how you can entertain easily and successfully with these fast-fix dishes.

Quick Glamor Tricks

ICE CREAM CAKE

A dazzling party cake—colorful as confetti and delicious, too

1 (10″) angel food cake
1 qt. strawberry ice cream
1 qt. chocolate ice cream
1 qt. pistachio ice cream
2 c. heavy cream

• Cut cool cake, made from packaged mix or bakery bought, crosswise in 4 equal layers.
• Spread tops of 3 bottom layers with ice cream, using a different flavor for each. (You can choose your favorites.) Do one at a time, starting with strawberry, and place immediately in freezer or refrigerator's freezing section. Proceed with chocolate ice cream; stack on top of strawberry in freezer. Then follow with layer spread with pistachio ice cream. Add top layer of cake. Work fast.
• Whip cream and use to frost cake. Store in freezer until serving time. (May be made several days ahead.) Makes 20 servings.

PEANUT CUPCAKES

School boy says they're favorites

½ c. peanut butter
⅓ c. shortening
1 tsp. vanilla
1½ c. brown sugar
2 eggs
2 c. sifted flour
2 tsp. baking powder
½ tsp. salt
¾ c. milk

• Cream together peanut butter, shortening and vanilla. Add brown sugar slowly and beat until light and fluffy. Add eggs, one at a time, beating after each addition.
• Sift flour, baking powder and salt together. Add to creamed mixture alternately with milk.
• Set paper baking cups in muffin-pan cups and fill half full of batter. Bake in moderate oven (375°) 20 minutes or until done. Makes about 24 cupcakes.
Note: Spread tops of cupcakes with peanut butter and sift on confectioners sugar.

QUICK HOLIDAY CAKE

Yuletide dessert gem: Plain cake with jeweled frosting broiled on top

2 tblsp. butter or margarine
⅓ c. firmly packed brown sugar
2 tblsp. undiluted evaporated milk
⅓ c. mixed candied fruits, chopped
⅓ c. broken nuts
⅓ c. flaked coconut
1 (8×8×2″) cake layer

• Blend together butter, sugar and milk. Add fruits, nuts and coconut.
• Put cake on baking sheet; spread fruit mixture over top. Place under preheated broiler until delicate brown and bubbly (about 2 to 3 minutes). Makes 9 to 12 servings.

CHERRY UPSIDE-DOWN CAKE

Serve it at its very best warm from the oven

2 tblsp. melted butter or margarine
2 tblsp. brown sugar
1 (1 lb. 8 oz.) jar cherry pie filling
1 egg, beaten
½ c. milk
½ tsp. almond extract
1 (11¾ oz.) pkg. cupcake mix

California Has Favored Chinese Dishes for years – now they've moved across USA, often via Chinatown restaurants. Chow Mein is on page 368.

Bean Cookery Varies by Regions of the U. S. We give you two baked bean recipes, pages 358 and 361, Chapter 24.

Superior Food Earns Money A Florida homemaker gets $1.50 per pound for this easy-to-make Date Pecan Loaf (no chopping). Recipe on page 335.

Another Money Maker – $2.50 for this Alabama Lemon Cheese Cake. It's called that – no cheese actually but lemon curd filling. Recipe on page 336.

• Measure butter and brown sugar into 9″ square pan. Pour filling over mixture. Place in moderate oven (350°) while preparing cake topping.
• Add egg, milk and almond extract to cake mix. Prepare according to package directions.
• Remove pan from oven; drop 1 c. batter by spoonfuls over fruit. Spread batter over top.
• Bake cake 35 to 45 minutes. Remove from oven; cool 5 minutes.
• Turn upside down on plate so fruit makes topping. Serve warm with whipped cream. Makes 8 to 10 servings.

Variations: Use 1 (1 lb. 5 oz.) can pineapple pie filling instead of cherries. For a quicker dessert, cook the pie filling as directed on label. Serve warm over slices of pound cake or squares of unfrosted bakery cake.

TOPSY-TURVY MINCEMEAT CAKE

2 tblsp. butter or margarine
1 c. sifted brown sugar, firmly packed
2 c. prepared mincemeat
1 (1 lb. 1 oz.) pkg. orange cake mix
1 c. heavy cream, whipped

• Put butter, sugar and mincemeat in 10½″ ring mold. Heat in moderate oven (375°) while making cake.
• Prepare cake batter as directed on package and pour over hot mincemeat mixture in pan. Bake in moderate oven (375°) about 25 minutes or until delicately brown and springs back to light touch.
• Let stand a few minutes; turn out upside down on chop plate. Or cool in pan and just before serving warm in slow oven (300°) 10 to 15 minutes. Place small dish of whipped cream in center. Makes 16 to 20 servings.

ORANGE-COCONUT CAKE

Simple to fix, easy to serve

1 c. flaked or shredded coconut
2 tblsp. orange juice
1 tblsp. grated orange rind
1 pkg. yellow cake mix
1 c. heavy cream

• Combine coconut, orange juice and rind. Let stand while cake bakes and cools.
• Prepare cake by package directions. Bake in a 9″ square pan; cool.
• Whip cream until very stiff. Fold in coconut mixture. Spread on cake. Chill several hours before serving. Makes 10 to 12 servings.

APPLE COFFEE CAKE

Apples and brown crumbs—sweet, spicy and crunchy—top this treat for a crowd

3 c. biscuit mix
½ c. sugar
½ tsp. salt
1 tsp. cinnamon
½ c. milk
2 eggs, slightly beaten
3 tblsp. oil or melted shortening
1 (1 lb. 4 oz.) can apple slices
½ c. brown sugar, firmly packed
¼ c. flour
1 tsp. cinnamon
¼ c. butter or margarine
⅓ c. walnuts, coarsely chopped

• Combine mix, sugar, salt and cinnamon.
• Mix together milk, eggs and oil; stir into dry ingredients. Spread batter in greased 8×12″ dish. Cover with apple slices.
• Blend together brown sugar, flour and cinnamon; coarsely cut in butter. Add nuts and sprinkle over top of apple slices.
• Bake in hot oven (400°) 35 minutes. Makes 12 servings.

Quick Cake Toppings

A luscious way to crown cake is to spread a buttery, sweet topping on it and broil until bubbly and hot. There's no better way to add your own glamor touch to fresh-baked or frozen cake in a jiffy. You need not take freshly baked cake from the pan before adding the topping, but you will want to thaw frozen cake about 20 minutes. The five toppings that follow are ample for an 8" cake layer, round or square.

PEPPERMINT CANDY TOPPING

Excellent on chocolate cake

¼ c. confectioners sugar
¼ c. flour
⅛ tsp. salt
2 tblsp. soft butter or margarine
2 tblsp. light cream
½ c. crushed soft peppermint candy

• Blend together sugar, flour, salt and butter; add cream and candy. Mix well.
• Spread mixture over cake.
• Broil until mixture begins to brown, 2 to 4 minutes. Cake makes 8 to 12 servings.

ROYAL CHERRY TOPPING

Cherries add bright color and marvelous taste

¼ c. confectioners sugar
½ tsp. ginger
3 tblsp. flour
⅛ tsp. salt
2 tblsp. soft butter or margarine
12 maraschino cherries, drained and chopped

• Blend sugar, ginger, flour, salt and butter until evenly crumbled. (Pastry blender or fork works fine.)
• Stir in cherries.
• Spread mixture over cake.
• Broil until mixture begins to bubble, 3 to 4 minutes. Cake makes 8 to 12 servings.

FRUIT-NUT TOPPING

Brown sugar and butter melt to goodness

2 tblsp. butter or margarine
⅓ c. sifted brown sugar
2 tblsp. light cream
⅓ c. mixed candied fruit
⅓ c. blanched, slivered almonds
⅓ c. flaked or shredded coconut
⅛ tsp. salt

• Cream butter and sugar together; add remaining ingredients.
• Mix lightly and spread on cake.
• Broil until bubbly and glazed, 3 to 5 minutes.

HONEYED COCONUT TOPPING

Adds glamor to white cake

2 tblsp. soft butter or margarine
⅔ c. flaked or shredded coconut
¼ c. honey
1 tsp. grated lemon rind
⅛ tsp. salt

• Spread top of cake with butter.
• Combine remaining ingredients, blend well. Spread over cake.
• Broil to just toast coconut lightly, 2 to 4 minutes. Cake makes 8 to 12 servings.

TOASTY PRALINE TOPPING

⅓ c. melted butter or margarine
½ c. brown sugar, firmly packed
¼ c. milk
¼ tsp. salt
½ tsp. vanilla
1 c. finely cut shredded or flaked coconut
½ c. chopped nuts

• Blend together all ingredients.
• Spread mixture over top of hot square cake layer. Broil slowly until golden—3 to 5 minutes. Watch carefully. Cake makes 8 to 12 servings.

Tricks with Cookie Mix

COOKIE SHORTCAKE

Red and white candy makes the dessert colorful—tastes as good as it looks

24 (about ½ lb.) chocolate wafer cookies
1 qt. vanilla ice cream
½ c. crushed peppermint stick candy

• Place a cookie on each dessert plate. Top with spoonful ice cream; sprinkle with 1 tsp. candy; top with second cookie. Press down gently on top cookie, add a second spoonful of ice cream, sprinkle with more candy, then cover with a third cookie.
• Serve at once with ice cream topped with candy sprinkle; or store in freezer before serving. Makes 8 servings.

Variation: Serve with chocolate sauce.

HALF-AND-HALF MACAROONS

They'll be the talk of the party!

1 (13 oz.) pkg. white coconut macaroon mix
¼ c. chopped maraschino cherries
¼ tsp. almond extract
1 (13 oz.) pkg. chocolate coconut macaroon mix

• Prepare white macaroon dough according to package directions for cherry macaroons, adding cherries and almond extract.
• In separate bowl prepare chocolate macaroon dough by package directions.
• With end of teaspoon, scoop up dab of chocolate dough to half fill spoon. Fill rest of spoon with cherry macaroon dough. Push off spoon onto paper-covered baking sheet; bake according to package directions. Makes about 4 dozen.

WALNUT BROWNIES

Old friends that are ever welcome

1 (1 lb.) pkg. brownie mix
Confectioners sugar frosting
36 walnut halves

• Prepare brownies according to package directions. Cool in pan.
• Spread with frosting made with 2 c. sifted confectioners sugar. Cut in 36 (1½") squares. Press walnut half on each. Makes 36 brownies.

LIBERTY BELL COOKIES

Fourth-of-July specialty

• Roll out molasses cookie dough (may use gingerbread mix following directions on package). Cut in bell shapes, bake and cool.
• Use thin confectioners sugar icing (1 c. sifted sugar to 2 to 3 tblsp. milk, depending on consistency desired) to make crack and to write 1776 on each bell. Use toothpick or pastry tube to write numbers and to draw crack on cool cookies. Makes about 6 dozen.

LAYERED BROWNIES

Pass these cookies to friends who drop in —a fine greeting

1 (1 lb.) pkg. fudge brownie mix
1 (1 lb.) pkg. blond brownie mix
4 eggs, unbeaten
½ c. water
Walnut halves

• Follow directions for cake-like brownies; divide each batter in half. Spread chocolate batter evenly in two well greased 8×8×2" pans; spread blond batter on top of chocolate. Garnish with walnuts. Bake in moderate oven (350°) about 35 minutes.
• Cool slightly; remove from pan. When cold, cut in 2" squares. Makes 32.

PENNSYLVANIA DUTCH HEARTS

The prettiest heart cookies you ever saw —and so easy to make

1 (11½ oz.) pkg. icebox cookie dough, any flavor
Bright colored sugars (red, yellow, blue, green, etc.)

• Roll dough thin on lightly floured surface. Cut cookies with heart cutter. (Dutch hearts are wider—pinch dough at tip to make fatter hearts.)
• With tip of small pointed spoon, drop colored sugar on hearts, leaving about ¼" margin around edges unsugared. Use one color or combinations, including multi-colored balls and silver dragees.
• To color sugar, put about ¼ cup sugar in covered jar. Add few drops food color, shaking after each addition to get desired color.
• Bake according to package directions, about 7 minutes or until lightly browned. Makes about 6 dozen.

CHRISTMAS COOKIE NIBBLES

Crisp, bite-size cookies all aglitter with colored sugars and candies

1 (11½ to 12 oz.) pkg. refrigerator cookies
Red and green sugars
Tiny multi-colored candy balls
Confectioners sugar

• Cut cookie dough (peanut, sugar, coconut or butterscotch) into slices ⅛" thick. Using floured small cutters, cut each slice into tiny cutouts. (For variety, cut slices with knife in fourths and circles with inside of doughnut cutter. Shape trimmings in hands to make small balls.)
• Roll in colored sugars or candies. (Leave some plain to shake in confectioners sugar after baking.)
• Bake on ungreased baking sheet in moderate oven (375°) about 4 minutes. Let cool 1 minute before removing. Makes about 9 to 10 dozen.

Desserts in a Hurry

NORTH POLE CHERRY PIE

Watch eyes light up at this festive, cherry-ice cream pie

1 qt. vanilla ice cream
1 baked (9") pie shell or crumb crust
1 (1 lb. 6 to 8 oz.) jar cherry pie filling

• Spread slightly softened ice cream in pie shell and freeze. (You may tint ice cream delicate green.)
• An hour before serving, spread filling over top. Return to freezer. Serve quickly. Makes 6 servings.

CRANBERRY CHIFFON PIE

Pink of perfection in new quick pie

1 c. cranberry juice cocktail
1 pkg. lemon chiffon pie filling
⅓ c. sugar
9" graham cracker crust

• Chill ½ c. cranberry cocktail.
• Heat remaining juice to boiling; stir into filling mix. Add chilled juice; beat until foamy with mixer at highest speed.
• Add sugar, beat until mixture stands in peaks—1 to 3 minutes. Spoon into pie shell. Chill until set (about 2 hours). Serve plain or with whipped cream. Makes 6 servings.

PASTRY TRICKS

Orange: Use orange juice instead of water in making pastry. Add ½ tsp. grated orange rind for 1-crust pie. Good with cranberry, raisin, orange and lemon pies.

Nuts: Add ¼ c. finely chopped nuts to pastry for 1-crust pie. Just right with cream and custard pies.

Shiny Tops: Brush top crust of 2-crust pies with milk before baking.

Sugary Tops: Moisten top crust with water, using fingers; sprinkle evenly with sugar and bake as usual.

LEMON COCONUT PIE

Busy-day pie wonder—with cake crust

1 (7 or 8 oz.) baker's loaf cake
½ c. flaked or shredded coconut
1 pkg. lemon flavor pudding and pie filling
2 eggs, separated

• Cut cake into 12 or 14 slices. Line sides and bottom of a 9" pie pan with them to make pie shell.
• Sprinkle half of coconut over cake slices.
• Prepare pudding according to package directions, using egg yolks. Pour immediately into pie shell.
• Make meringue from the egg whites, using 6 tblsp. sugar or as directed on pudding package. Spread over filling; sprinkle with remaining coconut. Bake in moderate oven (350°) 12 minutes or until lightly browned. Cool and cut. Makes 6 servings.

BROWNIE PUDDING

Chocolate with nuts—that means it's mighty fine eating

1 (1 lb.) pkg. brownie mix
1 or 2 eggs
½ c. chopped nuts
¾ c. brown sugar
¼ c. cocoa
1¾ c. hot water

• Mix batter according to directions for cake-like brownies, adding eggs and nuts as directed. Pour into greased 9×9×1½" pan.
• Mix together brown sugar and cocoa. Sprinkle over top of batter. Gently pour hot water over sugar mixture. (When baked, this topping makes a small amount of chocolate sauce in bottom of pan.)
• Bake in moderate oven (350°) 45 to 55 minutes until cake layer tests done. Serve warm or cold. Spoon into serving dishes. Serve with light cream or whipped cream. Makes 6 to 9 servings.

PINEAPPLE SUPREME

A dessert as inviting as Hawaiian sunshine—a snap to make

2 (13½ oz.) cans frozen pineapple chunks, partially thawed
1 c. (½ pt.) dairy sour cream
4 tsp. sugar
Freshly grated nutmeg

• Arrange pineapple in sherbet glasses.
• Blend cream with sugar; place generous spoonful on each serving of pineapple. Dust lightly with nutmeg. Makes 6 servings. Serve with coconut or chocolate-coconut macaroons made from packaged mix or other cookies.

Variation: Substitute strawberry or vanilla ice cream for sour cream topping.

BANANA-APRICOT DESSERT

So delicious to eat; so quick to make

3 tblsp. butter or margarine
1 (1 lb. 14 oz.) can apricot halves
1 tsp. cinnamon
2 tsp. cornstarch
¼ c. water
6 ripe, firm bananas
Whipped cream

• Melt butter in skillet. (You can cook in chafing dish or electric skillet at the table.)
• Pour can of apricots into skillet. Sprinkle with cinnamon.
• Mix cornstarch with water. Add slowly to liquid in skillet, stirring constantly. Bring to a boil; cook about 3 minutes.
• Peel bananas; cut in crosswise halves. (Use ripe bananas with yellow skins without brown flecks.) Place in pan with apricots. Heat together just long enough to warm fruit. Serve hot with a fluff of whipped cream. Makes 6 servings.
• Other canned fruits may be used in place of apricots—as sliced peaches, pears cut in sections, Queen Anne cherries, Bing cherries. If desired, a soft custard or vanilla sauce may be poured over. Or, try a fruit sherbet.

FRUITED TAPIOCA

A happy meal ending—the fruits blend their flavors successfully

1 (6 oz.) can grape juice concentrate
1½ c. hot water
¼ c. quick-cooking tapioca
¼ c. sugar
Dash of salt
1 tblsp. butter or margarine
2 tsp. lemon juice
1 (1 lb.) can pears, drained
Light cream

• Combine grape juice and hot water in saucepan; add tapioca, sugar and salt. Bring to a boil over medium heat, stirring constantly.

• Remove from heat. Blend in butter and lemon juice; cool to room temperature—need not be chilled.

• Spoon into serving dishes. Top with drained pear half. Serve with light cream sweetened with 1 tblsp. sugar. Makes 6 servings.

PEACHES IN LEMON SAUCE

Double quick—cream cheese melts beautifully

1 (1 lb. 4 oz.) can peach halves or slices
1 egg
2 tblsp. lemonade concentrate
½ c. syrup (from peaches)
1 tblsp. sugar
Dash of salt
1 (3 oz.) pkg. cream cheese

• Drain syrup from fruit. Spoon fruit into individual dessert dishes.

• Beat egg in top of double boiler. Add lemonade concentrate (don't add water), syrup, sugar and salt. Beat well.

• Place over boiling water; cook until thick and smooth, stirring occasionally, about 6 to 8 minutes.

• Add cream cheese. Beat with a rotary beater until smooth. Serve warm or cool over peach halves. Ginger snap cookies are good accompaniment, although any desired crisp cookie may be served. Makes 6 servings.

STRAWBERRY MERINGUES A LA MODE

Juicy, red-ripe berries in crisp meringues with ice cream topknots

½ (4.1 oz.) box meringue mix (2 in box—use 1 packet)
⅔ c. sugar
⅓ c. water
1 qt. strawberries, sliced
1 qt. strawberry ice cream

• Prepare meringue shells according to package directions, using sugar and water. Cool.

• To serve, fill center with strawberries and top with strawberry ice cream. Makes 6 to 8 servings.

Variations: Use half and half fresh pineapple or banana cubes and sliced strawberries. Top with strawberry or pineapple ice cream.

COCONUT CREAM PUDDING

You'll use the recipe for this quick and easy dessert often

2 (3¾ oz.) pkgs. instant pudding (coconut cream)
3 c. milk
1 c. light cream
4 tsp. grated orange rind

• Combine all ingredients in bowl.

• Beat until well blended, about 1 minute. Pour into bowl or pan; let stand about 5 minutes.

• Spoon into serving dishes. Garnish with orange sections or Rosy Rhubarb Sauce (recipe follows). Makes 6 servings.

Rosy Rhubarb Sauce: Put following ingredients in saucepan: 1 (1 lb.) pkg. quick frozen rhubarb or 1 lb. fresh rhubarb, cut in 1″ pieces, ¼ c. light corn syrup and dash of salt. Bring to slow boil; cook 5 minutes or until pieces are tender. Cool; chill. Spoon over coconut cream pudding. Makes about 2 cups.

RAISIN-RICE DESSERT

Whoever finds the whole almond in his serving wins a special gift

1 (5 oz.) pkg. quick-cooking rice
1 qt. milk
1 tsp. salt
¼ c. golden raisins
1 envelope unflavored gelatin
¼ c. cold milk
¾ c. sugar
1 c. heavy cream
½ tsp. almond extract
1 whole blanched almond
1 (1 lb. 4½ oz.) can pineapple spears, drained
Red Velvet Sauce (recipe follows)

• In heavy saucepan, bring rice, 1 qt. milk, salt and raisins to boil. Cover and simmer 20 minutes or until rice is tender and milk absorbed; stir occasionally with fork.
• Soften gelatin in ¼ c. milk. Stir with sugar into hot rice mixture. Spread in large shallow bowl; cover and chill.
• Whip cream stiff; blend in extract. Fold into rice mixture. (Add the whole almond!)
• Lightly oil 5 cup mold, preferably deep with fluted sides. Press pineapple spears against sides or into fluted ridges. Pour in rice mixture; cover; chill several hours.
• To serve, unmold dessert on plate. Garnish edge with remaining pineapple spears. Slowly pour a little Red Velvet Sauce on top. Serve immediately with remaining sauce. Makes 10 to 12 servings.

Red Velvet Sauce (prepare shortly before serving): Add 1 tblsp. lemon juice, ⅛ tsp. salt and enough water to pineapple syrup to make 2½ cups; stir in 1 pkg. Danish dessert mix (strawberry flavor). Cook according to package directions. Cool, but do not chill (sauce thickens too much when cold). Makes sauce for 10 servings.

WAFFLES à la MODE

1¼ c. sifted cake flour
1 tblsp. sugar
½ tsp. salt
1 tsp. baking powder
2 eggs, separated
1 c. light cream
1 tblsp. melted fat or oil
¼ c. chopped nuts
Ice cream
Chocolate sauce

• Sift flour; measure; sift again with sugar, salt and baking powder.
• Combine cream, egg yolks and fat, and beat well. Add nuts and dry ingredients; mix thoroughly.
• Beat egg whites until stiff; fold into batter.
• Pour batter onto hot grids of waffle iron. Makes 2 waffles or 8 sections. Serve at once topped with scoop of vanilla or your favorite ice cream. Top with fudge sauce from your grocer's shelf. If time permits, try this simple Chocolate Sauce.

Chocolate Sauce:

• Combine in top of double boiler: 1 (6 oz.) pkg. semi-sweet chocolate pieces, ½ c. light corn syrup, ¼ c. milk, 1 tblsp. butter or margarine, and ¼ tsp. vanilla.
• Place over hot water to heat; mix until smooth. Makes 1½ cups.

PEANUT-CHOCOLATE SAUCE

1 (4 oz.) pkg. chocolate pudding mix
¾ c. water
¾ c. corn syrup
¼ tsp. salt
1 tblsp. butter or margarine
⅓ c. peanut butter
½ tsp. vanilla

• Empty package contents into saucepan. Gradually add water, mixing until smooth. Add corn syrup and salt; mix well.
• Cook over medium heat, stirring constantly until mixture comes to a boil.
• Remove from heat and add butter, peanut butter and vanilla; stir until melted. Serve warm or cold over ice cream. Makes 1¾ cups.

Quick Breads, Sandwiches

SPANISH CORN BREAD

Mighty good and mighty filling—good with baked beans, chicken or pork

1 (12 oz.) pkg. corn muffin mix
1 (12 oz.) can whole kernel corn with sweet peppers
½ tsp. dry mustard
1 small onion, finely chopped
1 egg, beaten
⅔ c. milk

• Combine muffin mix, corn, mustard and onion. Add egg and milk; blend according to package directions.

• Spread in greased 8×8×2" square baking pan; bake in hot oven (400°) about 20 minutes or until corn bread tests done. Serve warm. Makes 9 to 10 servings.

SPICED RAISIN MUFFINS

Just pass these piping hot muffins and hear the compliments

2 c. prepared biscuit mix
¼ c. sugar
½ tsp. ground cinnamon
1 c. finely cut raisins
1 egg, slightly beaten
¾ c. milk

• Combine biscuit mix, sugar, cinnamon and raisins (if you cut them with scissors in mixing bowl, raisins distribute better).

• Blend together egg and milk; add to dry ingredients. Stir until batter is just moistened. Bake in hot oven (425°) about 15 minutes. Makes 12 muffins.

EASY PIZZA

Here's a new sandwich—something easy to fix for club refreshments

1 (10 oz.) pkg. brown-and-serve French bread (2 loaves)
¼ c. salad or olive oil
3 to 4 fresh tomatoes, sliced
Grated Parmesan cheese
½ (8 oz.) pkg. sliced Muenster, mild or sharp Cheddar cheese
1 (2 oz.) can anchovy fillets
½ tsp. dried oregano
½ tsp. dried basil
½ tsp. dried marjoram or thyme leaves

• Cut loaves in halves, lengthwise. Brush cut surfaces with part of oil. Cover with tomatoes.

• Sprinkle with grated cheese; top with cheese slices. Lay anchovy fillets on top.

• Combine herbs and sprinkle over each pizza. Drizzle with remaining oil. Bake on baking sheet in hot oven (400°) 15 to 20 minutes. Makes 6 to 8 servings.

Variation: Make little pizzas using refrigerated biscuits with pizza topping.

HOT BUTTERED BREAD

So good they'll think you made it

1 (1 lb.) loaf white bread
¼ c. butter or margarine

• Spread bread slices on one side with softened butter; put back in shape of loaf. Cut lengthwise halves and tie with string.

• Wrap loaf in foil and heat in moderate oven (375°) 20 to 25 minutes. Makes 10 to 12 servings.

CHILI-TOPPED CHEESE TOAST

Takes only 10 minutes to make this South-of-the-Border favorite

1 (1 lb.) can chili con carne with beans
8 slices bread
1 (8 oz.) pkg. sliced pimiento cheese

• Heat chili con carne slowly in saucepan.

• Toast bread on one side under broiler. Turn; cover untoasted sides with cheese slices. Broil until cheese melts.

• Cut toast in diagonal halves or quarters. Arrange on individual plates. Spoon hot chili over toast. Garnish with olive slices; serve at once. Makes 6 to 8 servings.

CRISP ONION WAFFLES

It's easy to bake them at the table—serve in quarters as a hot bread

2 c. pancake mix
2 eggs, well beaten
1⅔ to 2 c. milk
¼ to ⅓ c. melted shortening or oil
2 tblsp. dehydrated onion soup mix

• Make waffle batter according to directions on pancake mix package. Stir in onion soup mix. Bake as usual. (If waffles are not crisp enough, add about ¼ c. more milk to batter.)

• Cut large waffles in quarters. Makes about 12 quarters or 8 to 10 servings.

• These waffles make a fine base for creamed fish, chicken or dried beef.

Main Dishes with Little Effort

EASY-SERVE BAKED HAM

Just cut the string and presto—the big ham just falls apart in even slices!

1 (6 lb.) canned ham
1 (1 lb.) jar apricot preserves (about 1½ c.)
Whole cloves

• Slice ham and tie together with string. Your meat dealer may slice the ham on his slicer and tie it up for you.

• Place ham, fat side up, on rack in shallow baking pan. Spread apricot preserves over top. Stud with cloves.

• Heat in slow oven (325°) 15 minutes per pound. Baste with pan juices 3 or 4 times while baking.

• Place on platter to serve. Cut and remove string. Makes 15 to 20 servings.

VEGETABLE MEDLEY

Three vegetables in one generous dish—perfect with fried chicken

2 (10 oz.) pkgs. frozen peas
3 medium carrots, sliced and cooked
3 c. sliced celery, cooked
Seasonings
Butter or margarine

• Cook peas as directed on package. Simmer carrots and celery in just enough water to cover, until tender. Don't overcook; celery should be a bit crisp.

• Combine vegetables. Season with salt and pepper. Serve with melted butter. Makes 10 to 12 servings.

Good Vegetable Combination: Try buttered peas in fluffy, mashed winter squash cups.

QUICK BARBECUED FRANKS

Hard to resist when steaming hot

1 lb. frankfurters
½ c. ketchup
2 tblsp. prepared mustard
½ tsp. cloves
2 tblsp. oil
1 (3½ oz.) can French fried onions

• Drop frankfurters into kettle of boiling water; cover, heat 5 to 8 minutes; drain.
• Add ketchup, prepared mustard, cloves and oil to frankfurters. Simmer about 5 minutes.
• Heat onions as directed on can.
• Remove frankfurters to platter. Garnish with onions. Makes 6 servings.

BEEF STEW-IN-FOIL

The oven makes the meal; the foil cuts cuts down on dish washing

1½ lbs. boneless chuck, cut in pieces
4 large potatoes, peeled and quartered
6 large or 12 small onions, peeled
6 large carrots, cut in half
1 (8 oz.) can tomato sauce
Seasoned salt
Sweet marjoram

• For six servings, make double folds of regular (12-inch) foil or separate pieces of heavy-duty foil, each about 20″ long.
• Center equal portions of meat and vegetables on each foil wrap.
• Pour tomato sauce over each. Sprinkle with seasoned salt and pinch of marjoram. (Oregano may be substituted for marjoram.)
• Bring sides of foil together over food. Make several folds, pressing together firmly. Fold ends and press tightly.
• Store in refrigerator until an hour and a quarter before mealtime.
• Place packages on baking sheet or in shallow pan. Bake in moderate oven (350°) 1 to 1¼ hours.
• To serve, cut crisscross slits with scissors in top of foil. Fold back corners; fold down to make collar or rim around edge to hold in juices. Transfer, in foil, to individual serving plates. (Guard against steam burns!) Makes 6 servings.

QUICK BROILER MEAL

It takes only 20 minutes to fix—add a green salad or coleslaw

1 (1 lb. 4 oz.) can sweet potatoes, drained
2 (12 oz.) cans chopped ham
1 (1 lb. 3 oz.) can sliced pineapple, drained
French dressing or bacon fat
2 tblsp. brown sugar

• Split sweet potatoes lengthwise and place in broiler pan. Brush generously with syrup from pineapple.
• Arrange serving-size pieces of meat and pineapple slices on broiler rack. Brush both with French dressing or bacon fat. Sprinkle brown sugar over pineapple.
• Put broiler rack in pan and slide into broiler about 3″ below heat. Broil 10 to 15 minutes or until thoroughly heated. Serve at once. Makes 6 servings.

SHRIMP BISQUE

Serve with assorted crackers

1 (10½ oz.) can condensed cream of celery soup
1½ c. milk
1 (5 oz.) can shrimp
¼ c. chopped green pepper
3 drops Tabasco sauce

• Dilute soup with milk in saucepan.
• Chop shrimp, reserving some whole for garnish.
• Add shrimp, green pepper, and Tabasco sauce to soup.
• Heat and pour into soup bowls. Makes 6 servings.

Creamy Ham Soup: Add 1 (2¼ oz.) can deviled ham to 1 (10½ oz.) can condensed cream of mushroom soup. Then prepare by label directions. Or, add bits of cooked ham to canned cream of chicken soup.

SAVORY BEEF CAKES

Something different made with ground beef—quick and extra-good

1 (10½ oz.) can Scotch broth soup
1 egg, beaten
½ c. quick-cooking rolled oats
½ tsp. salt
1¼ lbs. ground beef
2 tblsp. melted fat or oil
1 medium onion
½ tsp. beef extract or ½ beef bouillon cube
½ c. water

• Empty soup into bowl. Add egg, oats and salt. Beat thoroughly to mix.
• Add beef; mix well. Dampen hands and form into 12 cakes.
• Heat fat in large skillet over moderate heat. Add meat cakes. Chop onion or cut into crosswise slices. Toss over meat. Brown beef, cooking 7 to 8 minutes on each side.
• Remove to hot platter. Add beef extract and water to pan drippings. Heat to boiling. Pour over beef. Makes 12 patties.

CORNED BEEF CASSEROLE

Your family will ask you to repeat this dish

4 oz. (half of 8 oz. pkg.) spaghetti, cooked
1 (10½ oz.) can condensed cream of mushroom soup
1 c. milk
½ tsp. prepared mustard
½ c. (4 oz.) shredded sharp process cheese
1 (12 oz.) can corned beef, chopped
1 (4 oz.) can sliced mushrooms
2 slices bread
1 tblsp. soft butter or margarine

• Break spaghetti in 2" lengths. Cook in boiling water without salt for 10 minutes.
• Blend together soup and milk until smooth. Add mustard, half the cheese, corned beef, drained mushrooms and cooked spaghetti.
• Pour into greased 1½ qt. casserole.
• Spread bread with butter. Put together sandwich style; cut into cubes and sprinkle over top with remaining cheese. Bake in moderate oven (350°) 25 minutes. Makes 4 servings.

FAST-FIX BRUNSWICK STEW

Shortcut to a great Southern main dish folks across country will enjoy

1 medium onion, chopped
1 green pepper, chopped
1 c. chopped celery
¼ c. butter or margarine
1 (1 lb.) can mixed vegetables
1 (8 oz.) can cut okra
1 (1 lb.) can cream style corn
1 (6 oz.) can tomato paste
1 tblsp. Worcestershire sauce
¼ tsp. Tabasco sauce
1½ tsp. salt
½ tsp. black pepper
1 (12 oz.) can roast beef
1 c. fine bread crumbs (optional)

• Sauté onion, green pepper and celery in butter over low heat until just tender.
• Mix in remaining ingredients except meat and crumbs. Add meat; cover and cook over low heat 30 minutes. If stew is not thick enough, stir in crumbs just before serving. Makes 6 to 8 servings.

BEANS WITH DEVILED HAM

These beans have a subtle spicy taste—extra fine with mustard pickles

2 (1 lb.) cans New England style pork and beans
2 (4½ oz.) cans deviled ham
⅛ tsp. ground cloves

• Place beans in saucepan over moderate heat. Blend ham and cloves thoroughly through beans. Heat about 10 minutes, stirring occasionally. Makes 6 to 8 servings.

BAKED PORK CHOPS

Million-dollar flavor in a fast-fix dish

6 rib or loin pork chops, 1" thick
1 tblsp. flour
1 (1½ oz.) pkg. dehydrated onion soup mix
2½ c. boiling water
1 c. dairy sour cream
Celery leaves or parsley

• Brown chops lightly in hot skillet. Remove to baking pan.
• Pour fat from skillet, leaving about 1 tblsp. in pan. Add flour and dehydrated onion soup mix. Blend in water. Pour over chops.
• Cover with foil; bake in moderate oven (350°) 30 minutes.
• Uncover; bake 30 or 40 minutes longer, or until tender.
• Remove from oven. Place chops on serving plate. Garnish with celery leaves.

To Make Gravy: Blend sour cream into liquid in pan and heat. Makes 6 servings.

SALMON-MACARONI BAKE

You'll be proud to serve this hearty main dish that's a real snap to make

2 (15 or 16 oz.) cans macaroni and cheese
2 tsp. prepared mustard
3 tblsp. grated Parmesan cheese (optional)
4 hard-cooked eggs
1 (1 lb.) can sockeye or pink salmon

• Grease 1½ qt. casserole. Empty 1 can macaroni and cheese into bottom. With a fork, break apart into layer.
• Dot layer with mustard and half Parmesan cheese. Add layer of 2 eggs, sliced or diced.
• Drain salmon and break into big chunks. Remove skin and bones. Place pieces in a strip across casserole and fill in on both sides with second can macaroni and cheese. (Or, if you like salmon mixed in, add a layer and cover with macaroni.)
• Sprinkle top with cheese. Cover; bake in moderate oven (350°) 30 minutes.
• Garnish top with 2 remaining eggs, cut in quarters. Makes 6 servings.

FISH PIQUANT

Try this for Friday's supper—it's a winner

2 lbs. frozen fish fillets (haddock, flounder or perch)
½ c. French dressing
2 tblsp. butter or margarine
1 small onion, chopped
1 lemon
Tartar sauce

• Thaw fish as directed on package.
• Dip pieces in French dressing.
• Heat butter in skillet. Add fish; sprinkle onion over top.
• Cook over moderate heat 7 or 8 minutes on each side, turning once.
• Serve with lemon wedges and tartar sauce. Makes 6 servings.

QUICK TARTAR SAUCE

Tops in easy preparation, good eating

1 c. mayonnaise
2 tblsp. pickle relish
1 tblsp. chopped onion
1 tblsp. minced parsley
1 tblsp. chopped pimiento

• Combine ingredients in order listed. Chill. Makes 1¼ cups.

HURRY-UP CHEESE SANDWICHES

• Make thin cheese sandwiches but do not let cheese come out to edges. Bake in hot waffle iron until golden brown, about 2 minutes. Serve hot off the grids with steaming vegetable soup, mixed fruit salad, cookies and milk or tea—you have a wonderful supper.

HASTY RAREBIT

Famous cheese dish in a new dress

2 (10½ oz.) cans condensed cream of celery soup
2 (6 oz.) links smoke-flavor cheese
8 slices toast

• Blend together soup and cheese over hot water. Serve immediately on toast. Garnish with parsley and stuffed olives. Makes 8 servings.

CHICKEN-TUNA PIE

Surprise—chicken and tuna baked between two flaky pastry crusts

1 (10 oz.) pkg. pie crust mix
¼ tsp. poultry seasoning
2 tblsp. yellow cornmeal
1 (10½ oz.) can condensed cream of chicken soup
2 tblsp. water
1 or 2 chicken bouillon cubes
1 (13 oz.) jar or can boned chicken, cut in large pieces (about 2 c.)
1 (7 oz.) can tuna, flaked

• Make pie crust by package directions for 2-crust pie; add seasoning and cornmeal, then liquid. Fit half pastry into 9" pie pan.
• Heat soup; blend in water and bouillon cubes. Add chicken and tuna; pour into pastry-lined pan. Cover with top crust, making slits in center.
• Roll out leftover pastry; cut into chicken shapes; place on top.
• Bake in hot oven (425°) until filling bubbles and crust is delicately brown, 30 to 40 minutes. Makes 6 servings.

Individual Pies: Double recipes of pastry and filling; use 5" tart pans. Fill with chicken-tuna mixture; roll pastry and cut into 6" circles; cover filling and flute edges. Bake in hot oven (425°) about 25 minutes. (Bake pastry chickens separately.) Makes 8 pies.

CHICKEN SOUFFLE

Almost too easy to believe—it's tall, light and tasty

1 (10½ oz.) can condensed cream of chicken soup
4 eggs, separated

• Blend together soup and well-beaten egg yolks. Beat whites until stiff but not dry; gently fold into soup mixture. Pour into greased 1½ qt. casserole.
• Bake in slow oven (300°) 1 hour. Serve at once with Jiffy Mushroom Sauce. Makes 4 servings.

Jiffy Mushroom Sauce: Blend 1 (10½ oz.) can condensed cream of mushroom soup and ½ c. milk. Heat thoroughly.

Variations: Use cream of celery or asparagus soup instead of chicken soup. Or use cream of mushroom soup for soufflé and cream of asparagus for sauce.

FESTIVE FRANKS

⅓ c. finely chopped onions
⅓ c. finely chopped celery
½ clove garlic, minced
3 tblsp. shortening
1 (10½ oz.) can condensed tomato soup
2 tblsp. brown sugar
2 tblsp. Worcestershire sauce
2 tblsp. lemon juice or vinegar
2 tsp. prepared mustard
4 drops Tabasco sauce (optional)
1 lb. frankfurters

• Brown onion, celery and garlic in shortening in heavy skillet. Stir in remaining sauce ingredients; simmer 3 to 5 minutes. Add frankfurters. Cover and simmer 20 minutes. Makes 4 to 5 servings.

Slick Tricks with Vegetables

BAKED GREEN BEANS

Crisp onion topping adds pleasing flavor and texture contrast

2 (10 oz.) pkgs. frozen green beans, French style
1 (10½ oz.) can condensed cream of mushroom soup
1 (3½ oz.) can French fried onions

• Partially cook green beans as directed on package. Mix with soup and pour into 1½ qt. baking dish. Top with onions.
• Bake in moderate oven (375°) 15 to 20 minutes or until beans are tender. Makes 6 servings.

TOMATO-BEAN CHOWDER

Hearty and just right on frosty days

1 (1 lb.) can pork and beans
1 (10½ oz.) can condensed tomato soup
1½ c. water
½ c. onion slices
½ c. chopped green celery
1 tsp. Worcestershire sauce
⅛ tsp. pepper
1 c. (¼ lb.) salami, cut in strips

• Combine ingredients and simmer 15 to 20 minutes. Makes 6 servings.

CREOLE BEANS

Homespun, but fine in flavor

8 slices bacon
2 (1 lb.) cans Blue Lake green beans
1 tblsp. dried onion soup mix
1 (1 lb.) can stewed tomatoes
1 tsp. sugar

• Sauté bacon until crisp; drain on paper toweling. Pour off all but 3 tblsp. drippings.
• Empty beans carefully into skillet; add onion soup mix; heat thoroughly.
• Snip bacon into small pieces; add half to beans, also add stewed tomatoes and sugar. Top with remaining bacon. Makes 8 servings.

POTATOES CHANTILLY

Puffed up and brown—fit for a king

1 (7 oz.) box instant mashed potatoes (2 envelopes)
1 c. heavy cream
½ c. grated sharp cheese
Salt and pepper to taste

• Prepare dehydrated potatoes as directed on package; place in greased shallow baking dish.
• Whip cream; fold in cheese. Season with salt, pepper. Spread over potatoes.
• Bake in moderate oven (350°) until golden, about 20 minutes. Serve immediately. Makes 8 servings.

BEEF SAUCE FOR VEGETABLES

3 tblsp. butter or margarine
2 tblsp. flour
1 (10½ oz.) can condensed beef broth
½ c. water
½ c. nonfat dry milk

• Melt butter; blend in flour.
• Add broth, water and dry milk. Bring to boil over low heat, stirring constantly. Cook 2 to 3 minutes. Makes about 2 cups.

21

Master Recipes with Variations

Most good cooks know the satisfaction of making more than one dish from a recipe. It's like making several different, good-looking dresses from one basic pattern. You feel you're putting on a sleight-of-hand performance in your kitchen—you start with a recipe, say cookies, make a few changes in the standard ingredients or method and turn out several exciting kinds. You're like the magician, who flourishes a red silk handkerchief, drops it into his tall, black hat and, after some hocus-pocus, pulls out a blue one, a yellow and a pink as well. Several-from-one recipes are an old trick of clever cooks and an easy way to introduce variety in meals.

Some of the most popular food stories in FARM JOURNAL have featured Master Recipes. No collection of our readers' favorites can overlook these. There are 20 in this chapter and they will make a minimum of 141 variations of the dishes. About the best description for a Master Recipe comes from one of our readers who called her basic cake "Quick Change" (see her recipe follows in this chapter).

Several of our first Master Recipes are for make-it-yourself mixes, farm women's forerunners of the handy packages now sold by the millions. Besides the Master Recipes grouped in this chapter, you will find a number of variations following many other recipes throughout this cookbook. That's because more-than-one-dish-from-a-recipe is a firmly established tradition with good farm cooks and with our Food Department.

Quick Coffee Cakes

About the best call to breakfast on Sunday morning, or any other day, is the spicy aroma of coffee cake drifting through the house. You can stir up this quick one in less time that it takes the hungry family to gather around the table. The secret is to keep the shortening and dry ingredients, mixed, in the refrigerator. You change the toppings to get variety. (The Pineapple-Apricot and Apple-Cheese take more time to fix; you may wish to serve them with the mid-morning coffee.)

COFFEE CAKE MIX

(*Master Recipe*)

8 c. sifted flour
4 tblsp. baking powder
1 tblsp. salt
2 tsp. cream of tartar
2 c. shortening, or 1⅔ c. lard

• Sift together flour, baking powder, salt and cream of tartar into large bowl.
• Cut in shortening with pastry blender, or use electric mixer at low speed 1 to 2 minutes. Overmixing will cream flour and shortening; mixture should be dry and crumbly, like coarse cornmeal.
• Store in tightly-covered container at room temperature; or in refrigerator, if lard is used. Will keep 4 to 6 weeks. Makes about 12 cups (enough for 6 coffee cakes—each cake uses 2 c. of the mix).

PLAIN COFFEE CAKE

2 c. mix
2 eggs
⅔ c. sugar
¾ c. milk

• Measure mix into bowl (pile lightly into measuring cup; level with spatula).
• Beat eggs until fluffy; gradually add sugar. Combine egg mixture with mix; beat 2 minutes until light and fluffy. Add milk, ¼ c. at a time, beating well after each addition.
• Spread batter in buttered 8×8×2" baking dish. Put on topping. Bake in moderate oven (350°) 35 minutes or until toothpick inserted in center comes out clean. Makes 6 to 8 servings.

BAKE-ON COFFEE CAKE TOPPINGS

Peach-Cinnamon:

¾ tsp. lemon extract
¾ tsp. almond extract
1 c. canned, cling peach slices, drained
½ c. sugar
½ tsp. cinnamon

• Add extracts to coffee cake batter. Arrange peaches over batter in pan and bake.
• Mix sugar with cinnamon. Sprinkle over warm coffee cake just before serving.

Brown Sugar-Cinnamon:

¼ c. butter or margarine
1 c. brown sugar
¼ tsp. salt
3 tblsp. flour
1½ c. chopped nuts
½ tsp. cinnamon
½ tsp. nutmeg

• Blend with fork butter, sugar, salt, flour and nuts.
• Add cinnamon and nutmeg to mix be-

fore adding liquids. Sprinkle topping over batter in pan and bake.

Honey-Pecan Variation: Use ½ c. brown sugar instead of 1 c. in recipe above and omit nuts. Sprinkle topping over batter, as above, then arrange 1 c. pecan halves over that. Pour 1 c. honey over all. Bake.

Cranberry-Orange:

2 c. cranberries, drained
1 c. sugar
2 tblsp. grated orange rind
¾ tsp. orange extract

• Butter 8×8×2" baking dish; cover bottom with cranberries. Sprinkle with sugar and orange rind.
• Add orange extract to batter.
• Spread batter over cranberries and bake. Cool 15 minutes. Turn out on platter.

Apple-Cheese:

¼ c. red cinnamon candies
1 c. water
¼ c. sugar
¾ c. brown sugar
1 large apple, peeled and cored
½ c. grated, sharp cheese
¾ c. sifted flour
½ c. quick-cooking rolled oats
¼ c. butter or margarine

• Combine in saucepan cinnamon candies, water, sugar and ¼ c. brown sugar.
• Cut apple into rings; cook in syrup until clear and shiny; drain.
• Add cheese tossed with ½ c. flour to mix for coffee cake.
• Mix rolled oats, ¼ c. flour, ½ c. brown sugar and butter; sprinkle over batter in pan. Top with candied apple rings and bake.

Toasted Coconut:

1 c. flaked or shredded coconut
½ c. sugar
1 tsp. cinnamon
¼ c. light cream
½ tsp. nutmeg

• Toss together coconut, sugar, ½ tsp. cinnamon and cream.
• Add ½ tsp. cinnamon and nutmeg to mix for coffee cake. Sprinkle topping over batter in pan and bake.

Pineapple-Apricot:

3 tblsp. butter or margarine
½ c. brown sugar
4 pineapple slices, drained
6 apricot halves, drained

• Melt butter in 8" round pan; sprinkle with sugar. Arrange pineapple and apricots on top of sugar. Spread batter over pineapple mixture and bake. Cool 15 minutes. Turn out on plate.

COFFEE CAKE RING

(Cinnamon Leaf Ring)

2 c. milk, scalded
2 pkgs. granular yeast
¾ c. shortening
¼ c. butter or margarine
½ c. sugar
2 tsp. salt
4 egg yolks or 2 eggs, beaten
6 c. sifted flour (about)

• Cool milk to warm (110°); sprinkle yeast over top. Let stand to soften.
• Cream shortening and butter; add sugar and salt. Cream together until light and fluffy. Add egg yolks, yeast-milk and enough flour to make soft dough. Knead until smooth and elastic on lightly floured cloth or board. Place in greased bowl; cover and let rise until doubled (about 1 hour).
• Roll dough thin (about ¼") and cut into rounds with 2" biscuit cutter. Dip each in melted butter or margarine (about 1 cup), then in cinnamon-sugar mixture (2 tblsp. cinnamon to 2 c. sugar). Stand up in two well buttered ring molds 8½" round and 2¼" deep, until rings are filled. Let rise until light (about ½ hour). Bake in moderate oven (350°) about 25 minutes. Cool slightly before turning out. Makes 20 to 25 servings. (Make rolls from any leftover dough. Variations follow.)

COFFEE RING VARIATIONS:

Kolaches: Make ½ recipe basic dough. Shape into small balls (about 1½") and place on greased baking sheets; let rise. Brush with melted butter or margarine. Make deep hole in center of each with thumb; then press out with forefinger to make hole larger. Fill them with a fruit filling (recipe follows). Bake in moderate oven (375°) about 15 minutes. Makes 4 dozen buns. To give a special occasion touch to the Kolaches, sprinkle a fine dusting of confectioners sugar over tops before serving.

Fruit Fillings: Cook together slowly, stirring until thickened: 2 c. dried apricots, cut fine (or 2 c. mashed cooked prunes), ¾ c. sugar, ¾ c. water and 1 tblsp. lemon juice. Cool.

Orange Twists: Make ½ recipe basic dough, adding 1½ tsp. grated orange rind to dough. Roll into rectangles 10×18". Spread with well-blended mixture of grated rind of 1 orange, ¾ c. sugar and ⅓ c. soft butter or margarine. Roll up lengthwise; cut into 1½" slices; with back of shears, indent center of each slice. Place on greased baking sheet and let rise. Bake in hot oven (400°) 15 to 20 minutes. Makes about 4 doz. rolls. While still warm, brush with following glaze: Bring to boil ½ c. sugar, ¼ c. white corn syrup and ¼ c. hot water; simmer 1 minute, stirring once or twice. Set aside to cool until rolls are removed from oven.

Cinnamon-Raisin and Currant Buns: Make ½ recipe basic dough. Roll into rectangles 9×18". Spread with mixture of 2 tsp. cinnamon and ½ c. sifted brown sugar; sprinkle with ½ c. seedless raisins or dried currants and drizzle with 2 tblsp. dark corn syrup. Roll up and cut into 1" slices. Place in very well greased muffin pans, each containing 1 tblsp. corn syrup; let rise. Bake in moderate oven (350°) 20 to 25 minutes. Makes about 4 dozen rolls.

Muffin Magic

Fluffy, tender muffins add a company touch to meals. And they are marvelous extenders when the remainder of the dinner is on the scanty side. You can use our Master Recipe to make these 17 different kinds from farm homes.

BASIC MUFFIN RECIPE

2 c. sifted flour
1 tblsp. baking powder
½ tsp. salt
3 tblsp. sugar
1 egg, beaten
1 c. milk
3 tblsp. oil or melted shortening

• Sift together flour, baking powder, salt and sugar.
• Combine in bowl egg, milk and oil; pour into dry ingredients all at once. Stir until dry ingredients are moist but still lumpy, about 17 to 25 strokes.
• Spoon batter into greased muffin pans, filling pans only ⅔ full. Bake in hot oven (425°) 20 to 28 minutes, depending on size of muffins. Makes about 18 medium-size muffins.

MUFFIN VARIATIONS:

Apple-Nutmeg: Peel and dice 1 medium-size apple. Sprinkle with 1 tsp. nutmeg and 2 tblsp. sugar. Stir into batter after liquid and dry ingredients have been partially mixed together.

Apricot-Nut: Thoroughly drain ½ c. cooked, finely chopped apricots. Combine with ½ c. chopped walnuts. Stir into batter after liquid and dry ingredients have been partially mixed.

Bacon-Mushroom: Fry 4 slices bacon with ½ c. chopped mushrooms until bacon is crisp and mushrooms browned. Thoroughly drain on paper toweling to remove extra fat. Crumble bacon into bits. Stir with mushrooms into liquid ingredients.

Celery Salt-Parsley: Combine ½ tsp. celery salt and 2 tblsp. finely chopped parsley. Stir into dry ingredients.

Cheese-Garlic: Combine 1 c. grated process cheese with ⅛ tsp. garlic salt. Stir into dry ingredients. Bake 20 to 25 minutes.

Cheese-Paprika: Stir 1 c. grated process cheese and ½ tsp. paprika into dry ingredients. Bake about 20 to 25 minutes.

Cherry: Thoroughly drain ¾ c. canned or freshly cooked red sour cherries. Add ¼ c. sugar and ⅛ tsp. cinnamon. (Do not let stand—more juice will form.) Gently fold into batter after mixing liquid and dry ingredients.

Cranberry-Orange: Combine ¾ c. chopped raw cranberries, 2 tblsp. grated orange rind and ¼ c. sugar. (Do not let stand—juice forms.) Gently fold into batter after liquid and dry ingredients have been combined.

Damson Preserves: Fill pans ½ full of batter. Put 1 tsp. preserves in each; top with batter so pans are ⅔ full. Strawberry jam is equally good.

Date-Nut: Combine ½ c. chopped walnuts, ½ c. chopped dates and 1 tblsp. lemon rind. Stir into batter after liquid and dry ingredients have been partially mixed.

Grapenut: Stir ½ c. grapenuts cereal into batter after liquid and dry ingredients have been partially mixed.

Ground Beef: Combine in a small frying pan: ½ lb. (1 c.) ground beef, ½ tsp. salt and ⅛ tsp. pepper. Fry slowly, stirring frequently, until meat is browned. Thoroughly drain meat on paper toweling to remove excess fat. Add 3 tblsp. ketchup to meat. Stir into liquid ingredients; mix with dry ones.

Lemon-Sugar: Combine ½ c. sugar with 2 tblsp. grated lemon rind. (Or use ½ c. chopped nuts with 2 tblsp. brown sugar.) Put enough batter in pans to fill ¼ full. Sprinkle with sugar mixture, then top with another layer of batter; fill the pans only ½ to ⅔ full (otherwise sugar will melt out and make muffins stick).

Mint Jelly: Fill pans ¼ full of batter. Place 1 tsp. mint jelly in each and top with a layer of batter. Pans should be ½ to ⅔ full. If more, jelly will boil out and stick.

Orange: In the basic muffin recipe, use only ¾ c. milk, and combine with ¼ c. orange juice. Grate 1 tblsp. orange rind, and stir into liquid ingredients.

Pineapple: Thoroughly drain 1 c. crushed pineapple. Stir into batter after liquid and dry ingredients have been partially mixed. Or substitute 1 c. well-drained, sweetened, stewed rhubarb for the pineapple and add 1 tblsp. grated orange rind.

Prune: Thoroughly drain enough chopped, cooked prunes to make 1 c. pulp. Stir into batter after liquid and dry ingredients have been partially mixed.

CRISPY WAFFLES

(Master Recipe)

2 c. sifted cake flour
1 tblsp. baking powder
1 tsp. salt
2 tblsp. sugar
3 eggs, separated
1½ c. milk
½ c. oil

• Sift dry ingredients together.
• Beat egg yolks. Mix in milk and oil. Add to dry ingredients; stir.
• Beat egg whites stiff; fold into batter.
• Bake in hot waffle iron to desired crispness. Makes 3 waffles.

WAFFLE VARIATIONS:

Fig Waffles:
Add ½ c. ground or chopped figs before folding in the egg whites. Serve with ice cream and lemon sauce.

Blueberry Waffles:
Use 1 c. of milk in regular waffle recipe. Add 1 c. drained, sweetened blueberries before folding in egg whites.

Orange Waffles:
Substitute ½ c. orange juice for ½ c. of milk in regular batter. Add 2 tsp. grated orange rind.

FLUFFY ORANGE SAUCE FOR ORANGE WAFFLES

½ c. orange juice
2 tblsp. grated rind
1 c. sugar
1 egg
1 c. heavy cream

• Cook all but cream over low heat, stirring constantly until thickened.
• Whip cream until stiff; fold into cooled orange mixture.

GRIDDLE CAKES

(Master Recipe)

2 c. sifted flour
5 tsp. baking powder
2 tsp. salt
3 tblsp. sugar
2 eggs, beaten
2 c. milk
6 tblsp. melted shortening or oil

• Sift together flour, baking powder, salt and sugar.
• Beat eggs in mixing bowl. Add milk, shortening and flour mixture. Stir until blended.
• Heat griddle or heavy frying pan slowly until moderately hot. Test temperature by sprinkling few drops of water on it. When drops stay round and bounce about, temperature is right. Or use an electric skillet or griddle set at temperature given in book of instructions.
• Grease very lightly before baking each batch. Ladle or pour about ¼ c. batter for each cake onto hot griddle. Bake until top side is full of bubbles that begin to break and edges are dry; turn; brown on other side.
• Makes 2½ dozen cakes 4″ to 5″ in diameter, or 1 dozen 6″ to 7″ in diameter.

Note: To make sour milk griddle cakes, substitute 2¼ c. sour milk or buttermilk for sweet milk. For leavening use 1 tsp. baking soda and 1 tblsp. baking powder.

GRIDDLE CAKE VARIATIONS:

Apple: Add 1 c. finely chopped unpeeled raw apples and 1 tsp. cinnamon.

Blueberry: Add 1 c. frozen sweetened blueberries, thawed and drained.

Banana: Add 2 mashed ripe bananas.

Date: Add 1 c. chopped dates.

Pineapple: Add 1 c. well-drained crushed pineapple.

Mincemeat: Add ½ to ¾ c. mincemeat.

Pecan: Add ½ c. chopped pecans.

Corn: Add 1 c. canned cream style corn.

Rice: Add 1 to 2 c. leftover rice (½ tsp. cinnamon or nutmeg peps up the flavor) and a little milk if batter needs thinning.

Cheese: Add ½ c. grated Parmesan cheese.

Deviled Ham: Add 1 (4½ oz.) can deviled ham.

Tuna: Add 1 (6½ or 7 oz.) can tuna, flaked.

FRITTER BATTER

(*Master Recipe*)

2 c. sifted flour
1 tblsp. baking powder
1½ tsp. salt
2 tblsp. sugar
4 egg yolks
⅔ c. milk
2 tblsp. melted butter or margarine
4 egg whites, stiffly beaten
1 to 2 c. chopped meat, fruit or vegetable

• Sift together flour, baking powder, salt and sugar.
• Beat egg yolks well, add milk. Stir into dry ingredients. Blend in butter. Carefully fold in egg whites and meat.
• Drop from tablespoon into deep hot fat (365° to 375°). Fry 4 to 5 minutes, or until crisp and brown. Makes 18 medium-size fritters.
• (For a sweeter dessert fritter, increase sugar in basic recipe from 1 to 3 tablespoons.)

FRITTER VARIATIONS:

Vegetable: Use 1 to 2 c. cooked or canned vegetables, drained. Take your choice of: corn, green beans, baby lima beans, diced carrots or peas.
• Fold vegetables and beaten egg whites in at the same time; season with ¼ tsp. paprika and 2 tblsp. chopped parsley.

Meat: Use 1 to 2 c. cooked or canned. Any of these makes good fritter flavor: chopped shrimp, cut-up frankfurters, crumbled sausage or chopped ham.

Vegetable-Meat Combinations: Use 1 to 2 c. cooked or canned. Try corn and chopped ham; peas and chopped shrimp; minced celery leaves and crumbled sausage; chopped asparagus and ham; or lima beans and diced frankfurters.

Orange Fritters: Use 2 c. diced oranges. Fold ½ c. sifted cake flour into beaten egg whites, then add oranges and 1 tblsp. grated orange rind. Fold into fritter batter.

ONION SAUCE

Serve with meat and vegetable fritters

3 onions, sliced
2 tblsp. butter or margarine
3 tblsp. flour
2 c. meat or vegetable broth

• Lightly brown onions in butter; cover tightly and simmer 5 minutes. Stir in flour. Slowly add meat broth. (If you have no broth on hand, dissolve 2 bouillon cubes in 2 c. boiling water.)
• Cook, stirring constantly, until thickened. If deeper brown is desired, add 1 tsp. bottled gravy flavor and color. Serve warm over hot fritters. Makes about 2 cups.

SPICY VANILLA SAUCE

Extra-good with apple fritters

1 c. sugar
2 tblsp. flour
¼ tsp. nutmeg
⅛ tsp. allspice
1 c. cold water
2 tblsp. butter or margarine
1 tsp. vanilla

• Mix together in saucepan sugar, flour, nutmeg and allspice. Stir in water; simmer until clear and thickened.
• Blend in butter and vanilla. Serve warm over hot apple fritters. Makes about 1⅓ cups.

ORANGE SAUCE

First choice for pineapple, banana and orange fritters

3 tblsp. sugar
1 tblsp. cornstarch
⅛ tsp. salt
1 c. orange juice
Grated rind of 1 orange

• Combine in pan sugar, cornstarch and salt. Gradually stir in orange juice and rind.
• Cook, stirring constantly, over low heat until thick and clear. Serve over hot fritters. Makes about 1¼ cups.

FEATHERY-LIGHT DUMPLINGS

(*Master Recipe*)

1 c. sifted flour
1½ tsp. baking powder
½ tsp. salt
2 tblsp. shortening
⅓ c. milk
1 egg, beaten

• Sift together in bowl: flour, baking powder and salt. Cut in shortening with pastry blender until mixture is crumbly.
• Pour in milk; add egg. Mix only until flour is dampened (dough should be lumpy). Drop by spoonfuls on top of boiling meat or fruit mixtures. Cover tightly and steam 12 minutes without removing cover. Makes 6 fluffy dumplings.

To Double Recipe: Increase milk to ¾ c. Use only 1 egg. Double other ingredients. Use a wide, shallow pan to provide more surface on which to cook 12 large dumplings.

DUMPLING VARIATIONS:

Parsley or Spinach Dumplings: For attractive color and good flavor, add ¼ c. minced parsley or young spinach leaves (use stems, too) to the flour and shortening mixture; then add milk and egg. Substitute mint leaves in dumplings with lamb stew.

Whole Wheat Dumplings: Decrease flour to ⅔ c. Add ⅓ c. whole wheat or graham flour to dry ingredients before cutting in shortening. These are special with veal stew.

Cornmeal Dumplings: Add the ⅓ c. milk to ½ c. fine cornmeal and let stand. Reduce flour to ⅓ c., sift with baking powder and salt, and cut in shortening. Add the beaten egg to the meal-milk mixture and stir. Fold flour mixture into cornmeal only until flour is dampened. Especially good with stews that contain a large amount of tomato.

Cheese Dumplings: Add ½ c. grated process cheese to flour and shortening mixture; then add liquids. Good with a combination of fresh vegetables.

Seed Dumplings: Add ½ to 1 tsp. poppy or caraway seeds to dry ingredients. After spooning dumplings into the pan, sprinkle with seeds. Attractive and good with cabbage dishes.

Meat Dumplings: To stretch a bit of chopped or ground cooked meat into a luncheon dish, add ½ c. of the meat to flour-shortening mixture before adding liquids. Steam, covered, on top of vegetables or soup, or on foil over any boiling mixture.

Fruit Dumplings: Add ½ c. finely chopped, cooked, sweetened and pitted prunes or apricots to flour-shortening mixture, before adding liquids. Nice with pork dishes.

Dessert Dumplings with fruit and sauce: Make Feathery-Light Dumplings, but add 3 tblsp. sugar to dry ingredients; use butter or margarine for shortening. Add 1 tsp. vanilla to the milk. Drop on simmering fruit, cooked this way: drain 5 c. sliced, canned peaches, berries or other fruits. Put in shallow kettle with 1 c. of the juice. Cover and simmer 3 minutes over direct heat before adding dumplings.

SWEET-MILK DOUGHNUTS

(*Master Recipe*)

4¼ c. sifted flour
3½ tsp. baking powder
1 tsp. salt
½ tsp. nutmeg
¼ tsp. cinnamon
3 eggs
1 tsp. vanilla
¾ c. sugar
3 tblsp. soft butter or margarine
¾ c. milk

• Sift together flour, baking powder, salt and spices.
• Beat eggs; add vanilla and sugar. Beat well. Mix in butter.
• Add milk and sifted dry ingredients alternately. Mix into a soft dough.
• Turn dough onto lightly floured board. Knead lightly for half a minute and roll out ⅓" thick. Cut with floured doughnut cutter. Remove trimmings.
• Lift each doughnut on a wide spatula and carefully ease into deep hot fat (375°). Put as many into fat at a time as can be turned easily.
• Fry about 3 minutes, until completely brown on both sides. Lift from fat with a long fork. Do not pierce.
• Drain on paper toweling.
• Form trimmings into a ball. Make into doughnut balls or re-roll and cut with doughnut cutter. Fry as above.
• Serve plain, sugared or frosted (see variations for doughnuts). Makes about 2 dozen.

DOUGHNUT VARIATIONS:

Dropped Doughnuts: Drop dough by spoonfuls into deep hot fat (375°). (Use 2 teaspoons which have been dipped into the fat first, so dough won't stick to them. Take a rounded portion of dough on one spoon, push off into fat with other spoon.)
• Or, roll dough in balls with floured hands and drop into fat. Turn as soon as they rise to top. Fry until golden brown on both sides.

Sugared Doughnuts: While doughnuts are still warm, dip into bowl of granulated sugar or mixture of sugar and cinnamon (½ c. sugar to ½ tsp. cinnamon). Or, when doughnuts have cooled, shake in paper bag containing confectioners sugar.

Frosted Doughnuts: Doughnuts frost best while still warm. Dip into plain frosting or any other flavors given below. For a special touch, dip top of frosted doughnut into dish of chopped walnuts, pecans, almonds or peanuts. Or dip into a dish of finely cut shredded coconut.

Plain: Mix together 1¾ c. sifted confectioners sugar, 3 tblsp. hot water, 2 tsp. melted butter or margarine and ½ tsp. vanilla.

Chocolate: Add to plain frosting, 1 sq. melted chocolate and an additional 2 tsp. hot water. Mix well.

Orange: Omit vanilla. Add to plain frosting in place of water, 3 tblsp. orange juice and 1 tsp. grated orange rind.

Maple: Omit vanilla. Add to plain frosting ¼ tsp. maple extract.

Peppermint: Omit vanilla. Add to plain frosting ¼ tsp. peppermint extract and 2 drops red food color.

QUICK-CHANGE CAKE

(Master Recipe)

1¼ c. sifted flour
⅞ c. sugar
1½ tsp. baking powder
⅛ tsp. salt
1 egg
1 c. heavy cream
1 tsp. vanilla

• Sift dry ingredients into mixing bowl. Add egg, cream and vanilla. Beat 2 minutes.
• Pour into lightly greased and floured 8×8×2" square pan. Bake in moderate oven (350°) 35 to 40 minutes.

CAKE VARIATIONS:

Sour Cream Cake: Substitute thick sour cream for heavy cream, but add ½ tsp. baking soda to dry ingredients.

Rhubarb Kuchen: Pour batter into lightly greased and floured 11×7×1½" pan. Scatter 1½ c. thinly sliced fresh rhubarb over batter. Bake in moderate oven (375°) 25 to 30 minutes. Remove from oven, sprinkle 2 tblsp. sugar over hot cake. Cut into squares or sticks.

Upside-Down Cake:

1 recipe Quick-Change Cake batter
¼ c. butter or margarine
½ c. brown sugar
5 pineapple slices, or pear or peach halves
Maraschino cherries
Nut halves
Whipped cream

• Melt butter in 8″ or 9″ skillet, or in 3″ deep baking pan. Add brown sugar.
• Place pineapple slices in a pattern in pan. Arrange cherries and nuts in pineapple centers and at sides.
• Gently spoon batter over fruit and nuts. Bake in moderate oven (350°) 45 to 50 minutes.
• Serve fruit side up with whipped cream or with sauce made from 1 c. fruit juice, ½ c. sugar, 1 tblsp. flour and 1 tblsp. butter or margarine. Cook together until syrupy.

Creamy Strawberry Cake:

A wonderful way to vary Quick-Change Cake

1 pkg. vanilla pudding mix
1¾ c. milk
1 qt. fresh strawberries
1 (8″) baked Quick-Change Cake
Confectioners sugar

• Prepare pudding according to package directions with 1¾ c. milk. Cool.
• Select a few large berries for garnish; slice remaining berries.
• Split cooled cake into 2 layers. Cover bottom layer with sliced strawberries. Spoon cooled pudding over berries.
• Place top layer over pudding. Sprinkle on confectioners sugar through a lace paper doily to make design. Garnish with whole strawberries.

Variation: Other berries or fruit may be used in place of strawberries. Interesting combinations, such as sliced sweetened peaches and blueberries, add color and flavor.

SPONGE CAKE ROLL

(*Master Recipe*)

¾ c. sifted cake flour
1 tsp. baking powder
¼ c. sugar
4 large eggs
¼ tsp. salt
½ tsp. cream of tartar
1 tsp. vanilla
½ c. sugar

• Sift together 3 times, cake flour, baking powder and sugar.
• Combine eggs, salt, cream of tartar and vanilla in large mixer bowl. Beat at high speed with electric mixer, until mixture stands in peaks. Add sugar, 2 tblsp. at a time. Continue beating at high speed until mixture again stands in peaks.
• Carefully fold dry ingredients into egg mixture.
• Line greased 10×15″ jelly roll pan with waxed paper so that paper extends above sides. Pour in batter. Bake in moderate oven (375°) 13 minutes. Cool on rack 1 minute.
• Loosen sides and turn out onto towel sprinkled with confectioners sugar. Trim edges with sharp knife. Peel off waxed paper. Fold towel over long side of cake and roll cake in towel to "set" roll while cake is warm.
• Cool, unroll and spread with Chocolate Filling (recipe follows) to within 1″ of edges. Roll up cake and chill 2 to 3 hours. Slice into 10 servings.
• Speedy and easy, when made with a mixer.

Chocolate Filling:

¾ c. milk
¼ c. sugar
2 tblsp. flour
⅛ tsp. salt
1 egg, slightly beaten
2 (1 oz.) squares unsweetened chocolate, melted
½ c. heavy cream
1 tsp. vanilla

• Scald milk in top of double boiler. Blend and add sugar, flour and salt. Add

egg. Cook over boiling water 5 minutes, stirring constantly.
• Blend in chocolate. Cover and cook 5 minutes longer; stir occasionally. Chill.
• Whip cream; add vanilla. Fold into chilled mixture.

SPONGE ROLL VARIATION:

Lemon Sponge Squares: Bake sponge roll; cut into 12 equal portions. Spread 6 squares with half of Lemon Filling. Place remaining 6 squares on top. Put a generous spoonful of Lemon Filling on each; sprinkle with ½ c. slivered toasted almonds. Makes 6 servings.

Lemon Filling:

¾ c. sugar
¼ c. cornstarch
¼ tsp. salt
1¼ c. boiling water
2 egg yolks, slightly beaten
¼ c. lemon juice
2 tsp. grated lemon rind
1 tblsp. butter or margarine
Dash salt

• Blend together sugar, cornstarch and salt. Slowly stir in boiling water. Bring mixture to boil; reduce heat, boil 1 minute, stirring to keep smooth.
• Remove from heat. Add slowly ⅓ of hot mixture to egg yolks, add egg mixture to portion in pan. Cook over low heat 2 minutes, stirring constantly. Remove from heat.
• Add lemon juice, rind, butter and salt. Stir until butter is melted and mixture is well blended. Cool before using.

CARAMEL BREAD PUDDING

(*Master Recipe*)

5 c. milk
10 slices day-old bread, cut into cubes
3 tblsp. butter or margarine
¾ c. brown sugar
¼ tsp. salt
4 eggs, beaten
1 c. sugar

• Scald milk in double boiler.
• Place bread in large bowl. Add butter, brown sugar and salt. Pour on hot milk; let stand 5 minutes.
• Beat eggs until fluffy; then beat bread mixture well. Cool; fold in eggs.
• Grease one 2 qt. mold, two 1 qt. molds, or two 9×4″ loaf pans.
• Cook 1 c. sugar in heavy skillet over low heat, stirring until it is caramelized (melted and light brown in color). Quickly pour into greased mold. Tilt mold to spread caramelized sugar evenly over bottom and sides. Let caramel coating cool slightly; add pudding mixture.
• Set in shallow pan of hot water. Bake in slow oven (325°) 1½ hours for 2 qt. mold; 1 hour for 1 qt. molds; or until knife inserted in center comes out clean.
• Cool slightly, then loosen edges with spatula and turn out on platter. The caramel makes a beautiful golden brown sauce over pudding. Serve slightly warm, with whipped cream, or pass cream. Makes 8 servings.

PUDDING VARIATIONS:

(Omit caramelized sugar from Master Recipe but add ½ c. sugar with brown sugar.)

Chocolate: Melt two (1 oz.) squares unsweetened chocolate in the hot milk.

Coconut: Stir in ½ c. coconut just before pouring pudding into mold.

Coffee: Substitute ½ c. evaporated milk and ½ c. freshly made coffee for 1 c. of the fresh milk.

Fruit: Fold in 1 c. thoroughly drained canned diced fruit or sliced apples just before pouring pudding into mold.

Dried Fruit: Soak 1 c. dried apricots, prunes, or peaches in small amount of cold water for several hours. Dice, and fold into pudding just before pouring into mold.

Peanut Brittle: Crush ½ c. peanut brittle; sprinkle over individual servings of bread pudding.

Gingerbread Dress-Ups

For a snack, warm gingerbread and glasses of cold milk have few equals. And maple syrup and sour cream gingerbreads taste just as wonderful as they did when Grandmother used to make them.

GINGERBREAD MIX

(Master Recipe)

8 c. sifted flour
2¼ c. sugar
2½ tsp. baking soda
2 tblsp. baking powder
3 tblsp. ginger
3 tblsp. cinnamon
1 tsp. cloves
1 tblsp. salt
2¼ c. shortening

• Sift together twice, all ingredients except shortening.
• Cut shortening into dry ingredients with two knives or pastry blender until mixture resembles cornmeal. Store in tightly covered jar or can in refrigerator. Makes enough mix for 6 (8") square pans of gingerbread. The mix will keep about 3 months (as long as the shortening stays fresh and sweet).

GINGERBREAD FROM MIX

These gingerbread recipes fit one 8" square pan; for a crowd, double recipe and bake in two pans or one 9×12"

2 c. gingerbread mix
1 egg, beaten
½ c. dark molasses
½ c. boiling water

• Put gingerbread mix in mixing bowl.
• Combine egg, molasses and water; stir half of mixture into gingerbread mix. Blend just until smooth. Add remainder of molasses mixture; blend until smooth.
• Pour batter into a greased, waxed paper-lined 8×8×2" pan. Bake in moderate oven (350°) 35 minutes.

VARIATIONS:

Mincemeat Gingerbread: Add 1 c. prepared mincemeat to the above recipe before stirring in liquid ingredients. Bake in moderate oven (350°) 50 minutes.

Gingerbread Orange Squares: Make up above gingerbread recipe and pour into an 8" square pan. Sprinkle with Orange Topping made by mixing 2 tblsp. melted butter, 3 tblsp. grated orange rind, ¼ c. sugar and ¾ c. chopped nuts. Bake in moderate oven (350°) 35 minutes.

Gingerbread Upside-Down Cake: Make gingerbread, reducing the molasses to ⅓ c. and the water to ¼ c. Cut 8 pear halves in halves again. Drain thoroughly. Melt 2 tblsp. butter in a 9" round pan; add ¼ c. brown sugar. Mix and spread over bottom of pan. Arrange pears over sugar-butter mixture; pour batter over pears. Bake in moderate oven (350°) 45 minutes.

Maple Gingerbread: Put 2 c. gingerbread mix in mixing bowl. Heat ⅔ c. maple syrup; combine with ⅓ c. sour cream and stir into gingerbread mix. Add 1 egg, well beaten. Pour into greased, waxed paper-lined 8×8×2" pan. Bake in moderate oven (350°) 40 minutes.

GINGERBREAD PANCAKES

1 egg, beaten
⅓ c. molasses
⅔ c. milk
2 c. gingerbread mix

• Combine egg, molasses and milk; add to gingerbread mix. Stir only until dry ingredients are dampened. Batter should be lumpy.
• Bake pancakes on greased griddle. Serve with melted butter and sprinkle with confectioners sugar. Makes 2 dozen.

VANILLA CREAM PIE

(*Master Recipe*)

¾ c. sugar
5 tblsp. flour
¼ tsp. salt
1½ c. milk
½ tsp. vanilla
2 egg yolks, slightly beaten
1 tblsp. butter or margarine
1 (8″) baked pie shell

• Combine sugar, flour and salt in top of double boiler. Mix with wooden spoon. Blend in milk, vanilla and egg yolks. Add butter.
• Place over rapidly boiling water; cook until thick and smooth, about 7 minutes, stirring constantly. Scrape down sides of pan frequently.
• Remove from heat. Scrape spoon and sides of pan. Set aside to cool in ice water in bottom part of double boiler. Do not stir.
• Slowly turn cooled filling into baked pie shell. Cover with meringue.

PIE FILLING VARIATIONS:

Cocoa: Add 4 tblsp. cocoa to first dry-ingredient mixture, and use 2 tblsp. butter or margarine.

Chocolate: Shave 1½ squares of chocolate and add to mixture before cooking. Chocolate melts as mixture cooks.

Butterscotch: Substitute ¾ cup firmly packed brown sugar for granulated sugar. Add 1 tsp. lemon juice with the butter.

Caramel: Use 2 tblsp. less milk. Caramelize ¼ cup of the sugar by placing in heavy pan over medium heat, and stirring until sugar melts and turns brown. Reduce heat and add ¼ cup boiling water. Cook until syrupy. Add to dry ingredients, with liquids, before cooking. Syrup may lump if milk and egg yolks are very cold, but it will melt and blend into mixture as it heats if stirred constantly. Add 1 tsp. lemon juice with butter.

Burnt Almond: Fold ½ cup chopped, blanched almonds (toasted, if desired) into above Caramel filling. To blanch almonds, pour boiling water over shelled nut meats. Let stand 20 minutes; skins will slip off easily between forefinger and thumb. Chop, then toast by browning almonds in melted butter in skillet. Drain on paper toweling.

Coconut: Use 9″ pie shell. Fold finely grated coconut into cooked vanilla filling (basic recipe)—1 to 2 cups (2 cups for lots of coconut!). Add part of it to meringue, if you like.

Pineapple: Use 9″ pie shell. Drain 1 (1 lb. 4 oz.) can crushed pineapple, pressing out all juice; substitute for ½ cup of milk. Reduce sugar to ½ cup. Omit vanilla; substitute pineapple juice for ½ cup milk. Add 1 tblsp. lemon juice. Just before turning cooked filling into pie shell, fold in the well drained, crushed pineapple.

Fruit: Slice 2 to 3 bananas into a 9″ pie shell. Cover at once with cooled vanilla, butterscotch or caramel filling. Top with meringue. Or use 1 cup fresh berries, sliced peaches or strawberries, chopped dates, or well drained canned fruit. Or try covering bottom of pie shell with jam or jelly before putting in vanilla filling.

Lemon: A truly different lemon pie! Perfect for the beginner cook, because there's no tricky blending of eggs and hot cornstarch mixture. It's made in one pan; cuts warm.
• Substitute lemon juice for part of the milk in these proportions: ¼ cup for mild, or ½ cup juice for tart lemon filling. Add grated rind of 1 lemon in either case. Thoroughly blend milk into dry ingredients, then add lemon juice and remaining ingredients. Cook same as basic filling.

Orange: Reduce milk to ¾ cup; blend well into dry ingredients. Add ¾ cup fresh orange juice and 2 tsp. grated orange rind. Add remaining ingredients and cook.

EIGHT-IN-ONE COOKIES

One of our most popular Master Recipes —a Farm Journal 5-star recipe

2 c. butter or margarine
2 c. sugar
1 c. brown sugar
4 eggs
6½ c. sifted flour
1 tblsp. cream of tartar
2 tsp. baking soda
¼ c. milk

• Cream butter and sugars together until smooth and fluffy. Stir in unbeaten eggs, one at a time.
• Sift dry ingredients together. Add to creamed mixture, alternately with milk. Mix thoroughly.
• Store (unflavored) dough, tightly covered, in refrigerator. Will keep 6 weeks. Makes 8 cups dough.
• Bake as needed, on greased baking sheet in moderate oven (375°) 10 to 15 minutes.

COOKIE VARIATIONS:

Chocolate: Knead into 1 c. cookie dough, 1 tblsp. cocoa and ⅓ c. semi-sweet chocolate pieces. Shape about 2 dozen round balls. Bake.

Coconut: Knead into 1 c. cookie dough, 1 c. flaked coconut and ¼ tsp. almond extract. Shape about 24 balls; place on greased baking sheet; press flat with spatula. Top each with piece of candied cherry. Bake.

Butterscotch: Knead into 1 c. cookie dough, ¾ tsp. caramelized sugar syrup and ⅓ c. finely chopped nuts. Shape into roll. Chill in refrigerator until it will slice thin, at least 3 hours. Bake. Makes about 12 cookies.

Ginger: Stir into 1 c. cookie dough, 1 tblsp. dark molasses and ¼ tsp. ginger. Shape about 24 balls, dip fingers occasionally in water so dough doesn't stick to hands. Bake.

Fruit 'n Spice: Stir into 1 c. cookie dough, ½ c. cooked, drained dried fruit; 2 tblsp. brown sugar; ¼ tsp. cinnamon; ⅛ tsp. cloves. Drop by teaspoonfuls on greased baking sheet. Bake. Makes 36.

Orange: Stir into 1 c. cookie dough, ¼ c. grated orange rind and ¼ c. sugar mixed with 4 tsp. orange juice. Bake as drop cookies. Makes 24.

Banana: Stir into 1 c. cookie dough, ¼ c. mashed ripe banana; ½ tsp. grated lemon rind; ¼ tsp. lemon juice. Drop 1 teaspoonful at a time into finely rolled corn flakes. Coat by turning gently with spoon. (Dough is very soft.) Bake on greased baking sheet. Watch carefully for scorching. Makes 24.

Gumdrop: Mix into 1 c. cookie dough, ½ c. gumdrops, cut fine. Shape into 24 balls; crisscross with fork. Bake.

SUGAR COOKIES

(*Master Recipe*)

½ c. butter or margarine
1 c. sugar
1 egg
½ tsp. vanilla
2 tsp. grated lemon rind
¼ tsp. salt
1½ tsp. baking powder
2 c. sifted flour
¼ c. milk

• Cream butter and sugar thoroughly. Add egg, vanilla and lemon rind. Beat until mixture is light and fluffy.
• Sift dry ingredients. Stir into creamed mixture together with milk.
• Divide dough in half. Chill 1 hour.
• Roll out half, on floured board, keeping the other chilled until ready to roll. Roll ¼″ thick.
• Cut into bars and place on greased baking sheet.
• Brush with slightly beaten egg white (optional) and sprinkle with sugar.
• Bake in moderate oven (350°) 12 to 15 minutes. Makes 24 large cookies.

SUGAR COOKIE VARIATIONS:

Chocolate Chip Cookies: Add ½ c. semi-sweet chocolate pieces to dough.
• Grease and flour 2 square 9×9″ baking pans. Spread half the dough in each. Bake in moderate oven (350°) 25 minutes, or until light brown.
• While still warm cut into 3″ squares. Makes 18 cookies.

Nut Sugar Cookies: Mix ½ c. finely chopped nuts into dough. Roll dough.

Coconut Cookies: Add ½ c. shredded coconut. Make drop cookies.

Raisin Cookies: Add ½ c. seedless raisins. Make drop cookies.

Spiced Sugar Cookies: Add ¼ tsp. nutmeg and ½ tsp. cinnamon to dough, omitting lemon rind. Roll dough.

Roll and Ball Cookies

COOKIE STARTER

(Master Recipe)

2¼ c. sifted flour
¾ tsp. salt
1 c. butter or margarine

• Sift flour and salt into bowl.
• Cut in butter (room temperature) until mixture resembles coarse bread crumbs.
• Store in clean jar with tight fitting lid. Keep in refrigerator or freezer. Makes 3 to 4 cups.

TIPS ON USING MIX:

• Let the crumbs reach room temperature before adding other ingredients. Loosen with a fork if mix is too compact. Your electric mixer can help you make cookie dough from the mix.
• To short-cut cookie making, shape dough into roll; wrap and chill thoroughly. Slice and bake cookies as desired. When dough is cold, allow more time for baking. To get a thicker cookie, shape teaspoonfuls of dough with fingers and roll in palms of hands into balls; stamp with flat bottomed glass and bake.
• When you bake and then freeze, wrap cookies in foil or plastic film, or store them in freezer containers.

OLD ENGLISH GINGER CRISPS

1 c. cookie starter
¼ tsp. baking soda
1½ tsp. ginger
¼ tsp. nutmeg
¼ tsp. cinnamon
¼ c. dark brown sugar
1 tblsp. dark molasses
1 tblsp. sour milk

• Mix ingredients well.
• Form dough into ball; chill 2 hours.
• Shape in 1″ balls. Roll in confectioners sugar, then pat very thin with glass dipped in confectioners sugar.
• Bake on greased baking sheet 3″ apart in moderate oven (350°) 4 minutes.
• Remove cookies while still hot. Twist over wooden spoon handle and sprinkle with sugar. Makes 1½ dozen.

BLIND DATES

1 (3 oz.) pkg. cream cheese
1 c. cookie starter
½ tsp. vanilla
2 tblsp. confectioners sugar
2 doz. dates, pitted

• Soften cheese to room temperature; combine with remaining ingredients, except dates. Form into 4 balls.
• Chill dough 2 hours.
• Work with one ball at a time, and roll ⅛″ thick on board dusted with confectioners sugar.
• Cut in 2 ½″ rounds with cutter.
• Place date in center of each round. (Date may be stuffed with nut, or use ½ date and 1 nut.) Seal edges; pinch ends to points.
• Place 1″ apart on baking sheet, seam side down. Bake 10 to 12 minutes in moderate oven (350°).
• Sprinkle with confectioners sugar. Cool. Makes 2 dozen.

ICE CREAM WAFERS

1 c. cookie starter
½ tsp. vanilla
1 egg yolk
⅓ c. sugar
½ tsp. baking powder

- Mix all ingredients.
- Chill dough thoroughly.
- Sprinkle board and rolling pin with confectioners sugar. Roll small amount of dough ⅛″ thick.
- Cut cookies and place 1″ apart on greased baking sheet. Bake in moderate oven (350°) about 6 minutes, until cookies are lightly browned.
- Dust with confectioners sugar. Makes 3 dozen.

WAFER VARIATIONS:

Chinese Almond Cookies:

- Make up Ice Cream Wafer recipe, adding ½ tsp. almond extract.
- Chill dough until firm enough to handle, about 1 hour.
- Shape into balls about 1″ in diameter. Flatten with glass dipped in confectioners sugar.
- Place cookies on lightly greased baking sheet, 3″ apart.
- Beat egg white with fork. Brush a little on each cookie.
- Decorate each cookie with slivered, blanched almonds to make flower.
- Bake in moderate oven (350°) about 12 minutes. Makes 2 dozen.

Orange and Lemon Wafers:

- Make up Ice Cream Wafer recipe omitting vanilla and adding grated rind of 1 orange and grated rind of ½ lemon.
- Roll out and cut cookies into different shapes. (Or roll into balls, using 1 teaspoon dough for each cookie. Dip fork into confectioners sugar and make waffle design by crisscrossing with fork. Don't mash cookies too flat.)
- Bake 1″ apart on lightly greased baking sheet in moderate oven (350°) 10 minutes. Decorate with strips of orange rind. Makes 1½ dozen.

Sesame Cookies:

In Charleston, South Carolina, they're called Benne Cookies—benne is the colloquial name for sesame seed.

- Make Ice Cream Wafer recipe, substituting ¼ tsp. baking soda and ½ tsp. cream of tartar for baking powder. Add ½ c. toasted coconut and ¼ c. sesame seeds (if none available add another ¼ c. toasted coconut).
- Mix ingredients well.
- Shape dough into roll. Chill 15 minutes.
- Slice and bake in moderate oven (350°) 15 minutes or until lightly browned. Makes 2½ dozen.

Victorian Spice Cookies:

- Make up Ice Cream Wafer recipe using brown sugar instead of white, and ¼ tsp. baking soda instead of baking powder. Add ½ c. chopped walnuts, 1 tsp. cocoa, ⅛ tsp. nutmeg, ½ tsp. cinnamon and ¼ tsp. allspice.
- Mix together all ingredients. Form into balls using 1 tsp. dough for each.
- Put on greased baking sheet 1″ apart. Make hole in centers of cookies with finger tip. Place ¼ tsp. firm jelly in each hole.
- Bake in moderate oven (350°) about 10 minutes, until cookies are firm. Makes 2½ dozen.

FREEZER ICE CREAM

(Master Recipe)

2 qts. heavy cream
1 pt. milk
4 eggs
½ c. sweetened condensed milk
1½ c. sugar
¼ tsp. salt
1 tsp. vanilla

• Heat 2 c. cream with milk in top of double boiler.
• Beat eggs slightly. Add sweetened condensed milk, sugar and salt. Blend in a little hot cream, then slowly add to mixture in double boiler.
• Cook 5 minutes, stirring, to 176° or until mixture just coats spoon. Cool.
• Stir in vanilla and remaining cream. Freeze in ice and coarse salt mixture. Makes 1 gallon.

VARIATIONS:

Chocolate: Omit 1 qt. cream. Melt 6 (1 oz.) squares chocolate in double boiler. Blend in ½ c. additional sugar. Slowly stir in 1 c. boiling water. Add to cooked base.

Peppermint: Omit 1 pt. cream and vanilla. Add 1 lb. crushed mints and tint with green food color, if you wish, before freezing.

Coffee: Omit 1 qt. cream and vanilla. Add 2 c. strong coffee with ¼ c. sugar.

Apricot: Omit 1½ qts. cream, 1 c. milk and vanilla. Add 2 qts. mashed apricot pulp, 1 pt. juice and 1 c. additional sugar.

Fresh Peach: Omit 1½ qts. cream, 1 c. milk and vanilla. Add 2 qts. sieved peach pulp, 1 pt. juice and 1 c. additional sugar.

Strawberry or Raspberry: Omit 1 qt. cream, 1 c. milk and vanilla. Add 2 qts. sieved berries with 1 c. additional sugar.

Peanut Brittle: Omit 1 pt. cream and vanilla. Add 1 lb. crushed peanut brittle.

VANILLA ICE CREAM

(Master Refrigerator-Tray Recipe)

6 eggs
1 c. sugar
2 c. milk
2 tsp. vanilla
½ tsp. salt
2 c. heavy cream, whipped

• Beat eggs until thick and lemon colored.
• Add sugar, milk, vanilla and salt; blend well. Fold into whipped cream. Pour into 2 cold freezer trays. Freeze until partially set.
• Break into chunks in large, chilled bowl. Beat until light and fluffy, but not melted.
• Return to tray; freeze until firm. "Mellow" it in the refrigerator section about 30 minutes before serving. Makes 8 servings.

ICE CREAM VARIATIONS:

Maple Nut: Substitute 2 tsp. maple flavoring for vanilla; add ½ c. hickory nuts or pecans at second beating.

Strawberry: Slice 2 c. fresh strawberries; sprinkle with ¼ c. sugar. Let stand while you make ice cream; omit vanilla. Add berries at second beating. (Mixer will chop up berries.)

Peppermint: Omit vanilla from basic ice cream recipe; decrease sugar to ½ c. Freeze partially. Beat in well ⅔ c. crushed peppermint candies. Measure out 1½ c. of the ice cream, add ⅛ tsp. red food color. Pour remaining ice cream in 9" square pan. Drizzle pink ice cream over plain, swirl with spatula. Freeze. Serve on squares of chocolate cake, baked from prepared mix.

Sherbets: Prepare basic recipe, decreasing milk to 1 c. At second beating: for orange, add 1 (6 oz.) can orange concentrate; for raspberry, add 1 c. red raspberry purée; for lime, add 1 c. water, 1 tsp. lime extract, and ¼ tsp. green food color.

Fruit Frosts

(A cross between ices and sherbets)

STRAWBERRY FROST

(Master Recipe)

Strawberries (enough for 1¾ c. purée—about 1 qt.)
¼ c. unsweetened applesauce
1 c. sugar
1 envelope unflavored gelatin
¼ c. cold water
¾ c. boiling water

• Put strawberries through food mill to make purée. Add applesauce and sugar.
• Soften gelatin in cold water. Dissolve in boiling water; add to fruit mixture and blend. Makes 1½ quarts.

To Freeze in Ice Cream Freezer: Fill 2 qt. can; place in packed ice and salt. Turn until mixture is fairly stiff. Remove dasher, cover can with waxed paper, and replace lid. Let ripen until firm.

FROST VARIATIONS:

Raspberry: Use 1¼ c. raspberry purée and ¾ c. applesauce.

Blackberry: Use 1¼ c. blackberry purée and ¾ c. applesauce.

Blueberry: Use 1½ c. blueberry purée and ½ c. applesauce. Add 1 tsp. lemon juice.

Elderberry: Use 1½ c. elderberry purée and ½ c. applesauce.

Cherry: Use 1¼ c. cherry purée and ¾ c. applesauce.

Cranberry: Use 1½ c. canned strained cranberry sauce, ½ c. applesauce and ½ c. sugar.

Rhubarb: Use 1½ c. sweetened rhubarb sauce and ½ c. applesauce.

Peach: Use 1¾ c. peach purée and ¼ c. applesauce.

Salad Bowl Variety

FRENCH DRESSING

(Master Recipe)

2 tsp. salt
2 tsp. sugar
½ tsp. dry mustard
¼ tsp. pepper
½ c. cider vinegar
1½ c. oil
Dash cayenne

• Combine all ingredients in a jar. Cover; shake well. Store in refrigerator. Shake again just before serving. Makes 2 cups.

DRESSING VARIATIONS:

(Add new ingredients at least an hour before serving and chill. Shake well when using.)

Curry Dressing:. Combine 1 c. of the basic dressing; 1 tsp. curry powder; ¼ tsp. dry mustard; 2 sieved hard-cooked egg yolks.

Indian Rose Dressing: Combine 1 c. of the basic dressing; 1 small cooked beet forced through a coarse sieve; 1 tsp. onion; ½ tsp. celery seed; dash cayenne.

Parisian Dressing: Combine 1 c. of the basic dressing; 2 tblsp. each chopped green pepper and chopped celery; 2 tsp. chopped onion; ½ tsp. Worcestershire sauce; ½ tsp. seasoned salt.

Roquefort Dressing: Combine 1 c. of the basic dressing with 3 tblsp. crumbled Roquefort cheese; 1 tsp. Worcestershire sauce; 1 tblsp. lemon juice; 1 tsp. paprika.

Spicy Red Dressing: Combine 1 c. of the basic dressing; ⅓ c. ketchup; 1 tsp. chopped onion; 1 tsp. Worcestershire sauce; 2 tblsp. India relish or chopped sweet pickle.

Spinosa Dressing: Combine 1 c. of the basic dressing; 2 tblsp. each chopped green olives and parsley; 1 tblsp. chopped chives; 1 tsp. paprika.

22

Money-Maker Recipes

Many good cooks make money at home for their own pocketbooks and to boost their contributions to church, club or school projects and other worthy causes. Our readers often sell dishes they make unusually well—frequently the ones their families and friends rave about. Some mother-daughter teams cook together to earn spending money for both. And most of them see that the food they sell uses several ingredients produced on their own farms. A beautiful example is the elegant pound cake in this chapter. The woman who enjoys a profitable business with it markets her butter, buttermilk and eggs in this tasty loaf.

Homemade taste is what sells foods prepared in home kitchens. And if a dish attracts customers, keeps them reordering and wins new purchasers, the tribute to the cook is real. For it's easier for people to compliment you on a pretty cake or loaf of bread you bake than to part with cash to buy it. Or as one of our readers put it: "Reorders are the test. If you have them, you can rejoice that your food is superior."

Among FARM JOURNAL's readers who make money at home by preparing and selling food, cakes, candies, cookies and breads are the best sellers. Home-canned relish specialties also are good earners, as are salads that may be ordered for special occasions. The colorful Ribbon Salad included in this chapter, for instance, is a beauty with a delightful mingling of flavors. No wonder an Ohio farm woman has become its caterer—town women like to order it for their luncheon parties. You may wish to try it next time you entertain your club or have a big family dinner.

This chapter gives recipes for foods that are on the best seller list in the country. All have been taste tested in our Countryside Kitchens. All rate "excellent" with the Food Department. We believe you, too, will like all of them.

Cakes Like Mother Made

Nothing equals a beautiful cake in capturing customers at food sales. Men snap them up in a hurry and proudly carry them home. Women's sales resistance is little stronger, for cake has a tantalizing appeal. Frequently the cakes offered for sale are the old-fashioned kind—generous, tempting loaves, or three gloriously big layers put together with rich filling.

These seven recipes have proved their worth by fine sales records. All of them make out-of-this-world cakes—take time to bake but they're luscious. You'll want to try them for special occasions.

COCONUT CAKE SUPREME

Handsome cake that men can't pass up when they see it at a food sale

4 egg whites, unbeaten
2¾ c. sifted cake flour
4 tsp. baking powder
¾ tsp. salt
¾ c. butter or shortening
1½ c. sugar
1 tsp. vanilla
1 tsp. almond extract
1 c. milk or coconut milk

• Place egg whites in bowl and bring to room temperature.
• Measure and sift flour, baking powder and salt three times.
• Cream shortening well, then add 1 c. sugar and blend well.
• Beat egg whites until fluffy. Gradually add ½ c. sugar, beating until stiff peaks form.
• Add flavorings to milk and add milk alternately with flour to creamed mixture. Beat well.
• Fold egg white mixture into batter. Pour into 3 greased round 8" layer pans.
• Bake in moderate oven (350°) 25 to 30 minutes. Cool on cake racks.

Coconut in Other Cakes: Fold ½ to 1 c. finely cut (with scissors) flaked or shredded coconut into angel food cake batter; ½ c. into devils food.

WHITE FROSTING

Snowy drifts shaggy with coconut

2 c. sugar
1 c. water
⅛ tsp. salt
1 tsp. white vinegar
3 egg whites
½ tsp. vanilla
½ lb. fresh (or frozen) coconut

• Combine sugar, water, salt and vinegar in a heavy saucepan. Cook over medium heat, stirring constantly until clear.
• Without stirring, cook until mixture forms a thin thread when dropped from spoon (242°).
• Beat egg whites until stiff. Add hot syrup, beating constantly. Continue beating until frosting holds shape. Add vanilla.
• Spread between layers, topping with fresh coconut. Cover top and sides of cake and pile with freshly grated coconut. Makes 8 to 10 servings.

Variation: For Creole Frosting, substitute 1 c. brown sugar for 1 c. white sugar. Fold in 1 c. toasted flaked or shredded coconut with the vanilla. To toast coconut, heat in shallow pan in moderate oven (350°) until light brown.

LAYER FRUIT CAKE

A Christmas special with many fans glad to pay money for it

1 c. shortening
2 c. sugar
1 tsp. cloves
1 tsp. cinnamon
1 tsp. nutmeg
1 tsp. allspice
1 c. milk
8 egg whites, unbeaten
4 c. sifted flour
1 tblsp. baking powder
¼ lb. candied cherries
1 c. nuts
1 lb. raisins
½ lb. currants
½ lb. citron

• Cream sugar and shortening. Add spices, milk and egg whites. Mix well.
• Sift flour and baking powder. Add fruit and nuts to flour mixture. Stir into creamed mixture. Blend well.
• Pour batter into 5 greased 8" round layer pans.
• Bake in slow oven (325°) about 40 minutes or until cake springs back when lightly touched with finger. Makes two 2-layer cakes and one 1-layer cake.
• Spread with Citrus Filling.

Citrus Filling:

Juice of 2 oranges
Rind of 2 oranges
Juice of 2 lemons
Rind of 2 lemons
1 large coconut, grated
2 c. sugar
1 c. boiling water
4 tblsp. cornstarch

• Combine all ingredients except cornstarch in saucepan. Bring to boil.
• Mix cornstarch with a little water. Stir into hot mixture. Continue cooking until thick enough to spread. Cool. Spread between layers and on top of Layer Fruit Cake.

DATE NUT CAKE

A Florida money maker—try it and you'll see why

4 eggs, unbeaten
1 c. sugar
½ c. oil
1 tsp. salt
1 c. sifted flour
1 lb. pitted dates
4 c. whole pecan halves

• Combine eggs, sugar and oil. Beat well.
• Add remaining ingredients, mixing well.
• Place in greased, floured 9×5×3" loaf pan. Bake in slow oven (300°) 2 hours. Cake must be started in cold oven. Makes 1 (3 pound) loaf.

CHOCOLATE NUT LOAF

Rich with chocolate, tender and moist—you'll enjoy every crumb

1 c. butter or margarine
2 c. sugar
5 eggs, well beaten
2 squares unsweetened chocolate, melted
1 tsp. vanilla
2½ c. sifted cake flour
1 tsp. baking soda
¼ tsp. salt
1 c. buttermilk
1 c. chopped walnuts

• Cream butter well, add sugar gradually. Beat until light and fluffy.
• Add eggs and melted chocolate. Blend well. Add vanilla.
• Add sifted dry ingredients alternately with buttermilk. Fold in nuts.
• Pour batter in 2 greased loaf pans, 8½×4½×2½". Bake in slow oven (325°) 1 hour.
• Sprinkle top with confectioners sugar or spread with your favorite white or chocolate frosting. In our Countryside Test Kitchens we filled ridges with confectioners sugar.

LEMON CHEESE CAKE

A Southern delicacy—contains no cheese, but buttery filling with hint of cheese-like curd adds color and luscious flavor

1 c. butter
2 c. sugar
1 tblsp. baking powder
3 c. sifted cake flour
¾ c. milk
6 egg whites, stiffly beaten

• Cream butter and sugar with mixer, beating until light and fluffy.
• Add sifted dry ingredients alternately with milk. Fold in egg whites. Pour into 3 greased round 8" layer pans.
• Bake in moderate oven (350°) 25 to 30 minutes, or until top springs back when lightly touched. Cool on racks.

Lemon Cheese Cake Filling:

½ c. butter
1 c. sugar
6 egg yolks
Grated rind of 2 lemons
Juice of 2 lemons

• Combine all ingredients in top of double boiler. Cook over hot water, stirring constantly until thick.
• Cool. Place between layers and on top of Lemon Cheese Cake. Sprinkle with coconut, if desired. White 7-minute icing may be used to frost sides of the cake.

POUND CAKE

Moist cake with silky grain keeps old customers and wins new ones

1 c. butter
2 c. sugar
4 eggs, unbeaten
1 tsp. vanilla
1 tsp. lemon extract
3 c. sifted flour
½ tsp. baking soda
½ tsp. baking powder
¾ tsp. salt
1 c. buttermilk

• Cream butter and sugar thoroughly. Add eggs, one at a time.
• Beat at medium speed with electric mixer 2½ minutes. Add flavorings.
• Sift dry ingredients together and add to creamed mixture alternately with buttermilk. Beat 3½ minutes at medium speed. Do not overbeat or cake will fall.
• Place in large greased loaf pan, 10×5×3" (may overflow smaller pan). Bake in slow oven (325°) 1 hour and 10 minutes, or until done.

CHOCOLATE TELEGRAM CAKE

A birthday cake that sells. Make one for Dad or Uncle Bill

⅓ c. lard
⅓ c. butter
1½ c. sugar
1 tsp. vanilla
3 eggs, separated
¼ c. cocoa
2 c. sifted flour
½ tsp. salt
1 c. milk
1½ tsp. baking soda
1 tblsp. vinegar

• Cream lard and butter thoroughly. Gradually add sugar. Beat well.
• Add vanilla and egg yolks, beating until light and fluffy. Add cocoa.
• Sift flour and salt together, add to creamed mixture alternately with milk in which the soda has been dissolved. Stir in vinegar.
• Beat egg whites until stiff but not dry. Fold into batter.
• Pour into greased 12×8½×2" pan. Bake in moderate oven (350°) about 40 to 45 minutes. Cool. Frost with your favorite chocolate frosting and decorate like a telegram, writing desired message with white frosting, using pastry tube.

Candle Decorations: On plain frosted cake casually arrange candles of several colors—yellow, green, white and pink (use your leftovers!). Write age of birthday child on cake with candles.

Breads That Lure Customers

Home baking may not be the universal art it used to be in home kitchens, but the fondness for beautifully browned loaves stays the same. Breads take a prominent place in bake sales, and frequently bring regular customers. These recipes have earned many dollars for country cooks.

BANANA BREAD

Freezer owners buy many loaves to keep on hand for quick sandwich making

⅓ c. shortening
¾ c. sugar
1 egg, well beaten
2 c. bran flakes
1½ c. sifted flour
2 tsp. baking powder
½ tsp. salt
½ tsp. baking soda
½ c. chopped walnuts
1½ c. mashed bananas
2 tblsp. water
1 tsp. vanilla

• Cream well shortening and sugar. Add egg and bran flakes.
• Sift together flour, baking powder, salt and soda. Add nuts.
• Combine bananas and water. Add to creamed mixture alternately with dry ingredients; stir in vanilla.
• Bake in greased 9×5×3″ pan in moderate oven (350°) 1 hour and 10 minutes. Makes 1 (1 lb.) loaf.

CINNAMON LOAF

Deliver these long, sweet-topped loaves warm for reorders

1 egg, well beaten
3 c. prepared biscuit mix
¾ c. milk
2 tblsp. butter
2 tsp. cinnamon
¼ c. sugar
¼ c. confectioners sugar
2 tblsp. warm water

• Combine egg, biscuit mix and milk. Mix well.
• Turn dough out onto floured board and knead lightly. Roll into loaf shape.
• Spread with butter. Sprinkle with mixture of cinnamon and sugar.
• Roll, beginning at long edge. Seal. Place on baking sheet. Make cuts with scissors 1″ apart.
• Bake in hot oven (400°) 20 minutes.
• Prepare glaze from confectioners sugar and warm water. Makes 10 to 12 slices.

MAPLE STICKS

In demand for coffee parties

½ c. butter or margarine
½ c. sugar
2 eggs, beaten
1 tsp. salt
2 pkgs. granular or compressed yeast
2 c. water
8 c. sifted flour
Confectioners frosting

• Cream margarine and sugar. Add eggs and salt.
• Sprinkle granular yeast over warm (110°) water, or compressed yeast over lukewarm (85°) water. Stir to blend. Add dissolved yeast with remaining water and flour to creamed mixture. Knead until smooth.
• Place in greased bowl and let rise until doubled. Turn out on floured board. Roll to ¼″ thick; cut into strips or circles. Let rise 1 hour.
• Fry in deep fat at 375°. Drain on paper toweling. Frost with confectioners sugar frosting, maple flavored. Makes 2 dozen.

RAISIN-BRAN BREAD

Some families buy this especially for baked bean suppers

2 c. buttermilk or thick sour milk
2 c. all-bran cereal
1¼ c. brown sugar
2 tsp. baking soda
1 tsp. salt
1 c. raisins or chopped dates
⅓ c. chopped walnuts
2 c. sifted flour

• Pour buttermilk over bran and let stand 10 minutes. Add sugar, baking soda and salt, stirring well.
• Mix fruit and nuts with flour. Stir into bran mixture.
• Bake in greased 9×5×3" pan in moderate over (350°) 1 hour. Makes 1 loaf.

MOLASSES OATMEAL BREAD

It has the homemade look and taste—both stimulate sales

1 c. rolled oats
⅓ to ½ c. molasses
¼ c. shortening
1 tblsp. salt
2 c. boiling water
2 pkgs. granular yeast
1 c. warm water
8 c. sifted flour

• Combine oats, molasses, salt, shortening and water. Set aside to cool.
• Sprinkle yeast over warm (110°) water. Stir to blend. Add to molasses mixture.
• Stir in flour, in two additions, mixing well. Place in large greased bowl, cover and set in a warm place until doubled, about 1½ hours. Punch down. Allow to rise until doubled two more times about 30 minutes each.

• Divide dough into 3 portions. Knead each portion. Form into loaves and place in greased loaf pans. Allow to rise until doubled.

• Bake in hot oven (425°) 10 minutes. Reduce heat and finish baking in moderate oven (350°) 30 to 35 minutes. Remove from pans at once. Brush tops of loaves with melted butter and cover lightly until cool. Makes 3 loaves.

CHEESE BREAD

Good salesmanship: Indicate what marvelous toast this bread makes

1¾ c. milk, scalded
3 c. shredded process cheese
4 tblsp. sugar
2 tsp. salt
2 tblsp. butter
1 pkg. granular yeast
¼ c. warm water
5½ c. sifted flour
Melted butter

• Combine milk, 2 c. cheese, sugar, salt and butter. Stir until cheese melts. Cool.
• Sprinkle yeast over warm (110°) water; stir to blend. Add to milk mixture. Let stand 3 minutes. Add 5 c. flour and additional cheese. Mix well.
• Turn out onto board which has been sprinkled with remaining flour.
• Knead until dough is smooth and satiny. Place in large bowl and brush with melted butter. Cover and let rise till doubled, about 1½ hours. Punch down and divide in thirds. Let rest 10 minutes covered with a towel.
• Shape into 3 loaves. Place in greased loaf pans. Cover and let rise till doubled.
• Bake in moderate over (375°) 45 minutes. Remove from pan to rack to cool. Makes 3 loaves.

Cheese Toast: Slice Cheese Bread, toast and butter. Use as a base for creamed chicken, turkey, eggs, tuna, salmon or dried beef. Or, spread toast with deviled ham and top with poached eggs and creamed peas or asparagus. For toast with a difference, bake unbuttered thin Cheese Bread slices in waffle iron until golden.

Candy Cooks Sell Their Sweets

Homemade candy stays on the best seller lists the year around. Many customers buy it by the pound—example: our Pulled Mints. The story of their sales success, printed in Farm Journal, brought an avalanche of letters to the Food Department, many requesting the recipe; others sending their own successful candy recipes. This candy has made hundreds of dollars for an Ohio farm woman, a member of Farm Journal's Family Test Group.

PULLED MINTS

Creamy candy that melts in the mouth

2 c. sugar
1 c. water
¼ c. butter or margarine
Pinch of cream of tartar
Few drops food color
4 to 5 drops oil of peppermint or wintergreen, lemon or cinnamon

• Combine sugar, water, butter and cream of tartar in saucepan. Stir over medium heat until sugar is completely dissolved.

• Cook, without stirring, over high heat until temperature reaches 260° or until a few drops of the mixture become brittle when dropped in cold water. Keep sugar crystals wiped from sides of pan with moist cheesecloth wound around fork tines, or a moist pastry brush.

• Pour onto greased marble slab or greased large shallow pan or tray. With greased hands, turn edges into center so they won't get hard. Let cool.

• When cool enough to handle, sprinkle over drops of food color and your choice of flavor. Pick up into a ball. Hold in one hand, pull out with other hand (as for taffy); fold back and pull again, working in color and flavor. Turn, to pull all parts evenly. Continue pulling like taffy until almost cold.

• Stretch out in a "ribbon" of even thickness (about ½" to ¾" wide). Cut off with kitchen shears in short lengths. Arrange in layers in a waxed paper-lined covered container, such as a 1 lb. coffee can. Candy will become soft and creamy in a few hours. Makes about 1 pound.

CARAMEL WALNUT ROLL

Crunchy walnuts coat buttery candy

1¼ c. light brown sugar
½ c. sugar
1⅓ c. dark corn syrup
6 tblsp. butter
1 c. evaporated milk
½ tsp. vanilla
⅛ tsp. salt
2 c. walnuts

• Combine sugars and syrup in heavy saucepan. Bring to a boil over medium heat, stirring constantly. Cook until syrup reaches 245° and is thick.

• Add butter, stirring to melt. Slowly add evaporated milk so mixture continues to boil, stirring constantly. Continue cooking until mixture again reaches 245°. Remove from heat, add vanilla and salt.

• Pour into greased 13×9×2" pan. Cool until candy is firm enough to handle.

• Spread walnut halves on waxed paper measuring the same size as pan. Turn candy out on top of walnuts and roll as for jelly roll, pressing walnuts into caramel.

• Divide roll into thirds and make 3 small rolls.

• May be wrapped in waxed paper in rolls, or individual pieces may be sliced from each roll. Wrap rolls or slices in waxed paper or transparent plastic film. Makes 3 small rolls or 3 dozen pieces.

STRAWBERRY DIVINITY

Always a drawing card

3 c. sugar
¾ c. light corn syrup
¾ c. water
2 egg whites, unbeaten
1 (3 oz.) pkg. strawberry flavor gelatin
½ c. flaked or shredded coconut
1 c. chopped pecans

• Combine sugar, corn syrup and water in heavy saucepan. Bring to a boil, stirring constantly. Reduce heat and continue cooking, stirring only occasionally, to hard ball stage (252°).
• Beat egg whites until fluffy, then add gelatin, beating until mixture forms peaks.
• Pour hot syrup in thin stream into beaten whites, beating constantly. Beat until candy loses gloss and holds shape.
• Fold in coconut and nuts.
• Pour into greased 9×9×1½" pan. Makes 5 dozen.

CHOCOLATE RIPPLE DIVINITY

Black and white beauty that will open pocketbooks

2 c. sugar
½ c. water
½ c. light corn syrup
⅛ tsp. salt
2 egg whites, unbeaten
1 tsp. vanilla
1 (6 oz.) pkg. semi-sweet chocolate pieces

• Combine sugar, water, syrup and salt in a heavy saucepan. Cook over low heat, stirring constantly until sugar is dissolved. Cook to hard ball stage (252°) without stirring.
• Beat egg whites until stiff. Pour hot syrup slowly over egg whites, beating constantly. Add vanilla. Continue beating until mixture loses gloss and will hold shape.
• Fold in chocolate bits quickly and drop from teaspoon onto buttered waxed paper. Makes 2 dozen.

BROWN SUGAR SEA FOAM

Fluffy candy loaded with nuts—good Christmas seller

2 c. sugar
1½ c. light brown sugar
¼ c. dark brown syrup
¾ c. hot water
⅛ tsp. salt
2 egg whites, stiffly beaten
1 tsp. vanilla
1 c. pecans
1 c. walnuts

• Combine sugars, syrup, water and salt in heavy saucepan. Stir over medium heat until dissolved. Bring to a boil without stirring, and boil to soft ball stage, about 235°. Remove from heat.
• When mixture stops bubbling, pour in a thin stream into egg whites, beating constantly.
• Add vanilla and nuts. When candy thickens, pour into greased pan. Makes 2 dozen 1½" squares.

FRUITED SEA FOAM

Mixed fruits sparkle in snowy candy and attract customers

3 c. sugar
⅔ c. water
½ c. light corn syrup
2 egg whites, stiffly beaten
⅛ tsp. salt
½ tsp. vanilla
1 c. candied mixed fruits

• Combine sugar, water and syrup in a heavy saucepan. Boil until mixture forms a hard ball when dropped in cold water, about 252°.
• Combine egg whites and salt, beat until stiff. Pour hot syrup over egg whites, beating constantly until mixture loses gloss.
• Add vanilla and beat until mixture forms peak. Fold in candied mixed fruit. Pour into greased 8×8×2" pan. Scatter mixed fruit on top, cut into squares. Makes about 24 pieces.

PEANUT BRITTLE

Boys' favorite—mothers who find it at church sales take some home

2 c. sugar
1 c. light corn syrup
½ c. hot water
1 tsp. salt
2 c. raw Spanish peanuts
1 tsp. butter
1 tsp. vanilla
1½ tsp. baking soda

• Combine sugar, syrup, water and salt in a heavy saucepan.
• Bring to a full boil and add peanuts. Cook until nuts snap and syrup begins to turn color.
• Add butter and vanilla. Cook until amber colored and continue cooking slowly to 300°, stirring occasionally.
• Remove from heat and add baking soda, stirring well.
• Pour immediately onto buttered hard surface (marble, porcelain) or baking sheet. Cool and pull out until very thin. Break into pieces. Makes about 1 pound.

CONFECTIONERS SUGAR FUDGE

So tempting few people can resist it

2 (1 lb.) pkgs. confectioners sugar
2 (6 oz.) cans evaporated milk
2 tblsp. butter
2 (6 oz.) pkgs. semi-sweet chocolate bits
6 tblsp. marshmallow crême
1 c. chopped nuts

• Combine sugar, milk and butter in heavy saucepan. Bring to a boil, stirring constantly. Boil 4 minutes.
• Add chocolate bits and marshmallow creme. Beat until chocolate melts and fudge thickens. Add nuts.
• Turn into buttered 8×8×2" pan. Makes about 3 pounds.

Cookies By the Dozen

Good homemade cookies always are in demand. These recipes bring repeat orders. Even young cooks can earn money with their baking talent. For example, Two-Way Cookies are made and delivered by a little girl who finds this a satisfactory way to earn spending money.

TWO-WAY COOKIES

As easy to bake two kinds as one—twice as easy to sell

4 c. sifted flour
1 tsp. salt
1 tsp. baking soda
1 c. margarine
1 c. sugar
1¼ c. light brown sugar, firmly packed
3 eggs, unbeaten
1 tsp. vanilla
½ tsp. orange extract
1 (6 oz.) pkg. semi-sweet chocolate pieces
1 (3½ oz.) can flaked coconut

• Sift dry ingredients.
• Cream margarine, gradually add sugars.
• Add eggs, one at a time, beating thoroughly after each addition. Add vanilla; blend.
• Add sifted dry ingredients. Mix well. Divide batter in half.
• Add orange flavoring and chocolate bits to one half dough and coconut to other half.
• Drop by spoonfuls onto greased baking sheet.
• Bake in a moderate oven (350°) 12 to 15 minutes. Makes 4 dozen.

NUT AND FRUIT BARS

For quick turnover offer these cookies for sale at Christmas—cash catchers

3 eggs, unbeaten
1 tsp. vanilla
1 c. sugar
1 c. sifted flour
½ tsp. salt
1 tsp. baking powder
1 c. chopped walnuts
1 (8 oz.) pkg. pitted dates
1 (6 oz.) jar maraschino cherries, drained

• Combine eggs and vanilla. Beat well. Add sugar and sifted dry ingredients; blend well. Stir in nuts and fruits.

• Bake in greased 15½×10½×1" pan 30 minutes in moderate oven (350°). Cool. Cut into squares. Sprinkle with confectioners sugar. Store in airtight box. Makes 2 dozen.

DOUBLE CREAM COOKIES

Tea-party tidbits—rich and dainty

1 c. soft butter
⅓ c. heavy cream
2 c. sifted flour

• Mix ingredients; chill thoroughly. Roll ⅛" thick and cut in 1½" rounds. Place on waxed paper heavily sprinkled with granulated sugar and turn to coat circles.

• Place on baking sheet; prick tops with fork in 3 or 4 places. Bake in moderate oven (375°) until puffy, but not browned, about 8 minutes. Cool. Put together in pairs with Creamy Frosting. Makes about 5 dozen double cookies.

Creamy Frosting: Blend together ¼ c. butter, ¾ c. sifted confectioners sugar, 1 egg yolk and 1 tsp. vanilla or ¼ tsp. almond extract.

LEMON BLOSSOM SNOWBALLS

Pure white cookies—perfect with tea

½ c. shortening or butter
⅔ c. sugar
2 tsp. grated lemon rind
1 egg, unbeaten
1¾ c. sifted flour
½ tsp. baking soda
¼ tsp. cream of tartar
3 tblsp. lemon juice
1 tblsp. water
½ c. chopped nuts

• Cream shortening, sugar and lemon rind until light and fluffy.

• Add egg. Beat until smooth.

• Sift together flour, baking soda and cream of tartar. Add to creamed mixture alternately with lemon juice and water.

• Stir in chopped nuts. Chill dough.

• With floured hands, form dough into small balls and place 1" apart on ungreased baking sheet.

• Bake in moderate oven (350°) 8 to 10 minutes. Remove from sheet and roll immediately in confectioners sugar. Makes 3½ dozen.

Orange Blossom Variation: Omit lemon rind and lemon juice. Substitute grated orange rind and orange juice. Use pecans for nuts.

CHOCOLATE OATMEAL COOKIES

Candy lovers buy these cookies

2 c. sugar
½ c. milk
¼ c. butter or margarine
⅓ c. cocoa
3 c. quick-cooking rolled oats
½ c. flaked or shredded coconut
½ c. peanut butter
1 tsp. vanilla

• Combine sugar, milk, butter and cocoa. Boil 1 minute. Remove from heat.

• Mix in rest of ingredients.

• Drop on waxed paper. Makes 30 cookies.

Successful Caterers' Recipes

In many communities women take orders for special food to be delivered for special occasions. Ribbon Salad is one example—it's much in demand for town women's luncheon parties. Sometimes customers for the homemade treasures of good cooks don't cook especially well themselves, but they know delicious food.

Home canned relishes always attract buyers. Barbecued Hamburgers sell well at farm sales. And there are the clubs, specialties which members make in quantity and sell to raise money for worthy causes. The Chicken Tamale recipe has been a gold mine for an Arkansas Home Demonstration group.

RIBBON SALAD

Party-pretty, two-tone salad—the kind caterers say are good sellers

2 (3 oz.) pkgs. lime flavor gelatin
5 c. hot water
4 c. cold water
1 (3 oz.) pkg. lemon flavor gelatin
½ c. miniature marshmallows, cut into pieces
1 c. pineapple juice
1 (8 oz.) pkg. cream cheese
1 (1 lb. 4 oz.) can crushed pineapple
1 c. heavy cream, whipped
1 c. mayonnaise
2 (3 oz.) pkgs. cherry flavor gelatin

• Dissolve lime gelatin in 2 c. hot water. Add 2 c. cold water. Pour into 14×10×2" pan. Chill until partly set.

• Dissolve lemon gelatin in 1 c. hot water in top of double boiler. Add marshmallows and stir to melt.

• Remove from heat. Add 1 c. drained pineapple juice and cream cheese.

• Beat until well blended and stir in pineapple. Cool slightly. Fold in whipped cream and mayonnaise. Chill until thickened.

• Pour in layer over lime gelatin. Chill until almost set.

• Dissolve cherry gelatin in 2 c. hot water. Add 2 c. cold water. Chill until syrupy. Pour over pineapple layer. Chill until firm. Makes 24 squares.

DATE PECAN PIE

A quick sell-out every time

Pastry:

1½ c. sifted flour
½ tsp. baking powder
½ tsp. salt
⅔ c. shortening
4 tblsp. cold water

Filling:

1 c. dairy sour cream
3 eggs, beaten
1 c. sugar
1 tsp. cinnamon
¼ tsp. salt
¾ c. dates, cut into pieces
½ c. chopped pecans
Whipped cream

• Prepare pie shell. Chill.

• Combine sour cream, eggs, sugar and seasonings in a bowl; mix well. Add dates and pecans. (Put dates and nuts through food chopper to save time.) Blend well. Pour into unbaked pie shell.

• Bake in a very hot oven (450°) 10 minutes; reduce heat to moderate (350°) and continue baking 35 to 40 minutes. Cool. Spread with sweetened whipped cream. Makes 8 servings.

Note: Because this pie is very rich, you may like to distribute the flavor with a small scoop or spoonful of vanilla ice cream, rather than whipped cream.

BARBECUED HAMBURGERS

A natural, to serve at farm sales

3 tblsp. shortening
3 lbs. ground beef
3 large onions, finely chopped
1 clove garlic, minced
1 tblsp. salt
1½ tsp. black pepper
½ tsp. red pepper
2 tsp. chili powder
2 tsp. Worcestershire sauce
¼ c. flour
1¼ c. canned tomatoes
¾ c. ketchup

• Melt shortening in heavy skillet. Combine ground beef, onions and garlic. Cook in skillet until lightly browned.
• Add seasonings. Stir in flour. Add tomatoes and ketchup, mixing well.
• Simmer 15 to 20 minutes until thickened. Spoon between split buns to make hot sandwiches. Makes 20 servings.

3-FRUIT MARMALADE

An eye-catcher at any food bazaar

Rind from 3 oranges
Rind from 2 lemons
2½ c. water
2½ c. sugar
2 c. canned crushed pineapple
1 (10½ oz.) jar maraschino cherries
1 pkg. powdered pectin

• Put rind through food chopper. Add water and let stand several hours or overnight.
• Place rind and liquid in heavy saucepan; boil 15 minutes. Add sugar, pineapple, quartered cherries and cherry juice.
• Boil all ingredients 15 to 20 minutes, until mixture has cooked down.
• Add powdered pectin. Bring to a boil, stirring constantly. Boil 1 minute. When thickened, pour into ½ pint jars and seal at once. Makes 5½ pints.

CHICKEN TAMALES

Popular group-meal dish in Arkansas

1 (4 to 5 lb.) chicken, cut up
1 large onion, chopped
1 clove garlic, minced or crushed
2 tblsp. oil
Paprika
Salt
Cayenne
Chili powder
Cumin powder
2 c. cornmeal
10 c. boiling chicken broth
1½ tsp. salt
Corn shucks
Oil

• Place chicken in large kettle; cover with water. Simmer until tender and meat falls from bones. Remove from broth; take meat off bones. Put through coarse blade of food chopper.
• Cook liver, heart and gizzard separately; grind.
• Cook onion and garlic in oil until soft and clear. Add chicken and seasonings.
• Bring chicken broth to boil. Prepare mush, using broth, cornmeal and salt.
• Trim and brush shucks for wrapping tamales. Rinse with cold water. Place in pan, and cover with boiling water. Let stand until soft and pliable. Drain on paper toweling. Grease with oil.
• On each shuck, place a layer of mush and a layer of chicken mixture. Roll as for jelly roll. Secure each end of shuck with string cut from corn "silk".
• Place tamales on rack in large kettle, over enough water in bottom of kettle to prevent burning. Cover kettle; steam tamales about 3 hours over low heat.
• More mush may be served with tamales. Makes 6 to 8 servings.

23

Old-Fashioned Recipes

Few farm women have the ingredients or time these busy days to fix the tedious dishes Grandmother used to make. But sometimes nostalgia nudges all of us to turn back the clock long enough to make a few old-time favorites to treat our families and friends. This chapter has some of the recipes that made Grandmother's kitchen such a wondrous, homey place, with goodness going into and coming out of kettles and ovens all day long.

When you've a lot of windfall apples, cook up some old-time apple butter—its appeal is difficult to resist, especially if you remember hot biscuits topped with this spicy, cider-flavored spread. Our recipe is for the oven type which requires less attention (less stirring), but it tastes like the apple butter made outdoors in big black iron kettles.

Pressed chicken was one of Grandmother's favorites, and when we made it in Countryside Kitchens we decided it also is one of ours. Teamed with flaky, sweet cream biscuits (both chicken and biscuit recipes are in this chapter), buttered peas or asparagus and a fruit salad, you have such a scrumptious guest luncheon that everyone at the table will let the rest of the world go by while they enjoy a truly great American meal.

Our mincemeat is food for the gods, as one farm woman so aptly put it, but minutes can't be precious in homes where it's made—it takes time. Apple-elderberry, currant and quince custard pies, the kind that came so temptingly from Grandmother's oven, taste just as delicious as of old. We have the recipes for them; if you have the ingredients, you're fortunate.

And there's corned beef—you can cure a piece of brisket by our directions if you have the urge. And if you do, we think you'll like our recipe that follows for Grandpa's delight, corned beef and cabbage.

If you can find the ingredients and time to try some of these recipes, we know you'll join in the Food Department's declaration: Grandmother was a wonderful cook.

ELDERBERRY APPLE PIE

Purple-black berries and windfall apples made this a thrifty pie—often it was served with cream

2 c. elderberries
1½ c. tart apples, peeled and chopped
1½ c. sugar
3 tblsp. quick-cooking tapioca
1 unbaked (9″) pie shell

• Wash and stem elderberries. (Hold berries in palm of hand and pull them off with wire egg beater, the kind shaped like tennis racquet.)
• Combine apples, sugar, tapioca and elderberries, crushing fruit with spoon. Fill pie shell with fruit mixture; top with pastry lattice. Bake in hot oven (425°) 10 minutes, reduce heat to moderate (350°) and bake 20 minutes longer.

AMBER PIE

From the recipe file of an Iowa farm woman who acquired a fondness for the pie at her grandmother's house

½ c. strawberry jam
½ c. sweet cream
¼ tsp. salt
3 egg yolks, slightly beaten
1½ tblsp. butter, melted
1 (9″) baked pastry shell
3 egg whites
⅓ c. sugar

• Combine first three ingredients with egg yolks. Add butter. Pour the mixture into the pastry shell. Bake in a slow oven (325°) 30 minutes or until the filling is thickened.
• Make meringue by beating egg whites until almost stiff and gradually adding sugar. Continue beating until the egg whites hold their shape. Pile the meringue on top of the pie, and bake in a moderate oven (350°) 10 minutes until it is a golden brown. Serve slightly warm.

Pie Bar: Have two, three or more kinds of pie. Let guests have their choice—adds fillip to your entertaining.

LEMON WHEY PIE

Delicate in flavor—a rare eating experience

1½ c. whey
1 c. sugar
3⅓ tblsp. cornstarch
2 egg yolks, slightly beaten
1½ tblsp. butter
½ tsp. salt
¼ c. lemon juice
1 tsp. grated lemon rind
1 (8″) baked pie shell
2 egg whites
¼ c. sugar

• Bring to boiling about 1 c. whey. Mix 1 c. sugar and cornstarch, and add to remaining cold whey to make a smooth paste. Combine mixture with hot whey and cook until thick, stirring constantly.
• Combine thickened mixture with egg yolks, butter, salt, lemon juice and rind.
• Cook 2 minutes. Pour into baked pie shell, cover with meringue made with egg whites and ¼ c. sugar; bake in slow oven (325°) until golden brown, 20 minutes.

CURRANT PIE

Good cooks' rule: Use lattice top with ripe currants; bake greener fruits between two crusts

3 c. red currants
1½ c. sugar
3 tblsp. quick-cooking tapioca
½ tsp. salt
Pastry for 2-crust (9″) pie

• Wash and stem currants. Crush slightly in bowl. Mix sugar, tapioca and salt; add to currants and stir until berries are coated with mixture.
• Pour into pastry-lined pan; top with lattice pastry. Bake in hot oven (425°) 10 minutes, reduce heat to moderate (350°) and bake 30 minutes longer, or until center is set. Top with sweetened whipped cream.

CONCORD GRAPE PIE

Many men eulogize this pie that Mother-used-to-make

5 c. Concord grapes
2 c. sugar
¾ c. flour
¼ tsp. salt
2 tblsp. lemon juice
Pastry for 2-crust (9") pie
Butter

• Seed grapes. Mix sugar, flour and salt and add to grapes. Add lemon juice. Let stand while pastry is made.
• Line pan with pastry, add grape mixture, dot with butter. Cover with pastry lattice top. Lay a pastry strip around edge of pie and crimp edges. This pastry "collar" will help hold in the juices.
• Bake in very hot oven (450°) 10 minutes, reduce heat to moderate (350°) and bake 20 to 30 minutes longer.

QUINCE CUSTARD PIE

Remembering how wonderful it tastes makes you long for homey kitchens you visited as a child

2 large ripe quinces
½ c. sugar
1 tsp. lemon juice
¼ tsp. nutmeg
¼ tsp. cinnamon
2 tblsp. melted butter or margarine
3 eggs, separated
1 c. milk
1 (9") unbaked pastry shell
⅓ c. sugar
⅛ tsp. salt

• Peel and quarter quinces. Cook until tender. Put through food mill (should yield 1 cup). Add ½ c. sugar, lemon juice, nutmeg, cinnamon and butter.
• Beat egg yolks until thick; add milk. Add to quince mixture. Pour into pastry shell.
• Bake in hot oven (425°) 10 minutes; reduce heat to moderate (350°) and bake 30 minutes or until custard sets.
• Make meringue from egg whites, ⅓ c. sugar and salt. Spread over pie. Brown in hot oven (400°) 5 minutes.

HONEY BAKED QUINCE

We give a blue ribbon to this dish

6 quinces, peeled and cored
2 tblsp. honey
⅛ tsp. grated lemon rind
1 tblsp. sugar
Water
Cream

• Place quinces in shallow baking dish. Fill each with honey with lemon rind added. Sprinkle with sugar. Add water to cover bottom of pan.
• Bake in moderate oven (350°) 1½ hours or until soft, basting occasionally. Serve with cream, plain or whipped. Makes 6 servings.

LEMON "CAKE" DESSERT

This cake-pudding makes its own sauce as it bakes

¼ c. flour
1 c. sugar
½ tsp. salt
3 egg yolks, well beaten
¼ c. lemon juice
1½ c. milk
1 tblsp. grated lemon rind
3 egg whites, stiffly beaten

• Sift together flour, sugar and salt.
• Blend together egg yolks, fruit juice, milk and rind.
• Combine liquid and dry ingredients; beat until smooth. Fold in egg whites.
• Pour into greased 8×8×2" pan; place in larger pan with hot water.
• Bake in slow oven (325°) 45 minutes. Serve warm or cold, cut in squares. Makes 6 servings.

APPLE PUDDING

Sugar and spice and everything nice—especially apples

1½ c. sifted flour
1½ tsp. baking powder
¼ tsp. salt
½ tsp. cinnamon
¼ c. butter
¾ c. sugar
2 eggs, beaten
¾ c. milk
2 c. thinly sliced apples

• Sift dry ingredients together.
• Cream butter with the sugar. Add eggs, then the dry ingredients alternately with the milk.
• Spread half of the batter in a greased 8″ to 10″ baking dish, cover with sliced apples and top with remaining batter. Bake in a moderate oven (375°) 30 minutes. Serve warm with Burnt Sugar Sauce. Makes 8 servings.

Burnt Sugar Sauce:

¾ c. sugar
2 tblsp. cornstarch
¼ tsp. salt
1 c. hot water
1 tsp. vanilla
2 tblsp. butter

• Caramelize ¼ c. sugar in heavy skillet until a light golden brown. (Do not burn.)
• Combine cornstarch, ½ c. sugar and salt, and add hot water, stirring until smooth. Cook over low heat until clear and thickened. Add hot caramelized sugar and continue cooking over low heat until well blended.
• Remove from heat, add vanilla and butter. Serve warm over apple pudding. Makes 1 cup.

Variation: Other sauces: vanilla sauce made from packaged pudding, lemon sauce, or any thickened fruit sauce.

DE LUXE MINCEMEAT

Time-consuming, but good. Some farm cooks substitute venison for beef. (See also Tomato Mincemeat in Garden chapter)

3 lbs. beef round
Water
½ lb. suet
2½ qts. apples, peeled and chopped
2 lb. seedless raisins
2 lb. dried currants
¼ lb. citron, diced
2 tblsp. candied orange peel, chopped
2 c. sugar
2 tsp. salt
4 tsp. cinnamon
2 tsp. nutmeg
2 tsp. allspice
2 tsp. ginger
1½ tsp. cloves
2 c. cider
2 c. pineapple juice
Grated rind of 1 lemon
Juice of 1 lemon
2 c. white corn syrup
¾ c. cider vinegar
¼ c. butter or margarine

• Simmer beef in small amount water until tender; remove, cool, discard bone or gristle and put meat through food chopper (medium blade). Cook down stock until ¾ c. remains.
• Grind suet fine. Combine meat, suet and apples in 2 gal. crock. Add raisins, currants, citron and orange peel.
• Combine in saucepan sugar, salt, spices, cider, pineapple juice, lemon rind, juice and syrup. Heat to boiling point. Add vinegar and butter; mix well. Add to ingredients in crock. Store, covered, in cool place 3 to 4 weeks, stirring every few days. Or package in desired amounts and freeze. Filling for 8 pies.

Mincemeat Pie:

Use 4 c. mincemeat for 2-crust (9″) pie. Bake in hot oven (400°) 25 minutes.

Apple Dumplings de luxe Crisp pastry surrounds juicy, tender fruit in this old-fashioned dessert. Dumpling recipes on page 212 in Apple chapter.

Happy Meal Endings Hostess favorites, Black Bottom Pie and refreshing Lime Parfait, page 377, are a Guest Cook's contribution (in that chapter).

Hearty Supper in a Dish Lima beans and pork sausages in bubbling hot tomato sauce. Lima Bean Barbecue recipe, page 49, in Eating Outdoors.

Cream-topped Peanut Butter Pie is one of those Dishes You Can Make Ahead (recipe in that chapter, page 295). Good traveler to community suppers.

Mincemeat Cookie Bars:

Work until crumbly ⅔ c. shortening, 1 c. light brown sugar, 2½ c. sifted flour, ½ tsp. salt and 1½ tsp. baking soda. Stir in 1½ c. quick-cooking rolled oats. Press half of mixture into greased 7×11" pan. Spread with 2 c. mincemeat. Press remaining oats mixture on top. Bake in moderate oven (375°) 25 minutes. Cut into 12 bars. Take from pan at once.

Mincemeat Pinwheels:

Roll out biscuit dough (made with 2 c. flour); brush with melted butter. Spread with 1 c. mincemeat. Roll up like jelly roll; cut in 1" slices. Place in greased muffin pans; brush with butter. Bake in moderate oven (375°) 15 minutes. Makes 12 pinwheels.

Doughnuts to Dunk

The family used to hang around the kitchen on doughnut frying days. Children settled for fried cakes with glasses of cold milk, but most adults poured coffee to go with this perfect food for dunking. While fewer doughnuts are homemade today, there are red letter occasions, such as Hallowe'en and Shrove Tuesday, when they come from kettles for quick tossing in paper bags of sugar. And the old description of well-received foods holds—they disappear like fried hot cakes!

NEW JERSEY DOUGHNUTS

Lemon-nutmeg flavor is a good cook's secret that wins compliments

½ c. butter
1 c. sugar
2 eggs
1 tsp. grated lemon rind
4½ c. sifted flour
2 tsp. baking powder
2 tsp. salt
2 tsp. nutmeg
1 c. milk

• Cream butter and sugar; add eggs and lemon rind; beat until light and fluffy.

• Sift flour with baking powder, salt, and nutmeg; add alternately with milk to creamed mixture. Mix well. Roll out on lightly floured board, and cut with doughnut cutter.

• Fry in hot fat (365°) 3 minutes. Drain on paper toweling. Makes 2 dozen.

CHOCOLATE CAKE DOUGHNUTS

Mashed potatoes make these extra good

1½ c. sugar
¼ c. melted butter or margarine
1 c. cold mashed potatoes
2 eggs, beaten
3 c. sifted flour
2 tblsp. baking powder
1 tsp. salt
1 tsp. nutmeg
½ c. cocoa
½ c. milk

• Stir sugar, butter and mashed potatoes into eggs; whip until creamy.

• Sift flour, baking powder (2 tblsp. is right), salt, nutmeg, and cocoa together; add alternately with milk to egg mixture. Mix well. Chill 2 hours.

• Roll ½" thick on lightly floured board. Cut with doughnut cutter; fry in hot fat (365°) 3 minutes. Drain on paper toweling. Makes 2 dozen.

JELLY DOUGHNUTS

We recommend this double-sweet doughnut for a coffee party

Substitute 1 c. whole wheat flour for 1 c. white flour in Spicy Raised Doughnuts. Make recipe as below, but cut dough with a 2" biscuit cutter—no hole in center. Put a teaspoonful of jelly on half of doughnuts, top with remaining doughnuts; pinch edges together. Fry in hot fat (365°) about 3 minutes. Drain on paper toweling. Sprinkle with confectioners sugar. Makes 2 dozen.

SPICY RAISED DOUGHNUTS

Sugared golden rings spiced just right—a Farm Journal 5-star recipe

2 pkgs. granular or compressed yeast
¼ c. sugar
¼ c. water
⅓ c. butter
1½ c. scalded milk
2 eggs, beaten
5 c. sifted flour
2 tsp. salt
2 tsp. nutmeg
½ tsp. cinnamon

• Sprinkle granular yeast and 1 tblsp. sugar over warm (110°) water; or crumble compressed yeast and 1 tblsp. sugar over lukewarm (85°) water; let stand 5 minutes.

• Put butter and remaining sugar in large bowl; pour in hot milk, stirring until butter melts; cool to lukewarm. Add yeast and eggs.

• Sift flour, salt and spices together, and stir into yeast mixture; mix well (this makes a soft dough). Cover with a dampened cloth; let rise in warm place until doubled.

• Turn out on lightly floured board; shape into a soft ball. Roll ½" thick; let rest 20 minutes. Cut with doughnut cutter.

• Fry 3 or 4 at a time in hot fat (365°) about 3 minutes. Drain on paper toweling; sugar while warm. Makes 3 dozen.

BAKED DOUGHNUT PUFFS

You bake these in muffin pans—no frying

2 tblsp. shortening
½ c. sugar
1 egg
2 c. sifted flour
½ tsp. salt
1 tblsp. baking powder
½ tsp. nutmeg
½ c. milk
½ c. chopped walnuts
¼ c. confectioners sugar
½ tsp. cinnamon
¼ c. melted butter

• Cream shortening, sugar and egg until light and fluffy. Sift together flour, salt, baking powder and nutmeg. Add alternately with milk to creamed mixture. Mix well (this will be a stiff dough). Stir in nuts.

• Drop from tablespoon into well greased small size muffin pans. Bake in hot oven (400°) 20 minutes.

• Combine confectioners sugar and cinnamon in paper bag. Dip top of doughnuts in melted butter; shake 2 or 3 at a time in sugar. Serve hot. Makes 1 dozen.

Old-Time Soups

WHEY TOMATO BOUILLON

Fortunate is the man who dips a spoon into a bowl of this soup

1½ c. strained tomato juice
½ small bay leaf
1 small onion, finely cut
2 whole cloves
1½ c. whey
½ tsp. salt
Dash of pepper
¼ tsp. celery salt
1 tblsp. butter
1 tblsp. whipped cream
1 tblsp. chopped parsley or paprika

• Combine tomato juice, bay leaf, onion and cloves. Bring to a boil, then turn to simmer 5 minutes.

• Add whey and strain the mixture through cheesecloth. Add seasonings and butter. Reheat bouillon and serve hot, garnished with whipped cream, chopped parsley or a dash of paprika. Makes 6 servings.

OXTAIL SOUP

One of the great beef soups, thick with vegetables

1 large oxtail (about 2½ lb.)
Flour
Fat or oil
3 qts. cold water
1 tblsp. salt
⅛ tsp. black pepper
1 bay leaf
2 sprigs parsley
½ c. chopped onion
½ c. diced turnips
½ c. chopped celery
½ c. diced carrots
1 tsp. Worcestershire sauce

• Have oxtail cut between joints. Singe to remove hairs; wash and dry. Dredge with flour and brown on all sides in hot fat in soup kettle. Add water, salt, pepper, bay leaf and parsley. Bring to boil and boil 10 minutes. Skim; cover and simmer 2 or 3 hours, or until meat is tender. Remove meat from bones and add meat to broth (or serve joints in soup if you are short of time).
• Add vegetables and simmer until they are tender. Stir in Worcestershire sauce. Serve very hot. Makes 6 to 8 servings.

Luncheon Menu: Oxtail soup, toast or crackers, hard-cooked egg and shredded lettuce salad, oatmeal cookies and applesauce.

Crisp Crackers to Serve with Soup: Brush crackers with soft butter and sprinkle with celery seeds and paprika. Brown lightly in broiler or moderate oven (350°). Poppy seeds may be substituted for celery seeds.

BORSCH

Spoon on whipped sour cream

2 lbs. beef or veal knuckle
4 cups diced beets
¼ c. lemon juice
3 medium onions, sliced
15 whole allspice
8 sprigs parsley
1 bay leaf
½ c. chopped green pepper
3 c. diced potatoes
4 c. chopped cabbage
2 c. canned tomatoes
Salt
Pepper

• Cover meat with water and simmer about 3 hours, or until rich broth is formed. Stir occasionally. Remove bone and skim fat from broth.
• Mix beets with lemon juice; add onions, allspice, bay leaf, parsley and green pepper. Add to broth and simmer 20 minutes. Add potatoes, cabbage and tomatoes and simmer until potatoes are tender. Season. Makes 10 servings.

BEAN SOUP

Pep up with grated horse-radish

2 c. dried beans
1 ham bone or 1½ lb. ham butt
½ c. chopped onion
1 c. chopped celery and leaves
1 qt. canned tomatoes
¾ c. diced potatoes
1 tsp. salt
⅛ tsp. pepper

• Wash beans, add 6 c. water and boil 2 minutes. Remove from heat and let stand 1 hour. Simmer beans without draining until tender, about 2 hours, adding more water if necessary.
• In meantime simmer ham in water to cover. Skim fat from broth and add tender beans. Stir in remaining ingredients and simmer until potatoes are tender, about 20 minutes. Makes 10 servings.

Cakes Made with Lard

CHOCOLATE CAKE

Perfect escort for vanilla ice cream

½ c. lard
2 tblsp. milk
2 c. sifted cake flour
⅔ c. cocoa
1⅓ c. sugar
1 tsp. baking powder
¾ tsp. salt
½ tsp. baking soda
1 c. thick sour milk
2 eggs
3 drops red food color

• Whip the lard and 2 tblsp. milk together, until light and fluffy, 2 minutes with mixer at medium speed.
• Add sifted dry ingredients to lard with ⅔ of the sour milk. (To make sweet milk sour, subtract 1 tblsp. milk, add 1 tblsp. vinegar.) Beat until smooth (1 minute with mixer at medium speed).
• Blend in eggs, remaining milk and food color. Beat 1 minute.
• Pour into 2 greased and floured 8″ layer pans. Bake in moderate oven (350°) 25 to 30 minutes.

WHITE CAKE

Lard gives cake old-fashioned richness

½ c. lard
1 c. milk
1 tsp. vanilla extract
1 tsp. almond extract
2¼ c. sifted cake flour
1 tblsp. baking powder
1 tsp. salt
1¼ c. sugar
3 egg whites

• Add to the lard 2 tblsp. of the milk, vanilla and almond extracts. Whip until light and fluffy, or 2 minutes with mixer at medium speed.
• Add sifted dry ingredients to lard mixture with ⅔ of the milk. Beat until smooth, or about 2 minutes with electric mixer at medium speed.
• Add remaining milk and unbeaten egg whites. Beat until smooth.
• Pour into two greased and floured 8″ layer pans. Bake in moderate oven (350°) 25 to 30 minutes.

Gold Cake: Use white cake recipe, substituting 3 unbeaten egg yolks for the 3 egg whites, and ½ tsp. lemon extract for the almond and vanilla.

SPICE CAKE

Women say it's a good keeper; men beg to eat it right away

1 c. milk
½ c. lard
1 tsp. vanilla
2¼ c. cake flour
1 tblsp. baking powder
1 tsp. salt
1¼ c. sugar
1 tsp. cinnamon
½ tsp. allspice
½ tsp. cloves
½ tsp. nutmeg
2 eggs, unbeaten

• Whip 2 tblsp. milk with lard and vanilla; cream until light (2 minutes with mixer at medium speed).
• Add sifted dry ingredients to lard mixture with ⅔ milk. Beat until smooth (2 minutes with mixer at medium speed). Add remaining milk and eggs. Beat until smooth(2 minutes). Pour into 2 greased 8″ layer pans.
• Bake in moderate oven (375°) 35 minutes. Turn on racks to cool. Frost with Mocha Frosting.

Mocha Frosting:

½ c. butter
1 egg yolk
2 tblsp. strong coffee
2 squares unsweetened chocolate
2½ c. confectioners sugar

• Cream butter; add egg yolk, coffee, melted chocolate. Mix well, gradually adding sugar.
• Blend until smooth. Makes frosting for 2 (8″) layers.

Old-Fashioned Homemade Meats

Fewer farmers butcher meat at home in this freezer and locker era, but what cook doesn't like once-in-a-blue-moon to cure and fix small quantities of old-time favorites? These recipes for corned beef, pork sausage and head cheese are classic examples of family treasures brought out occasionally in country kitchens when seasonal meat preparation is underway. They're treats any cook can be proud to serve. And what table talk they stimulate!

PORK SAUSAGE

Southern cooks like to serve fried apples with this—a fine combination

9 lbs. lean pork
¾ tsp. red pepper
3 tblsp. salt
1½ tblsp. pepper
1½ tblsp. crushed fresh sage (1 tsp. dried sage)

• Cut raw meat into cubes; grind fine in food chopper.
• Sprinkle seasonings over meat and mix well. Refrigerate or freeze. Makes about 9 lbs.

Some good cooks shape and wrap sausage in rolls that resemble refrigerator cookie dough. It's easy to slice off circles the thickness you like.

CORNED BEEF

New Englanders omit the saltpeter

1½ c. salt
1 c. sugar
¾ tsp. saltpeter
8 to 10 lbs. beef brisket

• Mix together salt, sugar and saltpeter. Cut meat in 5″ chunks. Work on heavy brown paper; rub each piece of meat thoroughly with salt mixture.
• Pack meat tightly into 2 gal. crock or enamel pan. Spread remaining salt mixture over top of meat. Cover with plate that fits tightly and weight it down. (Tight packing and salt bring juices from meat, making a curing solution. Sugar improves flavor; saltpeter gives meat a reddish color.)
• Shift top pieces to bottom after 7 days. Keep crock in refrigerator or other cool place at least 24 days before using. Then use meat within 3 weeks, washing well in cold water before cooking. Leave unused meat in cure (dilute with ½ its volume of boiling water).

CORNED BEEF WITH CABBAGE

Please pass horse-radish sauce

5 lbs. corned beef
Cold water
½ clove garlic
2 peppercorns
3 carrots, peeled and quartered
3 onions, peeled
1 head cabbage, cut in wedges

• Wash brine from corned beef, using 3 or 4 waters. Cover with cold water; add garlic and peppercorns. Simmer until meat is tender (1½ hours for young beef; up to 5 hours for older beef).
• Add carrots and onions for last hour of cooking, cabbage the last 20 minutes. Serve corned beef on platter, with vegetables around it. Makes 6 to 8 servings.

HEAD CHEESE

Hominy and hogshead cheese are musts for Christmas and New Year's breakfast in Charleston, South Carolina

1 pig's or calf's head
1 large onion, quartered
4 whole cloves
6 celery tops
4 sprigs parsley
1 carrot
1 bay leaf
12 peppercorns
2 tsp. salt
Cayenne pepper
Sage
Nutmeg (optional)

• Clean head, removing snout and reserving tongue and brains. Scrub well and place in large kettle. Cover with water; add onion, stuck with cloves, and tongue. Tie celery, parsley, carrot, bay leaf and peppercorns in cheesecloth and drop into kettle. Add salt.

• Bring to boil, skim carefully and simmer slowly about 4 hours, or until meat is tender and falls easily from bones. Remove tongue from water after it has cooked 1½ hours.

• Lift head onto a large platter. Strain and reserve liquid in kettle. Remove all rind from head; cut the meat and tongue, skin removed and excess tissue from root end, trimmed, into tiny pieces. (Some women like to put meat through food chopper.) Place in large bowl.

• Drop brains into a little of the cooking liquid; simmer, covered, 15 minutes. Remove, drain and add to meat and tongue. Season lightly with cayenne, sage and nutmeg. Toss to mix well.

• Pack mixture into 9×5×3" loaf pan or mold, pressing firmly. Pour ½ c. cooking liquid, cooled until lukewarm, over mixture. Cover pan or mold and put weight on it. Chill at least 48 hours before using. Slice to serve. Makes 18 ½" slices or 8 servings.

PRESSED CHICKEN

Grandmother teamed the chilled chicken with brown-crusted biscuits hurried from the oven

3 (3½ lb.) chickens
6 to 8 c. hot water
8 tsp. salt
1 carrot, quartered
1 c. celery, chopped
12 parsley sprigs
¾ tsp. savory
1 medium onion

• Cut chicken in pieces. Put in large kettle and add all remaining ingredients. Bring to boil; simmer until chicken is very tender.

• Remove chicken from kettle and strain broth. Return broth to heat and simmer until reduced to half its measure. Remove meat from bones; leave it in small pieces.

• Add chicken to cooked-down broth; simmer 5 minutes. Pour into 9×5×3" loaf pan, cover and weight down to press. Chill overnight. To serve cut in ½" slices. Makes 18 slices.

Old-Time Hot Breads

SWEET-CREAM CORN BREAD

This is New England johnnycake—serve with plenty of butter

¾ c. yellow cornmeal
1¼ c. sifted flour
1 tblsp. baking powder
½ tsp. salt
¼ c. sugar
2 eggs, beaten
1 c. heavy cream

• Sift dry ingredients together. Add eggs and cream. Beat vigorously until smooth. Pour into 9" square pan. Bake in hot oven (425°) about 30 minutes. Makes 8 servings.

DROP BISCUITS

Help yourself to two; split, insert butter so it can be melting in the second while you eat the first

2 c. sifted flour
1 tblsp. baking powder
1 tsp. salt
2 eggs, beaten
¾ c. heavy cream

• Sift dry ingredients together. Add eggs and cream. Stir to mix (dough should be lumpy and soft). Drop from tablespoon onto baking sheet. Bake in hot oven (400°) 15 minutes. Makes 12 large biscuits.

AM-NOR PANCAKES

Bake in waffle iron for extra-crisp waffles. They were christened Am-Nor by an American cook of Norwegian origin

1½ c. buttermilk
3 egg yolks
¼ c. shortening, melted
1½ c. sifted flour
1 tblsp. baking powder
½ tsp. baking soda
¼ tsp. salt
3 egg whites, beaten stiff

• Combine buttermilk, yolks and shortening in bowl.
• Sift together dry ingredients and add buttermilk mixture, stirring only until smooth. Fold in egg whites.
• Bake on lightly greased hot griddle, using 2 tblsp. batter for each cake and browning on both sides. Makes 18 pancakes.

TWENTIETH-CENTURY HOMINY

Grandmother used wood ashes to make hominy—a trick learned from the Indians. We've modernized the recipe

1 qt. shelled corn
2 tblsp. baking soda
1 tsp. salt

• Wash corn, add 2 qt. cold water and soda; cover and soak overnight.
• In morning bring to boil (in enamel kettle) in water in which corn soaked. Cook 3 hours or until hulls loosen. Add more water if necessary.
• Drain off water; wash corn in cold water, rubbing vigorously until hulls are removed. Bring corn to a boil with 2 qts. cold water, drain. Repeat. Add salt. Makes 1 quart. Butter and serve hot or pass gravy to ladle over hominy. Some good cooks like to fry hominy in a skillet with bacon drippings added.

OVEN APPLE BUTTER

Everyone used to take a turn stirring the purple-russet goodness

2 qts. water
2 tblsp. salt
6 lbs. apples, cored, peeled and sliced
2 qts. sweet cider
3½ to 4 c. sugar
1 tsp. cinnamon
½ tsp. cloves
½ tsp. allspice

• Combine water and salt. Add apples. Drain well but do not rinse slices.
• Grind through finest blade of food grinder. Measure pulp and juice (should be 2 qts.).
• Combine with cider. Place in large enamel pan. Center pan in moderate oven (350°). Let mixture simmer until cooked down about half and is thick and mushy (about 3 to 3½ hours). Stir thoroughly every half hour.
• Put mixture through sieve or food mill; should yield 2¼ to 2½ quarts.
• Combine sugar and spices; add to sauce and return to oven. Continue simmering about 1½ hours or until thick, stirring every half hour. To test, pour small amount onto cold plate. If no liquid oozes around edge, apple butter is cooked.
• Pour into hot, sterilized jars and seal at once. Makes 2 quarts.

How to Make Cottage Cheese

Pioneer families who kept cows used milk and cream in every possible way, and one of the favorite—but time-consuming—activities was cheese-making. Our files have a number of old-time recipes but we chose cottage cheese as something you might occasionally make for real homemade flavor. A farm homemaker (home economist) who still makes it shared her recipe with us. She—and we agree—thinks this art should not be lost.

HOMEMADE COTTAGE CHEESE

1. Pasteurize 2 gallons of skimmed milk. Cool the milk to about 75° F. in can under running water. (Without a pasteurizer, heat milk to 165° F. for 30 minutes; then cool to 75°.)

2. Transfer milk to enameled pan with cover to heat curd. Add 1 c. starter. For homemade starter, sour small amount fresh (unpasteurized) skim milk by holding at room temperature 12 to 24 hours. If cheese is made regularly, save 1 c. clabbered milk before heating curd. Keep covered in cool place.

For commercial starter, buy lactic acid culture from dairy or commercial culture laboratory. Add this to pasteurized skim milk which has been cooled to 75°. As the starter has the organisms necessary for clabbering, its use is optional; however it is a must with pasteurized milk and you get more uniform results.

3. After milk with starter has stood overnight at room temperature (70° to 75°), a firm clabber forms and a little whey appears on the surface. If it stands too long, cheese may be rubbery and strong. In cooler weather, may take 12 to 18 hours for milk to clabber.

4. Cut curd into ½″ squares by passing a long knife or spatula through it lengthwise and crosswise of the container. Don't change pans to cook curd—breaks it up too much!

5. Set pan of clabbered milk in a larger pan containing hot water—double boiler style. Heat slowly to separate whey and make small firm curds. Stir gently for even heating and avoid matting. Avoid breaking curd in unnecessarily small pieces.

6. Carefully check temperature with thermometer as it nears 100° F. Test curd by gently rubbing between fingers —should feel slightly granular. (For firmer curd, heat to 110°. Family approval will tell you when to stop.) For a rather soft curd, heat to 100° F., then keep it at that temperature until curd feels grainy. Avoid overheating!

7. Pour mixture immediately into colander lined with cheesecloth. Drain 1 to 2 minutes. Shift curd on cloth by gently lifting 1 corner.

8. Rinse curd thoroughly with cold water to wash out all whey. (Dip cheesecloth with curd in ice water to cool faster.)

9. Remove curd from cloth; add 2 tsp. salt (1 tsp. for each lb. of curd). Blend. Store, tightly covered, in cold place.

10. At serving time, fold in cream—amount depends on personal preferences. A gallon of milk makes about 1 quart cottage cheese.

24

Regional Dishes

Along the Eastern Seaboard, regional dishes developed in home kitchens of our early colonists. Mainly of English and German (Pennsylvania) ancestry, the dishes were thoroughly Americanized by the foods available and by the influence of friendly Indians.

A different type of cooking developed in the Southwest, which extends from West Texas westward to the Pacific Ocean. Even before Virginia and Massachusetts were settled, Santa Fe was founded. The favorite dishes started out as a combination of Spanish and Indian stand-bys, modified by local conditions.

Southern Louisiana is the home of our brand of Creole cooking, which originated along the Gulf of Mexico and is predominantly French with Spanish and Indian accents. The rest of the South became famous for a style of country cooking that made lavish use of the foods produced in abundance on the plantations. Put these styles of cooking together and you have the foundation for Southern regional foods that are used today.

The Midwest and West have few truly regional dishes because they were settled later by people from other areas of the United States. For instance, New Englanders emigrating to Kansas introduced Yankee dishes, just as Southerners carried their favorites next door to Missouri. Nationality groups also had a tremendous influence on Midwestern cooking—especially on breads and cookies. Some of the best foods of the Central regions still resemble their Northern European origins.

Few people today recognize the influence of native Indians on our cookery. Some of the classic national treats introduced by Indians and refined by early settlers: wild rice, baked beans, Indian pudding, corn breads, succotash, hominy, maple sugar, pinto beans, chili peppers.

You will find the regional recipes that follow grouped into four areas that correspond to the four regional editions of FARM JOURNAL— East, Central, South and West.

Recipes from Our Eastern Region

BOSTON BAKED BEANS

Salt pork in the bean pot—traditionally New England

2 lbs. pea beans (navy) (1 qt.)
1 tblsp. salt
2 to 4 tblsp. brown sugar
½ c. molasses
1 tsp. dry mustard
½ to ¾ lb. salt pork

• Wash and soak beans overnight in water to cover. Drain, place in saucepan, cover with water and simmer until skins burst, 1½ to 2 hours.
• Turn beans into bean pot or heavy casserole without draining. Combine salt, brown sugar, molasses and mustard with 1 c. boiling water; pour over beans.
• Scrape pork rind and cut gashes in fat ½" apart. Press into beans leaving only rind exposed.
• Cover pot and bake in very slow oven (275°) 6 to 8 hours without stirring, but adding more water as needed to keep beans moist. Remove cover last ½ hour of baking. Makes 8 servings.

Vermont Baked Beans: Omit brown sugar and molasses and add ½ c. maple syrup. Put an onion in bottom of pot before adding beans.

BOSTON BROWN BREAD

Spread the hot slices with butter

1 c. rye flour
1 c. yellow cornmeal
1 c. white flour
2 tsp. baking soda
1 tsp. salt
¾ c. molasses
2 c. thick sour milk or buttermilk

• Mix dry ingredients; stir in molasses and milk, mixing well, but do not beat. Fill 1½ qt. mold ⅔ full.
• Cover with tight-fitting lid or aluminum foil. Steam 3 to 3½ hours on rack in tightly-covered kettle, containing a small amount of boiling water. Makes 8 to 10 servings.

ANADAMA BREAD

Extra-special when toasted

2 c. milk
½ c. yellow cornmeal
2 tsp. salt
½ c. light or dark molasses
3 tblsp. shortening or oil
⅓ c. water
2 pkgs. granular or compressed yeast
5 c. sifted flour (about)

• Combine milk, cornmeal and salt in saucepan; heat to boiling, stirring constantly. Reduce heat; cook 5 minutes.
• Add molasses and shortening; blend. Cool to lukewarm.
• Sprinkle granular yeast over warm (110°) water or crumble compressed yeast into lukewarm (85°) water. Add softened yeast to cool cornmeal mixture.
• Add 2 c. flour; beat thoroughly.
• Add enough remaining flour to make stiff dough.
• Turn dough out on lightly floured board; let rest 10 minutes. Knead until smooth and elastic—about 10 minutes.
• Place in well greased bowl; turn once to bring up greased side. Cover; set in warm place (80° to 85°) to rise until doubled, about 40 minutes.
• Without punching down, turn out on floured board. Divide in half; shape into 2 loaves. Place in greased 9×5×3" pans.
• Cover, and let rise again until doubled, about 40 minutes.
• Bake in moderate oven (375°) about 50 minutes. Turn out of pans, cool on rack. Makes 2 loaves.

BOSTON CREAM PIE

Cinderella of American desserts—plain one-egg cake in glamorous dress

2 c. sifted cake flour
1¼ c. sugar
2½ tsp. baking powder
1 tsp. salt
⅓ c. shortening
1 c. milk
1 tsp. vanilla
¼ tsp. almond extract (optional)
1 egg, unbeaten

• Sift dry ingredients into mixing bowl. Add shortening, milk, vanilla and almond extract. Beat 2 minutes (mixer at medium speed) or 300 strokes by hand.
• Add egg; beat 2 minutes as before. Pour into two greased 8" or 9" round layer pans.
• Bake in moderate oven (350°) 25 to 30 minutes. Makes 2 layers. Use one to make Boston Cream Pie; freeze the other.
• Split cooled cake layer in crosswise halves. Spread Custard Cream Filling over lower half. Cover with top half. Dust with confectioners sugar. Or spread with Chocolate Icing.

Custard Cream Filling:

Smooth as velvet and one of the great delicacies of country kitchens

1 c. milk, scalded
½ c. sugar
3 tblsp. cornstarch
⅛ tsp. salt
2 eggs, slightly beaten
1 tblsp. butter or margarine
1 tsp. vanilla

• Gradually add milk to mixture of sugar, cornstarch and salt. Cook slowly, stirring constantly, until mixture thickens (about 10 to 15 minutes).
• Add about ½ c. hot mixture to eggs and blend; carefully combine both mixtures and cook about 3 minutes, stirring constantly.
• Remove from heat; blend in butter and vanilla. Cool. Makes 1¼ cups.

FILLING VARIATIONS:

Banana: Spread custard filling between halves of split cake layer. Cover custard with banana slices (1 medium to large banana, sliced and sprinkled with lemon juice) and top with remaining cake.

Pineapple: Combine 1 c. cooled filling with ½ c. drained crushed pineapple just before spreading between split cake. Pineapple may also be added to all the following variations.

Orange-Pineapple: Add 1 tsp. grated orange rind to pineapple filling.

Coconut: Add ⅔ c. flaked or cut shredded coconut to custard filling.

Chocolate Icing:

When this frosting tops the dessert in Boston, it's called Chocolate Cream Pie

2 tblsp. butter or shortening
2 squares melted chocolate
¼ tsp. salt
½ tsp. vanilla
2¼ c. sifted confectioners sugar
¼ to ⅓ c. milk

• Blend together shortening, chocolate, salt and vanilla. Add sugar alternately with milk. Beat until smooth. If thinner glaze is desired, add a little more liquid.

HURRY-UP BOSTON CREAM PIE

• Use 1 (1 lb. ½ oz.) package Boston Cream Pie, containing packets for: yellow cake mix, cream filling mix and chocolate icing mix. Follow directions in package for preparing each and for combining. Makes one 8" or 9" cake.

WASHINGTON PIE

• Bake cake as for Boston Cream Pie. Put cool, split layers together with jelly; sprinkle top generously with confectioners sugar. Serve cut in wedges like pie.

LITTLE INDIAN PUDDING

Family-size recipe—you may wish to double it

⅓ c. yellow cornmeal
⅓ c. cold water
1 qt. whole milk
½ tsp. salt
½ tsp. cinnamon
½ tsp. ginger
½ c. molasses

• Combine cornmeal and water. Scald milk, add cornmeal mixture, stirring to prevent lumps. Cook 20 minutes or until thickened. Add salt, spices and molasses.
• Pour into a 1½ qt. greased casserole or baking dish; bake in slow oven (325°) at least 2 hours. Serve warm with heavy cream, vanilla ice cream or hard sauce. Makes 6 servings.

ELECTION DAY CAKE

Spicy, raisin coffee bread—traditionally served in Hartford, Connecticut on Election Day

Sponge:

¾ c. milk
1 pkg. granular or compressed yeast
¼ c. water
1 tsp. sugar
1 c. sifted flour

Cake:

½ c. butter or margarine
1 c. brown sugar
1 egg, beaten
1 c. raisins
⅓ c. citron, chopped
1½ c. sifted flour
1 tsp. cinnamon
¼ tsp. cloves
¼ tsp. nutmeg
1 tsp. salt

• Scald milk; cool until lukewarm.
• Sprinkle granular yeast over warm (110°) water or crumble compressed yeast into lukewarm (85°) water. Stir in sugar. Let stand until yeast mixture is bubbly, about 5 minutes. Add to milk. Stir in flour, beat until smooth; let stand in warm place (85°) until doubled.
• Cream butter and brown sugar; add egg and beat well. Stir in raisins and citron. Sift together dry ingredients and stir into creamed mixture, beating well.
• Mix sponge and cake batter until well blended. Turn into greased 5½×9½" loaf pan (pan should be no more than half full). Let rise in warm place until doubled.
• Bake in moderate oven (375°) 45 minutes. Frost while warm with confectioners sugar frosting. Makes 16 servings.

RED FLANNEL HASH

Quick version of the traditional hash—with coleslaw and apple pie, it's a complete dinner

4 c. chopped cooked potatoes
1½ c. chopped cooked beets
½ c. chopped onions, peeled
1 clove garlic, minced or crushed
1 (12 oz.) can diced cooked corned beef
½ c. light cream
½ tsp. salt
⅛ tsp. pepper
½ tsp. dry mustard
6 eggs
Seasonings
Chopped parsley

• Mix all ingredients but eggs and parsley. Place in greased 2 qt. casserole.
• Bake, covered, in moderate oven (350°) 25 minutes.
• Remove cover; shape 6 holes in hash with back of spoon. Drop 1 egg in each. Season. Bake 20 minutes more. Sprinkle with parsley. Serve hot. Makes 6 servings.

PHILADELPHIA SCRAPPLE

Buckwheat flour is the secret of its fine flavor—plus slow browning

2 lbs. lean bony pork
2 qts. water
1 tblsp. salt
Pepper
½ tsp. sage or poultry seasoning
⅛ tsp. mace
1 c. fine cornmeal
½ c. buckwheat flour

• Put meat in kettle; add 1½ qts. water, salt and pepper; simmer until meat is very tender. Skim fat from top, strain off broth and set aside.

• Remove meat from bones and chop it fine (do not grind). Pour broth into saucepan; add meat, sage and mace and bring to boil.

• Combine cornmeal and buckwheat; slowly stir 2 c. cold water into mixture. Add a little at a time to meat, keeping it simmering continuously. Stir until mixture reaches the consistency of soft mush. Lower heat so scrapple will not scorch (or cook over boiling water 1 hour), stirring occasionally.

• Pour into two 9×5×3" pans, rinsed with cold water. Chill.

• To cook, turn scrapple out of pan and cut in ¼" to ½" slices. Lay them, so slices do not touch, in a cold, heavy skillet. Set over moderate heat; let brown slowly but thoroughly on one side; repeat for other side. It may take about 30 minutes to brown scrapple properly. Makes 8 to 14 servings.

For extra flavor, add 2 slices pork liver, chopped, with pork.

Good Eating—Central USA

HOME-STYLE BAKED BEANS

When you travel west from the Atlantic shore, a taste of baked beans will tell you when you have reached the Midwest. Here they carry the flavor of tomatoes and, as if that were not enough, ketchup is served with them. Ohio is the first state where you'll find the tomato-bean combination.

HOOSIER BEAN SUPPER

Baked Beans — Baked Ham
Coleslaw
Chili Sauce — Mixed Pickles
Hot Rolls
Apple Pie
Milk — Coffee

BAKED BEANS

2 lbs. navy or pea beans (1 qt.)
1 tsp. salt
3 tblsp. brown sugar
⅓ c. molasses
2 tsp. dry mustard
2 (1 lb.) cans tomatoes (1 qt.)
1 medium onion, sliced
¾ lb. fat salt pork

• Cover beans with cold water and soak overnight. Drain, add cold water to cover and simmer until skins burst, 1 to 1½ hours. Turn into heavy casserole or bean pot without draining.

• Combine salt, brown sugar, molasses, mustard, tomatoes and onion; add to beans. If liquid does not cover beans, add hot water.

• Scrape salt pork rind and cut deep gashes in fat ½" apart. Press into beans leaving only rind exposed. Cover and bake in slow oven (275°) 6 to 8 hours, adding more water as needed to keep beans covered. Remove cover during last half hour of baking. Serve with ketchup or chili sauce. Makes 8 to 12 servings.

WILD RICE

A delicacy with wild duck, pheasant or barnyard fowls—harvested by Minnesota and Wisconsin Indians, so much enjoyed across country it's become a luxury

1 c. rice
4 c. boiling water
1 tblsp. salt
Butter
Salt
Pepper

• Cover rice with water; let stand uncovered 20 minutes. Drain and repeat 3 times, using fresh boiling water each time, adding salt the last time. Add butter, salt and pepper to season. Keep warm in oven or double boiler until last minute before serving. Makes 3 cups.

PERSIMMON DATE PUDDING

This is the dessert they're dreaming about when they sing: Back Home Again in Indiana

1¼ c. sifted flour
1½ tsp. baking soda
1½ tsp. baking powder
½ tsp. salt
1 c. sugar
½ c. soft bread crumbs
1 c. native persimmon pulp (skinned)
1 c. chopped dates
1 c. chopped walnuts
1 tsp. vanilla
1½ tblsp. melted butter
½ c. milk

• Sift together flour, soda, baking powder, salt and sugar. Combine and add all dry ingredients. Mix well.
• Add remaining ingredients.
• Line one 8½×4½×2½" loaf pan with brown paper and grease. Spoon in pudding mixture.
• Bake in moderate oven (350°) 1½ hours. Serve hot or cold with hard sauce, ice cream or whipped cream. Makes 10 to 12 servings.

Pudding keeps 2 to 3 weeks in refrigerator or it may be packaged and frozen. (See directions for freezing persimmons in Freezer Chapter.)

WISCONSIN CRANBERRY PUDDING

Come Thanksgiving or Christmas in Wisconsin and steaming cranberry puddings, drenched with rich butter sauce, will end thousands of festive family dinners. The dessert caught on in early days, for the bright red berries grew wild in many areas of the Badger state. Now they're an important commercial crop. The recipe:

CRANBERRY PUDDING

1⅓ c. flour
½ c. molasses, mild flavored
2 c. whole raw cranberries
¼ c. chopped nuts
2 tsp. baking soda
⅓ c. hot water

• Combine flour, molasses, cranberries and nuts in a bowl.
• Add soda to the hot water and pour into bowl. Mix lightly.
• Pour into greased 1 qt. mold. Cover tightly with foil. Steam over boiling water 1½ hours. Serve warm with Vanilla Sauce. Makes 6 servings.
• Double recipe for a larger mold. Add another hour of steaming.

Vanilla Sauce: Combine 1 c. sugar, 2 tsp. flour, ½ c. butter or margarine and ½ c. light cream. Bring to boil over low heat. Cook 2 to 3 minutes. Add ¼ tsp. vanilla. Serve hot.

Variation: Brown sugar and butter sauce is the traditional holiday companion in Wisconsin to Cranberry Pudding. To make it, melt ½ c. butter, add ½ c. brown sugar and ½ c. heavy cream. Bring to a boil; add ½ tsp. vanilla. Serve warm. Makes about 6 servings.

Corn's Popping

Popcorn and winter evenings go together in the Midwest. Muffled sounds of kernels bursting inside the popper are tantalizing music. Popcorn balls make ideal party food for youngsters. The following recipes for fun-time popcorn come from farm kitchens.

POPCORN BALLS

Packages of the snowy white balls go from home to youngsters away at school

5 qts. popped corn (20 c.)
4 c. sugar
2 tsp. salt
1 c. water
2 tblsp. butter or margarine
¼ tsp. cream of tartar

• Turn popped corn into bowl. Cook other ingredients to firm ball stage (245°). Pour syrup over corn, stirring gently to coat kernels.
• Butter hands and quickly shape corn into 2″ balls. Makes 20 balls.

CHOCOLATE POPCORN BALLS

Here's just the snack for nibblers with a sweet tooth

1 c. sugar
½ c. water
⅓ c. corn syrup
3 tblsp. butter or margarine
3 squares unsweetened chocolate, melted
5 c. popped corn

• Bring first five ingredients to a boil and cook to the hard ball stage (254°). Pour slowly over popped corn in large bowl. Mix quickly. Butter hands and shape into 2″ balls. Makes 12 balls.

MOLASSES POPCORN BALLS

An old-fashioned treat—always welcome

1¾ c. light molasses
2 c. sugar
⅔ c. water
2 tsp. vinegar
½ tsp. baking soda
3½ qts. popped corn, salted

• Combine molasses, sugar, water and vinegar. Cook to hard ball stage (250°). Remove from heat; wipe crystals off pan.
• Add soda; stir to mix thoroughly. Pour over corn, mixing well. Shape into balls. Makes 12 balls.

TRICKS WITH POPPED CORN

Cheese: Add ⅓ c. dry, grated sharp cheese to ¼ c. melted butter. Pour over freshly popped, salted corn, toss lightly and serve at once.

Peanut: When melting butter to pour over hot popped corn, add a spoonful of peanut butter. It blends with the butter and gives a pleasing flavor.

Popcorn Valentine: Press popped corn, coated with syrup, into heart-shaped mold or molds while it is warm and pliable. Allow to cool. Turn out on plate. Slice to serve. Syrup may be tinted pink before it is poured over corn.

Quick Caramel Corn: Melt ½ lb. light caramel candy with 2 tblsp. water over boiling water; stir to make smooth sauce. Pour mixture over 2 qts. salted popcorn to coat kernels; spread on lightly greased baking sheet. Cool; break apart.

Popcorn-On-Sticks: Grease hands lightly; then form popcorn cylinders to put on sticks. You can make cylinders by lightly pressing syrup-coated corn into small, greased juice cans. Remove can bottoms to push out cylinders. Insert a wooden skewer into every cylinder of popped corn.

From Good Cooks in Dixie

SOUTHERN PECAN PIE

A young cousin of chess pie

1 c. pecan halves
1 (9") unbaked pie shell
3 eggs
1 c. light corn syrup
1 tblsp. melted butter or margarine
½ tsp. vanilla
1 c. sugar
1 tblsp. flour

• Arrange nuts in pie shell.
• Beat eggs; add and blend corn syrup, butter and vanilla.
• Combine sugar and flour. Blend with egg mixture and pour over nuts in pie shell. Let stand until nuts rise, so they'll get a nice glaze during baking.
• Bake in moderate oven (350°) 45 minutes.

CHESS PIE

It originated in England, was adopted in the South and is the dessert folks from Dixie long for when they're up North

1 c. brown sugar, packed
½ c. granulated sugar
1 tblsp. flour
2 eggs
2 tblsp. milk
1 tsp. vanilla
½ c. butter, melted
1 c. pecans, chopped
1 (8") unbaked pastry shell

• Mix sugars and flour; thoroughly beat in eggs, milk, vanilla and butter. Fold in pecans. Bake in moderate oven (375°) until just set. Serve slightly warm, plain or with whipped cream.

Note: There are many ways to make Chess Pie. This recipe came from a Southern farm kitchen.

PEANUT PIE

Selected from a recipe collection of a good North Carolina cook

1 c. dark corn syrup
3 eggs, unbeaten
3 tblsp. flour
2 tblsp. melted butter
¼ tsp. salt
1 c. whole toasted peanuts
1 (8") unbaked pastry shell

• Combine syrup, eggs, flour, butter and salt in mixing bowl. Beat with rotary beater 60 turns only.
• Spread toasted peanuts in bottom of unbaked pastry shell. Pour liquid mixture over top. Bake in moderate oven (350°) 30 minutes.

To Toast Peanuts: Place shelled nuts in shallow pan in moderate oven (350°) about 10 minutes, or until nuts are slightly brown.

PEANUT SOUR CREAM CANDY

You'll hunt a long time before you find a better-tasting sweet

2 c. sugar
⅛ tsp. salt
1 c. dairy sour cream
⅛ tsp. cinnamon
½ tsp. vanilla
3 drops almond extract
1 c. peanuts

• Mix sugar, salt and cream, and boil gently, without stirring, to firm ball stage (245°). Cool to lukewarm; add flavorings and beat until creamy.
• Fold in peanuts, and pour into buttered shallow pan. When cool, cut into squares. Makes 48 squares.

SKILLET TOASTED PEANUTS

• Sauté 1 c. raw, shelled peanuts in 2 tblsp. butter or margarine about 5 minutes. Drain on paper toweling and salt.

CRISP PEANUTS

Heat salted peanuts in moderate oven (350°) before serving. Cool to crisp. Toss with raisins if you like. Unshelled peanuts also may be heated to crisp.

Peanut Pointers:

• Blend ½ c. ground peanuts into 2 c. of tangy cheese sauce for baked macaroni and cheese.

• Blend together ¾ c. applesauce, ½ c. peanut butter, and ½ c. prepared marshmallow whip for a yummy filling between cake layers. Frost whole cake with plain white icing.

• Add ½ c. peanut butter to your regular graham cracker pie crust recipe—it's different and delicious!

• Cover your favorite coffee cake batter with this Peanut Crunch Topping: Combine and blend together until fine like crumbs, ¾ c. flour, ½ c. sugar, 3 tblsp. butter and 1 c. finely ground peanuts.

• Add 2 c. coarsely ground peanuts to ½ gallon Vanilla Ice Cream recipe for Peanut Ice Cream.

SPOONBREAD

Rush it to the table

1 c. white cornmeal
3 c. milk
1 tsp. salt
2 tblsp. butter or margarine
4 eggs, separated

• Mix cornmeal, milk and salt together in top of double boiler. Cook over boiling water to a thick mush, about 15 minutes, stirring constantly at the finish.
• Add butter. Cool mixture slightly and add beaten egg yolks. Fold in stiffly beaten egg whites.
• Pour mixture into a well greased 12×8×2" shallow baking dish. Bake in hot oven (400°) 30 minutes. Serve immediately with butter, spooning right from the baking dish. Makes 8 servings.

OLD VIRGINIA SALLY LUNN

Rich, light, tender almost cake-like bread, yet not sweet—A Farm Journal 5-star recipe

2 c. milk
1 c. shortening
2 pkgs. granular or compressed yeast
3 eggs, beaten
4 tblsp. sugar
2 tsp. salt
6 c. sifted flour

• Scald milk, add shortening to melt. Cool. Add yeast when warm (110°) if granular yeast, when lukewarm (85°) if compressed yeast.
• Stir in beaten eggs, sugar, and salt. Mix well. Stir in flour and beat thoroughly. Cover and let rise in warm place (80° to 85°) until doubled, about 1 hour.
• Punch down. Spoon into greased 9" ring mold or tube pan; let double again.
• Bake in moderate oven (350°) 1 hour. Makes 16 servings.

HUSH PUPPIES

They star in fish fries

2 c. white cornmeal
1 tblsp. flour
½ tsp. baking soda
1 tsp. salt
1 egg, beaten
3 tblsp. finely chopped onion
1 c. buttermilk

• Mix dry ingredients; add beaten egg, onion and buttermilk. Mix well and drop by tablespoonfuls into deep hot fat (360° to 375°). When they float, they are cooked. Remove from kettle and drain. Serve hot. Makes 20 to 25 hush puppies.

LANE CAKE

Good cooks in Georgia and Alabama say this is the finest cake developed in Southern kitchens

Cake:

1 c. butter or margarine
2 c. sugar
3¼ c. sifted cake flour
2 tsp. baking powder
1 c. milk
1 tsp. vanilla
8 egg whites, stiffly beaten

Filling:

½ c. butter or margarine
1 c. sugar
8 egg yolks, beaten
1 c. seeded raisins, chopped
1 c. chopped pecans
1 tsp. vanilla

Frosting:

2½ c. sugar
⅛ tsp. salt
⅓ c. dark corn syrup
⅔ c. water
2 egg whites, beaten until foamy
1 tsp. vanilla

• Cream butter and sugar for cake. Sift flour and baking powder and add to creamed mixture alternately with milk and vanilla. Fold in egg whites. Pour into three 9" layer pans. Bake in moderate oven (350°) until golden brown.
• Cream butter and sugar for filling. Add egg yolks, and cook in double boiler until thick. Add remaining ingredients and spread between cooled layers of cake.
• To make frosting, dissolve sugar, salt and syrup in water. Cook mixture; when it reaches boiling point, pour 3 tblsp. into egg whites. Continue beating eggs until stiff but not dry. Add vanilla. Boil syrup mixture to 240°, or until it spins a thread at least 10" long when dropped from edge of spoon. Then pour syrup slowly over egg whites, beating until frosting is thick, cool and of good spreading consistency. Spread over cake. If the frosting becomes hard, add a drop or two of hot water to the mixture. This frosting does not form a crust that cracks when cake is cut. Makes enough frosting for a 3-layer (9") cake.

TENNESSEE TURKEY HASH

Here's a famous southern dish to salvage left over turkey

2 to 3 tblsp. butter or margarine
¼ c. chopped green pepper
¼ c. chopped celery
2 c. cut up cooked turkey
3 c. gravy, made with water
½ tsp. onion juice
2 tblsp. sharp cheese, grated
2 hard-cooked eggs, sliced

• Melt butter in heavy skillet and lightly brown green pepper and celery. Add turkey (you may include cut up giblets), gravy and onion juice.
• Bring mixture to boil; simmer gently 10 to 15 minutes to blend flavors. Just before serving, add cheese and eggs. Makes 6 servings.

SCALLOPED OYSTERS

Superb Sunday supper main dish—enjoyed along the Atlantic Seaboard

2½ c. coarse cracker crumbs
1 pt. oysters, drained
¼ c. oyster liquor
¾ c. cream or top milk
1 tsp. Worcestershire sauce
½ tsp. salt
⅛ tsp. pepper
⅓ c. butter or margarine

• Arrange ⅓ of the crumbs in well buttered, shallow 1 qt. baking dish. Cover with ½ of oysters; repeat layer of crumbs and remaining oysters.
• Blend liquids and seasonings; pour over oysters. Cover with remaining crumbs and dot with butter.
• Bake in moderate oven (350°) about 45 minutes. Makes 5 servings.

Good Food from West of the Rockies

ORIENTAL PERSIMMONS

This is the fruit that in autumn brightens fruit counters with its lantern-shape glow. These persimmons have been favored in China and Japan for centuries; they are now grown commercially in California and Florida. Select fully ripe fruit for best flavored dishes. A ripe persimmon is very soft and its salmon-pink skin is darker at the top.

PERSIMMON-GRAPEFRUIT SALAD

California's Thanksgiving salad

6 Oriental persimmons
3 grapefruit
1 avocado

• Wash and peel persimmons. Peel and section grapefruit. Peel and slice avocado, dipping slices in grapefruit juice to prevent darkening.
• Arrange fruit on salad greens on individual plates. Makes 6 servings.

OREGON PEAR PIE

Northwestern cooks team their magnificent pears with brown sugar

1 (9") baked pastry shell
6 pear halves, drained
⅓ c. brown sugar
5 tblsp. flour
⅛ tsp. salt
¼ tsp. cinnamon (optional)
2 c. milk, scalded
2 eggs, separated
4 tblsp. sugar

• Use either canned or freshly cooked pears. Slice or cut in quarters. Let drain while preparing custard.
• Mix dry ingredients. Pour milk over dry mixture. Slowly add beaten egg yolks. Cook and stir over low heat or in double boiler until mixture thickens. Remove from heat; cool.
• Arrange pears in baked pastry shell; carefully pour egg yolk mixture over them.
• Top with meringue made by beating egg whites, gradually adding sugar. Bake in slow oven (325°) 25 to 30 minutes.

Variation: Substitute canned apricot halves for pears.

DATE BUTTER

Californians use this rich sweet in many appealing dishes

2 (7 oz.) pkgs. pitted dates
¾ c. water

• Chop or cut up dates. Add water.
• Cover; cook over medium heat until mixture boils; reduce heat, cook about 10 minutes or until dates are mushy. Stir occasionally. Makes 1¾ cups.

DATE CANDY

Coconut and cherries add bright contrast to dates

2 c. date butter
½ c. chopped nuts
½ c. flaked coconut
¼ c. sliced candied cherries

• Blend ingredients; chill. Shape into balls, then roll in additional coconut. Makes about 30 candies.

DATE TURNOVERS

• Place pitted date on 2" circles biscuit dough (¼" thick), fold over, press edges together. Bake in hot oven (450°) 12 to 15 minutes.

CHOW MEIN

1½ lbs. lean pork, thinly sliced
¼ c. cornstarch
2 tsp. sugar
5 tblsp. soy sauce
2 tblsp. oil
2 tblsp. fat
2 c. water
½ tsp. monosodium glutamate
1½ c. celery, sliced
1 c. onions, chopped or sliced
1 tblsp. molasses
1 (8 oz.) can water chestnuts, sliced
1 (1 lb. 4 oz.) can bean sprouts (2 c.)
1 (4 oz.) can sliced mushrooms, drained
Salt and pepper
1 bunch small green onions
Toasted whole blanched almonds

• Cut meat into thin strips.
• Combine 2 tblsp. cornstarch and sugar; blend in 1 tblsp. soy sauce and oil. Let meat stand in this mixture 10 minutes. Brown lightly on all sides in hot fat; add remaining soy sauce, 1½ c. water and monosodium glutamate; simmer 45 minutes. Add celery and onion; simmer 10 to 15 minutes.
• Blend remaining cornstarch and ½ c. water; stir into meat mixture. Add molasses, water chestnuts, bean sprouts and mushrooms; heat thoroughly. Season with salt and pepper.
• Garnish with green onions, cut in lengthwise strips, and toasted whole almonds. Serve with canned crisp fried noodles. Makes 6 to 8 servings.

Two Hawaiian Meats

Good cooks in Hawaii are clever at harmoniously blending Western and Oriental recipes. Fresh pineapple is used extravagantly and deliciously. Long spears of the honey-colored fruit make stirrers for glasses of iced tea. And white layer cakes, covered with soft, cooked frosting, literally drip with fresh coconut. The two recipes that follow illustrate how Hawaiians cook meat.

HAWAIIAN SPARERIBS

No sweet-sour spareribs surpass these

2 lbs. spareribs
2 tblsp. shortening
1 clove garlic, chopped
1 tsp. ginger
¼ c. soy sauce
½ c. vinegar
2 tblsp. sugar
2 c. hot water
Cornstarch

• Cut ribs in 2" pieces; brown in hot shortening. Combine garlic, ginger, soy sauce, vinegar and sugar and pour over ribs. Add hot water.
• Simmer until meat is tender, about 45 minutes. Remove meat and thicken liquid in pan with cornstarch (about 2 tblsp.). Reheat ribs in gravy and serve with rice. Makes 6 servings.

HAWAIIAN SOY STEAK

Serve hot in buns for tasty sandwiches

2 lbs. sirloin or sirloin tips
2 tblsp. dry ginger root or 1 tsp. ground ginger
⅓ c. soy sauce
⅔ c. water
3 tblsp. sugar
1 clove garlic, crushed
6 tomatoes
3 green peppers

• Pound meat, score by slashing against the grain and cut in thin strips ½" thick ×4×3". Mix in bowl, ginger, soy sauce, water, sugar and garlic. Add steak strips; chill at least 1 hour.
• At mealtime slice tomatoes and green peppers into broiler pan; broil 5 minutes. Then put meat above them on rack. Cook 4" from heat until meat browns on both sides, about 5 minutes.

Variation: Substitute lamb chops for the steak.

Southwestern Dishes

South-of-the-Border influences show up in Southwestern cooking and one is the use of chili peppers (made from the hot peppers with pointed ends). They're as universal in kitchens of the Southwest and California as salt. The following recipes are from Southwestern ranch kitchens. Let your conscience and your palate be your guide!

CHILI CON CARNE

Pinto beans make this an authentic dish of Colorado and New Mexico

1 lb. pinto beans
¼ c. chopped onion
2 cloves garlic, minced
3 tblsp. fat
¼ c. chili powder
1 tblsp. flour
1 tblsp. salt
3 lbs. ground or cubed beef
1 qt. canned tomatoes, strained
1 tsp. oregano

• Soak beans overnight; cook tender.
• Brown onion and garlic in fat.
• Blend chili powder, flour and salt; add to onion and garlic. Add beans and meat. Cover and cook 1 hour.
• Add tomatoes, oregano. Cover, simmer 1½ hours. Makes 8 to 10 servings.

SOPAIPILLAS

A heritage from good Mexican cooks

2 c. sifted flour
1 tsp. baking powder
1 tsp. salt
1 tblsp. shortening
¾ c. cold water (about)

• Sift dry ingredients. Cut in shortening, add water, shape into a ball.
• Form dough in 6 balls.
• Roll each into very thin rounds. Cut in wedge shapes and fry in hot fat (375°) about 4 minutes, or until puffed and golden brown. Makes 3 dozen.

TORTILLAS

An adapted recipe for the big, thin cornmeal tortillas of the Southwest

½ c. cornmeal
¾ c. prepared pancake mix
1⅓ c. milk
1 egg, slightly beaten

• Combine cornmeal and pancake mix.
• Blends liquids; add to dry ingredients.
• Drop by spoonfuls on hot greased griddle. Spread batter out with spoon, pancake size. Turn when lightly brown. Place on pan and put in warm oven until serving time. Makes 1½ dozen.

ENCHILADAS

Stack 3 tortillas to make enchiladas for a woman, 5 for a hungry man

2 (8 oz.) cans tomato sauce
1 c. water
1 tsp. chili powder
1½ dozen tortillas
1½ c. grated process cheese
1½ c. onion rings
9 eggs, scrambled
1½ c. shredded lettuce

• Combine tomato sauce, water and chili powder; bring to a boil.
• Dip 6 tortillas in sauce. Place on flat baking pan. Sprinkle with ⅓ of the cheese and onions. Dip 6 more tortillas in sauce; place on top of first layer. Repeat, using remaining cheese, onions, and tortillas.
• Heat in hot oven (400°) 10 minutes.
• Cook scrambled eggs.
• Remove pan from oven. Top each stack with lettuce and eggs.
• Heat remaining sauce to serve with enchiladas. Makes 6 servings.

Variation: Circle enchiladas with shredded lettuce and dabs of guacamole.

TOSTADOS

This hearty dish calls for a tossed green or pineapple salad

1 lb. bulk pork sausage
1 (1 lb. 4 oz.) can kidney beans, drained
⅛ tsp. Tabasco sauce
½ tsp. dry mustard
½ tsp. salt
6 tortillas
1 c. process cheese

• Break up sausage with a fork and brown in frying pan. Remove the meat. Drain off all but about 2 tablespoons of fat. Fry beans. Add sausage and seasonings, and mix.

• Lay tortillas on baking pan. Spread each with sausage mixture. Sprinkle with cheese, shredded or grated.

• Bake in hot oven (400°) 10 minutes, or until cheese melts. Makes 6 servings.

GUACAMOLE

Our choice of the many good recipes for this Mexican favorite

2 large avocados, mashed
1 large ripe tomato, peeled, finely chopped and drained
1 large onion, finely chopped
1 clove garlic, grated (optional)
3 tblsp. mayonnise or salad dressing
1 tblsp. oil
2 tsp. chili powder
2 tsp. sugar
Salt
Pepper

• Blend all the ingredients together. Serve on lettuce, on tomato slices, as spread for toast (top with crisp bacon), as dip for corn and potato chips and with Mexican dishes. Makes 1¼ to 1½ cups.

MEXICAN BEAN POT

Mighty good—serve tomato or pineapple salad, too

2 c. dried kidney beans (or 4 c. cooked or canned)
1 tblsp. salt
6 slices bacon
4 tblsp. drippings or shortening
1 clove garlic, minced or crushed
Pinch of thyme
Small bay leaf
2 whole cloves
2 tsp. dry mustard
⅛ tsp. cayenne
2 tblsp. vinegar
½ c. spicy juice (from sweet pickles, spiced fruit)
¼ c. strong coffee
6 onion slices

• Cover beans with 6 c. water. Boil 2 minutes; then soak 1 hour, or overnight.

• Fry bacon until half cooked; drain fat to make 4 tblsp. Add fat to beans (fat keeps beans from foaming).

• Simmer until tender, about 2 hours.

• Drain beans; combine with other ingredients except bacon, coffee and sliced onion.

• Place in 1½ qt. casserole. Bake in moderate oven (350°) 1 hour.

• Pour coffee over beans. Garnish top with bacon and onion slices.

• Bake in hot oven (400°) about 20 minutes, until bacon is crisp. Makes 6 servings.

25

Guest Cooks in Our Test Kitchens

An air of excitement invades our Countryside Kitchens when we're expecting a Guest Cook to demonstrate some of her best dishes. Not only does the food staff gather 'round, but as aromas drift down the corridors, the whole editorial staff offers taste-testing services!

Farm women we have invited to visit us through the years are known in their neighborhoods, counties or parishes as top cooks. Frequently we meet them through Home Demonstration Agents. Many of them, too, are members of FARM JOURNAL's Test Group of 500 farm and ranch families. Guest cooks have come to us from all regions and many states to represent farm women in their respective areas. And what pleasant surprises they bring from their farms!

Visits of gifted country cooks are friendly days in our Countryside Kitchens. There's lots of neighborly chatting and recipe swapping. These women not only prepare dishes for us, but they tell us how they entertain. We learn about cooking problems and the kind of recipes they like to see in FARM JOURNAL.

We believe you'll agree that the recipes in this chapter are exceptional. For instance, there's a nut loaf, introduced to us in our Kitchens by an Iowa woman back in 1951. It's now a FARM JOURNAL 5-star recipe. You'll find a chicken recipe from a Guest Cook who lives on the banks of the Delaware River; a Thanksgiving dinner from Virginia's Shenandoah Valley; desserts from a Mississippi plantation; barbecued pot roast from Colorado's western slope; rice ice cream from Arkansas—but there's no need to enumerate further the delights that follow. You'll want to see for yourself.

Holiday Buffet Supper

One of our Guest Cooks from the Midwest reproduced her attractive Christmas buffet supper in our Test Kitchens. She brought along two charming helpers, her young daughters, and the merry trio of good cooks set out a tempting array of country foods. Much of the food can be made ready in advance.

We give you her menu, main dish and nut loaf recipes.

BUFFET SUPPER

Scalloped Chicken
Asparagus with Cheese Sauce
Frosty Fruit Salad
Pickles and Jams
Orange Coverleaf Rolls
Coffee Milk
Nut Loaf

ALICE'S SCALLOPED CHICKEN

Cook the chicken days in advance, discard bones and store meat in freezer

- **1 (5 to 6 lb.) stewing hen**
- **1 c. chicken fat**
- **1⅛ c. flour**
- **1 tblsp. salt**
- **¼ tsp. white pepper**
- **4½ c. chicken broth**
- **2 c. rich milk**
- **4 c. day-old bread, toasted and cubed**
- **¼ c. chopped onion**
- **1 c. chopped celery**
- **1 tsp. salt**
- **½ to 1 tsp. sage**
- **⅓ c. melted butter or margarine**

• Simmer chicken in salted water to cover, or pressure cook until tender. Remove meat from bones.

• Melt fat in heavy skillet; blend in flour, salt and white pepper. Cook on low heat until bubbly, stirring constantly.

• Slowly stir in liquids; boil 3 minutes, stirring constantly.

• Lightly toss together bread cubes, onion, celery, salt, sage and butter. Arrange in two 2 qt. baking dishes. Top with chicken; cover with white sauce. Mix with fork to moisten dressing. Bake in moderate oven (350°) 1 hour. Makes 16 servings.

NUT LOAF

Now a Farm Journal 5-star recipe

- **1½ c. sifted flour**
- **1½ c. sugar**
- **1 tsp. baking powder**
- **1 tsp. salt**
- **2 lbs. pitted dates**
- **1 (8 oz.) bottle maraschino cherries, drained**
- **2 lbs. shelled walnuts**
- **1 lb. shelled Brazil nuts**
- **5 large eggs**
- **1 tsp. vanilla**

• Sift together flour, sugar, baking powder and salt. Add (do not chop) dates, cherries and nuts. Stir to coat nuts and fruit with flour.

• Beat eggs well; stir in vanilla. Mix into flour-nut mixture (easiest to do with hands).

• Spoon into three 8½×4½×2½" greased loaf pans. Bake in slow oven (325°) 1 hour or until browned. Cool before slicing. Makes 3 loaves.

Exciting Rice Dishes

When people say there is nothing new under the sun, our rebuttal starts with rice dishes—these unusual, tasty ones our Guest Cook brought from Arkansas to make in our Test Kitchens. She's the wife of a rice grower and knows that one way to promote the crop her husband grows is to find interesting, different ways to use it. These three recipes are samples of her accomplishments.

RICE ICE CREAM

Pineapple and rice—different ice cream

1½ c. cooked rice
2 c. milk
1 c. cream
4 eggs, well beaten
2 (15 oz.) cans sweetened condensed milk
⅛ tsp. salt
1 qt. milk
1 (1 lb. 4 oz.) can crushed pineapple
4 tblsp. lemon juice (or 1 lemon)

• Mash the rice while hot with a fork. Place in saucepan with milk and cream.
• Add beaten eggs to hot rice mixture. Cook about 1 minute, stirring constantly. Add condensed milk and salt. Stir well.
• Pour into gallon freezer. Stir in 1 qt. milk, or as much as needed to make the freezer ¾ full.
• Freeze until mushy.
• Add pineapple and lemon juice. Continue freezing until firm. This can be stored in home freezer. To tray-freeze Rice Ice Cream in your refrigerator use ½ recipe. When mushy turn into bowl, beat thoroughly; stir in pineapple and lemon juice. Freeze.

FARMER JONES' SPECIAL

Men like this hearty main dish

1 c. chopped celery
1 c. chopped onion
1 tblsp. butter or margarine
1 c. tomato juice
1 lb. ground beef
1 tsp. salt
1 can tomato paste
1 c. natural brown or white long grain rice
⅓ c. grated Parmesan cheese

• Cook celery and onion in butter or margarine until golden brown. Cover; cook until vegetables are tender.
• Add tomato juice, ground beef, salt and tomato paste. Simmer 10 minutes.
• In the meantime, cook rice according to package directions.
• Place rice while hot in large 12" ovenware pie plate. Put meat mixture over top of rice; sprinkle with cheese.
• Broil for 2 or 3 minutes. Makes 8 servings.

RICE AND CHICKEN JAMBALAYA

Meal-in-a-dish—extra good

½ c. chopped onion
1 c. diced celery
½ c. butter, margarine or chicken fat
4 c. chicken broth
1 c. uncooked rice
1½ tsp. salt
⅛ tsp. pepper
4 to 5 lb. stewing chicken, cooked and diced
1½ c. diced carrots
1 c. chopped parsley

• Cook onion and celery in butter until golden brown in 2 qt. saucepan.
• Add chicken broth, rice and seasonings.
• Cover; cook over low heat about 20 minutes. Add chicken and carrots and cook 15 minutes more.
• Sprinkle with chopped parsley. Makes 8 servings.

Minnesota Raspberry Favorites

Who knows better what the most delicious raspberry dishes are than the wife of a berry grower, who is an exceptionally good cook? When a gracious Minnesota Guest Cook made her desserts in our Countryside Test Kitchens, everyone who sampled them, had a one-word response—wonderful! And each year since, when summer and red berries arrive, we say: Oh, to be in Minnesota, now that raspberries are ripe. We share two of her recipes with you.

OPEN-FACE RASPBERRY PIE

Unusual but has an enthusiastic following

1 tblsp. lard
3 eggs
2 c. milk
1 tsp. salt
2 c. sifted flour
1 qt. raspberries
1 c. sugar

• Put lard into 12×9×2" pan. Heat in oven until lard is sizzling hot.
• In the meantime, beat eggs very well. Stir in milk, salt and flour. This will make a very thin batter. Pour batter into sizzling hot pan. Sprinkle berries over top, then sprinkle with sugar.
• Bake in hot oven (425°) about 45 minutes. Batter will rise then fall. Makes 12 servings.

RASPBERRY CRISP

Luscious, crowned with whipped cream

1 qt. raspberries
⅓ c. sugar
¼ c. butter
⅓ c. flour
⅓ c. brown sugar
¾ c. rolled oats

• Sprinkle raspberries with sugar in 9" square pan.
• Blend butter, flour, brown sugar and rolled oats. Sprinkle over raspberries.
• Bake in moderate oven (350°) about 30 minutes. Makes 6 servings.

Prize-Winning Chicken

One of our Guest Cooks who lives on a farm overlooking Delaware Bay, came to our Test Kitchens to show us how to fix her Company Chicken. It had just won the blue ribbon in a national chicken cooking contest. And before our Food Department had time to stop raving about her prize fried chicken, she was fixing another of her favorite recipes, Lemon-Broiled Chicken, which we give you here.

LEMON-BROILED CHICKEN

For the best brown flavor you ever tasted, and it's simple

2 plump young broilers (not over 2½ lbs.)
1 lemon, quartered
¼ c. melted butter or margarine
2 tsp. salt
¼ tsp. pepper
½ tsp. paprika
2 tblsp. sugar

• Rub chicken halves inside and out with lemon; brush with butter.
• Mix together salt, pepper, paprika and sugar; sprinkle lightly over chickens.
• Place chickens in broiler pan, skin side down. Place pan in bottom of broiler. Turn chickens after 20 minutes and raise closer to heat. Baste occasionally to insure even browning. Broil until pink color at bone disappears. Makes 4 servings.

Thanksgiving Specialties

Our Guest Cook from the historical Shenandoah Valley of Virginia made her family's favorite Thanksgiving Dinner dishes in our Test Kitchens. Two of her choice recipes follow.

BAKED DRESSING

To bake in turkey or in a pan like pudding—Virginians like it pudding-style

3 eggs
2 c. milk
1 c. chicken broth and fat
1 chopped onion
¼ c. chopped celery leaves
1½ tsp. salt
¼ tsp. pepper
2 qts. day-old bread cubes

• Beat eggs in large bowl. Add milk, broth, onion, celery leaves, salt, pepper.
• Add bread cubes and mix lightly.
• Pour into greased baking dish 8×8×2". Bake in moderate oven (350°) 45 to 50 minutes, or until puffy and golden brown. Makes 8 servings.

FROZEN AMBROSIA

A light dessert to follow Thanksgiving Dinner's turkey and trimmings

4 c. orange juice
½ c. lemon juice
3 c. sifted confectioners sugar
2 c. heavy cream
2 tblsp. sugar
2 tsp. vanilla

• Mix together orange juice, lemon juice and confectioners sugar.
• Whip cream; blend in sugar, vanilla.
• Pour fruit juice into 2 refrigerator trays. Spoon whipped cream over top, but do not mix together (juice and cream will be separate layers). Freeze firm.
• Spoon into sherbet dishes or a compote; top with slivered salted almonds or with peanuts. Makes 8 to 10 servings.

Peach Pie and Pork Chops

A Guest Cook from Iowa who dotes on her freezer whetted the appetites of everyone near our Countryside Kitchens. She baked a pretty peach pie and barbecued browned, lean pork chops. Her recipes:

PEACH PIE

Top shows off yellow peaches with cherry centers; freezes well

½ c. sugar
5 tblsp. cornstarch
2 tblsp. quick-cooking tapioca
⅛ tsp. salt
1 c. peach juice
½ tsp. almond extract
1 qt. sliced fresh or frozen peaches
Pastry for 2-crust (9") pie
2 tsp. butter or margarine
6 peach halves
6 maraschino cherries

• Combine sugar, cornstarch, tapioca and salt. blend in peach juice and almond extract. Pour over sliced peaches.
• Mix well and turn into pastry-lined pie pan. Dot with butter. Place 6 peach halves, hollow side up, on top.
• Place pastry strips across surface between peach halves. Bake in very hot oven (450°) 10 minutes; reduce to moderate (350°) for 20 to 30 minutes. Cool and place maraschino cherry in hollows.

BARBECUE SAUCE FOR PORK CHOPS

½ c. ketchup
1 tsp. salt
1 tsp. celery seed
½ tsp. nutmeg
⅓ c. vinegar
1 c. water
Bay leaf

• Combine all ingredients and pour over browned pork chops. Cover and simmer until chops are tender. Makes 1½ cups, or enough for 6 to 8 pork chops.

Colorado Barbecued Pot Roast

A young cattleman's wife, an active member of the Colorado Cowbelles, responded to our invitation to demonstrate in our Countryside Kitchens some of the choice beef dishes Western women make in their ranch kitchens. We selected her pot roast with dumplings as one of the most rewarding dishes for a man to come home to.

COLORADO POT ROAST

Rich brown roast barbecued in a kettle on the kitchen range—a Western treat

2 tblsp. flour
1 (4 lb.) beef pot roast
1 c. canned tomatoes
1 c. water
2 cloves garlic
1 tblsp. salt
½ tsp. pepper
1 c. sliced onions
¼ c. vinegar
¼ c. lemon juice
¼ c. ketchup
2 tblsp. brown sugar
1 tblsp. Worcestershire sauce
1 tsp. mustard
¼ tsp. paprika

• Rub flour on meat; brown well on all sides in heavy kettle. Slip rack under meat. Add tomatoes, water, garlic, salt and pepper. Cover, simmer 2 hours.
• Combine remaining ingredients. Pour over meat; cover and simmer until tender, 1 to 1½ hours.
• To serve, remove meat to hot platter; keep warm while dumplings steam.

Dumplings:

Serve pronto—dumplings never wait

¾ c. sifted flour
½ c. cornmeal
1½ tsp. baking powder
½ tsp. salt
½ c. milk
2 tblsp. melted shortening or oil

• While meat is cooking, sift together flour, cornmeal, baking powder and salt.
• Shortly before serving time, stir in milk and shortening just until dry ingredients are moistened. Drop by large spoonfuls into boiling pot roast sauce. Cook uncovered over low heat 10 minutes, then tightly covered 10 minutes.
• Serve at once with sliced pot roast and sauce. Makes 6 servings.

Festive Puddings

Puddings, as made by our Guest Cook from Michigan, become glamour desserts. As this young homemaker prepared them in our Test Kitchens, she told the Food Editor about her incentive, when she was a little girl, to learn to be a good cook. It came from her mother—now her husband's enthusiasm encourages her. You'll want to try two of her puddings.

CHOCOLATE-MINT TOWER

¾ c. sugar
6 tblsp. flour
¼ tsp. salt
3 c. milk
3 (1 oz.) squares unsweetened chocolate, grated
1 tsp. vanilla
½ c. heavy cream
1 tblsp. sugar
1 to 2 drops green food color
1 to 2 drops peppermint extract

• Combine sugar, flour and salt in top of double boiler. Slowly add milk; stir until well blended. Add chocolate.
• Place over boiling water; cook until thickened, stirring constantly. Continue cooking 10 minutes. Add vanilla. Chill (keep pudding covered so film doesn't form on top).
• Whip cream. Add sugar, food color and peppermint extract.
• Alternate layers of pudding and whipped cream in sherbet glasses. Garnish with mint leaves. Six servings.

HOLIDAY STEAMED PUDDING

3 tblsp. shortening
⅓ c. sugar
1 tsp. vanilla
1 egg yolk
½ c. chopped dates
¼ c. chopped candied cherries
¼ c. chopped walnuts
2 c. honey graham cracker crumbs
1 tsp. baking powder
¼ tsp. salt
½ c. milk
1 egg white

• Cream together shortening, sugar and vanilla.
• Beat egg yolk and add to creamed mixture. Stir in dates, cherries and nuts.
• Combine cracker crumbs, baking powder and salt. Add alternately to fruit mixture with milk.
• Beat egg white until stiff and fold in.
• Fill 6 greased custard cups ⅔ full. Cover tightly with aluminum foil or double thickness of waxed paper. Steam 30 minutes in covered kettle. Or in pressure saucepan, steam 10 minutes without indicator weight, then 10 minutes at 10 lbs. pressure. Serve with hard sauce. Makes 6 servings.

Company Desserts

These recipes are from a charming, young Guest Cook who came to our Countryside Test Kitchens to demonstrate how she makes hostess desserts in her own kitchen on a Mississippi Delta cotton plantation. We selected two:

LIME PARFAIT

2 egg yolks, beaten
½ c. sugar
½ c. light corn syrup
1 c. scalded milk
2 egg whites, beaten
⅓ c. lime juice
1 tsp. grated rind of lime
Few drops green food color
1 c. light cream

• Combine egg yolks, sugar, corn syrup and milk. Cook over boiling water, stirring constantly, until thickened. Cool. Fold in egg whites.
• Add lime juice, rind, food color and cream. Spoon into freezer tray. Freeze.
• Break into chunks with wooden spoon; turn into chilled bowl. Beat until fluffy and smooth with electric or rotary beater. Return to cold tray; freeze firm.
• Alternate in parfait glasses with your favorite fresh or frozen fruit and whipped cream. Makes 6 servings.

BLACK BOTTOM PIE

Top-ranking pie in states bordering on the Gulf of Mexico

3 c. milk
1 c. sugar
¼ c. flour
4 eggs, separated
1 envelope unflavored gelatin
¼ c. cold water
1 (1 oz.) square unsweetened chocolate, cut up
2 tsp. vanilla extract
1 (10″) baked pie shell
½ c. heavy cream, whipped
1 (1 oz.) square chocolate, grated

• Scald milk. Mix ¾ c. sugar and flour thoroughly; stir into milk.
• Beat egg yolks until lemon colored; gradually add milk mixture, stirring constantly. Cook over low heat, stirring until mixture thickens.
• Soften gelatin in cold water; add to mixture and stir until dissolved.
• Divide mixture into two parts. To one, add the cut-up square of chocolate. Stir until melted; add 1 tsp. vanilla. Cool. Turn into baked pie shell.
• Beat egg whites, adding ¼ c. sugar while beating, until mixture holds peaks. Add second tsp. vanilla.
• Fold egg whites into remaining cooled mixture; spread over chocolate filling. Chill 4 to 6 hours. Just before serving spread top of pie with whipped cream; sprinkle with grated chocolate.

Shrimp at Its Best

Gourmets the world over consider Creole cookery one of America's most distinctive types. And no one disputes the top popularity of shrimp in the seafood class. It's not surprising we invited a Guest Cook from Acadian country in southern Louisiana to visit our Test Kitchens and show us how she cooks shrimp. We recommend with pride these three recipes:

TO BOIL AND CLEAN SHRIMP

• Drop 1 lb. shrimp into 1 pt. boiling water with 1 tsp. salt added. (You also may add 1 small onion, sliced, a few parsley sprigs and 4 peppercorns.) Simmer, covered, until shrimp are pink and tender, about 8 to 10 minutes. Drain, remove shell and black vein along outside curve of shrimp with sharp pointed knife. (You may shell and de-vein shrimp before cooking, reducing cooking time to 3 to 5 minutes. Always remove black vein from canned shrimp before using.)

CREOLE SHRIMP SAUCE

A snappy sauce that's just right for boiled or fried shrimp

4 tblsp. mayonnaise or salad dressing
4 tblsp. Worcestershire sauce
4 tblsp. ketchup
1 tsp. prepared horse-radish
¼ tsp. garlic juice
½ tsp. salt
⅛ tsp. black pepper
1 egg yolk, cooked

• Combine all ingredients and chill thoroughly. Sprinkle grated egg yolk over top just before serving. Makes about ¾ cup.

Rice Duet: Serve Shrimp Creole with two kinds of rice, such as brown and white, or white and wild rice. Easy to do and gives everyone his choice.

SHRIMP CREOLE

Serve with a tossed salad, crusty French bread and dessert, for a super meal

¼ c. oil or shortening
¼ c. flour
4 cloves garlic, minced
½ c. chopped celery
½ c. chopped green pepper
2 (8 oz.) cans tomato sauce
1½ tsp. salt
½ tsp. black pepper
¼ tsp. red pepper
1½ lbs. raw shrimp, (fresh or frozen)
3 c. hot cooked rice

• Heat oil; add flour, stirring constantly until smooth and golden brown.
• Add garlic, celery and green pepper; cook until tender. Add tomato sauce and seasonings; cook 20 minutes, stirring frequently.
• Add shrimp and simmer 15 to 25 minutes more. Serve in rice ring or over mound. Makes 6 servings.

SHRIMP SALAD

Main dish salad rave—it's the peppy seasoning that's so different

1 lb. shrimp, cooked or 2 (5 oz.) cans, cleaned
1 c. celery, coarsely chopped
2 hard-cooked eggs, coarsely chopped
3 tblsp. dill pickles, diced
½ c. mayonnaise or salad dressing
1 tblsp. lemon juice
1 tblsp. ketchup
½ tsp. Worcestershire sauce
¾ tsp. salt
¼ tsp. pepper
Lettuce

• Chill shrimp and if large, cut in halves or quarters.
• Toss together shrimp, celery, eggs and pickles with mayonnaise which has been combined with lemon juice, ketchup, Worcestershire sauce and seasonings. Serve on crisp lettuce and salad greens. Garnish top with shrimp and egg. Makes 4 servings.

Index

A

Alice's Scalloped Chicken 372
Almond(s)
  Acorns 19
  Bars 86
  Butter Balls 89
  Fruit Roll 20
  Moons 98
  Pastry 7
Amber
  Grape Marmalade 265
  Pie 346
Ambrosia
  Chiffon Cake 4
  Cupcakes 300
  Frozen 375
  Refrigerator Dessert 294
Am-Nor Pancakes 355
Anadama Bread 358
Anchovy Butter Sauce 268
Apple(s) 203–214
  Butterscotch Baked 214
  Cabbage with 231
  Cake Pie 213
  Caramel 214
  Cheese Salad 210
    Chip 210
    Grapefruit 210
    Poinsettia 211
    September 211
  Coffee Cake 301
  Company Cake 209
  Cranberry Relish 29
  Dumplings 212
    Old-Time 212
  Fudge Squares 86
  Green Chutney 266
  Griddle Cakes 207
  Honey Dressing 22
  Honeyed 221
  Hot Punch 214
  Layer Cake 209
    Nobby 210
  Mystery Dessert 213
  Nut Bread 207
    Fresh 206
  Oven Butter 355
  Pie
    Deep-Dish 204
    Elderberry 346
    Favorite 204
    Frosted Raisin 205
    Orange 8
    Quick 204
    Sour Cream 205
  Pudding 348
    Virginia 211
  Rosy Spring 63
  Scalloped Sweet Potatoes and 156
  Spicy Bars 87
  Treat Cake 207
  Walnut Crisp 212
Applesauce
  Cake à la Mode 5
  Fruit Cake 208
  Pink Glaze 63
  Tricks 209
Apricot
  Apple Ring 206
  Banana Dessert 305
  Biscuit Ring 81
  Meringue Pie 10
  Prune Tarts 9
  Quick Chiffon 35
  Sticks 20
Asparagus
  Casserole 32
  Mushroom Sauce 160
  Saffron 228

Asparagus (*Continued*)
with Mock Hollandaise 61
Avocado
Grapefruit Salad 293
Guacamole 370
Salad Dressing 292

B

Bacon
Baked Bass with 275
Flounder 275
Cabbage Casserole 232
Cheese Sauce 195
Tangy 232
'n Egg Salad Bowl 238
Baked
Bass with Bacon 275
Beans 361
Bean and Salami Filling 256
Cauliflower 234
Chicken Legs 28
Deviled Tomatoes 247
Doughnut Puffs 350
Dressing 62, 375
Eggplant with Ham 236
Filled Zucchini 248
Fish au Gratin 276
Flounder with Bacon 275
Green Beans 314
Ham Timetable 116
Honey Custard 218
Lima Beans 228
Pork Chops 312
Potatoes 49
Stuffed 145
Potato Slices 44
Spareribs 119
Trout 275
Turnips with Peanuts 248
Bake-on Coffee Cake Toppings, with Variations 316, 317
Banana(s) 260
Apricot Dessert 305
Bread 337
Devils Food Cake 67
Layer 259
Milk Shake 189
Orange Drink 83
Split 71
Barbecue (d)
Cheese Sandwiches 196
Chicken Special 46
Fried Chicken 131
Hamburgers 344
Lima Bean 49
Quick Franks 310
Sauce 65, 67, 131, 375
Fruit 129
Short Ribs 106
Skillet Franks 253
Spareribs 48, 120
Southern Chicken 65
Texas 131
Basic Muffin Recipe (Master Recipe) 318
Variations 319
Basil 240
Bean(s) (*See* Vegetables)
Beanburgers 109
Cheese 109
and Frankfurter Soup 255
Lima Bean Barbecue 49
Spanish 27
Porridge 229
Rice Salad 32
and Sausage 114
Mexican style 74
Soup 351
Tomato-Bean Chowder 314
with Deviled Ham 311
Beef
Beefburger Broiler Meal 114
Braised Pot Roast 103
Colorado 376

Beef (*Continued*)
Rolled 103
Savory 103
Seasonings 103
Broiled Patties 48
Sirloin 51
Dinner Pie 252
Dried Beef Sprinkles 126
with Eggs 126
Jellied Mold 289
and Ketchup Filling 256
Lemon Baked Beefsteaks 105
Loaf 26
Pie Supreme 108
Pilau 30
Potato Pot Pie 147
Pressed 289
Roll 145
Sauce for Vegetables 314
Sauerbraten 182
Savory Cakes 311
Shish Kabobs 54
Short Ribs with Dumplings 106
with sour Cream 252
Standing Rib Roast 102
Steak, Broiled
Kitchen 53
Outdoor 51
Time Table 53
Steak with Tomato Sauce 104
Go-withs 52
Swiss Steak 104
Tender Brown Cubes 251
Stew in Foil 310
Beefeater's Kidney Beans 254
Beet(s) (*See* Vegetables)
Perfection Salad 31
Relish 269
Best-Ever Cheese Cake 184
Beverage(s)
Coffee, Swedish Style 54
Cranberry Spike 17
Currant Juice 260
Fruit Punch 73
Good Luck Punch 72
Half-and-Half Cooler 84
Hot Apple Punch 214
Spicy Punch 72
Tomato Juice 83
Lemonade Cooler 42
Mulled Apricot Nectar 17
Orange-Banana Drink 83
Pineapple-Cranberry Cocktail 62
Raspberry Float 17
Spiced Tomato Juice 17
Thirst Quencher 84
Tomato Cocktail 287
Big Irish Lamb Stew 124
Biscuit
Apricot Biscuit Ring 81
Biscuit Sticks 76
Chicken and Sweet Cream 178
Double Cheese 195
Drop 355
Potato Puff Buns 83
Stickies 76
Black Bottom Pie 377
Black Cherry Chiffon Pie 168
Black Walnut
Cake 36
Cookies 98
Blind Dates 329
Bluebarb Jam 262
Blueberry
Betty 15
Buckle 78
Fresh, Pie 8
Spiced Jam 263
Treat 295
Blue Cheese Ball 196
Blue Devil Butter 275
Bologna Cheese Sandwiches 197
Borsch 351
Boston Baked Beans 358
Brown Bread 358
Cream Pie 359

Braised Pot Roast 103
Brazil Nut Bars 87
Brazilian Lace Cookies 89
Bread
  Anadama 358
  Apple Nut 207
  Banana 337
  Blueberry Buckle 78
  Boston Brown 358
  Bran 80
  Caraway 81
  Cheese 338
    Crackers 196
    Toast 338
  Chili-Topped 309
  Cinnamon 82, 250
    Loaf 337
  Coffee Cake Mix (Master Recipe), with Variations 316, 317
    Cranberry 84
    Date Streusel 84
    Dutch Plum 79
    Marmalade 80
    Pineapple 81
    Plain 316
    Ring (Master Recipe), with Variations, 317, 318
  Corn
    Quick 188
    Skillet 187
    Spanish 308
    Sweet Cream 354
  Date Turnovers 367
  Delicious Stuffing 141
  French 50
    Toast 76
    Deep-Fat-Fried 76
    Oven or Broiler 76
    Waffle Iron 76
  Fresh Apple 206
  Fritter Batter 321
  Fruit Nut 291
  Graham Prune 291
  Honey Buns 219
  Honey Rye 33
  Hot Buttered 308
  Hush Puppies 365
  Jam Twists 78
  Maple Sticks 337
  Molasses Oatmeal 338
  Nut Loaf 372
  Oatmeal 33
  Old Virginia Sally Lunn 365
  Orange Date 79
  Peanut Dainties 77
  Pizzas, Individual 79
  Prune Pinwheels 80
  Puff Shells 60
  Quick Butterhorn Rolls 250
  Raisin-Bran 338
  Sopaipillas 370
  Spoonbread 365
    Virginia 69
  Tortillas 369
  Twice-Baked 250
  Whole Wheat 34
    Tart Shells 257
Bread and Butter Pickles 272
Broccoli (*See* Vegetables)
  au Gratin 29
  Soufflé 230
Broiled
  Beef Patties 48
  Chicken 130
  Corn in Husks 235
  Fish 274
  Ham and Yams 154
  Lamb Patties 123
  Sirloin 51
Brown
  Butter Frosting 95
  Gravy 122
  Potato Soup 149
  Stew 104
  Sugar Cookies 95

Brown (*Continued*)
Sugar Drops 96
Browned Potato Loaf 147
Brownies 100
Pudding 305
Brunswick Stew 68, 69
Buffet Supper 372
Burnt Sugar Sauce 348
Butter 171–184
Almond, Cookies 89
Blue Devil 275
Brazil Nut 234
Brown, Frosting 95
Date 367
Frosting 58, 173
Coffee 173
Flavored Spreads 175
Herb 45
How to Make 174
Molasses Butterballs 89
Oven Apple 355
Sauce 51
Sponge Cake 172
Buttered Carrot Sticks 233
Butterhorn Rolls 64
Buttermilk Bran Muffins 187
Butterscotch
Baked Apples 214
Chocolate Frosting 16
Drops 92
Meringue Pie 222
Pecan Pie 11
Sauce 214
Sundae Sauce 39

C

Cabbage (*See* Vegetables)
with Apples 231
Casserole 231
Bacon 232
Tomato 233
with Cheese 231
Slaw with Mustard Mold 233
Cake(s)
Ambrosia Chiffon 4
Apple Cake Pie 213
Apple Coffee 301
Apple Layer 209
Applesauce
à la Mode 5
Fruit 208
Apple Treat 207
Apricot-Apple Ring 206
Banana Devils Food 67
Banana Layer 259
Best-Ever Cheese 184
Black Walnut 36
Boston Cream Pie 359
Butter Sponge 172
Caramel 224
Champion Angel Food 59
Cherry Custard Shortbread 191
Cherry Upside-Down 300
Chocolate 352
Angel Food 166
Loaf 16
Nut Loaf 335
Sticks 77
Telegram 336
Cider and Spice 208
Coconut Cake Supreme 334
Company Apple 209
Cookie Shortcake 303
Cupcakes
Ambrosia 300
Tea-Time 3
Whole Wheat 77
Date-Nut 335
Devils Food 38
Election Day 360
Formal Wedding 56
Frozen Fruit 14
Fruited Honey 218
Fudge 2

Cakes (*Continued*)
Hickory Nut 38
Holiday Cake Special 4
Honey-Cheese 219
Honey-Filled Coffee 217
Honey-Fruit 220
Honey-Lemon Layer 220
Hurry-Up Boston Cream Pie 359
Ice Cream 300
Ice Cream Layer 258
Individual Coffee Cakes 250
Informal Wedding 58
Jeweled Pound 172
Lane 366
Large Dark Fruit 226
Layer Fruit 335
Lemon "Cake" Dessert 347
Lemon-Cheese 336
Lemon Refrigerator 296
Maple Upside-Down 223
Nobby Apple 210
Orange 259
Orange-Coconut 301
Pink Party Roll 258
Poinsettia Cheese 202
Poppy Seed Layer 3
Potato Chocolate 37
Pound 336
Prune 38
Prune Spice 37
Pumpkin 2
Quick-Change (Master Recipe) 323
Creamy Strawberry 324
Rhubarb Kuchen 323
Sour Cream 323
Upside-Down 324
Quick Holiday 300
Refrigerator 296
Ribbon 173
Sour Cream 183
Spice 352
Sponge Cake Roll (Master Recipe) 324
Chocolate Filling 324
Lemon Filling 325
Lemon Sponge Squares 325
Strawberry Angel 294
Strawberry Meringue 168
Sunshine Ice Cream 166
Sunshine Layer 166
3-Way Gold 259
Topsy Turvy Mincemeat 301
Twin Wedding Ring 59
Whipped Cream 173
White 352
White Fruit 5
White Wonder 165
Yellow Angel 167
Yellow Lard 73
Cake Topping 221
Camp-Style Eggs and Corn 162
Candies
Brown Sugar Sea Foam 340
Caramel Walnut Roll 339
Chocolate Ripple Divinity 340
Confectioners Sugar Fudge 341
Date 367
Date-Pecan Candy Roll 40
English Toffee 39
Fruited Sea Foam 340
Never-Fail Fudge 73
No-Cook Candy 221
Peanut Brittle 341
Peanut-Sour Cream 364
Pulled Mints 339
Raisin Peanut Fudge 40
Strawberry Divinity 340
Caper Sauce 277
Caramel
Almond Sponge 225
Bread Pudding (Master Recipe) 325
Chocolate 325
Coconut 325

Caramel (*Continued*)
Coffee 325
Dried Fruit 325
Fruit 325
Peanut Brittle 325
Cake 224
Candy Apples 214
Cream Frosting 225
Custard 190
Custard Pie 225
Flavored Custard 225
Quick Caramel Corn 363
Sundae Sauce 225
Walnut Roll 339
Caramelized Syrup 224
Caraway Bread 81
Carrots (*See* Vegetables)
Casserole (*See also* Main Dishes)
Beans and Sausage, Mexican Style 74
Broccoli and Onions, Curried 281
Cabbage 231
Cabbage-Bacon 232
Cabbage-Tomato 233
Cheese and Noodle Ring 192
Chicken 136
Chicken-Almond 135
Chicken Crunch 136
Chicken Tamales 344
Corned Beef 113, 311
Farmer Jones' Special 373
French Hunter's Dinner 69
Friday 70
Ham and Noodles 288
Ham-Noodle 28
Lima-Sausage 114
Parsnips 242
Pork Savory 74
Rice and Chicken Jambalaya 373
Rutabaga-Potato 245
Salmon 280
Salmon Loaf 280
Sausage-Flower Casseroles 164
Sweet Potato 153
Thirty-Minute Chop Suey 121
Tuna Fish Pie 280
Turkey-Oyster 28
Cauliflower, Baked 234
Cauliflower Salad 234
Celery
in Carrot Rings 269
Rhubarb Salad 291
Stuffing 139
Champion Angel Food Cake 59
Charcoal Broiled Chicken 42
Cheese
Apple-Cheese Salad 210
Bacon and Cheese Sauce 195
Barbecue Sandwiches 196
Bean Burgers 109
Best-Ever Cheese Cake 184
Blue Cheese Ball 196
Bologna Cheese Sandwich 197
Bonbons 40
Bread 338
Cabbage with Cheese 231
Cherry Cheese Pie 202
Chili-Topped Cheese Toast 309
with Corn and Beans 195
Corned Beef with Cheese Yams 156
Cottage Cheese Dressing 222
Cottage Cheese and Fruit Salad 198
Cottage Cheese Salmon Loaf 193
Crackers 196
Cranberry Cheese Pie 199
Cream Cheese and Clam Dip 195
Creamed Eggs with Cheese 162
Double Cheese Biscuits 195
Dried Beef Filling 200
Fondue 193
Fruit Cottage Cheese Ring 201
Fruited Cheese Pie 202
Ham Casserole 28
Ham-Egg-Cheese Sandwich 200
Harvest Cheese Sandwich 197
Heart-of-Gold Cheese Pie 202

Cheese (*Continued*)
Homemade Cottage Cheese 356
Honey Cheese Cake 219
Honey Cheese Frosting 220
Lemon Cheese Cake 336
Lime Salad 293
Meat Loaf 107
Mincemeat Cheese Cookies 98
Molded Cheese and Pineapple Salad 201
and Noodle Ring 192
Pie 200
Pineapple Cheese Pie 202
Pineapple Salad 175
Poinsettia Cheese Cake 202
Popcorn 363
Potato-Cheese Scallop 26
Potato-Cheese Soup 149
Refrigerator Cheese Pie 198
Soufflé 193
Strata 194
Strawberry Cheese Pie 199
Stuffed Hamburgers 110
Toast 338
Tomato-Cheese Rarebit 194
Tomato-Cheese Sauce 200
Topped Potatoes 145
Tuna Macaroni and Cheese 194
Tuna Surprise 197
Turnips in Cheese Sauce 248
Velvety Cheese Soup 186
Chef's Salad 71
Cherry
Black Cherry Chiffon Pie 168
Cheese Pie 202
Custard Shortbread 191
North Pole Cherry Pie 304
Pie au Gratin 44
Pie Special 6
Royal Cherry Topping 302
Sauce 177
Sour Cherry and Pineapple Jam 263
Sour Cherry Preserves 264
Upside-Down Cake 300
Chess Pie 364
Chicken (and Other Poultry) 127–142
Alice's Scalloped 372
Almond Casserole 135
Baked Chicken Legs 29
Barbecue Fried Chicken 131
Barbecued Chicken Special 46
Broiled 130
Bundles 48
Casserole 136
Charcoal Broiled 42
Company 254
Company Chicken Salad 138
Creamed 137
Crisp Baked 128
in Crumb Baskets 137
Crunch Casserole 136
Crusty Fried 128
Deviled 131
with Dressing 136
Dumplings 133
with Dumplings 134
Frenched Chicken Sandwich 134
Fried Chicken Creole Style 130
Fruited Chicken Salad 138
Glazed Broiled 129
Gumbo 133
Hot Chicken Salad 138
Lemon Broiled 374
Livers De Luxe 180
Loaf 132, 288
Maine Chicken Pie 132
Molded Chicken 60
Molded Chicken Loaf 286
Oven Fried 128
Pan Fried 128
Paprika 130
and Pickle Filling 256
Pineapple Salad 61
Pressed 354
Rice and Chicken Jambalaya 373
and Rice Salad 138

Chicken (*Continued*)
Sandwich Filling 134
Sauce with Peas 160
Scalloped 70
Smothered 130
Soufflé 313
Southern Barbecued 65
Supper Dish 132
Supreme 134
and Sweet Cream Biscuits 178
Tamale Pie 133
Tamales 344
Tetrazzini 135
Texas Barbecued 131
Tuna Pie 313
Upside-Down Chicken Dinner 137
Chili
con Carne 30, 70, 369
Dumpling Stew 105
Sauce 239
with Tomatoes 32
Topped Cheese Toast 309
Chinese
Chews 86
Mutton Stew 125
Chocolate
Angel Food Cake 166
Angel Pie 15
Butterscotch Chocolate Frosting 16
Cake 352
Cake Doughnuts 349
Chip Torte 15
Creamy Chocolate Frosting 259
Creamy Chocolate Icing 38
Filling 324
Hermits 93
Lime Chocolate Pie 297
Loaf Cake 16
Macaroons 92
Malted Milk 189
Marshmallow Cookies 46
Meringues 13
Mint Pie 16
Mint Tower 376
Minted Chocolate Pie 288
Nut Drops 218
Nut Loaf 335
Nut Waffles 23
Oatmeal Cookies 342
Peanut Chocolate Sauce 307
Peanut Clusters 76
Peppermint Pie 12
Popcorn Balls 363
Potato Chocolate Cake 37
Ripple Divinity 340
Sauce 307
Sticks and Variations 77
Sundae Sauce 39
Super-Duper Chocolate Cookies 91
Telegram Cake 336
Walnut Cookies 88
Chops Baked in Soup 29
Chowder
Corn 186
Fish 279
Potato-Salmon 150
Tomato-Bean 314
Vegetable 255
Chow Mein 368
Christmas
Cookie Nibbles 304
Drop Cookies 93
Cider
Creamy Cider Icing 208
Filling 208
Shimmy 214
and Spice Cake 208
Stew 104
Cinnamon
Bread 82, 250
Favorites 91
Loaf 337
Pecan Rolls 78
Rolls 54
Circle Sandwiches 196

Citrus
Filling 335
Fruit Custard 297
Clear Watermelon Pickles 270
Cobbler, Two-Fruit 205
Cocoa
Doughnut Balls 83
Frosting 46
Coconut
Cake Supreme 334
Cream Pudding 306
Honey-Coconut Cake Topping 221
Ice Cream 219
Lemon Coconut Pie 305
Lemon Coconut Squares 100
Orange Coconut Cake 301
Coffee
Butter Frosting (with variations) 173
Cake Mix 316
Cake Ring (Master Recipe) 317
Cinnamon, Raisin and Currant Buns 318
Kolaches 318
Orange Twists 318
Ice Cream 298
Swedish Style 54
Coleslaw, with Fish and Game 283
Colorado Pot Roast 376
Company
Apple Cake 209
Chicken 254
Chicken Salad 138
Creamed Potatoes 147
Meat Balls 24
Concord Grape Pie 347
Confectioners Sugar Frosting 87, 205
Confectioners Sugar Fudge 341
Confections
Almond Acorns 19
Almond Fruit Roll 20
Apricot Sticks 20
Orange Walnuts 20
Pear Pinwheels 19
Prune Crystal Balls 20
Conserve, Plum 263
Cooked Peas in Pod 243
Cookies 85–100
Almond Bars 86
Butter Balls 89
Moons 98
Apple Fudge Squares 86
Black Walnut Cookies 98
Blind Dates 329
Brazilian Lace Cookies 89
Brazil Nut Bars 87
Brownies 100
Brown Sugar Cookies 95
Drops 96
Butterscotch Drops 92
Chinese Chews 86
Chocolate Hermits 93
Macaroons 92
Nut Drops 218
Oatmeal Cookies 342
Peanut Clusters 76
Walnut Cookies 88
Choco-Marshmallow Cookies 46
Christmas Cookie Nibbles 304
Drop Cookies 93
Cinnamon Favorites 91
Cookie Bonbons 91
Cookie Starter (Master Recipe) 329
Blind Dates 329
Ice Cream Wafers 330
Old English Ginger Crisps 329
Tips on Using Mix 329
Corn Flake Cookies 94
Crackle-Top Ginger Cookies 90
Crisp Molasses Cookies 96
Crisscross Cookies 92
Date and Nut Macaroons 90
Date-Nut Bars 88
Double Cream 342

Cookies (*Continued*)
Dream Bars 88
Eight-In-One Cookies
(Master Recipe) 328
Banana 328
Butterscotch 328
Chocolate 328
Coconut 328
Fruit 'n Spice 328
Ginger 328
Gumdrop 328
Orange 328
Fancy Spritz 99
Favorite Honey Bars 216
Frosted Molasses Creams 87
Fruit Bars 100
Fruity Gumdrop 94
Ginger 97
Gingersnaps 90
Half-and-Half Macaroons 303
Holiday Fruitcake 95
Honey Wafers 217
Ice Cream Wafers 330
Chinese Almond 330
Orange and Lemon Wafers 330
Sesame 330
Victorian Spice 330
Layered Brownies 303
Lemon 98
Lemon Blossom Snowballs 342
Lemon-Coconut Squares 100
Mincemeat Cheese 98
Cookie Bars 349
Pinwheels 349
Molasses Butterballs 89
Cookies 97
Ginger 90
Whole Wheat 226
Nut Bars 86
and Fruit Bars 342
Oatmeal Molasses 96
Refrigerator 99
Old English Ginger Crisps 329
Orange 94
Carrot 96
Peanut Molasses 94
Pecan Drops 92
Pennsylvania Dutch Hearts 304
Raisin-Carrot 93
Raisin-Sour Cream 91
Refrigerator 99
Salted Peanut 16
Some-Mores 49
Sour Cream Ginger Squares 183
Spicy Apple Bars 87
Molasses Balls 89
Sugar 97
Sugar Cookies (Master Recipe) 328
Chocolate Chip 329
Coconut 329
Nut Sugar 329
Raisin 329
Spiced Sugar 329
Super-Duper Chocolate 91
Toffee Cookie Squares 88
Two-Way 341
Walnut Brownies 303
Corn (*See* Vegetables)
and Beans with Cheese 195
Cakes 234
Chowder 186
on the Cob 49
Flake Cookies 94
'n Peas with Savory 236
"Oysters" 236
Pie 235
Relish 267
Stuffed Tomatoes 247
Waffles 235
Corned Beef 353
with Cabbage 353
Casserole 113, 311
with Cheese Yams 156
Eggs with Corned Beef Hash 113

Corned Beef (*Continued*)
Hearty Corned Beef Salad 287
Relish and Onion Filling 256
Cottage Cheese
Coleslaw 44
Dressing 222
and Fruit Salad 198
Salmon Loaf 193
Country Fried Potatoes 145
Crackle-Top Ginger Cookies 90
Cranberry
Apple Relish 29
Cheese Pie 199
Chiffon Pie 304
Coffee Cake 84
Jellied Cranberry Mold 291
Marmalade Relish 267
Mince-Cranberry Pie 34
Nut Glaze 199
Nut Pie 11
Orange Relish 29
Pineapple-Cranberry Cocktail 62
Pineapple Relish 29
Pudding 362
Raisin Pie 35
Relish Salad 29
Salad 21
Spike 17
Turkey-Cranberry Salad 140
Wisconsin Cranberry Pudding 362
Cream Cheese
and Clam Dip 195
Dried Beef Filling 256
Creamed
Chicken 137
Eggs with Cheese 162
Kale and Onions 241
Onions 241
Peas and Deviled Ham 243
Shrimp 160
Cream of Potato Soup 149
Creamy
Carrots 234
Chocolate Frosting 259
Chocolate Icing 38
Cider Icing 208
Frosting 342
Fruit Dressing 178
Creole
Beans 314
Pork Chops 118
Shrimp Sauce 378
Crisp
Baked Chicken 128
Molasses Cookies 96
Onion Waffles 309
Peanuts 365
Crispy Waffles (Master Recipe) 319
Blueberry 320
Fig 320
Orange 320
Crisscross Cookies 92
Crumb Crust 295
Crusty
Fried Chicken 128
Sausage Cakes 121
Cucumber
Cabbage Mold 287
Sauce 277
Currants 260
Juice 260
Pie 346
Sauce 187
Curried Egg Canape 162
Custard
Baked Honey 218
Caramel 190
Custard Pie 225
Flavored Custard 225
Citrus Fruit 297
Cream Filling 359
Fruit 170
Lemon Custard Pudding 13
Perfect Baked 170
Perfect Soft 170
Quince Custard Pie 347

Custard (*Continued*)
Pie 167
Rich Custard Sauce 170
Sauce 213
Cutting the Bride's Cake 57, 59

D

Dad's Best Relish 268
Date(s)
Butter 367
Candy 367
Cream Filling 2
Nut Bars 88
Nut Cake 335
Nut Macaroons 90
Pecan Candy Roll 40
Pecan Pie 343
Persimmon Pudding 362
Steamed Pudding 14
Streusel Coffee Cake 84
Turnovers 367
Orange Bread 79
Deep-Dish Apple Pie 204
Deep-Fat-Fried French Toast 76
Delicate Garden Lettuce 238
Delicious Bread Stuffing 141
Delicious Dills 271
De Luxe Mincemeat 348
Desserts
Ambrosia Refrigerator 294
Apple Mystery 213
Apple Walnut Crisp 212
Banana Apricot 305
Blueberry Betty 15
Blueberry Treat 295
Caramel Almond Sponge 225
Chocolate Chip Torte 15
Cider Shimmy 214
from Freezer 49
Frozen Ambrosia 375
Fruited Tapioca 306
Hearty Shortcake 252
Lemon Cake 347
Lemon Snow 167
Lime Treat 190
Lime Parfait 377
Mincemeat Brown Betty 213
Miniature Pecan Tarts 9
Orange Marmalade Bavarian 190
Peaches in Lemon Sauce 306
Pineapple Supreme 305
Pink Party Roll 258
Prune-Apricot Tarts 9
Pumpkin Tarts 257
Raisin Rice 307
Raspberry Crisp 374
Raspberry Tarts 7
Rhubarb Ambrosia 245
Rhubarb Crunch 244
Rice Delight 175
Robins' Nests 64
Schaum Torte 169
Strawberry Bavarian 175
Strawberry Parfait Ring 18
Strawberry Revel 294
Swiss Strawberry Rice 176
Deviled
Chicken 131
Eggs 162
Different Eggs 126
Devils Food Cake 38
Banana 67
Different Fried Fish 274
Dilled Okra Pickles 272
Dilly Beans 272
Dinner Beef Pie 252
Dips, Cream Cheese and Clam 195
Double Cheese Biscuits 195
Double Cream Cookies 342
Doughnuts
Baked Puffs 350
Chocolate Cake 349
Cocoa Balls 83
Glazed 82

Doughnuts (*Continued*)
Jelly 350
Mashed Potato 82
New Jersey 349
Raised 82
Raised Orange 82
Spicy Raised 350
Sugared 82
Sweet Milk 322
Chocolate 323
Dropped 323
Frosted 323
Maple 323
Orange 323
Peppermint 323
Plain 323
Sugared 323
Dream Bars 88
Dried Beef
with Eggs 126
Sprinkles 126
Dried Fruit Lollipops 83
Drop Biscuits 355
Duck(s)
Fried 142
Roast 142
Wild 282
Dumplings
Apple 212
Chicken 133
Chicken with 134
Colorado 376
Egg 105
Feathery-Light (Master Recipe) 322
Cheese 322
Cornmeal 322
Dessert 322
Fruit 322
Meat 322
Parsley or Spinach 322
Seed 322
Whole Wheat 322
Old-Time Apple 212
Potato 106
Dutch Plum Cake 79

E

Easy
Burgers 110
Hollandaise Sauce 134
Lemon Pie 167
Pizza 308
Baked Ham 309
Egg(s) 157–170
à la Suisse 163
Bacon 'n Egg Salad Bowl 238
in a Basket 161
Benedict 158
in Buttercups 159
Camp-Style and Corn 162
with Corned Beef Hash 113
Creamed with Cheese 162
Curried Canape 162
Deviled 162
Different 126
Special 161
Dried Beef with 126
Dumplings 105
Filling 290
Ham-Cheese Sandwich 200
Molded Salad 289
Omelet
Extra Special 159
Hasty 161
Pancakes 161
Puffy 159
Waffle 160
Oven-Cooked 163
Pickled, Pennsylvania Dutch Style 272
Platter 163
Poached in Hash 158
Potato Scrapple 149

Egg(s) (*Continued*)
Sauce 277
Scrambled 158
Perfect 159
in Spanish Sauce 163
in Toast Rings 164
Eggplant (*See* Vegetables)
Clam Bake 236
with Ham 236
Soufflé 237
Steaks 238
Eight-In-One Cookies (Master Recipe) 328
Elderberries 260
Apple Pie 346
Election Day Cake 360
Elisabeth's Fruit Salad 31
Enchiladas 369
English Toffee 39

F

Fancy Frankfurters 54
Fancy Touches 47
Farmer Jones' Special 373
Fast-Fix Brunswick Stew 311
Favorite Apple Pie 204
Favorite Honey Bars 216
Feathery-Light Dumplings 322
Variations 322
Festive Franks 313
Festive Rice Pudding 169
Fillet Mignyam 155
Fillets Supreme 276
Filling(s)
Cake
Chocolate 324
Cider 208
Citrus 335
Custard Cream 359
Date Cream 2
Honey 217
Lemon 165
Lemon Cheese 336
Sour Cream 183
Sandwich
Baked Bean and Salami 256
Beef and Ketchup 256
Chicken and Pickle 256
Chinese Dried Beef 200
Corned Beef, Relish and Onion 256
Cream Cheese-Dried Beef 256
Egg 290
Ham 290
Sardine and Pimiento 256
Fish 274–280
Anchovy Butter Sauce 268
Baked
Bass with Bacon 275
Fish au Gratin 276
Flounder with Bacon 275
Trout 275
Broiled 274
Chowder 279
Cream Cheese and Clam Dip 195
Fillets Supreme 276
Pan Fried 276
Fried, Different 274
Oven 276
Garnishes for Fried Fish 275
in Cream 274
Molded 277
Salmon Salad 280
Tuna 60
Oyster
Oven Fried 279
Pie 279
Sandwiches 279
Scalloped 366
"Stretcher" Stew 150
Turkey-Oyster Casserole 28
Vegetable Stew 186
Pickle 274
Piquant 312

Fish (*Continued*)
Salmon
Casserole 280
Cottage Cheese Loaf 193
Layer 193
Loaf 280
Macaroni Bake 312
Oyster Pie 279
Seafood Sauce 278
Soup 278
Trout au Bleu 277
Tuna
Cheese Surprises 197
Chicken Pie 313
Fish Pie 280
Macaroni and Cheese 194
Mounds 286
Onion Salad 293
Potato Bake 24
Spaghetti 253
with Sour Cream 180
Five Day Sweet Chunk Pickles 271
Flavored Butter Spreads (Master Recipe) 175
Fluffy
Beets 230
Frosting 172
Hard Sauce 14
Horse-Radish Sauce 289
Orange Sauce 320
Yams with Prunes 154
Foil Fish Fry 49
Formal Wedding Cake 56
How to Assemble 57
Frankfurter(s)
and Bean Soup 255
Fancy 54
Festive 313
Broiler Meal 113
Flapjacks 113
Quick Barbecued 310
Relish 269
Savory Macaroni and 112
Skillet Barbecued 253
Special 46
Freezer Ice Cream 331
Variations 331
French
Bread 50
Ways to Serve 50
Dressing (Master Recipe) 332
Curry 332
Indian Rose 332
Parisian 332
Roquefort 332
Spicy Red 332
Spinosa 332
Dressing 239
Fried Potatoes 151
Hunter's Dinner 69
Onion Soup 255
Peas 243
Toast 76
Toast in Oven or Broiler 76
Frenched
Chicken Sandwiches 134
Green Beans 229
Fresh
Apple Bread 206
Blueberry Pie 8
Peach Shake 189
Friday Casserole 70
Fried Chicken Creole Style 130
Duckling 142
Fritter
Batter (Master Recipe) 321
Meat 321
Orange 321
Vegetable 321
Vegetable-Meat 321
Frosted
Apple-Raisin Pie 205
Molasses Creams 87
Frosting(s)
Brown Butter 95
Butter 58, 173

Frosting(s) (*Continued*)
Butterscotch Chocolate 16
Caramel Cream 225
Cocoa 46
Coffee Butter 173
Confectioners Sugar 87, 205
Creamy 342
Creamy Chocolate 259
Fluffy 172
Fudge 2
Golden Glow 96
Harvest Moon 3
Honey-Cheese 220
Lemon Cream 165
Mocha 73, 352
Orange 77, 166
Orange Satin 4
Ornamental 57
Peanut 183
Pineapple 179
Quick 5
Sea Foam 37
Seven-Minute 59
Sour Cream 3
White 334
Frozen
Ambrosia 375
Christmas Salad 292
Fruit Cake 14
Fruit Salad 257
Salads in Orange Shells 257
Salads Supreme 292
Fruit
Banana Apricot Dessert 305
Barbecue Sauce 129
Bars 100, 342
Cake
Applesauce 208
Frozen 14
Holiday Cookies 95
Honey 220
Large Dark 226
Layer 335
White 5
Citrus Custard 297
Cobbler, Two-Fruit 205
Creamy Dressing 178
Custard 170
Dressing, Tangy 31
Dried Lollipop 83
Frost
Blackberry 332
Blueberry 332
Cherry 332
Cranberry 332
Elderberry 332
Peach 332
Raspberry 332
Rhubarb 332
Strawberry 332
Nut Bread 291
Topping 302
Persimmons 260
Date Pudding 362
Grapefruit Salad 367
Pie, Oregon Pear 367
Punch 73
Salad
Cottage Cheese and, 198
Cottage Cheese Ring 201
Elisabeth's 31
Frozen 257
Molded 31
Plate 22
Watermelon Syrup 271
Fruited
Cheese Pie 202
Chicken Salad 138
Honey Cake 218
Sea Foam 340
Tapioca 306
Fruity Gumdrop Cookies 94
Fudge
Apple Fudge Squares 86

Fudge (*Continued*)
  Cake 2
  Frosting 2
  Never-Fail 73

G

Game 281–284
  Pheasant Menu 281
  Pheasant with Rice 281
  Pressure Cooked 284
  Rabbit, Onion-Stuffed 283
  Roast Raccoon 283
  Roast Wild Duck 282
  Roast Wild Goose 282
  Stuffed Pheasant 284
  Venison
    How to Roast 282
    Scallopine 283
    Steaks 284
  Wild Rabbit 284
Garden Salad Loaf 47
Garlic
  Dressing for Beef 54
  Olives 32
Garnishes
  Fancy Touches 47
  for Fried Fish 275
  for Potato Soups 150
  Rosy Spring Apples 63
  Whipped Cream 19
Ginger
  Cookies 97
  Crackle-Top Cookies 90
  Gingersnaps 90
  Molasses 90
  Quince 264
  Sour Cream Squares 183
Gingerbread
  Maple 223
  Mix (Master Recipe) 326
    Maple 326
    Mincemeat 326
    Orange Squares 326
    Upside-Down 326
  Pancakes 326
  Waffles 23
Glaze
  Cranberry-Nut 199
  Honey 44
  Mustard 44
  Pink Applesauce 63
  Sweet for Ham 115
Glazed Doughnuts 82
Golden Ember Sauce 42
Golden Glow Frosting 96
Golden Glow Ice Cream 18
Good Luck Punch 72
Good Vegetable Combination 309
Goose
  Roast Wild 282
  Steam Baked 141
Gooseberry Pie 6
Goulash with Noodles 253
Graham Prune Bread 291
Grandma's Turnips 245
Grape(s)
  Amber Grape Marmalade 265
  Concord Pie 347
  Cream Sherbet 182
  Ketchup 265
  Spiced Jelly 264
Grapefruit Salads
  Apple 210
  Avocado 293
  Molded 292
Grated Potatoes 144
Gravy
  Brown 122
  Jelly 126
  Sour Cream 182
  Turkey 140
Green
  Apple Chutney 266
  Bean(s)
    with Chives 229

Onions Star on Platter Cooked in pickled-peach juice their spiciness enhances plump veal birds. Veal Bird Platter recipe, page 112, is with Meats.

Perfect Coffee Go-With Let everyone break off his serving of Honey-Filled Coffee Ring. Recipe for gala bread, page 217, in Special Sweetenings.

Punch Makes the Party Let it float berries and pink ice cubes. Recipe for festive Raspberry Float with gelatin base, page 17, is a Company Special.

Help-Yourself Dessert Assemble several kinds of cheese and pear or apple slices on tray, set out assorted crackers. Easy on the hostess (see page 196).

Green (*Continued*)
with Dill 229
Soup 229
in Sour Cream 181
Sweet 'n Sour 46
Gage Plum Salad 21
Pea Medley 244
Peppers to freeze 260
Salad 238
Tomato Chutney 266
Tomato Mincemeat 266
Griddle Cakes (Master Recipe) 320
Apple 207, 320
Banana 320
Blueberry 320
Cheese 320
Corn 320
Deviled Ham 320
Mincemeat 320
Pecan 320
Pineapple 320
Rice 320
Tuna 320
Grilled Frankwiches 112
Grilled Snacks 77
Guacamole 370

H

Half-and-Half Cooler 84
Half-and-Half Macaroons 303
Ham
Baked 309
Honey-Glazed 115
Timetable 116
Boiled and Yams 154
Cheese Casserole 28
Deviled
with Creamed Peas 243
with Beans 311
Egg Cheese Sandwich 200
Eggplant with 236
Filling 290
Harvest Balls 116
Loaf 116
Mustard 27
Party 26
Macaroni Roll-Ups 118
Molded 60
and Noodles 288
Pinwheels 290
and Potato Salad Ring 287
Salad 60
Sandwich 51
Slice 116
Honeyed 44
Spicy 117
Tamale Pie 117
Vegetable Scallop 117
Hamburgers
Barbecued 344
Beefburger Broiler Meal 114
Cheese Bean 109
Cheese Stuffed 110
Easy 110
Delight 110
Jumbo 53
Mixy 110
Harvest
Cheese Sandwich 197
Moon Frosting 3
Sandwich Special 165
Hash
Browned Potatoes 151
Meat Potato 148
Poached Eggs in 158
Red Flannel 360
Tennessee Turkey 366
Hasty
Omelet 161
Rarebit 313
Hawaiian
Soy Steak 368
Spareribs 368
Head Cheese 354
Heart-of-Gold Cheese Pie 202

Hearty
  Corned Beef Salad 287
  Shortcake 252
Heavenly Rice 224
Herbs 260
  Butter 45
Hickory Nut Cake 38
Holiday
  Broccoli 230
  Cake Special 4
  Fruit Cake Cookies 95
  Steamed Pudding 377
Hollandaise Sauce 158
  Easy 134
  Mock 61, 134
Holland Hot Salad 239
Home-Cooked Tomato Sauce 252
Homemade Cottage Cheese 356
Hominy, Twentieth-Century 355
Honey
  Baked Custard 218
  Baked Quince 347
  Buns 219
  Cakes
    Cheese 219
    Filled Coffee 217
    Fruit 220
    Fruited 218
    Lemon Layer 220
  Cheese Frosting 220
  Coconut
    Cake Topping 221
    Ice Cream 219
    Topping 302
  Dressing
    Apple-Honey 22
    Lime-Honey 292
    Honey 221
    Honey Fruit 222
  Favorite Bars 216
  Filling 217
  Glaze 44
  Glazed Baked Ham 115
  Lemon Rhubarb Pie 216
  Orange Sauce 221
  Rose Geranium Jelly 221
  Rye Bread 33
  Wafers 217
Honeyed
  Apples 221
  Coconut Topping 302
  Ham Slices 44
Horse-Radish
  Beets 230
  Cream Sauce 182
  Fluffy Sauce 289
  Jelly 269
  Pickled 268
  Tomato Sauce 269
  Sauce 269
Hot
  Apple Punch 214
  Buttered Bread 308
  Chicken Salad 138
  Dog Relish 267
  Spicy Punch 72
  Tomato Juice 83
How To
  Assemble Formal Cake 57
  Boil and Clean Shrimp 378
  Make Butter 174
  Roast Venison 282
Hurry-Ups
  Boston Cream Pie 359
  Potatoes 144
Hush Puppies 365

I

Ice Cream
  Banana Split 71
  Cake 300
    Layer 258

Ice Cream (*Continued*)
- Coffee 298
- Freezer (Master Recipe) 331
  - Apricot 331
  - Chocolate 331
  - Coffee 331
  - Fresh Peach 331
  - Peanut Brittle 331
  - Peppermint 331
  - Raspberry 331
  - Strawberry 331
- Golden Glow 18
- Honey Coconut 219
- Lemon 298
- Lemon Apricot 191
- Orange Pekoe 18
- Pies 11, 12
  - Raspberry 258
- Rice 373
- Robins' Nests 64
- Rhubarb 298
- Snowballs 258
- Strawberry Snowballs 19
- Sunshine, Cake 166
- Vanilla (Master Recipe) 331
  - Maple Nut 331
  - Peppermint 331
  - Sherbets 331
  - Strawberry 331
- Wafers (Master Recipe) 330
  - Chinese Almond 330
  - Orange Lemon 330
  - Sesame 330
  - Victorian Spice 330

Icing
- Creamy Chocolate 38
- Creamy Cider 208

Individual
- Butterfly Coffee Cakes 250
- Meat Loaves 250
- Pizzas 79

Informal Wedding Cake 58

J

Jam(s)
- Bluebarb 262
- One-Minute Red Raspberry 262
- Plum-Raspberry 262
- Sour Cherry and Pineapple 263
- Spiced Blueberry 263
- Spiced Peach 263

Jam Twists 78

Jellied Beef Mold 289
- Cranberry Mold 291

Jelly(ies)
- Doughnuts 350
- Gravy 126
- Horse-Radish 269
- Rose Geranium-Honey 221
- Spiced Grape 264

Jeweled Pound Cake 172

Jumbo Hamburgers 53

K

Kabobs
- Beef Shish 54
- Lamb 45
- Wyoming Lamb 123

Kale, Creamed and Onions 241

Ketchup Sauce 269

Kidney Beans and Onions 228

Kitchen Broiled Steak 53

Kris Kringle Wreath Salad 21

L

Lamb
- Chops 126
  - Marinade 122
- Curry 125
- Kabobs 45
  - Wyoming 123
- Patties 123

Lamb (*Continued*)
Broiled 123
Roast Leg of 122
and Sausage Roll 126
Shanks in Tomato Sauce 125
Shoulder Roast with Stuffing 122
Stew
Big Irish 124
Chinese Mutton 125
Little Irish 124
Peruvian 124
Lane Cake 366
Large Dark Fruit Cake 226
Layered Brownies 303
Layer Fruit Cake 335
Lemon
Baked Beefsteak 105
Blossom Snowballs 342
Broiled Chicken 374
Butter Topping 123
Cake
Cheese Cake 336
Dessert 347
Honey Layer 220
Refrigerator 296
Carrot Marmalade 265
Coconut Squares 100
Cookies 98
Cream Frosting 165
Custard Pudding 13
Filling 165
Ice Cream 298
Apricot 191
Orange Marmalade 264
Orange Rind 260
Pie
Chiffon 296
Coconut 305
Easy 167
Honey Rhubarb 216
Meringue 10
Quick 10
Snow 10
Whey 346
Sauce
Peaches in 306
Sherbet 298
Snow 167
Lemonade Cooler 42
Lettuce, Delicate Garden 238
Lima Bean(s)
Barbecue 49
Sausage Casserole 114
Lime
Cheese Salad 293
Dessert Treat 190
Honey Salad Dressing 292
Parfait 377
Pie
Chocolate 297
Meringue 10
Pineapple Sherbet 22
Little
Indian Pudding 360
Irish Lamb Stew 124
Liver
Burgers 111
Lyonnaise 111
Puffs 111
Louis Sauce 276
Louisiana Yam Muffins 156
Lyonnaise
Potatoes 144
Liver 111

M

Macaroni
Ham Roll-Ups 118
Meat Ball Soufflé 24
Salmon Bake 312
Tuna 194
Savory, and Frankfurters 112
Main Dishes
Chow Mein 368
Cottage Cheese Salmon Loaf 193

Main Dishes (*Continued*)
  Dinner Beef Pie 252
  Easy Pizza 308
  Enchiladas 369
  Goulash with Noodles 253
  Molded Chicken Loaf 286
  Skillet Supper 120
  Tamale Pie 253
  Tostados 370
Maine Chicken Pie 132
Make-at-Home Club Sandwiches 136
Maple
  Gingerbread 223
  Pie Topping 223
  Sticks 337
  Upside-Down Cake 223
Marjoram 240
Marmalade
  Amber Grape 265
  Coffee Cake 80
  Lemon-Carrot 265
  Orange-Lemon 264
  Fruit 344
Marshmallow
  Popcorn Balls 39
  Sauce 71
Mashed Potato
  Balls 150
  Doughnuts 82
  Salad 146
Meat(s)
  Balls in Tomato Sauce 30
  Barbecued Short Ribs 106
  Bean Burgers 109
  Beef (*See* Beef)
  Beef Pie 108
  Bologna Cheese Sandwiches 197
  Cheese Loaf 107
  Company, Balls 24
  Grilled Frankwiches 112
  Ham (*See* Ham)
  Hawaiian Soy Steak 368
  Hawaiian Spareribs 368
  Head Cheese 354
  Individual Meat Loaves 250
  Lamb (*See* Lamb)
  Liverburgers 111
  Liver Lyonnaise 111
  Liver Puffs 111
  Loaf 106
  Loaf Ring 107
  Macaroni Meat Ball Soufflé 24
  Norwegian Pie 108
  Oxtail Soup 351
  Pork (*See* Pork)
  Pork Sausage 353
  Potato Burgers 109
  Potato Hash 148
  Puffs 109
  Quick Meat Loaf 107
  Rolled Stuffed Flank Steak 107
  Savory Meat Balls 109
  Savory Meat Loaf 107
  Short Ribs 106
  Sooner Meat Balls 109
  Stuffed Meat Roll 108
  Tongue with Spicy Sauce 110
  Twin Meat Loaves 107
  Veal Loaf 112
    Platter 112
  Wyoming Lamb Kabobs 123
Meringue
  Chocolate 13
  Pies
    Apricot 10
    Butterscotch 222
    Lemon 10
    Lime 10
  Shells
    Pastel 13
    Strawberry 306
    Strawberry, Cake 168
Mexican Bean Pot 370
Milk 185–202
Miniature Pecan Tarts 9

Mincemeat
  Brown Betty 213
  Cheese Cookies 98
  Cookie Bars 349
  Cranberry Pie 34
  de Luxe 348
  Green Tomato 266
  Pie 348
  Pinwheels 349
  Topsy Turvy Cake 301
Mint Sauce 123
Minted
  Chocolate Pie 288
  Mayonnaise 201
  Walnuts 39
Minute Red Raspberry Jam 262
Mixed Beet Relish 267
Mixy-Burgers 110
Mocha Frosting 73, 352
Mock Hollandaise Sauce 134
Molasses
  Butterballs 89
  Cookies 97
  Frosted Creams 87
  Ginger Cookies 90
  Oatmeal Bread 338
  Oatmeal Cookies 96
  Peanut Cookies 94
  Popcorn Balls 363
  Spicy Balls 89
  Whole Wheat Cookies 226
Molded
  Cheese and Pineapple Salad 201
  Chicken Loaf 286
  Cucumber-Cabbage 287
  Egg Salad 289
  Fish 277
  Fruit Salad 31
  Grapefruit Salad 292
  Ham, Chicken 60
  Jellied Beef 289
  Jellied Cranberry 291
  Salmon Salad 280
Mornay Sauce 278
Mother-Daughter Dinner
  Market Order 64
  Menu 62
Muffins
  Basic Recipe 318
    Apple-Nutmeg 318
    Apricot-Nut 318
    Bacon-Mushroom 318
    Celery-Parsley 319
    Cheese-Garlic 319
    Cheese-Paprika 319
  Buttermilk Bran 187
  Louisiana Yam 156
  Spiced Raisin 308
Mulled Apricot Nectar 17
Mustard
  Butter Sauce 278
  Ham Loaf 27

N

Never-Fail Fudge 73
New Ham Sandwich 51
New Jersey Doughnuts 349
New Potatoes 63
  au Gratin 194
Nippy Pork Chop Platter 118
Nobby Apple Cake 210
No-Cook Candy 221
Noodle(s)
  Goulash with 253
  Ham and 288
  Ham Casserole 28
North Pole Cherry Pie 304
Norwegian Meat Pie 108
Nut(s)
  Apple Walnut Crisp 212
  Baked Turnips with Peanuts 248
  Brazil Nut Butter 234
  Bread
    Apple Nut Bread 207

Nuts (*Continued*)
Cinnamon Pecan Rolls 78
Fruit Nut Bread 291
Nut Loaf 372
Cake
Black Walnut 36
Chocolate Nut Loaf 335
Date Nut 335
Hickory Nut 38
Candy
Almond Acorns 19
Almond Fruit Roll 20
Caramel Walnut Roll 339
Date Pecan Roll 40
Minted Walnuts 39
Orange Walnuts 20
Peanut Brittle 341
Peanut Sour Cream 364
Raisin Peanut Fudge 40
Caramel Almond Sponge 225
Cookies
Almond Bars 86
Bars 86
Black Walnut 98
Brazil Nut Bars 87
Butter Balls 89
Chocolate Drops 218
Chocolate Walnut 88
Date and Nut Macaroons 90
Date Bars 88
and Fruit Bars 342
Moons 98
Peanut Molasses 94
Pecan Drops 92
Salted Peanuts 16
Walnut Brownies 303
Cranberry Glaze 199
Crisp Peanuts 365
Fruit Topping 302
Miniature Pecan Tarts 9
Peanut Chocolate Sauce 307
Peanut Frosting 183
Peanut Popcorn 363
Pie
Date Pecan 343
Peanut 364
Toasty Pecan 35
Southern Pecan 364
Walnut 179
Skillet Toasted Peanuts 364

O

Oatmeal
Bread 33
Molasses 338
Cookies
Chocolate 342
Molasses 96
Refrigerator 99
Old
English Ginger Crisps 329
Fashioned Sour Cream 239
Time Apple Dumplings 212
Virginia Sally Lunn 365
Omelet
Extra-Special 159
Hasty 161
Pancakes 161
Puffy 159
Waffle 160
Onion(s) (*See* Vegetables)
Pie 241
Sauce 321
Parsley 242
Stuffed Rabbit 283
with Savory Sage Stuffing 242
Open-Face
Raspberry Pie 374
Sandwiches (Dried Beef) 126
Orange
Banana Drink 83
Cake 259
Coconut Cake 301

Orange (*Continued*)
Cookies 94
Carrot 96
Date Bread 79
Frosting 77, 166
Satin 4
Frozen Salad in Orange Shells 257
Marmalade
Bavarian 190
Lemon 264
Pekoe Tea Ice Cream 18
Pie
Apple 8
Rhubarb Cream 244
Relish
Cranberry 29
Rind 260
Sauce 321
Fluffy 166
Honey 221
Stuffing 142
Tapioca à la Mode 14
Walnuts 20
Oregano 240
Salad Dressing 281
Oregon Pear Pie 367
Oriental Persimmons 367
Ornamental Frosting 57
Outdoor Broiled Steak 51
Oven
Apple Butter 355
Cooked Eggs 163
Cooked Peas 244
Fried Chicken 128
Fried Fish 276
Fried Oysters 279
Fried Potatoes 152
Overnight Salad 176
Oxtail Soup 351
Oyster (*See* Fish)
Pie 279
Sandwiches 279

P

Pancakes
Am-Nor 355
Apple 207, 320
Banana 320
Blueberry 320
Cheese 320
Corn 320
Date 320
Deviled Ham 320
Frankfurter Flapjacks 113
Mincemeat 320
Omelet 161
Pineapple 320
Potato 148
Rice 320
Sour Milk 207
Swedish Style 187
Tuna 320
Pan Fried Chicken 128
Pan Fried Fillets 276
Panned Cabbage de Luxe 231
Paprika Chicken 130
Parsley-Onion Sauce 242
Parsnip Casserole 242
Patties 242
Party Ham Loaf 26
Pastel Meringue Shells 13
Pastry
Almond 7
Crumb Crust 295
Rich 6
Tricks 304
Peach(es)
Chutney 266
Fresh, Shake 189
in Lemon Sauce 306
Pie 375
Purée 260
Spiced Jam 263
Peanut
Brittle 341

Peanut (*Continued*)
Butter Chiffon Pie 295
Chocolate Sauce 307
Dainties 77
Frosting 183
Molasses Cookies 94
Pie 364
Popcorn 363
Sour Cream Candy 364
Pear
Chutney 265
Pinwheels 19
Peas (*See* Vegetables)
and Green Onions 243
with cream 177
Pecans (*See* Nuts)
Pennsylvania Dutch Hearts 304
Peppermint
Candy Topping 302
Chiffon Pie 296
Milk Shake 189
Peppers (*See* Vegetables)
Perfect Baked Custard 170
Perfect Scrambled Eggs 159
Perfect Soft Custard 170
Persimmons 260
Date Pudding 362
Grapefruit Salad 367
Peruvian Lamb Stew 124
Pheasant with Rice Stuffing 281
Philadelphia Scrapple 361
Pickled Eggs, Pennsylvania Dutch Style 272
Horse-Radish 268
(*See also* Relishes)
Pickles
Bread and Butter 272
Clear Watermelon 270
Delicious Dills 271
Dilled Okra 272
Dilly Beans 272
Fish Pickle 274
5-Day Sweet Chunk 271
Sweet Dills 272
Sweet-Sour Dills 271
Watermelon 270
Picnic Potato Salad 43
Picture-Pretty Relishes 269
Pie(s)
Amber 346
Apple
Cake 213
Deep Dish 204
Elderberry 346
Favorite 204
Frosted Raisin 205
Orange 8
Quick 204
Sour Cream 205
Apricot Meringue 10
Chiffon 35
Black Bottom Pie 377
Black Cherry Chiffon 168
Blueberry, Fresh 8
Butterscotch Meringue 222
Caramel Custard 225
Cheese 200
Cranberry 199
Fruited 202
Heart-of-Gold 202
Pineapple 202
Refrigerator 198
Strawberry 199
Cherry
au Gratin 44
Black Chiffon 168
Cheese 202
North Pole 304
Special 6
Chess 364
Chicken Tuna 313
Chocolate
Angel 15
Lime 297
Mint 16
Minted 288

Pie(s) (*Continued*)
Coconut, Lemon 305
Concord Grape 347
Corn 235
Cranberry
Cheese 199
Chiffon 304
Mince 34
Raisin 35
Currant 346
Custard 167
Quince 347
Date Pecan 343
Elderberry Apple 346
Gooseberry 6
Honey-Lemon Rhubarb 216
Ice Cream 11
Lemon
Easy 167
Chiffon 296
Coconut 305
Honey-Lemon Rhubarb 216
Meringue 10
Quick 10
Snow 10
Whey 346
Lime
Chocolate 297
Meringue 10
Mince-Cranberry 34
Mincemeat 348
Onion 241
Peach 375
Peanut 364
Butter Chiffon 295
Pear, Oregon 367
Pecan
Date 343
Southern 364
Toasty 35
Peppermint Chiffon 296
Pineapple
Cheese 202
Strawberry 8
Potato, Topsy Turvy 242
Prune Plum 35
Pumpkin 8
Tawny 36
Quince Custard 347
Raisin 7
Cranberry 35
Frosted Apple 205
Sour Cream 36
Raspberry
Ice Cream 258
Open-Face 374
Sour Cream 181
Refrigerator 179
Cheese 198
Rhubarb Orange Cream 244
Honey-Lemon 216
Sour Cream
Apple 205
Raisin 36
Raspberry 180
Strawberry
Cheese 199
Pineapple 8
Vanilla Cream Pie 327
Burnt Almond 327
Butterscotch 327
Caramel 327
Chocolate 327
Cocoa 327
Coconut 327
Fruit 327
Lemon 327
Pineapple 327
Walnut Cream 179
Washington 359
Pineapple
Cake
Coffee 81
Cranberry
Cocktail 62

Pineapple (*Continued*)
Relish 29
Frosting 179
Lime Sherbet 22
Milk Shake 189
Pie
Cheese 202
Strawberry 8
Salad
Cheese 175
Chicken 61
Molded Cheese and 201
Sour Cherry and, Jam 263
Supreme 305
Pink Applesauce Glaze 63
Pink Party Roll 258
Pizza
Easy 308
Individual 79
Plain Coffee Cake 316
Plank Dinner 228
Plum(s)
Conserve 263
Dutch Cake 79
Green Gage 21
Prune Pie 35
Raspberry Jam 262
Poached Eggs in Hash 158
Poinsettia Cheese Cake 202
Salad 211
Popcorn 54
Balls 363
Chocolate 363
Marshmallow 39
Molasses 363
Cheese 363
on-Sticks 363
Peanut 363
Quick Caramel 363
Valentine 363
Poppyseed
Layer Cake 3
Rolls 34
Salad Dressing 293
Pork
Chops
Baked 312
in Soup 29
Continental 180
Creole 118
Nippy Platter 118
Stuffed 118
Yam 153
Roast
Loin of 63
with Spicy Apricot Glaze 115
Sausage 353
Savory 74
Rolls 119
Spareribs
Baked 119
Barbecued 48, 120
with Orange Stuffing 119
Sweet-Sour 120
Pot Roast Seasonings 103
Potato(es) 143–156
Baked 49
Slices 44
Stuffed 145
Beef Roll 145
Pot Pie 147
Burgers 109
Chantilly 314
Cheese
Scallop 26
Topped 145
Chocolate Cake 37
Chowder, Salmon 150
Creamed
Company 147
Skillet 144
Dumplings 106
Egg Scrapple 149
Fried
Country 145
French 151

Potato(es) (*Continued*)
Oven 152
Grated, Panbroiled 144
Hash Browned 151
Hurry-Up 144
Loaf, Browned 147
Lyonnaise 144
Mashed
Balls 150
Doughnuts 82
Meat, Hash 148
New 63
au Gratin 194
Pancakes 148
Pie, Topsy Turvy 242
Provincial 146
Puff Buns 83
Puffed-Up 151
Rutabaga Casserole 245
Salad, Picnic 43
Ham and, Ring 287
Mashed 146
Sweepstakes 146
Savory 147
Scalloped 188
Skillet 144
Soup
Brown 149
Cheese 149
Cream of Potato 149
Garnish for 150
Sunflowers 152
Toads 246
Tuna
Bake 24
Puffs 148
Waffles 148
Poultry 127–142
(*See* Chicken, Duck, Goose and Turkey)
Pound Cake 336
Jeweled 172
Pressed
Beef 289
Chicken 354
Pressure-Cooked Game 284
Provincial Potatoes 146
Preserves
Sour Cherry 264
Tomato 264
Prunes
Apricot Tarts 9
Bread, Graham 291
Cake 38
Spice 37
Crystal Balls 20
Fluffy Yams with 154
Pinwheels 80
Plum Pie 35
Puffed-up Potatoes 151
Puff Shells 60
Puffy Omelet 159
Pulled Mints 339
Pumpkin
Cake 2
Nut Waffles 23
Pie 8
Tawny 36
Tarts 257
Pudding(s)
Apple 348
Brownie 305
Caramel Bread (Master Recipe) 325
Coconut 325
Coffee 325
Chocolate 325
Dried Fruit 325
Fruit 325
Peanut Brittle 325
Coconut Cream 306
Chocolate Mint Tower 376
Cranberry 362
Festive Rice 169
Fruited Tapioca 306
Heavenly Rice 224

Pudding(s) (*Continued*)
Holiday Steamed 377
Lemon Custard 13
Little Indian 360
Orange Tapioca à la Mode 14
Persimmon-Date 362
Steamed Date 14
Surprise 182
Virginia Apple 211
Wisconsin Cranberry 362
Yam 155
Punch (*See* Beverages)
Fruit 73
Good Luck 72
Hot Apple 214
Mulled Apricot Nectar 17
Raspberry Float 17
Spicy 72

Q

Quick
Apple Pie 204
Apricot Chiffon Pie 35
Barbecued Franks 310
Broiler Meal 310
Butterhorn Rolls 250
Caramel Corn 363
Change Cake (Master Recipe) 323
Creamy Strawberry 324
Rhubarb-Kuchen 323
Sour Cream 323
Upside-Down 324
Frosting 5
Holiday Cake 300
Lemon Pie 10
Meat Loaf 107
Raised Corn Bread 188
Seafood Sauce 268
Soups 255
Stew 251
Tartar Sauce 312
Tomato Sauce 268
Quince
Custard Pie 347
Ginger 264
Honey Baked 347

R

Raised Doughnuts 82
Orange 82
Raisin
Bran Bread 338
Carrot Cookies 93
Cranberry Pie 35
Frosted Apple, Pie 205
Peanut Fudge 40
Pie 7
Rice Dessert 307
Sour Cream Cookies 91
Sour Cream Pie 36
Spiced Muffins 308
Rarebit
Hasty 313
Tomato-Cheese 194
Raspberry
Crisp 374
Float 17
Ice Cream Pie 258
1-Minute Jam 262
Open-Face Pie 374
Plum Jam 262
Tarts 7
Sour Cream Pie 181
Red Flannel Hash 360
Refrigerator
Cake 296
Cheese Pie 198
Cookies 99
Pie 179
Relishes
Beet 269
Bread and Butter Pickles 272

Relishes (*Continued*)
Carrot 226
Clear Watermelon Pickles 270
Corn Relish 267
Cranberry(ies)
Apple 29
Marmalade 267
Orange 29
Pineapple 29
Relish Salad 29
Dad's Best 268
Delicious Dills 271
Dilled Okra 272
Dilly Beans 272
Fish Pickle 274
5-Day Sweet Chunk Pickles 271
Frankfurter 269
Garlic Olives 32
Grape Ketchup 265
Green Apple Chutney 266
Green Tomato Chutney 266
Hot Dog 267
Mixed Beet 267
Onion Parsley Sauce 242
Peach Chutney 266
Pear Chutney 265
Picture-Pretty 269
Sandwich Spread 268
Sweet Dills 272
Sweet-Sour Dill Chunks 271
Tomato Horse-Radish Sauce 269
Watermelon Pickles 270
Rhubarb
Ambrosia Betty 245
Celery Salad 291
Crunch 244
Ice Cream 298
Pie
Honey-Lemon 216
Orange Cream 244
Swirls 245
Ribbon
Cake 173
Salad 343
Sandwich Loaf 290
Rice
Bean Salad 32
Delight 175
Duet 378
and Chicken Jambalaya 373
Chicken Salad 138
Festive Pudding 169
Heavenly Rice 224
Ice Cream 373
Raisin, Dessert 307
Savory Sausage 26
Stuffing (with Pheasant) 281
Supreme 176
Swiss Strawberry 176
Wild 362
Rich Pastry 6
Rind (orange and lemon) 260
Roast
Beef (Standing Rib) 102
Duck 142
Leg of Lamb 122
Pork
with Apricot Glaze 115
Loin 63
Raccoon 283
Turkey 61, 139
Wild Duck 282
Wild Goose 282
Robins' Nests 64
Rolls
Butterhorn 64
Cinnamon, Toasted 54
Cinnamon Pecan 78
Poppy Seed 34
Twice-Baked 250
Quick Butterhorn 250
Rolled
Pot Roast 103
Stuffed Flank Steak 107
Roquefort Dressing 239
Rose Geranium-Honey Jelly 221

Rosy
Spring Apples 63
Rhubarb Swirls 245
Royal Cherry Topping 302
Russian
Dressing 239
Eggplant 237
Rutabaga-Potato Casserole 245
Rye
Honey Bread 33

S

Saffron Asparagus 228
Salad(s)
Apple Cheese 210
Chip 210
Grapefruit 210
Bacon 'n Egg Bowl 238
Beet Perfection 31
Bowl 52
Cauliflower 234
Cheese Lime 293
Pineapple 175
Chef's 71
Chicken and Rice 138
Company 138
Pineapple 61
Coleslaw 283
Cottage 44
Cottage Cheese and Fruit 198
Cranberry 21
Relish 29
Cucumber-Cabbage 287
Delicate Garden Lettuce 238
Elisabeth's Fruit 31
Frozen Christmas 292
Fruit 257
In Orange Shells 257
Supreme 292
Fruit-Cottage Cheese Ring 201
Fruit Plate 22
Fruited Chicken 138
Garden Loaf 47
Grapefruit Avocado 293
Green 238
Green Gage Plum 21
Ham 60
and Potato Ring 287
Hearty Corned Beef 287
Holland Hot 239
Hot Chicken 138
Kris Kringle Wreath 21
Mashed Potato 146
Molded
Cheese and Pineapple 201
Egg 289
Fruit 31
Grapefruit 292
Ham, Chicken 60
Salmon 280
Overnight 176
Persimmon-Grapefruit 367
Picnic Potato 43
Poinsettia 211
Rhubarb-Celery 291
Ribbon 343
Rice-Bean 32
September Apple 211
Shrimp 378
Sweepstakes Potato 146
Sweet-Sour Cabbage Slaw 178
Tomato Aspic 246
Tuna Onion 293
Turkey-Cranberry 140
Vegetable Ribbon 63
Winter Bowl 183
Yam Fruit 154
Yuletide 176
Salad Dressing 239
Apple-Honey 22
Avocado 292
Cottage Cheese 222
Creamy Fruit 178

Salad Dressing (*Continued*)
French 239
Master Recipe 332
Honey 221
Fruit 222
Lime 292
Minted Mayonnaise 201
Old-Fashioned Sour Cream 239
Oregano 281
Poppy Seed 293
Roquefort 239
Russian 239
Sour Cream 181
Tangy Fruit 31
Thousand Island 239
Salmon
Cottage Cheese Loaf 193
Fondue 164
Loaf 280
Macaroni Bake 312
Oyster Pies 279
Potato Chowder 150
Salted Peanut Cookies 16
Sandwich(es)
Bologna Cheese 197
Broiled 197
Cake 290
Cheese Barbecue 196
Chicken Filling 134
Circle 196
Frenched Chicken 134
Ham Pinwheels 290
Egg-Cheese 200
Harvest Cheese 197
Special 165
Make-at-Home Club 136
New Ham 51
Open-Face (Dried Beef) 126
Oyster 279
Ribbon Loaf 290
White and Gold 202
Sardine and Pimiento Filling 256
Sauce(s)
Anchovy Butter 268
Asparagus-Mushroom 160
Bacon and Cheese 195
Barbecue 65, 67, 131, 375
Beef Vegetables 314
Brazil Nut Butter 234
Burnt Sugar 348
Butter 51
Butterscotch 214
Caper 277
Caramel Sundae 225
Cherry 177
Chicken with Peas 160
Chili Dressing 239
Chocolate 307
Creole Shrimp 378
Cucumber 277
Currant 187
Custard 213
Egg 277
in Spanish Sauce 163
Fluffy
Hard 14
Horse-Radish 289
Orange 166, 320
Fruit Barbecue 129
Golden Ember 42
Hollandaise 158
Easy 134
Mock 61, 134
Home-Cooked Tomato 252
Honey Orange 221
Horse-Radish 269
Cream 182
Ketchup 269
Lemon Butter 123
Louis 277
Marshmallow 71
Meat Balls in Tomato 30
Mint 123
Mornay 278
Mustard Butter 278

Sauces (*Continued*)
Onion 321
Parsley 242
Orange 321
Peaches in Lemon 306
Peanut Chocolate 307
Quick Tartar 312
Tomato 268
Rich Custard 170
Satin 179
Seafood 278
Spaghetti Meat 251
Spicy Vanilla 321
Steak Supreme 52
Sundae 39
Sweet-Sour 212
Tangy Bacon 232
Texas Special 52
Tomato
Cheese 200
Cream 268
Curry 234
Horse-Radish 269
Vanilla 362
Sauerbraten 182
Sausage
Beans and 114
Mexican Style 74
Crumbles 121
Crusty Cakes 121
Flower Casseroles 164
Frizzles 121
Lamb Roll 126
Lima Casserole 114
Loaf 121
Pork, Old-Fashioned 353
Savory Rice 26
Squash and 246
Savory
Beef Cakes 311
Broiled Tomatoes 247
Dressing 240
Macaroni and Frankfurters 112
Meat Balls 109
Meat Loaf 107
Pork Rolls 119
Potatoes 147
Pot Roast 103
Sausage Rice 26
Scalloped
Cabbage 188
Chicken 70
Oysters 366
Poatoes 188
Sweet Potatoes and Apples 156
Scallopine of Venison 283
Schaum Torte 169
Scrambled Eggs 158
Scrapple
Philadelphia 361
Potato-Egg 149
Sea Foam Frosting 37
Seafood Sauce 278
Seasoned Butters 51
September Apple Salad 211
Seven-Minute Frosting 59
Shakes
Banana 189
Chocolate malted 189
Fresh Peach 189
Peppermint 189
Pineapple 189
Strawberry 189
Sherbet
Grape Cream 182
Lemon 298
Lime-Pineapple 22
Short Ribs 106
Shrimp
Bisque 310
Creamed 160
Creole 378
Sauce 378
How to Boil and Clean 378
Salad 378

Skillet
  Barbecued Franks 253
  Corn Bread 187
  Creamed Potatoes 144
  Scalloped Potatoes 144
  Supper 120
  Toasted Peanuts 364
Smothered Chicken 130
Snacks, Grilled 77
Snow Balls 258
Some-Mores 49
Sooner Meat Balls 109
Sopaipillas 369
Soufflés
  Cheese 193
  Chicken 313
  Eggplant 237
  Sweet Potato 153
  Swiss 200
Soup(s)
  Bean 351
    and Frankfurter 255
  Borsch 351
  Chicken Gumbo 133
  Chops Baked in 29
  Fish 278
  French Onion 255
  Green Bean 229
  Oxtail 351
  Potato
    Brown 149
    Cheese 149
    Cream of 149
    Garnish 150
  Quick 255
  Super Stock 254
  Velvety Cheese 186
  Vichyssoise 177
  Water Cress 186
  Whey Tomato Bouillon 350
Sour Cherry
  Pineapple Jam 263
  Preserves 264
Sour Cream
  Apple Pie 205
  Beef with 252
  Beets 181
  Cake 183
  Dressings 181
  Filling 183
  Fish with 180
  Frosting 3
  Ginger Squares 183
  Gravy 182
  Green Beans in 181
  Old-Fashioned Dressing 239
  Peanut Candy 364
  Raisin Cookies 91
  Raisin Pie 36
  Raspberry Pie 181
Sour Milk Griddle Cakes 207
Southern
  Barbecued Chicken 65
  Pecan Pie 364
Spaghetti
  Meat Sauce 251
  Tuna Bake 253
Spanish Limas 27
  Corn Bread 308
Spareribs with Orange Stuffing 119
Special Deviled Eggs 161
  Frankfurters 46
Spices (and Herbs)
  Basil 240
  Herbs 260
  Marjoram 240
  Oregano 240
  Savory 240
  Tarragon 240
  Thyme 240
Spice Cake 352
  Prune 37
Spiced
  Blueberry Jam 263
  Grape Jelly 264
  Peach Jam 263

Spiced (*Continued*)
Raisin Muffins 308
Tomato Juice 17
Spicy
Apple Bars 87
Buttered Beets 230
Ham Slice 117
Molasses Balls 89
Pumpkin Pie 11
Raised Doughnuts 350
Topping 205
Vanilla Sauce 321
Sponge Cake (Master Recipe)
Roll 324
Lemon Squares 325
Waffles 23
Spoonbread 365
Spreads
Flavored Butter 175
Onion 45
Relish Sandwich 268
Seasoned Butters 51
Take-Along Cheese 33
Squash
Medley 246
with Sausage 246
Standing Rib Roast 102
Steak (*See* Beef and Meats)
Go-withs 52
Sauce Supreme 52
with Tomato Sauce 104
Steam-Baked Goose 141
Steamed Date Pudding 14
Stew
Beef in Foil 310
Big Irish Lamb 124
Brown 104
Brunswick 68, 69, 311
Chili Dumpling 105
Chinese Mutton 125
Cider 104
Little Irish Lamb 124
Peruvian Lamb 124
Quick 251
"Stretcher" Oyster 150
Vegetable 186
Turnip 248
Stickies 76
Strawberry
Angel Cake 294
Bavarian Cream 175
Cheese Pie 199
Divinity 340
Frost (Master Recipe) 332
Blackberry 332
Blueberry 332
Cherry 332
Cranberry 332
Elderberry 332
Peach 332
Raspberry 332
Rhubarb 332
Meringues à la Mode 306
Meringue Cake 168
Milk Shake 189
Parfait Ring 18
Pineapple Pie 8
Revel 294
Snowballs 19
Swiss Rice 176
Vanilla Pie 12
Stretcher Stew 150
Stuffed
Baked Potatoes 145
Cabbage Leaves 232
Eggplant 237
Meat Roll 108
Peppers 250
Pork Chops 118
Tomatoes 27
Stuffing
Baked Dressing 62, 375
Celery 139
Delicious Bread 141
Garlic 54
Onion (Rabbit) 283

Stuffing (*Continued*)
- Onions with 242
- Orange 142
- Rice with Pheasant 281
- Savory 240
- Orange (with Spareribs) 119

Sugar Cookies 97
- (Master Recipe) 328
- Chocolate Chip 329
- Coconut 329
- Nut 329
- Raisin 329
- Spiced 329

Sugared Doughnuts 82

Sugar, Brown
- Cookies 95
- Drops 96

Sundae Sauces
- Butterscotch 39
- Chocolate 39

Sunshine
- Ice Cream Cake 166
- Layer Cake 166

Super-Duper Chocolate Cookies 91

Super Soup Stock 254

Surprise Pudding 182

Swedish Style Pancakes 187

Sweepstakes Potato Salad 146

Sweet
- Cream Corn Bread 354
- Dills 272
- Glazes for Ham 115
- Milk Doughnuts (Master Recipe) 322
  - Chocolate 323
  - Dropped 323
  - Frosted 323
  - Maple 323
  - Orange 323
  - Peppermint 323
  - Plain 323
  - Sugared 323
- Potato(es)
  - Balls 152
  - Broiled Ham and Yams 154
  - Casserole 153
  - Chips 153
  - Corned Beef with Cheese and 156
  - Dress-Ups 155
  - Filet Mignyam 155
  - Fluffy, with Prunes 154
  - Louisiana Muffins 156
  - Pie 155
  - Scalloped, and Apples 156
  - Soufflé 153
  - Yam Chops 153
  - Yam Flowerettes 154
  - Yam Fruit Salad 154
  - Yams with Lemon Slices 156
  - Yam Pudding 155

Sweet-Sour
- Cabbage 178
- Dill Chunks 271
- Green Beans 46
- Pork 120
- Sauce 212

Sweet 'n Tart Lemon Pie 11

Swiss
- Cheese Soufflé 200
- Steaks 104
- Strawberry Rice 176

T

Take-Along Cheese Spread 33

Tamale Pie 253

Tangy
- Bacon Sauce 232
- Fruit Dressing 31

Tarragon 240

Tart Scalloped Cabbage 232

Tartar Sauce, Quick 312

Tawny Pumpkin Pie 36

Tea-Time Cupcakes 3

Tender Brown Beef Cubes 251

Tennessee Turkey-Hash 366
Texas
  Barbecued Chicken 131
  Special Sauce 52
Thirst Quencher 84
Thirty-Minute Chop Suey 121
Thousand Island Dressing 239
Three-Fruit Marmalade 344
3-Way Gold Cake 259
Time Table for Broiling 53
Tips
  for the Cake Baker 57
  from Good Cooks 105
Toasty
  Pecan Pie 35
  Praline Topping 302
Toffee
  Cookie Squares 88
  English 39
Tomato(es)
  Aspic 246
  Baked-Deviled 247
  Bean Chowder 314
  Broiled 247
  Cabbage Casserole 233
  Cheese Rarebit 194
  Cocktail 287
  Corn Stuffed 247
  Green, Chutney 266
    Mincemeat 266
  Juice, hot 83
  Preserves 264
  Sauce
    Cheese 200, 278
    Cream 268
    Curry 234
    Home-Cooked 252
    Horse-Radish 269
    Quick 268
  Stuffed 27
  Tasty Bake 247
  Whey Bouillon 350
Tongue with Spicy Sauce 110
Toppings
  Bake-on Coffee Cake 316
    Apple-Cheese 317
    Brown Sugar-Cinnamon 316
    Cranberry-Orange 317
    Honey-Pecan 317
    Peach-Cinnamon 316
    Pineapple-Apricot 317
  Cake 221
  Fruit Nut 302
  Honey-Coconut 221, 302
  Maple Pie 223
  Peppermint Candy 302
  Royal Cherry 302
  Spicy 205
  Streusel 37
  Toasty Praline 302
Topsy Turvy
  Mincemeat Pie 301
  Potato Pie 242
Tortillas 369
Tostados 370
Trout au Bleu 277
Tuna
  Fish Pie 280
  Macaroni and Cheese 194
  Mounds 286
  Onion Salad 293
  Spaghetti Bake 253
  Potato Puffs 148
Turkey
  Cranberry Salad 140
  Divan 141
  Giblets and Neck 62
  Gravy 62, 140
  Hash 366
  Oyster Casserole 28
  Roast 61, 139
  Surprise 140
  Tetrazzini 140
Turnips (*See* Vegetables)
  in Cheese Sauce 248
  Stew 248

Twentieth-Century Hominy 355
Twice-Baked Rolls 250
Twin
  Meat Loaves 107
  Wedding Ring Cakes 59
Two
  Fruit Cobbler 205
  Way Cookies 341

U

Upside-Down Chicken Dinner 137

V

Vanilla
  Cream Pie (Master Recipe) 327
  Ice Cream (Master Recipe) 331
  Sauce 362
Veal
  Chops Baked in Soup 29
  Loaf 112
  Platter 112
Vegetables (s) 227–248
  Asparagus
    Casserole 32
    Mushroom Sauce 160
    Saffron 228
    with Mock Hollandaise Sauce 61
  Bean (s), Dried
    and Frankfurter Soup 255
    Baked 361
      Boston 358
      Vermont 358
    with Deviled Ham 311
    Mexican, Pot 370
    Porridge 229
    Soup 351
  Bean (s), Green
    Baked 314
    with Chives 229
    Corn and, with Cheese 195
    Creole 314
    Dilly 272
    Frenched 229
    Soup 229
    in Sour Cream 181
  Bean (s) Lima, Baked 228
    in Cream 177
    Sausage Casserole 114
  Bean (s) Kidney
    Beefeater's 254
    and Onions 228
  Beet (s)
    Fluffy 230
    Horse-Radish 230
    Mixed Relish 267
    Perfection Salad 31
    Relish 269
    Sour Cream 181
    Spicy Buttered 230
  Broccoli
    au Gratin 29
    Casserole of Curried, and Onions 281
    Holiday 230
    Soufflé 230
  Cabbage
    with Apples 231
    with Cheese 231
    Corned Beef 353
    Casserole (s) 231
      Tomato 233
      Bacon 232
    Panned de Luxe 231
    Scalloped 188
      Tart 232
    Slaw with Mustard Mold 233
    Stuffed Leaves 232
  Carrot (s)
    Buttered Sticks 233
    Rings, Celery in 269
    in Cream 177
    Creamy 234
    Lemon Marmalade 265
    Orange Cookies 96
    Raisin Cookies 93

Vegetable(s) (*Continued*)
Relish 226
Cauliflower, Baked 234
Cauliflower Salad 234
Celery
in Carrot Rings 269
Rhubarb Salad 291
Stuffing 139
Chowder 255
Corn
and Beans with Cheese 195
Broiled in Husks 235
Cakes 234
Cakes 234
Camp-Style Eggs and 162
Chowder 186
Flake Cookies 94
on-the-Cob 49
"Oysters" 236
and Peas with Savory 236
Pie 235
Relish 267
Stuffed Tomatoes 247
Waffles 235
Cucumber
Cabbage Mold 287
Sauce 277
Eggplant
Baked with Ham 236
Clam Bake 236
Russian 237
Soufflé 237
Steaks 238
Stuffed 237
Green Salad 238
Ham Scallop 117
Hominy, Twentieth-Century 355
in Cream 177
Carrots 177
Lima Beans 177
Tomatoes 177
Turnips 177
Kale, Creamed and Onions 241
Lettuce, Delicate Garden 238
Medley 309
Onion(s)
Casserole of Curried Broccoli 281
Creamed 241
and Kale 241
Crisp Waffles 309
French Soup 255
Green, and Peas 243
Kidney Beans and 228
Parsley Sauce 242
Pie 241
with Savory Sage Dressing 242
Stuffed Rabbit 283
Oyster Stew 186
Parsley-Onion Sauce 242
Parsnip
Casserole 242
Patties 242
Peas
Chicken Sauce with 160
Cooked in Pod 243
Corn and, with Savory 236
with Cream 177
Creamed and Deviled Ham 243
French 243
Green, Medley 244
and Green Onions 243
Oven Cooked 244
Peppers
Green 260
Stuffed 250
Potato(es) 143–156
and Rutabaga Casserole 245
Scalloped 188
Quince
Custard Pie 347
Ginger 264
Honey Baked 347
Rhubarb (*See* Rhubarb)
Orange Cream Pie 244
Rosy Swirls 245
Ribbon Salad 63
Rutabaga Potato Casserole 245
Squash 246

Vegetable(s) (*Continued*)
Medley 246
with Sausage 246
Tomato (*See* Tomatoes)
Turnips
Baked with Peanuts 248
in Cheese Sauce 248
Grandma's 245
Stew 248
Water Cress Soup 186
Wild Rabbit with 284
Zucchini, Baked Filled 248
Velvety Cheese Soup 186
Venison
Scallopine of 283
Steaks 284
Vermont Baked Beans 358
Vichyssoise 177
Virginia Apple Pudding 211
Virginia Spoon Bread 69

W

Waffles
à la Mode 307
Chocolate 23
Corn 235
Crisp Onion 309
Crispy (Master Mix) 319
Blueberry 320
Fig 320
Orange 320
French Toast 76
Gingerbread 23
Omelet 160
Potato 148
Pumpkin Nut 23
Sponge Cake 23
Walnut(s) (*See* Nuts)
Brownies 303
Cream Pie 179
Orange 20
Washington Pie 359
Water Cress Soup 186
Watermelon
Pickles 270
Syrup 271
Whey
Lemon Pie 346
Tomato Bouillon 350
Whipped Cream
Cake 173
Garnish 19
White
Cake 352
Fruit Cake 5
Frosting 334
and Gold Sandwiches 202
Wonder Cake 165
Whole Wheat
Bread 34
Cupcakes 77
Tart Shells 257
Wild
Rabbit with Vegetables 284
Rice 362
Winter Salad Bowl 183
Wisconsin Cranberry Pudding 362
Women's Luncheon 201
Wyoming Lamb Kabobs 123

Y

Yams (*See* Sweet Potatoes)
Chops 153
Flowerettes 154
Fruit Salad 154
with Lemon Slices 156
Pudding 155
Yellow
Angel Cake 167
Lard Cake 73
Yuletide Salad 176

Z

Zucchini, Baked 248